a village and its double

Urban Planning Manual

Olympic and Paralympic Games

Paris 2024

Dominique Perrault

Table of Contents

#6# A Word to Readers

This manual gathers all the documentation produced between 2018 and 2020 submitted to the Société de livraison des ouvrages olympiques (SOLIDEO) under the framework of the urban project management contract of which Dominique Perrault Architecture is the agent.

If the idea to organize and present all this information in the form of a "manual" on urbanism prevailed, it is precisely because the wealth and diversity of the documents presented go beyond elements that are commonly admitted in urbanism to show the sensitive work that nurtures the creation of an Olympic district. It is the "making of" so to speak of a workshop on urbanism, the point of convergence of some thirty designers and construction companies that were going to build the Athletes' Village.

This book aims to make available the greatest number of the fruits of an original urban design process in the heart of a Grand Paris undertaking its renewal.

I would like for the reader to retain the fact that what is still possible is as valuable as what has already been achieved. It is an invitation to project ourselves "further" in the heritage of the Olympic event, not as a legacy but as a gift. It is both a wish and a challenge.

Dominique Perrault

Scientific Workshops
CIO
International Olympic Committee
Group HYSPLEX
AMO Sustainable Development
SOLIDEO
MAITRISE D'OUVRAGE
Olympic Works Delivery Company
Organizing Committee for the 2024 Summer Olympic and Paralympic Games
PARIS 2024
Paris City Council
Interministerial Delegation for the Olympic and Paralympic Games
Metropole du Grand Paris
SGP
Société du Grand Paris
Île-de-France region
RTE
Transmission System Operator
CD93
Comité Départemental de Seine-Saint-Denis
City of Saint-Denis
City of Saint-Ouen-sur-Seine
City of L'Île-Saint-Denis
Établissement public territorial Plaine Commune
SEM Plaine Commune Développement
INSTITUTIONS
LOCAL AUTHORITIES

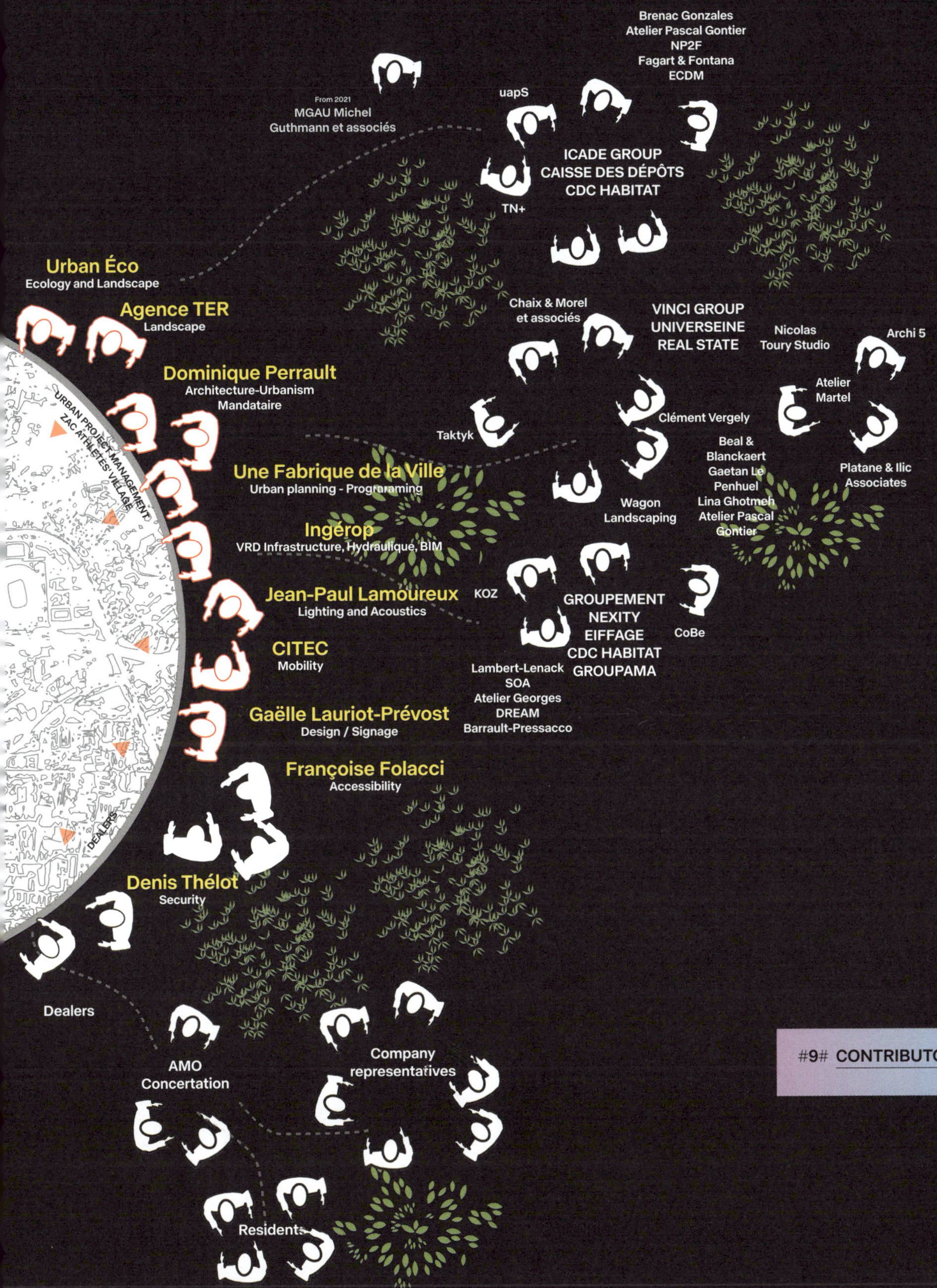

Brenac Gonzales
Atelier Pascal Gontier
NP2F
Fagart & Fontana
ECDM
From 2021
MGAU Michel
Guthmann et associés
uapS
ICADE GROUP
CAISSE DES DÉPÔTS
CDC HABITAT
TN+
Urban Éco
Ecology and Landscape
Agence TER
Landscape
Chaix & Morel
et associés
VINCI GROUP
UNIVERSEINE
REAL STATE
Nicolas
Toury Studio
Archi 5
Dominique Perrault
Architecture-Urbanism
Mandataire
URBAN PROJECT MANAGEMENT
ZAC ATHLETES' VILLAGE
Atelier
Martel
Taktyk
Clément Vergely
Beal &
Blanckaert
Gaetan Le
Penhuel
Lina Ghotmeh
Atelier Pascal
Gontier
Platane & Ilic
Associates
Une Fabrique de la Ville
Urban planning - Programing
Wagon
Landscaping
Ingérop
VRD Infrastructure, Hydraulique, BIM
Jean-Paul Lamoureux
Lighting and Acoustics
KOZ
GROUPEMENT
NEXITY
EIFFAGE
CDC HABITAT
GROUPAMA
CoBe
CITEC
Mobility
Lambert-Lenack
SOA
Atelier Georges
DREAM
Barrault-Pressacco
Gaëlle Lauriot-Prévost
Design / Signage
Françoise Folacci
Accessibility
DEALERS
Denis Thélot
Security
Dealers
AMO
Concertation
Company
representatives
Residents

#11# **THE TEAM**

A WORKING TEAM SERVING THE OLYMPIC AND PARALYMPIC VILLAGE

The Paris Olympics is an exceptional sporting, media, and tourist event. In 2024, Paris will host delegations from over 200 countries, 10,500 Olympic athletes, and 4,300 Paralympic athletes. Hosting this globally significant event and designing the future village represent a considerable challenge.

With a shared vision of the Metropolis and through a complementarity of confirmed expertise, the Urban Master Planning team is highly mobilized to support SOLIDEO and all relevant communities in achieving a rare challenge in the metropolitan area: building a piece of city within 73 months, towards which the eyes of 4 billion viewers will be turned, and which will constitute, in its Legacy phase, a benchmark neighborhood rooted in its territory. The team comprises established entities with proven operational experience, and their production capabilities are tailored to the dynamics of such a large-scale project.

#13# **THE TEAM**

THE VILLAGE WORKSHOPS

To ensure the proper coherence of the urban project, the DPA / Une Fabrique de la Ville / TER consortium, with the support of INGEROP, aimed to make the city-making process a determining element of its design.

Common exchange sessions among the various design teams are therefore essential to ensure the definition of a coherent narrative and to avoid a "catalog" effect of decontextualized architectures for this new neighborhood that will emerge in less than 3 years.

An exceptional aspect for an urban project of such magnitude in Europe, the implementation of the Athletes' Village project is concentrated within an extremely short period, two to three times shorter than usual development operations.

An intense approach of "workshops" has thus guided the entire consultation phase of the consortia on sectors D and E, and exchanges with the teams responsible for sectors A and B. This iterative approach has continued and accelerated during the refinement phase of the winning projects.

#15# THE TEAM

THE VILLAGE WORKSHOPS

Photographs of the village workshops with the designers, SOLIDEO, and project owners during workshops and sample meetings.

Opening Interview #17#

conversation

between

Frédéric Prot

_historian

Dominique Perrault

_urban planner

Fréderic Prot : You designed the Athletes' Village for the upcoming Paris Olympic and Paralympic Games. Your experience led you to write a manual on urbanism.

Dominique Perrault : Yes, but without intending to make a magisterial statement. This manual presents the wealth of a vast project of urbanism. Through a series of drawings, photographs, models, maps, collages, visuals, and excerpts of texts; a whole arsenal of methods for representing the city. Everyone will be able to discover a thousand ways to write about the city and the material of which it is composed that I wish to make available to all.

FP : It seems to me that the idea of a manual rather than a monograph is linked to the meaning you give to the notion of heritage, highlighted by the Paris 2024 Olympic Games organizing committee and the client, the SOLIDEO Company. The term heritage is a formidable polysemy in that it can be associated either with the inertia of an inheritance, or the dynamicity of a transmission. It will in fact be at the end of the Olympiads when everything will begin, that the decisive transformation of the Village will get underway. At the end of an approximately two-year phase, the Grand Paris will receive its genuine heritage of the Games, that is a new, connected, integrated and mixed-use district. The Olympic Village is programmed to pivot on its axis and mutate. Its future, you say, is "beyond itself," beyond the Games and beyond its perimeter.

DP : This book facilitates our understanding of the city and the way it develops; a process that has been accelerated by the Games.

FP : Your manual of urbanism gathers the materials collected and elaborated for this project. A bracing material, I would say, and not a documentary archive. In this sense, I see the book as a database and an example of applied methodology for a anyone who seeks to understand how a new territory, a bit of the city, is conceived.

DP : Documents on urbanism are, in general, dry and quickly focus on a body of rather technocratic regulations intended for city planning. The representation they form lacks a sensitive dimension. What seems totally enthralling about this manual is that through these pages we enter an immersive space of creation, liberty, and perception.

Its visual apparatus, the methods of representation it enhances are going to enable sharing our way of working, the district's urban and metropolitan geographic tensions.

FP : Here, we have access to material for thought, to hypotheses, to possible attitudes in relation to the site, to the variety of its development programs, and to its architecture. The book is in an imaginative and stimulating format. A sort of workroom of urbanism's potential which starts with a precise analysis of a place, its history, and geography. There are no cursed places, as you like to say.

DP : Conducting research is a process of elaborating the strands of hypotheses that are going to last for varying periods of time. Hypotheses that are related and opposed to each other. Working in this way ensures strength because it is a holistic approach; everything is mutually nourishing. We produce critical material that we are going to evolve, adapt, and transpose. It is an intellectual process. Everything that is conceived intuitively or through reasoning is reread, rewritten, and reinterpreted to produce a book.

FP : This manual provides a window into the living material of an urban planning agency.

— — — — — — —

DP : The aim is to show that the production of this type of object, in this case an Olympic "Village" that can then revert to a metropolitan district, is a sensitive artistic and cultural undertaking.

— — — — —

FP : That too is related to the making-of.

DP : In the preparation of a film, there are always many rushes. The cinematographic metaphor is quite accurate. It is a question of dynamic images and editing. That is why the format of this manual, its mockup, lends itself to the intention driving us forward. Each of us is invited to appropriate it in our own way. In general, an urban masterplan always boils down to an aerial view of a site plan and to section drawings defining building heights. That is not how we work. We make sketches and models, and then test our ideas to define the project that best responds to the question posed.

— — — — —

Urbanism must spark transformations, the installation of new populations, and the development of new economies. That is how it becomes part of life.

— — — — — — — —

FP : This book is a data source, gathering informative and creative material to serve spatial planning. The research forms the basis for the work of assemblage and metabolization.

DP : Developments operate in an arborescent form. It is a rather exhilarating thing, even if the work is demanding, because thousands of documents had to be created, synthesized and collated in a very short timeframe for studies.

FP : The operation of fictionalizing a site, upstream from an urbanism project, is integral to the geographic understanding of a place. I am thinking about the development study that you conducted in Caen in the 1990s on the former site of the Société Métallurgique de Normandie. It involved renewing ties between nature and architecture, rethinking the polarity between the Orne Valley and the plateau of the steel mill, reviewing the network

Redevelopment of the Unimetal Site

Caen, France

Urban Studies and Project Management Assistance, International Competition, 1994-1997.

The challenge here is more geographical than historical. The disappearance of a wealth such as the Société Métallurgique de Normandie can generate new contributions that would give nature to the city. Identifying the riches or potentials of the place, and from there, defining what the future could be. Along the Orne River, a wide tree-lined avenue is just waiting to be bordered by the continuity of city buildings. On the plateau, the traces of the old SMN facilities guide and prefigure the lines that intertwine countryside and urbanization. At the top of the valley, the layout of an old road that crossed the factory only asks to be connected to neighboring districts. Trying to extract from each place what is most essential. Designing a large-scale project that combines different activities and can introduce other relationships with nature. The relationship between the plateau and the valley deserves protection, respect, and development. The problem is not absence but an abundance of land. The project of enhancing the city extends to the riverbanks and hillsides, and, by the same token, to the entire site.

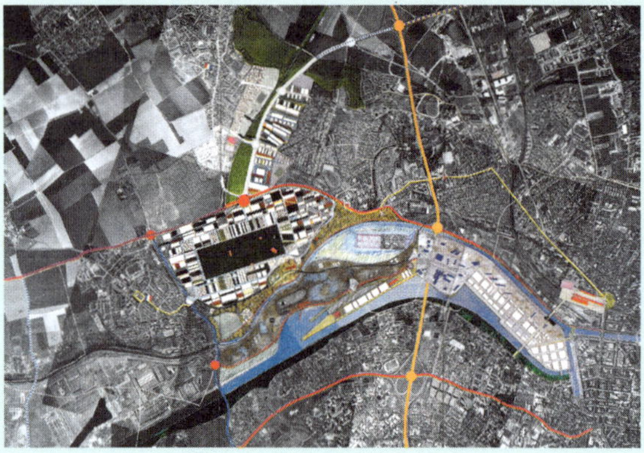

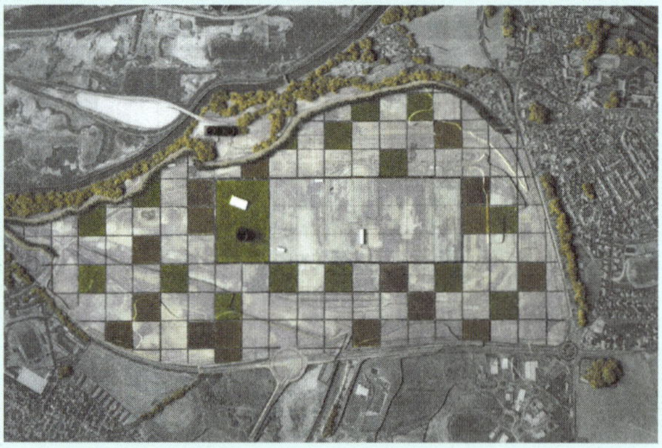

of links, the layout, and reconnecting the site with neighboring districts. Here, you already dealt with some of the issues later encountered at the Athletes' Village.

DP : But in other dimensions, because the site is spread across 200 hectares, or four times the area of the Village. We sought to reveal the most essential aspects with collages for example, showing how causing the Orne to leave its riverbed could result in a reconciliation between nature and the former industrial plateau. These fictions expressed a strategy, an attitude regarding the site.

FP : Here, positioning questions the relationship between urbanism and architecture.

DP : That is an important point. I would say that to define and write a city plan, one must be an architect to integrate and set up the architectural systems of such a plan. The design of the Village is situated in the realm of disciplinary mediation.

— — — — — —

I would speak of triggering urbanism that only an architect can implement. It is through this articulation that one can prefigure large-scale objects, as this book seeks to show.

— — — —

FP : Development fictions are decisive elements for representing the dimensions of a site.

DP : The stories we imagine are tools for understanding our "playing field." For example, "flooding" the Orne Valley is an act on a geographic scale. The valley lies in counterpart to the plateau where Unimétal stands. It plays a role in the general story and in the way to specify the site. Our manual of urbanism shows how to develop the overall shape of a project. We cannot launch the programming of hundreds of apartments without prefiguring them first, especially regarding the short timeframes imposed by the Village construction project. We must transmit the templates, to the builders of this housing stock and define the volumes, and placements so they can then freely develop their respective architecture and landscapes. It is a genuinely creative practice of urbanism.

FP : The challenge of the Village is the renewal of a site, more than the enhancing the value of land or buildings, and more than the renewal of spaces. It is not a question of reinitializing it, of undertaking a reset by starting with a blank page, but rather one of restoring a territory's links using another syntax. I see this reactivation as a process of reconnecting a place with its history, topography, broader geography, and landscapes. In this way, we can say that what changes it is architectural urbanism.

DP : The spirit of our Olympic entry was to take the Seine as the guiding thread and element unifying the different projects. The Village is one of the main projects that reveals it. There was no longer any relationship with the river. Everything was covered in concrete. Where was the Seine? The gash of the Route Departementale1 perpendicularly cut the riverbank off from the ensemble of the built complex. Unfortunately, this is still the case.

— — — — — —

The industrial infrastructure had flattened and erased the relief, leaving the topography unreadable. We enabled it to reemerge.

— — —

There is a 15-meter drop from the Saint-Denis–Pleyel hill-train station, currently being built by architect Kengo Kuma, down to the banks of the Seine. This is the natural incline. It is the rediscovery of the river and the original surface. You "descend" toward the Seine. So, I sought to create inviting and gently sloping perspectives, like the Mail Finot, which, with its terraced, splayed and green form is one of the main elements of the urban plan. Like the Allée de la Seine. Our work here aimed to create a calming effect. Thus, before redesigning the territory the land had to be reconfigured.

FP : The Village repairs a broken link by opening onto the wider river landscape. Restoring life to the river in the imaginary of Ile-de-France is an important metropolitan challenge. As are enhancing its visibility and accessibility, enlivening its banks, and reviving an urban sociability to promote the well-being of inhabitants. The decision to have the opening ceremony parade of athletes on the Seine is quite a symbol. In a way, the Olympic Village also fulfills the wish for a reconciliation between infrastructures, landscape and architecture.

DP : The Ile-de-France has a highly developed hydrographic system consisting of the river, its tributaries, canals, lakes, and ponds. It is a marvelous asset and resource for the metropolis of Grand Paris and its identity, culture, and economy. There are more than sixty commercial ports and marinas. If we think in terms of a sustainable metropolis, we can only deplore the spoiled sections of its riverbanks, owing to geographic dissension, and a poor culture of the city and the territory. Landscape continuities are often incomprehensible. Yet there is extraordinary potential for mutations along the 200 kilometers of the Seine, Marne, Oise, and Yonne as well as the canals, along which the activity and habitat of Ile-de-France are concentrated.

FP : Among the fictions presented in the book, we can see that residential and business islands transpose the image of great urban vessels, at their moorings.

DP : JI was absolutely determined to reconnect and increase the number of perpendicular links with the river. It was not a question of morphology, or forms, but rather of integrating architecture that could draw on the preexisting geography we had just revealed. Everything is enhanced by elements of the programs as well as research on environmental performance.

We had to be stubborn about the layouts of places because they were growing out of an older plan. A network began to emerge from this, manifesting itself through these city blocks marching down to the river.

FP : The landscaped grid of the Athletes' Village is comprised of two grand perpendicular paths to the Seine and two parallels that strengthen the urban continuity with the southwest part of old Saint-Ouen and its Dockyards, and the Pleyel district to the east. The Village road network echoes the site's earlier industrial grid. We can also see the correlation of the city block templates with the industrial buildings that structured the site in the 20th century.

DP : The aim of the mission entrusted to us was the transformation of an industrial brownfield into a new urban district straddling the towns of Saint-Denis and Saint-Ouen. The location is interesting in that it engages the entire region. It speaks to us of history because on this former industrial site, there are major and perfectly preserved infrastructures, interesting architecture, like the Halle Maxwell, and what is today the Cité du Cinéma.

FP : The electrical industry grew up in this area of Saint-Ouen / Saint-Denis to take advantage of the river as a logistics tool for materials and merchandise transport, beginning as early as 1830. That was the period when the Saint-Ouen docks were built. Loading cranes stood along the quays where the barges moored. Thus, organically linking the industrial heritage to the river required a specific analysis of the site.

DP : One of the resources comprising a development plan is what already exists onsite. This includes remaining structures, the street grid, the context with all its components. The approach is to "do with" and abandon nothing. Here, the entire territory is interested in the repurposed and celebrated project. The other source is city planning, or the programming of the site in anticipation of its evolution. In the first phase of its existence, the Village will welcome some 14,500 athletes and their entourages.

From the urban design phase, the objective was to simultaneously prefigure a mixed-use district that would not be retrenched inside its perimeter but connected to its immediate surroundings and that would also host the Olympic family.

FP : Historically, this receptivity of the Village to its own mutation into a metropolitan district is a rare, almost unheard project for Olympic villages.

DP : The long-term intention is for it to dissolve into the urban fabric, be a participant, lead it forward, and nurture it in a way that integrates it into the territory, like a successful graft.

FP : Dealing with what is "already there," building the city atop the city, means metabolizing certain elements of identity – whether visible or erased – inside a form, and with a language that will reimagine them without paraphrasing them. Here, it is a set of gaps inside a system of agreements. Architectural events and urban improvements are going to be subtracted from the root system of this "already there," and which are, in some way, the possible futures extracted from it. To repurpose a place is to imbue it with affects that resonate with new uses.

— — — — — — —

DP : We can only dialogue with a site if we do so with a critical vision. Only then can the work begin in earnest. We decide everything with this attitude! If it is sincere, an architectural and urbanistic statement is a critical act.

— — —

FP : The Bibliothèque Nationale de France is one of your most emblematic achievements. This project, which you drove from 1988 on, was paired with a grand urban redevelopment plan for the east side of Paris, from the Gare d'Austerlitz to the beltway.

DP : Yes, it gradually revealed over 2.5 kilometers of riverbank. Prior to that there was only the rail network, warehouses and vacant lots. The project was part of a public policy of rebalancing the capital between the east and the west sides. The political agreement involving the mayor of Paris, Jacques Chirac, and then President François Mitterrand, led to the cession of municipal property for the purpose of building the future grand national library and to develop a larger district around it along the banks of the Seine. At the time, close to a quarter of the riverfront's length inside Paris proper was not at all urbanized.

— — — — — — —

FP : During the same period, you were working on issues of urban integration and metropolitan identities and lifestyles in two other cities. First in Nantes, between 1992 and 1995, followed by Bordeaux. Their challenges are at the intersection of the those treated at the BnF and the Village.

— — — — — — — —

DP : For Jean-Marc Ayrault, the young mayor of Nantes, the necessity arose for a redeployment of the city. The project grew out of a critical analysis that set out to reconquer the city's islands. At the time, Nantes was traumatized by the closure of its shipyards. Thousands of jobs were lost. The sites were abandoned. The goal here was to regenerate the Ile de Nantes, future heart of the modern city, by integrating it into a strategic vision in terms of urbanism, which was to enhance this historical city by projecting it into its metropolitan dimension. Thus, new peripheral zones will be marshalled to transform the urban entity and its method of governance.

Urban Redevelopment of Ile Sainte-Anne

Nantes, France

Competition, Winning Project 1992, Development Mission 1992-1999

To define an approach and an urban design capable of guiding the future of Ile Sainte-Anne, facing the historic center of the city and at the head of the Loire estuary, Mr. Jean Marc Ayrault, Member of Parliament, and Mayor of Nantes, decided to launch a study mission. The exploratory study aims, first and foremost, to gather and organize the reference principles that will guide the debates and reflections prompted by such a subject. This prospective approach indeed concerns a very important territory and particularly significant issues for the city and its river. The proposals formulated are based on a comprehensive analysis of historical and geographical data, on the measurement of the site and on several aspects of its landscape. They are also informed by the examination of previous studies and by hearing from representatives of the relevant institutions, companies, and resident associations. The deep objective pursued here is to initiate a progressive and dynamic urban planning approach, open to future contributions and demanding in terms of the cultural and social values that will guide future transformations.

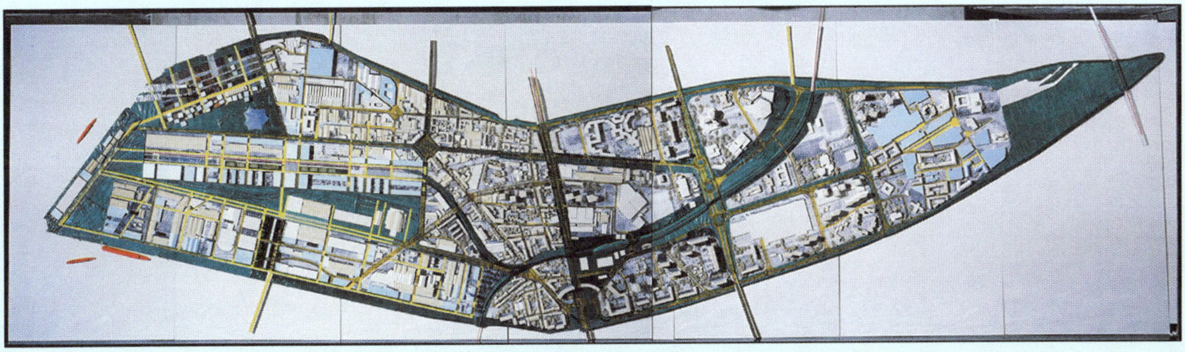

Development of the Two Banks of the Garonne

Bordeaux, France

Consultation for the Winning Project, Development Mission 1992-1999

Urban development concept for both banks of the Garonne, downtown development of the right bank through the revitalization of industrial wastelands (400 hectares). Establishment of a database (studies, interviews); urban analysis (history and geography); urban project: 12 intervention sequences along the Garonne; development of the master plan for the study area (Urban Community of Bordeaux). Development of the land use plan for different sectors (City of Bordeaux). This study led to a public exhibition inaugurated by Jacques Delmas, Mayor of Bordeaux, in 1994 at Arc en rêve, Center for Architecture.

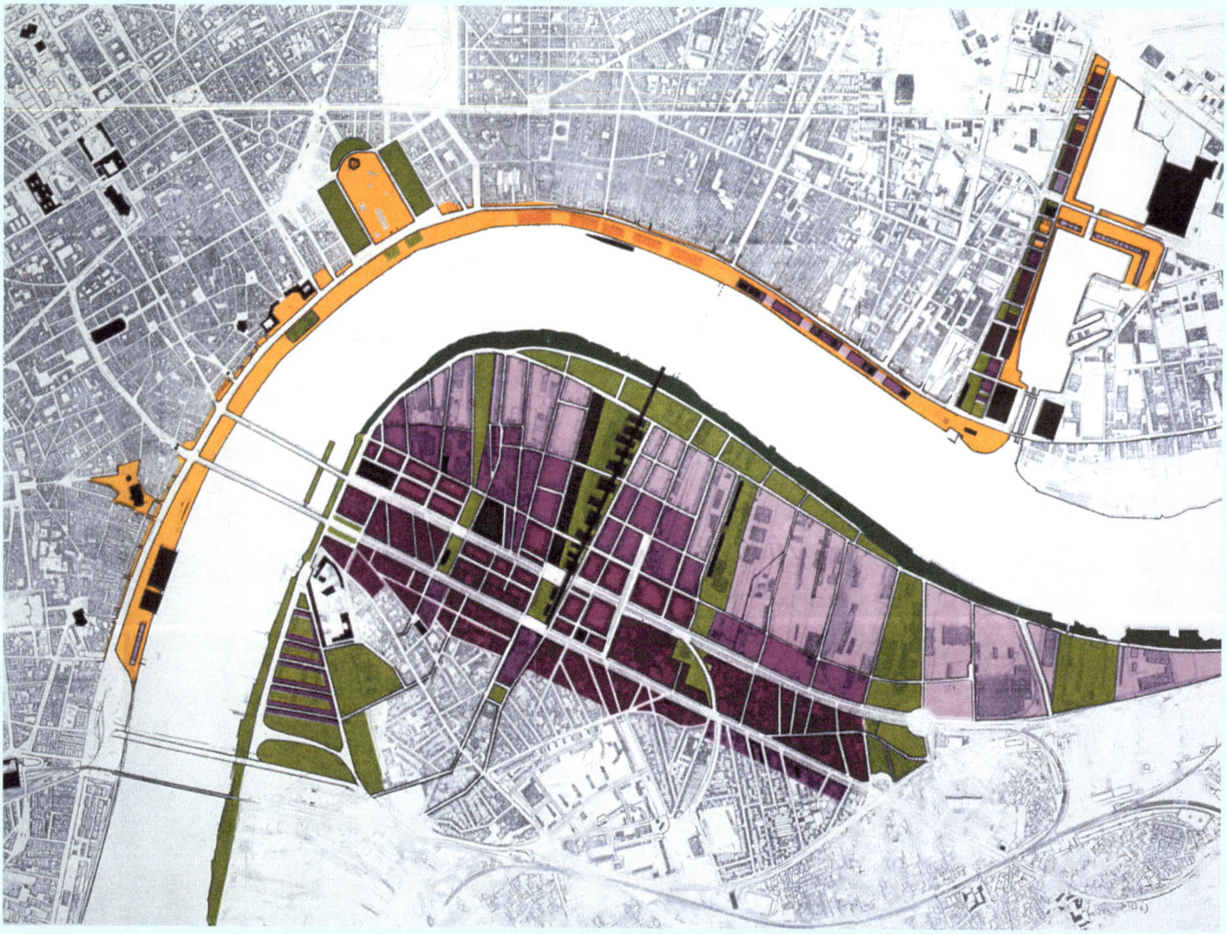

FP : Several planning and development studies that you conducted questioned the synergy between river and metropolitan restructuring, in urban configurations that remind one of the Olympic Village. You articulate development and optimization of riverfronts and landscapes, enhancement of the industrial heritage and urban ecology, like the pilot project “Bordeaux des deux rives” (both riverbanks of Bordeaux), which is comparable to the project in Nantes, and facing similar challenges..

DP : In Bordeaux, the aim was to reconquer nearly 500 hectares of brownfields on the right bank of the Gironde. The masterplan was imagined with the objective of organizing the view in relation to the limestone city on the left bank opposite. Like in Nantes, the city is destined to expand onto new lands, or perhaps to even reach its final limit. Here, the core issue was the metropolitan challenge of integration and rescaling. Indeed, this program is underway in all French metropolises, respecting their geographic diversity. It is noteworthy that their modes of governance are clearer, more democratic, and citizen-based than that of Grand Paris, where governance functions arduously.

FP : In both Nantes and Bordeaux, the public commission emanated from genuine planning-oriented governance, to which the future of the Athletes' Village still depends for its completion as a mixed-use and sustainable district. Development studies methodize the work of renewing urban zones that lack territorial integration, or that have fallen to the state. This is precisely the challenge of the Village.

DP : Urbanism engages the full range of past, present and future arrangements that can be implemented to increase the possibilities for cooperating on issues concerning the shared territory. We can view this as a process for creating an endlessly renewing purpose. It is also geography being organized around mobility networks of diverse and varied intensities.

For example, the Grand Paris Express is an infrastructure that will serve over one hundred stations slated for construction. A bus, metro, tramway and cycling network will cover the map of the metropolis, creating a new tissue of root systems.

Here, we are speaking about something totally new and innovative. The rapid emergence of the Village will take advantage of the future Saint-Denis–Pleyel train station. Thus, urbanism focuses more on the spaces between things than on the things themselves.

FP : In both architecture and urbanism, spacing and its precise positioning is the key to ensuring that everything holds together.

DP : Urban planning is political. It is concerned with spacing, and is the

Exposition "Metro! Le grand Paris en mouvement"

Paris, France

Exhibition at the Cité de l'architecture et du patrimoine, November 2023 – June 2024

Dominique Perrault, alongside Francis Rambert, is the co-curator of the exhibition 'Metro! The Grand Paris in Motion,' presented from November 8, 2023, to June 2, 2024, at the City of Architecture and Heritage. Dedicated to the Grand Paris Express, this exhibition will reveal to visitors one of the most significant infrastructure and architectural projects in the world. All arts, from illustration to cinema, are summoned to narrate, through the prism of the metro, the construction of the Grand Paris and the transformation of this territory in the era of ecological transition.

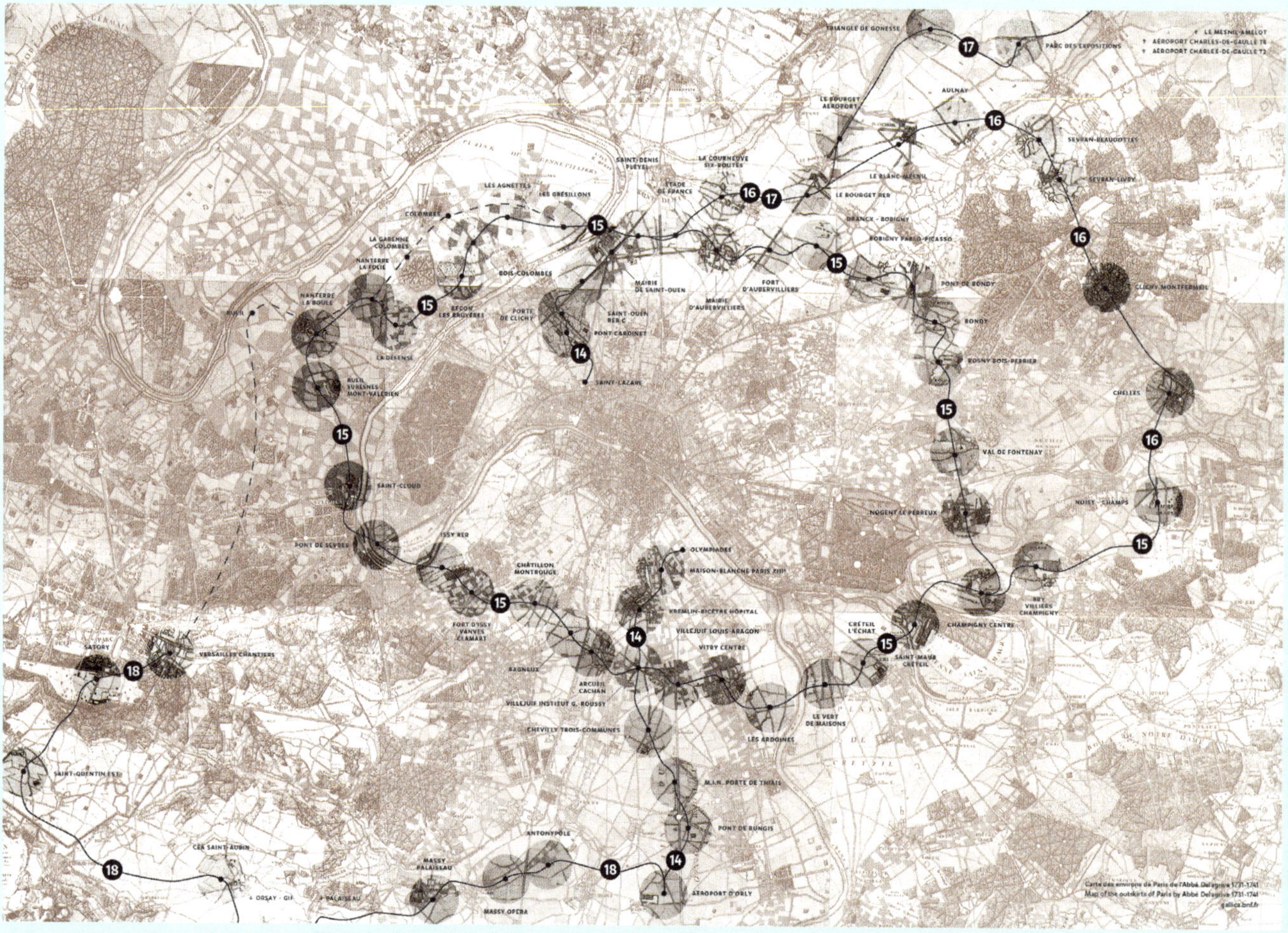

programming of the plan. Therefore, it is linked to the commission, to the extent planning exist.

— — — — — — —

Urban design on the other hand is closer to us. It is used to implement urban strategies, the presence of nature, and systems complementing what exists, either to strengthen them, or to produce solutions for new uses.

— — — — —

How do we weave these links and connect them in a durable way?

FP : Among your projects— built or unbuilt, past and present— are Olympic. I am thinking about the Berlin Velodrome and Swimming Pool when that city was competing to host the 2000 Summer Games. The terrain chosen was at the intersection of mobility networks and urban fabrics. The challenge was to achieve the junction of these systems to weld together the capital's East and the West.

DP : Architectural programs do not in themselves generate urban qualities. Planning is indispensable for supervising their placement. This was the case in Berlin. The two Olympic facilities you cite, in the Prenzlauer Berg district, were part of a pro-active metropolization plan for this sector of the capital, celebrating the fall of the Wall and unification.

FP : Reminder. In 2007, Madrid was vying to hold the 2016 Summer Games. You won the competition to build the future Olympic Tennis Center— la Caja mágica, the Magic Box— whose construction was completed in May 2009. A focus on the landscape guided this project as much as on the equally spectacular London VeloPark in 2012. In July of 2016, you participated in the international competition to design and build the future Beijing Olympic Ice-skating Rink for the 2022 Winter Games. This work represents an exceptional urban opportunity because the challenge is to create a new gateway to the Forested Park of the Chinese capital and to the city's central axis. Here more than a new architectural object, you designed a landscape. Beyond the Games, one of the objectives of this sports facility is also to stimulate the city's social life of in this place. We know that since 1992 in Barcelona, the Olympic Games are seen as accelerators of urban transformation and metropolitan development. The Games boost the development of the territory, becoming part of their heritage.

DP : It must be noted that the Olympic deadline is not in synch with the pace of the city. It is only several years after the Olympic flame is extinguished that we will be able to evaluate the success of this type of program and its territorial organicity. The history of the games demonstrates that Olympic villages have always been complexes designed to revert almost immediately after the athletes' departure to the regular real estate market.

Velodrome and Olympic Swimming Pool

Berlin, Germany

International competition, winning project 1992, completion of velodrome November 1997 / swimming pool November 1999

This project is linked to the reunification of the two Germanies and the candidacy of a city poised to become the capital, Berlin, for the 2000 Olympic Games. The chosen site is located at the intersection of urban networks and fabrics. To successfully connect these systems, the two buildings housing the velodrome and the Olympic swimming pool disappear. With the question of form thus removed, the project could address other concerns. The urban idea is to create a green space of a significant scale and within this green space, to implant... let's call them buildings. In Berlin, there is a deposit of a mixture of nature and architecture. And this mixture is a form of work that can be developed in the city. The idea was to create an orchard. That is, to plant apple trees. When approaching this orchard, one discovers, embedded in the ground, protruding to about one meter in height, two tables... One round, the other rectangular, covered with a metallic fabric that vibrates with the sunlight and resembles more water features than buildings.

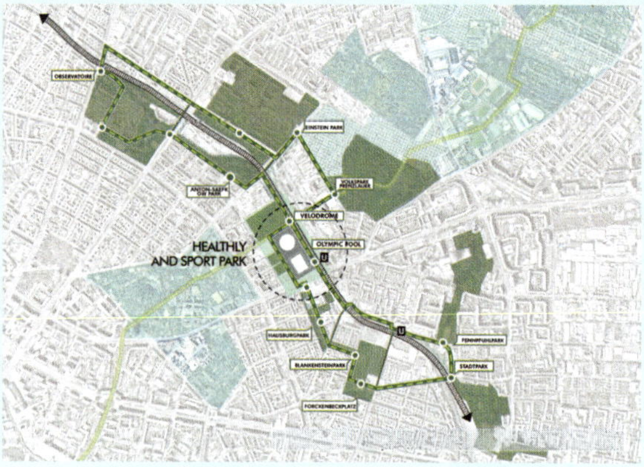

Lu Jia Zui Financial District of Pudong

Shanghai, China

International competition, 1992-1993 – won urban planning scheme

An iconic visual approach in Lujiazui concentrates office buildings into two narrow strips of skyscrapers, forming an L-shaped structure that mirrors the curve of the Huangpu River. The project highlights the old Bund on the west bank, embracing the curvature of the Huangpu with its rectilinear modernism.

Program:

- Urban development (urban analysis, urban development schemes)
- Riverside development in Pu Dong
- Development of a new central business district in the city of Shanghai.

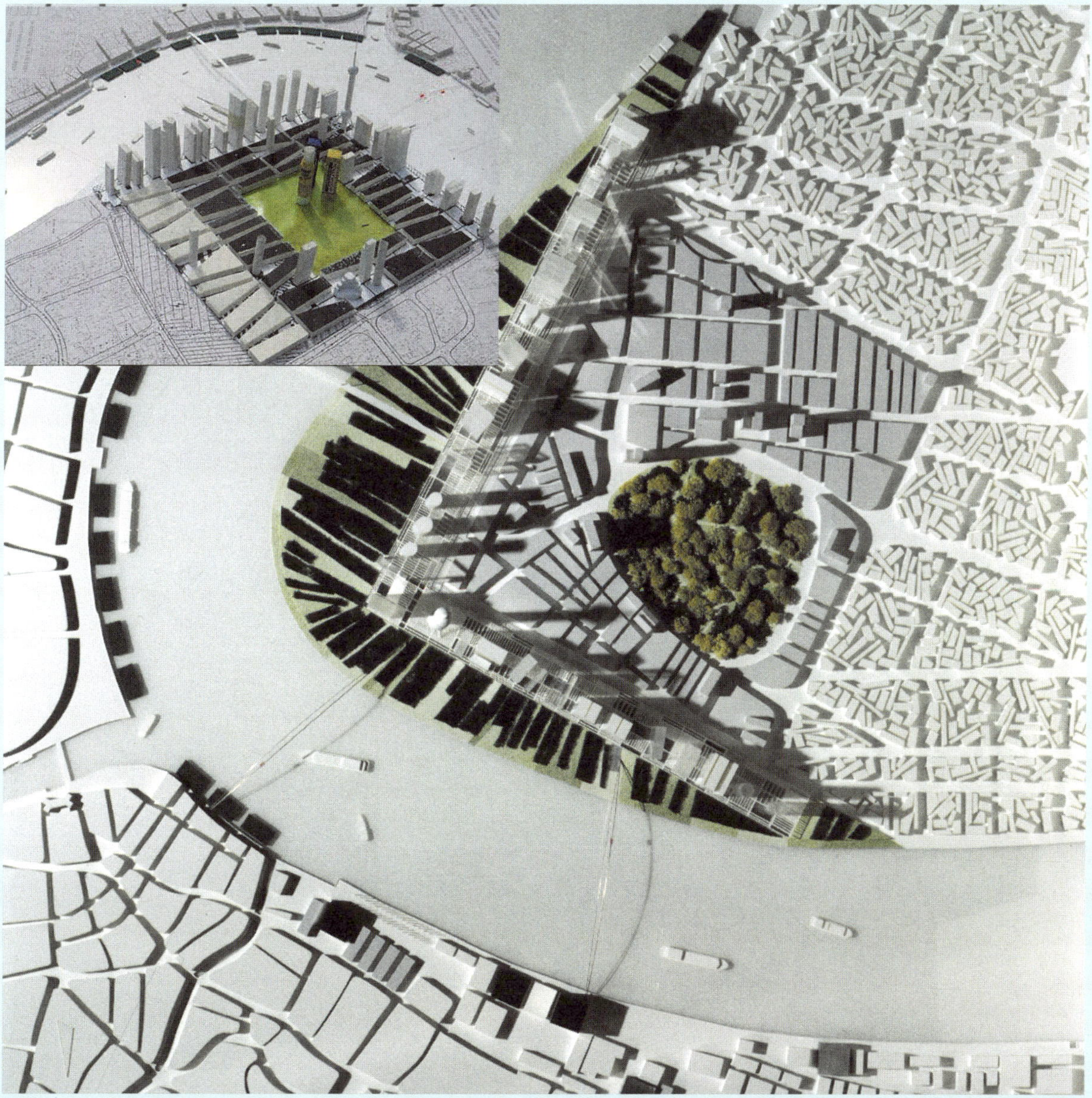

Exhibition "Metropolis",

Venice Architecture Biennale

Venise, Italy

French Pavilion of the Venice Architecture Biennale, 2010

In 2010, Dominique Perrault was appointed as the commissioner of the French Pavilion at the 12th Venice Architecture Biennale. By choosing "Metropolis" as the theme, Perrault proposed a reflection and interpretation that underpinned and nourished the genesis of the 21st-century metropolis. Firstly, by highlighting the transition from the City (urban unity, defined space, built form) to the Metropolis, a territory alternating between fullness and emptiness. Secondly, by demonstrating that emptiness is a space that connects much more than it separates; it appears as the building material of the metropolis. Finally, by illustrating his argument through 5 urban territories undergoing profound transformation, offering a fantastic catalogue of "possibilities".

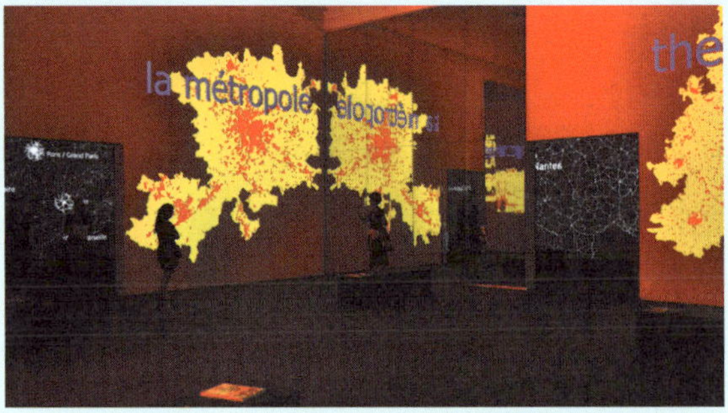

Our approach is substantially different on the Saint-Ouen/Saint-Denis site because it is during the design phase that the program's reversibility is organized into a metropolitan district. Here, we enter the open-ended phase of urbanism.

FP : Contrary to the Potemkin villages lacking integration with urban life that characterized several past Olympic projects, this district is a referent for a forward-looking Grand Paris. The mutations in the department of Seine-Saint-Denis are turning it into one of the most remarkable projects on their territory. In this geographic zone, its success will depend on the ability of public authorities to eradicate poverty, property fallen to the state, and exclusionary inequalities. An important part of the destiny of Grand Paris will depend on how we deal with these issues.

DP : Absolutely. Whether it is in investment or operations, as the developer and awarding authority, 80% of the SOLIDEO's public financing is directed toward the department of Seine-Saint-Denis. This is the department where 47 of the 64 built, supervised or renovated Olympic facilities are concentrated.

FP : The Athletes' Village is exemplary in several ways, including its reversibility, performance, metropolitan character, continuum, and size.

DP : The Village commission brief was very clear. It required the completion of a circumstance-specific site to host athletes with the further aim of a Heritage phase. Building envelopes will remain the same, but the entire interior functioning, layouts and cellular structure of the athletes' housing are going to be redesigned to create apartments, studios, offices and places for a range of activities.

We succeeded in implementing genuine flexibility in an adaptable and receptive urban structure without exorbitant investments. The reversible Village will be the heritage bequeathed by the Games but I would add it is the whole question of reversibility in architecture and urbanism as well. It participates in our cites' future and is expected at the end of the track.

FP : In August 2018 your firm won the competition to manage the Olympic and Paralympic Village project. The pace was more than brisk., You had to build an urban architectural ensemble of outsize dimensions, in less than two years.

DP : The transition from the design phase to the operational one took place in a continuum. We advanced from the plan to the construction of the plan by gathering the architects, landscape architects, engineers, construction companies, investors and developers around the table.

FP : The mission consisted of placing in the urban plan of the municipalities of Saint-Ouen–Saint-Denis the work of the nineteen firms selected to build the Village. The task of this project phase was to define the public spaces, the four superblocks of housing and activities, and to determine the programmatic adaptability of the built area in its Olympic phase and its reversibility in its Heritage phase. The key step was the filing of twenty-seven applications for construction permits, drawn up between April and June of 2020. Dual-status permits were invented by the territorial public authority of the Plaine Commune. This secured private investors by making it possible by means of a single and unique authorization, to simultaneously build an Olympic village and immediately project its post Games mutation into a district of the city.

DP : The filing of construction permit applications was the intersection where everyone involved came together. All companies participating in the building of the district, all project managers, had to meet to set up the process organizing how the district would be built and the construction of the facilities. The district designer's role ended there.

FP : Did you worry about a heterogeneity of architectural projects, a sort of "World's Fair" syndrome with buildings designed as architecture firms' flagship pavilions? What room for maneuver did you have to ensure that everyone could participate in a comprehensive urbanism project?

DP : No. The masterplan presented a very clearly traced out vision with this image of big buildings like ships organized perpendicular to the river.

For each big ship, or big building, there was a captain, or rather an architect, whose mission was to harmonize and ensure the cohesion and coherence of the team and the block.

Thus, these superblocks were a unifying element the same way the ground floor podiums were going to condition, install and finally create, a sort of base for the buildings. That is how everything was able to function without harming the specific character of each ensemble.

FP : You took the initiative to create a workshop on urbanism and architecture so that team synergy could ensure the cohesion of multiple works.

DP : The platform was a place enabling all actors to meet and work together. The workshop proved to be effective not only for managing the Village building program but also for the two municipalities. Like a double trigger, it could be handed over to them as a shared heritage. I am thinking here about the Plaine Commune. This workshop existed because we insisted upon it and because it was necessary. In the rush of execution, each firm, architect, and project head focused on his or her own project, without knowing what was being done "across the street." What each one was imagining and building could not be reduced to the scale of a building.

— — — — — —

That is why I created this "thousand hands" urbanism workshop, so the forty of us could come together and the architects could bring their models and discuss their projects. Our role was to support and facilitate sharing this overarching vision, and enable each of to be nurtured in an iterative way. It was a thoroughly unique experience.

— — — — — — —

FP : Through its visual data, way of perceiving, designing, and proceeding, the methodology resulting from this workshop also perfectly translates your urbanism manual. The Athletes' Village is currently France's main mono-site construction project. I readily appreciate it as a double case study. On one hand it is part of an innovative, mixed-use pilot district where the livability of future metropolises is being imagined, while on the other, a model of an urbanism project struggling with the shortcomings, contradictions, planning deficiencies, governance mechanisms, and urban culture of the commission. In this, the Village is having the effect of revealing enclaves, which is not the least significant part of its heritage. You once told me that these obstacles needed to be removed with a crowbar. We understand this necessary work of extraction regarding development policy. Beyond the Village, the aim is to overcome obstacles to building the city and the metropolis.

— — — — — —

DP : This district is making it possible to restructure several elements and to implement a sort of update. It obliges us to take another step forward, or to the side, in our questioning of its territorial connections, as an antidote to a zoning policy.

— — — — — —

FP : The notion of tension is crucial in your urbanist's analysis of the territory. The dialectic, polarities, and connections. Developing the territory requires eliciting structures in tension and intensifications. In 2013, you produced an Atlas of 100 metropolitan tensions; 100 examples of urban ecosystems that could thrive with greater autonomy; 100 interventions aiming for a cohesive and inclusive Grand Paris. Can we not also design the Olympic Village as a "Hôtel Métropole" with the purpose of becoming a catalyst for urban and metropolitan identities and lifestyles?

In the masterplan you designed for the development of the Hangang District, which you already spoke about – and which notably won you the international competition launched by the city of Handan in 2020 – you talk about a methodology that can be transposed to other sites and other contexts. Among this masterplan's four main principles of intervention, I notice the development

"Hotel Metropole" -AIGP

Paris, France

International Workshop
of Greater Paris, 2012

Dominique Perrault has been a member of the scientific council of the AIGP since 2012. The proposal of the "Metropolis Hotel" device is the result of various reflections on the metropolis: the assertion that the metropolis is not a city, the analysis of dwelling, the tensioning of what is already there, and the ambition to develop a device that can accompany the metropolitan phenomenon both urgently and cautiously. "The Metropolis Hotel" is a minimal device in terms of resources, accommodating existing land, pending their potential mutation, allowing the testing of the potential of a fabric, trying to gently infiltrate urbanity, rather than imposing a city model a priori.

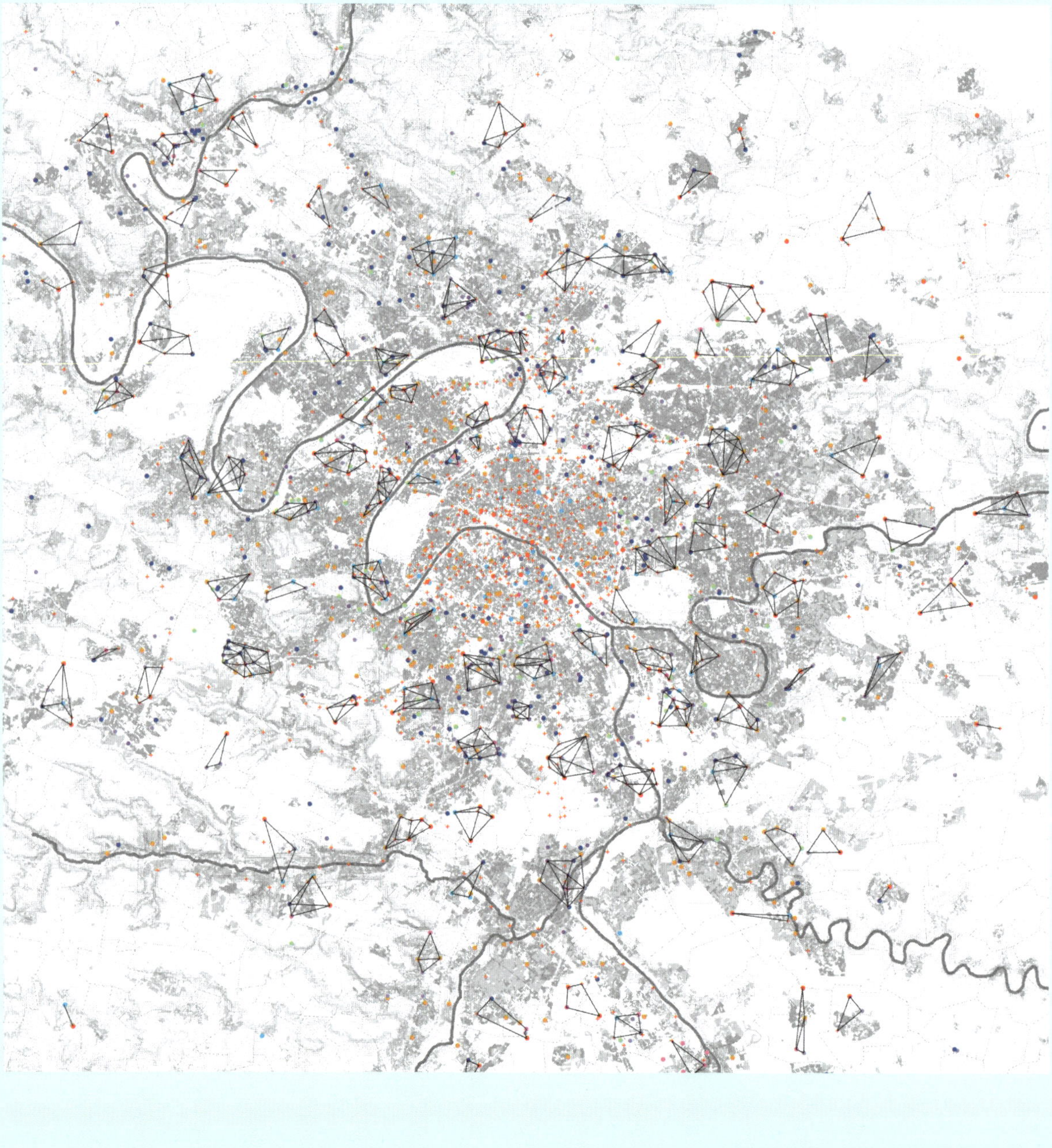

of mixed-use, connected, and flexible programs relying precisely on this concept of the "Hôtel Métropole." What interested me in this approach to city planning is the idea of using it to generate an ecosystem, gently infiltrating urban life rather than imposing an a priori city model. To be more specific, the Hôtel Métropole is a place of temporary residence for populations of varying profiles, including students, foreign researchers, young families, business tourists, and mobile workers. Therefore, the Olympic Village is related to this concept in that it welcomes international athletes and their entourage. You also define the Hôtel Métropole as an incubator of urban lifestyles and a strategy of resilience for the entire Ile-de-France region through the implementation of a network. Notably, how does one invent a district through its public spaces? They represent nearly half the area the Olympic Village that will become the future metropolitan district.

— — — — — — —

Residents are the interpreters of these places. It is they who bring them to life. The urbanist develops an open work, available for possible futures, which nevertheless has its specific character and logic of construction that gives it coherence.

— — — — —

Let us say that its structures are both complete and unfinished. Without a final definition. The urban fabric reacts like an interpreting organism.

Disons que ses structures sont à la fois complètes et inachevées. Sans définition ultime. Le tissu urbain réagit comme un organisme à l'action de l'interprète.

DP : To ensure availability in the plan, for this interpretation of the map, we must venture "beyond" the question of development stricto sensu.

— — — — — — —

I wish this manual of urbanism to provide an overview of the freedom and multiplicity of expressions that elaborate a project for a district. This going beyond the subject, which we are calling the "double," nurtures all the thinking and representations of the creative work underlying the masterplan.

— — —

This new map, posing the new district in its area, can only be understood through the process that brought it into being. The book A Village and its double describes an epiphany. In this manual, designed for everyone, missing, or forgotten pages can be added by others. Unfinished, because the process is not intended to stop, but on the contrary, to grow. New populations and generations will come and integrate the multipolar metropolis.

Master Plan of the Hangang District

Handan, China

International Invitational Competition, Winning Project 2020

The study conducted by Dominique Perrault develops a strategy for urban development that is both adaptable and flexible. The area in question, which represents approximately a quarter of the historical city's area, consists of highly heterogeneous built elements and significant industrial heritage. This heritage formed the starting point of the urban project, as did the geographical reality of the site, which guided the design process and the functioning of the new district. The proposal does not seek to standardize, but rather to coexist and interact a variety of elements to compose a new coherent territory. The project primarily highlights the urban aspect of the industrial heritage: the rehabilitation and reuse of the site's old circulation routes in particular define a new network for the district. The study particularly emphasized the feasibility and phasing of the development of the sector, as well as soil decontamination strategies.

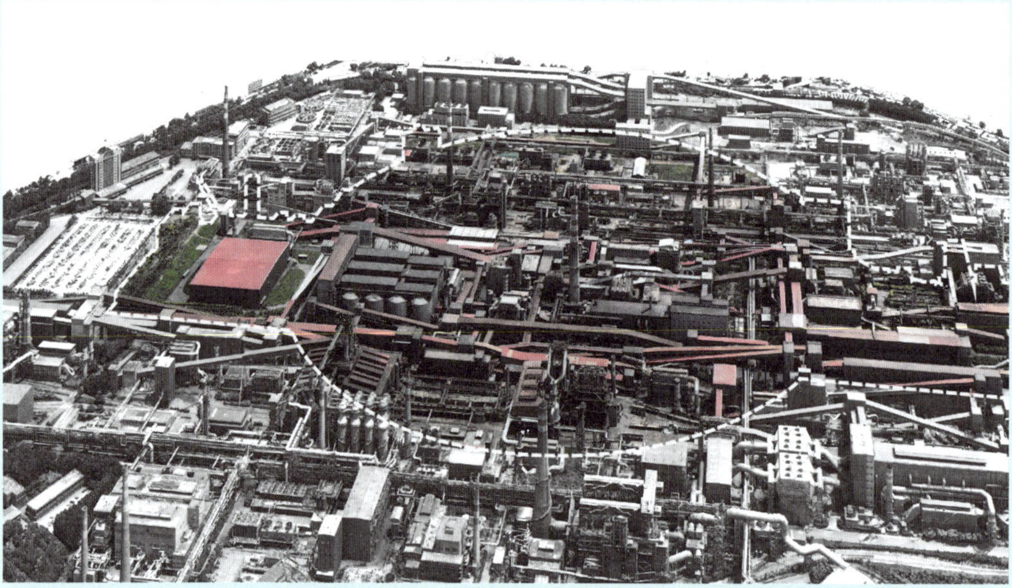

Olympic Village

Kitzbühel, Austria

International Competition, September 1997

Bid for the 2006 Winter Olympic Games. The planning principle involves organizing a public space around each building, such as a square, an esplanade, or a mall. This concern to accompany each of the developments with urban planning adds quality to the site during the Olympic Games period but also outlines the urban composition lines for the neighborhood after the Games. This gathering place can be used for events and activities planned around the sporting competitions. Similarly, to provide a pleasant landscaped environment for each of the sites, trees will be planted in geometric shapes, as if to "grow" the city with its building blocks around the sports facility and its esplanade. (Extract from the 1997 competition text)

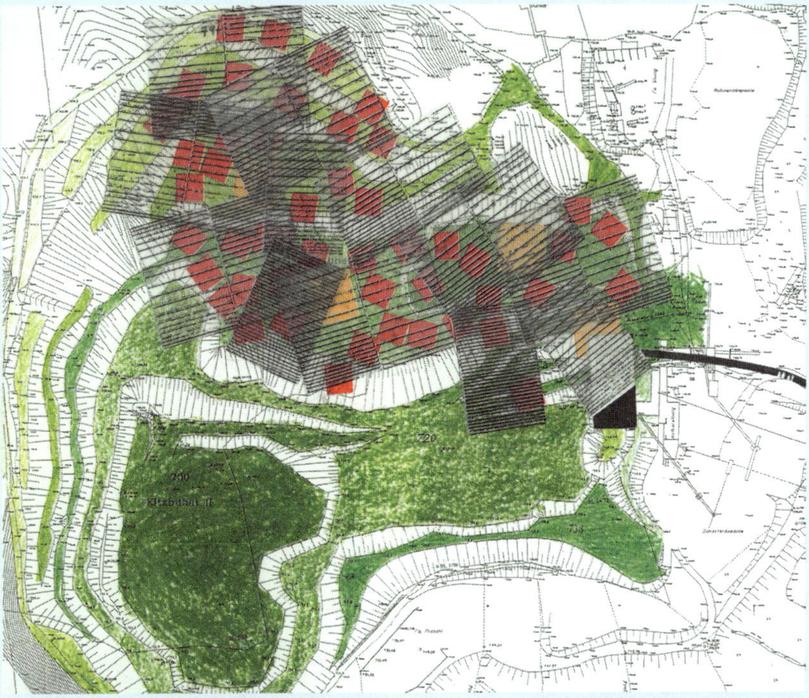

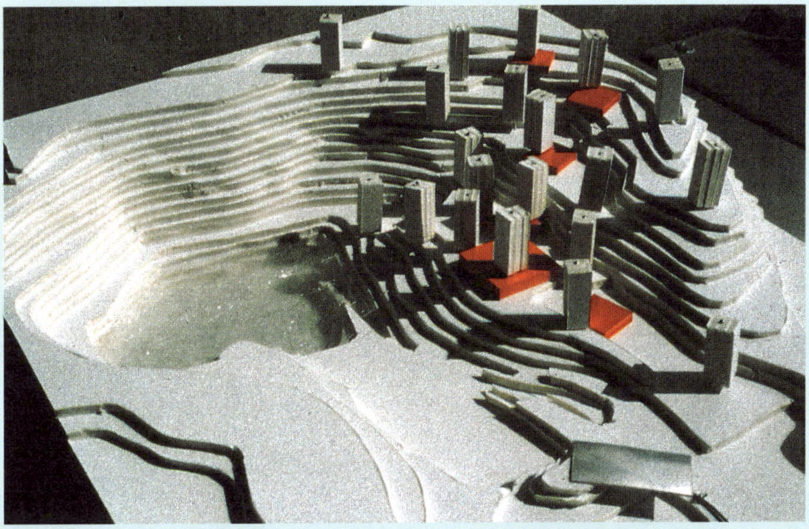

The Proposal #41#

The Athlete's Village

Ambitious Goals

As part of Paris' sustainability strategy for the facilities built for Paris 2024, public spaces are designed with the aim of adapting the city to the climate of 2050. The project meets ambitious sustainability goals: its carbon footprint is controlled, its design integrates climate issues (such as flooring, presence of vegetation and water in public spaces...) and aims to contribute to the enhancement and development of ecosystems.

Furthermore, the choice of materials for public spaces aims to limit the urban heat island effect and presents the best compromise between architectural intent, cost, maintenance, durability, permeability, and ease of access for people with reduced mobility. The issue of soil sealing has been addressed upstream of public spaces, contributing to the orientation of architectural and landscaping choices, with the goal of improving stormwater management.

Beyond work on public spaces, the urban morphology of the blocks also contributes to the cooling of public spaces by promoting air currents. The layout of public spaces alternates between sunny and shaded areas, well-ventilated areas, and areas open to a variety of uses.

Thirteen ambitions guided the project.

#45# **THE PROPOSAL**

First models, 1:1000, 2019.

#49# **THE PROPOSAL**

MIPIM model, 2019.

The 13 design points of the Olympic and Paralympic Village

Ambitious Goals

As part of Paris' sustainability strategy for the facilities built for Paris 2024, public spaces are designed with the aim of adapting the city to the climate of 2050. The project meets ambitious sustainability goals: its carbon footprint is controlled, its design integrates climate issues (such as flooring, presence of vegetation and water in public spaces...) and aims to contribute to the enhancement and development of ecosystems.

Furthermore, the choice of materials for public spaces aims to limit the urban heat island effect and presents the best compromise between architectural intent, cost, maintenance, durability, permeability, and ease of access for people with reduced mobility. The issue of soil sealing has been addressed upstream of public spaces, contributing to the orientation of architectural and landscaping choices, with the goal of improving stormwater management.

Beyond work on public spaces, the urban morphology of the blocks also contributes to the cooling of public spaces by promoting air currents. The layout of public spaces alternates between sunny and shaded areas, well-ventilated areas, and areas open to a variety of uses.

Thirteen ambitions guided the project.

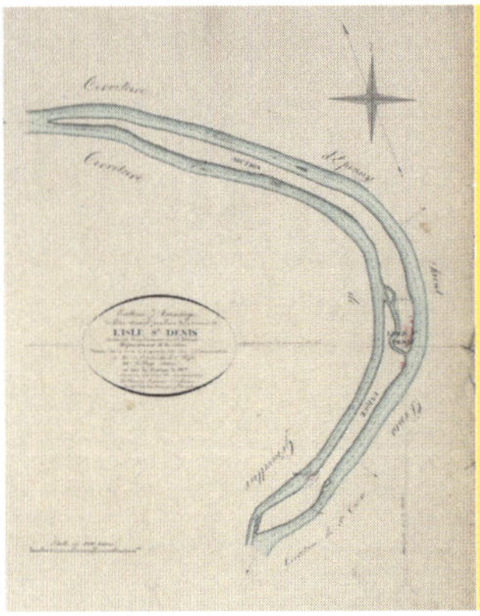

#54#

AMBITION 1
TERRITORIAL ANCHORING

#54#

AMBITION 2
URBAN IDENTITY

#54#

AMBITION 3
THE REVERSIBLE CITY

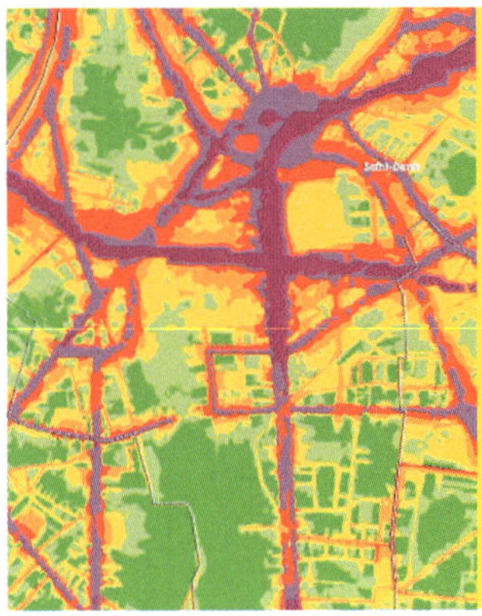

#54#

AMBITION 4-5
CLIMATE IN 2050
&
CARBON FOOTPRINT MANAGEMENT

#54#

AMBITION 6
ENERGY AND PRODUCTIVITY IN THE CITY

#54#

AMBITION 7
MOBILITY AND UNIVERSAL ACCESSIBILITY

#55#

AMBITION 8
WATER AND SOIL

#55#

AMBITION 9
BIODIVERSITY IN URBAN AREAS

#55#

AMBITION 10
SPORT IN THE CITY

#55#

AMBITION 11
URBAN FURNITURE AND LIGHTING 2050

#55#

AMBITION 12
CHORAL ARCHITECTURE

#55#

AMBITION 13
THE HEART OF THE HEART

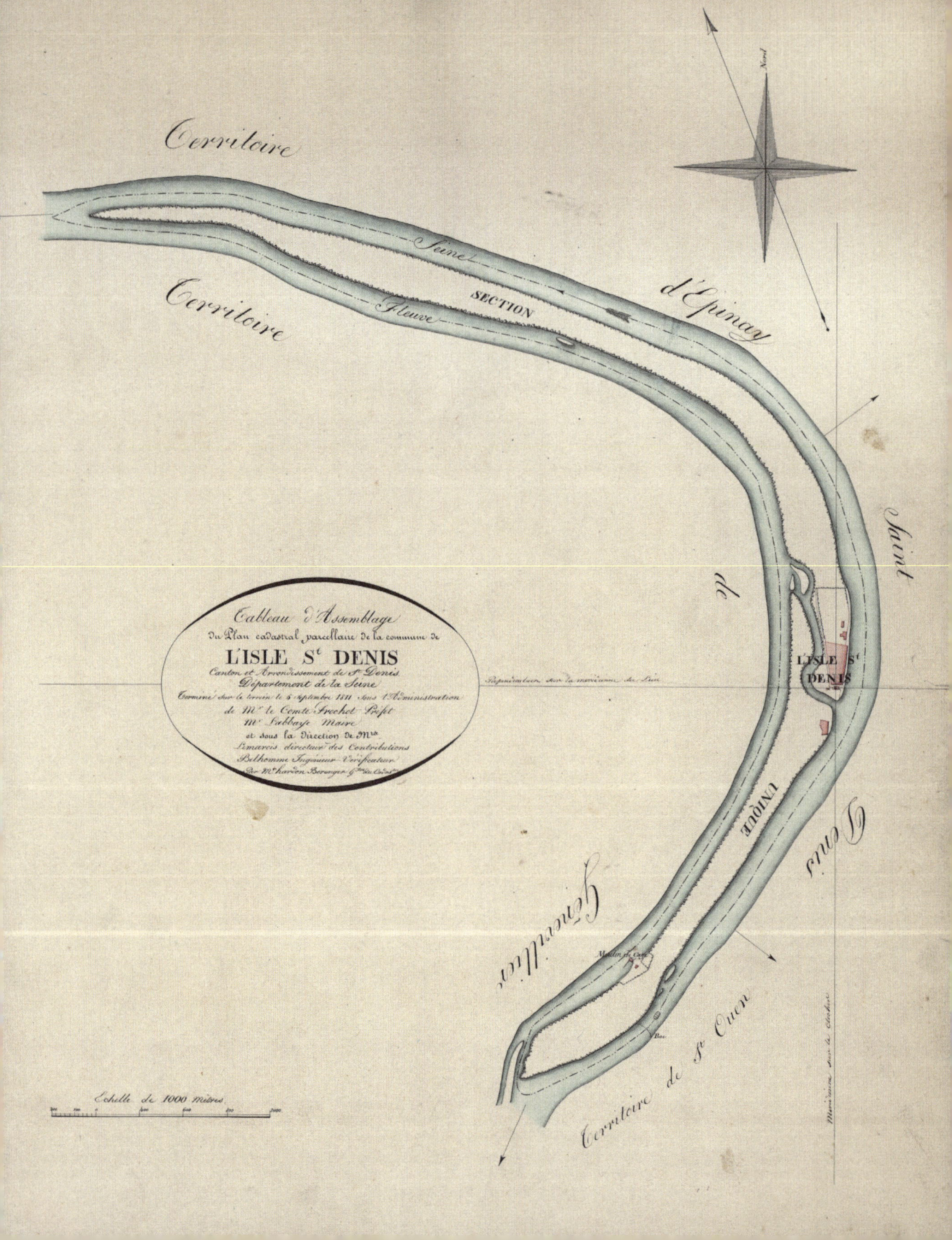
Tableau d'Assemblage
du Plan cadastral parcellaire de la commune de
L'ISLE St DENIS
Canton et Arrondissement de St Denis
Département de la Seine
Terminé sur le terrein le 5 septembre 1811 sous l'Administration
de Mr le Comte Frochot Préfet
Mr Labbaye Maire
et sous la Direction de Mrs
Limarcis directeur des Contributions
Belhomme Ingénieur Vérificateur
Nord
Territoire
Territoire
d'Epinay
Seine
Fleuve
SECTION
UNIQUE
L'ISLE St DENIS
Saint
Denis
de
Territoire de St Ouen
Echelle de 1000 mètres

AMBITION 1

TERRITORIAL ANCHORING

The Athletes' Village is exemplary in several ways. At its root, is a bigger project than itself, extending beyond the Olympic scope to the metropolis of Grand Paris. The increase in scale sets the horizon. After hosting the sports delegations, it is programmed to pivot on its axis and engage its transformation into an integrated metropolitan district. The future of the Village resides beyond itself, the Olympics and its perimeter. Reversibility is its performance, and metropolitan character, its continuum, its dimension.

Anchored in a territory revealing its metropolitan qualities, straddling the municipalities of Saint-Denis, Saint-Ouen and Ile-Saint-Denis, the future district is designed to translate and intensify the energy of Grand Paris, through an interactive relation with its immediate environment. Located 10 kilometers from the center of the capital and with an area of 51 hectares, 7 of which along the Seine, the Joint Development Zone of the Olympic and Paralympic Village is part of the downstream sector of the Seine. Identified in the preceding regional masterplan as strategic for rebalancing the dense, suburban belt of the Ile-de-France region, there is an important zone of high-potential sites here, that will greatly benefit from geographic, historic, and cultural assets.

In many respects, the Village in its Olympic phase is related to the concept of the Hôtel Métropole, developed by the Dominique Perrault Architecture firm while participating in the Greater Paris International Workshop. The Hôtel Métropole concept is one of a transitory, flexible and connected habitat and activities system aiming to dynamize metropolitan energies by unifying hybrid programs with short- and medium-term housing solutions. In this sense, the Hôtel Métropole is an incubator of urban living, a tensor and an activator of zones not ordinarily considered for housing typologies. Everything is available, everything is possible.

The metropolitan region's growth is constantly blocked by its discontinuities and its fractures in conflict with the urban fabric of the capital. The Games are hastening the work of integration, interaction and the stitching together of these areas, on the local and regional scale. A symbol of this is the new steel footbridge connecting the banks of Saint-Denis and the Ile-Saint-Denis, more effectively linking the two sites of the Olympic Village and extending the project of the Grand Paris Express on the Pleyel site. This new "emblematic" train station is destined to become one of the most important multimodal hubs of Ile-de-France. Some 250,000 daily voyagers will transit through the intersection of metro lines 14, 15, 16, and 17, connecting above ground with the RER D suburban line. This new architectural transport hub is already generating a high level of integrated urban living in the surrounding neighborhood adjacent to the current Olympic Village. This will help meet the demand for housing. One of the new centralities of the metropolis of Grand Paris is congealing here. We should add to this the proximity of the two A1 and A86 highways. The later encloses the northeast sector of the Village.

The new open and connected and neighborhood of "Pleyel – Berges de Seine" is the missing piece of an "archipelago" of development projects requiring a holistic view in the Territorial Development Contract and in the planning documents of Plaine Commune. Here as elsewhere, the challenge is precisely to have planning that is comprehensible, sharable and appropriable by all citizens; a "shared process" for building the city.

Mantes
Meulan
Triel
Gargenville
Rangiport
Epônes
la Falaise
Aubergenville
Flains
Medan
Villaines
Poissy
S. Germain
Marly

#61# **AMBITION 1**

TERRITORIAL ANCHORING

Geography of the Seine Valley

S.t Denis.

#63# **AMBITION 1**

TERRITORIAL ANCHORING

Engraving of Saint-Denis, 17th Century.

The site of the future Olympic and Paralympic Village is exceptional in that it stretches along both sides of the banks of the Seine, a river that is deeply linked to the image of Paris and Greater Paris. What is more, it will have to contend with a unique industrial heritage, that of the power plants built at the beginning of the 19th century to supply electricity to the Paris metro. the Paris metro.

Part of this heritage, the Cité du Cinéma, has already been restored to its former glory. The chosen site also offers a unique opportunity to reconcile the area with the historic centre of Saint-Denis, which has an exceptional wealth of heritage that is little known.

REPUBLIQUE FRANÇAISE
5c
POSTES
Saint-Ouen illustré
laisirs d'Été. - Une joyeuse Partie de Canotage autour de l'Ile
P. SUDAN édit. - St-Ouen

REPUBLIQUE FRANÇAISE
10c
POSTES

Profp. de la V: St

 AMBITION 1

TERRITORIAL ANCHORING

Geography of the Seine Valley.

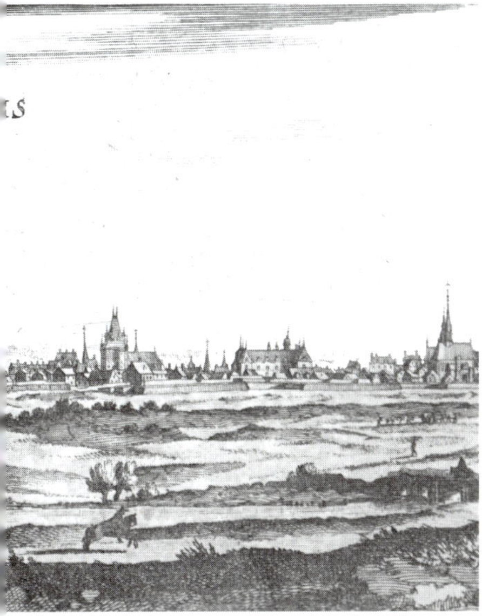

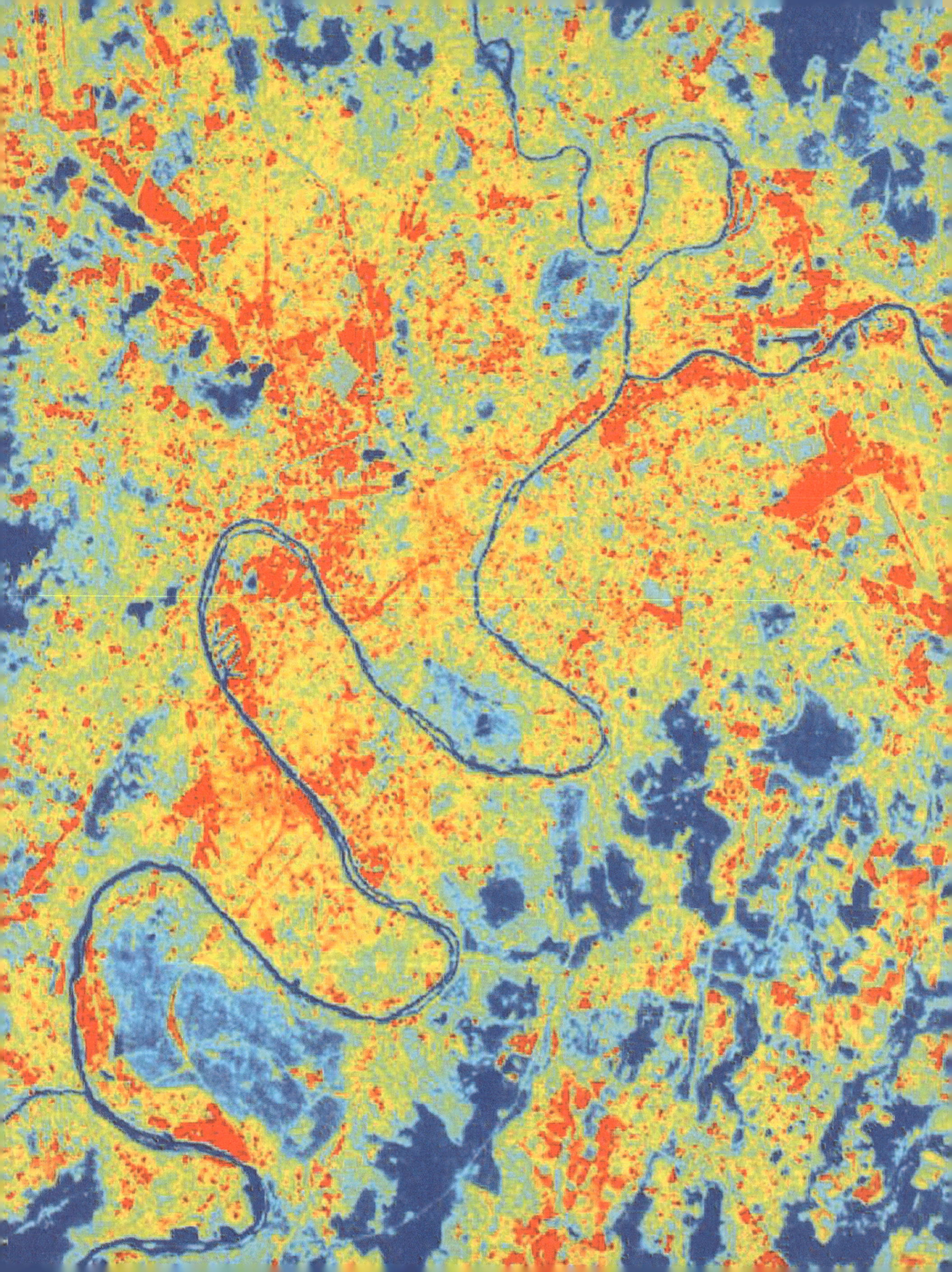

#67# **AMBITION 1**

TERRITORIAL ANCHORING

Geography of the Seine Valley.

Summer thermography and height of vegetation.

#69# **AMBITION 1**

TERRITORIAL ANCHORING
Artistic Representation.

The Pleyel site from an aerial view in 1926
© CAF / IGN

Axonometry / Collage
© SOLIDEO / Dominique Perrault / Ingérop / Une Fabrique de la Ville / CITEC / Agence TER / UrbanEco / Jean-Paul Lamoureux

Construction site of the Saint-Denis therm
power station on 4 April 1932
© Copyright - Archives départementales de la Seine-Saint-Denis

Aerial view of the Pleyel site in 1926
© CAF / IGN

Photograph 29/04/1969. Overall view of the Île des Vannes stadium construction site. Henri Baranger - Archives départementales de la Seine-Saint-Denis

1912, Société d'électricité de Paris. - Saint-Denis factory - Machine room
© Archives municipales de Saint-Denis

A street in the Olympic villa
Olympic Games © 1924 / IO

Cross-section of public spaces, across Route Départementale 1, banks of the Seine, 2019© SOLIDEO / Dominique Perrault / Ingérop / Une Fabrique de la Ville / CITEC / Agence TER / UrbanEco / Jean-Paul Lamoureux

Saint-Ouen - The church, the Château, 1905-1925© All rights reserved - éditions Flamery / Archives départementales de la Seine-Saint-Denis

Saint-Denis. - Electrical sectors of the city of Paris, 1900-1940
© Archives municipales de Saint-Denis

Saint-Denis - Aerial view c
© All rights reserved - Co
editions / Archives dépar

1966-1975 Saint-Ouen/L'île Saint-Denis© All rights reserved - éditions Raymon / Archives départementales de la Seine-Saint-Denis

Visual of Mail Finot, 2020. © SOLIDEO / Dominique Perrault / Ingérop / Une Fabrique de la Ville / CITEC / Agence TER / UrbanEco / Jean-Paul Lamoureux

Construction site of the Saint-Denis thermal power station on 4 April 1932
© All rights reserved - Archives départementales de la Seine-Saint-Denis

Ant
sho
© D

v taken at Île-Saint-Denis. NFC - Brioude - Journal des
mes editions
rchives départementales de la Seine-Saint-Denis

Saint-Ouen - Summer pleasures - A merry canoeing trip around the island (1905-1910)
© All rights reserved - éditions P. Sudan / Archives départementales de la Seine-Saint-Denis

Section through public spaces, across Route Départementale 1, banks of the Seine, 2019
© SOLIDEO / Dominique Perrault / Ingérop / Une Fabrique de la Ville / CITEC / Agence TER / UrbanEco / Jean-Paul Lamoureux

"Le Petit Bras dans l'Ile de Saint-Denis"
; d 19th century. © Alfred Taiee - Printed by Alfred Cadart / Archives départementales de la Seine-Saint-Denis

s, during the 1924 Paris

Construction site of the Saint-Denis thermal power station, 28 April 1932
© Rights reserved - Archives départementales de la Seine-Saint-Denis

View of the first Olympic village in Colombes under construction for the 1924 Paris Olympic Games © 1924 / IOC

Saint-Ouen - The bridge, view from the island 1925-1935
© All rights reserved - éditions Berthaud Frères / Archives départementales de la Seine-Saint-Denis

#71# AMBITION 1
TERRITORIAL ANCHORING

Pleyel, 1925
ne française (CAF)
la Seine-Saint-Denis

Plan of the Athletes' Village, 2020© SOLIDEO / Dominique Perrault / Ingérop / Une Fabrique de la Ville / CITEC / Agence TER / UrbanEco / Jean-Paul Lamoureux

New factory, Seine side, 1930-1940
Photography by Collection Douzenel. Archives municipales de Saint-Denis

Site model, 2018. © SOLIDEO / Dominique Perrault / Ingérop / Une Fabrique de la Ville / CITEC / Agence TER / UrbanEco / Jean-Paul Lamoureux

l published by Bioulac of the Carrefour Pleyel in Saint Denis,
el musical instrument factory at the beginning of the 20th century
c

Quai de Saint-Ouen. In 1929, the "factory with eighteen chimneys" Photograph Collection Douzenel. © Archives municipales de Saint-Denis

Saint-Denis thermal power station, now the Cité du Cinéma and offices - General view circa 1980
© Archives Seine Saint Denis / Direction régionale de l'équipement Île-de-France5

L'île Saint-Denis, Alfred Sisley, oil on canvas, 1872
Collection Musée d'Orsay. © Domaine public

#73# **AMBITION 1**

TERRITORIAL ANCHORING

Industrial History.

Power stations, 1933.

#75# **AMBITION 1**

TERRITORIAL ANCHORING

Aerial View of Saint-Denis, 1933.

#77# **AMBITION 1**

TERRITORIAL ANCHORING

Built, Human and Social Context.

#79# **AMBITION 1**

TERRITORIAL ANCHORING

Built, Human and Social Context.

L'Isle de France.
PARISIENSIS AGRI DESCRIP.
SEPTEMTRIO.
PICARDIE.
Fr. Guilloterius Biturix Viu. describebat, et CL.V. Petro Pithoeo I.C. dedicabat.
SENLIS
VALOIS.
LA GOELE.
LE MULTIEN.
L'AULNAY.
LA FRANCE.
LE PARISIS.
MEAUX
PARIS
LA BRIE.
OCCIDENS.
ORIENS.
MERIDIES.
Cum Privilegiis decennali Imp. Reg. et Brab. 1598.
Scala Leucarum

NOUVELLE DESCRIPTION DU TERRITOIRE ET BANLIEUEE DE LA VILLE CITTE ET UNIVERSITES DE PARIS
SEPTENTRION
S. DENIS
Argenteuil
PLAINE DE S. DENIS
S. Clou
VERSAILLE
OCCIDENS
ORIENS
MIDY

#81# **AMBITION 1**

TERRITORIAL ANCHORING

Maps of the Historic Site.

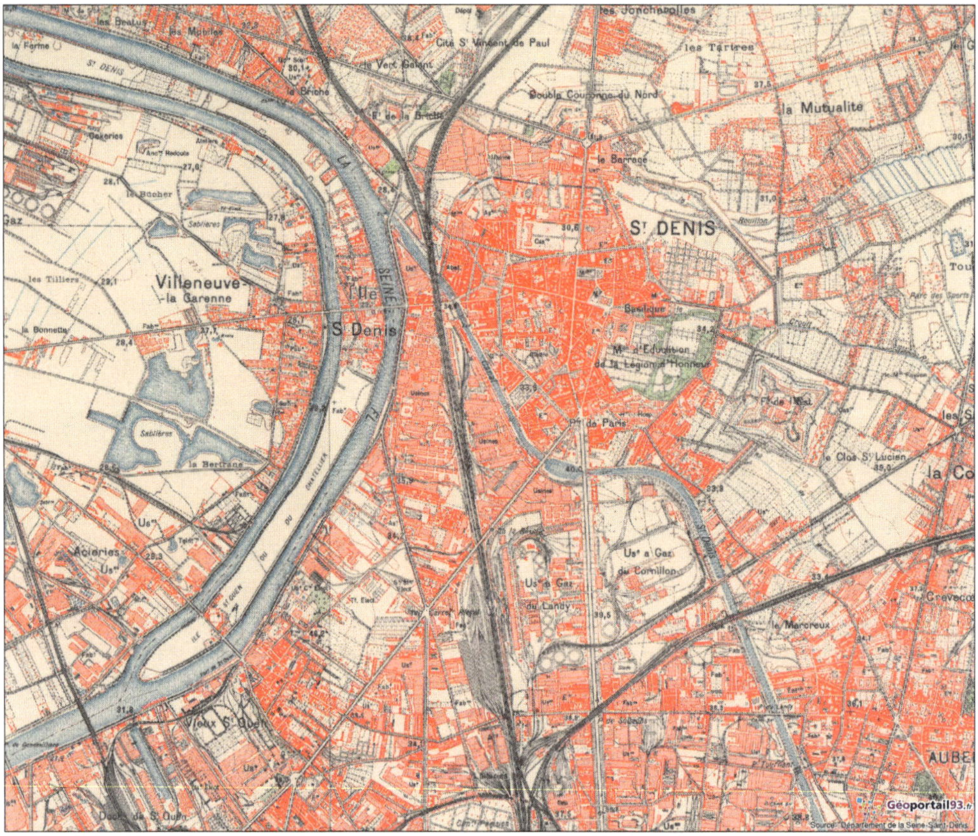

les Joncherolles
Cité St Vincent de Paul
les Tartres
Double Couronne du Nord
la Mutualité
le Barrage
St DENIS
Villeneuve-la Garenne
Ile St Denis
SEINE
Basilique
Mon d'Éducation de la Légion d'Honneur
Pte de Paris
le Clos St Lucien
Usne à Gaz du Cornillon
Usne à Gaz du Landy
Aciéries
la Bonnette
les Tilliers
le Bûcher
la Bertrane
Sablières
le Marcreux
Vieux St Ouen
Docks de St Ouen
AUBE
Géoportail93.fr
Source : Département de la Seine-Saint-Denis

St-Lazare
les Joncherolles
Cité St-Vincent-de-Paul
les Tartres
Double Couronne du Nord
la Mutualité
le Barrage
Zone industle
Chantiers navals
le Bûcher
Sablières
VILLENEUVE-LA GARENNE
St-DENIS
Maison Nationale de la Légion d'Honneur
St-Denis
Fort de l'Est
les Six Routes
les Hautes Noëlles
le Franc Moisin
Usine à Gaz du Cornillon
Usine à Gaz du Landy
Carrefour Pleyel
Aciérie
les 4 Chemins
ILE DES VANNES
le Vieux St-Ouen
Docks de St-Ouen
la Plaine St-Denis
AUBERVILLIERS
Géoportail93.fr

#83# **AMBITION 1**

TERRITORIAL ANCHORING

Maps of the Historic Site.

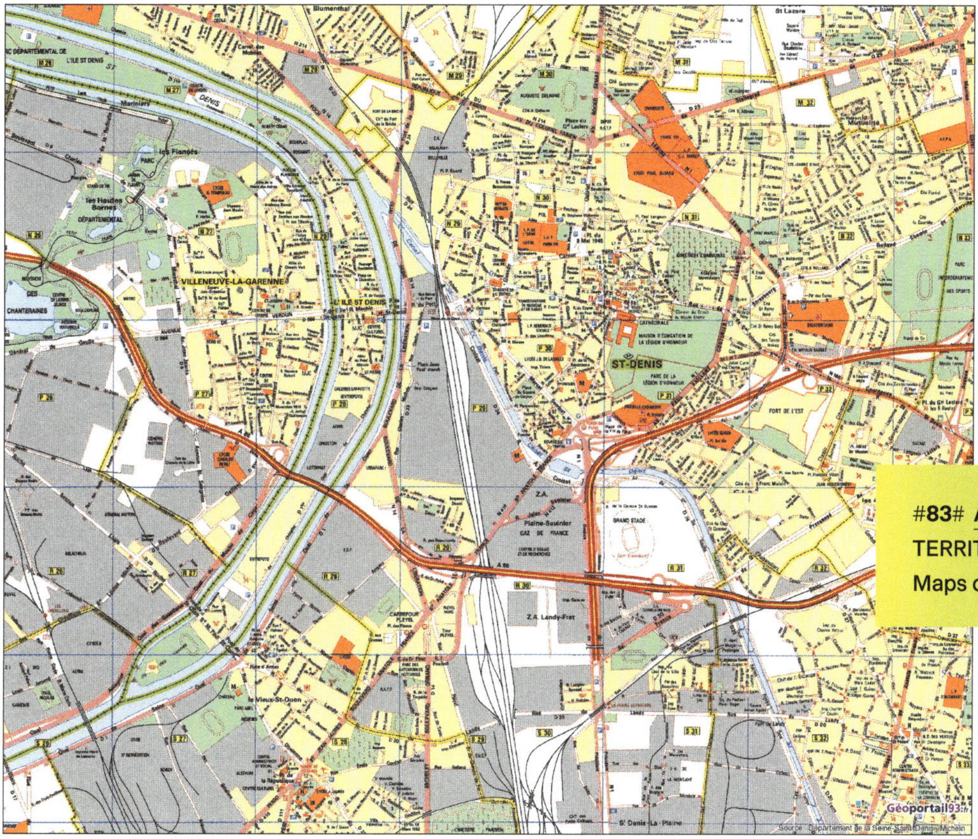

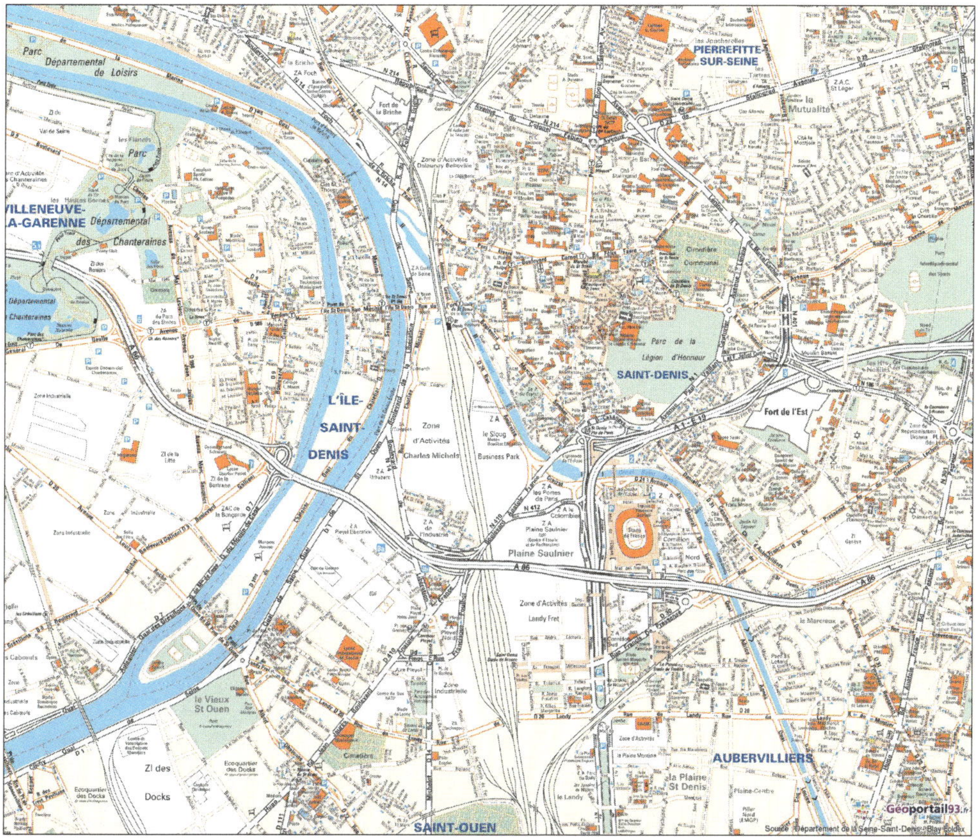

#85# **AMBITION 1**

TERRITORIAL ANCHORING

Aerial View of Saint-Denis Before Renovations, 2010.

The establishment of this new neighborhood from a vast industrial wasteland that, for decades, disregarded its geography and topography, presents an opportunity to reconnect with the natural terrain and the fifteen meters of elevation that separate the Pleyel district from the banks of the Seine. This river around which the life of the city has been organized since the Middle Ages, which witnessed the construction of the Basilique Saint-Denis, until the 19th century and the rise of Impressionist painting that made its hills famous.

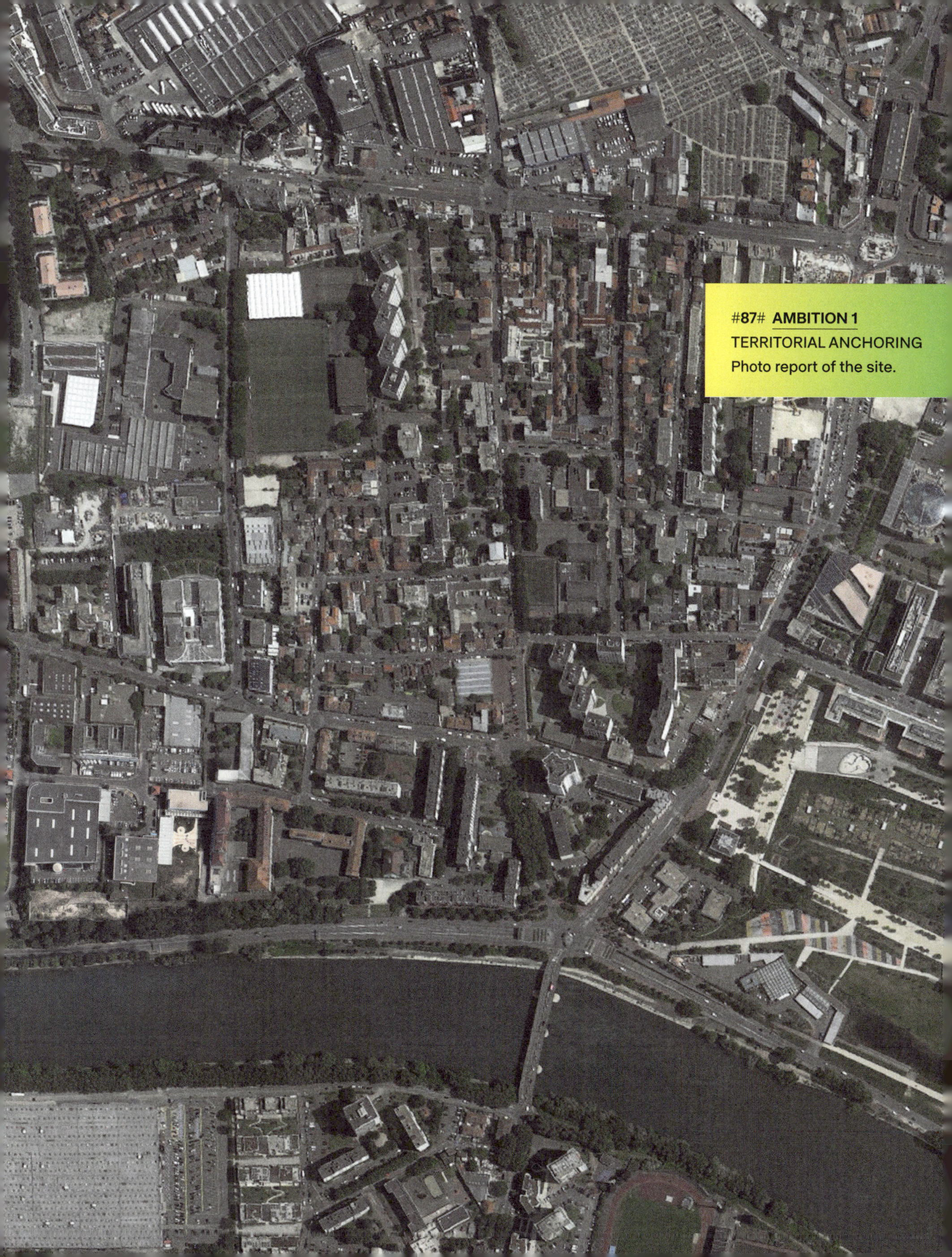

#87# **AMBITION 1**
TERRITORIAL ANCHORING
Photo report of the site.

#89# **AMBITION 1**

TERRITORIAL ANCHORING

In our view, the thinking behind the Olympic and Paralympic Village is first and foremost a long-term urban reflection on the creation of a city anchored in its territory and geography. The site chosen for the Village, and the context in which it will be built, carry within them and in their relationships, the seeds of this project.

The Seine, the city's 'artery' if ever there was one, runs through the Village, lending its banks and its stretch of water to all kinds of fun, festive, sporting and landscaping activities. The river and its redeveloped banks should act as a link between the neighbouring municipalities, forming a continuous, walkable blue and green network.

It establishes a link, both physical and mental, between the Ile de la Cité, at the historic heart of Paris, and the Ile-Saint-Denis, at the heart of Plaine Commune, the future territory of Greater Paris, bringing a strong and rich image to this international event of the 2024 Games, which must be those of Paris and Seine-Saint-Denis.

#91# **AMBITION 1**

TERRITORIAL ANCHORING

The Olympic and Paralympic Village project offers a unique opportunity to reconcile this area with its riverbanks and with the historic centre of Saint-Denis, which has an exceptionally rich and little-known heritage.

Opening views towards the river, particularly from the "domesticated" hillsides "the RD1 and 1bis, creating physical access to the Petit and Grand Arms to the Petit and Grand Arms, and the construction of a new crossing, the redeployment of uses on the water (leisure, logistics and even economic) will help to renew economic) will help to renew the area's links with the river.

#93# **AMBITION 1**

TERRITORIAL ANCHORING

Photo report of the site.

THE SEINE

THE RIVERBANKS

#95# **AMBITION 1**

TERRITORIAL ANCHORING

The site before work began.

A86
Villeneuve-la-Garenne
Ile Saint Denis
Cité du Cinéma
Olympic and
Paralympic Village
Saint Ouen

#97# **AMBITION 1**

TERRITORIAL ANCHORING

Reinvention of the site, beyond the perimeter.

Going beyond the boundaries of the study.

PORT HERITAGE
On the Saint Denis bank, you
will find the old slipway, the l
quay and the river vegetation.
ENERGY PRODUCTION
Public sports areas on the Ile
des Vannes are self-sufficient.
le parc productif
les terrasses
RIVER LOGISTICS
The old port of Saint Ouen
is actively involved in the
development of the district.

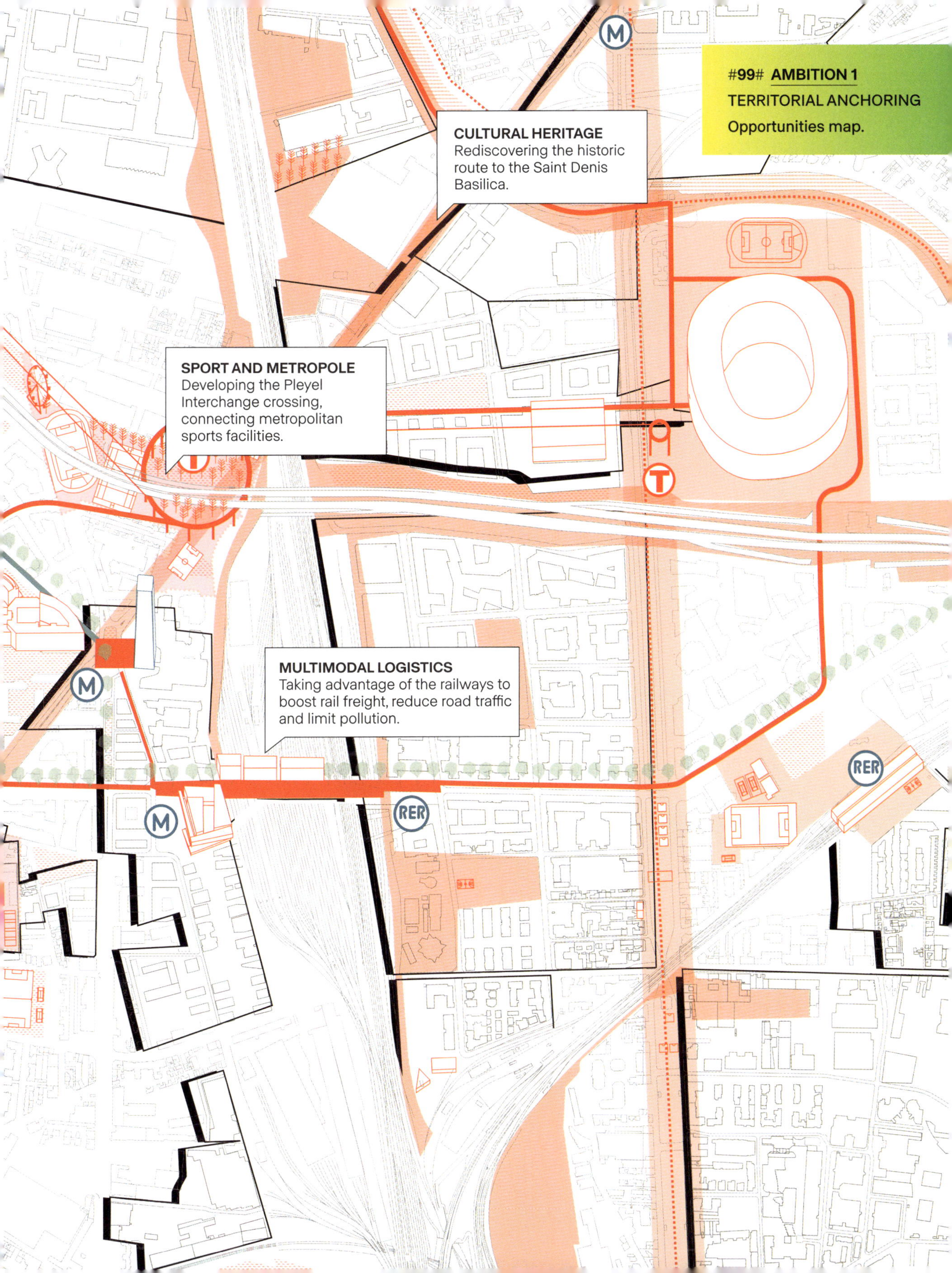

#99# **AMBITION 1**

TERRITORIAL ANCHORING

Opportunities map.

Heritage district - Current status of the ZAC

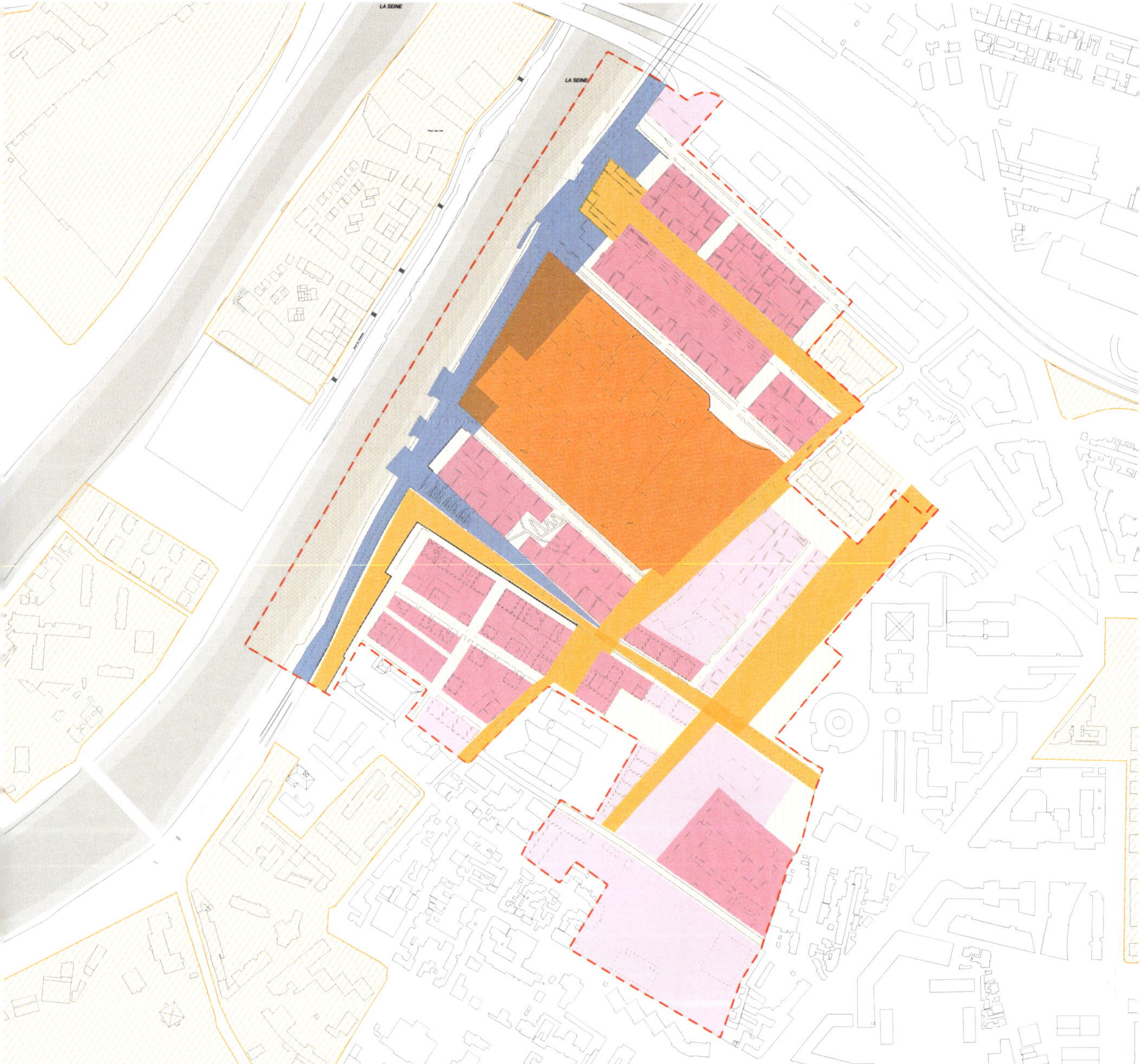

Projects under study

Projects in progress

Hors Mission -
The Cité du Cinéma

Village entrances

Banks of the Seine

Metropolitan location - An adjoining urban environment

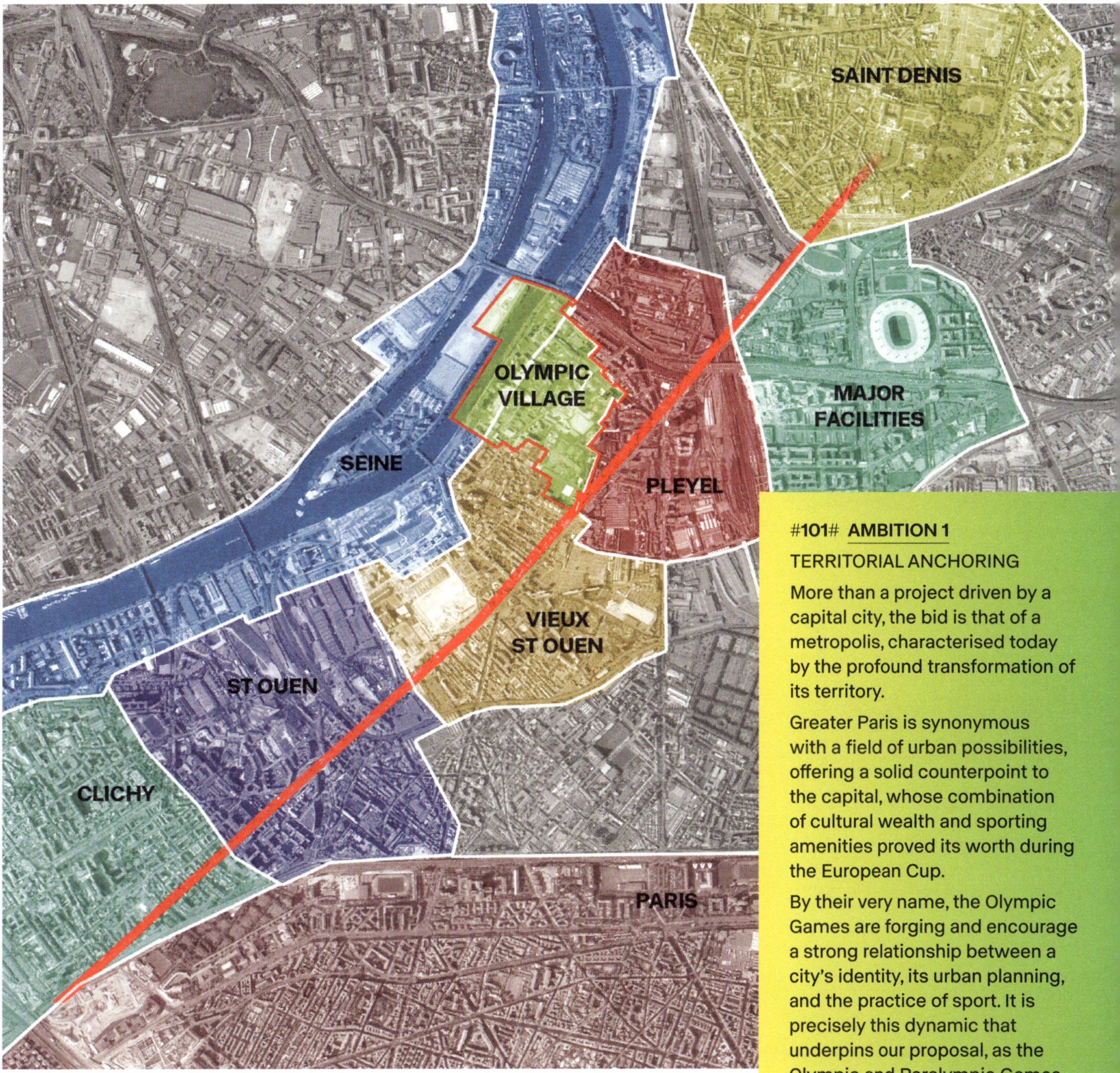

#101# **AMBITION 1**

TERRITORIAL ANCHORING

More than a project driven by a capital city, the bid is that of a metropolis, characterised today by the profound transformation of its territory.

Greater Paris is synonymous with a field of urban possibilities, offering a solid counterpoint to the capital, whose combination of cultural wealth and sporting amenities proved its worth during the European Cup.

By their very name, the Olympic Games are forging and encourage a strong relationship between a city's identity, its urban planning, and the practice of sport. It is precisely this dynamic that underpins our proposal, as the Olympic and Paralympic Games are factors in intensifying the development of Greater Paris.

Paris Olympic Village
2024 final report, November

Urban project - Going beyond the boundaries of the study

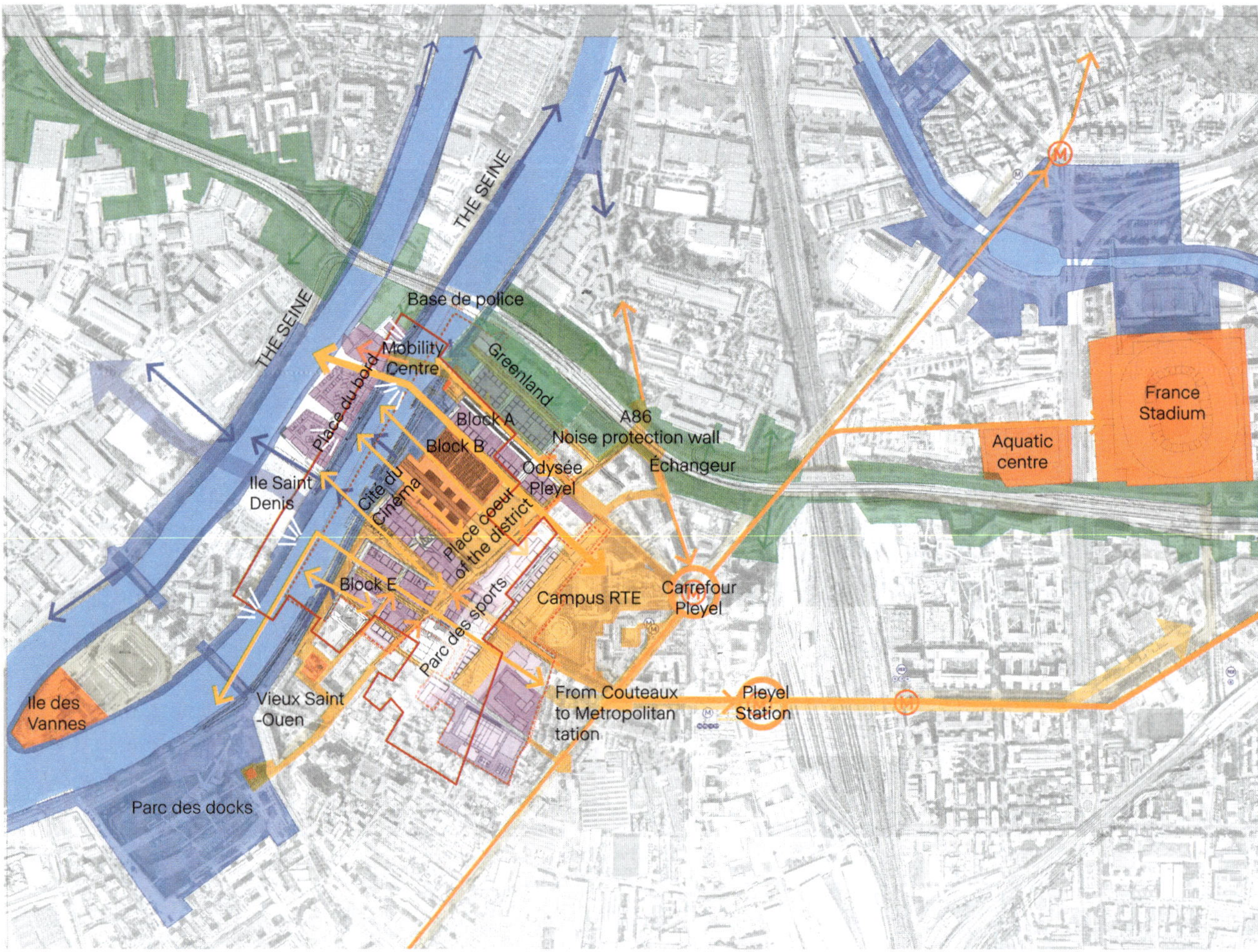

#103# **AMBITION 1**

TERRITORIAL ANCHORING

Reinvention of the site, beyond the perimeter.

"SITE"

AMBITION 2

URBAN IDENTITY

The Olympic site has an architectural past – an already there – that determines its morphology. Beginning in 1903, the electricity generating industry settled here to meet the capital's growing demand for electrical power, linked to urban lighting and the new subway system. This industry gradually faded away during the 1990s. Since then, the site has gradually been developing service sector industries, first by receiving public and private educational activities.

The urban planning of the new city blocks and public spaces of the Village maintain an echo of the heritage of this former industrial grid of the site and integrate its exceptional pieces of architecture. The industrial features that have disappeared from the site include fuel depots, transformer stations and merchandise warehouses, but two emblematic buildings remain. The Halle Maxwell (1907) is a former thermal power station responsible for supplying the north side of the Paris metropolitan area. The Cité du Cinéma, following a conversion overhaul undertaken from 2010 to 2012, now transposes in its structure and plan the appearance of another power station built between 1931 and 1933. The fully preserved monumental nave of the latter, housed the huge electric turbines. Athletes will dine here during the Games. Also noteworthy is the former "engineers' house" (Copernic pavilion) that will house the media center and, at the edge of the Village, the Devatting Hall, a concrete and glass fortress dating from the 1930 where transformer maintenance was performed and which will become a show venue.

The idea of district generates a dialogue between public intervention and the history of architecture, urbanism and cities. The requirement of the territorial development policy was that the Olympic Village of Saint-Denis–Saint-Ouen not be created ex nihilo on an abandoned zone (except for the industrial brownfield sector), but rather one lacking in "urbanity" and "metropolity", i.e., varied urban and metropolitan life and amenities. If the Cité du cinéma as well as a few companies (now relocated) were developed here on this site when the construction program began in 2019, this urban zone was not literally inhabited then. Along its perimeter, the intermunicipal area benefits from a relatively dense educational offering: two elementary schools, a middle school, a high school, an engineering school and the Ecole Louis-Lumière, preparing students for jobs in industries of cinema, photography and sound. The Universeine complex, built by Vinci group completes the Village site on its north side.

The template chosen for the Village's city blocks of housing and activities is the lot. Its morphology meets the criteria of being evolutive, adaptable and mixed use (apartments, offices, hotel, student housing, shops, etc.) in a balanced rapport between density, intensity and airy inhabitability for 6,000 inhabitants and the 6,000 workers that will set up here in the district. The fourth criterion is sustainability, ensured by the resilience of the built environment, in terms of modularity and flexibility. The mixed areas are more robust than those in the restrictive program, which were still being sacrificed, until just a few years ago, to the concept of "zoning" promoted by the Athens Charter of 1933. It organized urban areas based on four functions conceived of as attributions: inhabit / work / recreate / circulate. Deprived of a fruitful link with the city owing to transportation infrastructures that kept it deeply cut off, the specialized zones that began to sprout (shops, industries, offices, housing or parks) suffer from a sever lack of urbanity. "Zoning" and "tying in" are in complete contradiction.

Urbanity is a civility that the architect-urbanist is obliged to foster. These two interrelated notions aggregate notions of city-dwelling citizenship and hospitality, and the beneficial sharing of public space. Today, urbanity is also understood to include the proximity of services available to all. Thus, the idea of connection is generic: developing society and neighborhood; generating an integrating and integrated space, acknowledging desires and connecting the city; facilitating the meeting of all, and serving well-being. Here we are speaking of shared policies and shared services. There is indeed a right to urbanity, whose reverberations are democratic, republican, societal, environmental, economic, and territorial. The notion of urbanity crystalizes and unites. The metropolis of Grand Paris fully engages its entire program.

Facilitating and promoting appropriation of the public space as a place of freely interpretable potentialities and inclusive exchange is a key challenge for architecture with an urban dimension. Architects and urbanists work to ensure the evolution, adaptability, availability, durability, livability, readability and the attractivity of the spaces they build and develop.

The design of the Athletes' Village and the future district have all that. It is interesting here to emphasize the effect of the continuity between Olympic values and those of urbanity.

Sociability is not a mathematical equation. Nevertheless, it was incumbent upon the Village's project management and teams of architects to implement geometry of interior and exteriors spaces that encourages urbanity and the flourishing of integrated social life. Among other examples, the animation of ground floors was a key point of the project study and the Masterplan. The conviction was unanimous. Conceived as "active podiums," they condition the energy of the future district. Though strategic in the urban space, the base of buildings in many cities and many buildings tend toward non mixed uses and a form of inertia entirely detrimental in every way. Urbanity comes out the big loser. Public authorities, developers and urbanists must accurately take this into account. In this regard, the urban planning code ought to introduce certain dispositions aimed at promoting diversity of ground floor occupations. Thus, some 3,000 m² of commercial spaces are programmed on the site of the Village, and 17,700 m² of activities and services.

Energy transition and adaptability to climate change tie in with great social and economic mutations. The city is entering a redefinition phase. The concept of eco-urbanity and social sustainability extends to the sphere of integrated community life.

There is no need to recall the strategic dimension of the housing issue, a "time bomb" whose impact on other interlocking crises (economic, environmental without overlooking the one linked to modes of governance) is patently obvious. Planning is necessary, which is not only quantitative (70,000 units of housing annually) but closely linked to territorial development policies and the metropolitan question of the habitat, to remedy phenomena of relegation, segregation and social insecurity, and overcome geographic disparities in terms of habitat quality. This involves proposing methods of intervention in the metropolis answering urgent social needs. Action on housing, densification and intensification of the city are the levers of urbanity. Added to this is the necessity of adapting the housing offer to new lifestyles by promoting new, notably flexibles and evolving typologies, at reasonable cost (construction or renovation).

Financial issues are linked to these property issues. Municipal authorities lack the financial means and techniques for meeting these objectives. Thus, a metropolitan authority must take charge, by implementing prior corrective equalizations of territorial fractures; in sum, a development policy!

As a public development authority, the SOLIDEO amiably acquired 80% of the property of the Olympic Village in 2019. If the future district answers the metropolitan demand for housing, the tension is high between potential gentrification and social integration, a challenge for future acquisition processes (for starter homes or block purchases) and rental dwelling spaces. The underprivileged district of Stratford, on the east side of London, was chosen as the main place for the sites of the 2012 Olympic Games. The candidacy brief promised to renew this urban space, surrounded by marshes and vacant land and very poorly served by public transportation. The authorities undertook a construction program of 40,000 new units of moderate rent housing. Though today, four underground lines and one rail line connect Stratford to the City in less than fifteen minutes, sadly only 11% offer affordable rents for more modest households. Apartments with terraces and bay windows of new luxury buildings require income well above the purchasing power of former inhabitants. Rent on a tiny studio reaches EUR 2,200. Gentrification swept through.

To guard against this logic of property development, because the price of a square meter is in the region of EUR 7,000, the state, SOLIDEO and the developers made a commitment to social integration. 32% of housing units will be assigned to the social housing rental stock on the sector of Saint-Denis–Saint-Ouen and 48% on the L'Ile-Saint-Denis. The balance between private programs and public social programs is negotiated by project managers (private, public and quasi-public). From a level higher than the mandatory rate of 20 to 25% imposed by the Law on Solidarity and Urban Renewal (loi SRU), the figures of the Village match the share of social housing in the three municipalities of Saint-Denis (32%), Saint-Ouen (37%) and Ile-Saint-Denis (61%). The Village must also welcome between 500 and 600 units of student housing. Those of the Institut supérieur de mécanique (Supméca) have already moved in – provisionally, until the opening of the Games.

Ile Saint Denis
Seine
Reconnecting with the river
Promenade along the banks of the Seine
The Jardins Olympic Place
The Terrasses
The Coteaux
THE COURS
THE VERRIÈRES
THE STUDIOS
CITÉ du CINÉMA
THE QUINCONCES
MAIL FINOT
THE BELVÉDÈRES
THE VILLAS
Sports ground
PARC CENTRAL

#109# **AMBITION 2**

URBAN IDENTITY

A Territory in the Process of Being Revealed

The future district is one of the "islands" in an archipelago of projects that have been decided on without any real coherence between them. This situation highlights the essential need, not only for this area but for the whole of France, for planning that is comprehensible, shared and appropriated by all citizens.

An almost continuous mosaic of development projects covers the site and its surroundings, tending towards densification without any architectural direction or concerted planning.

The project's ambition, on the other hand, was to make the neighbourhood part of a sustainable, integrated, and sustainable community. area of influence much wider than just the Athletes' Village.

Several elements of the metropolis have also been considered in the design of the project: the A86 motorway, the main ring road of Greater Paris, the future Pleyel station, the Plaine Saulnier mixed development zone, the Olympic Aquatic Centre, the Seine, and its river traffic, as well as the many large-scale development projects.

Thinking about the legacy of the Village means preparing all its relationships with the wider area - architectural, landscape, urban, historical, social, and economic relationships.

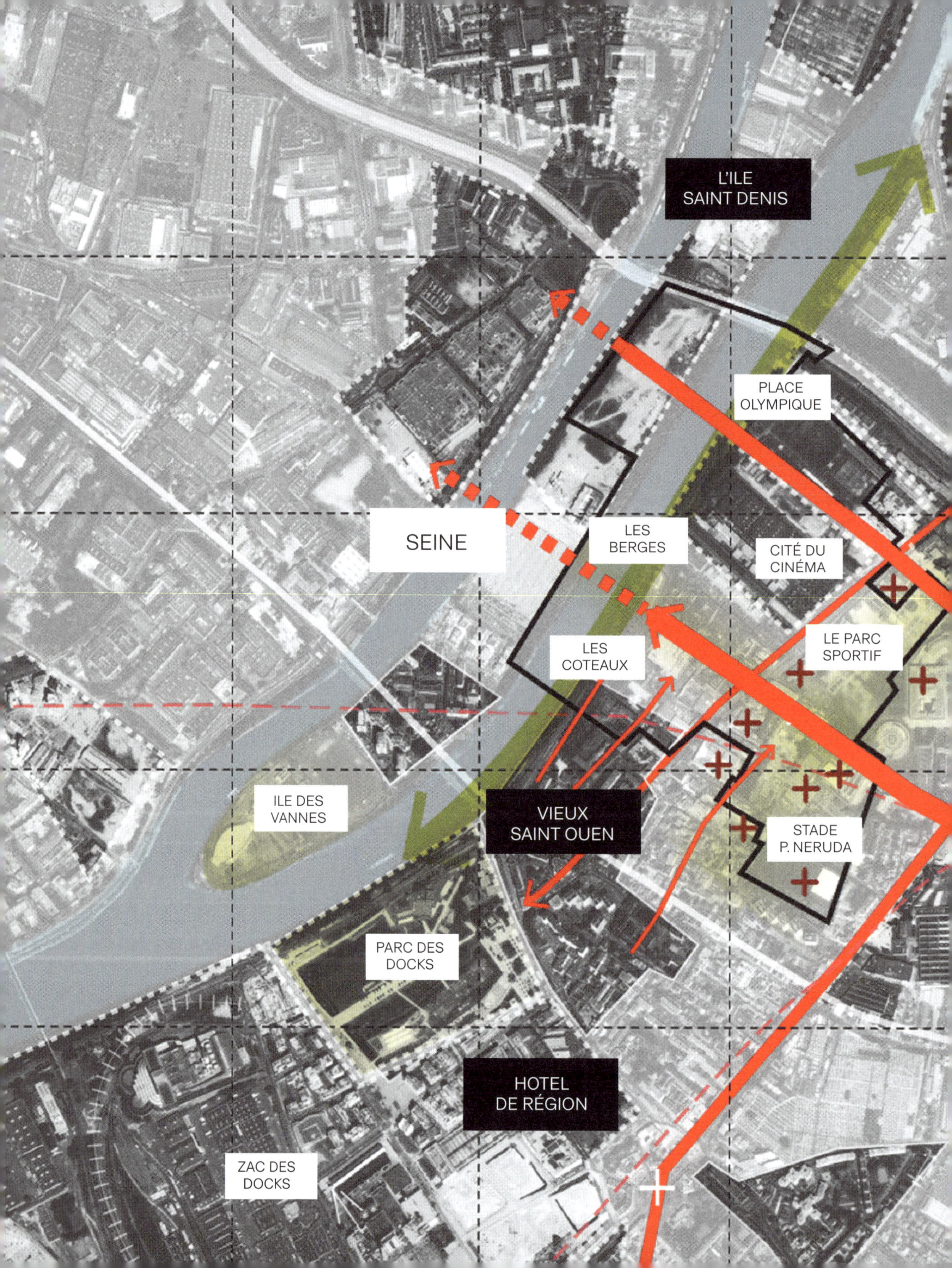
L'ILE SAINT DENIS
PLACE OLYMPIQUE
SEINE
LES BERGES
CITÉ DU CINÉMA
LES COTEAUX
LE PARC SPORTIF
ILE DES VANNES
VIEUX SAINT OUEN
STADE P. NERUDA
PARC DES DOCKS
HOTEL DE RÉGION
ZAC DES DOCKS

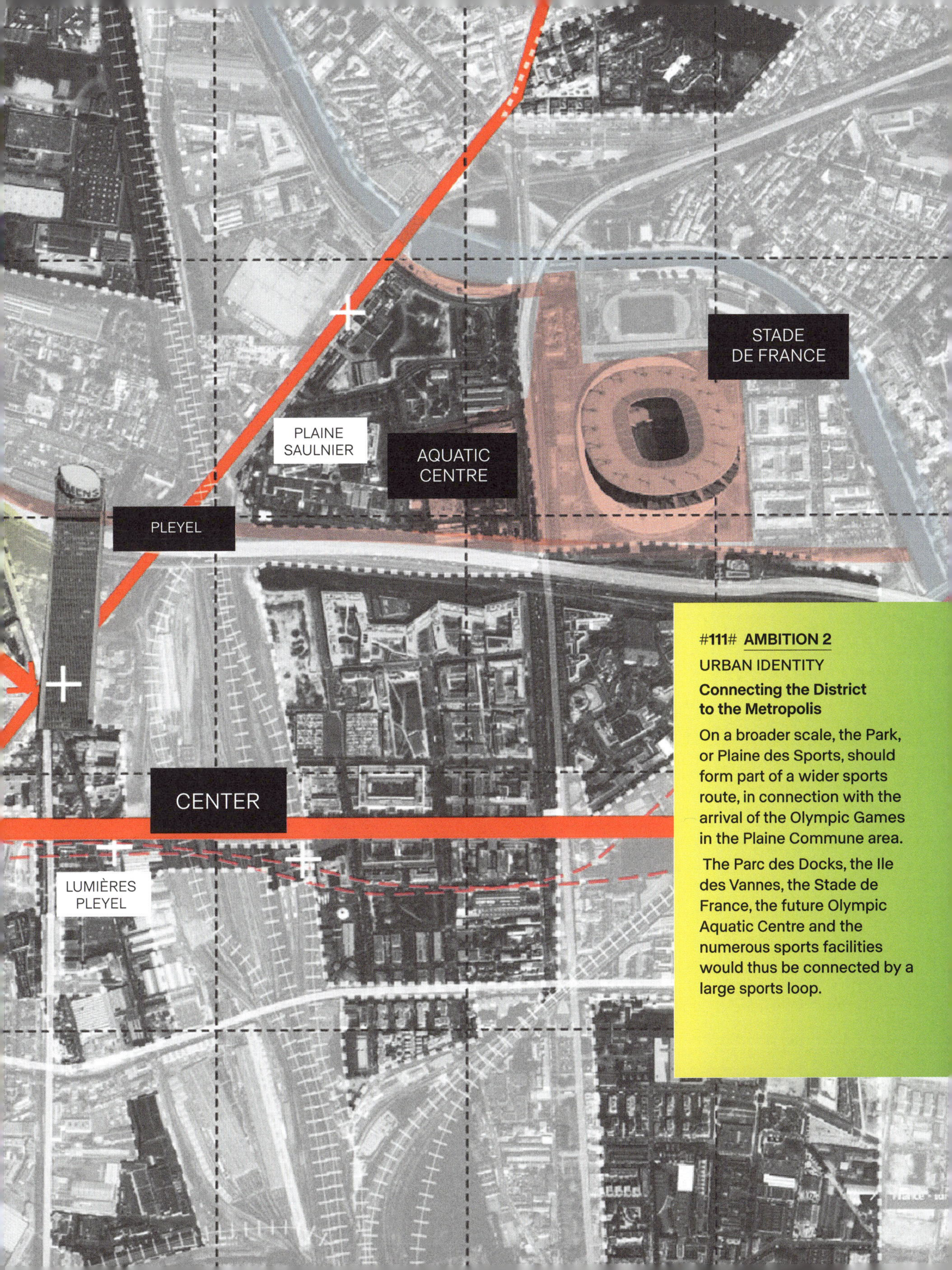

#111# **AMBITION 2**

URBAN IDENTITY

Connecting the District to the Metropolis

On a broader scale, the Park, or Plaine des Sports, should form part of a wider sports route, in connection with the arrival of the Olympic Games in the Plaine Commune area.

The Parc des Docks, the Ile des Vannes, the Stade de France, the future Olympic Aquatic Centre and the numerous sports facilities would thus be connected by a large sports loop.

A86
Villeneuve-la-Garenne
Ile Saint Denis
Cité du Cinéma
Olympic and
Paralympic Village
Saint Ouen

#113# **AMBITION 2**

URBAN IDENTITY
An Optimal Location

The future Olympic Village will be spread over 51 hectares, scattered across Ile-Saint-Denis, Saint-Denis and Saint-Ouen.

The urban project aims to improve interaction between the site, the Seine and the metropolis. This location minimises the need for athletes to travel. The Stade de France and the nautical centre are just a few minutes away by bus, and the Saint-Denis Pleyel station, 800m from the site, provides links to the centre of Paris on lines 14, 15, 16 and 17 of the Grand Paris Express, and line 13 of the metro.

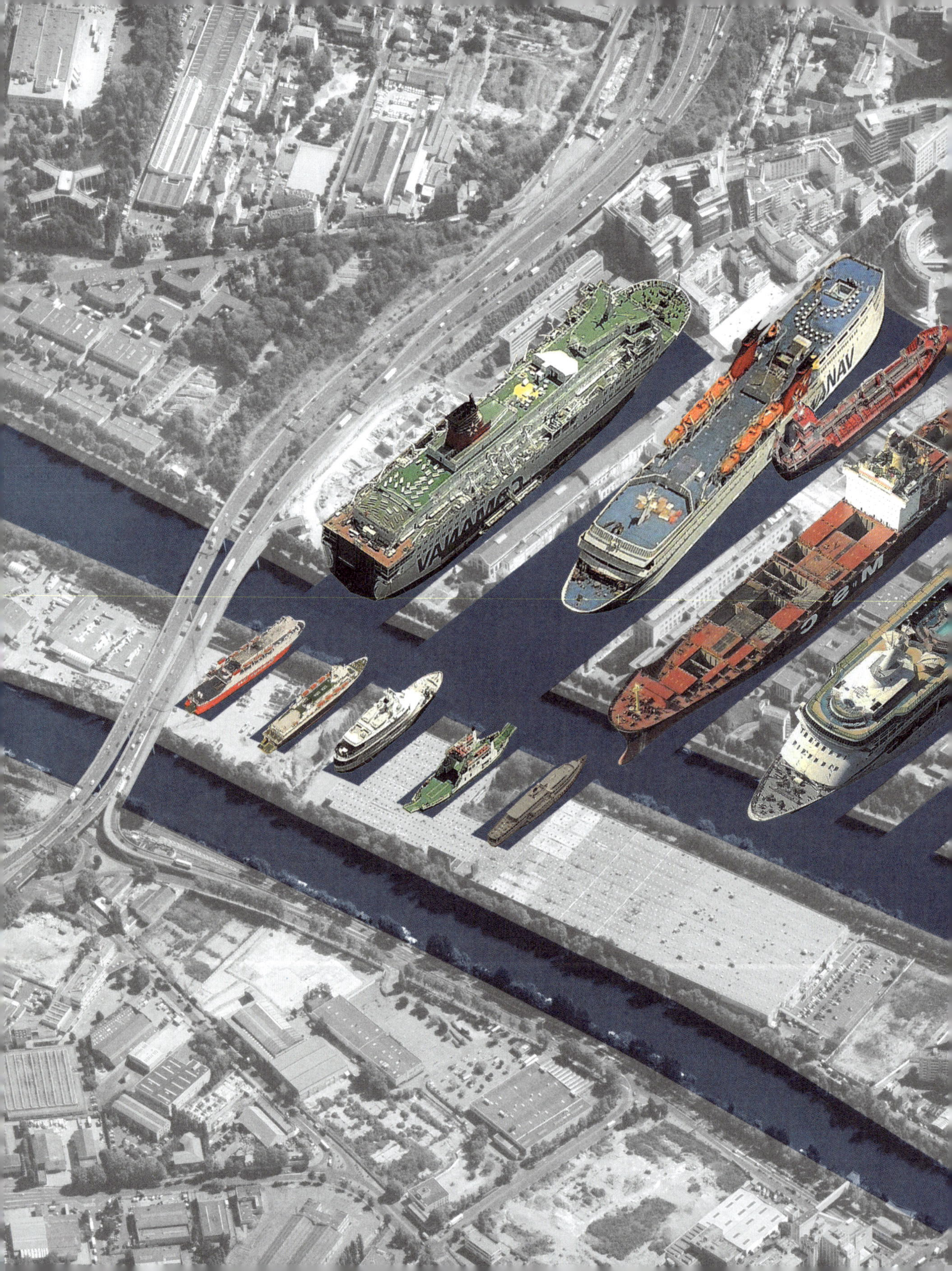

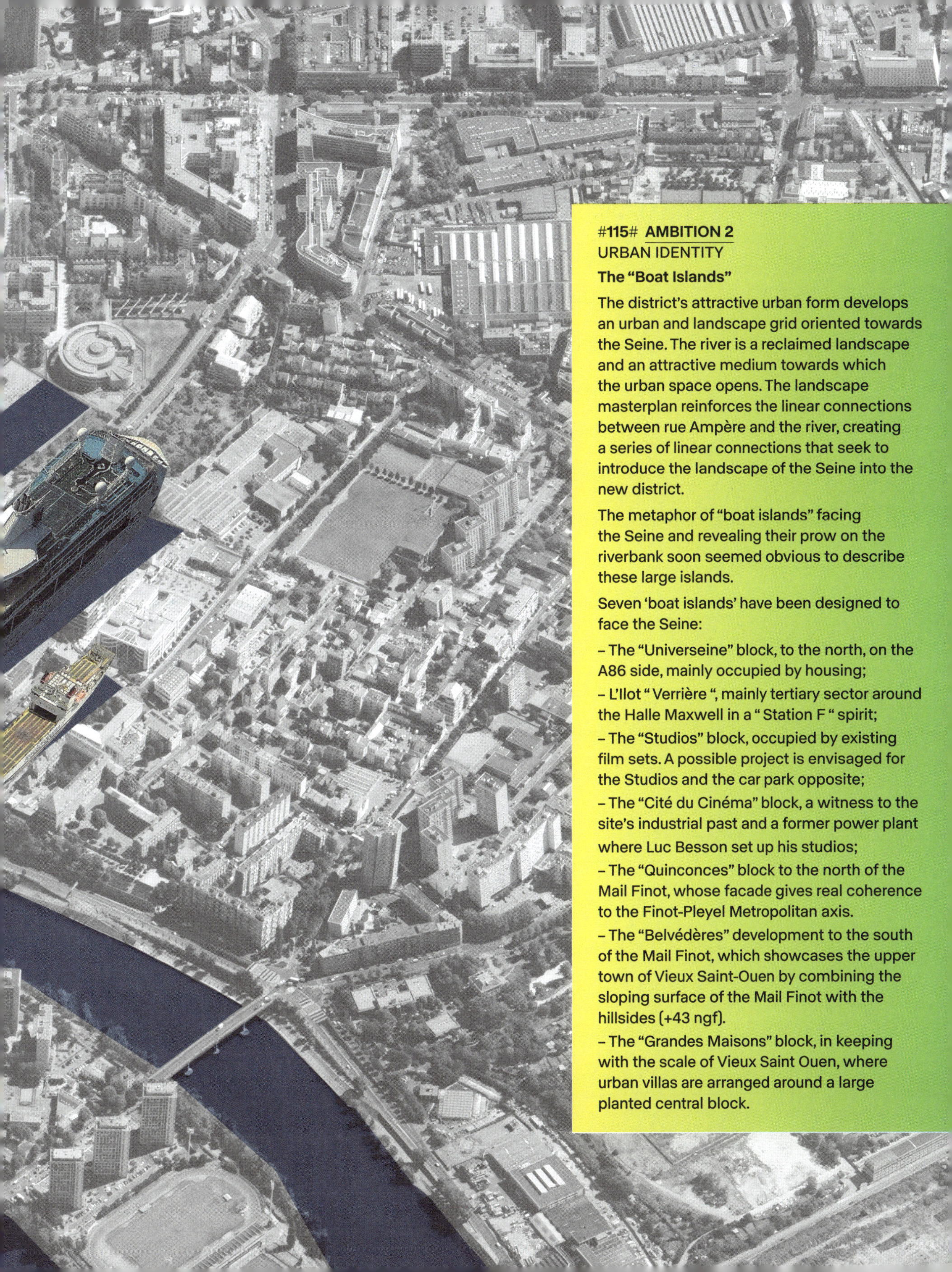

#115# **AMBITION 2**
URBAN IDENTITY

The "Boat Islands"

The district's attractive urban form develops an urban and landscape grid oriented towards the Seine. The river is a reclaimed landscape and an attractive medium towards which the urban space opens. The landscape masterplan reinforces the linear connections between rue Ampère and the river, creating a series of linear connections that seek to introduce the landscape of the Seine into the new district.

The metaphor of "boat islands" facing the Seine and revealing their prow on the riverbank soon seemed obvious to describe these large islands.

Seven 'boat islands' have been designed to face the Seine:

- The "Universeine" block, to the north, on the A86 side, mainly occupied by housing;
- L'Ilot " Verrière ", mainly tertiary sector around the Halle Maxwell in a " Station F " spirit;
- The "Studios" block, occupied by existing film sets. A possible project is envisaged for the Studios and the car park opposite;
- The "Cité du Cinéma" block, a witness to the site's industrial past and a former power plant where Luc Besson set up his studios;
- The "Quinconces" block to the north of the Mail Finot, whose facade gives real coherence to the Finot-Pleyel Metropolitan axis.
- The "Belvédères" development to the south of the Mail Finot, which showcases the upper town of Vieux Saint-Ouen by combining the sloping surface of the Mail Finot with the hillsides (+43 ngf).
- The "Grandes Maisons" block, in keeping with the scale of Vieux Saint Ouen, where urban villas are arranged around a large planted central block.

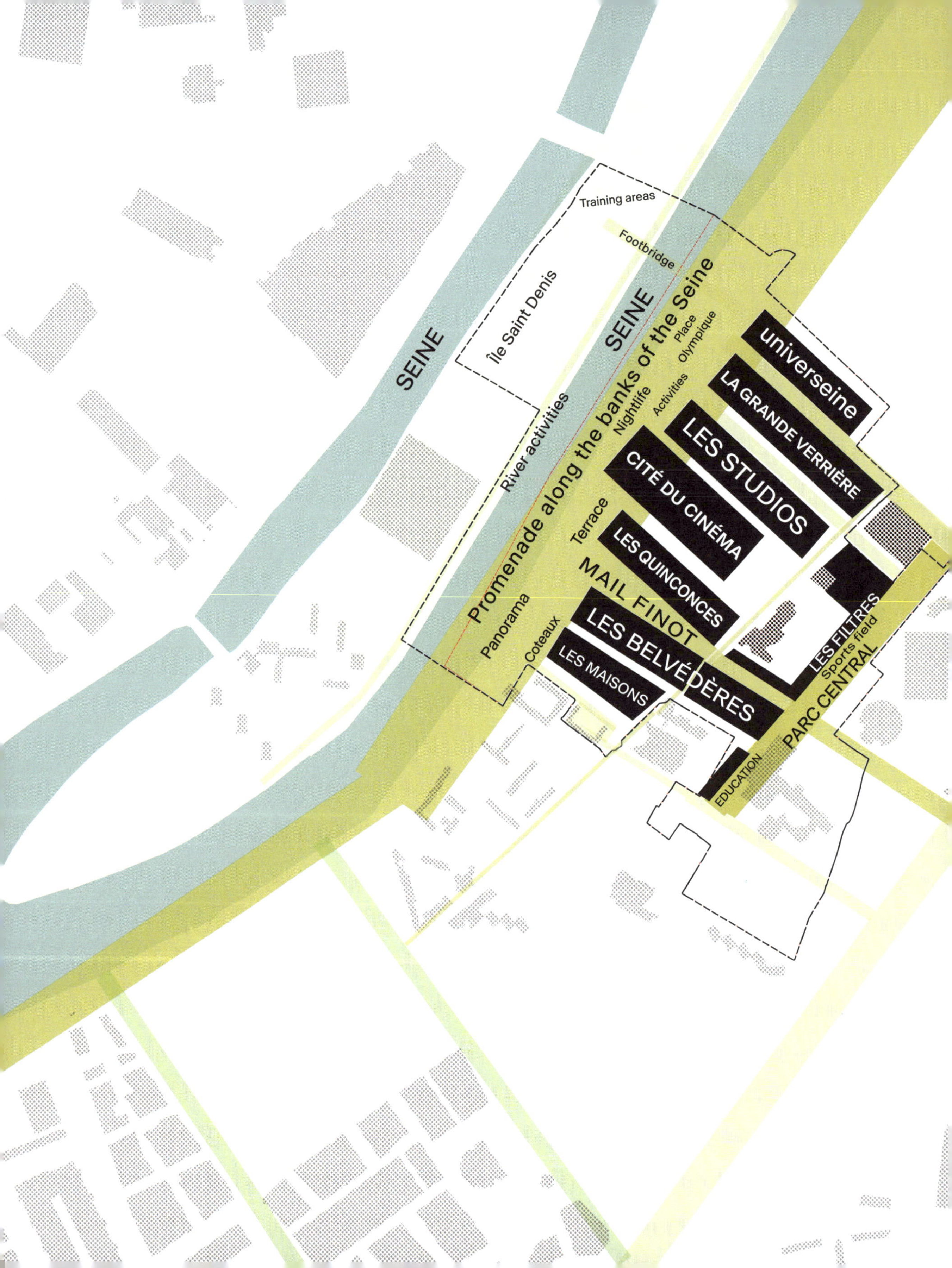
SEINE
Training areas
Footbridge
Île Saint Denis
SEINE
Promenade along the banks of the Seine
River activities
Place Olympique
Nightlife
Activities
universeine
LA GRANDE VERRIÈRE
LES STUDIOS
CITÉ DU CINÉMA
Terrace
LES QUINCONCES
MAIL FINOT
Panorama
Coteaux
LES BELVÉDÈRES
LES MAISONS
LES FILTRES
Sports field
PARC CENTRAL
EDUCATION

#117# **AMBITION 2**

URBAN IDENTITY

Guiding concept.

LES VILLAS
LES BELVÉDÈRES
LES QUINCONCES

#119# **AMBITION 2**

URBAN IDENTITY

Back to the Seine.

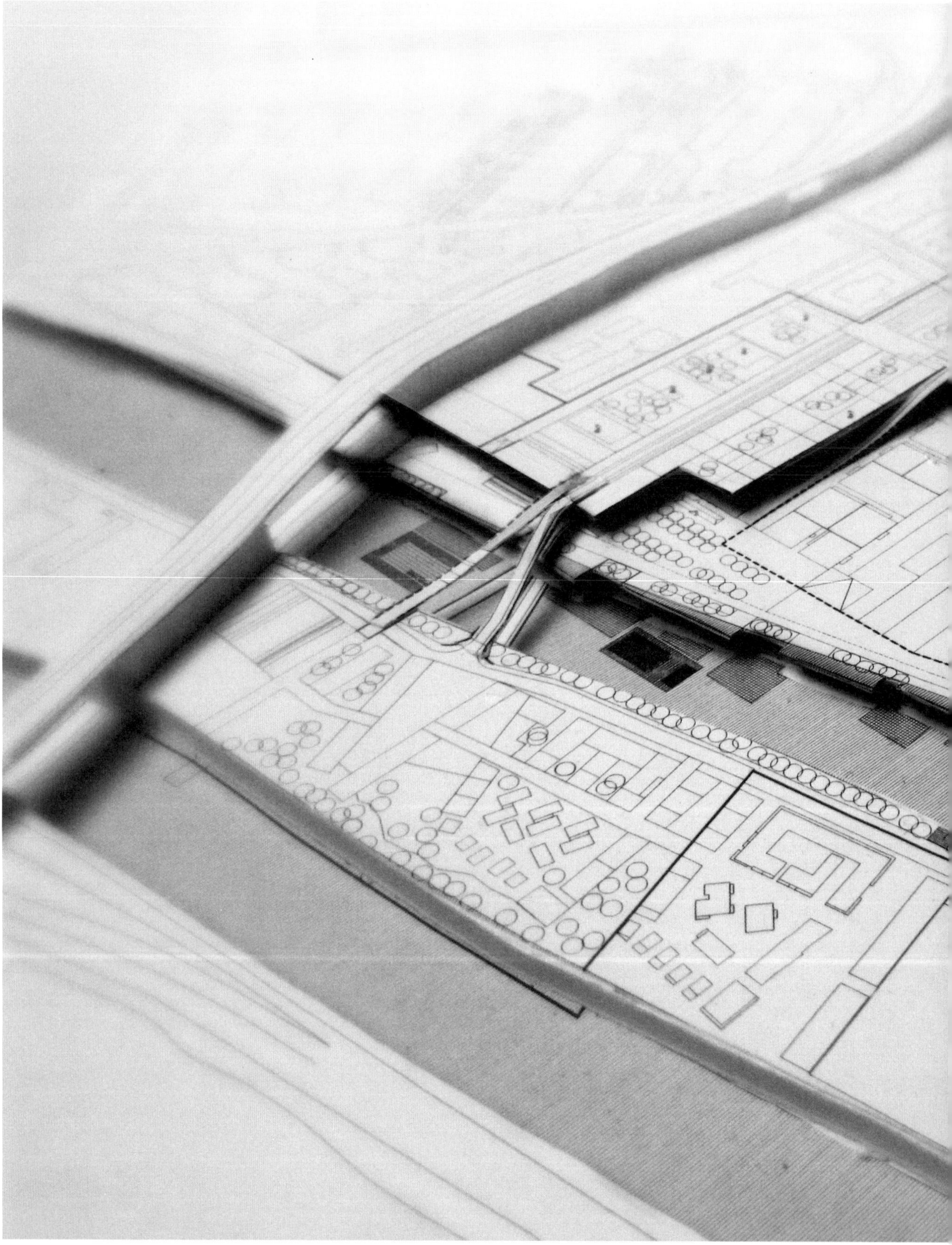

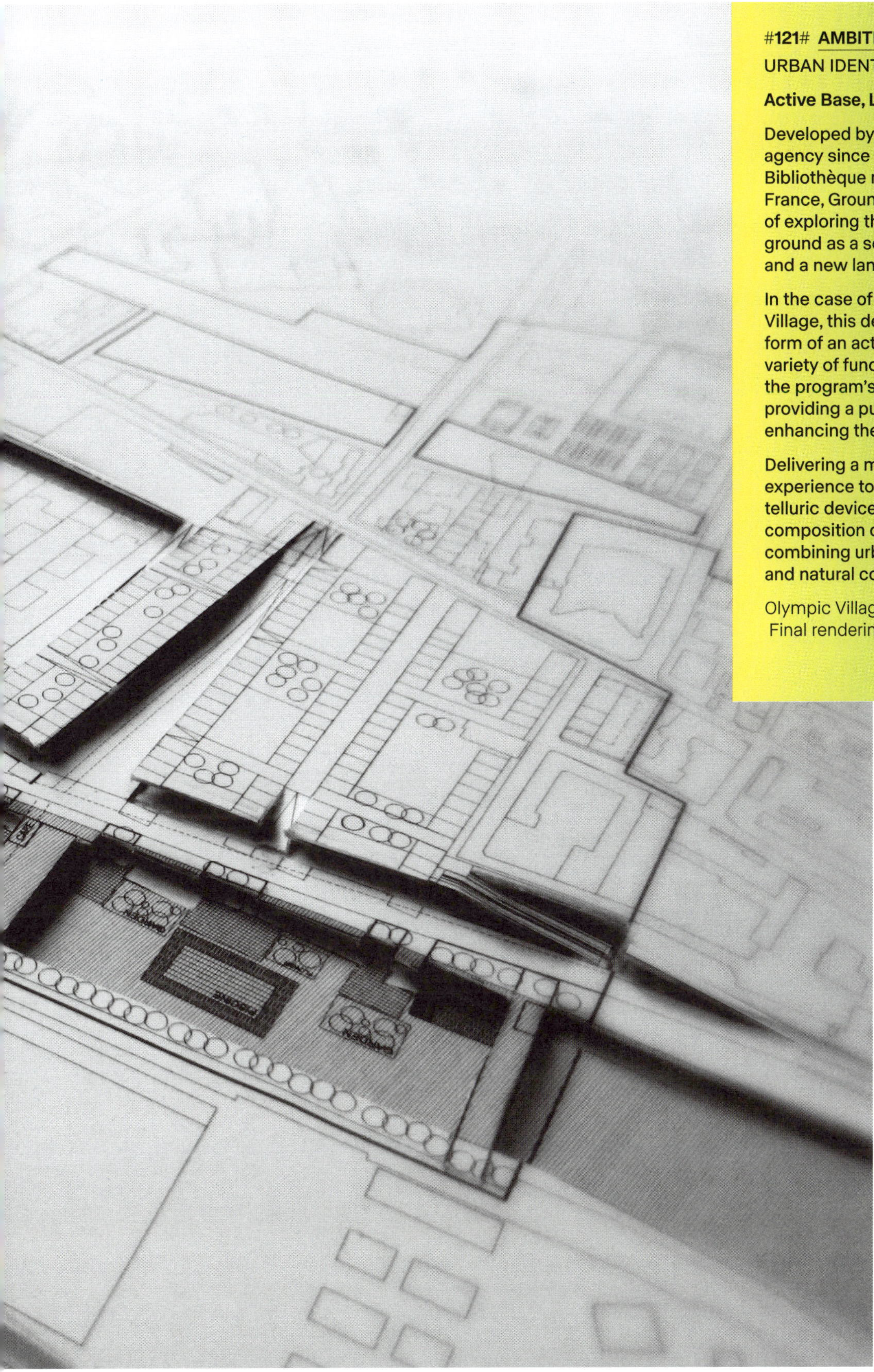

#121# **AMBITION 2**

URBAN IDENTITY

Active Base, Levelling

Developed by the DPA agency since 1989 and the Bibliothèque nationale de France, Groundscape is a way of exploring the thickness of the ground as a source of potential and a new landscape to explore.

In the case of the Olympic Village, this device takes the form of an active plinth with a variety of functions: sheltering the program's service areas, providing a public space, and enhancing the geography.

Delivering a memorable spatial experience to its users, this telluric device calls for the composition of a landscape combining urban, architectural, and natural components.

Olympic Village. Paris 2024
Final rendering, November 2016

Guide plan - Volumetric research

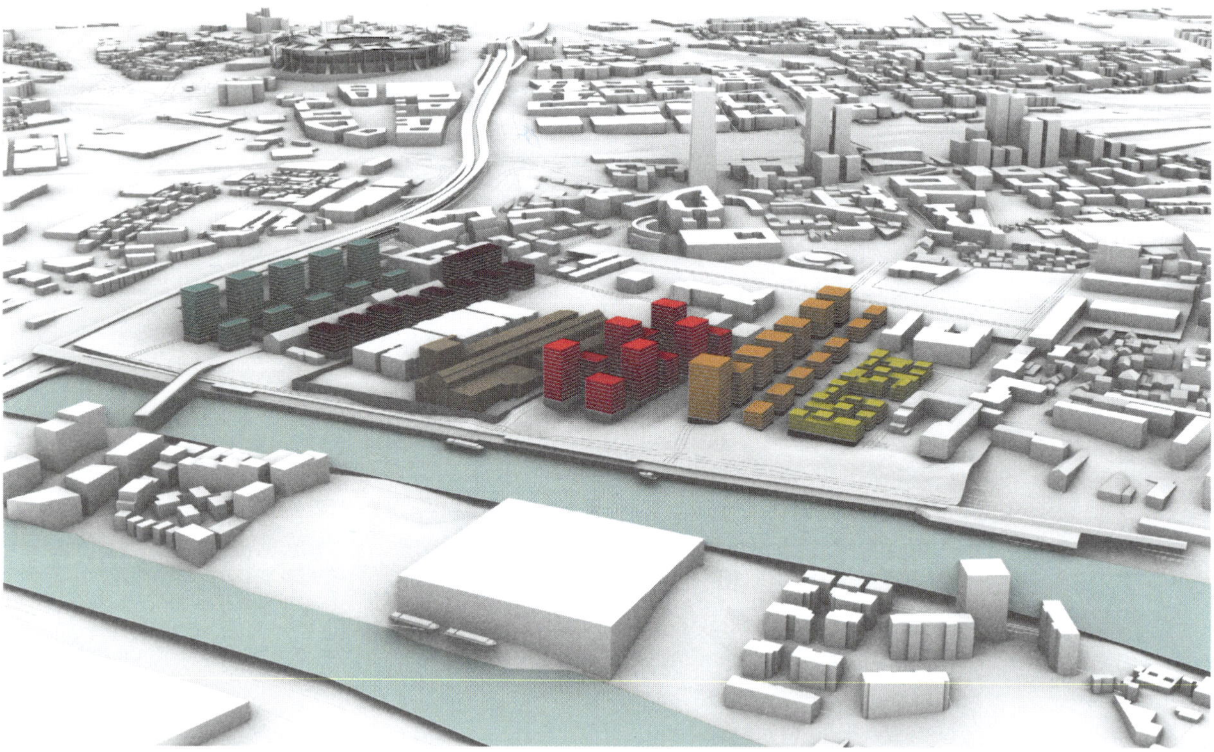

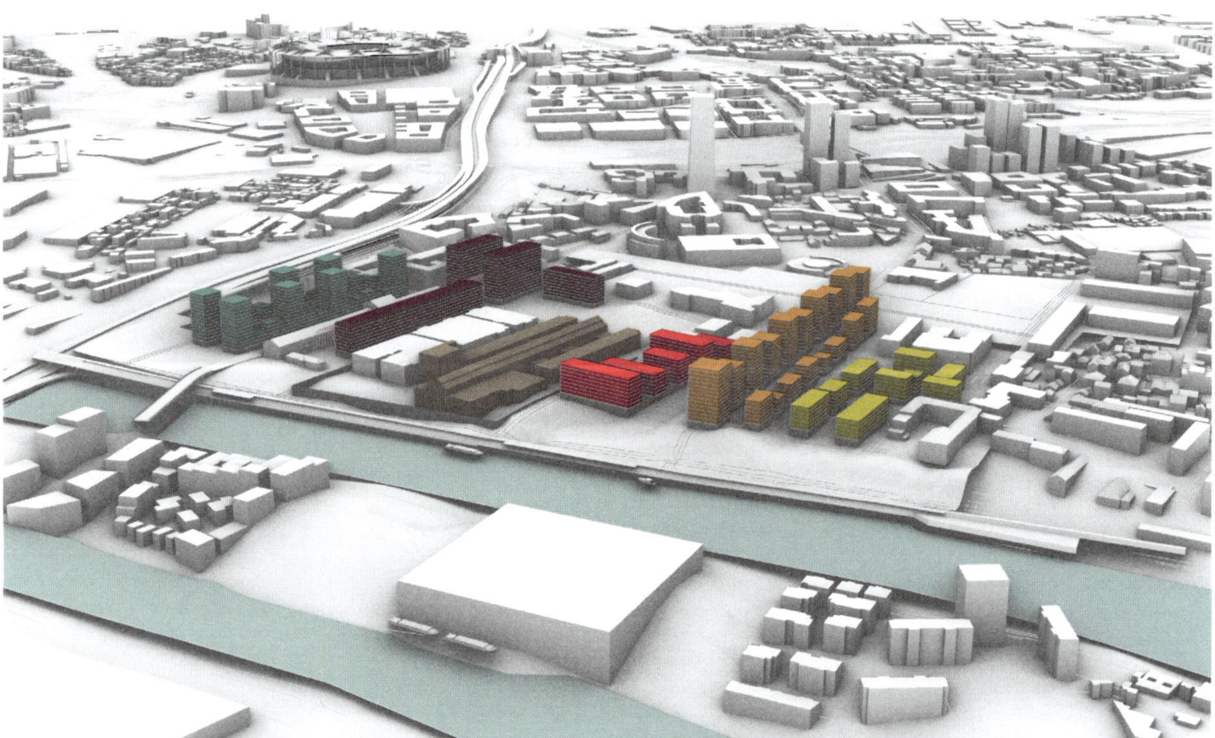

#123# **AMBITION 2**

URBAN IDENTITY

Urban morphology and form studies.

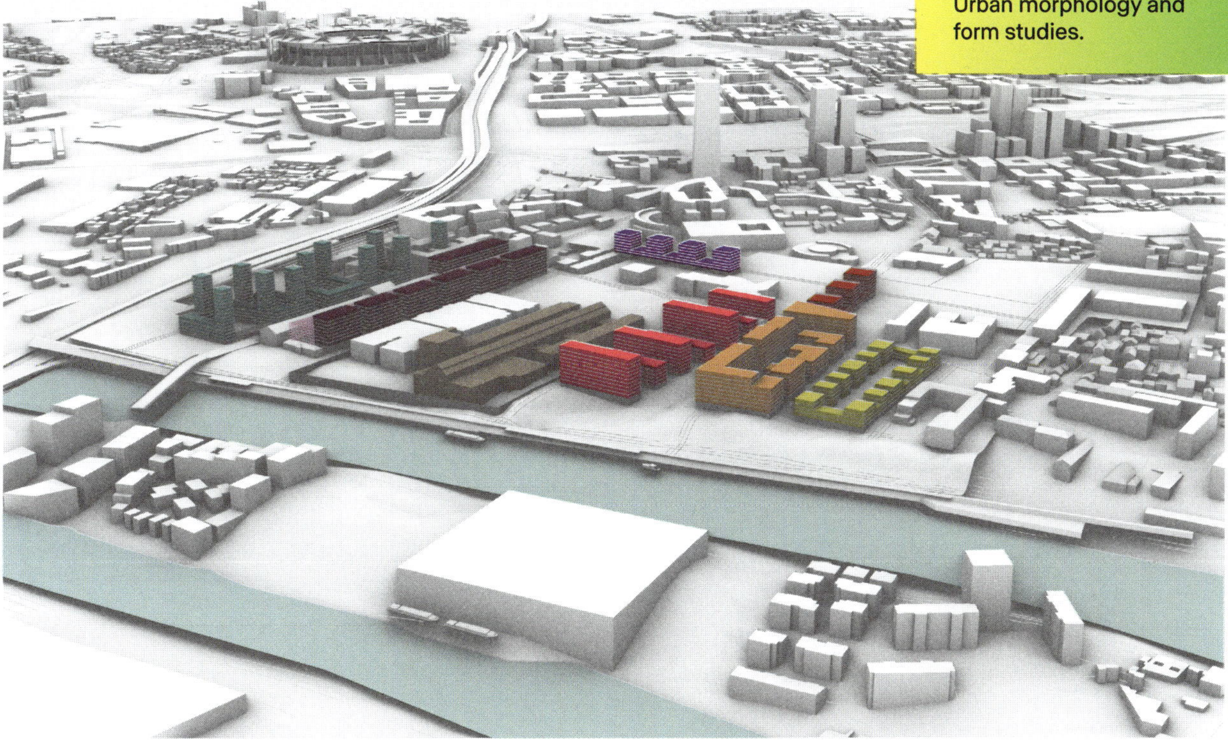

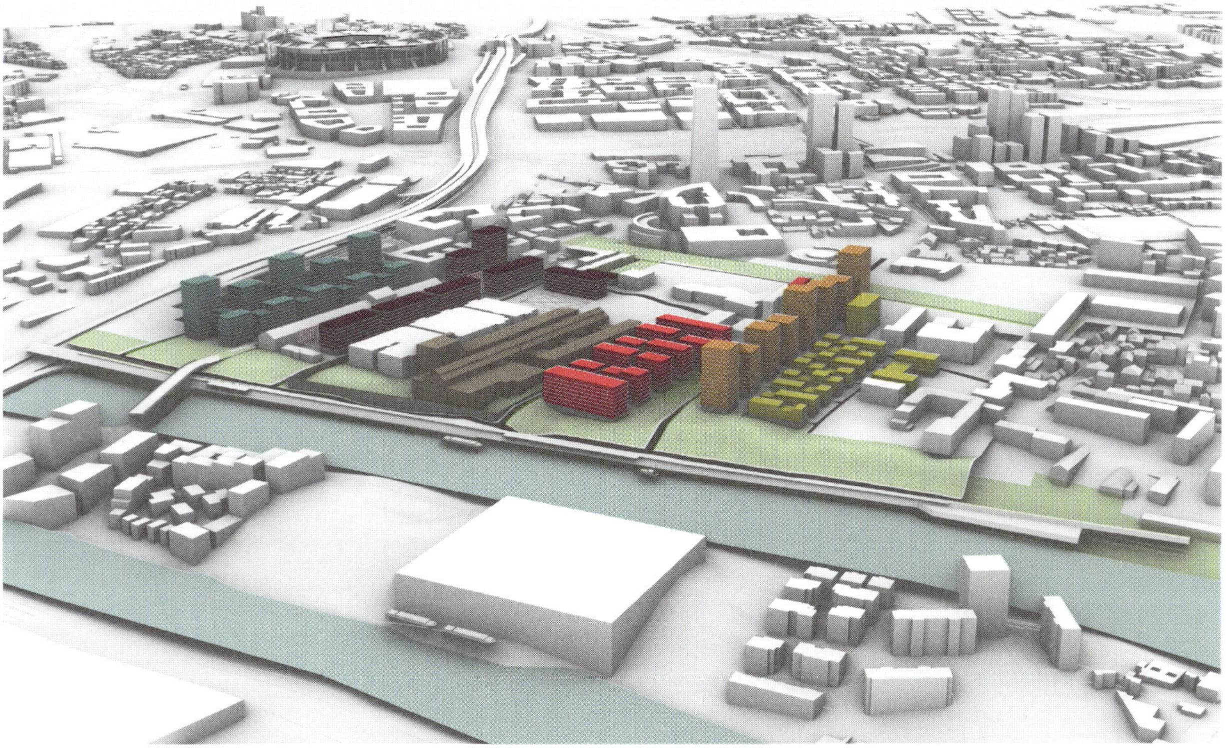

Sun exposure

VIEW FROM THE EAST

VIEW FROM THE WEST

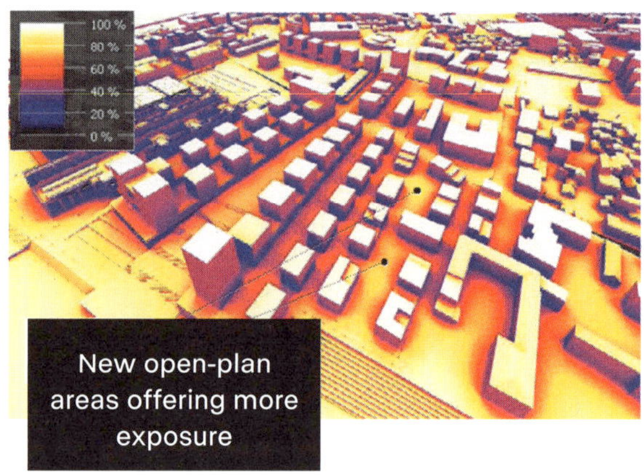

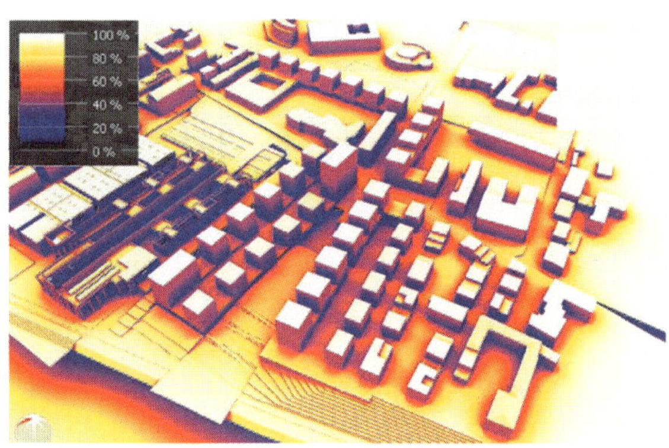

Simulation of prevailing winds

#125# AMBITION 2

URBAN IDENTITY

Urban morphology and form studies.

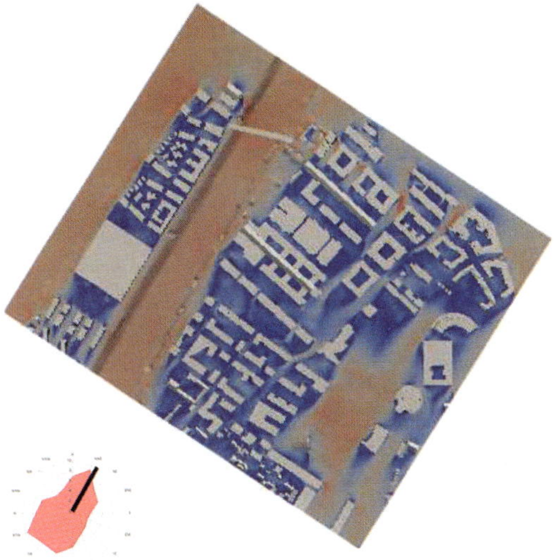

30°

This is a prevailing summer wind, but also occurs in winter. It is strongly accelerated in all the streets of Universeine and on the tower esplanade. Wind corridors are created along the axis of rue Ampère. The faults in the St Ouen section also create noticeable accelerations.

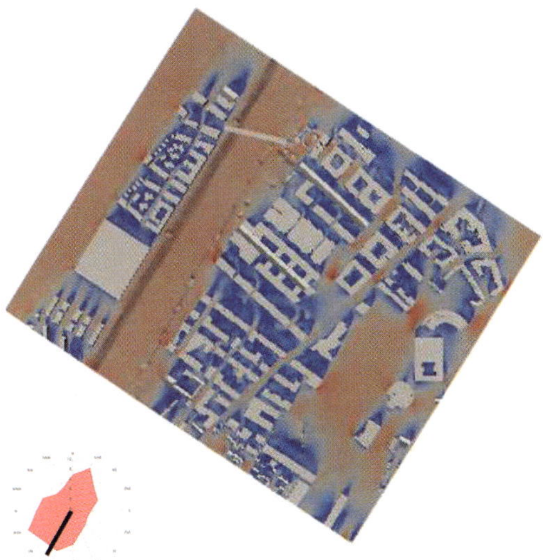

210°

The prevailing south-westerly wind, particularly in winter, rushes into the Seine canyon where it picks up speed. Gare Routière and Rue Ampère and its parallel. The result is significant corner acceleration along these corridors, which will no doubt require special treatment. Universeine is particularly affected by this direction, even though it is protected from it by the hall, as the few openings follow this direction.

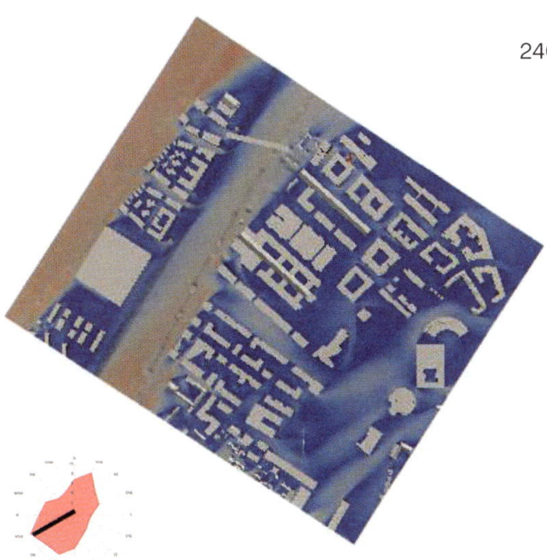

240°

This equally dominant direction moves very differently in the district because it is less accelerated by the Seine. Runoff is less concentrated at certain points.

In these two dominant directions (210 and 240), the Finot Mall is well protected. In the first direction, it is more protected, but with strong acceleration in front of the faults, whereas in the second direction the velocities are greater but less irregular (with, as a result, probably less discomfort felt).

U Magnitude

8m/s
28.8 km/h
15.5 knots
6 m/s
21.6 km/h
11.6 knots
4 m/s
14.4 km/h
7.7 knots
2 m/s
7.2 km/h
3.8 knots
0%

View from the North

View from the South

#127# **AMBITION 2**

URBAN IDENTITY

Urban morphology and form studies.

View from the East

View from the West

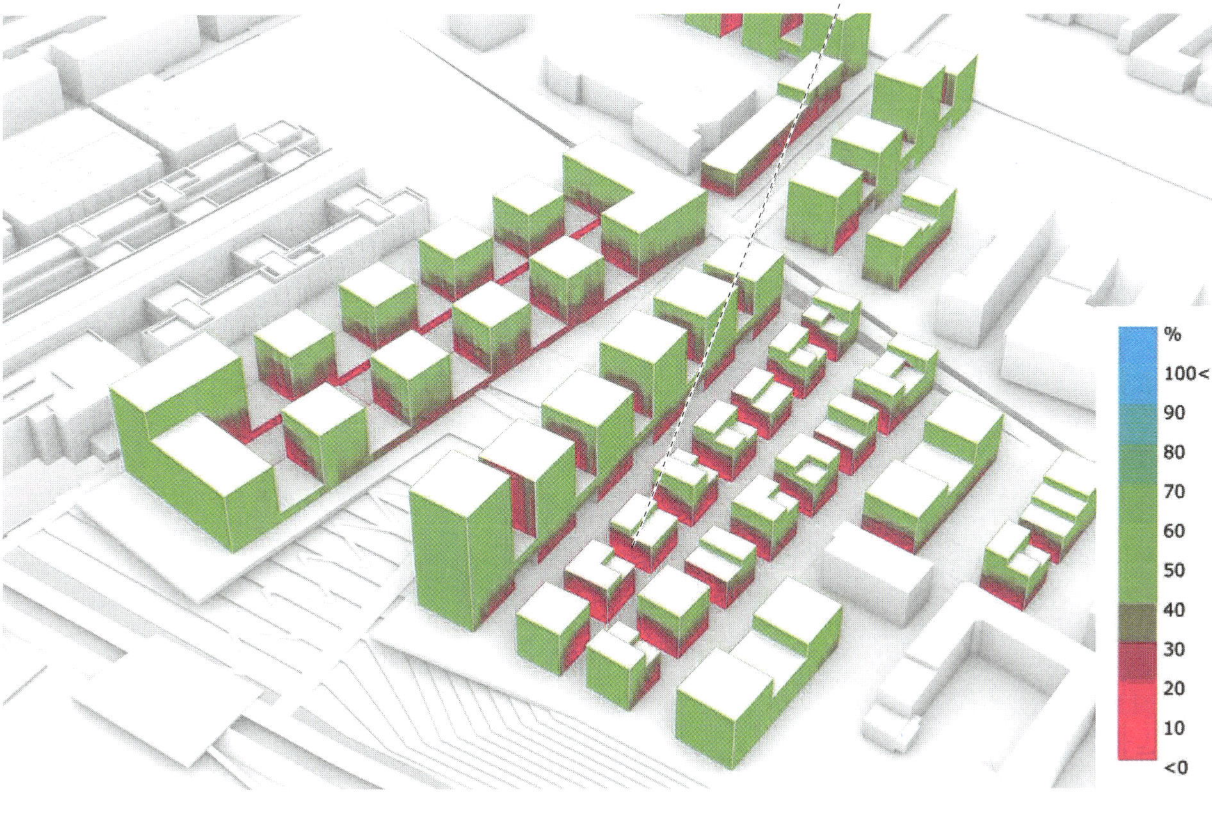

#129# **AMBITION 2**

URBAN IDENTITY

The experience of athletes in the Olympic and Paralympic Village.

#131# **AMBITION 2**

URBAN IDENTITY

The experience of athletes in the Olympic and Paralympic Village.

Summer Sunshine - Plan View

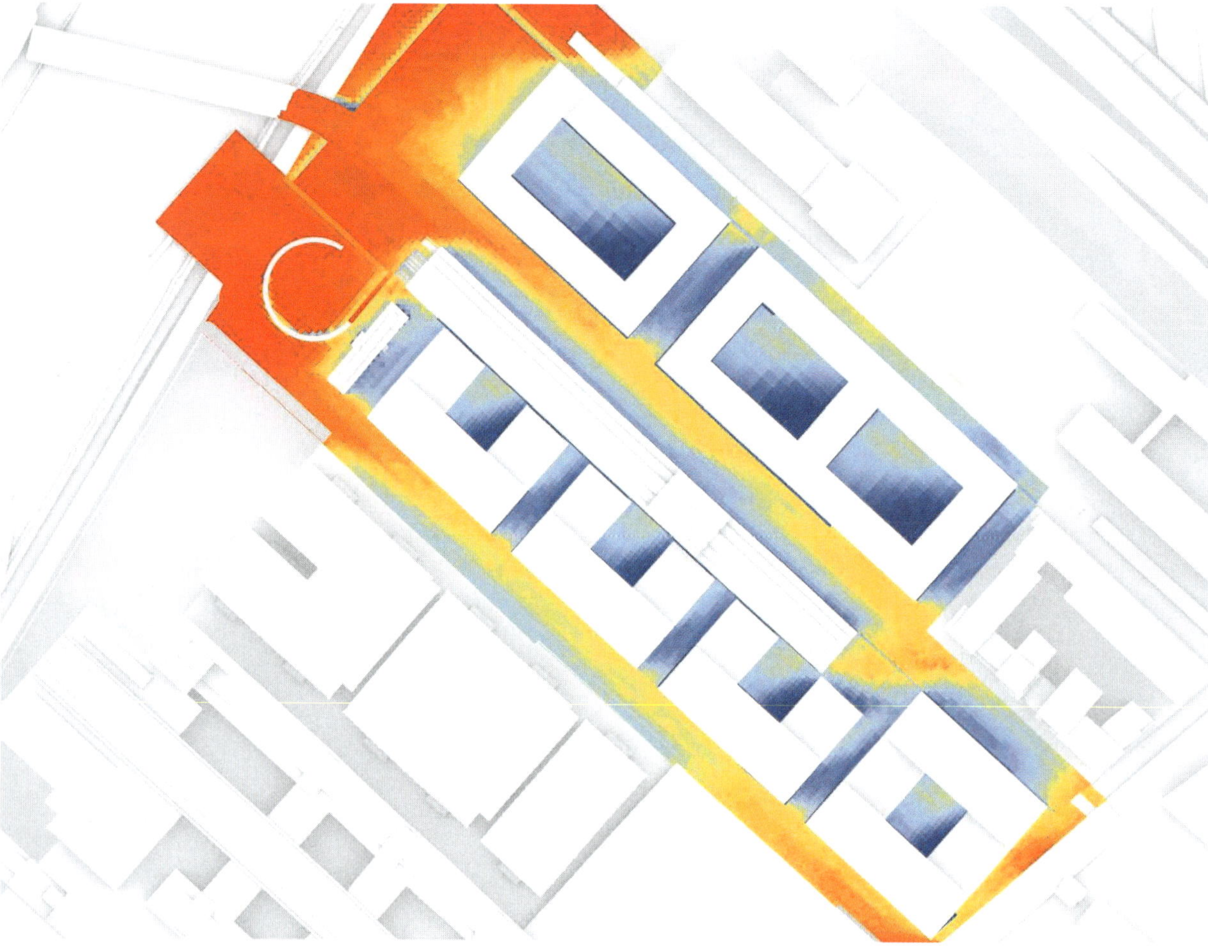

Summer sunshine from the facades

View from the North

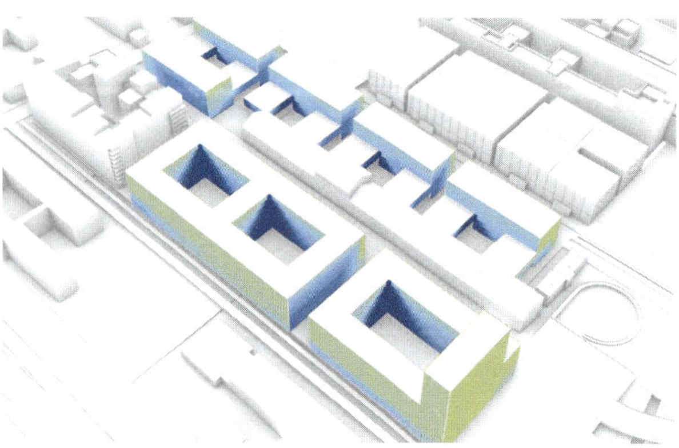

View from the South

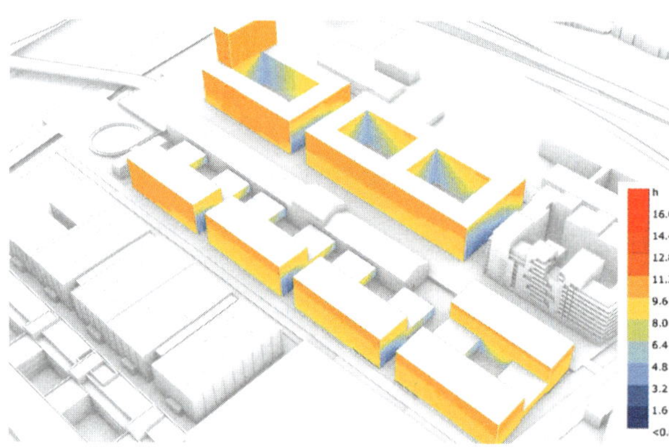

Heights and volumes - Organisation of programs

Detailed plan

Offers - December 2019

#133# AMBITION 2

URBAN IDENTITY

Urban morphology and form studies.

While they work best for natural light, courtyards maintain a presence of shade in the summer that should help keep them cool.

The question of the treatment of the eastern points of the Seine remains an issue for summer comfort, which can be dealt with by the place of open ground and vegetation (possibly with watering) and the choice of materials.

Offers - July 2020

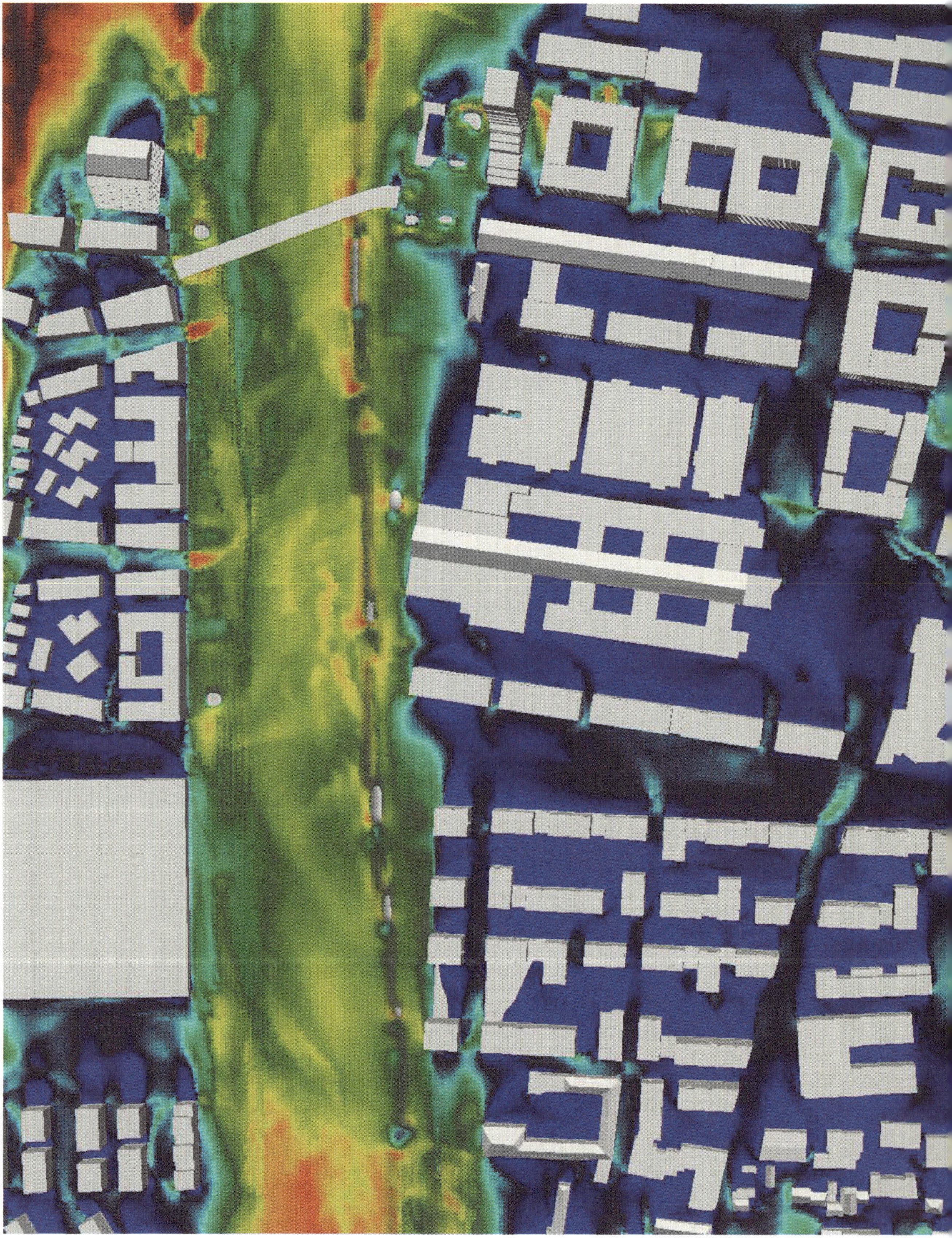

Probability of aeraulic discomfort

Possible uses	Probability of wind greater than 3.6m/s
Discomfort	40%
Active modes	30%
Normal walking	20%
Standing	10%
Seated	0%

PARIS 2024

#137# **AMBITION 2**

URBAN IDENTITY

Changes in General Volume

Architectural and urban development took place throughout the study of the master plan. The final proposal is the result of a work in which the 1000th scale model was used as an essential design tool. Numerous volumes were tested for each of the islands.

The volume representation helped to represent oneself and the model thus allowed the different participants, with different skills and knowledge, to visualize the spatial impact of the different scenarios represented. This tool allows you to

Easily compare different scenarios in parallel, making it an excellent discussion medium.

#139# **AMBITION 2**

URBAN IDENTITY

First models, 1:1000, 2019.

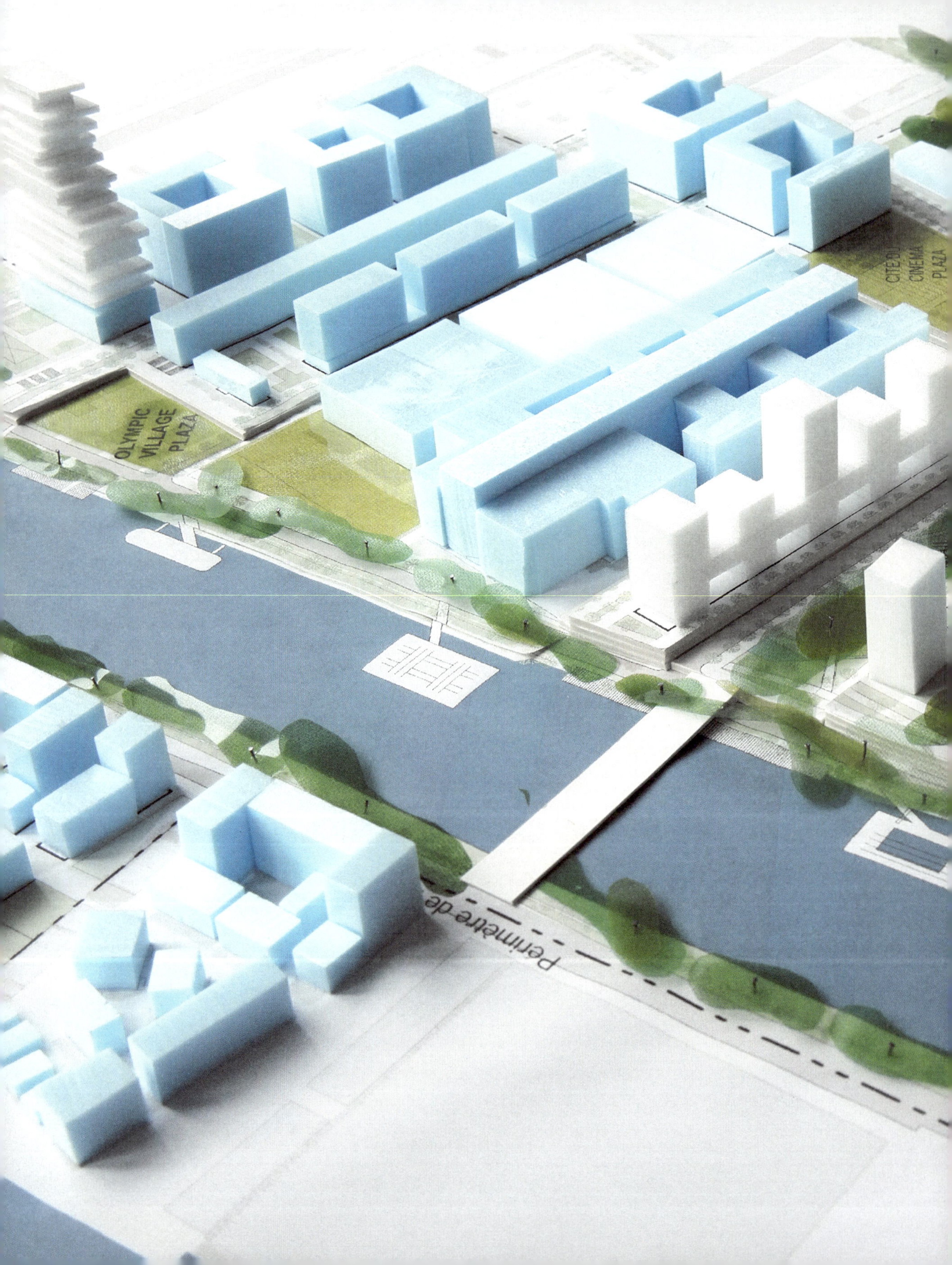
OLYMPIC VILLAGE PLAZA
CITE DU CINEMA PLAZA
Perimètre de

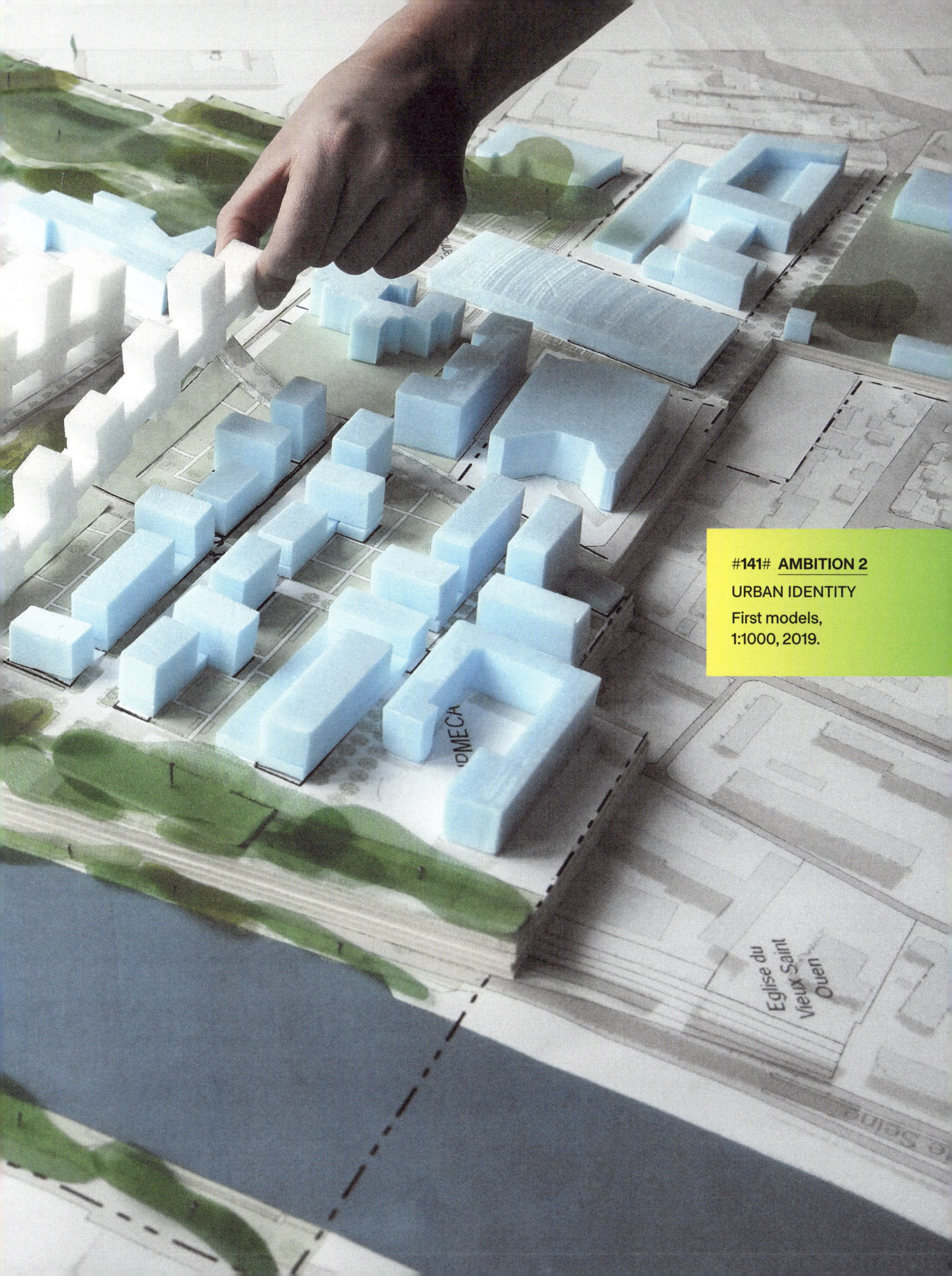

#141# **AMBITION 2**

URBAN IDENTITY

First models, 1:1000, 2019.

#143# **AMBITION 2**

URBAN IDENTITY

MIPIM model, 2019.

ESPAÑA
ESPAÑA
TÜRKIYE
TÜRKIYE
JAPAN

#145# **AMBITION 2**

URBAN IDENTITY

Public Space

The grid of public spaces is the structuring element of the village's urban project. It forms the backbone of the neighbourhood and helps to give it its identity. It also facilitates connections with neighbouring communities such as the southern district of Ile-Saint-Denis, Vieux-Saint-Ouen, and Pleyel. Beyond the Seine, the heart of the district, the structuring public spaces are:

The large perpendicular to the Seine, major links between Pleyel and the river: The Mail Finot, which gives a clear legibility to the Seine - Finot - Pleyel - Saint-Denis axis, The Allée de Seine, in the extension of the future pedestrian bridge that will span the Seine, future essential link in the link between the Universeine district, the river eco-district and the Pleyel cluster.

The two main parallels to the Seine: Rue Ampère, the backbone of the district, the main service road, and an essential link with the Vieux Saint Ouen district, the Parc Central, Parc Ampère and the Plaine des Sport, a large 2.5-hectare park around which several sports and cultural facilities are gathered.

In addition to these structuring public spaces, there must also be the central place of the Cité du Cinéma, which was conceived during the application phase and is now being called into question by land issues. Its function as a public space, a central square and the heart of a neighbourhood should not be set aside, but pushed back to a more distant time.

#147# **AMBITION 2**

URBAN IDENTITY

Public Space

The future public spaces of the Athletes' Village must be thought of on a double scale, that of the district and its immediate context, but also on the scale of the metropolis and this rapidly changing piece of territory.

The central location of the district in the Greater Paris area, its location in relation to the Seine, the challenges of integration into the existing urban and social fabric and the ambition to think of it as a laboratory for sustainable innovations (environmental excellence issues, maintenance and development of biodiversity, universal accessibility, among others) are the guiding principles on which our reflection for the preliminary design of public spaces is based.

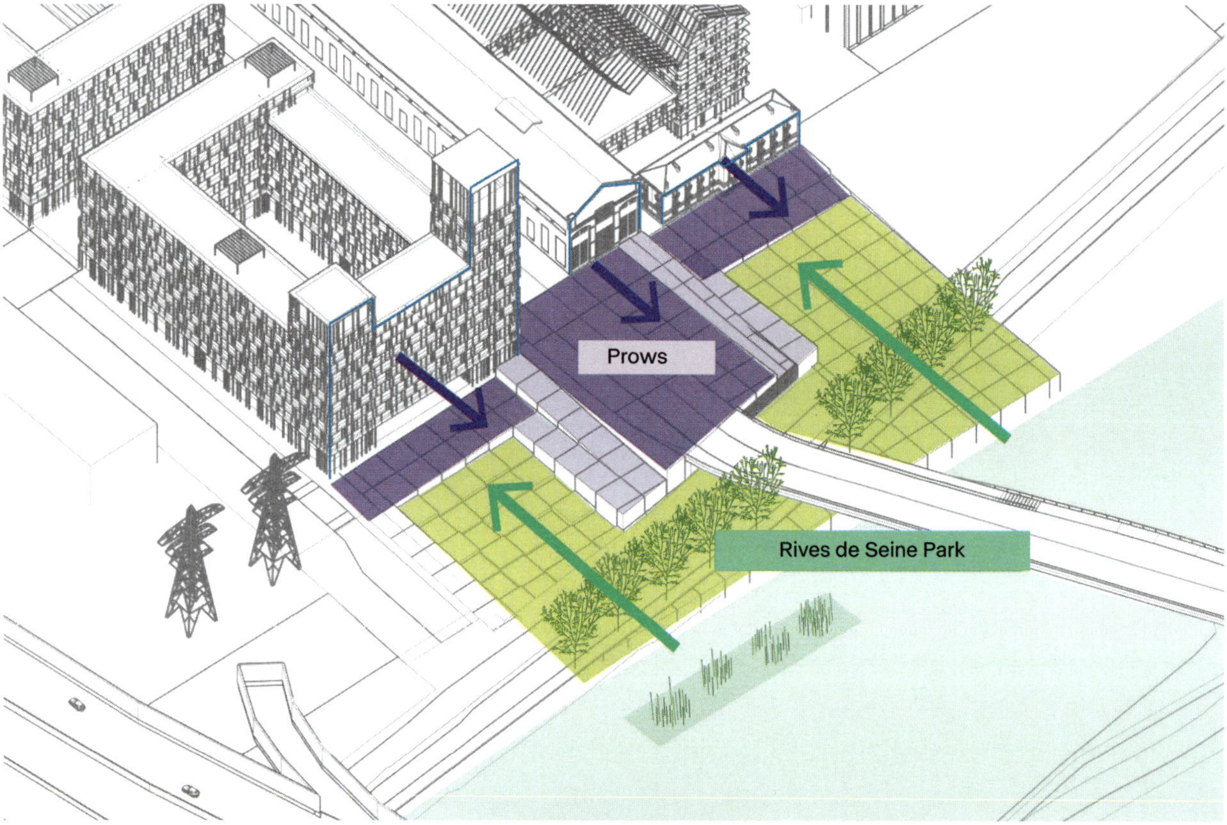

Prows
Rives de Seine Park

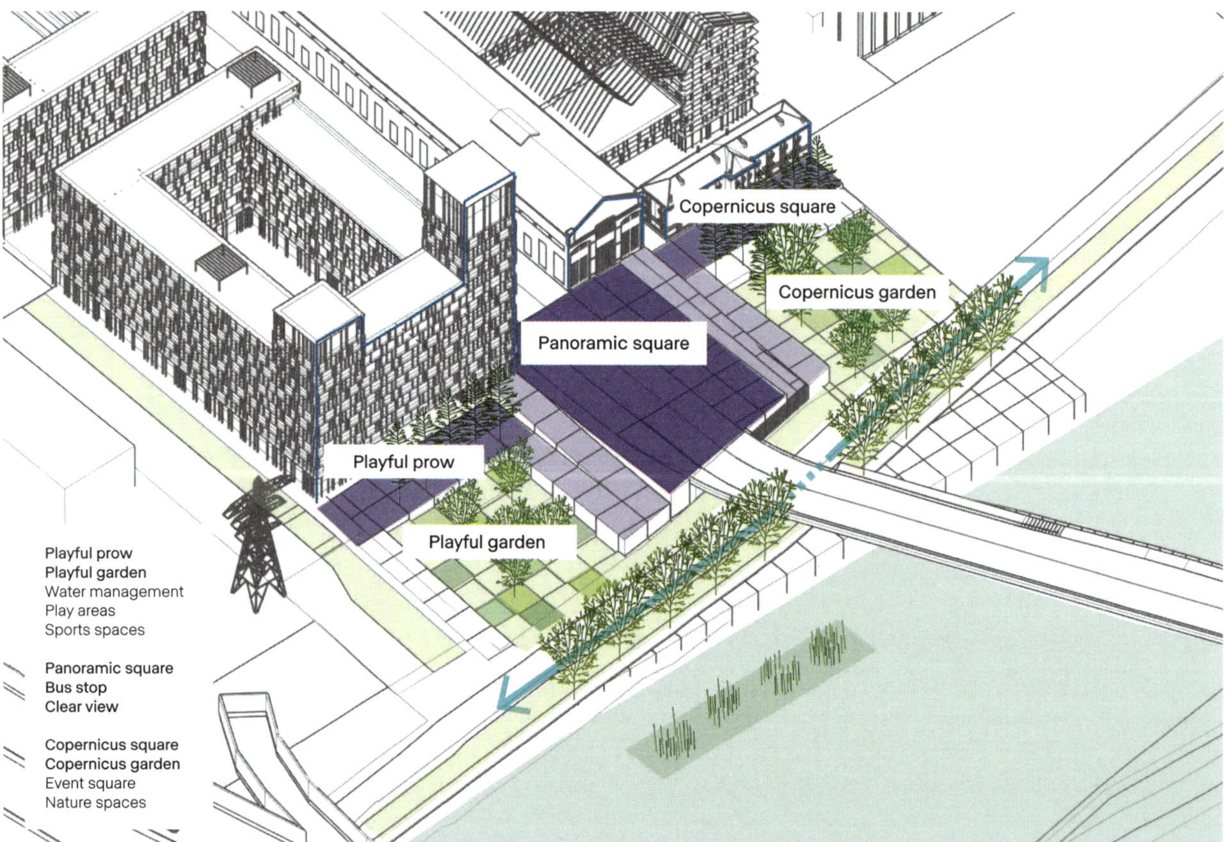

Copernicus square
Copernicus garden
Panoramic square
Playful prow
Playful garden
Playful prow
Playful garden
Water management
Play areas
Sports spaces
Panoramic square
Bus stop
Clear view
Copernicus square
Copernicus garden
Event square
Nature spaces

#149# **AMBITION 2**
URBAN IDENTITY
OVP and Allée de Seine.

#151# **AMBITION 2**

URBAN IDENTITY

Mail Finot

The Mail Finot is the major element in the conception of the relationship and descent to the Seine of the "great Dionysian territory", and of the link to the Gare Pleyel. It is also the central element of opening the banks to the city.

#153# AMBITION 2

URBAN IDENTITY

Mail Finot

Model, 1:200, 2020.

RDC programmes - Mail Finot

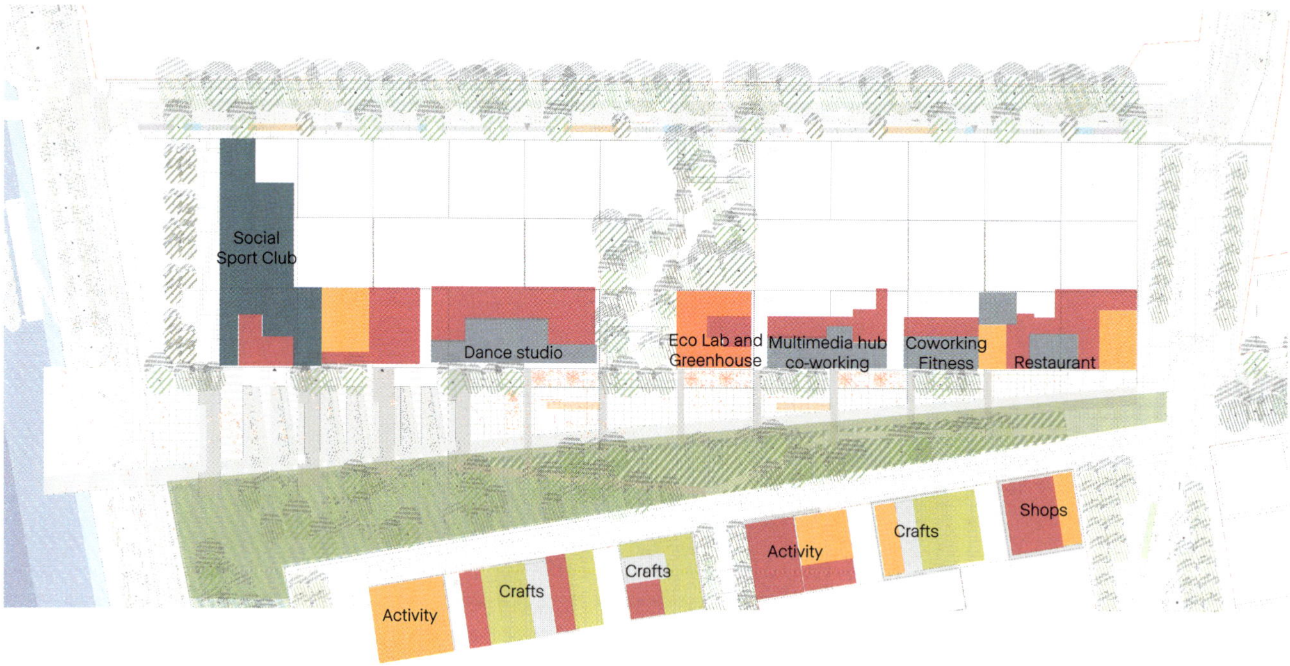

Openings in public spaces - Mail Finot

Sport programmes

Common areas

Business premises
Restaurants

Eco Lab

Crafts

N

#155# **AMBITION 2**
URBAN IDENTITY
Mail Finot
Visual master plan. 2019

#157# **AMBITION 2**

URBAN IDENTITY

An emblematic silhouette along the Mail Finot

Opening onto the Mail Finot, the active building bases open onto planted terraces facing south. The plinth crossing the shops and activities is raised by twelve 21x21m "pedestals" (two rows of six pedestals) of identical geometry and arranged in staggered rows to reduce the impression of mass, create visual openings towards the heart of the block and enjoy the views of the Seine.

Mobility

The Quinconce block is built around two key axes. The main one is the Mail Finot, a wide, traffic-free opening onto the Seine. Firemen's entrances have been integrated into the pathways. Finally, the creation of the street along the Cité du Cinéma will make it possible to provide the necessary access to the car parks, address the various buildings and ensure the continuity of the road axis towards the departmental road.

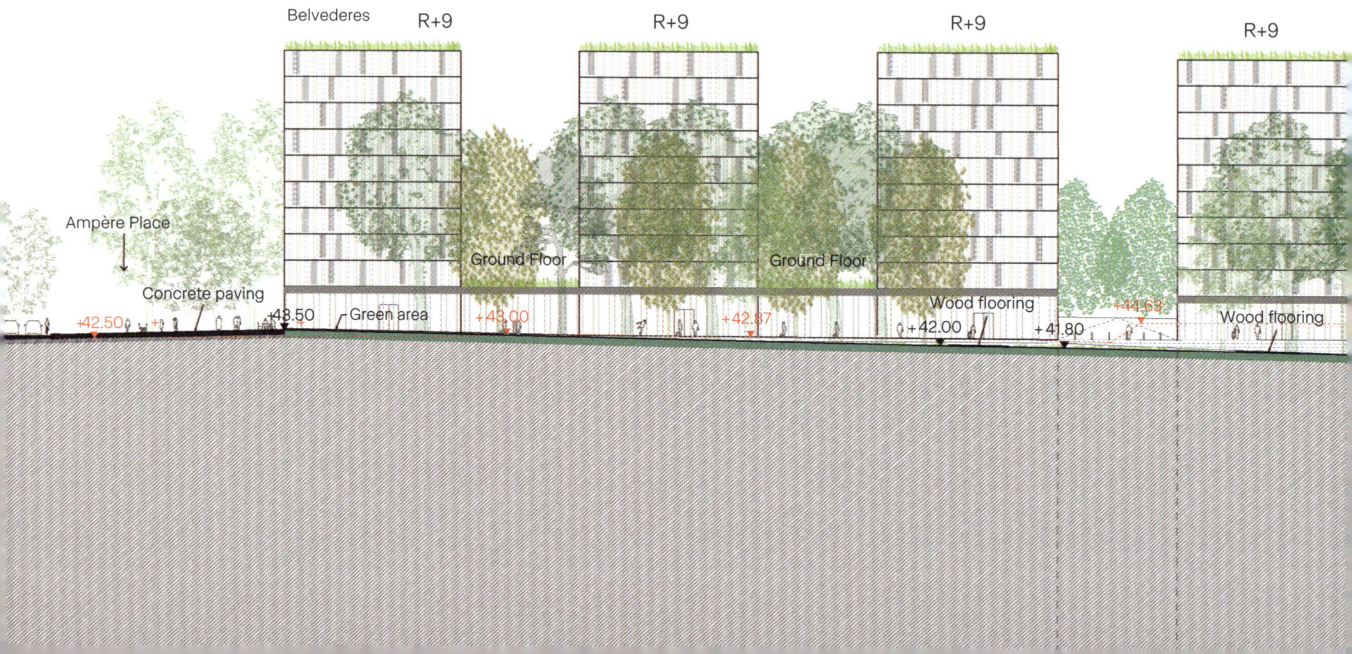
Belvederes
R+9
R+9
R+9
R+9
Ampère Place
Ground Floor
Ground Floor
Concrete paving
+42.50
+43.50
Green area
+43.00
+42.87
Wood flooring
+42.00
+41.80
+44.63
Wood flooring

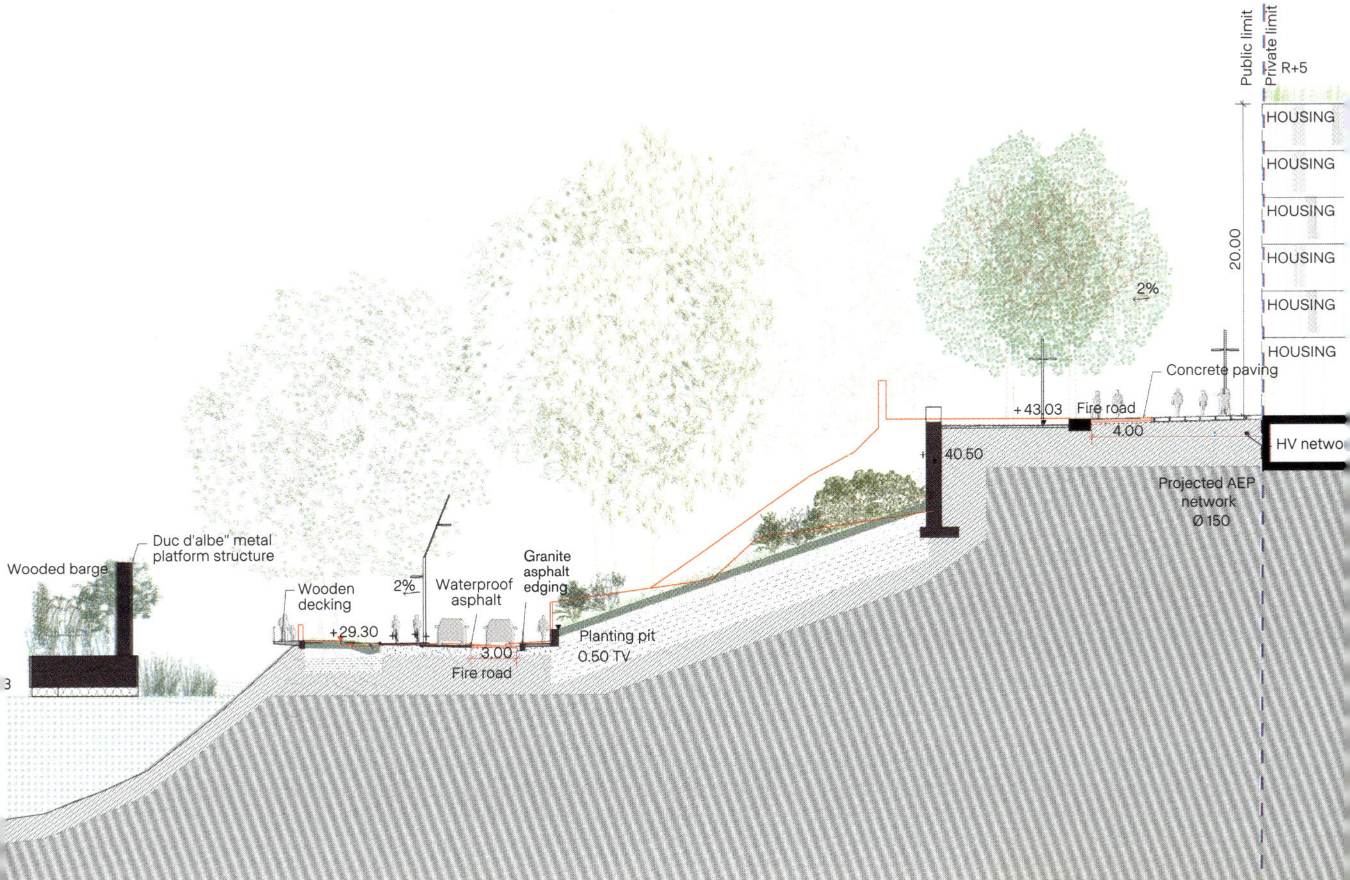

#159# **AMBITION 2**

URBAN IDENTITY

Mail Finot.

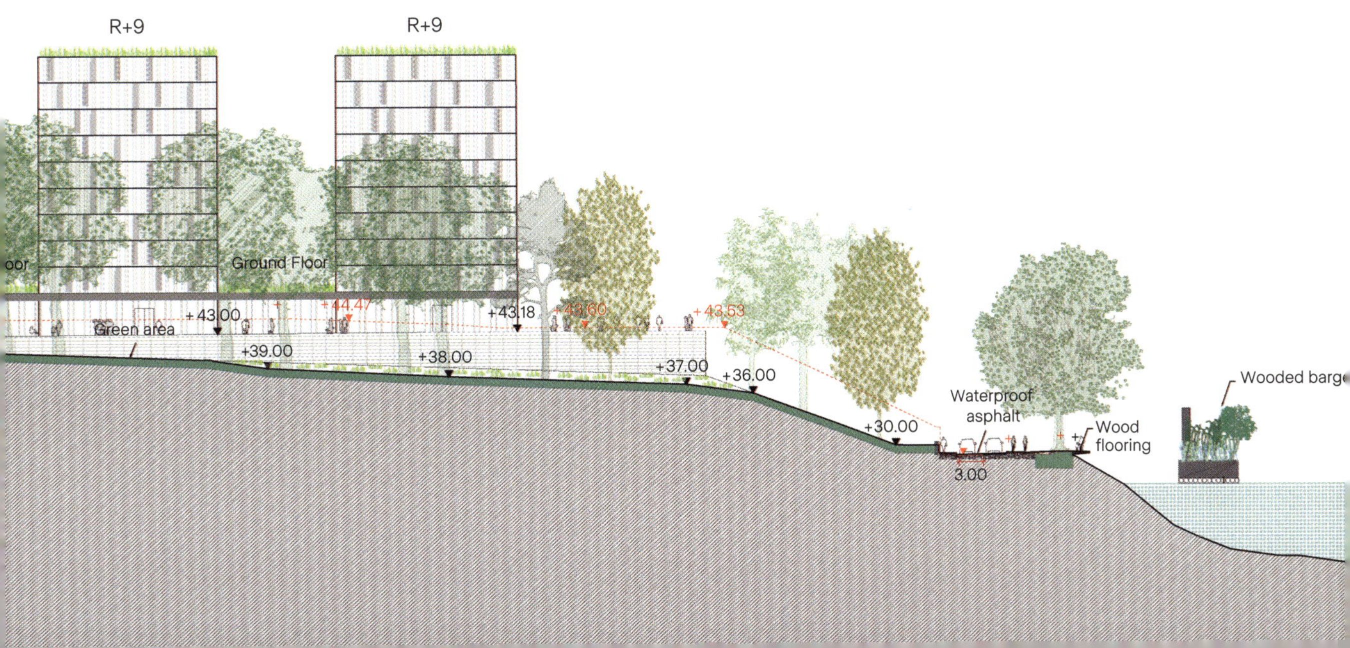

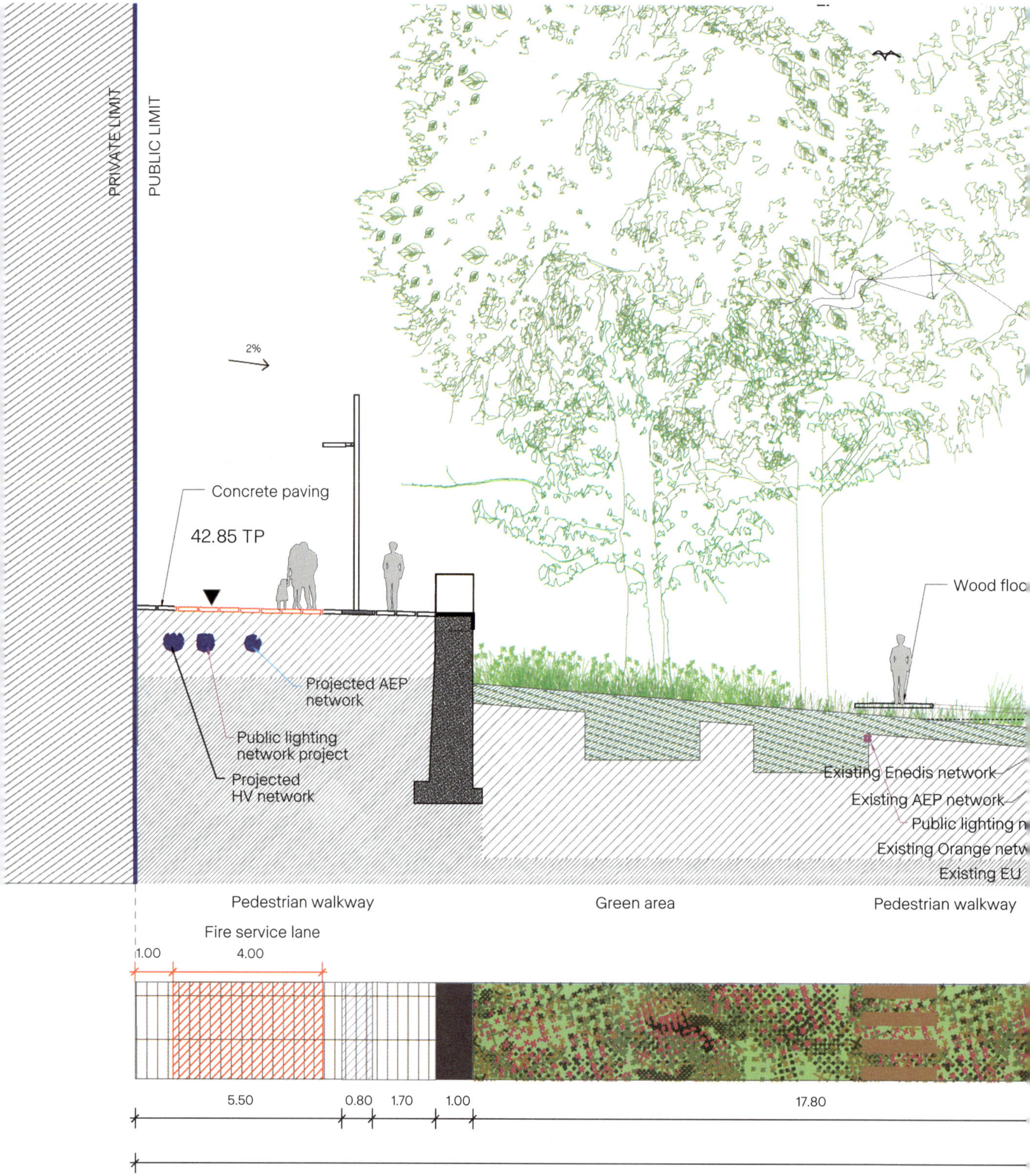
PRIVATE LIMIT
PUBLIC LIMIT
2%
Concrete paving
42.85 TP
Wood floo
Projected AEP network
Public lighting network project
Projected HV network
Existing Enedis network
Existing AEP network
Public lighting n
Existing Orange netw
Existing EU
Pedestrian walkway
Green area
Pedestrian walkway
Fire service lane
1.00
4.00
5.50
0.80
1.70
1.00
17.80

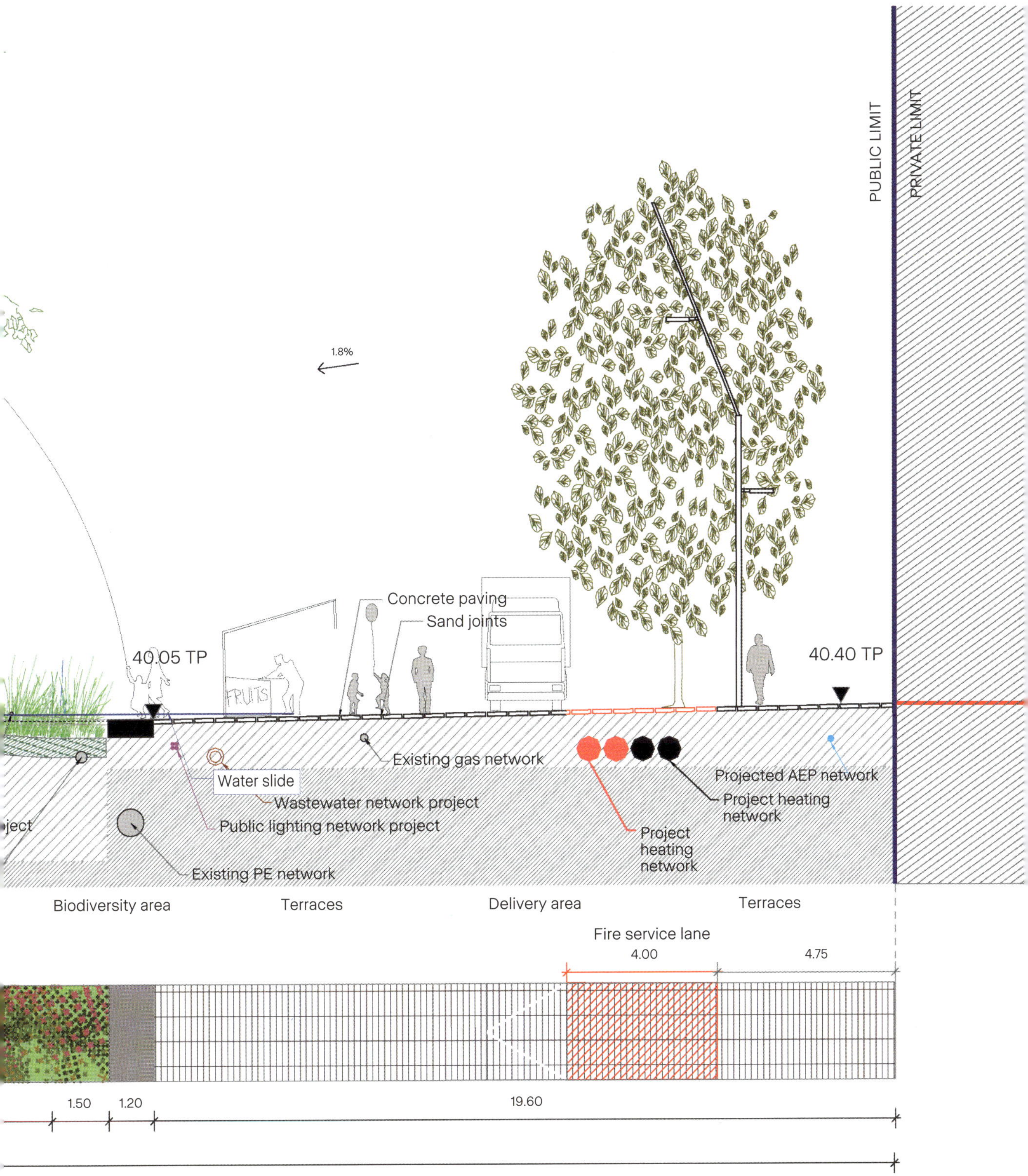
PUBLIC LIMIT
PRIVATE LIMIT
1.8%
Concrete paving
Sand joints
40.05 TP
40.40 TP
FRUITS
Existing gas network
Projected AEP network
Project heating network
Water slide
Wastewater network project
ject
Public lighting network project
Project heating network
Existing PE network
Biodiversity area
Terraces
Delivery area
Terraces
Fire service lane
4.00
4.75
1.50
1.20
19.60

PARIS

Mail Finot.

#165# **AMBITION 2**

URBAN IDENTITY

Mail Finot
Cross sections.

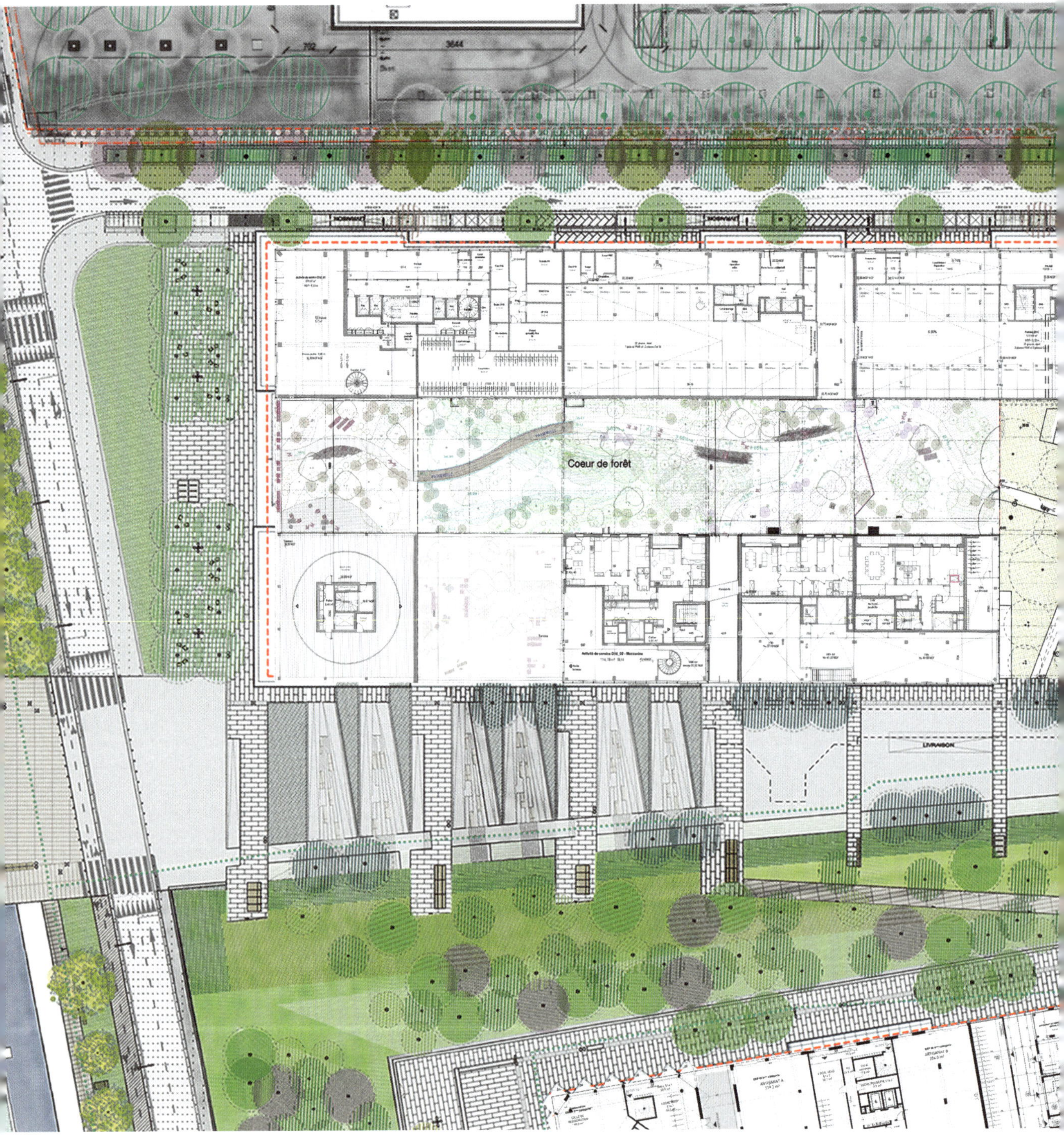
Coeur de forêt
LIVRAISON

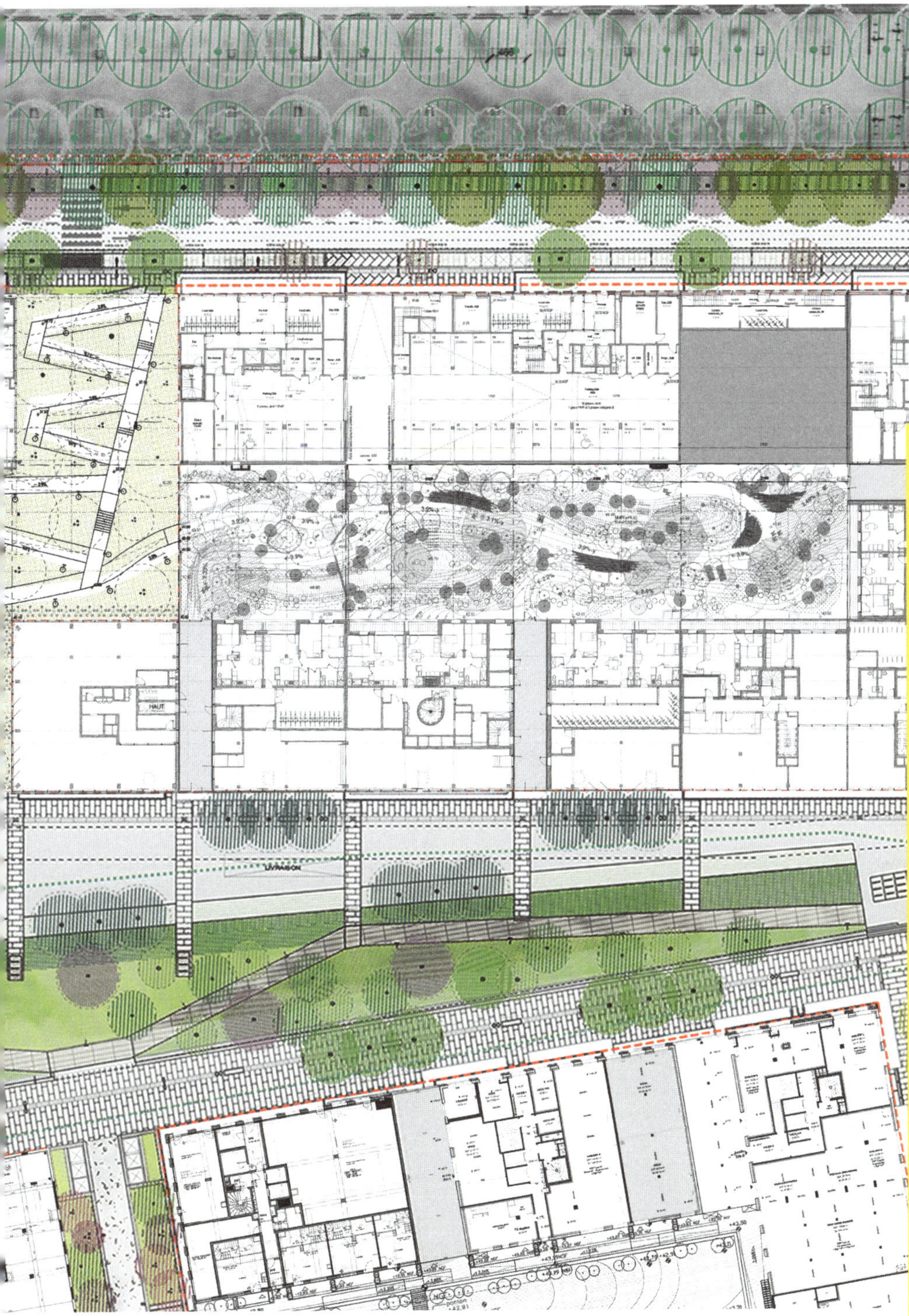

#167# **AMBITION 2**

URBAN IDENTITY
Mail Finot

Plan of public areas

All facades face due south onto the Mail Finot public space. R+9 on the Cité du Cinéma side, R+6 on the Mail Finot side, to ensure maximum sunlight for the heart of the block.

The block is punctuated to the north by an emergence of R+14. This building marks the address of the block on Rue Ampère and reinforces the commercial and business centre. It provides a degree of density and creates a landmark to mark the start of the descent to the Seine. A student residence has been designed as the bow of the development, opening onto the Seine.

The generous gaps between each plot (21 m between each 21x21m block) creates a rhythm in the facade, reducing the prominence of the building and filtering views while preserving light and space.

PARIS

#169# **AMBITION 2**

URBAN IDENTITY

The Cité du Cinéma

The Cité du Cinéma is built around public facilities that were previously untouched by urban development. The aim is to create a complex on the edge of the park, giving it a frontage and forming the main entrance to the future district.

In view of the loss of m2 of the block in front of the Cité du Cinéma (21,000 m2 SDP under consideration), and the absence of an urban façade on the Park, it is proposed to build housing on the southern façade of the Park.

The loss of m2 of green space (compared with the bid project) is offset by a significant gain in m2 of green space on the banks of the Seine. The morphology of this block creates different links between the public spaces. The need for construction also allows the integration of existing buildings without urban facades.

AMBITION 3

THE REVERSIBLE CITY

Once the Games are over, the road map for the long-term life of this new metropolitan mixed-use district of the Athletes' Village will unfold. The principle of full reversibility was key to the entire public commission. From the departure of the nearly 14,500 athletes and their entourages, a 2-year project will begin to transform bedrooms, living areas, bathrooms, and welcoming facilities for the sports delegations into apartments and offices. The receptivity of the Village to its mutation into a mixed-use district required all our energy and inventiveness. The project was a first in the history of Olympic Villages. The modularity of interior spaces of the city blocks is also at the service of the district's future adaptability, which must be made available for other uses over time.

In an open work, the author (here the architect-urbanist) leaves it up to the interpreter (the inhabitant) to determine the possibilities for multiple, coherent forms of intervention. The author cannot anticipate everything. However, as the work is endowed with a constructive logic and precise and constant structural properties, it will continue to grow and mutate through unforeseen uses. Its structures are both complete and unfinished. The inhabitant-interpreter must perform the architecture of the Village, triggering it with each new use. The project management aims for this availability of the built environment to its future potential.

To do this, we had to innovate through legal regulations. The Etablissement public territorial de Plaine Commune invented the "dual status permit" – two nested construction permits – programming future mutations, to secure private investment with the proof of planning. This reversibility offers avenues for designing new types of property investment products.

The approximately 2,400 apartments to come and a floor area of 119,000 m² for businesses, services, offices, and facilities are destined to form a new district in Seine-Saint-Denis in 2025, when approximately 8,000 inhabitants are expected. This is what the legacy of the Paris Games must be.

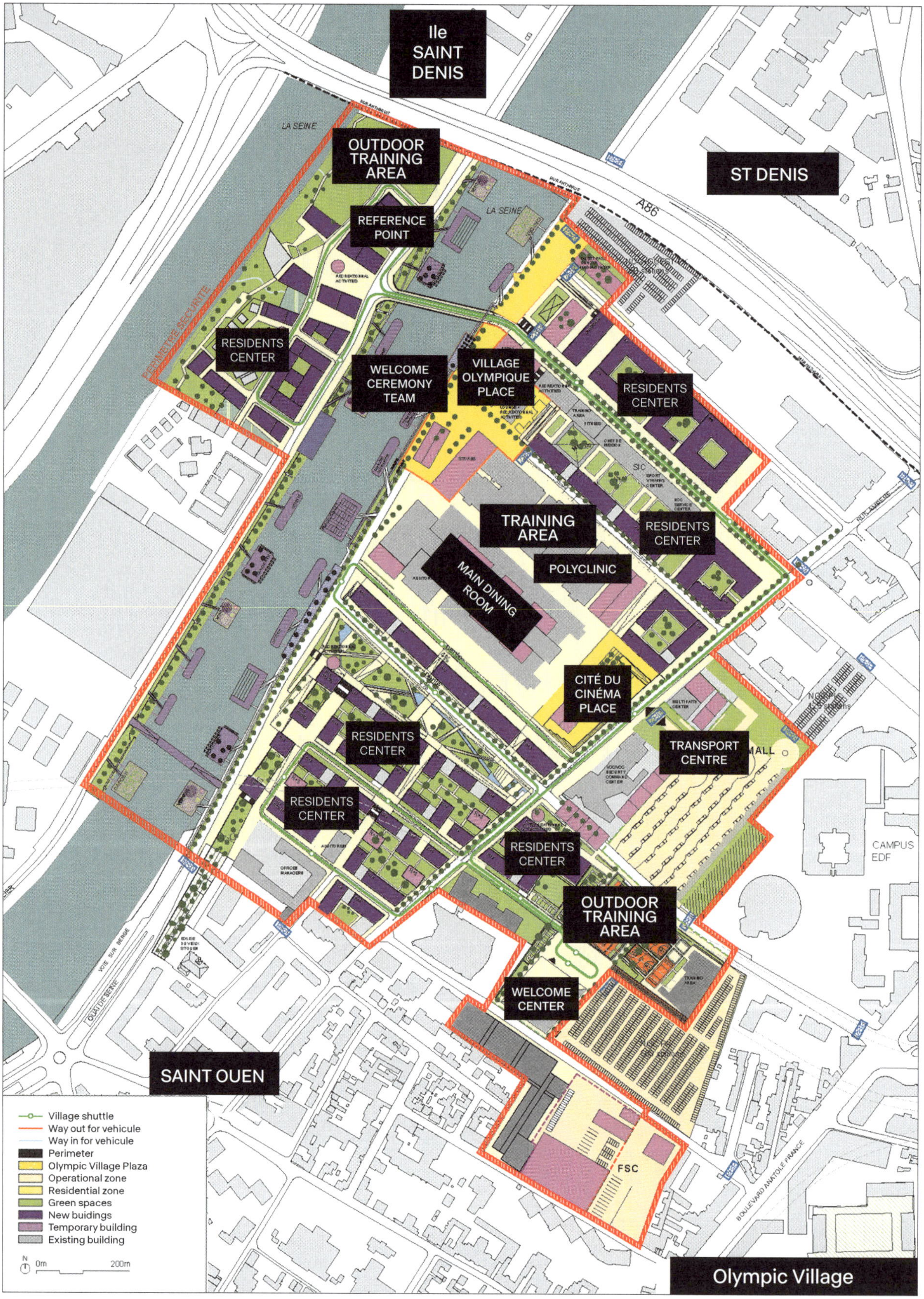

Ile SAINT DENIS
ST DENIS
OUTDOOR TRAINING AREA
REFERENCE POINT
RESIDENTS CENTER
WELCOME CEREMONY TEAM
VILLAGE OLYMPIQUE PLACE
RESIDENTS CENTER
TRAINING AREA
RESIDENTS CENTER
POLYCLINIC
MAIN DINING ROOM
CITÉ DU CINÉMA PLACE
TRANSPORT CENTRE
RESIDENTS CENTER
RESIDENTS CENTER
RESIDENTS CENTER
OUTDOOR TRAINING AREA
WELCOME CENTER
FSC
CAMPUS EDF
SAINT OUEN
LA SEINE
A86
Village shuttle
Way out for vehicule
Way in for vehicule
Perimeter
Olympic Village Plaza
Operational zone
Residential zone
Green spaces
New buidings
Temporary building
Existing building
0m
200m
Olympic Village

#175# **AMBITION 3**

THE REVERSIBLE CITY

The urban project designed for the Village offers great flexibility and allows for the reversibility of the facilities after the event. It is currently a mixed territory in terms of its functions and is undergoing a major transformation.

The urban strategy undertaken is above all a long-term reflection. The aim is to create a new sustainable neighbourhood, a piece of the city offered to all, anchored in its territory and geography.

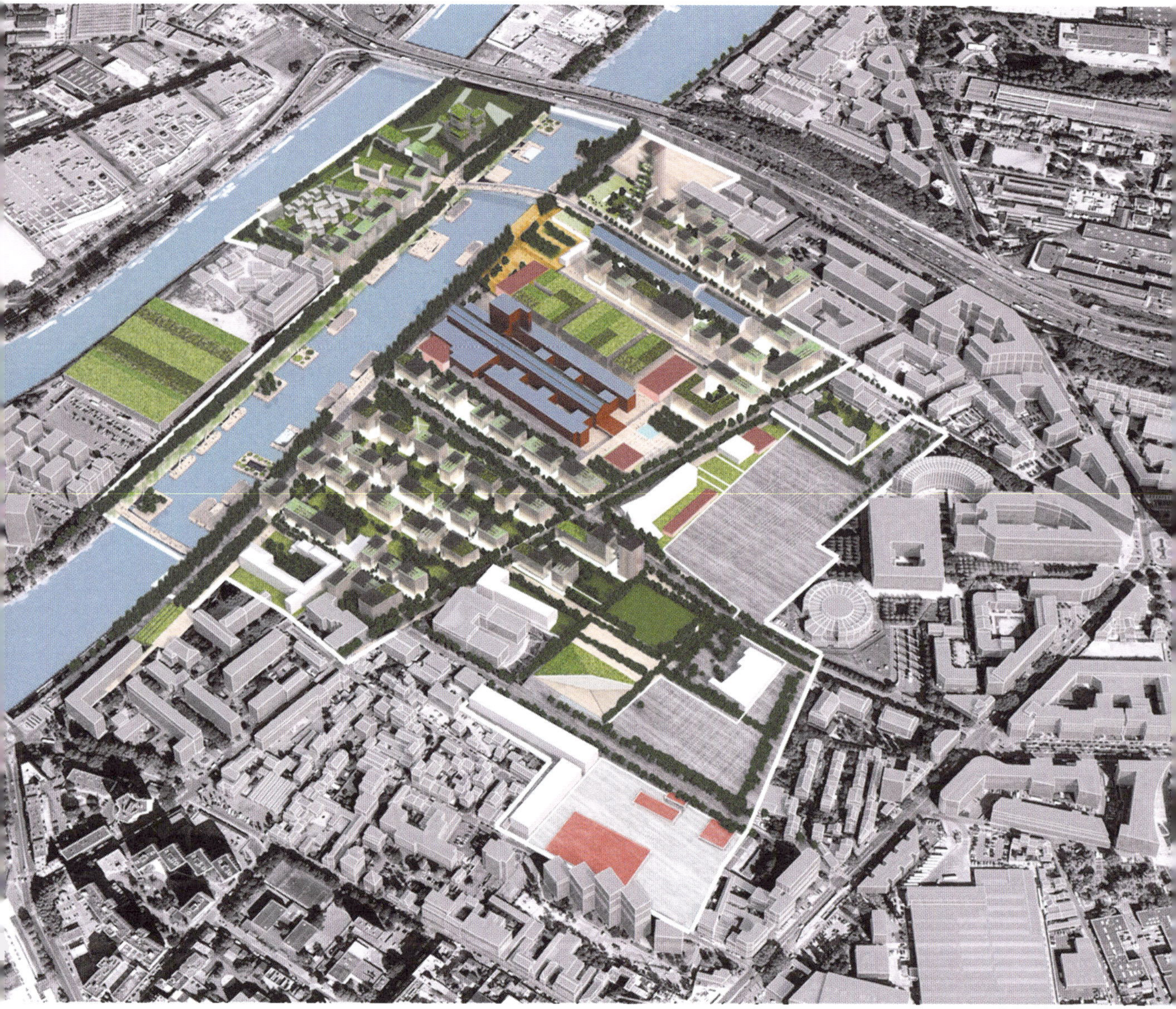

#177# **AMBITION 3**

THE REVERSIBLE CITY

Urban form and reversibility.

Qualities of an urban form.

The concept of the village.

The village during the Olympic Games.

The post-Olympic Games village.

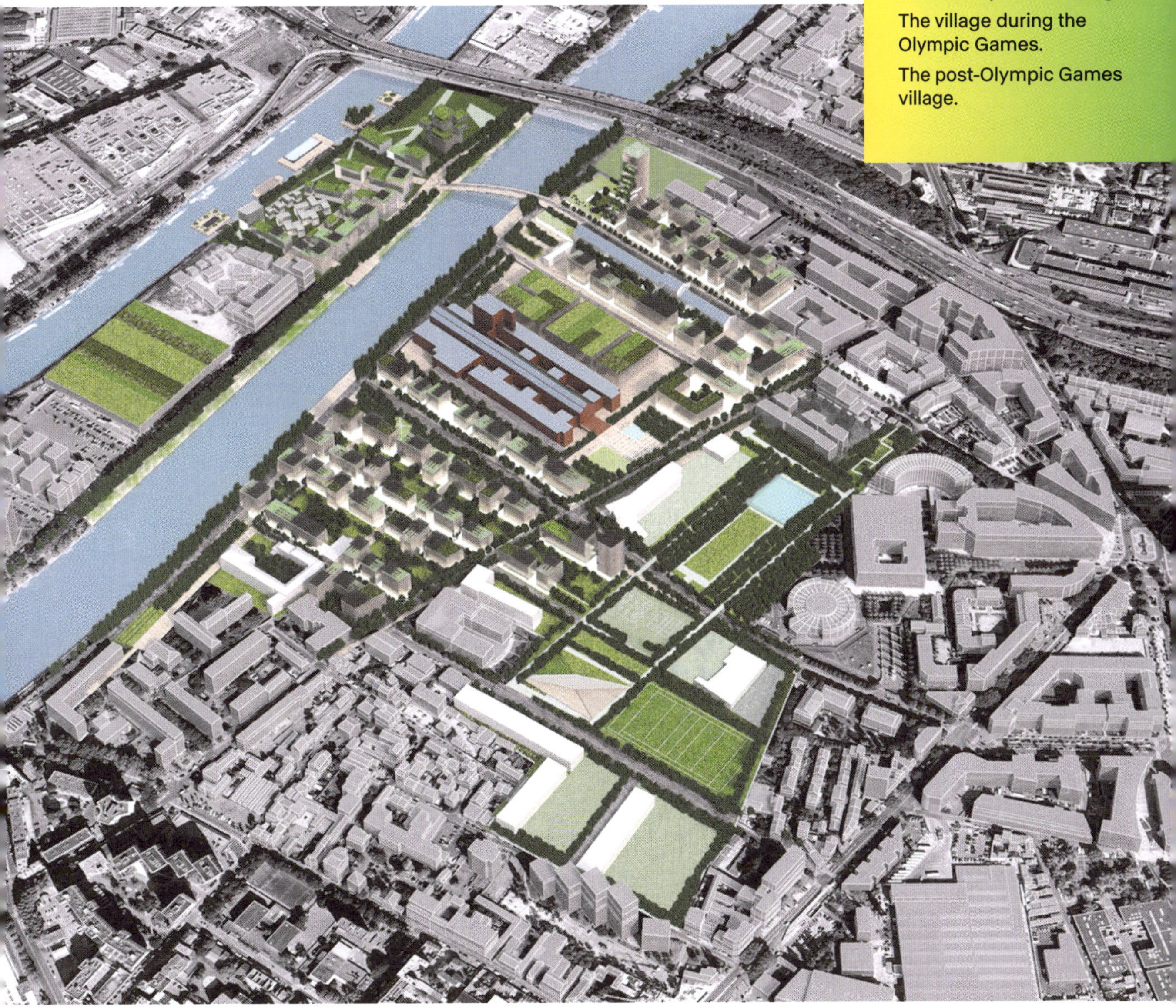

2026

#179# **AMBITION 3**

THE REVERSIBLE CITY

Scalable public spaces.

SAINT DENIS
LA SEINE
HALLE MAXWELL
ILOT A2
ILOT A3
ILOT B1
ILOT B2
STUDIOS
CITE DU CINEMA
ILOT D1
ILOT D2
ILOT E4
ILOT E5
SUPMECA
GYMNASE
COMPLEXE SPORTIF
PABLO NERUDA

#181# AMBITION 3

THE REVERSIBLE CITY

Evolution of Plan 04A
PRO 2020 - LEGACY PHASE

Evolution of Plan 04B
PRO 2020 - PHASE JOP 2024

SP01
SP02
SP03
SP04
SP05
SP06
SP07
SP08
SP10
SP11
SP12
CITE DU CINEMA
LYCEE
Platforms
SP01
SP02
SP03
SP04-SP06
SP04 TENTE
SP05
SP05 TENTE
SP07
SP08
SP05
SP05 TENTE
SP11
SP11 TENTE
SP12

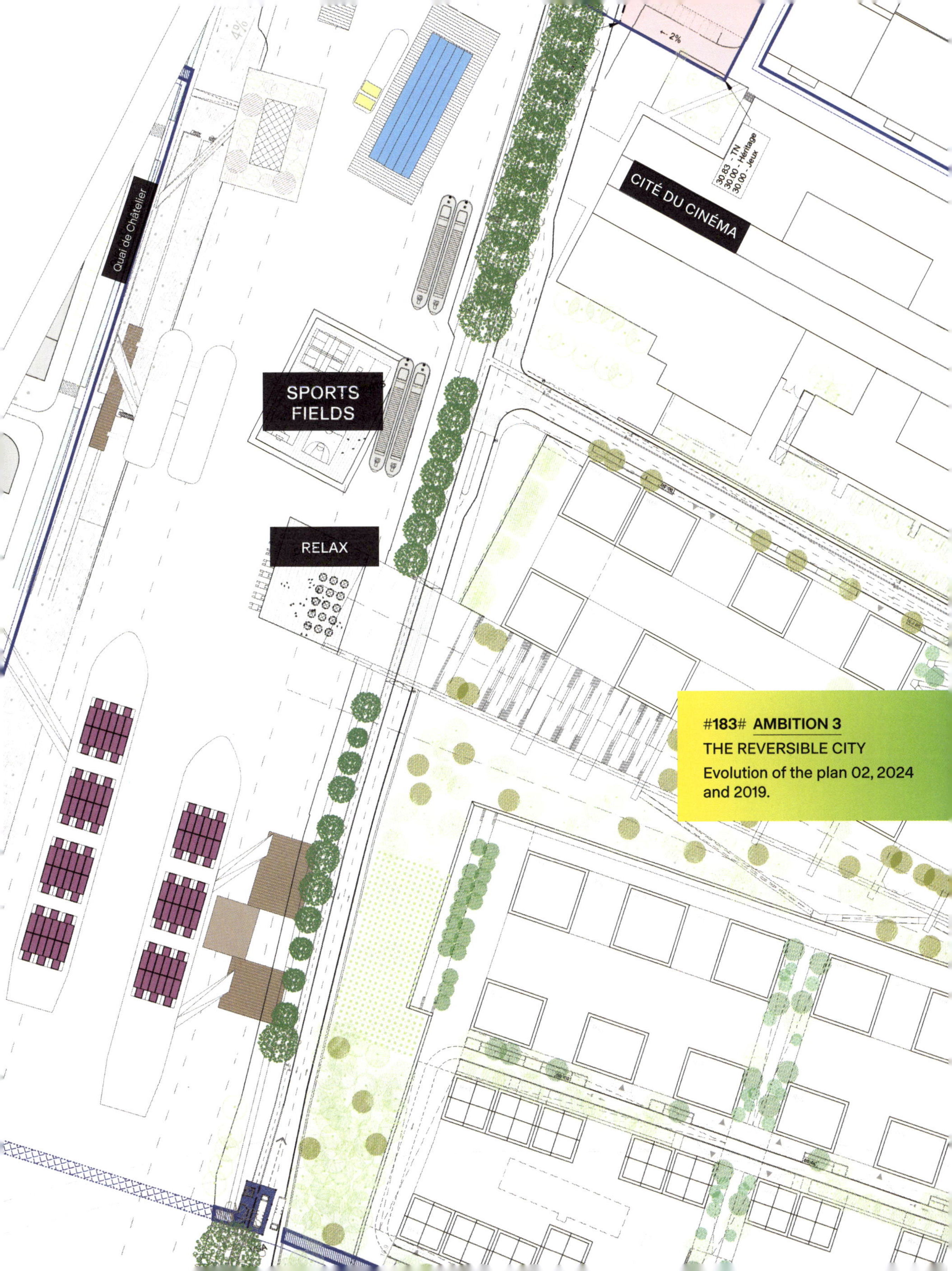

#183# **AMBITION 3**

THE REVERSIBLE CITY

Evolution of the plan 02, 2024 and 2019.

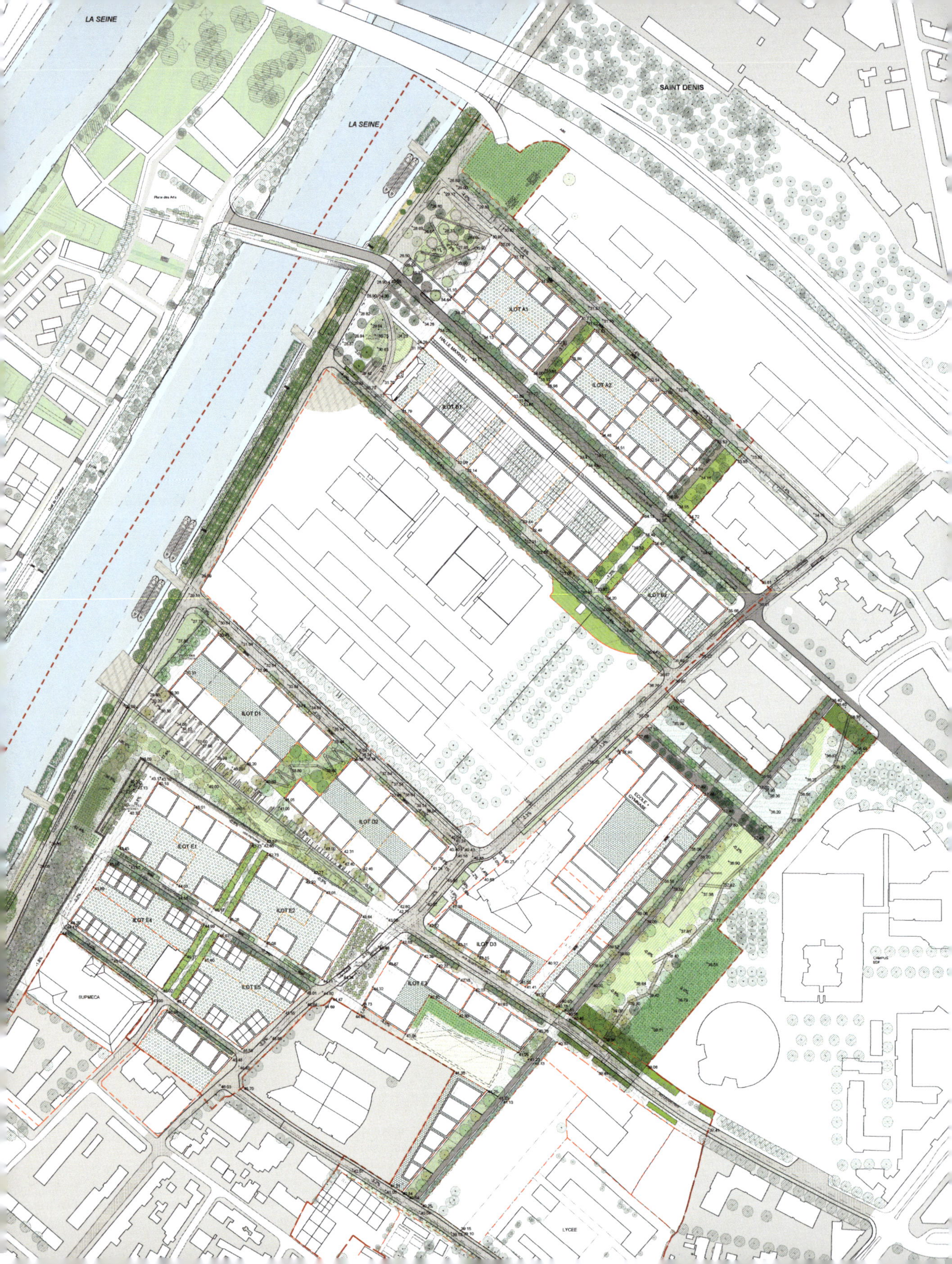
LA SEINE
LA SEINE
SAINT DENIS
HALLE MAXWELL
ILOT A1
ILOT A2
ILOT B1
ILOT B2
ILOT D1
ILOT D2
ILOT D3
ILOT E1
ILOT E2
ILOT E3
ILOT E4
ILOT E5
SUPMECA
LYCEE
ECOLE + GYMNASE

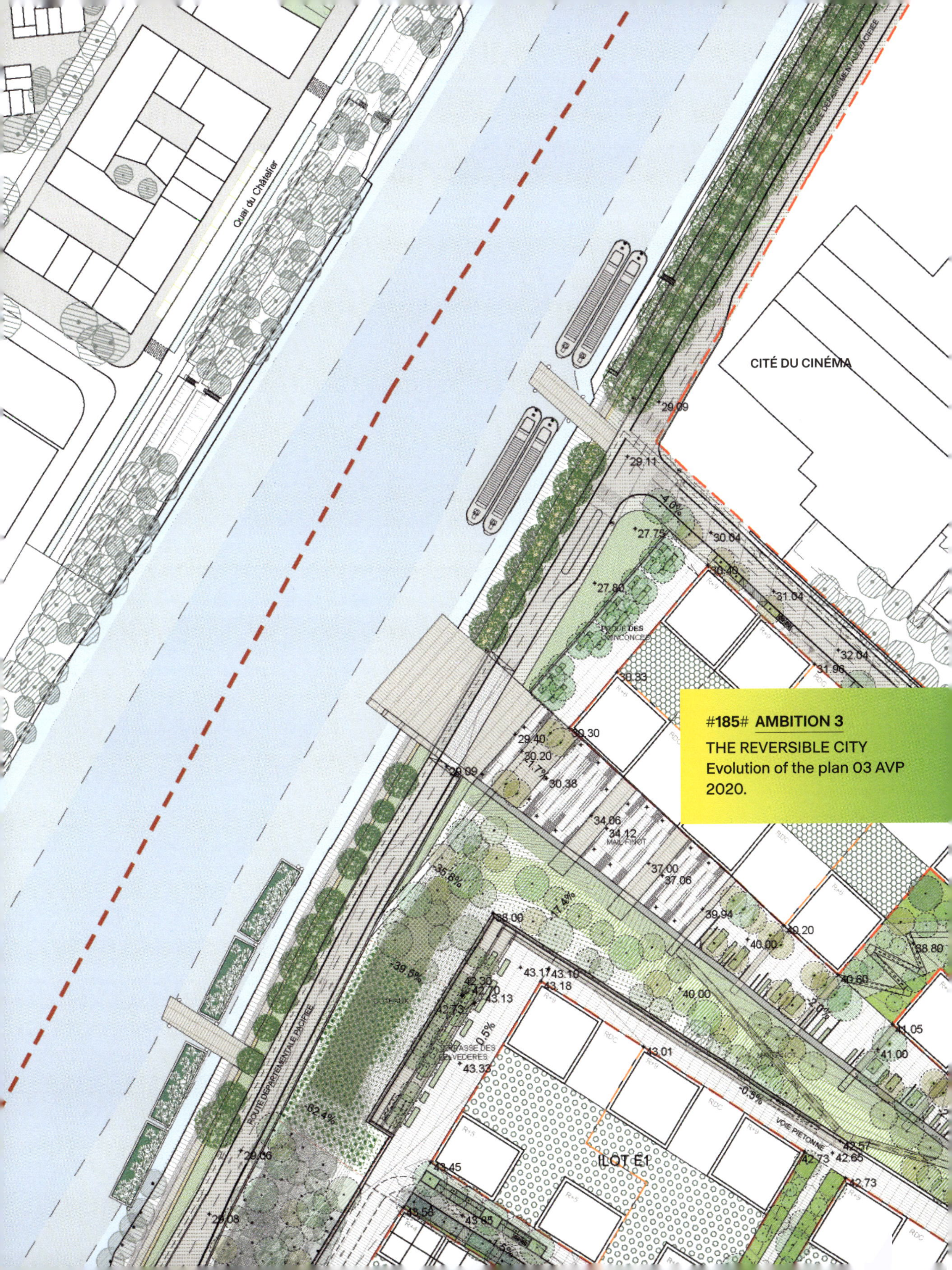

#185# AMBITION 3

THE REVERSIBLE CITY
Evolution of the plan 03 AVP 2020.

#187# AMBITION 3
THE REVERSIBLE CITY
Efficient public spaces.

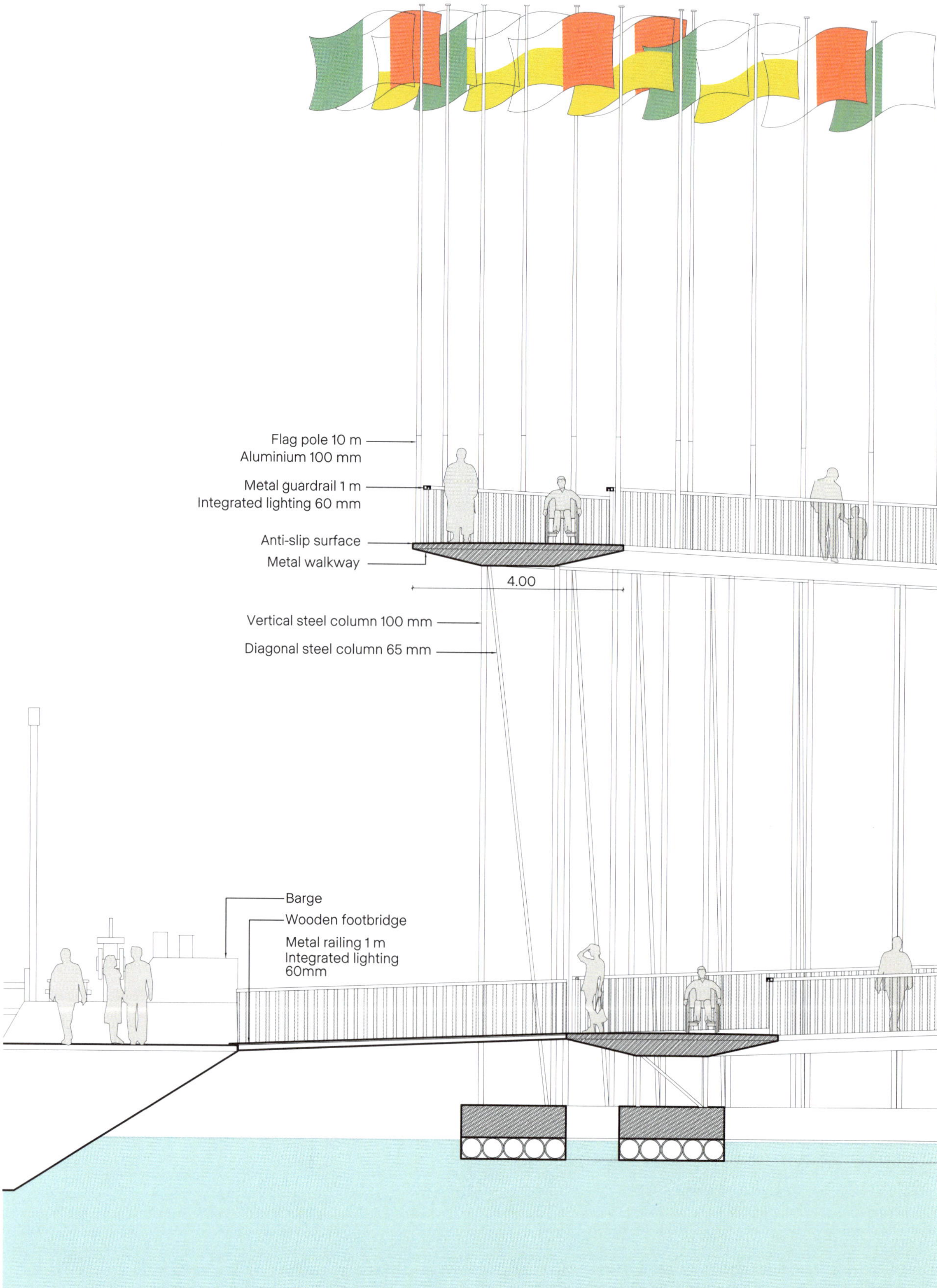
Flag pole 10 m
Aluminium 100 mm
Metal guardrail 1 m
Integrated lighting 60 mm
Anti-slip surface
Metal walkway
4.00
Vertical steel column 100 mm
Diagonal steel column 65 mm
Barge
Wooden footbridge
Metal railing 1 m
Integrated lighting
60mm

#189# **AMBITION 3**

THE REVERSIBLE CITY

Efficient public spaces.

#191# AMBITION 3

THE REVERSIBLE CITY

Efficient public spaces.

PLACE DES ATHLETES

#193# **AMBITION 3**

THE REVERSIBLE CITY

PARIS
PARIS
PARIS

#195# **AMBITION 3**

THE REVERSIBLE CITY

Family housing - I Saint Ouen I Les Belvédères : The Villas

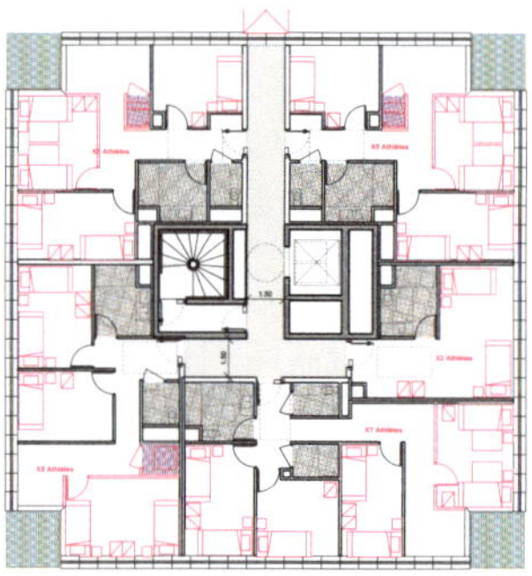

A I OLYMPIC GAMES

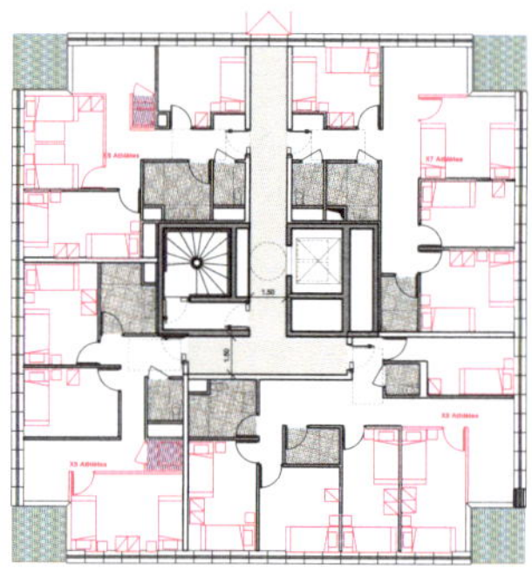

B I OLYMPIC GAMES

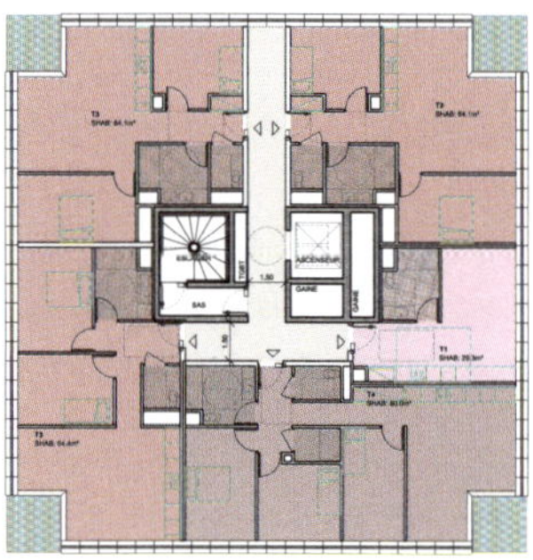

A I HERITAGE

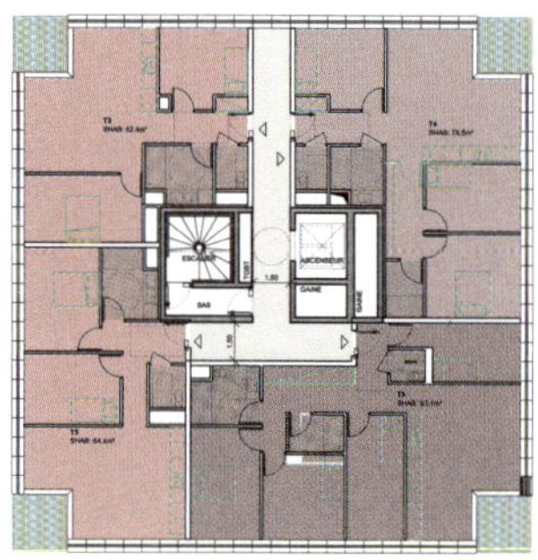

BI HERITAGE

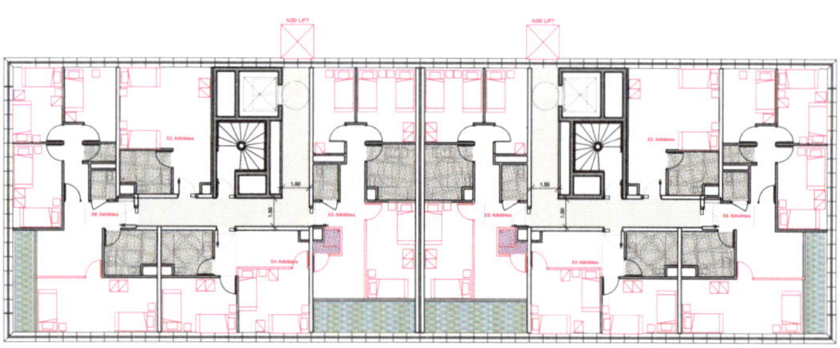

FLOOR PLAN I OLYMPIC GAMES

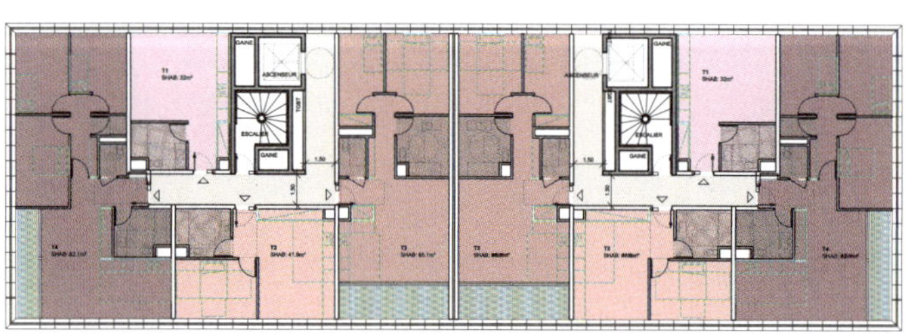

FLOOR PLAN I HERITAGE

The Offices

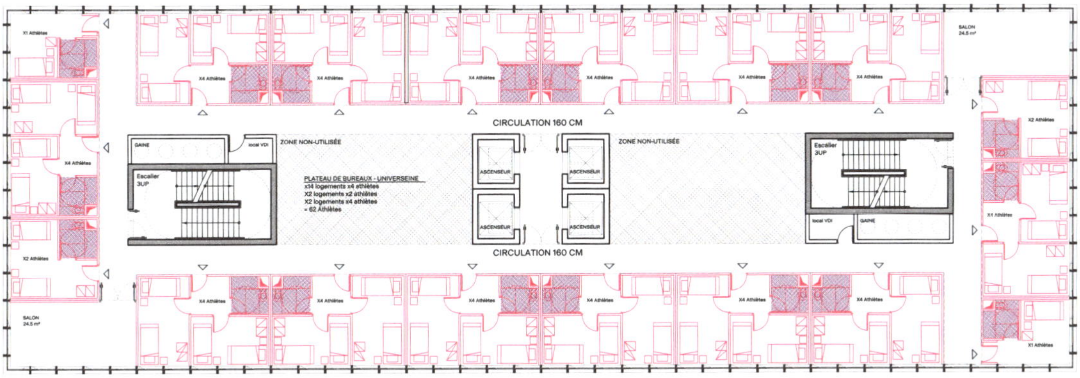

FLOOR PLAN I OLYMPIC GAMES

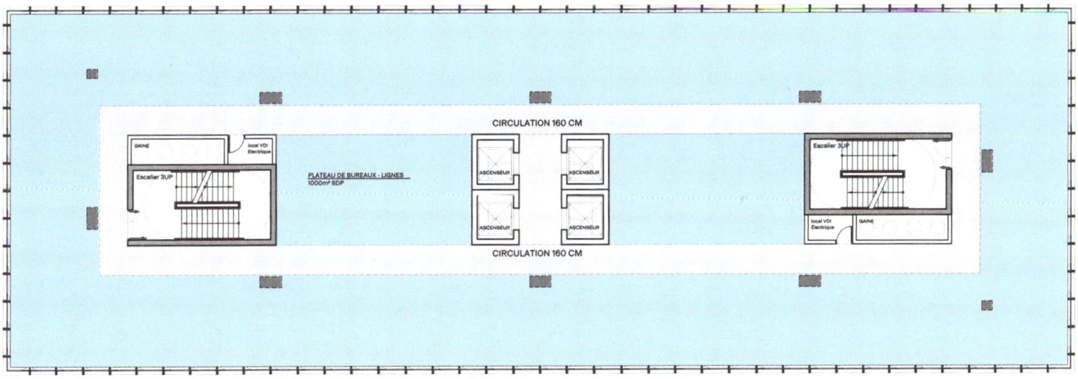

FLOOR PLAN I HERITAGE

#199# **AMBITION 3**

THE REVERSIBLE CITY

The Offices

The reversibility of the office is the one that requires the most innovation. We started with a classic heritage volume, a floor of about 900m² to which we add the most efficient typology, and get closer to a hotel. These repeated cells are two-room rooms with a bathroom. The shared spaces are spread over the plateau, a few rooms for a single athlete are provided.

This proposal makes it possible to rationalize the volumes built and minimize the technical constraints because they are all treated in the same way.

We propose to preserve the raised floor so that the shower can be at the same level as the floor.

The question of fluids can be dealt with in several ways, either by diverting it into a false floor or by a false ceiling or in the plenum on the ground floor. It is the latter proposal that we will favour.

SINGLE HOME
"Quinconces + Belvederes
Saint Ouen
T1

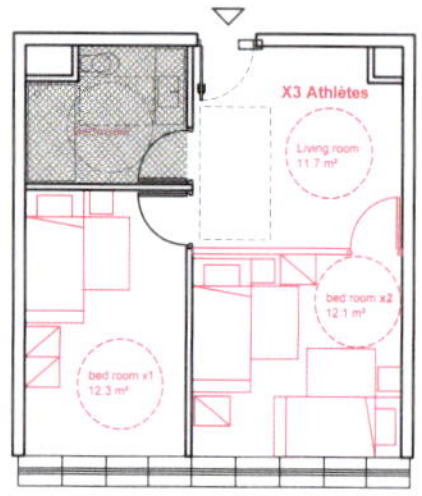

T1 I PARALYMPIC

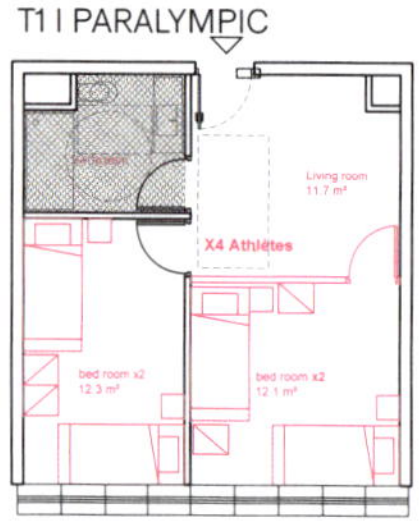

T1 I OG

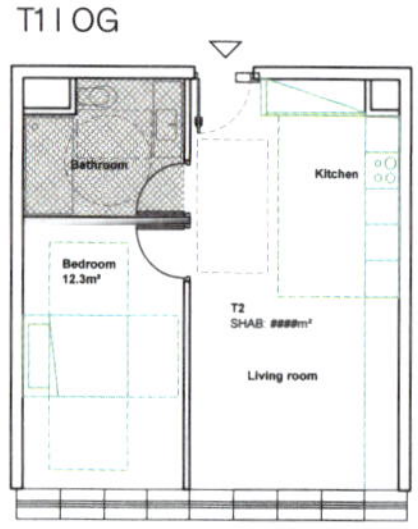

T1 I HERITAGE

SINGLE HOME
"Quinconces + Belvederes
T2
1.100th

T2 I PARALYMPIC

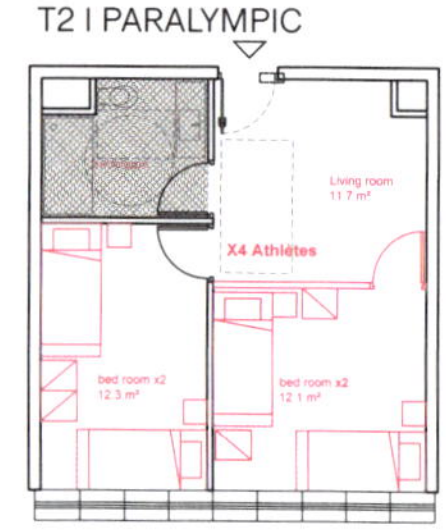

T2 I OG

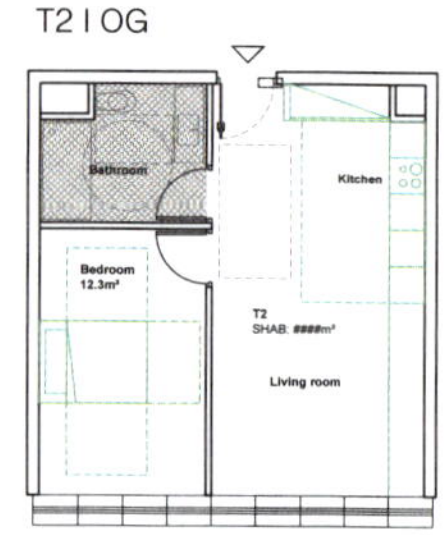

T2 I HERITAGE

SINGLE HOME
"Quinconces + Belvederes
T3
1.100th

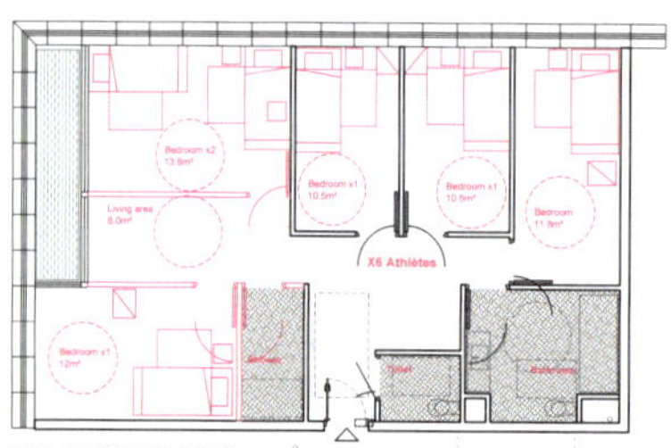

T1 I PARALYMPIC

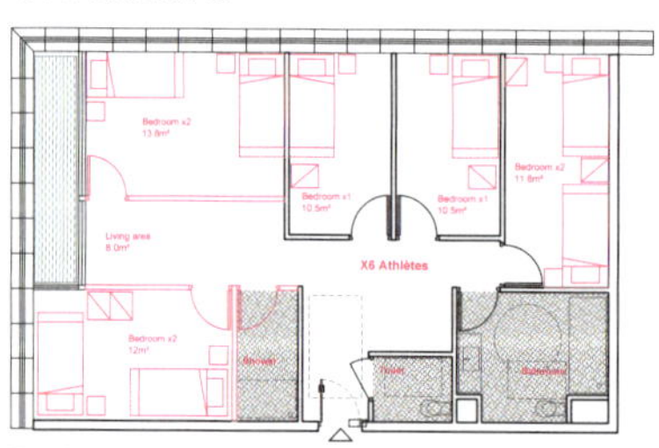

T1 I OG

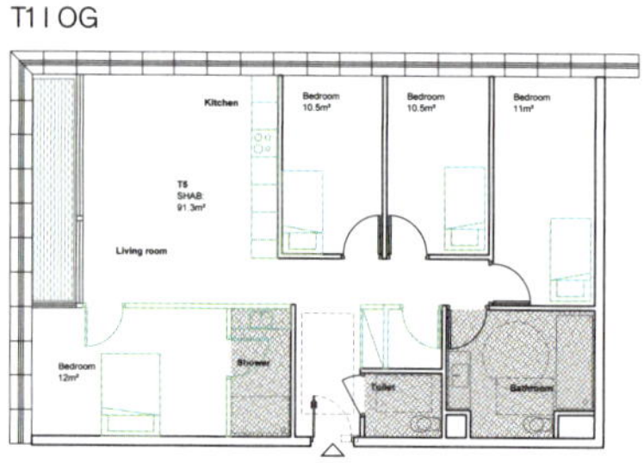

T1 I HERITAGE

#201# **AMBITION 3**

THE REVERSIBLE CITY
A group of families

The reversibility study follows the urban layouts and templates projected in the studies of the development plan for the Olympic and Paralympic Village.

The project is therefore associated with two distinct urban structures, one in Saint-Denis and the other in Saint-Ouen. The Ile-Saint-Denis sector is not covered by this study.

The urban morphology of the master plan differs between the two communes, but remains homogeneous when we focus on each of the blocks. Families of buildings stand out and extend over the entire study area, including office programmes, family housing, student and social residences and a hotel.

We can therefore put together a set of theoretical model plans that will enable us to analyse the consequences of reversibility.

SINGLE HOME
Saint Denis
T1
1.100th

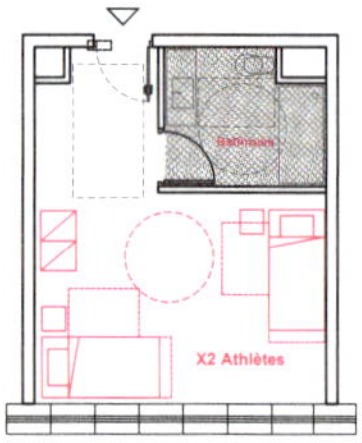

T1 I PARALYMPIQUE

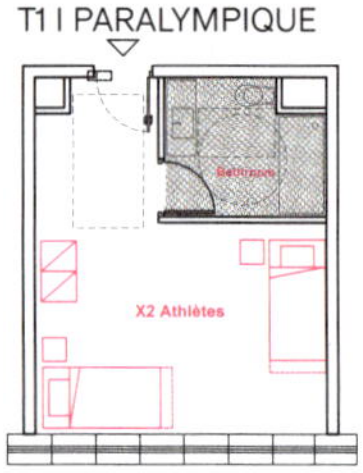

T1 I OG

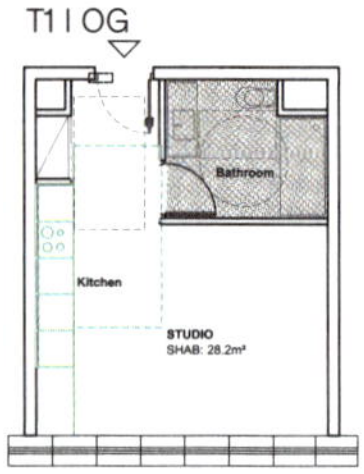

T1 I HERITAGE

SINGLE HOME
Saint Denis
T2
1.100th

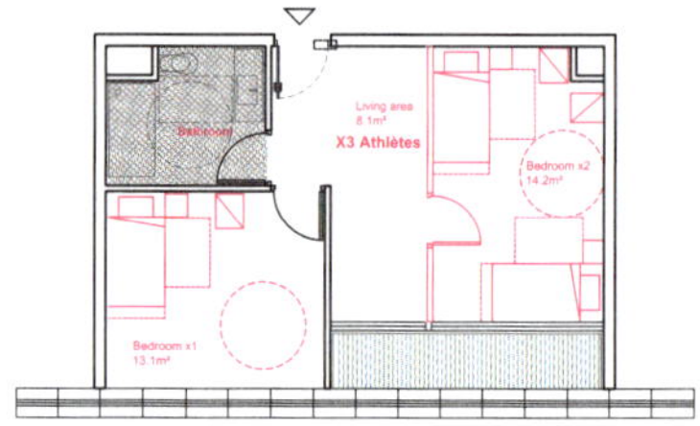

T2 I PARALYMPIQUE

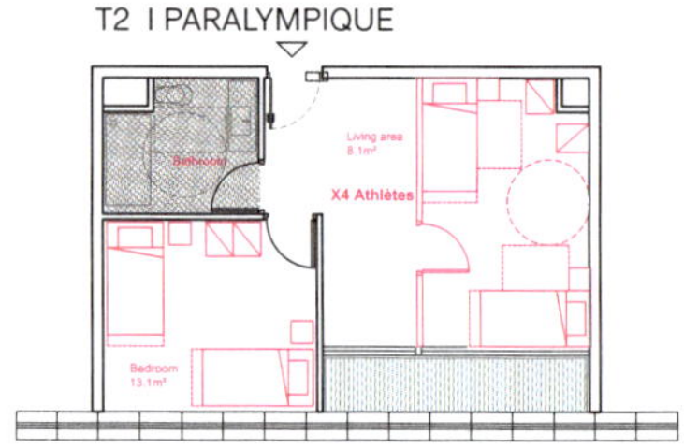

T2 I OG

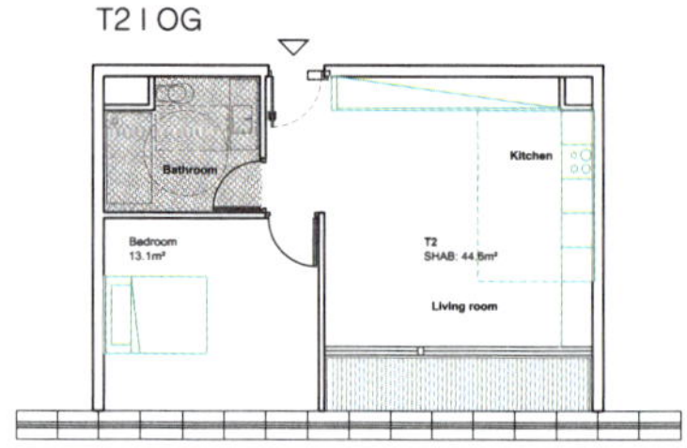

T2 I HERITAGE

SINGLE HOME
Saint Denis
T3
1.100th

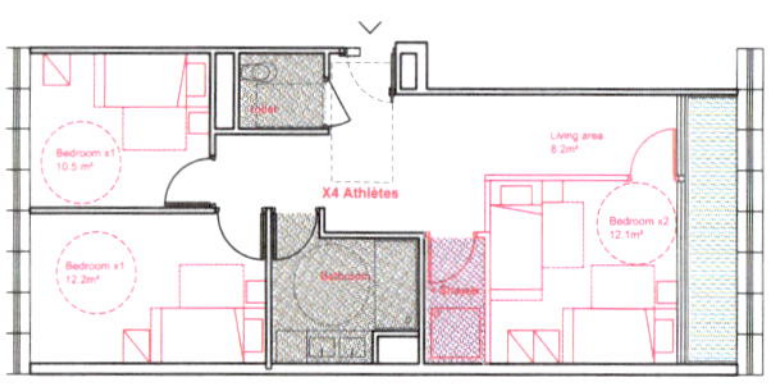

T3 I PARALYMPIC

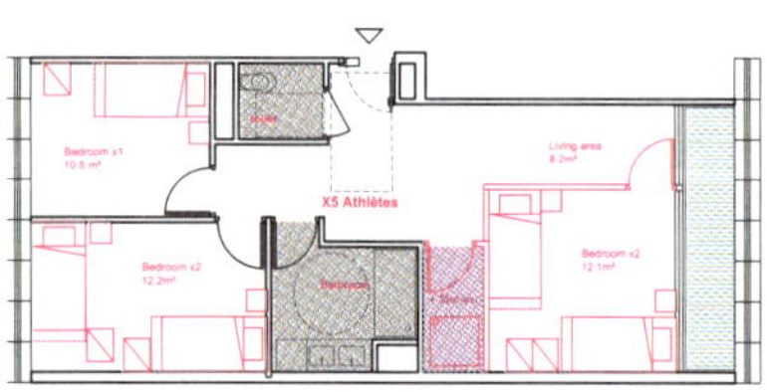

T3 I OG

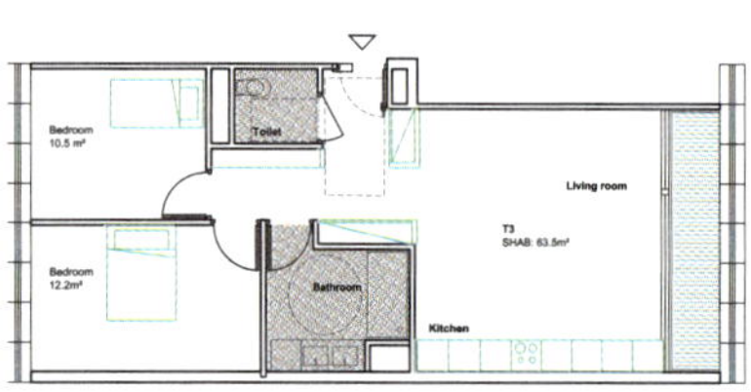

T3 I HERITAGE

SINGLE HOME
Saint Denis
T4
1.100th

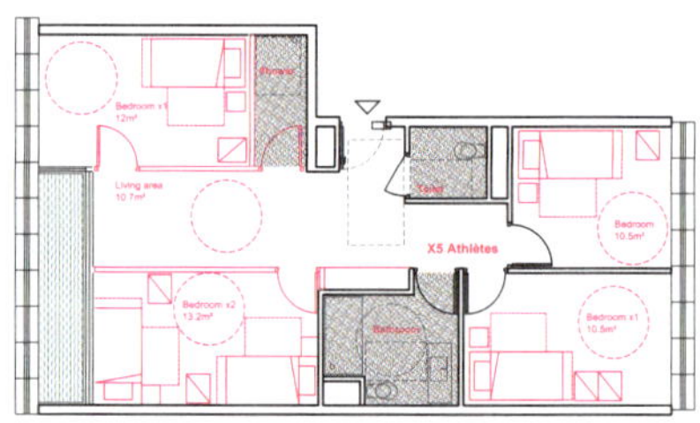

T4 I PARALYMPIQUE

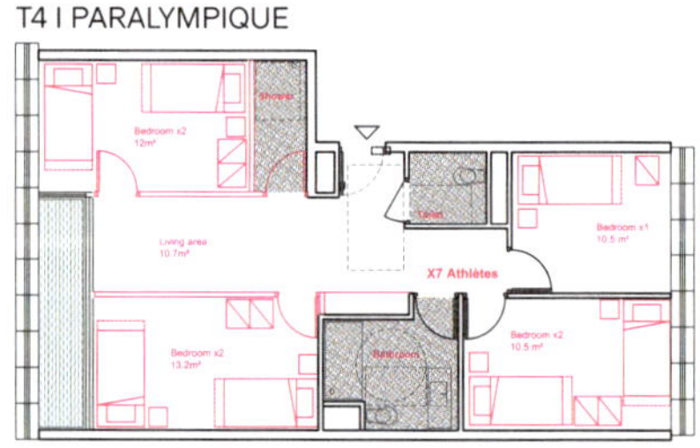

T4 I JO

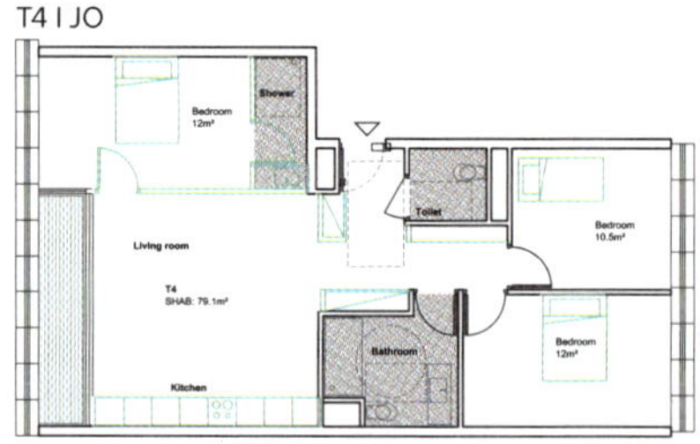

T4 I HÉRITAGE

The Hotel

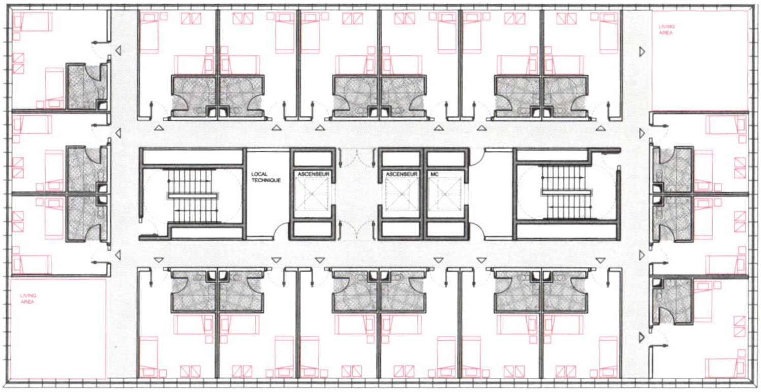

FLOOR PLAN I OLYMPIC GAMES

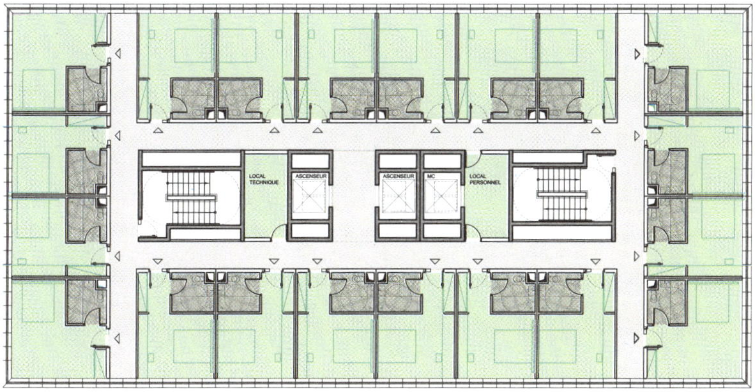

CURRENT FLOOR PLAN I HERITAGE

#203# AMBITION 3

THE REVERSIBLE CITY

The Hotel

We imagined the hotel rooms along the same lines as the student residences, with two athletes per room.

However, the hotel is the project for which we have the least information to date, and whose forecasts are the least clear. Even if room dimensions are consistent with a hotel program, the size of a room depends on its category and its operator. Several other room types may be proposed to complete the standard layout, and most hoteliers do not guarantee accessibility to all rooms for people with reduced mobility. In this case, we are aiming for 10% accessibility at room level: there will therefore be 18 rooms per floor during the JO phase, 2 of which will be accessible.

This is important in order to complete the Olympic capacity.

#205# **AMBITION 3**

THE REVERSIBLE CITY
Closing of the Olympic Games.

PARIS 2024
Les
Ateliers
Participati fs
CAUTION

The fence, a place of connection rather than separation

The interface between the various sectors of the Olympic and Paralympic Village itself and the surrounding neighbourhoods must be given special consideration.

On a finer scale, the "enclosure" of the Village, whether related to the construction site in the first instance or to the security of the Games, is one of the major issues to be considered in order to ensure that the Games are appropriated by all.

Securing the Village both during the construction phase and during the Games must not, however, give rise to a feeling of remoteness or unease among the local population due to the inaccessibility of the site and, above all, to the concentration of resources that will be committed to the Paris 2024 Olympics to the detriment of other public investments.

For us, the question is how to make the site's 'fence', before and during the Games, an active urban element, constituting not a border but rather a place in itself.

The work on this element must be approached sensitively both before and during the Games, so that the site can eventually be reopened and this former border can become a link.

With this in mind, right from the start of the bid, we proposed a number of ways of appropriating the site that could be undertaken rapidly in conjunction with the consultation process, with a view to developing an artistic approach.

During and before the Games, the border is hermetic, but it doesn't have to be "mute". Pavilions outside the Village, projection areas and project presentation media can be used for events surrounding the Games and to highlight the existence of the Village in the region, as well as to act as a place of mediation between SOLIDEO / Paris 2024 and the region's residents.

As early as the bid file submitted in November 2016, we emphasised the challenge of working on the Village's closure. Successfully bringing it to life and making it a place for sharing and linking up with neighbouring districts and their residents will be a guarantee of inclusion. Our team, in conjunction with the service providers appointed by the SOLIDEO, is putting forward proposals to liven up the site fences with appropriate communications that reflect the themes of the Territory of Culture and Creation, as well as youth and sport (values of the Territory and the Paris 2024 Games).

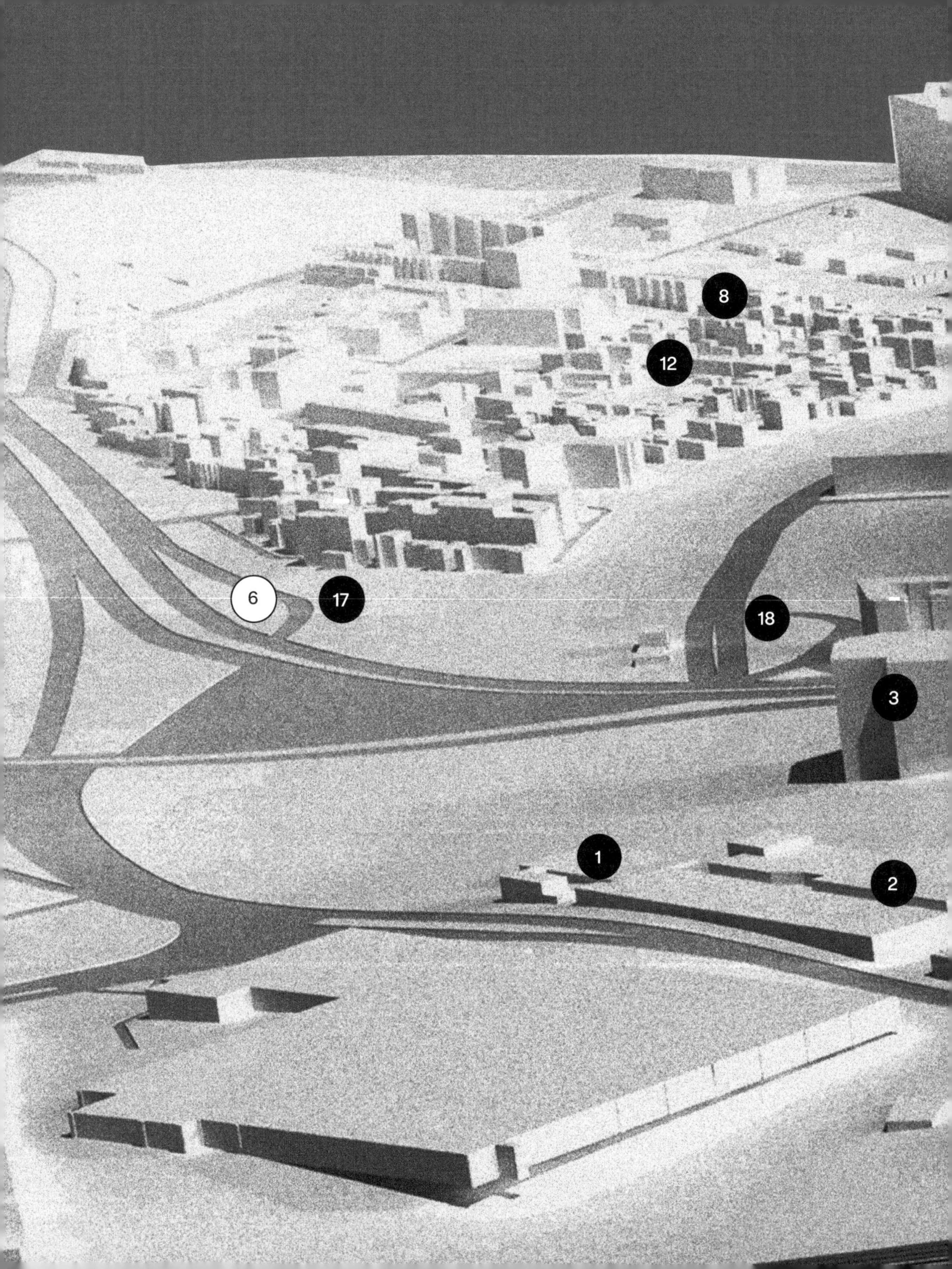
8
12
6
17
18
3
1
2

#209# **AMBITION 3**

THE REVERSIBLE CITY
19 proposals for doubles.

1 **The Seine and its double**
Developing the Seine as a space for leisure activities and biodiversity, but also as an axis for river logistics. How can the economic dimension of the river be integrated into the relationship with public space?

2 **The banks of the Seine and their dual role**
Transform the departmental road into a major pedestrian promenade linking the mouth of the Saint Denis canal to the Parc des Docks de Saint Ouen. Widen the park and provide pontoons on the Seine.

3 **The Cité du Cinéma and its double**
Transform the former EDF power station into a new metropolitan factory facing the Seine. Reinvesting and showcasing an industrial heritage similar to that of Battersea Power Station in London. Take advantage of basements that open directly onto the Seine. Imagining a central square at the heart of the district. Linking the underside of the Cité to the Quinconces bloc. Living in the courtyards of the Cité by covering them with glass roofs.

4 **The Olympic event and its double**
Imagine an Olympic Village with a flexible perimeter to allow for flexibility between now and 2024, in part floating. Take advantage of the Games to experiment with concepts such as clean, productive barges and floating urban farms.

5 **The fence and its double**
In progress. Design a fence that will serve as a place of entertainment, communication and exhibition during the event. Putting in place an ambitious scheme during the construction period.

6 **The landmark and its double**

7 **The Mail Finot and its double**
Extend the Mail Finot as a bridge between the two banks of the island. Linking the shores of the Olympic Village to the shores of Ile Saint Denis and Gennevilliers. Rethink the perspective from Pleyel by imagining a project for Marques Avenue.

8 **The interchange and its double**
Use surplus land from the Village to create a new topography and a new sports park under the Pleyel interchange. Link the district to the aquatic centre, the Stade de France and the Plaine Saulnier. Take advantage of the redevelopment of the interchange to improve transport links.

9 **The Ile des Vannes and its double**
Provide a metropolitan gateway to the area from the Seine. Use the infrastructure of the sports complex during the Games, integrating the island into the area under consideration. Develop a new symbolic square on the tip of the island: Place des Sports.

10 **The Parc Ampère and its double**
Extend the Park onto the Region's land to make it a genuine sports and landscaped strip.
Imagine a large service park with a metropolitan dimension, where different uses coexist: a network hub, a place for mobility, sport, facilities, a place for logistics and production in the basement.

11 **The Bus Station and its double**
Imagine a two-storey bus station during the Games to free up space and keep a park during the event, and imagine a reversible structure similar to the High Line in NYC, where the station becomes a belvedere park on several levels.

12 **The A86 and its double**
Question the links between the different operations, turning the constraint of the infrastructure on its head to turn it into a vector of social links, an urban opportunity. Imagine the A86 as a major ecological corridor. Imagine a cable car network above the infrastructure.

13 **Car parks and their duplicates**

14 **The ground floors and their doubles**

15 **Cap Ampère and its double**
Imagining a large energy campus. Integrating the 90,000 m2 and 4,000 people into the neighbourhood.

16 **The hillsides and their doubles**
Imagine access to the hillsides from the banks of the Seine via a large urban escalator integrated into the topography.

17 **The pylons and their doubles**
Keep the pylons and design an artistic installation. Install the Olympic rings on the pylons, visible from the motorway and in the distance.

18 **The studios and their doubles**
Install a large photovoltaic roof over the studios to produce part of the district's energy.

19 **The entrances to the neighbourhood and their doubles**
Develop the entrances to the Village, ADVLP.

#211# **AMBITION 3**

THE REVERSIBLE CITY

The Village and its Double.

100 years after the first Olympic Village: Paris 1924

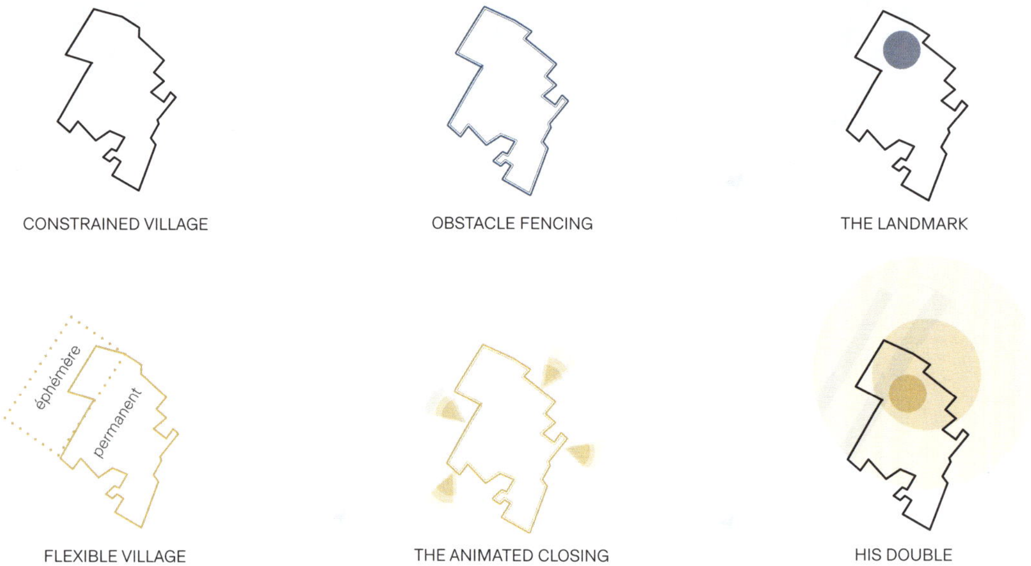

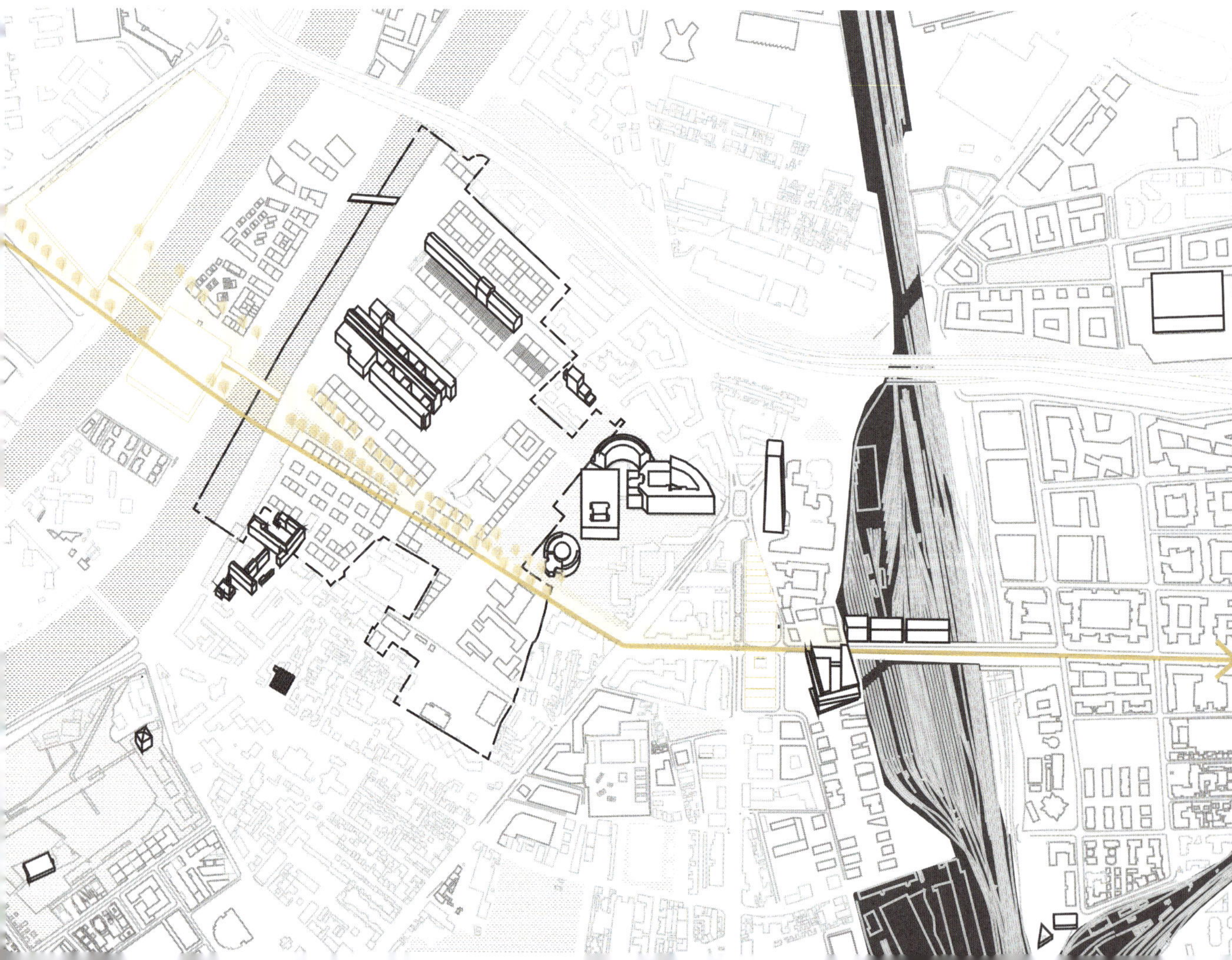

Paris 2024: The Olympic Event

After the 1900 Paris Games as part of the Universal Exhibition, the Paris site was chosen again in 1924 at the instigation of Baron Pierre de Coubertin, who was then President of the IOC.

This Olympiad, which ran from 5 July to 27 July 2024, brought together just over 3,000 athletes. It was the first to include a Village for the athletes. In 2024, the Games will mark 100 years of Village experience - with just over twenty Villages built (the 1940 and 1944 Games having been cancelled). The town of Colombes was therefore the site of the first Olympic Village, made up of wooden barracks. Louis Faure-Dujarric, the architect of the Colombes stadium, was appointed to build the "village" to house the athletes.

This "village" adjoined the stadium. It consisted of simple wooden huts with three-bedded rooms. The boundary of the "village" is marked by a simple sign at the entrance. It includes a hairdressing salon, a laundry, an infirmary, a guard post, a newspaper kiosk and a post office. A restaurant serves 3 meals a day.

The Americans did not live at the Village, but at Château de Rocquencourt. The Village was completely demolished after the games. A century ago, the Olympic Village was already made of wood. the 1900 Universal Exhibition.

Special features of the Paris 2024 Village. A built site and a unique geography.

In our view, the thinking behind the Olympic and Paralympic Village is first and foremost a long-term urban reflection on the creation of a city anchored in its territory and its unique geography, that of the Seine Valley. The site chosen for the Village, and the context in which it is set, carry within them and in their relationships, the seeds of this project.

The Olympic Village is exceptional in that it is located on both sides of a major river, deeply linked to the image of Paris and Greater Paris. It is not being built on a clean slate. It is fortunate that it has to deal with a landscape heritage and industrial heritage of exceptional quality, and with a very marked topography. The Seine, the city's "artery" if ever there was one, runs through the Village, lending its banks and waterfront to all kinds of recreational, festive, sporting and landscaping activities. The river and its redeveloped banks should be able to act as a link between the neighbouring communes, forming a continuous and practicable blue and green grid and the main continuity in terms of biodiversity.

It establishes both a physical and mental link between the historic heart of Paris and L'Ile-Saint-Denis, at the heart of Plaine Commune, the future territory of Greater Paris, bringing a strong and rich image to this international event of the 2024 Olympics, which must be those of Paris and Seine-Saint-Denis.

The Olympic and Paralympic Village project offers a unique opportunity to reconcile this area with both its riverbanks and the historic centre of Saint-Denis, which boasts a wealth of heritage and a dynamism that is little known.

In addition to the link with the river and the historic centre of Saint-Denis, the Olympic Village project (the future "Pleyel - Coteaux - Berges de Seine" district) is the missing piece in an "archipelago" of projects designed to be consistent with each other. It is the missing piece in an "archipelago" of projects designed to be consistent with each other through the synthesis of studies set out in the Territorial Development Contract and Plaine Commune's planning documents.

In addition, its compactness and urban form are unique. By 2050, the district should form a robust and legible urban fabric, based on a "linking urbanism "This will enable it to be fully integrated into an urban fabric on a metropolitan scale.

OLYMPIC GAMES
1956
M
ABC TV 3
1948
Londres
1932
Los Angeles
1952
Helsinki
1936
Berlin

#215# **AMBITION 3**

THE REVERSIBLE CITY

The long experience of the Olympic Villages and, more broadly, the history of the formation of the city should enable us to learn from this experience of the rapid construction of new districts.

The issue of rapid construction has often imposed rather monolithic villages, with very repetitive architectural forms.

The result has often been unmixed neighbourhoods where life has been slow to take hold and ground floors slow to be occupied.

The Paris 2024 Olympic and Paralympic Village will be the first to raise the question of using office buildings to house athletes and offer a strong programmatic mix.

The question of construction methods will be a particularly sensitive issue, as will be developed below. Similarly, discussions The same applies to the retail sector, which will need to be addressed quickly in order to deal with the issue of occupancy timescales.

Sydney
1988
1980
Moscou
1984
Séoul
Los
Angeles
USA
1992
Barcelone

#217# **AMBITION 3**

THE REVERSIBLE CITY

Olympic villages that set the standard for legacy

From an urban point of view, some villages have had a greater impact on the cities that have hosted the Games than others.

In 1992, the Barcelona Games transformed the city's image and put it on the list of European tourist destinations. The city, which turned its back on the sea, took advantage of the Games to reclaim its coastline.

The designers, MBM - Martorell-Bohigas-Mackay, extended Cerdà's urban fabric right down to the sea, transforming the seafront and creating a marina.

An architectural commissioning process giving preference to Spanish architects, and above all Catalan architects, who won the Premi FAD.

#219# **AMBITION 3**

THE REVERSIBLE CITY

100 years after the first village

In 1924, just a few kilometres from the future Athletes' Village, the municipality of Colombes hosted the very first Olympic Village in the history of the modern Games.

Temporary, it was made up of around sixty wooden houses separated by dirt paths and connected to running water and electricity.

Overlap between the Olympic venues 1924 and 2024

Source: Hélène Caroux, "Fabrique et usages des sites des JO dans le Grand Paris de 1924. Les leçons d'une histoire", Métropolitiques, June 10, 2019

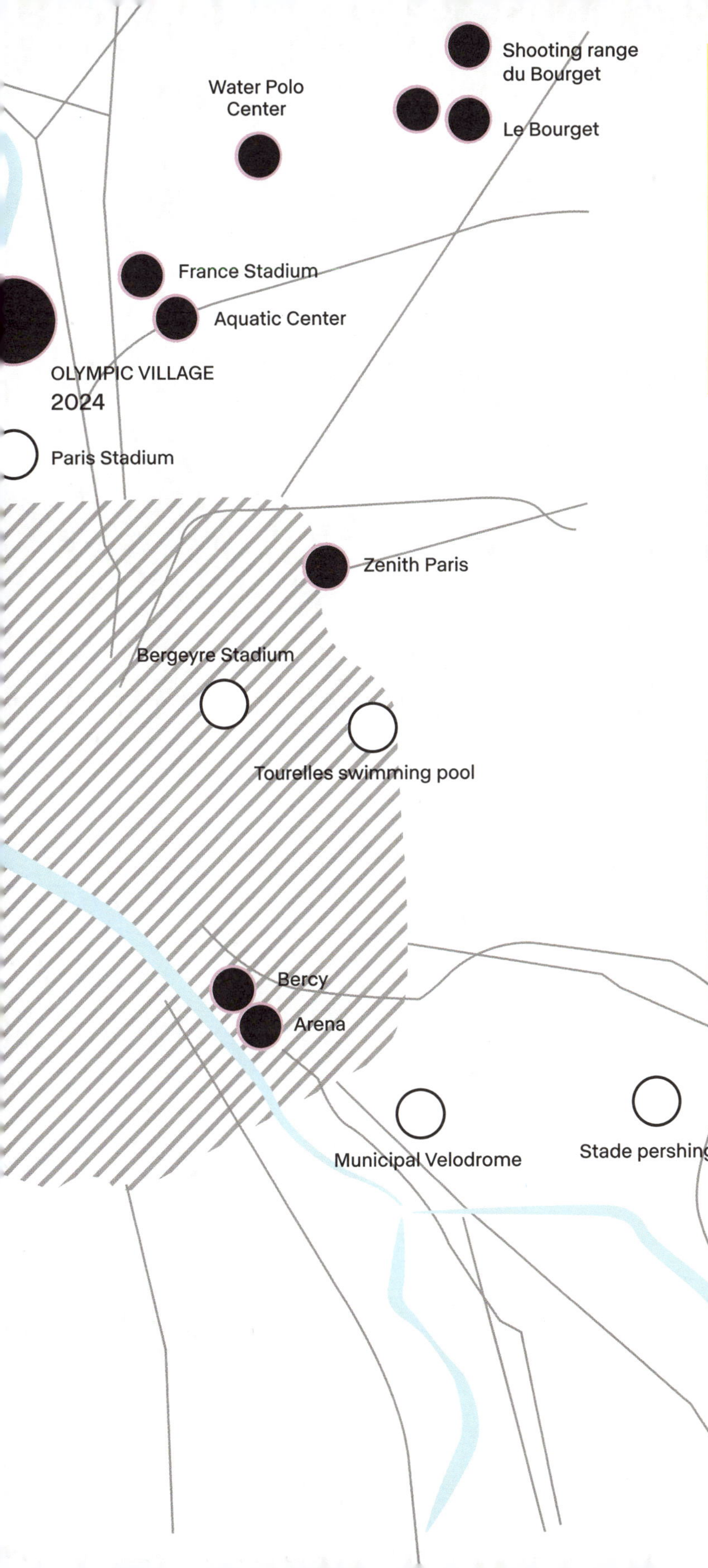

#221# **AMBITION 3**

THE REVERSIBLE CITY

In 1924, most Olympic venues were in the suburbs

Compared to 1924, the number of venues in Paris has also increased and These included the Eiffel Tower (beach volleyball, triathlon, marathon), Les Invalides (archery) and the Champs-Élysées (road cycling).

A compact Olympic and Paralympic Village - Benchmark of the Villages

01 ATHENES - 2004

02 PEKIN - 2008

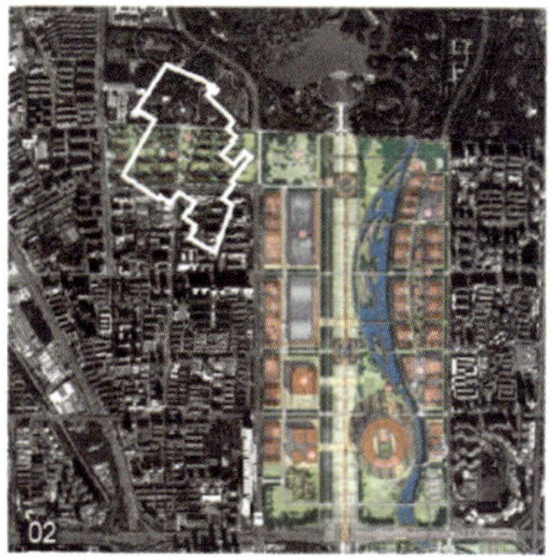

03 VANCOUVER - 2010

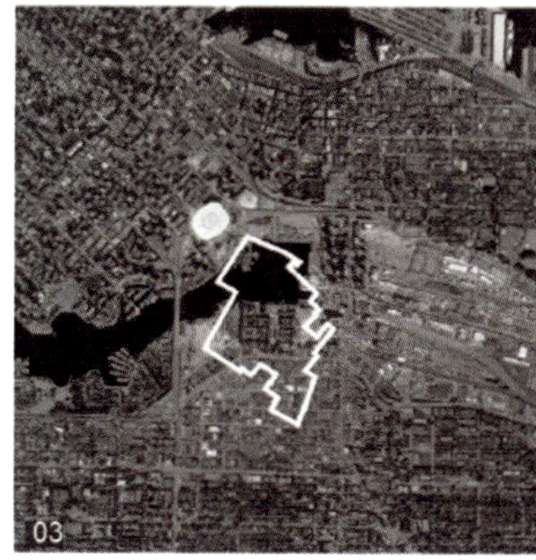

MEXICO CITY 1968

112 Countries - 5,516 Athletes

MUNICH 1972

121 Countries - 7,134 Atlethes

MONTREAL 1976

113 Countries - 6,084 Atlethes

BARCELONA 1992

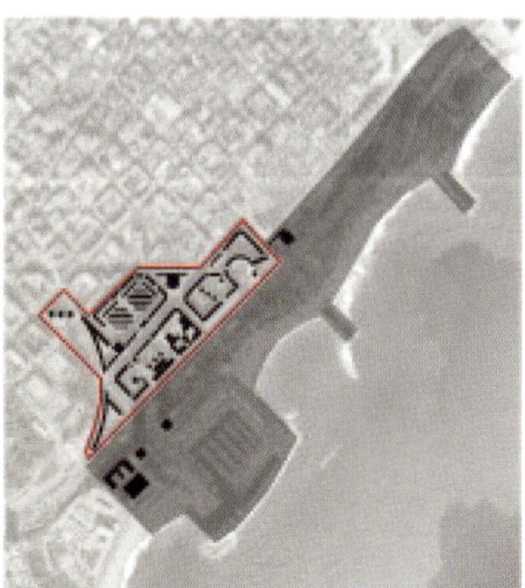

169 Countries - 9,356 Atlèthes

ATLANTA 1996

197 Countries - 10,318 Atlethes

SYDNEY 2000

199 Countries - 10,651 Atlethes

04 LONDRES - 2012

05 SOTCHI - 2014

#223# **AMBITION 3**

THE REVERSIBLE CITY

Scale comparisons.

A compact Olympic Village.

MOSCOW 1980

81 Countries - 5,179 Atlethes

SEOUL 1988

159 Countries - 8,391 Atlethes

ATHENS 2004

201 Countries - 10,625 Atlethes

BEIJING 2008

204 Countries - 11,028 Atlethes

Why not use the Village's surplus land to create a new topography and a new park under the Pleyel interchange?
Less than a kilometer between the Village and the Olympic Aquatic Center... How can the two metropolitan projects not be connected? Why not redevelop the Pleyel interchange?
Sport and the Metropolis? A sports park to link the stadium aquatic center and the Village?

The redevelopment of the interchange a an **urban opportunity** to improve soft mobility?

Use the derelict Viaduc space between the A86 and Boulevard Anatole to **promote** pedestrian routes and **enhance** our heritage?

The sports loop as a **link** between the metropolitan facilities of Greater Paris?

#225# **AMBITION 3**

THE REVERSIBLE CITY

The exchanger and it double.

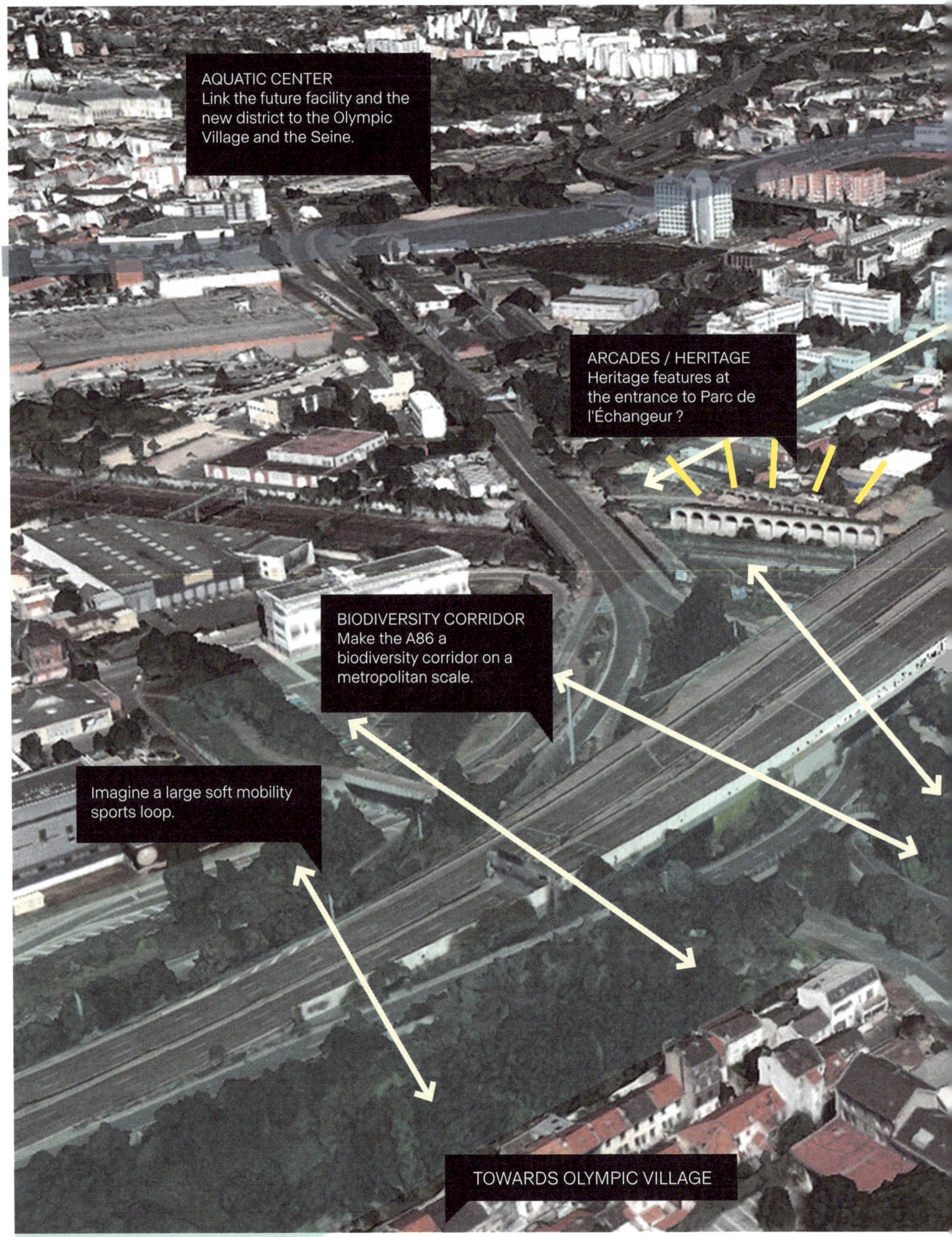
AQUATIC CENTER
Link the future facility and the new district to the Olympic Village and the Seine.
ARCADES / HERITAGE
Heritage features at the entrance to Parc de l'Échangeur ?
BIODIVERSITY CORRIDOR
Make the A86 a biodiversity corridor on a metropolitan scale.
Imagine a large soft mobility sports loop.
TOWARDS OLYMPIC VILLAGE

THE GREAT STADE
Linking the metropolitan facility to the wider area and to the Seine - by promoting soft modes of transport.
TOWARDS PLEYEL POLE

Ile des Vannes isolated

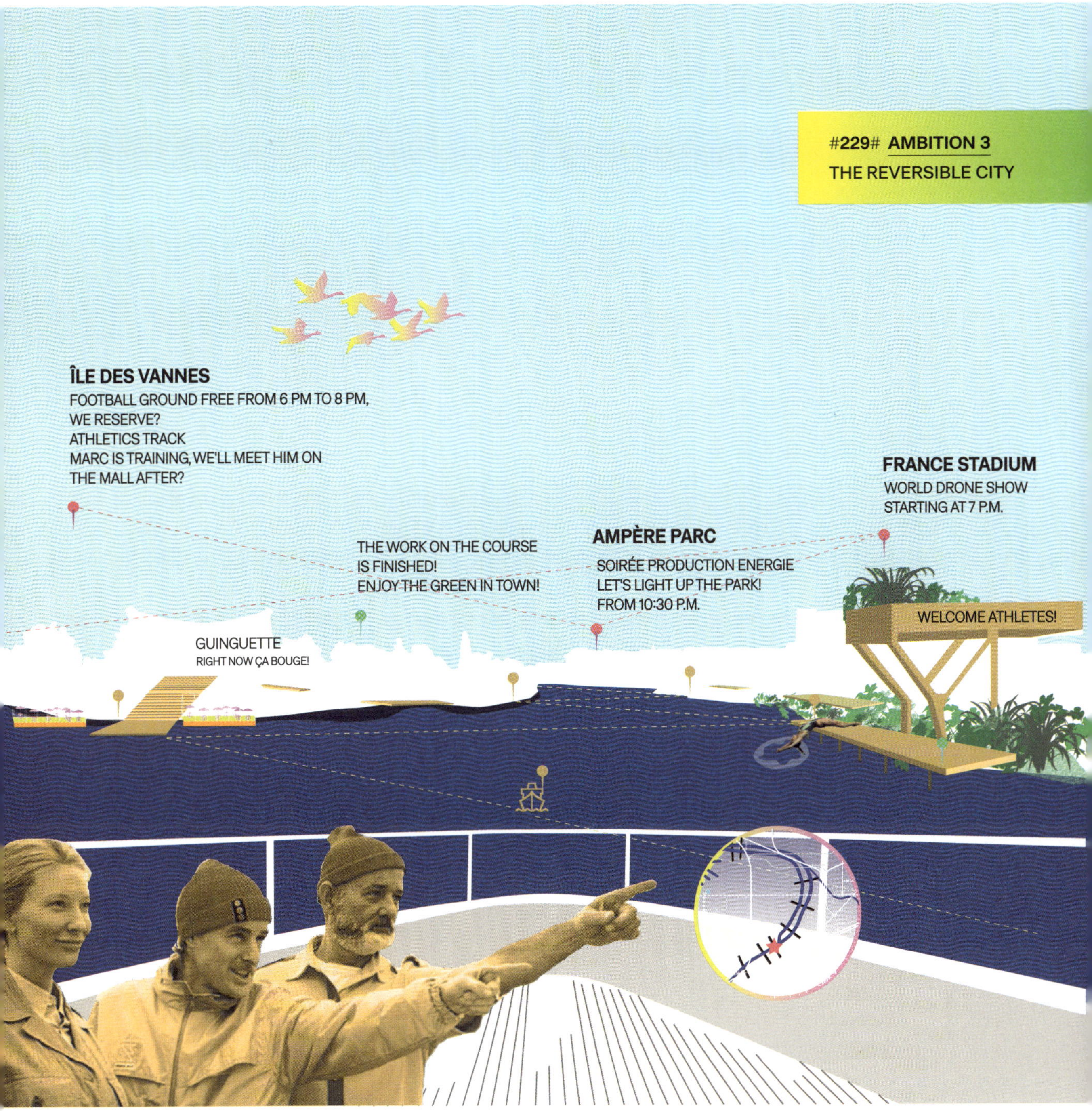

Ile des Vannes connected

Why not take advantage of the Games to experiment with concepts such as energy-producing, pollution-removing barges, floating urban farms and modular bridges?
Why not imagine an itinerant, floating Olympic Village?

Why not take advantage of the Seine to imagine a partly floating Olympic Village?
Ephemeral? Whose infrastructures would be relocated at the end of the Games?
What about the landmark during the Games?
Why not imagine a simplified, flexible village perimeter that allows for flexibility between now and 2024?

Olympic Village construction site
Earthworks 85 000 m3
Earthworks 175 500 m3
Reuse of excavated material for Parc de l'Échangeur

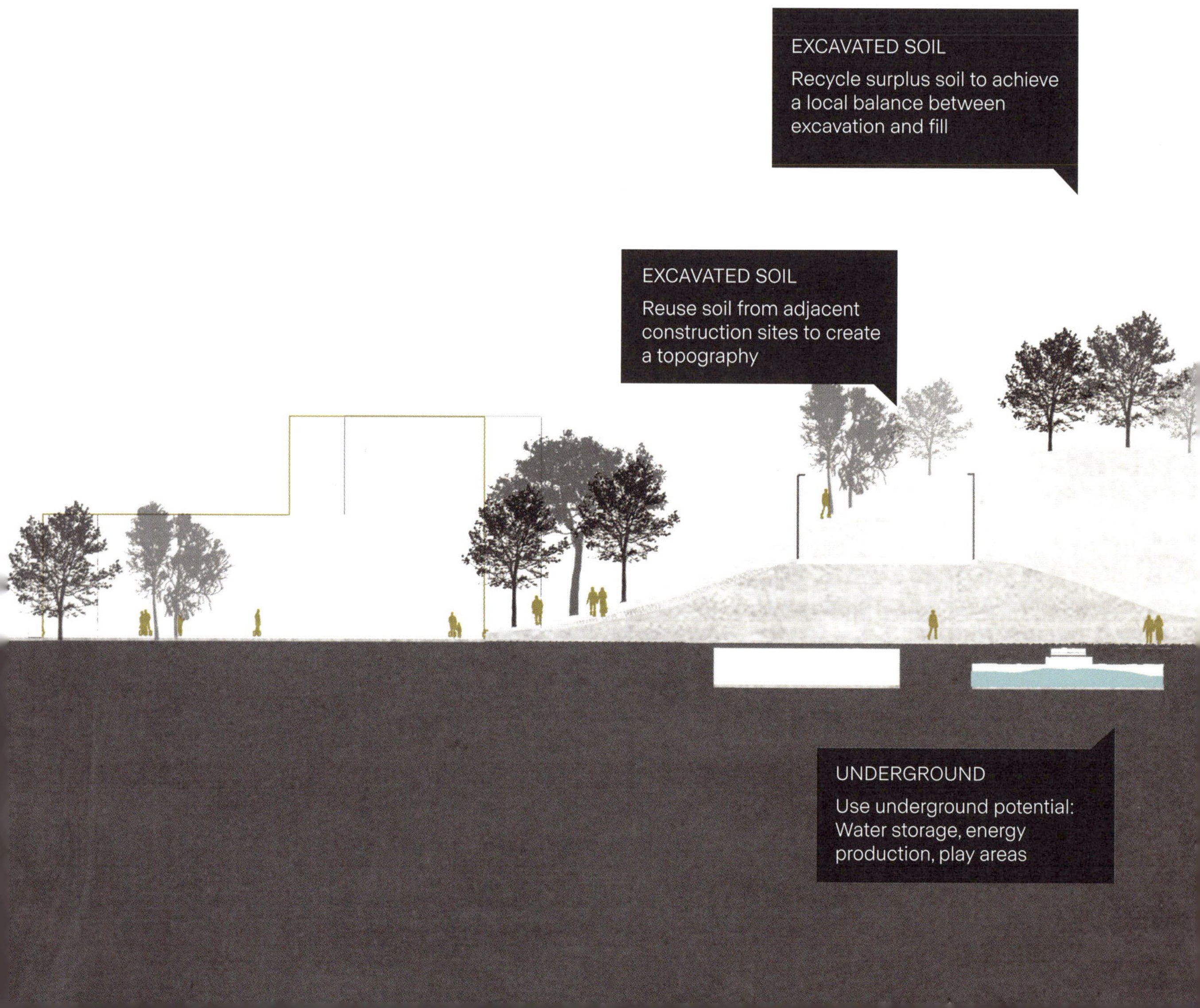
EXCAVATED SOIL
Recycle surplus soil to achieve a local balance between excavation and fill
EXCAVATED SOIL
Reuse soil from adjacent construction sites to create a topography
UNDERGROUND
Use underground potential: Water storage, energy production, play areas

#233# **AMBITION 3**

THE REVERSIBLE CITY

Crossing the A86: interchange sports park.

SANY
PARIS
PARIS

PARIS

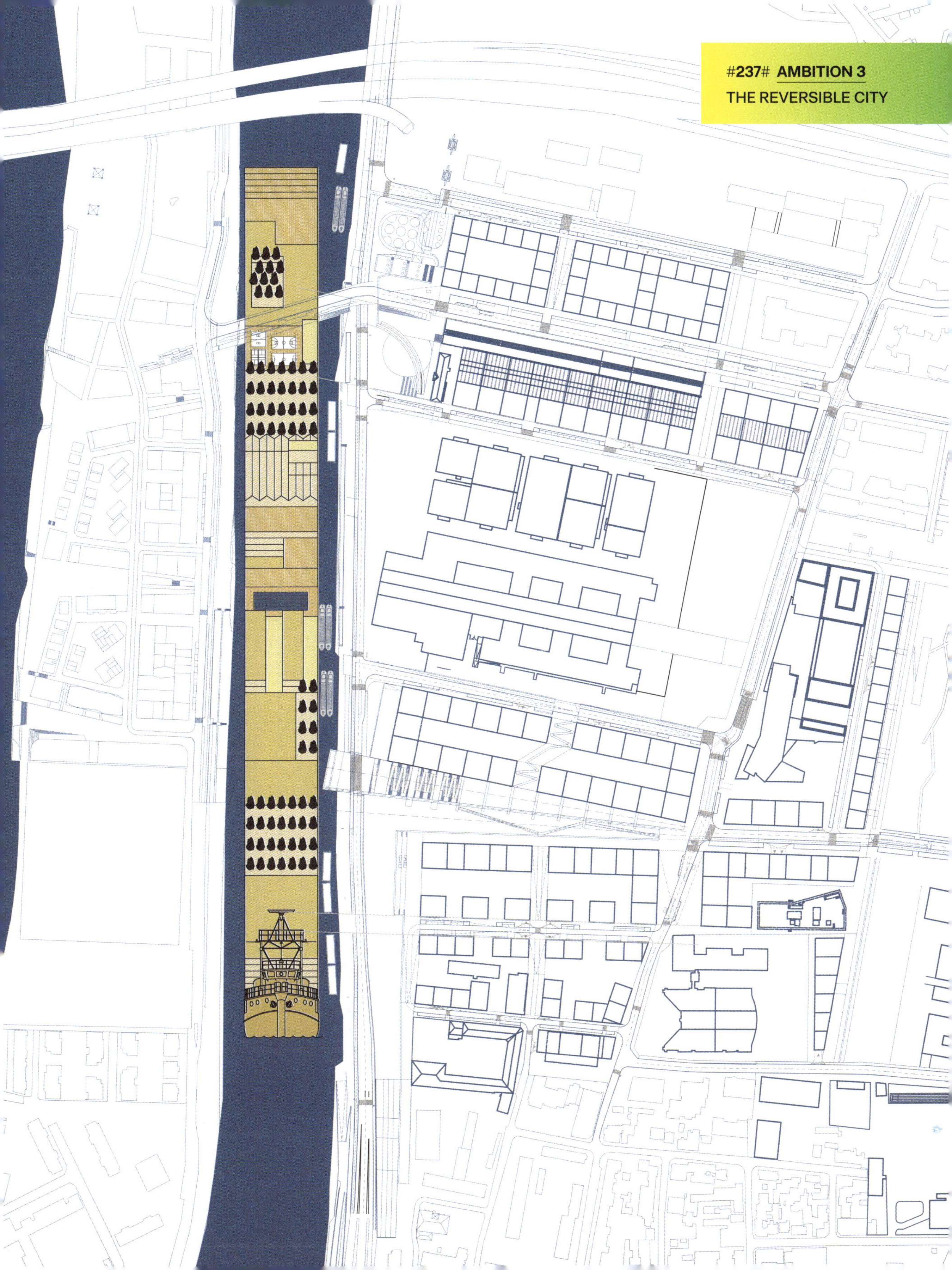

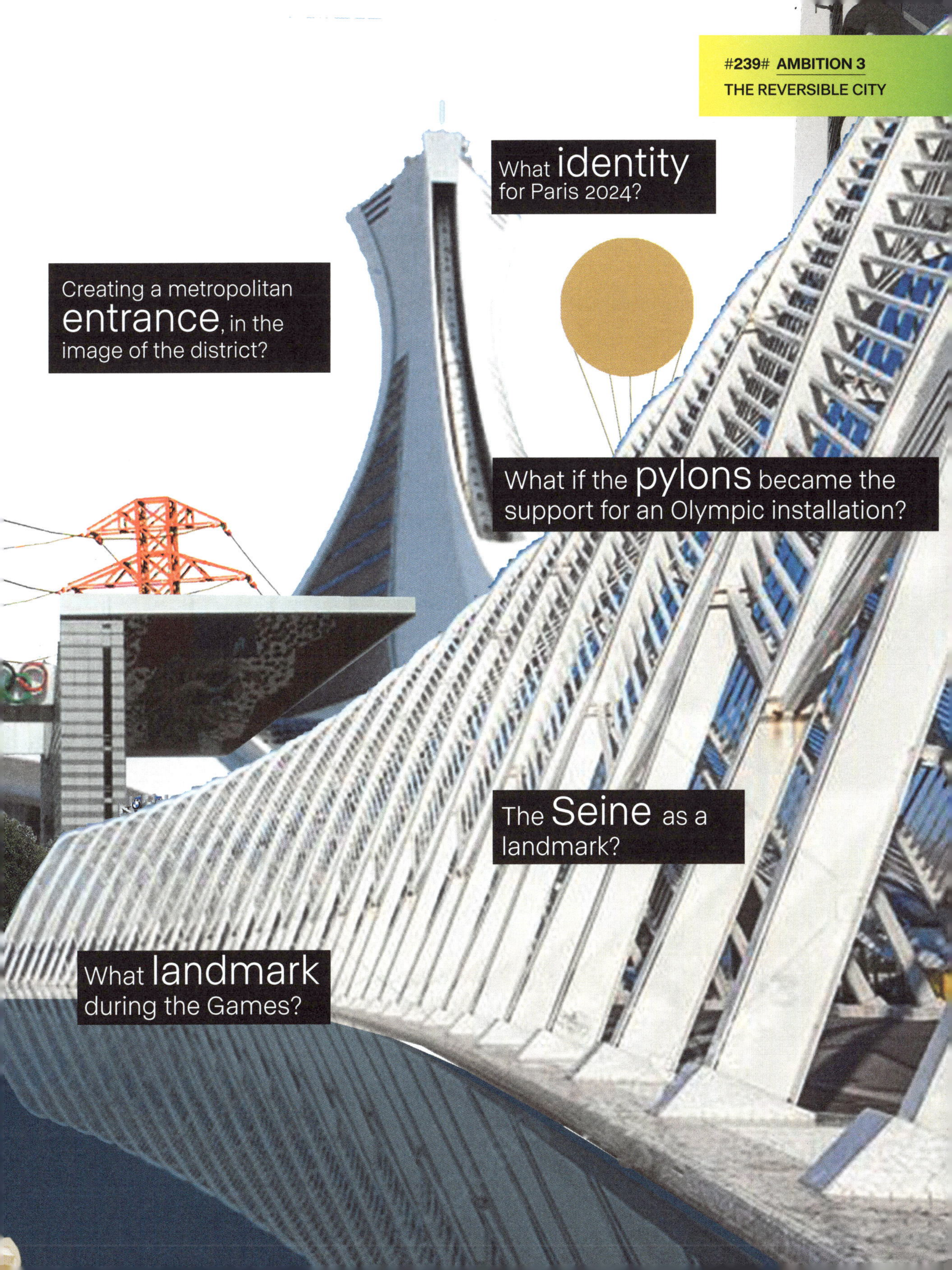
What identity for Paris 2024?
Creating a metropolitan entrance, in the image of the district?
What if the pylons became the support for an Olympic installation?
The Seine as a landmark?
What landmark during the Games?

Why not use the infrastructure of the sports complex: an indoor stadium, a swimming pool, an outdoor stadium, a rowing club and a bowling green during the Games?
How to link the great nave of P. Chazanoff, A. Kopp to the neighbourhood?

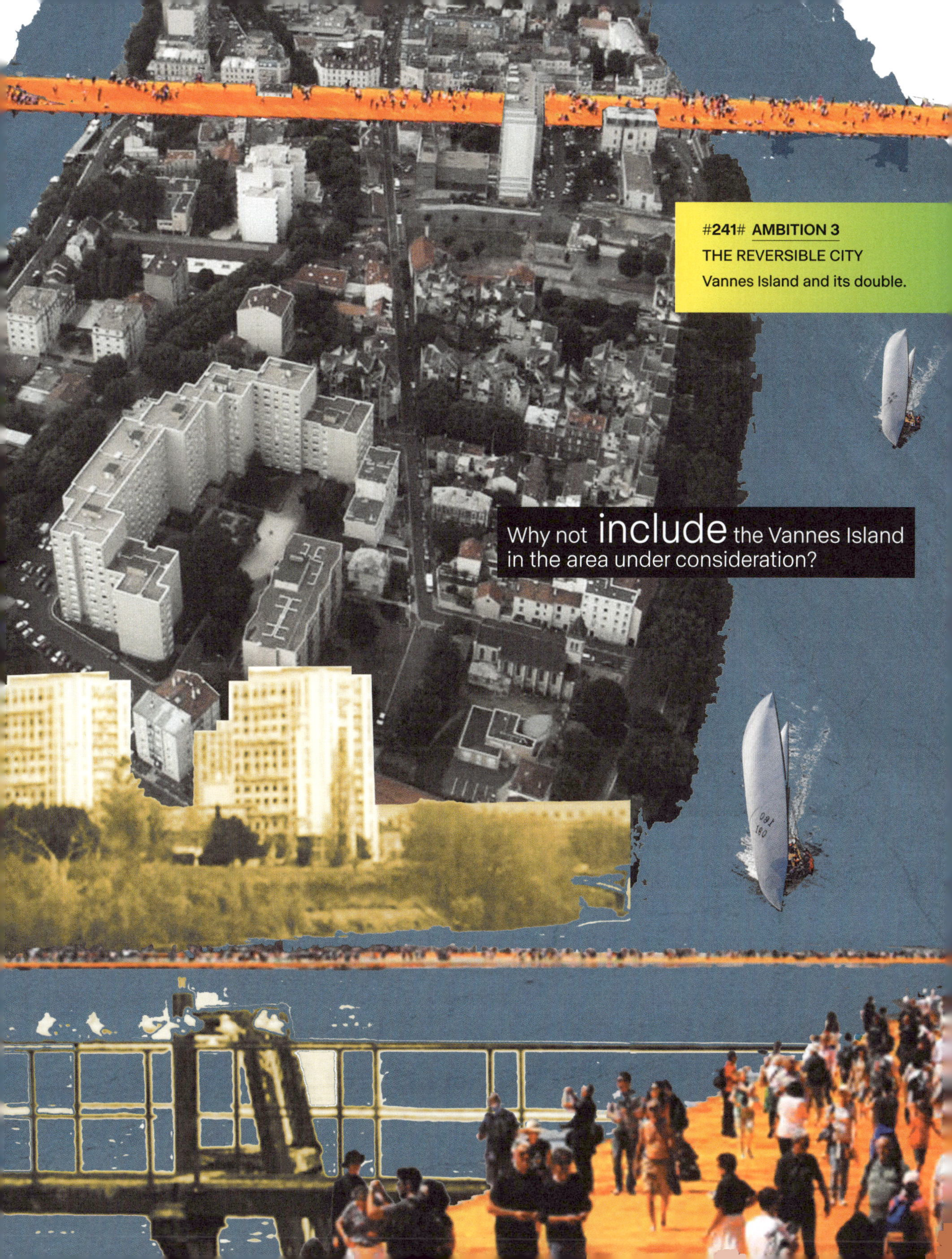

#241# AMBITION 3

THE REVERSIBLE CITY

Vannes Island and its double.

Why not **include** the Vannes Island in the area under consideration?

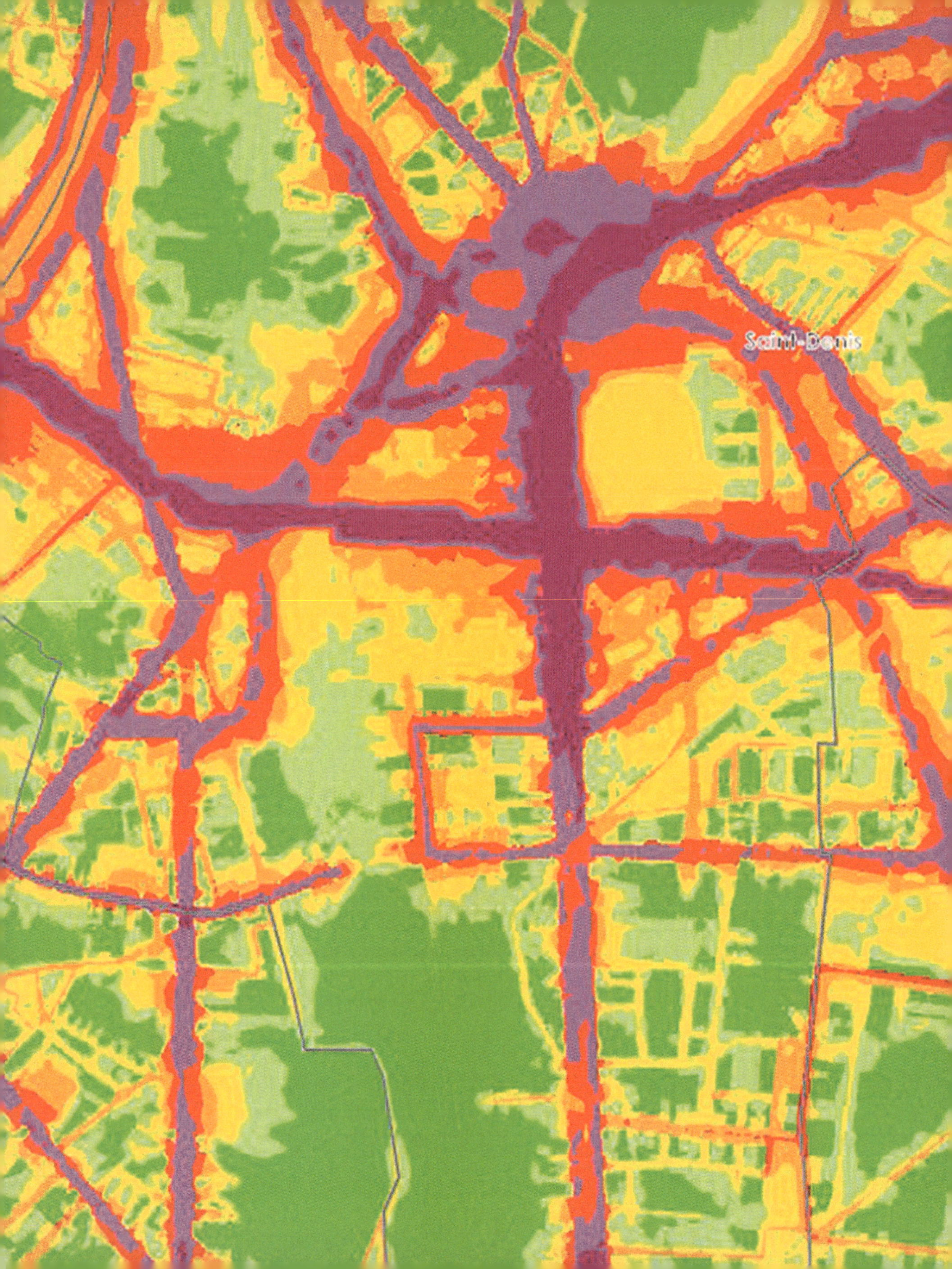
Saint-Denis

AMBITION 4-5

CLIMAT 2050 AND CARBON FOOTPRINT MANAGEMENT

Resilience is a word for our times, a symptomatic word of the Anthropocene epoch. A programmatic word, so capable of serving as system that it predicts the future of human societies facing climate shock, with these watchwords: assimilate, endure, react, subsist. Applied to the city and the metropolis, resilience speaks accurately about the necessity for them to adapt to the vagaries and perils with an enlightened response to the risks. The resilient city is a biotope of another order of nature than the original one. Between it and us, a new ecological link is developing— a vital relationship. The city is becoming our "living environment."

The climate trajectory of the Paris metropolis and its consequences can be predicted with a high degree of accuracy. The future holds recurring summer heatwaves, the intensification of winter rains, increasing risks of flooding and inundations exacerbated by impermeabilized land surfaces, vertiginous and exponential collapse of biodiversity, multiplication of heat islands, the imperative of revegetation (including urban canopies), economy of scarcity regarding the supply of water and energy, the urgency of collective cooling networks, and vast geo-engineering of geothermal and geo-cooling systems, capable of heating and cooling buildings and districts.

The inner ring of suburbs, more than Paris proper, will be impacted most by rising temperatures, owing to their lack of vegetation capable of slowing evapotranspiration – resulting, here again, from massive impermeabilization of land surfaces and the privileged use of concrete. The gap can reach between one and eight degrees. On the territory of the Greater Paris Metropolis, this massive impermeabilization of land reaches 32% versus 7% at the regional scale. With 87% of urbanized surface, the dense and mineralized metropolis threatens to become a furnace. In addition, between 1982 and 2017, parcel by parcel, it has lost over half of its farm lands – the most fertile in the national. The preservation of natural and semi-natural species is not always a priority. Densification of the built environment is driving speculative pressures on the last available lands, like the Aubervilliers workers' gardens. The dilemmas are legion between policies on employment-housing-services and environmental defense, as seen in Val-de-Marne, where the program of mixed-use districts around the future train station of Bry-Villiers-Champigny has come into conflict with the challenge of preserving a fragile ecological corridor.

Among all the potential futures of the metropolis, there is one about which there is no longer the slightest lingering doubt. The arsenal of proof submitted by the scientific community is unequivocal. The state no longer hesitates to include summer scenarios projecting France at +4°C, and +5°C in the country's southeast. Several phenomena that were only predicted to arrive by 2050 will already be a reality by 2030. The rarefaction of hydric resources is alarming. The "Explore 70" report from France's Bureau of Geological and Mining Research announces, for the horizon of 2046-2065, a reduction of "effective rainfall," diminishing groundwater recharge, a decline in the average annual flow of rivers and severely worsening low-water thresholds, occurring earlier and lasting longer in the long term. Summer flows should drop by 30 to 60%. Agriculture and other swaths of the economy will be deeply affected.

We know that it is urgent to act to halt rising temperatures as the limit of +2°C in relation to the preindustrial era, the target of the 2015 Paris Agreement, will be largely exceeded. Some predictions are for a global increase of +3 to +4°C. But it is even more important to begin to implement adaptation policies. Here, we must emphasize the commitment of the Greater Paris Metropolis to fight against climate disruption. It is doing this through its Metropolitan Climate Air Energy Plan. Adopted in 2018, for the seven million French inhabitants concerned, spread over the 131 member municipalities of this body, it is among the most ambitious in France. It aims to promote renewable energy, obtain a diversified and low carbon energy mix – with the objective of reaching carbon neutral in 2050— control energy consumption, reduce greenhouse gas emissions by 80% (with the year 2005 as reference point) as well as energy dependance, improve air quality (by reducing the level of fine particulates and nitrogen dioxide), given highly alarming epidemiological studies, and facilitate city and territorial programs of adaptation and resilience tackling short-medium- and long-term climate change.

The development activity of the entire territory must be rethought with ecological parameters. In this case, the mobilization of municipal authorities around the challenge of adaptation is judged unequal and weak overall in the 2019 senatorial report. The action of municipalities to tackle issues related to climate change have barely begun. Pioneering communities are still relatively rare. Therefore, the genuine, territory-wide implementation of policies driving adaptation must be forcefully encouraged. Setting this up is complex and requires a major paradigm shift.

Thermal performance is a stated objective of the new Olympic district. The insulating materials used and technologies employed must guarantee a maximum temperature of 28°C with moderate use of air-conditioning systems. Frugal energy consumption is the aim. To fight against the urban heat island effect, the future metropolitan district of the Village has set the goal of reducing the ambient exterior temperature by two degrees. Here, surfaces planted with vegetation are a lever ensuring well-being, preservation and resilience through the creation of cool islands. Urban furniture, designed by Gaëlle Lauriot-Prévost for the Olympic Village, is aimed at this performance. We should also remember that more than a quarter of Metropolitan inhabitants suffer from insufficient access to green spaces. Here, the Village is an example of how to respond to the grave poverty of the offer.

The Village is already ten years ahead in the stages of the trajectory toward Carbone neutrality inscribed in the 2050 agenda of the Paris Agreement and in the Metropolitan Climate Air Energy Plan. The carbon footprint per square meter was ambitiously reduced by more than 47% compared with current construction standards, and in a very short timeframe. Thus, the Village offers an economic model for housing and office development, without reliance on subsidies. This success becomes part of its heritage. One of the keys to achieving this was the use of wood and low-carbon concrete – even if the ecological impact of concrete production is still disputed. The equations are indeed complex. Including for wood. Although the SOLIDEO imposed its optimal use in buildings with heights under 28 meters, the "fireman's rule" regarding the use of biosourced and combustible materials exposed to risk of fire generates greater costs for construction of wooden buildings rather than a blend of materials. At the Olympic Village, the SOLIDEO obtained acceptance as a current technique the installation of three types of cladding (terracotta, metal, and render on exterior insulation) on the façades with a wooden framework; a technique that was implemented on 80 to 90% of buildings. Thus, the construction site is delivering lessons for future iterations of the Building Code. 100% of Village construction materials are biosourced, and 100% of its new buildings are passive or energy positive – meaning they produce more energy than they consume to operate. 80% to 100% of construction waste is recycled.

29.7 °

on 15/07/1910

32.9 °

on 12/07/1924

33 °

on 18/07/1955

36.5 °

on 29/06/2019

#247# **AMBITION 4**

CLIMATE IN 2050

Climate change in Paris

Climate change is visible in the Ile-de-France region and, of course, in Paris, where the urban heat island phenomenon is amplifying the rise in temperatures. With its very dense urban fabric, the city of Paris influences its meteorological environment by generating a microclimate: the "urban heat island". This results in night-time temperature differences of around 2.5°C on average over the year between Paris and neighbouring rural areas. These differences can reach 10°C in anticyclonic conditions with light winds and clear skies, such as heatwaves.

Average temperatures and rainfall on the rise

A study of the climate in Paris over the long term shows several notable changes:

- rising temperatures: around 0.3°C per decade
- rising rainfall

13% increase in annual rainfall

- less sunshine

Record temperatures in Paris (Montsouris station)

The future climate in France

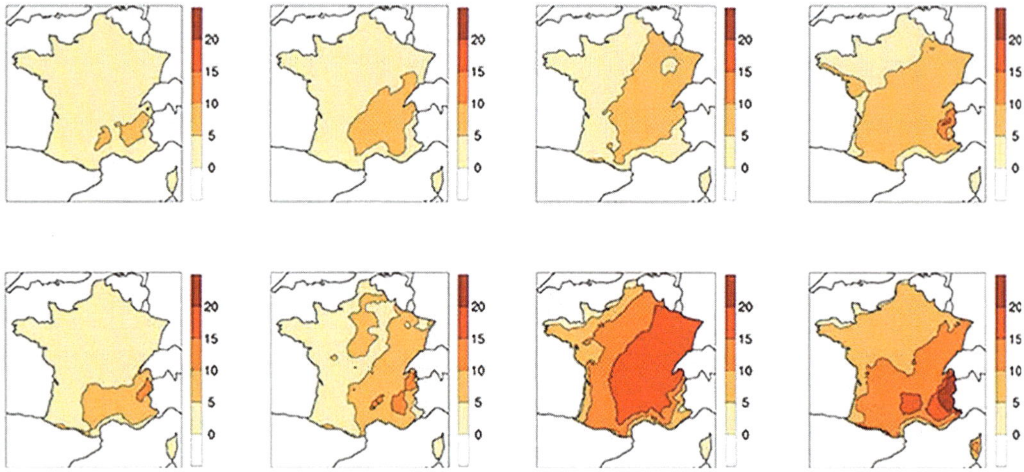

Anomaly in cumulative rainfall: difference between the period under consideration and the reference period [mm], Météo-France/CNRM2014: Météo-France Aladin model

Annual average

Emissions scenarios Reference (1976-2005) | Near horizon (2021-2050) | Medium horizon (2041-2070) | Distant horizon (2071-2100)

Scenario RCP2.6

Scenario RCP4.5

Scenario RCP8.5

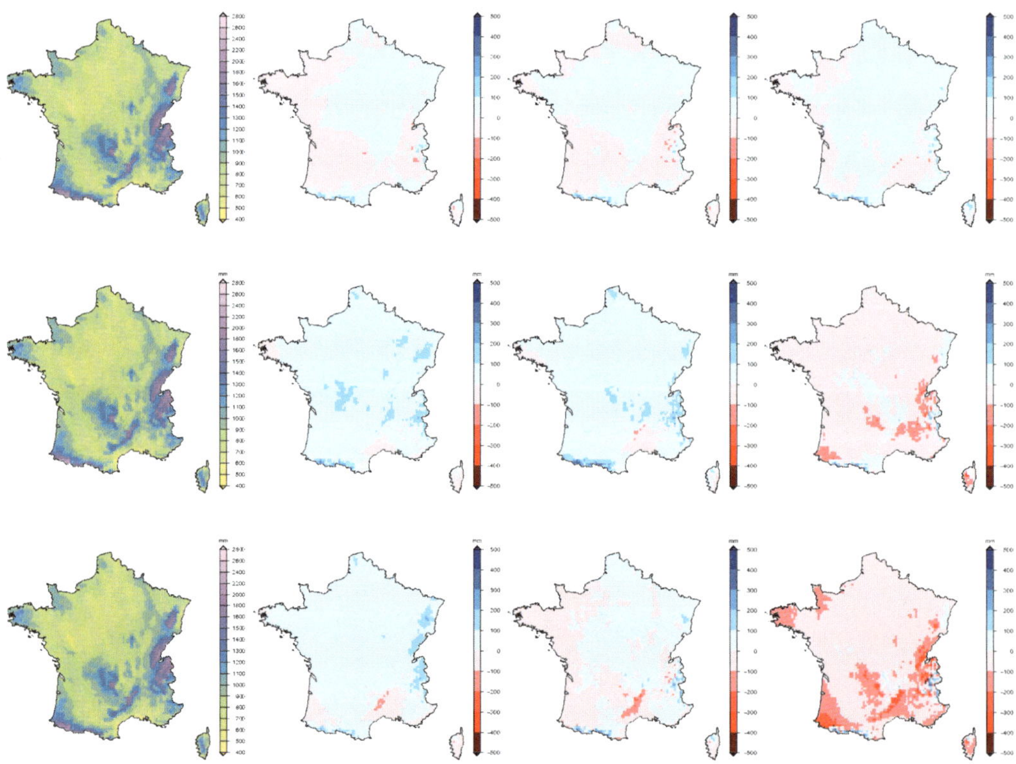

Soil moisture drought indicator (SSWI) from the ISBA model , Météo-France/CLIMSEC - CERFACS/SCRATCH08: Météo-France stretched Arpege-V4.6 model

Intermediate socio-economic development scenario (A1B)

Reference (around 1970) | Mid-term horizon (around 2055)

Year

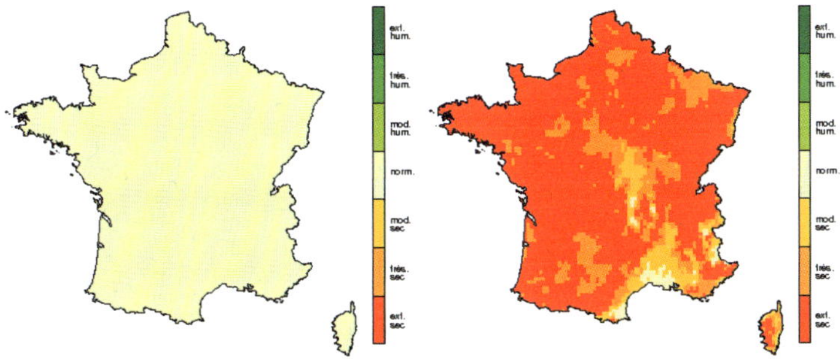

Daily mean temperature anomaly: difference between the period under consideration and the reference period [°C] , Météo-France/CNRM2014 : Météo-France Aladin model

Annual average

Emissions scenarios Reference (1976-2005) | Near horizon (2021-2050) | Medium horizon (2041-2070) | Future horizon (2071-2100)

Scenario RCP2.6

Scenario RCP4.5

Scenario RCP8.5

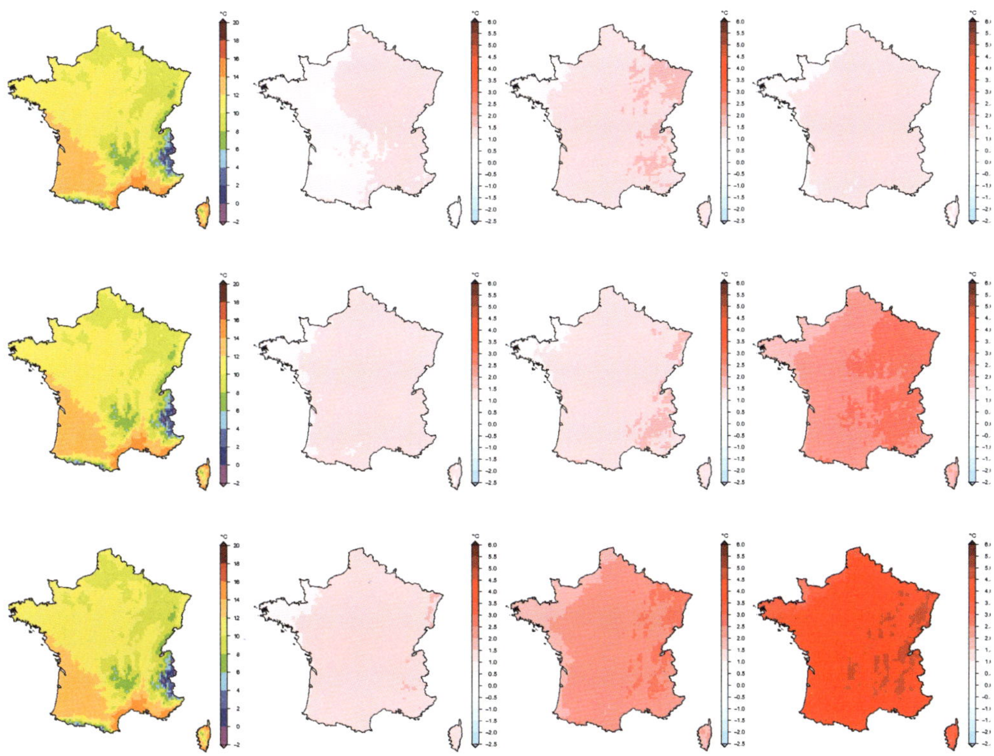

Chronological graphs of climate simulations for several scenarios in metropolitan France

Annual average

Mean annual temperature in mainland France at reference 1976-2005. Climate simulations of the past and future for three scenarios RCP 2.6, 4.5 and 8.5

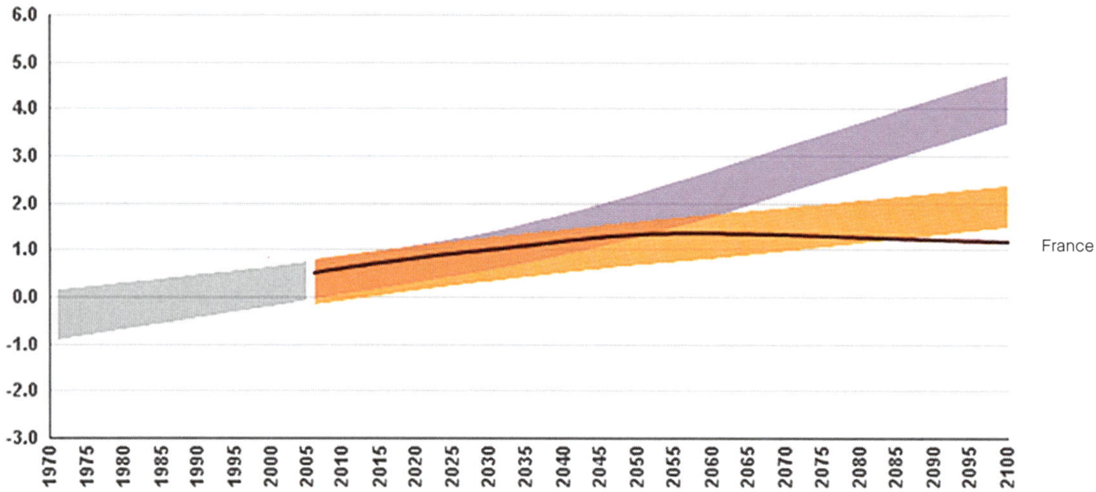

Deviation from reference for past and future climate simulations RCP 2.6, 4.5 and 8.5

Aladin RCP 2.6 simulation reference deviation

Annual average

Number of hot days in Ile-de-France. Climate simulations of the past and future for three scenarios RCP 2.6, 4.5 and 8.5

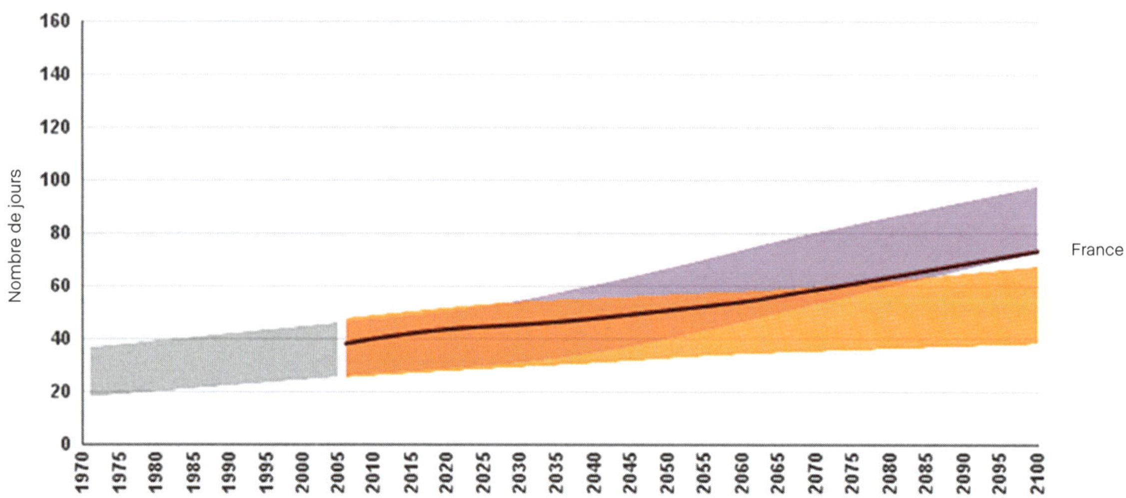

Number of days for past and future climate simulations RCP 4.5 and 8.5

Number of days for the Aladin RCP 2.65 simulation

Chronological graphs of climate simulations for several scenarios for metropolitan France

The graph on the right shows temperature trends simulated by a range of regional climate models. The results are presented for the past (grey plume) and for the 21st century for several socio-economic development scenarios (the RCP - coloured plumes and curved plumes). For each socio-economic development scenario, the most likely simulations fall within the corresponding-coloured plume.

In mainland France, climate projections show a continuation of annual warming until the 2050s, whatever the scenario. Over the second half of the 21st century, the change in mean annual temperature differs significantly depending on the scenario considered. The only scenario that stabilises warming is the RCP2.6 scenario (which includes a climate policy aimed at reducing CO2 concentrations). According to RCP8.5 (a scenario with no climate policy), warming could reach 4°C by 2071-2100.

The graph below shows temperature trends simulated by a range of regional climate models. The results are presented for the past (grey plume) and for the 21st century for several socio-economic development scenarios (the RCP scenarios - coloured plumes and curve). For each socio-economic development scenario, the most likely simulations fall within the corresponding-coloured plume.

In the Paris Region, climate projections show an increase in the number of hot days as warming continues.

Over the first part of the 21st century, this increase is similar from one scenario to another. By 2071-2100, this increase would be around 16 days compared with the 1976-2005 period according to the RCP4.5 scenario (scenario with a climate policy aimed at reducing greenhouse gas emissions), and 45 days according to RCP8.5 (scenario without a climate policy).

The choice of materials and the positioning of furniture and lighting must take account of the constraints involved in managing and maintaining the public space. Modular pavements at the foot of facades (HV networks, IRVE, TEL). Asphalt or concrete pavements. Principle of the technical strip.

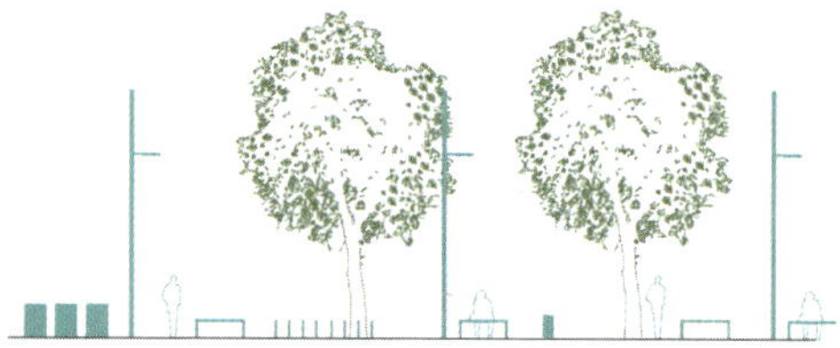

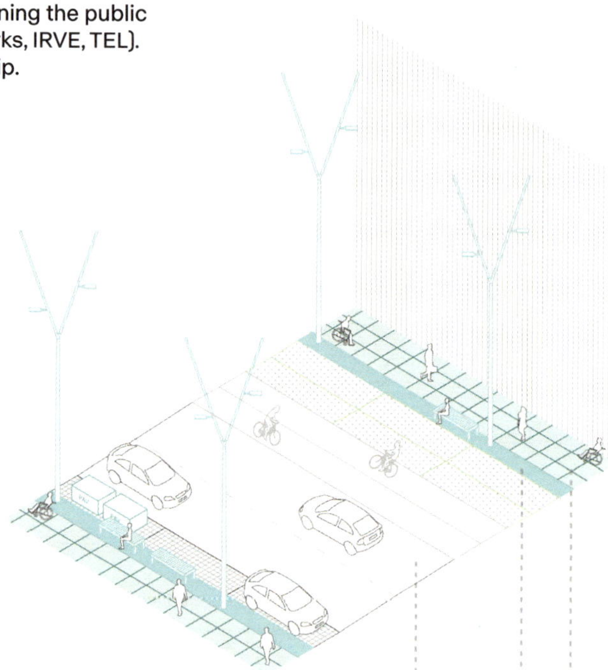

Rue Volta

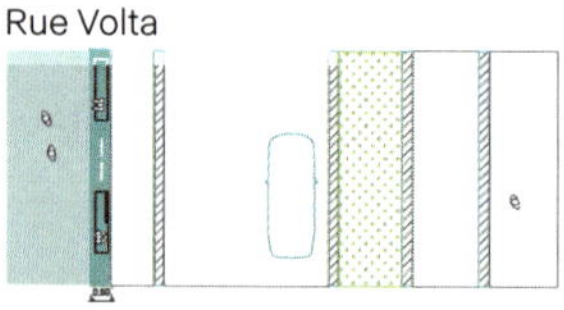

Rue Quinconces

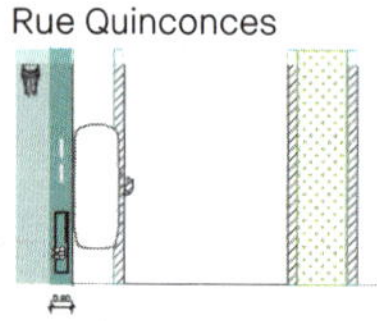

Allée de Seine

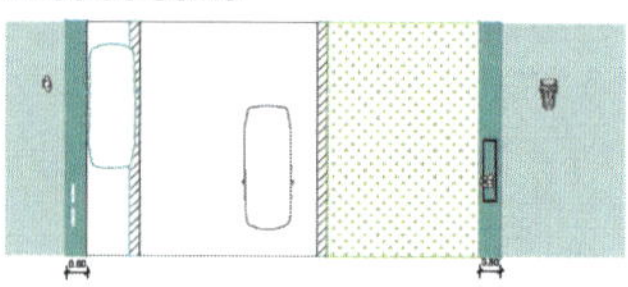

Rue Coteaux

Rue Ampère

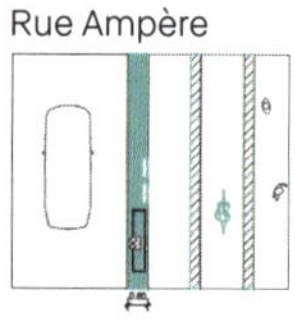

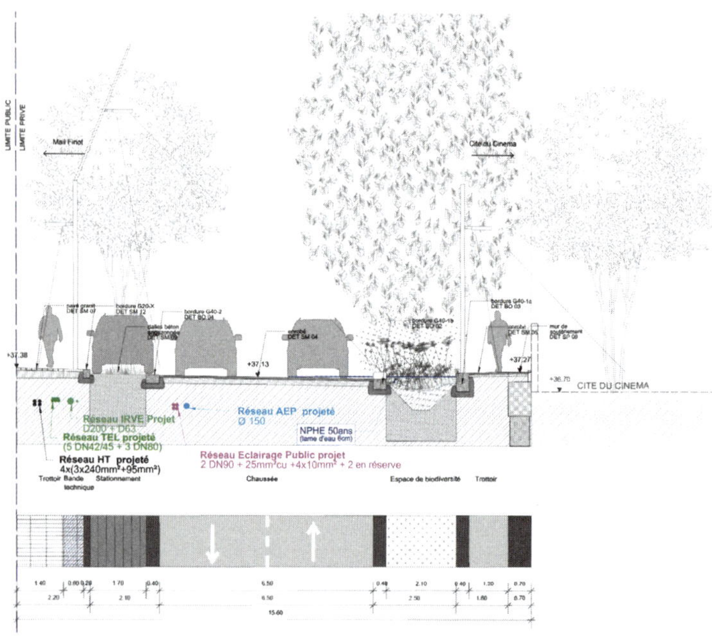

Section on rue de Quinconces

BELVEDERE

Rue des Villas
Pavement: modular granite
Footpaths: granite modular

Rue Belvedere
Footpaths: granite modular

UNIVERSEINE

Rue des Villas
Pavement: modular granite
Footpaths: granite modular

Rue Volta
Pavement: asphalt
Footpaths: granite modular on universeine side
Asphalt on RTE side

To guarantee urban comfort in the climate of 2050, by offering shaded, cool, high-quality spaces. Mitigating the effects of urban heat islands, guaranteeing nearby cool islands for every resident.

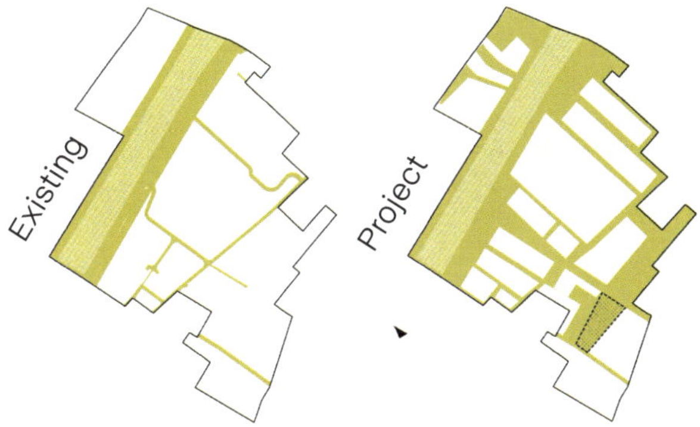

29.7 ° On 15/07/1910

32.9 ° On 12/07/1924

33 ° On 18/07/1955

36.5 ° On 29/06/2019

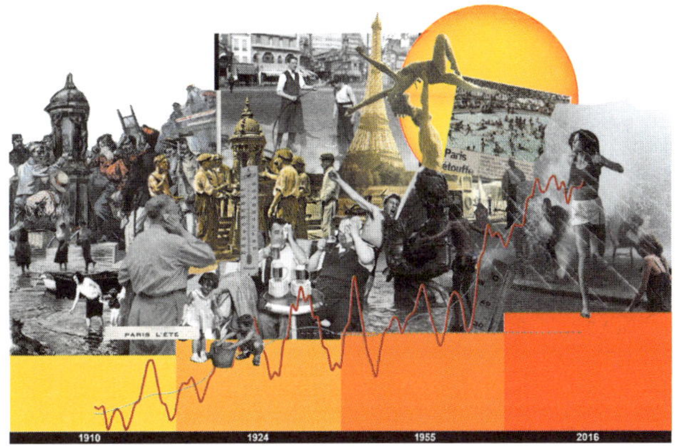

15 ha
Public spaces

18.000 m²
Area naturalised and/or natural habitat reconstituted

-2°
The district's objective in combating the urban heat island

1700 m²
Temporary flood zones in the neighbourhood

1600 m³
Linear storage spaces in the neighbourhood

100%
Water requirements for watering and cleaning public spaces covered by rainwater and raw water

30
Different tree species

1150
Newly planted trees

5 min
Time taken for residents to move away from a cool area

0
Net waterproofing

0
Discharge of rainwater into the network

7ha
Surface area of the Seine in the Olympic Village

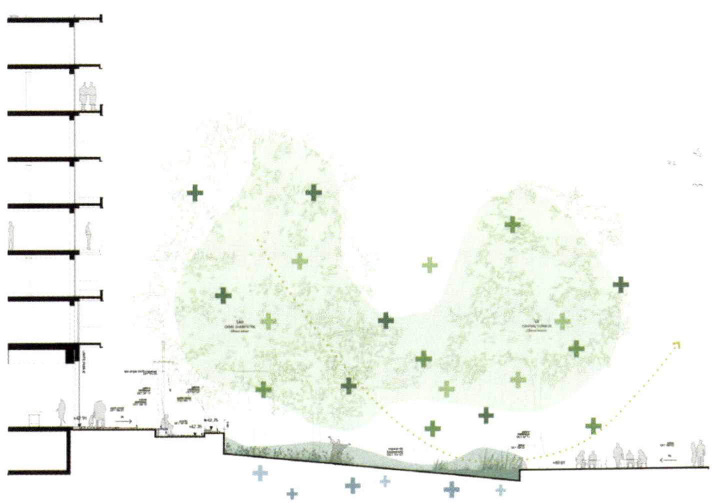

Relating to the climate - Learning from the current

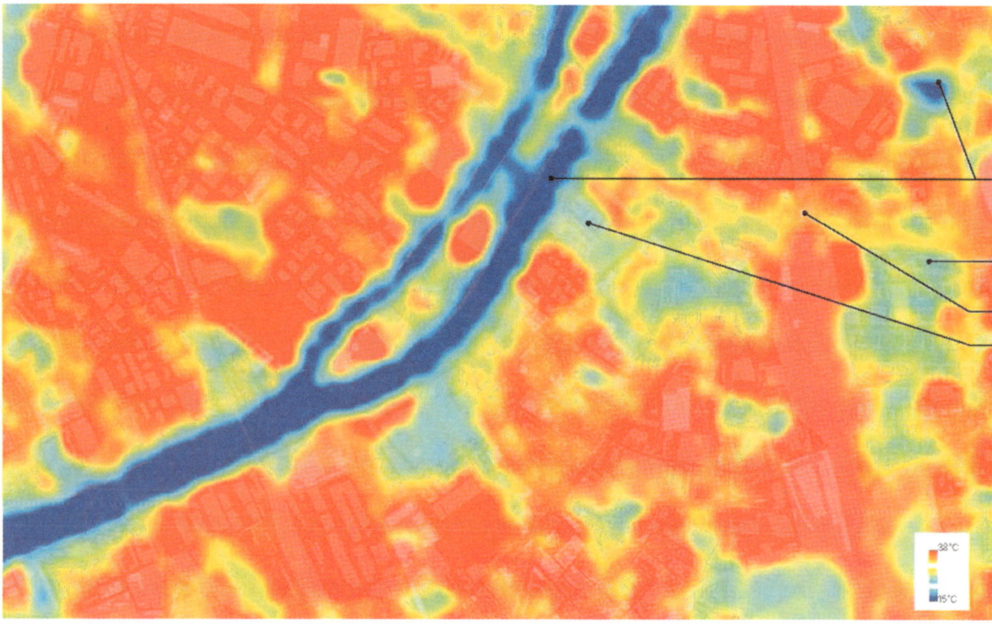

Thermography, August 2010 (APUR)

Some coverings are less suited to heat than others

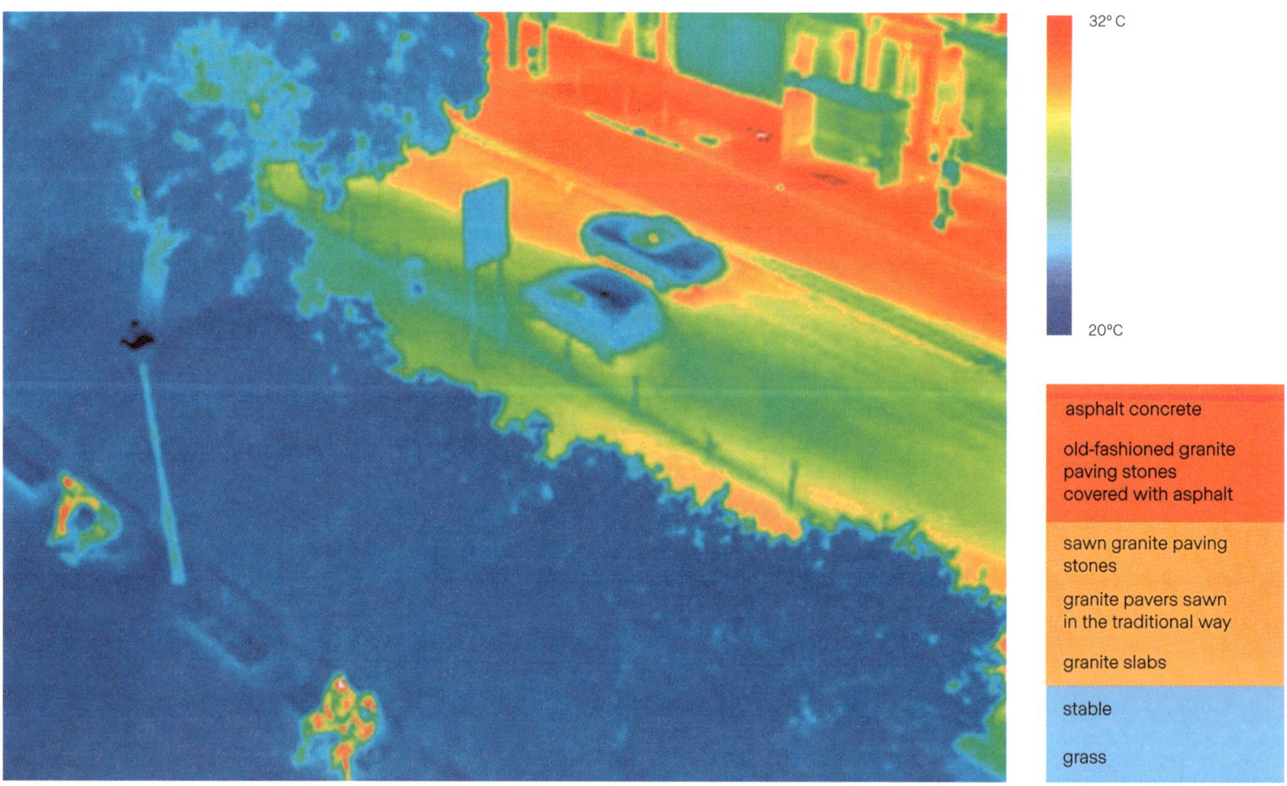

Wind circulation - The annual wind rose

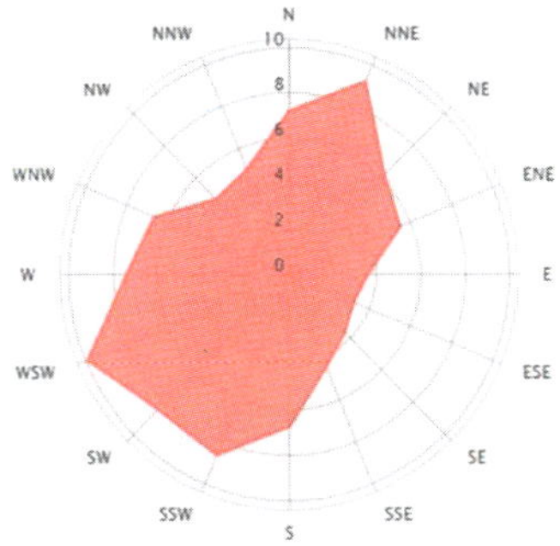

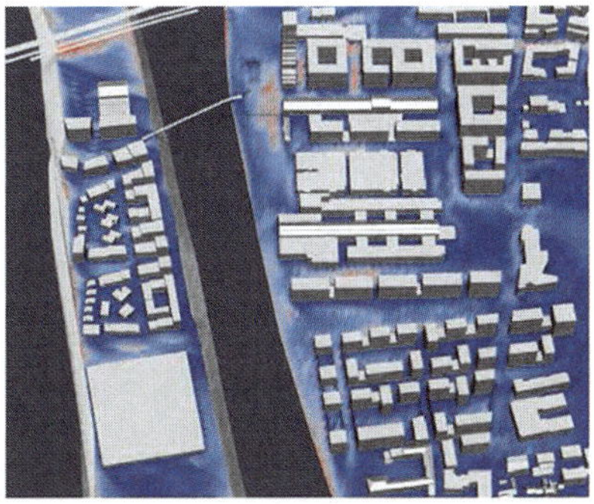

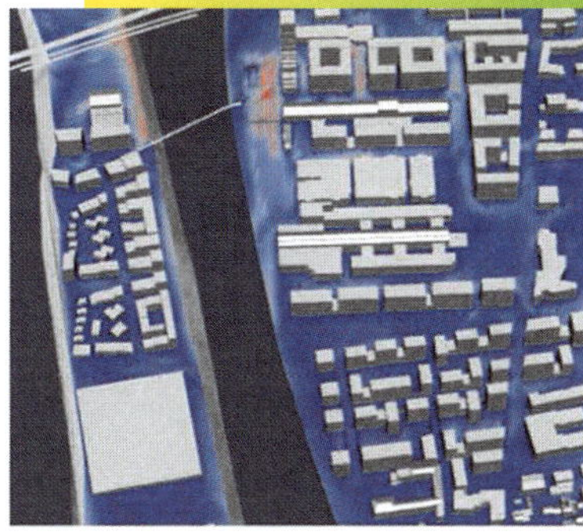

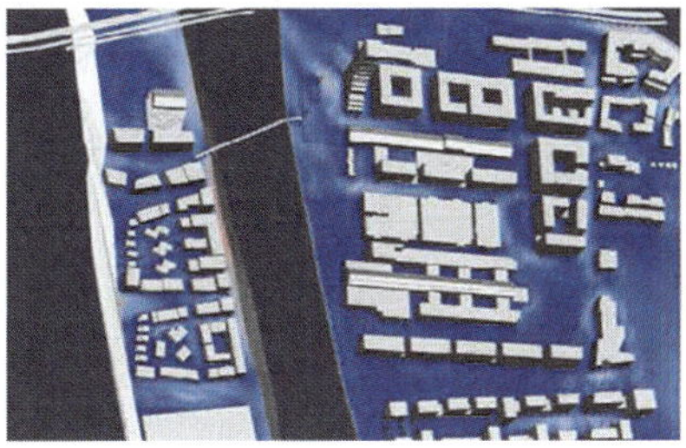
U180°

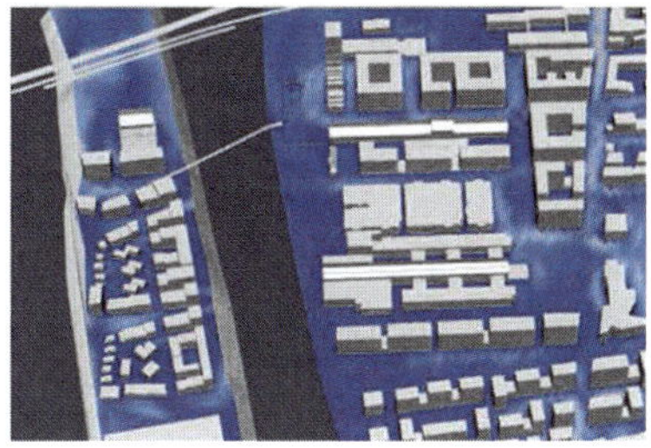
U210°

Sunshine - Summer solstice / not including trees

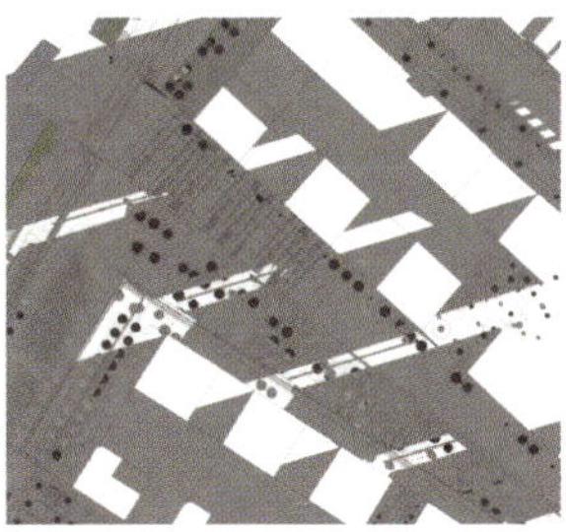
06H50

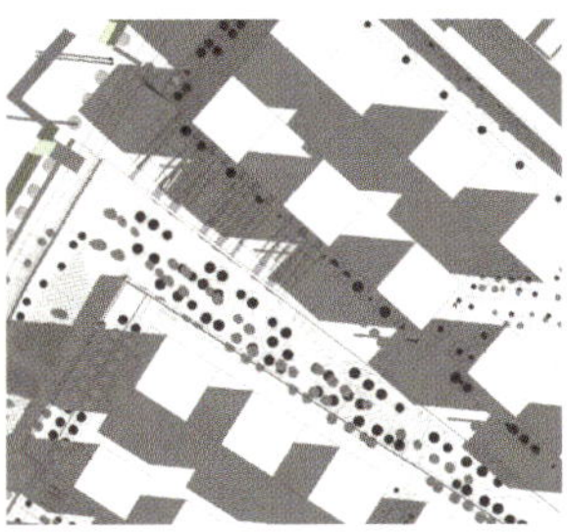
08H50

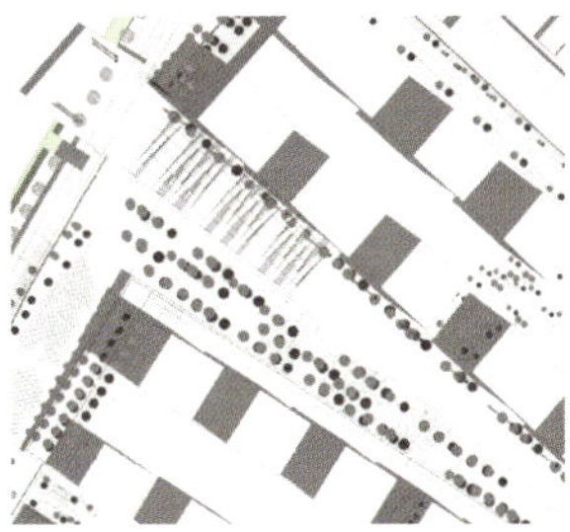
16H50

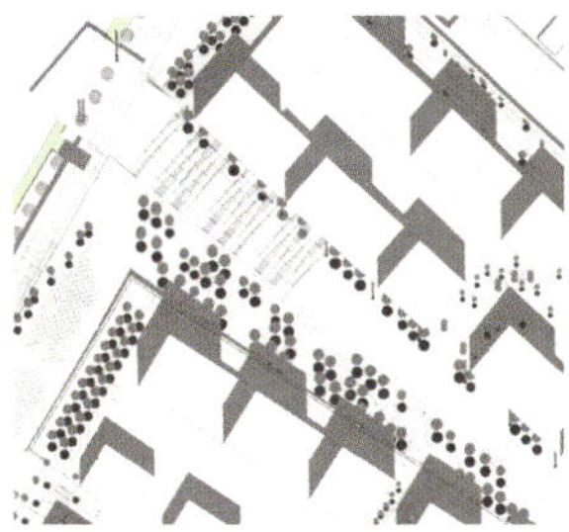
12H50

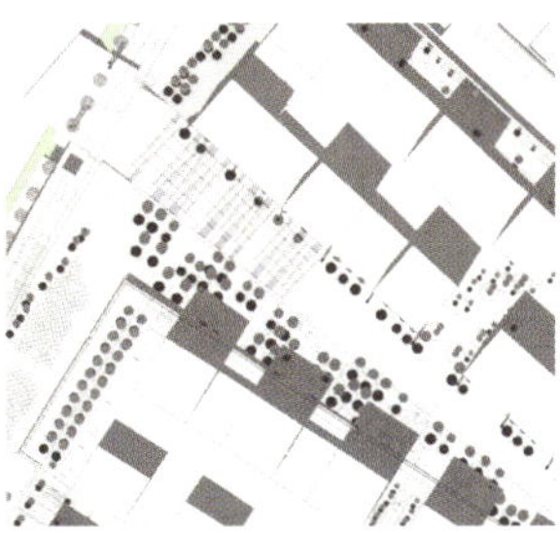
14H00

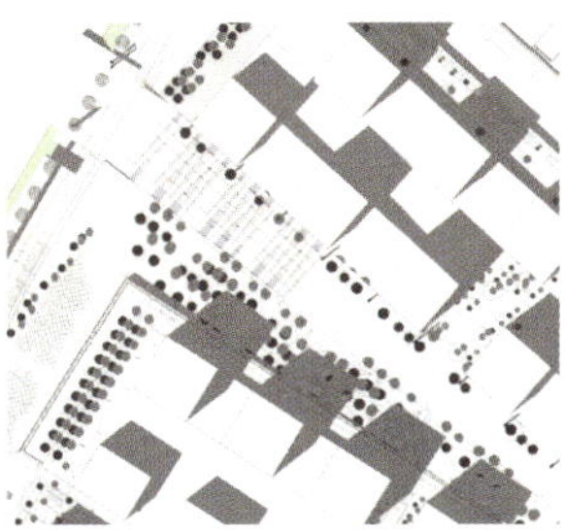
14H50

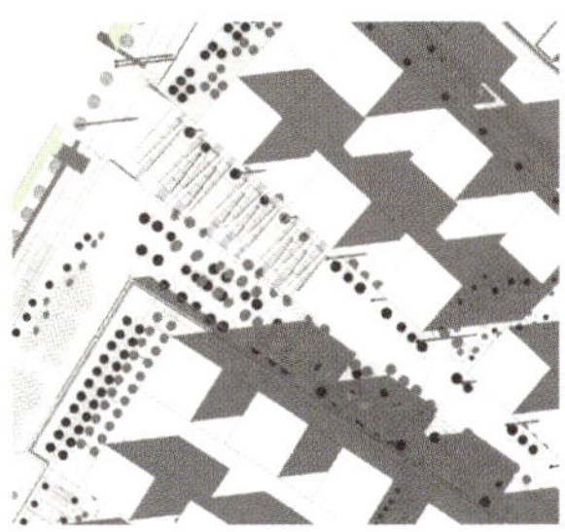
16H50

18H50

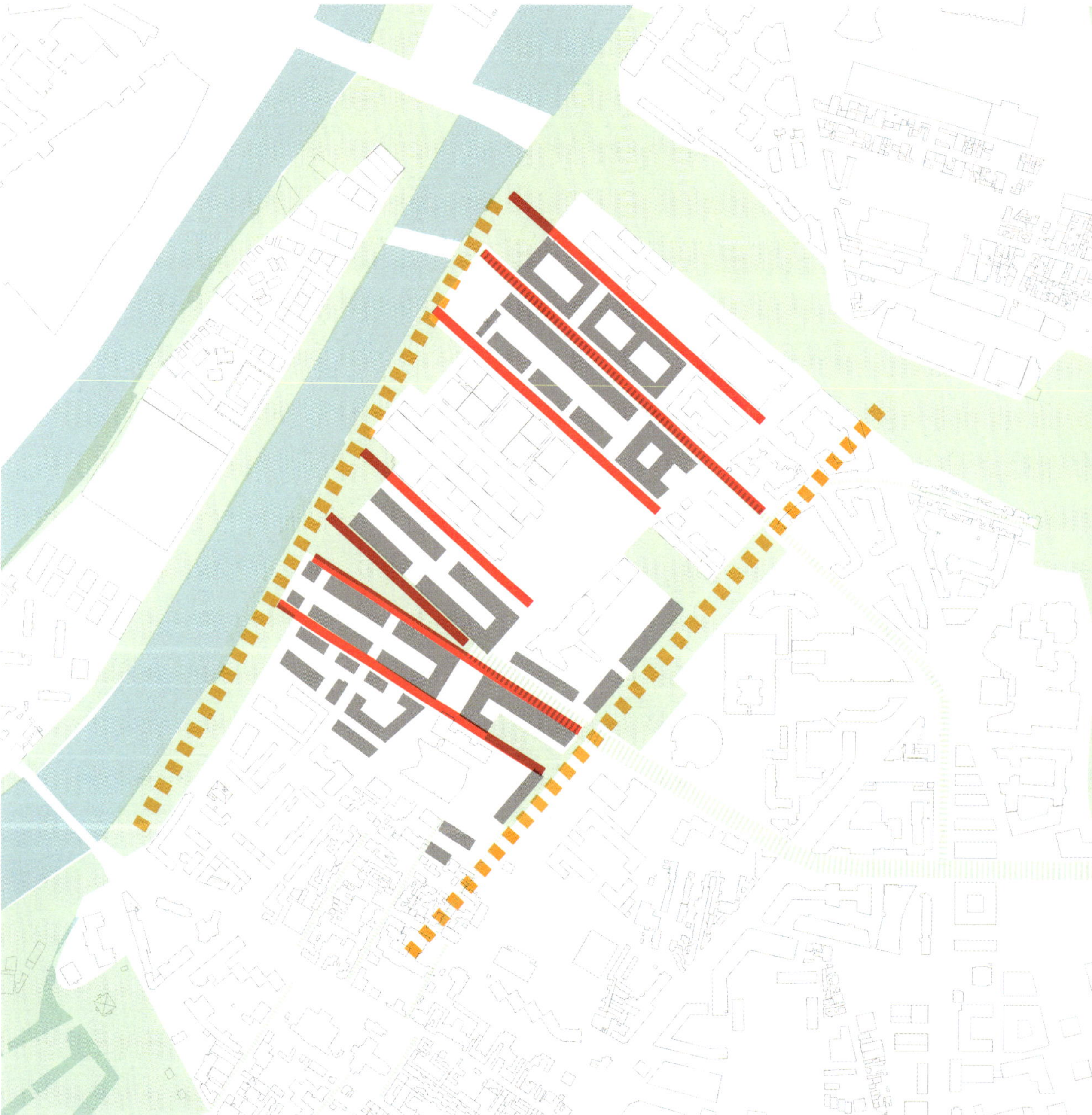

#257# **AMBITION 4**

CLIMATE IN 2050

Orientated public spaces.

East-west orientation of the urban grid

The orientation of the public roads within the district defines a duality due to the sunshine that these linear spaces receive:
a sunny side, pleasant for strolling in spring and summer, and a shady side, cool and refreshing in summer.

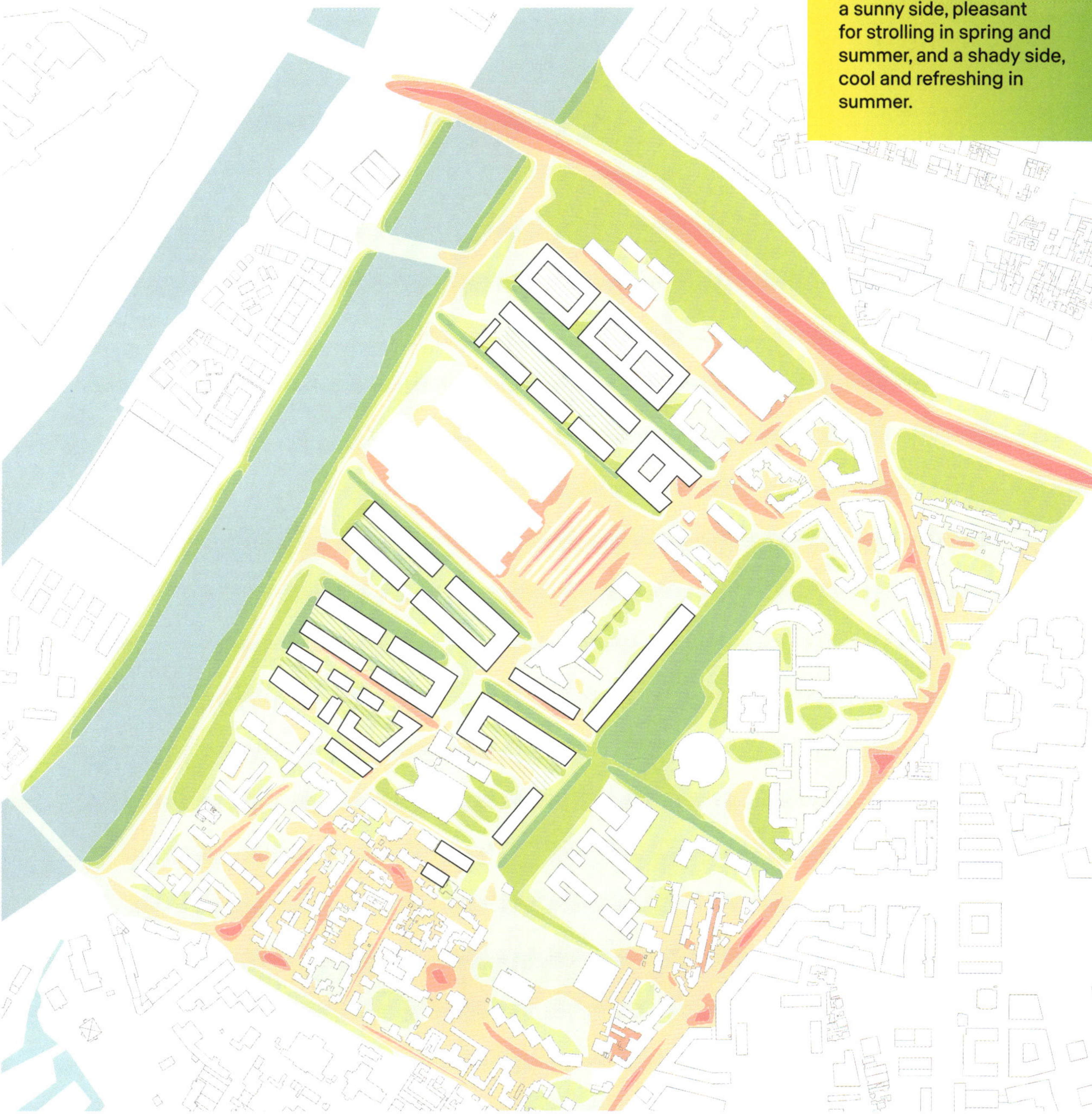

#259# **AMBITION 4**

CLIMATE IN 2050

Marianne Levinsen landscape, Lindevangs park, Frederiksberg.

TVK, Place de la République, Paris. LATZ + PARTNER, Place Flagey, Ixelles.

Michel Crajoud, Place de la Bourse, Bordeaux.

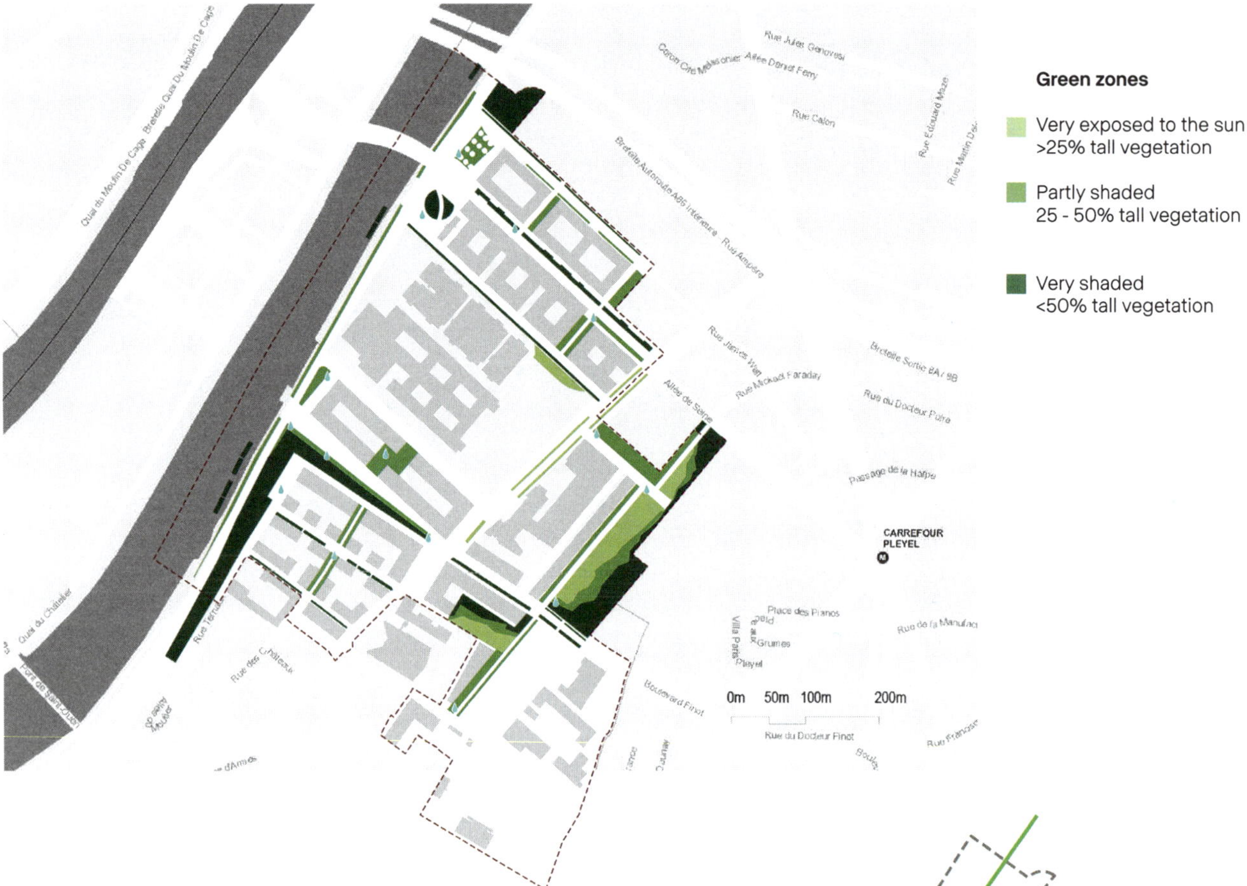

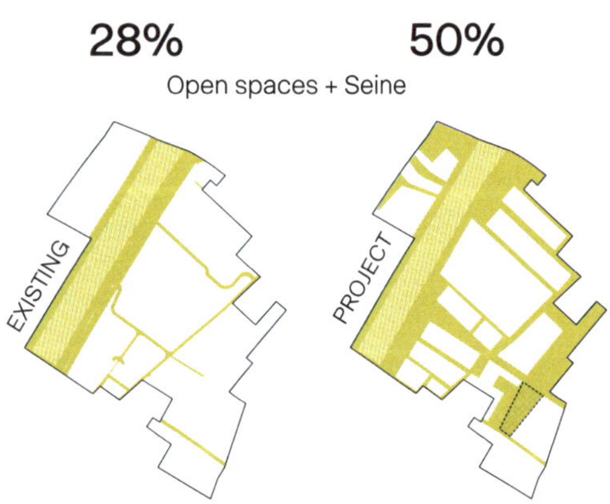

15 ha
Public spaces

18.000 m²
Area naturalised and/or natural habitat reconstituted

-2°
The district's objective in combating the urban heat island effect

30
Different tree species

1150
New trees planted

5 min
Time taken for residents to move away from a cool area

MAIL FINOT Cross-section 01
1/50

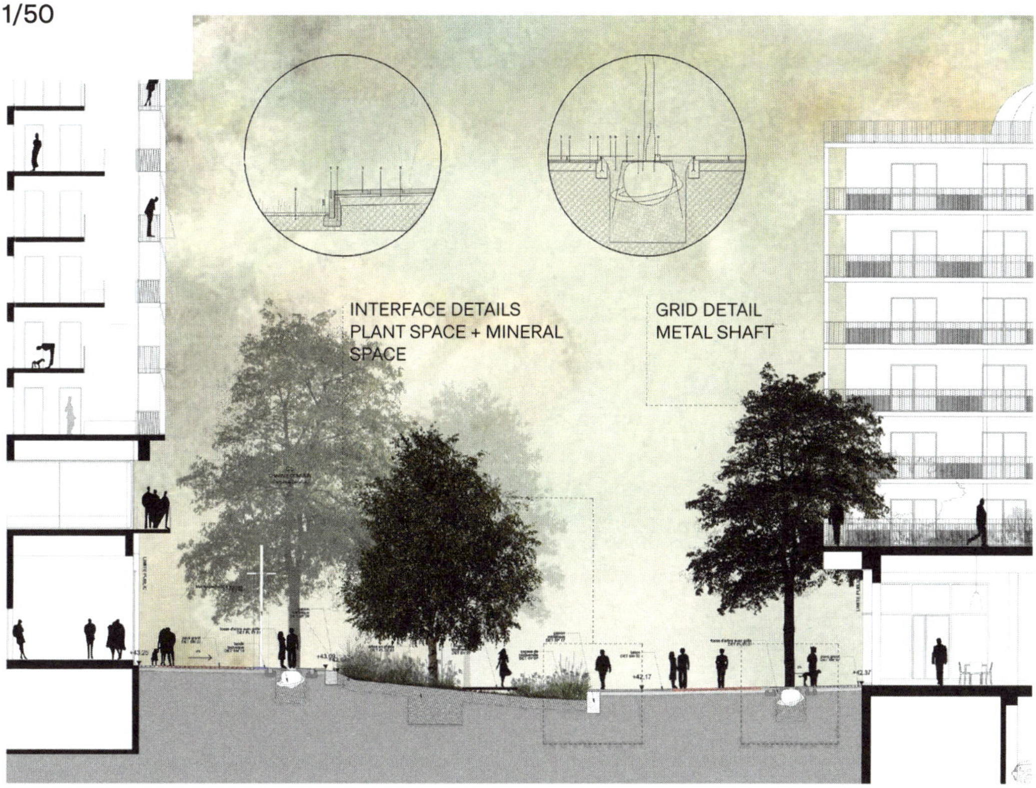

Quantifying ecosystem services

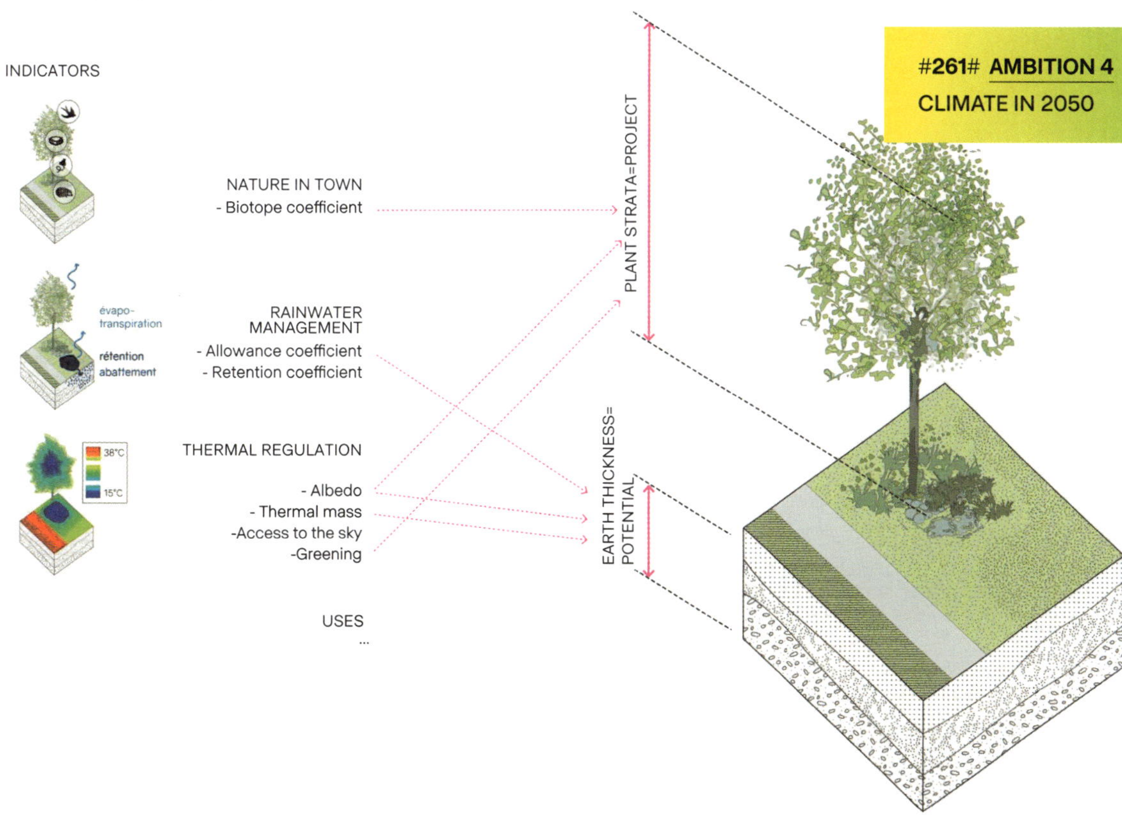

#263# **AMBITION 4**

CLIMATE IN 2050

Modular flooring - Light shade
Paves granit, Place de la Basilique, Saint Denis Evreux, Desvigne

Cast concrete - Light shade

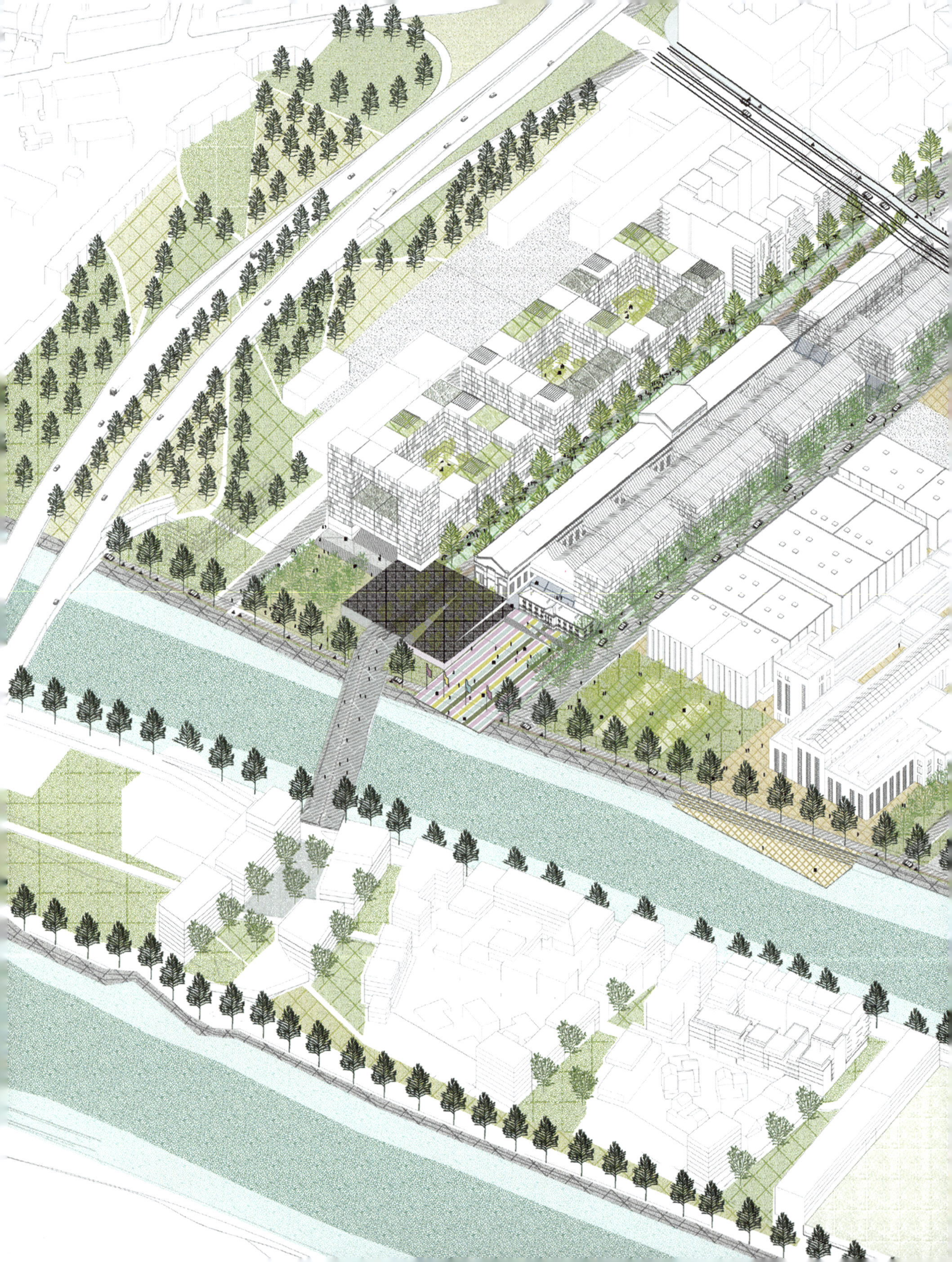

#265# AMBITION 4
CLIMATE IN 2050

#269# **AMBITION 4**

CLIMATE IN 2050

New record temperature in Paris!

47.1 degrees. That is the temperature recorded by Météo France stations on 12 August 2040.

Like every summer, the heatwave is sweeping across Europe, and France is once again being hit by it. Everyone in the neighbourhood has access to a within 5 minutes' walk. Thanks to the "Îlots" application, they can access a map to find places where "temperatures are cooler than in the surrounding area".

How the district functions during hot spells

The storage of running rain in the underground part of the open-air storage structures allows some of the rainwater to be retained in the ground. The aim is to make use of this water in hot weather to combat urban heat islands, by encouraging the natural phenomenon of evapotranspiration to act as an "urban air conditioner".

30.2 M **32.7 M**

2009 **2012**

2009 **2012**

32.4 M

2015

40 M

2017

#271# AMBITION 4

CLIMATE IN 2050

Beyond the ring road: Saint Denis, the new tourist destination?

Paris attracted more than 40 million tourists in 2017.

The Games are an international promotional tool for the host country, thanks to their resonance and media impact (3.7 billion television viewers, 25,000 journalists).

In Barcelona in 1992, the Games made it possible to develop the coastline and open the city to the sea.

In Sydney in 2000, they contributed to the creation of a new leisure, living, and working space, Homebush, where 130 companies now employ 12,000 people.

In 2012, in London, they helped to develop and revitalise an entire district, East London, which is now home to Europe's largest shopping centre.

In 2024, in Saint Denis, won't the Village become a new metropolitan landmark that people come to visit?

2015 2018

#273# AMBITION 4

CLIMATE IN 2050

Booming tourist numbers

The Village has become a tourist attraction, an urban landmark. Tourists come from all over the world to visit, observe and photograph!

The world's most widely covered media event has been a success. The area is a magnet for tourists, who come to enjoy the banks of the Seine and the Olympic square, to follow in the footsteps of the athletes and observe the aesthetic quality of the public space and the architecture.

#275# **AMBITION 4**

CLIMATE IN 2050

Extinction of species in the Paris Region

The Village as a specific and controlled reservoir of biodiversity, which makes it possible to maintain specific endogenous habitats that are essential to the regional metabolism.

Notion of biomimicry (using processes that exist in nature in our urban spaces to minimise our environmental impact).

0.1%

taking biodiversity into account in land-use planning

2011

#277# **AMBITION 4**

CLIMATE IN 2050

Taking biodiversity into account in regional planning.

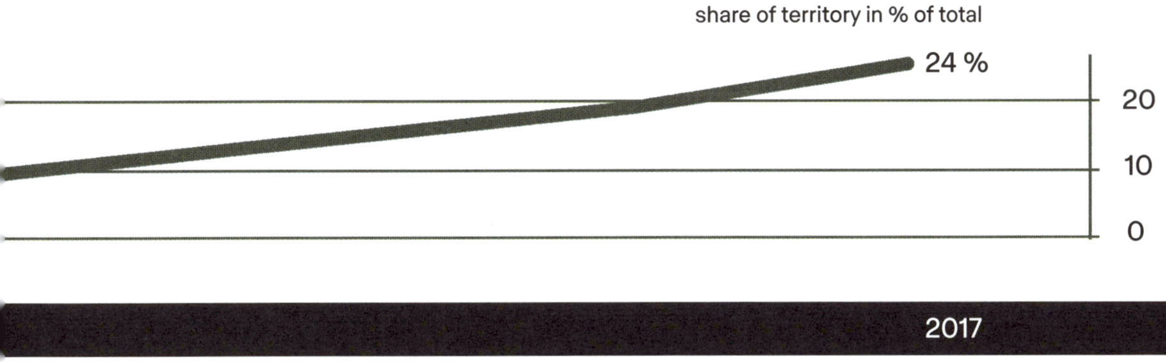

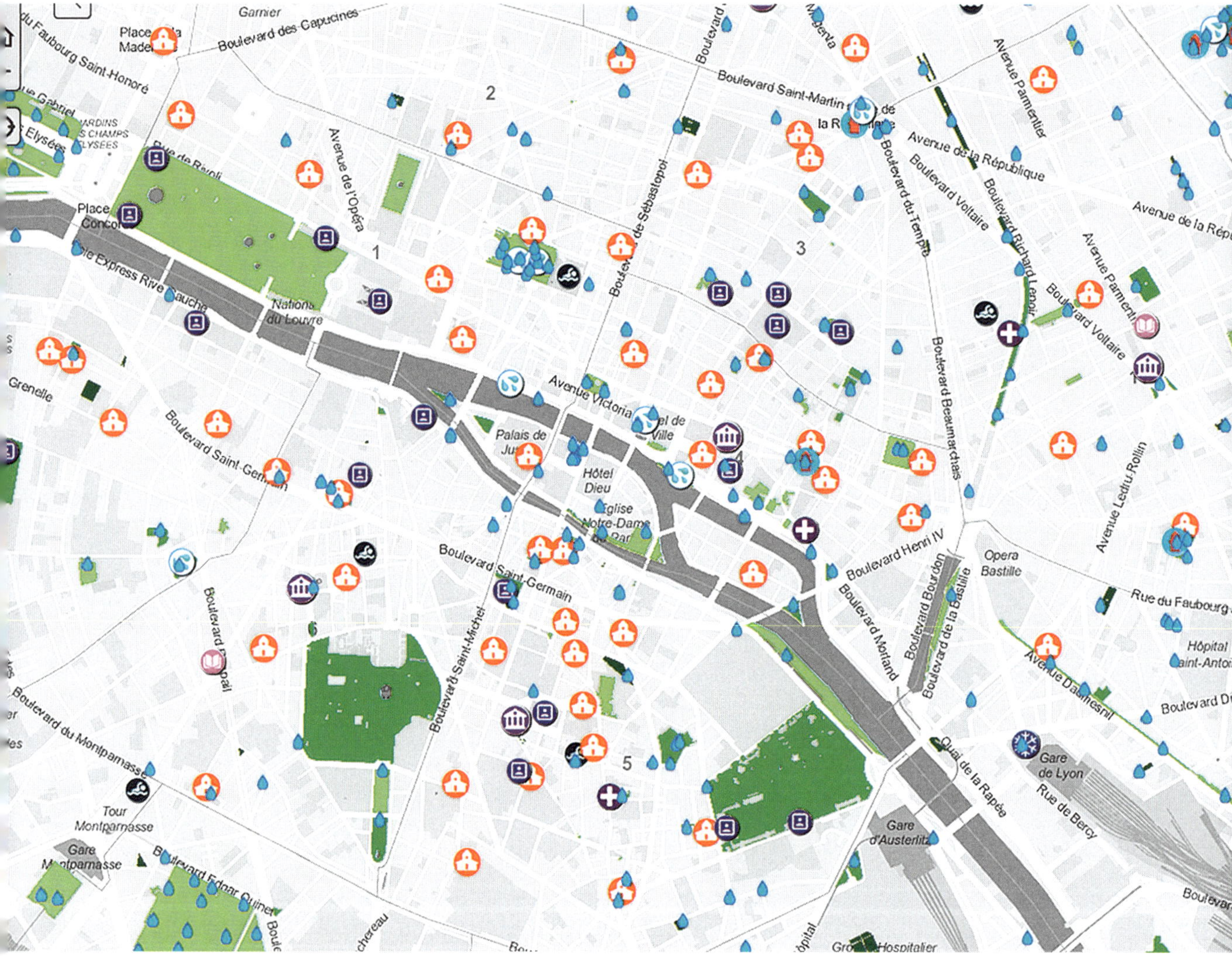

Islands of urban freshness

Drinking fountains

Cooling equipment

Fountains and misters

Ephemeral fountains and misters (2 in 1)

Fresh stop

Activities

Outdoor swimming

Swimming pool

Library

Museum

Places of worship

Administrative facilities

Borough Hall

EHPAD : Club/restaurant

Green spaces

Very sunny, therefore rather warm (less than 25% tall vegetation)

Partly shaded, therefore moderately cool (25-50% tall vegetation)

Very shaded, therefore cool (over 50% tall vegetation)

#279# **AMBITION 4**

CLIMATE IN 2050

Map of urban freshness areas in Paris (source: APUR).

Projection on the Olympic Village site (DPA).

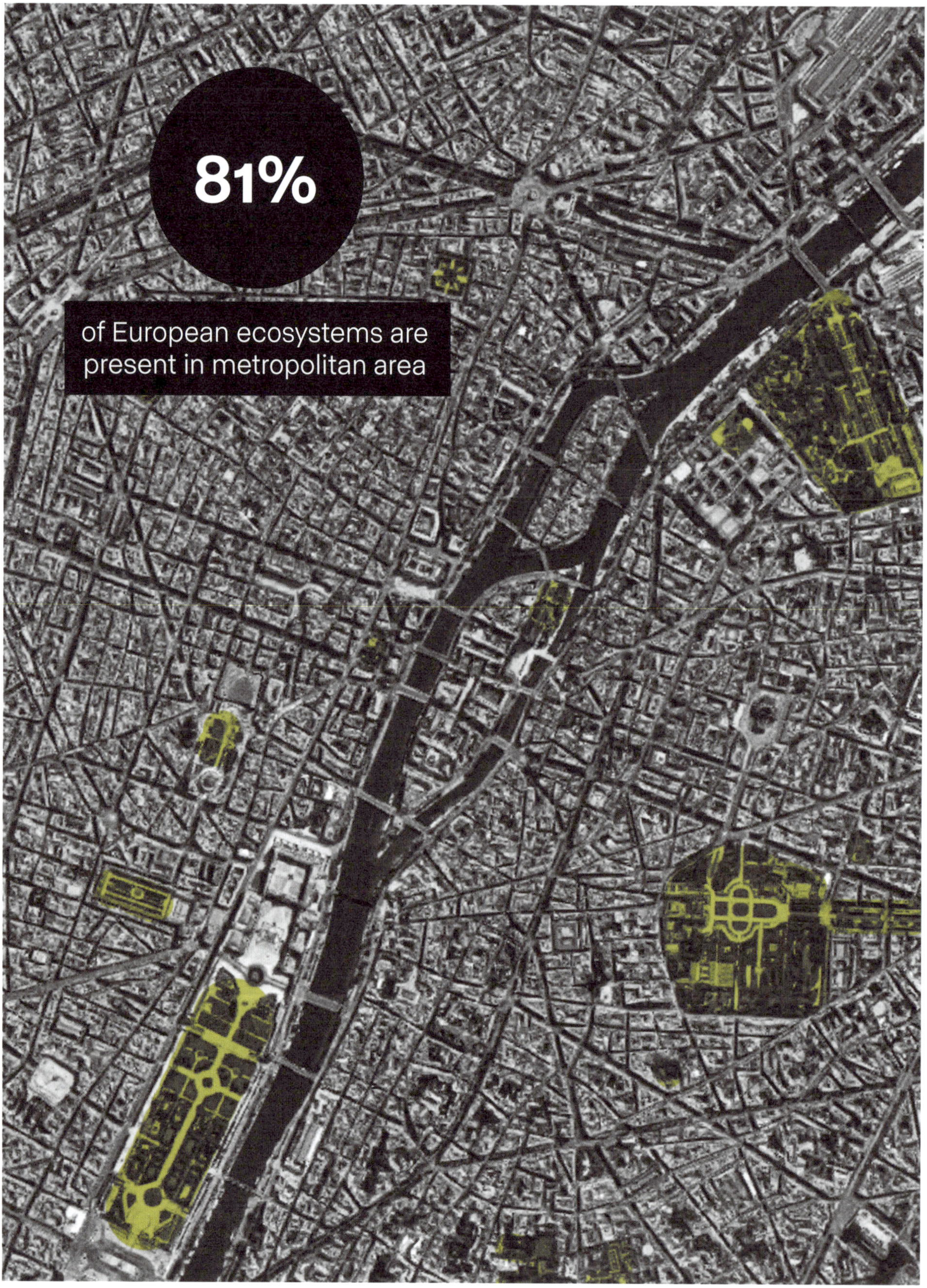
81%
of European ecosystems are present in metropolitan area

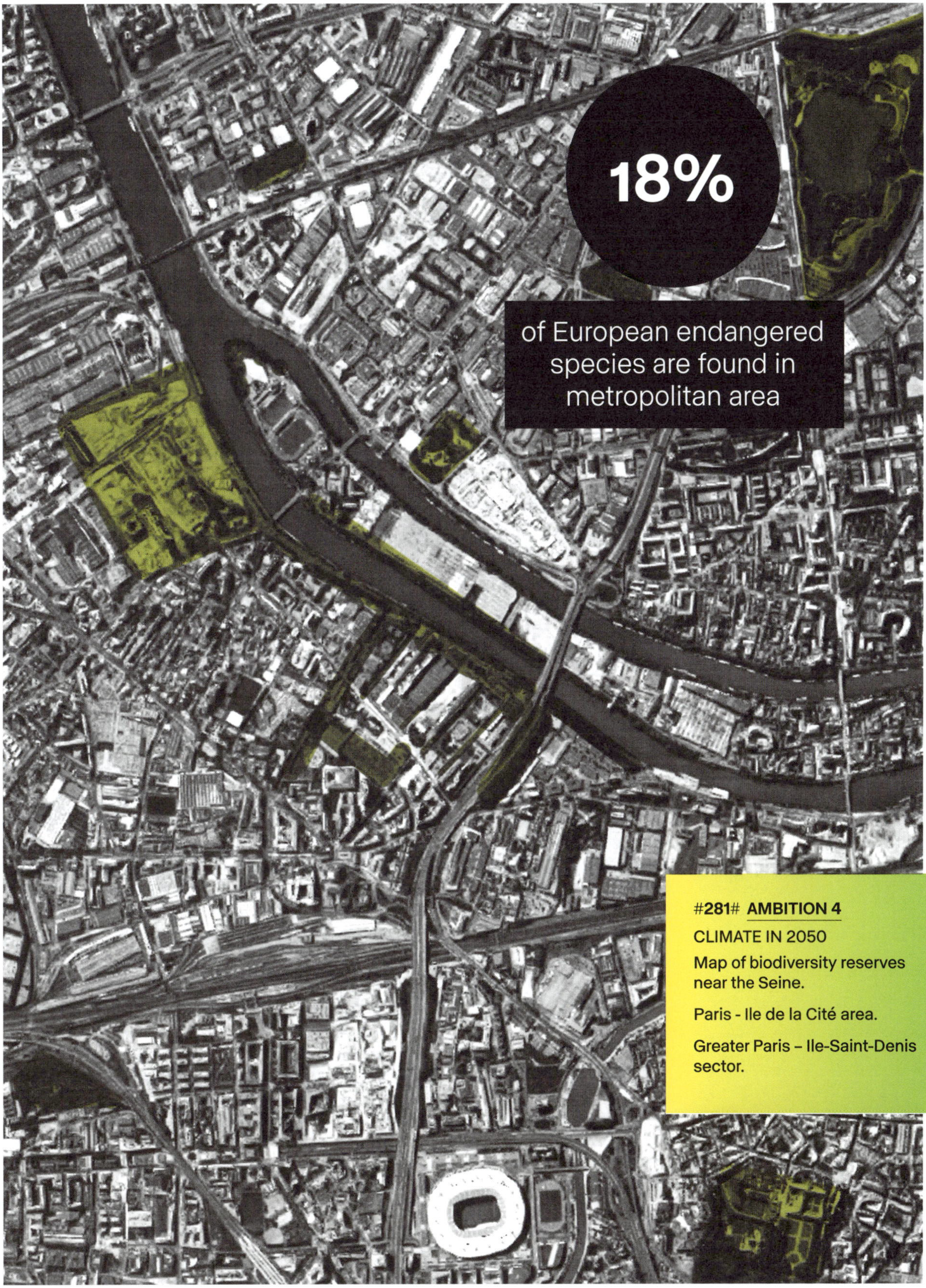

#281# **AMBITION 4**

CLIMATE IN 2050

Map of biodiversity reserves near the Seine.

Paris - Ile de la Cité area.

Greater Paris – Ile-Saint-Denis sector.

0.5 ha

Surface area
of mail Finot

0.4 ha

Place des
Athlètes

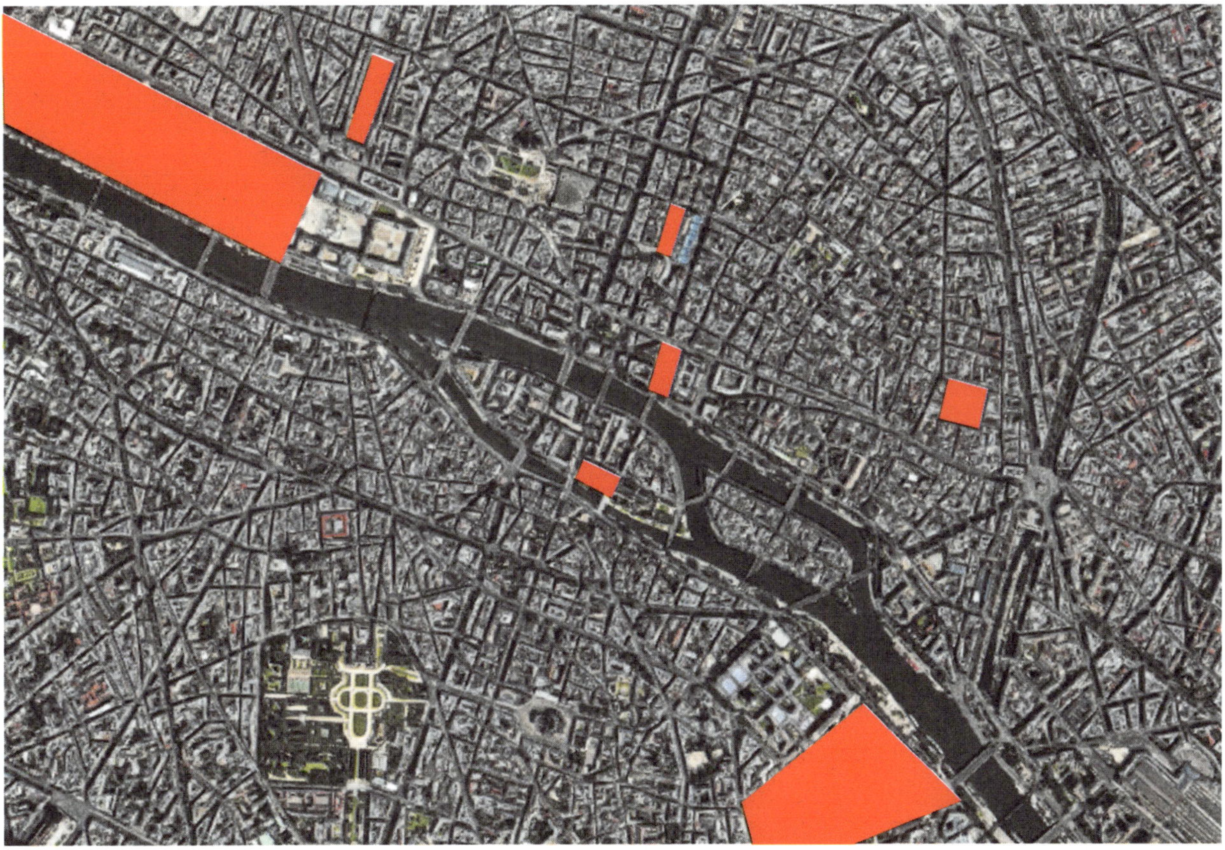

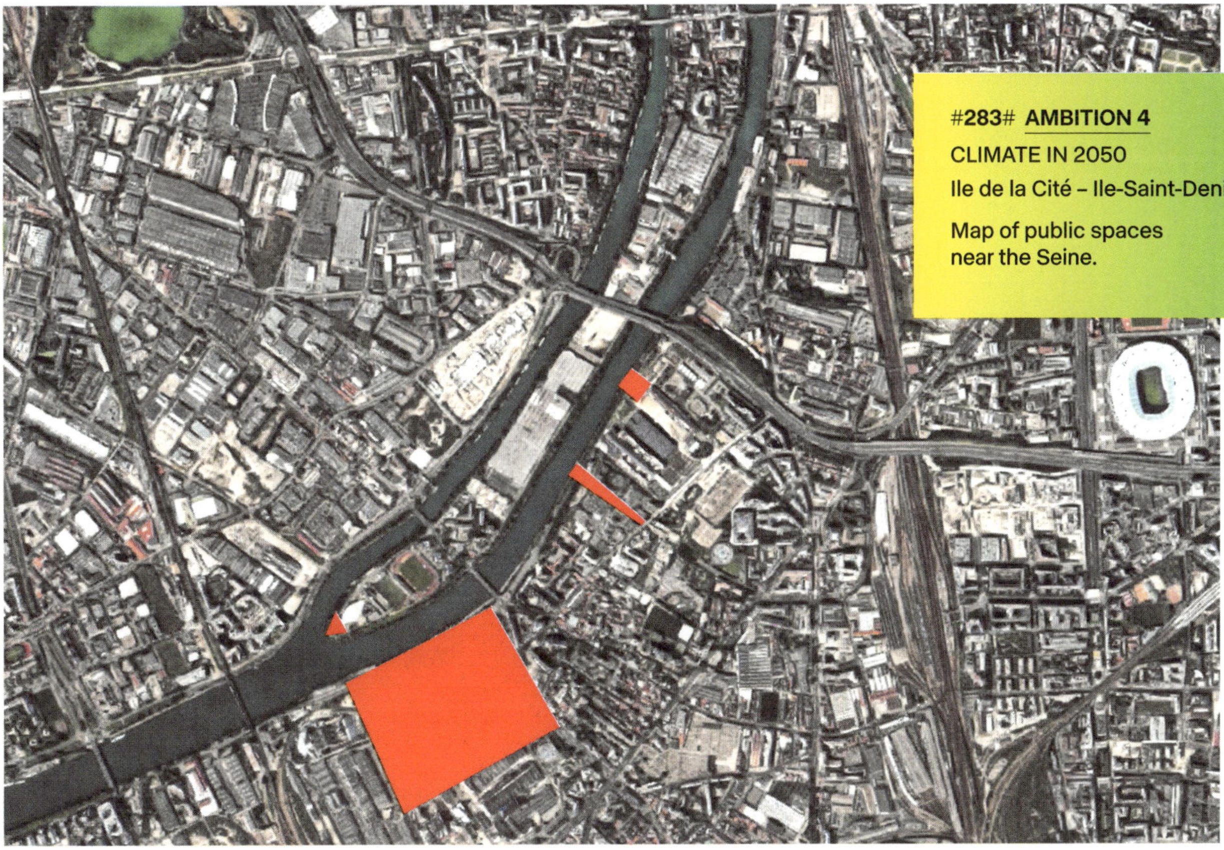

#283# **AMBITION 4**

CLIMATE IN 2050

Ile de la Cité – Ile-Saint-Denis.

Map of public spaces near the Seine.

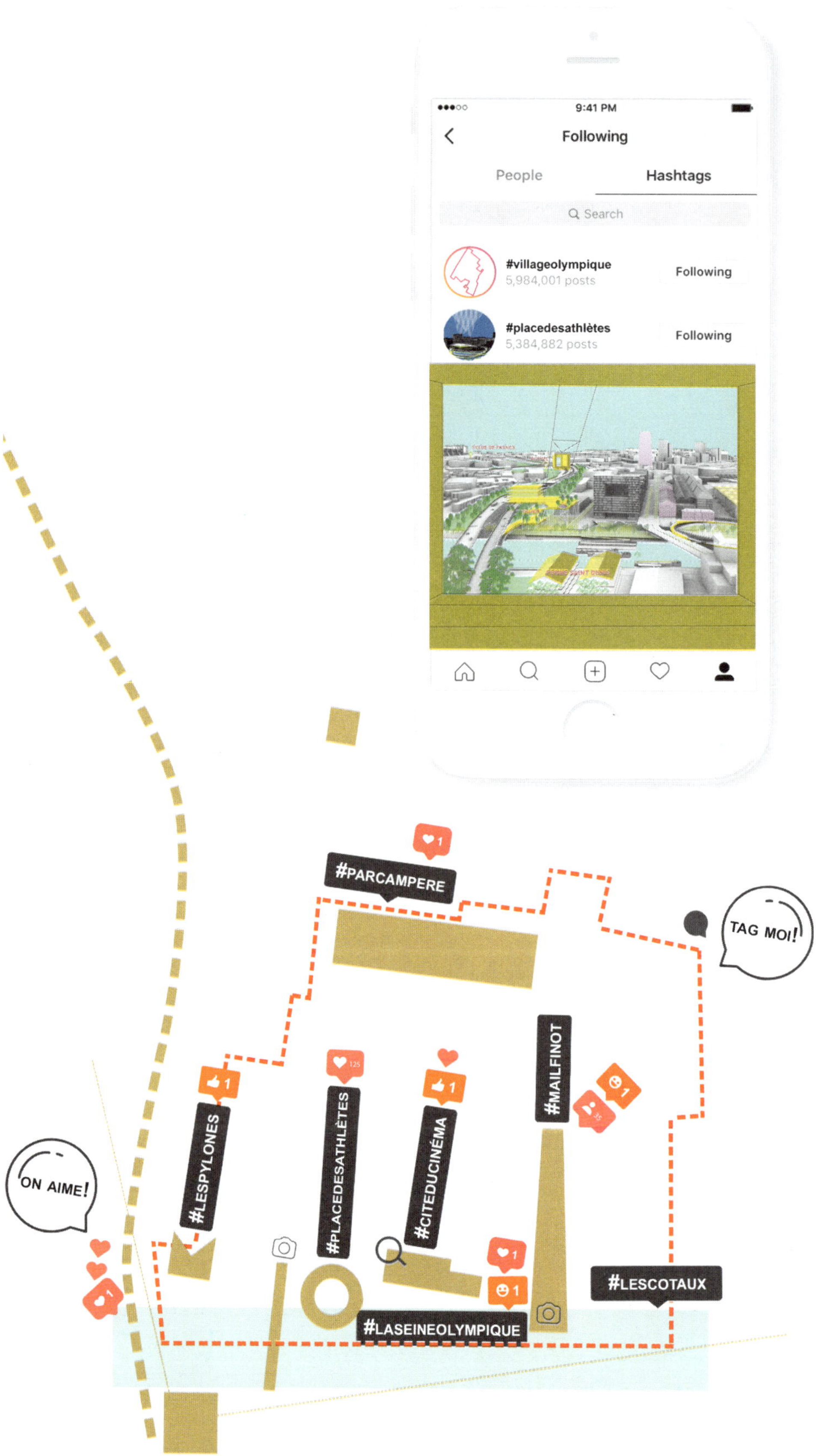
9:41 PM
Following
People
Hashtags
Search
#villageolympique
5,984,001 posts
Following
#placedesathlètes
5,384,882 posts
Following
#PARCAMPERE
TAG MOI!
#MAILFINOT
#LESPYLONES
#PLACEDESATHLÈTES
#CITEDUCINÉMA
ON AIME!
#LESCOTAUX
#LASEINEOLYMPIQUE

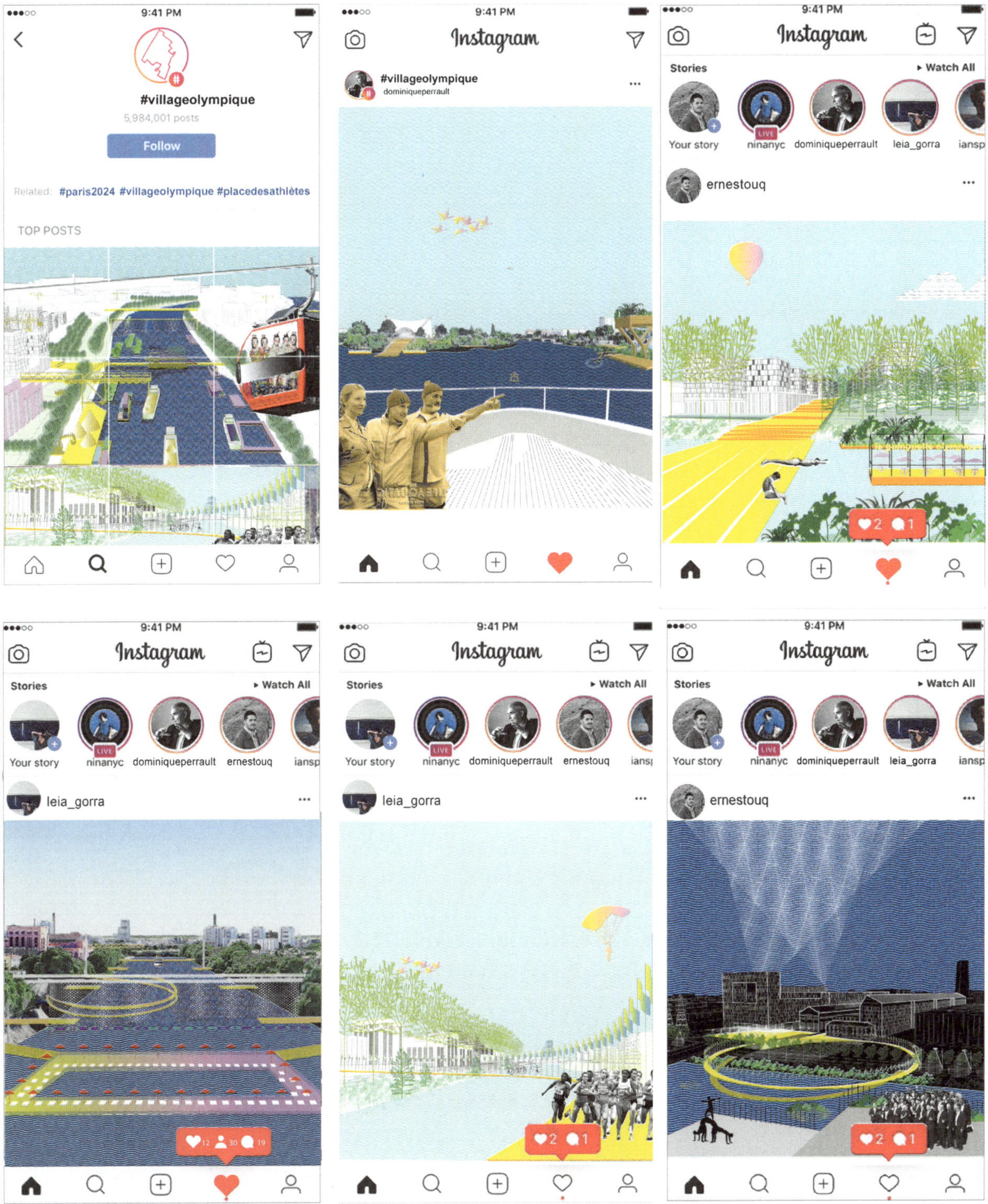
9:41 PM
#villageolympique
5,984,001 posts
Follow
Related: #paris2024 #villageolympique #placedesathlètes
TOP POSTS
Instagram
#villageolympique
dominiqueperrault
Stories
▸ Watch All
Your story
ninanyc
dominiqueperrault
leia_gorra
ernestouq
leia_gorra
2
1
12
30
19

#287# **AMBITION 4**

CLIMATE IN 2050

The Seine is expected to rise to 7.20 m this weekend!

Since the weekend, 20,000 people have been evacuated by the emergency services throughout France.

The Seine is expected to rise to 7.20 m this Saturday! Ile-Saint-Denis has practically disappeared under the water and the Parc des Rives de Seine is flooded.

But the îlots bateaux are aptly named! Open to the Seine, the large gardens and areas of biodiversity that border them can absorb a large part of the water!

A development designed to improve resilience to exceptional rainfall events.

During exceptional rainfall events, stormwater is managed as a "river street" flowing towards the Seine, protecting private plots from flood risks, and preserving urban functions as far as possible, particularly the continuity of pedestrian walkways.

8,62 m

1910

7,32 m

1924

7,1 m **6,1 m**

1955 **2016**

#289# **AMBITION 4**

CLIMATE IN 2050

The great flood of January 1910

20,000 buildings flooded in the capital, 30,000 houses affected in the suburbs, 150,000 people affected: the floods of January 1910 are regarded as a major natural disaster for Paris and the surrounding region. A disaster on the same scale in the Paris region would cost €30 billion today, according to the OECD (compared with €2 billion at the time).

The brief but intense flood of 1924

Heavy rain and cold weather caused the Seine to rise rapidly. On 6 January 1924, the river reached a maximum level of 7.32 metres at Paris-Austerlitz.

The controlled flood of January 1955

Snow, a sudden thaw followed by heavy rain caused rivers to overflow their banks in the Ile-de-France in January 1955. The flood peaked on 23 January at 7.12 metres at the Pont d'Austerlitz.

The spring flood of 2016

The Seine reached a level of 6.10 metres in Paris on the night of 3 to 4 June. Metro, train and RER stations were closed.

THE
MUSN'T
GO ON
SOS
BATS-TOI POUR
LE CLIMAT
Eh! De Rugy?
On fait quoi pour
le CLIMAT?
MARCHEZ
AUJOURD'HUI
OU
NAGEZ DEMAIN
NOUS
Flower

#291# **AMBITION 4**

CLIMATE IN 2050

Political areas

Politicalevents

The Village is the venue for a week of 24/7 events promoting a regional river logistics strategy?

Event uses and symbolism of spaces. Living spaces, political spaces, gathering spaces, social spaces.

Why not imagine the Seine as the hub of Greater Paris? The RD1 no longer needs to exist, the riverbanks are widened, and large pontoons extend out onto the river. All kinds of uses coexist here: as a mobility axis, a leisure area, a biodiversity reserve, the Seine would also remain a major logistics axis.

Why not imagine a river shuttle system to link Ile des Vannes to the region?

Why not create **a port** in the **neighborhood** to facilitate construction? How to keep the infrastructure as a legacy?

#293# **AMBITION 4**
CLIMATE IN 2050
THE SEINE AND ITS DOUBLE

What is the **swimmable Seine?**

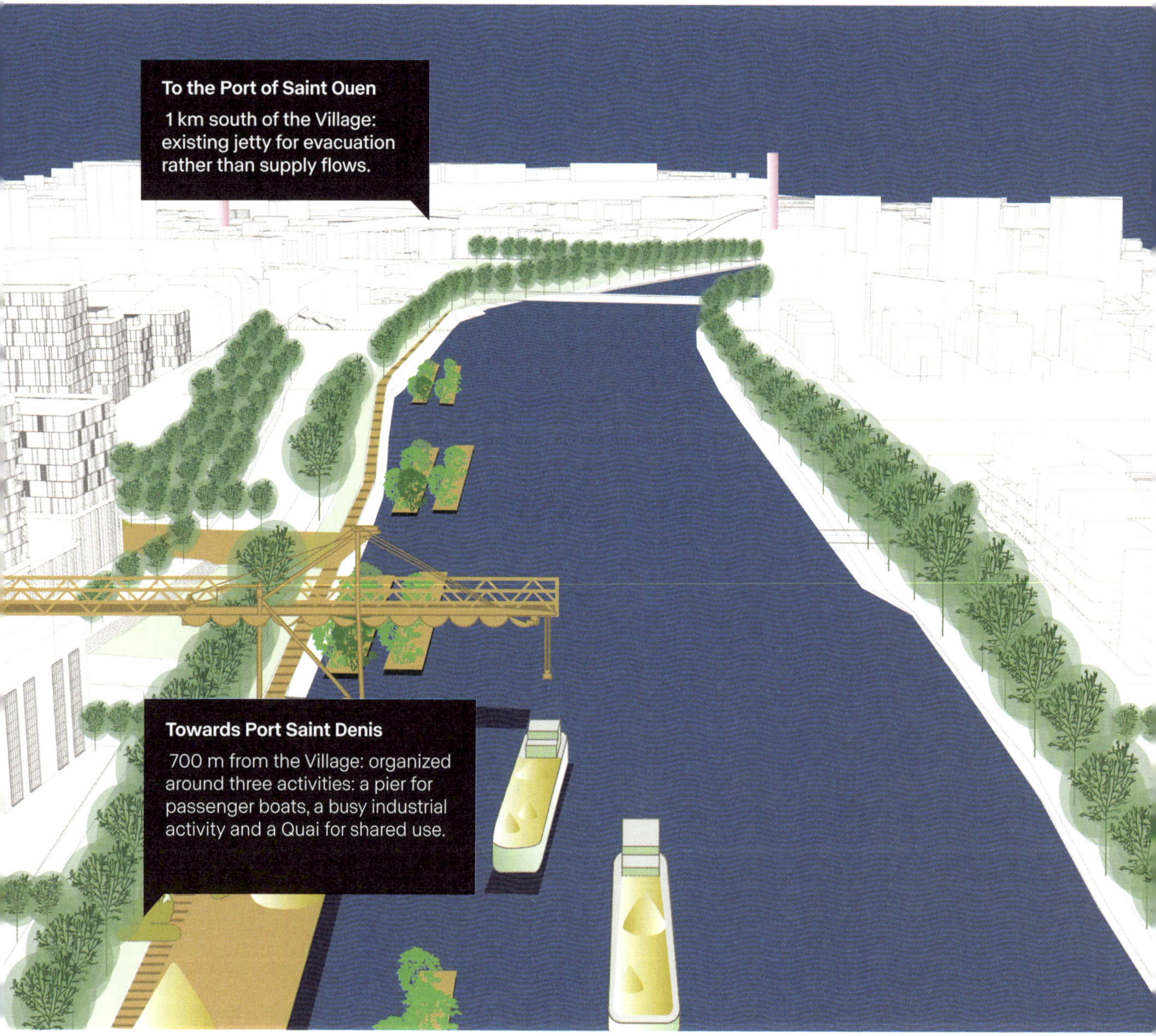
To the Port of Saint Ouen
1 km south of the Village: existing jetty for evacuation rather than supply flows.
Towards Port Saint Denis
700 m from the Village: organized around three activities: a pier for passenger boats, a busy industrial activity and a Quai for shared use.

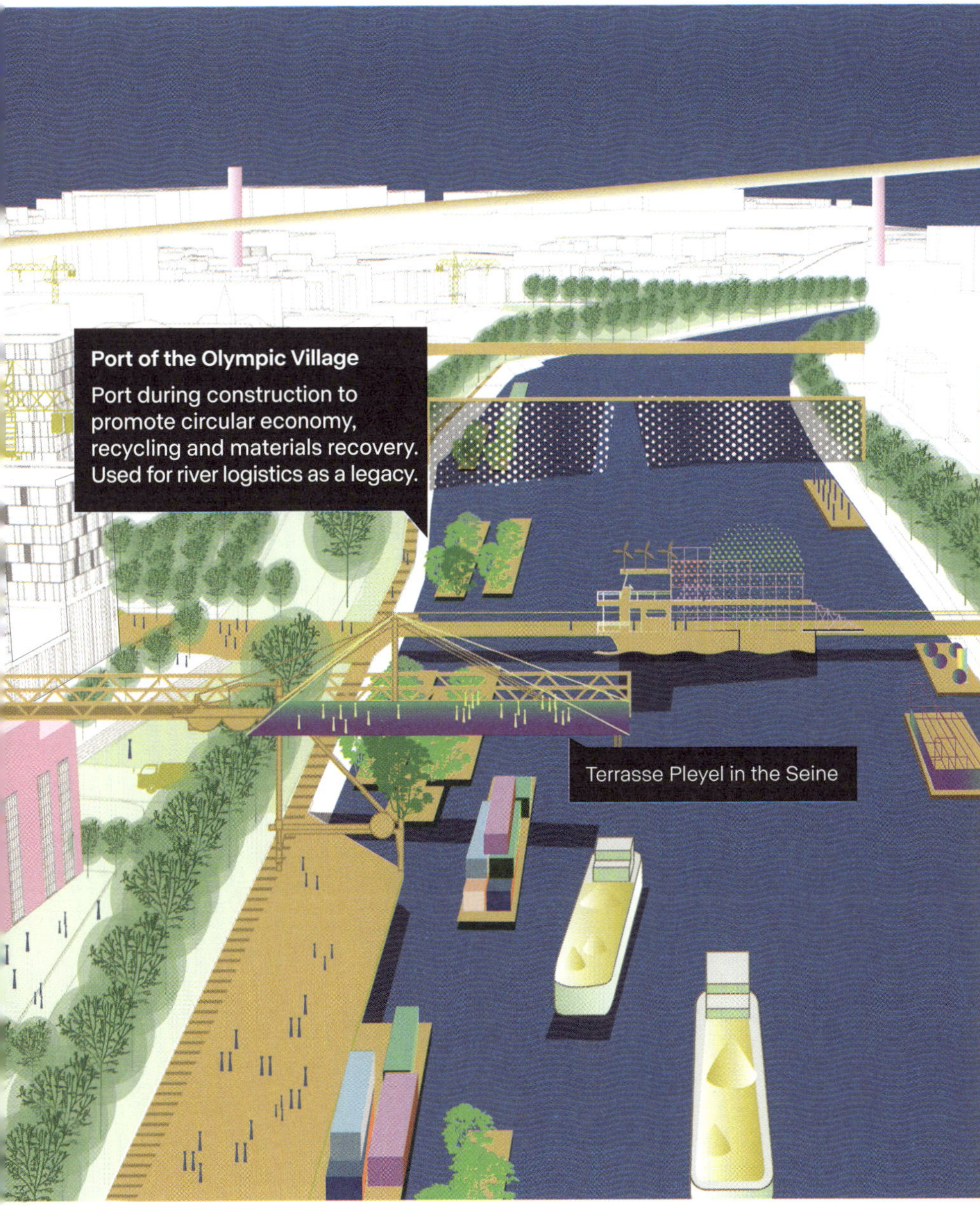

#295# **AMBITION 4**

CLIMATE IN 2050

The Seine 2019

The development of the banks of the Seine is part of a more general revaluation of the relationship with the Seine. It must become the structuring element for Greater Paris capable of connecting territories through new landscape continuities.

Today, the Seine is also a major source of industrial and economic activity. The ports of Saint Denis and Saint Ouen are close to the site.

Its double in 2050

What if the Seine were a public space where mobility, logistics and leisure activities coexisted?

Why not imagine a temporary port opposite each island to facilitate management?

Why not imagine a platform in front of the Cité du Cinéma that could remain after the construction work and serve as an access point for river shuttles, as a delivery point, as an exchange point, etc.?

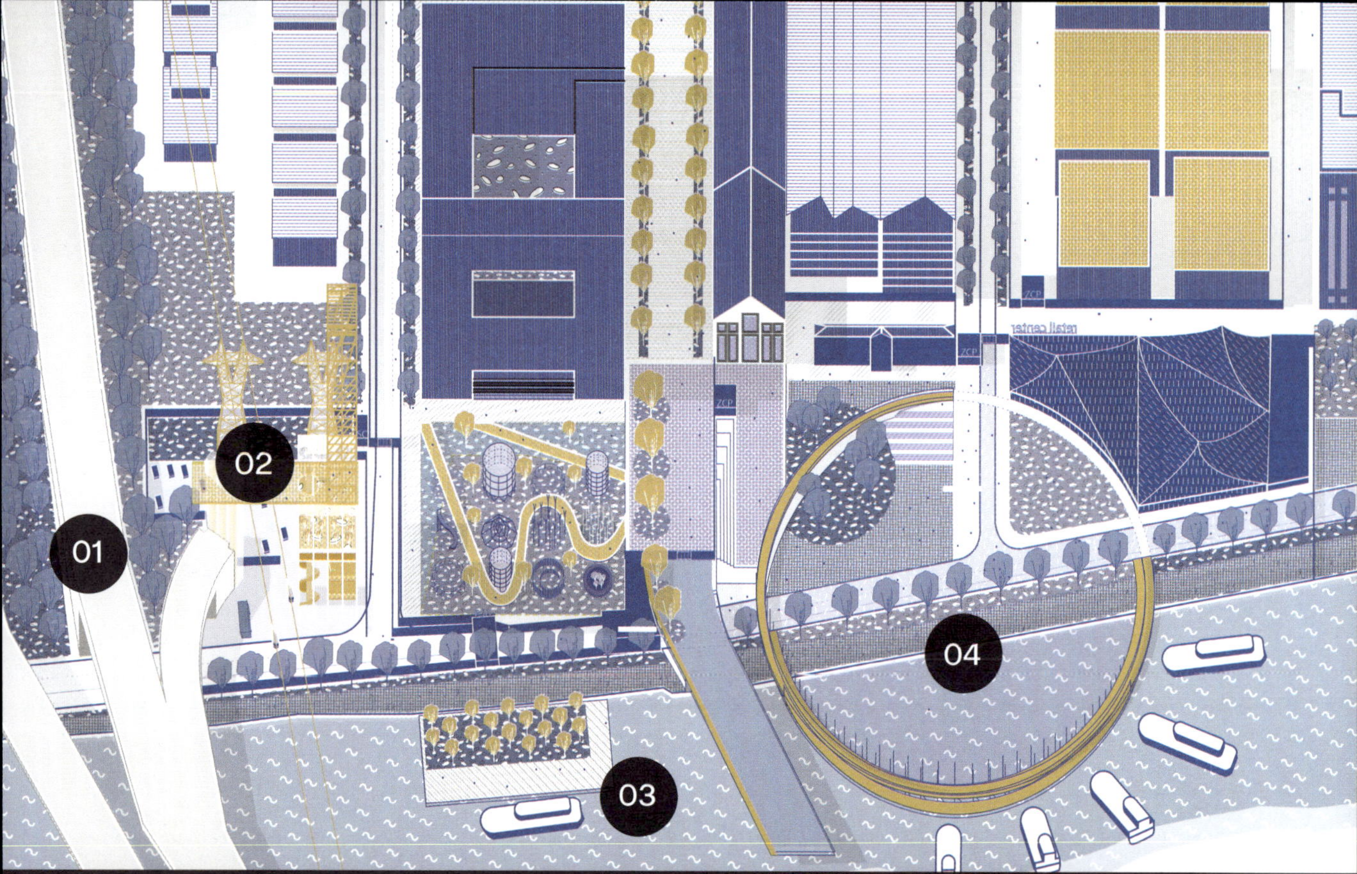

01. A86
The motorway as an ecological corridor? A paradox? Some of the excavated material from the project has been stockpiled on the site in order to "build" a planted embankment. Integrating the village safety centre into the motorway embankment?
The motorway as a key route for soft mobility?
A cable car along the A86 linking Ile Saint Denis, Pleyel and the Stade de France?

02. The entrance
A new kind of tower along the A86? How can we make the most of our industrial heritage? A section of motorway and electricity pylons are part of the landscape of many suburbs. They can be used to support projects and demonstrate the renewal of an industrial area.

05
06
07

Coatings - principles
4 materials - 4 identities

Carbon footprint
Le Quartier - Current state

Kg CO2
By type of material

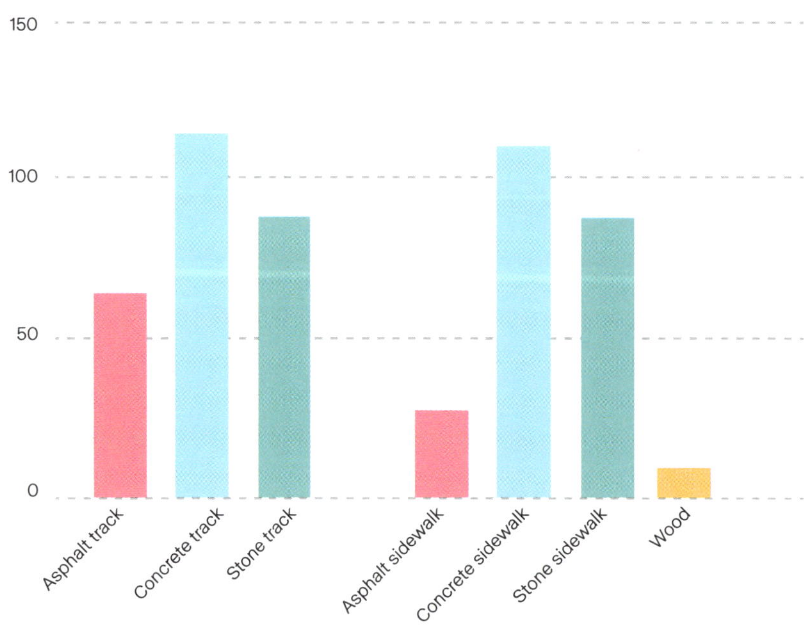

How can we reduce our carbon footprint?

Carbon footprint
Le Quartier - Projected state

Kg CO_2
By type of material

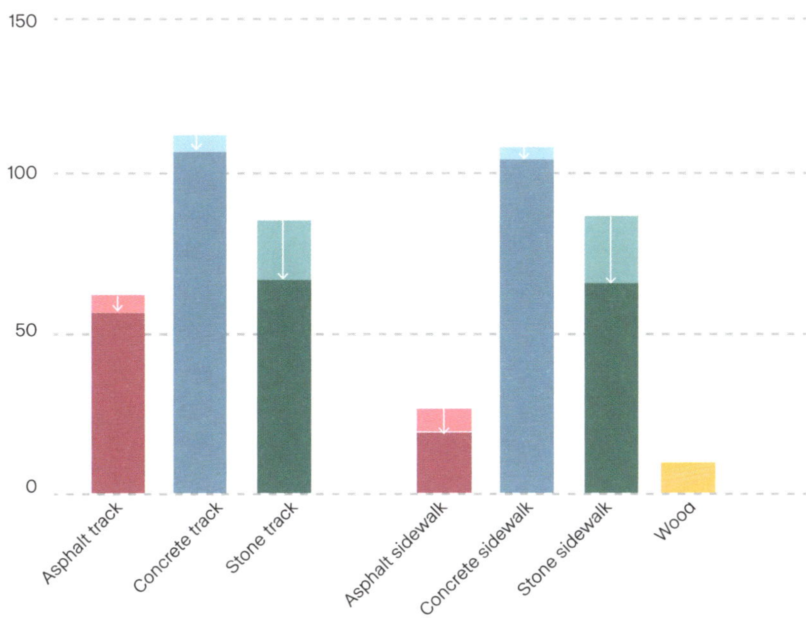

How can we reduce our carbon footprint?

If GNT made from recycled materials = 10% carbon savings

#299# AMBITION 5

CARBON FOOTPRINT MANAGEMENT

Materials for public spaces.

Carbon footprint
Le Quartier - Projected state

Kg CO_2
By type of material

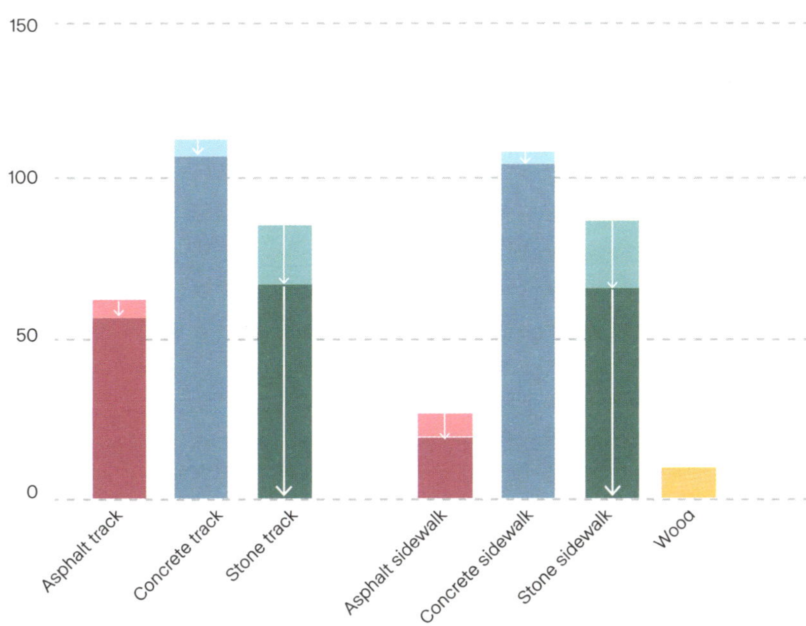

How can we reduce our carbon footprint?

If GNT made from recycled materials

Reuse of pavers (Bonneuil site) = 30% carbon savings
Additional savings if all stones come from Bonneuil

	Modular stone natural sand joint	Modular stone sand-jointed Reuse	Modular concrete sand joint	Modular stone natural grass joint	Modular concrete natural joint grass- Reuse	Modular concrete grass joint
Maintenance	2,0	2,0	2,0	2,0	2,0	2,0
Time to install	1,0	1,0	1,0	1,0	1,0	1,0
Permeability	1,0	1,0	1,0	2,0	2,0	2,0
Accessibility	2,0	1,0	2,0	-	-	-
Investment cost	-	2,0	1,5	-	2,0	1,5
Carbon footprint	1,0	3,0	2,0	1,0	3,0	2,0
UHI control	3,0	3,0	2,0	3,0	3,0	2,0
Architectural quality	3,0	3,0	3,0	3,0	3,0	3,0
Average	1,9	2,3	2,1	1,7	2,3	1,9

Modular sand-jointed natural stone

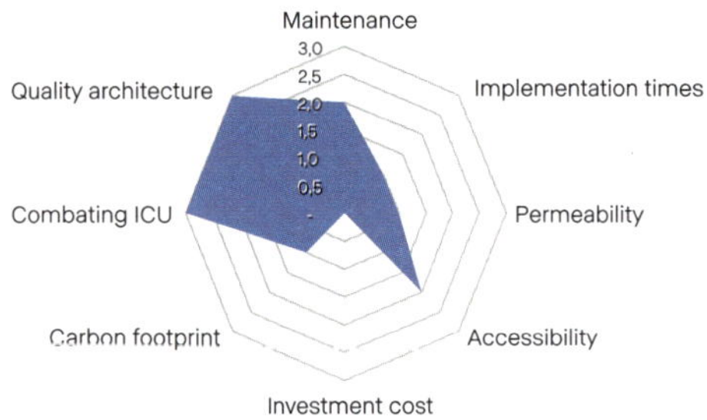

Modular sand-jointed natural stone - Reuse

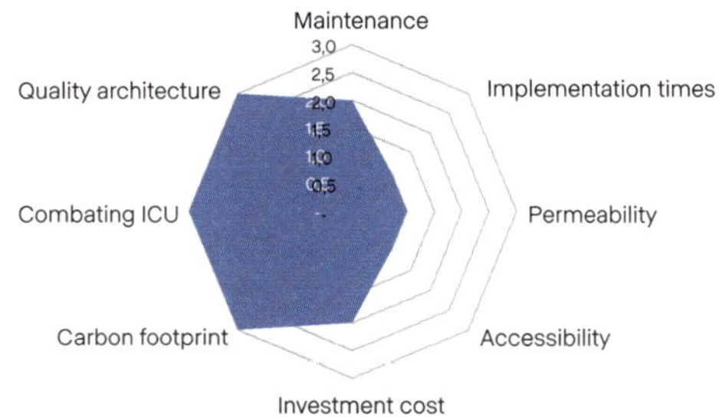

Modular grass joint natural stone

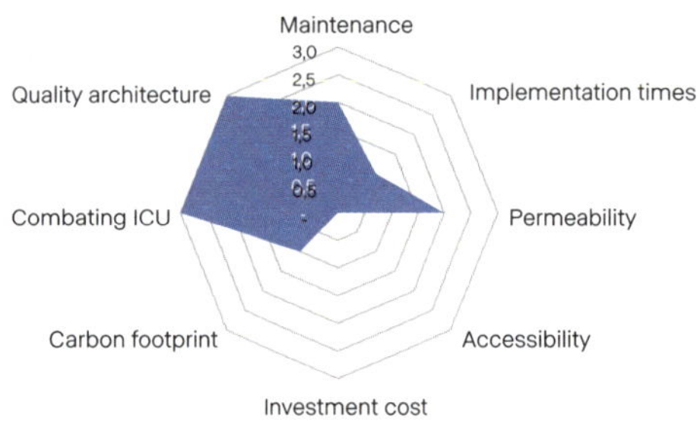

Modular grass joint natural stone - Réemploi

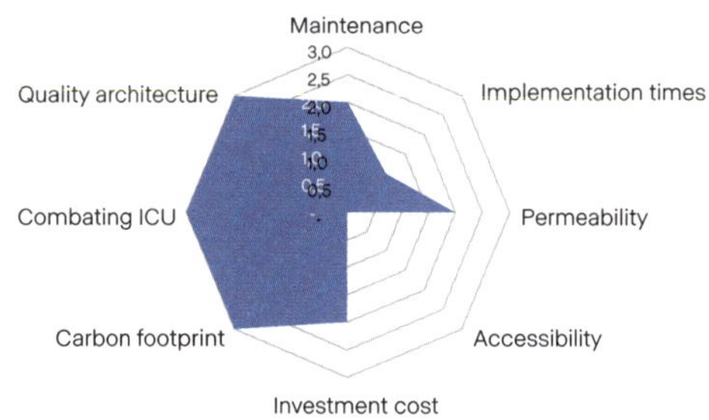

Black asphalt

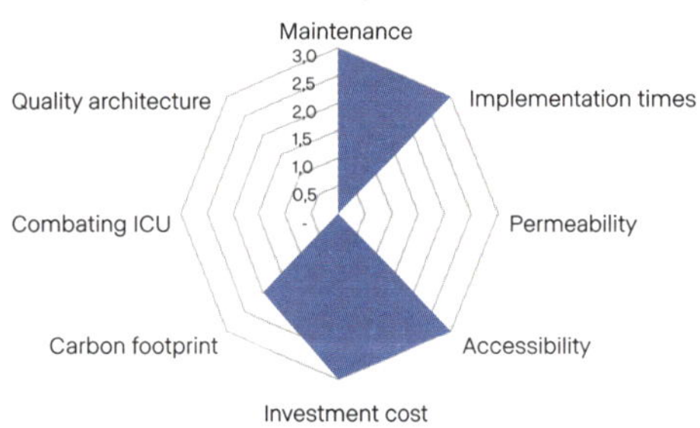

Drainage asphalt

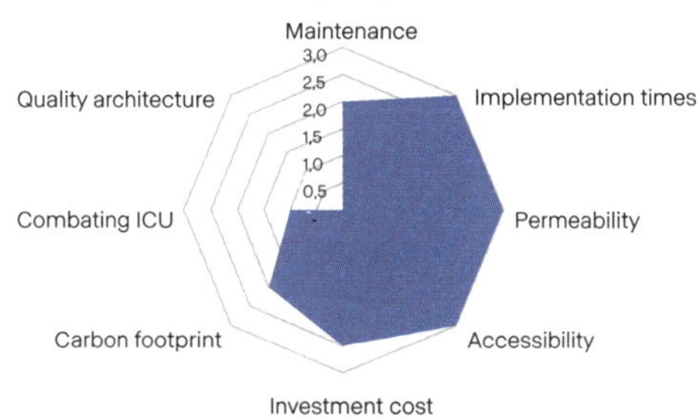

Concrete

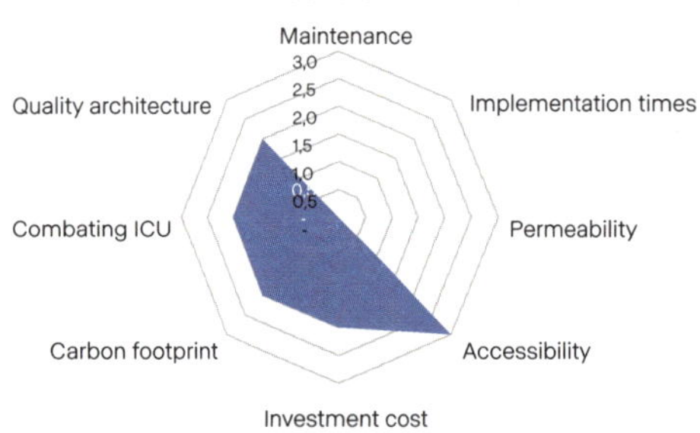

Porous concrete

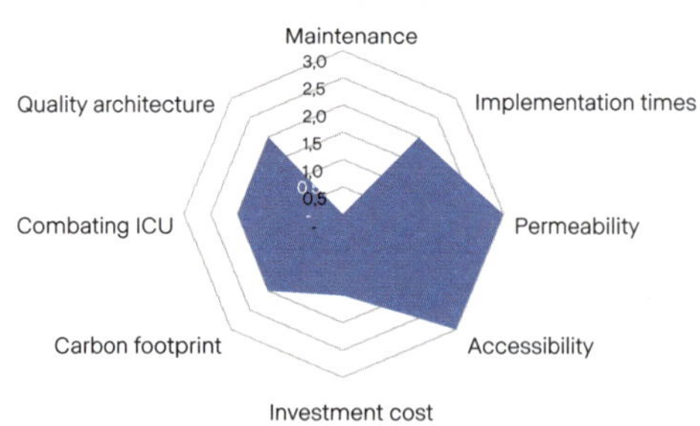

Black asphalt	Drainage asphalt	Light-coloured asphalt	Black asphalt + Surface treatment	Concrete	Béton poreux	Stabilisé
3,0	2,0	0,5	3,0	-	-	3,0
3,0	3,0	3,0	2,5	-	2,0	3,0
-	3,0	-	-	-	3,0	1,0
3,0	3,0	3,0	3,0	3,0	3,0	-
3,0	2,5	2,0	2,5	2,0	1,5	3,0
2,0	3,0	2,0	2,0	2,0	2,0	-
-	1,0	1,5	1,5	2,0	2,0	2,5
-	-	1,5	1,0	2,0	2,0	1,5
2,0	2,4	1,9	2,2	1,6	2,2	2,0

Modular concrete join sand

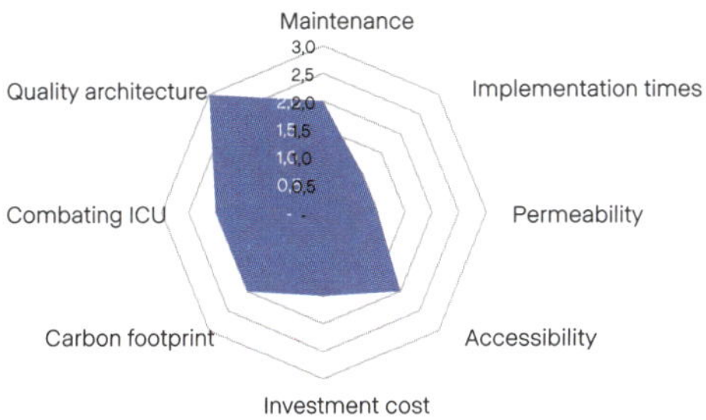

Modular concrete join grass

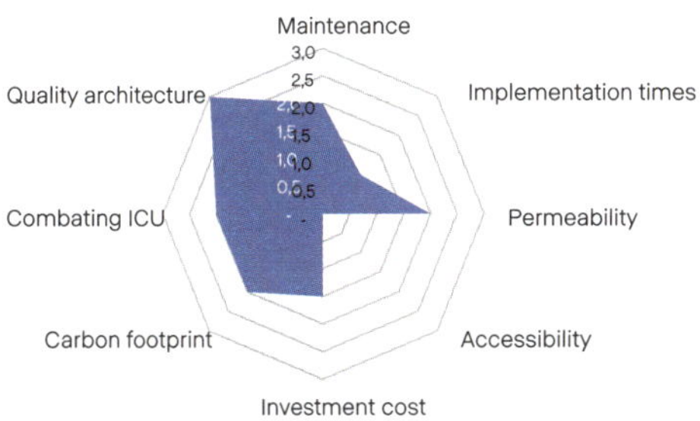

#301# **AMBITION 5**

CARBON FOOTPRINT MANAGEMENT

Materials for public spaces.

Light-colored asphalt

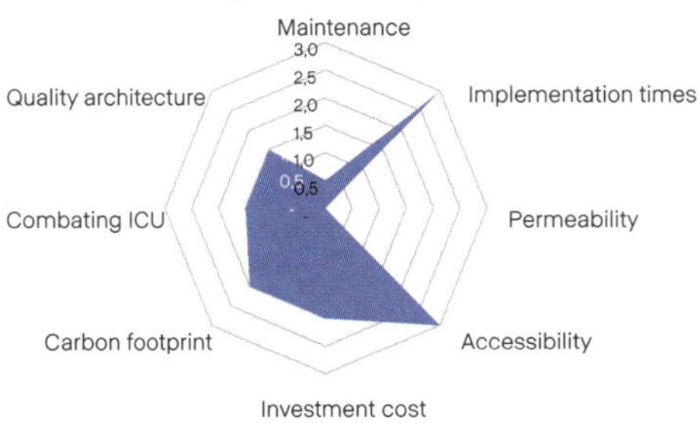

Black asphalt + surface treatment

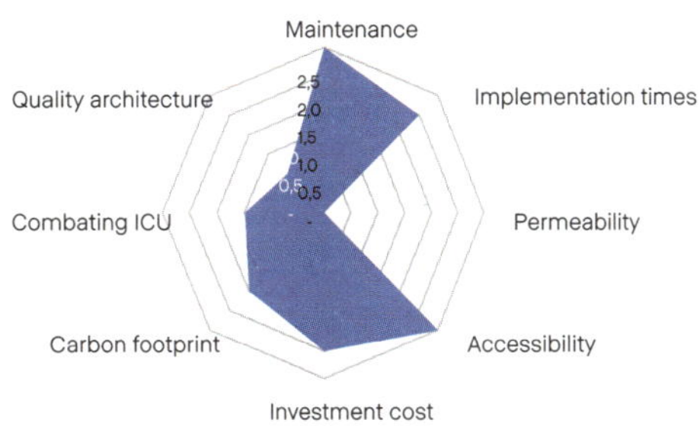

Affirming boat islands
Surfacing strategy

IDENTIFY
MODULAR GRANITE

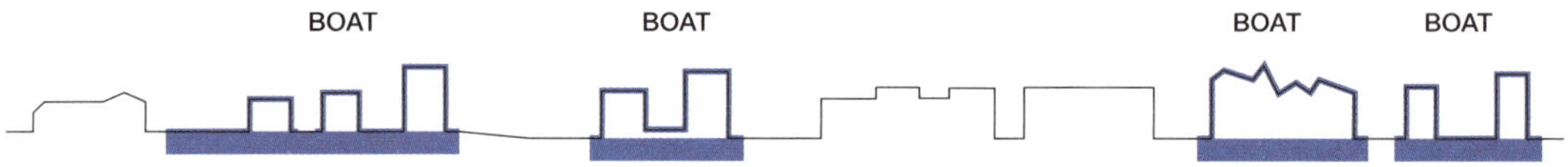

CLARIFY
LIGHT GRAY CONCRETE

CLARIFY

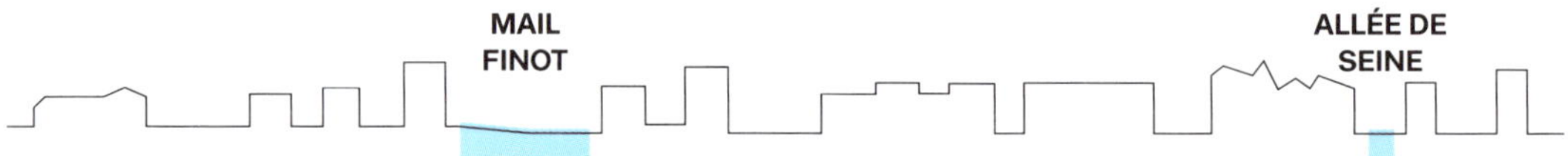

CONNECT
LIGHT GREY ASPHALT

CONNECT

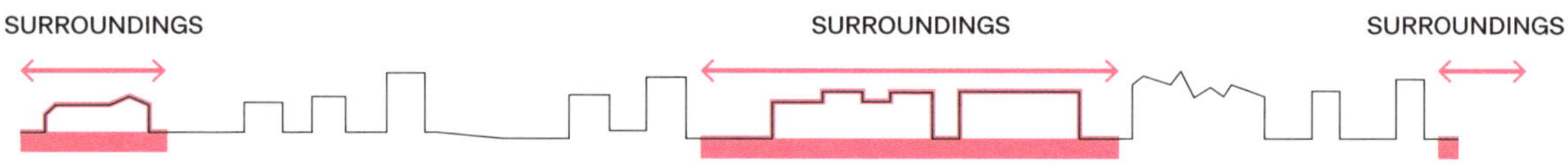

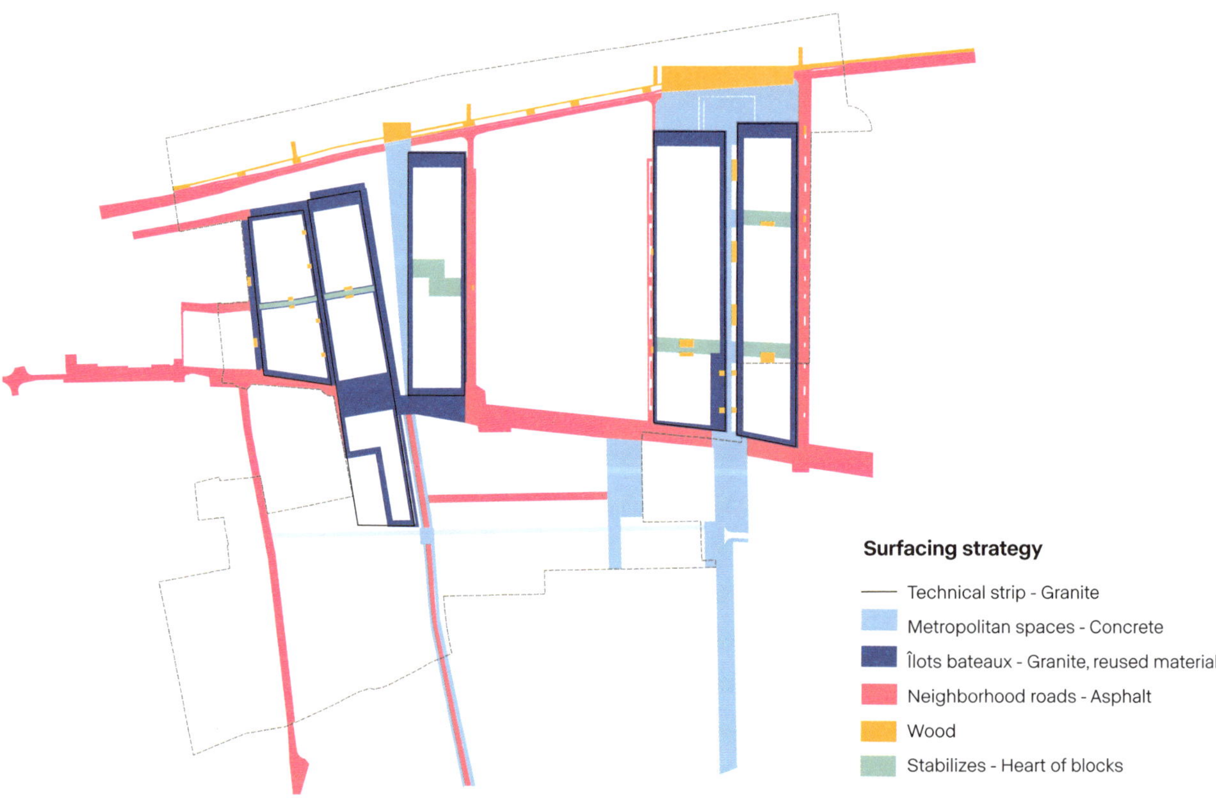

#303# **AMBITION 5**

CARBON FOOTPRINT MANAGEMENT

Materials for public spaces.

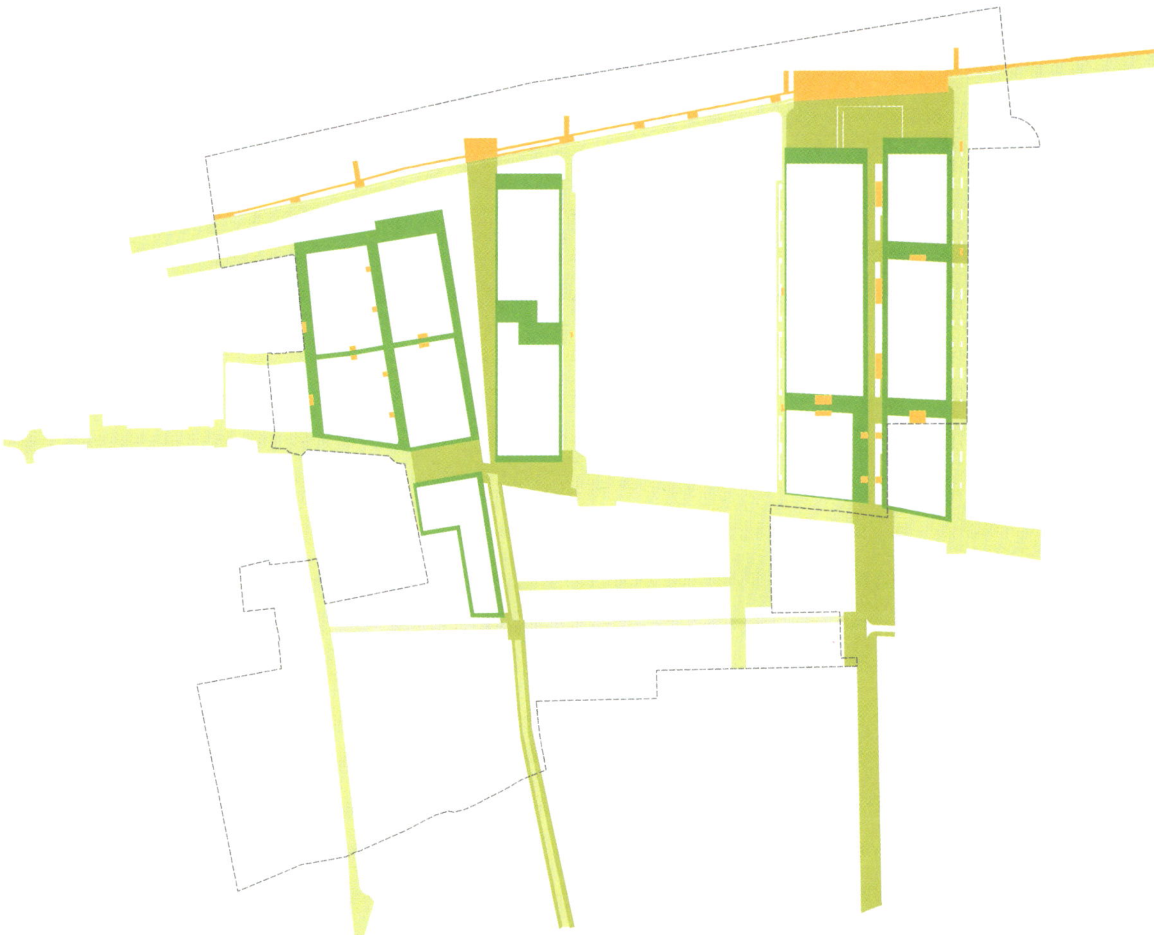

Surfacing strategy

- Recycled concrete
- Reemployment
- Recycled asphalt
- Wood

Phase 1

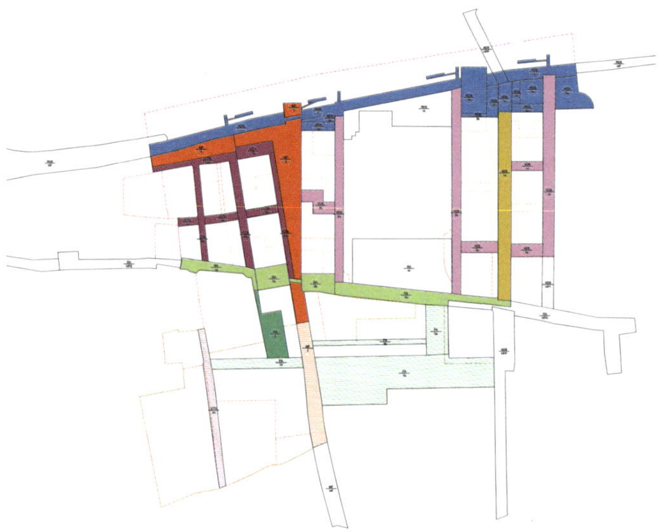

Phase 2

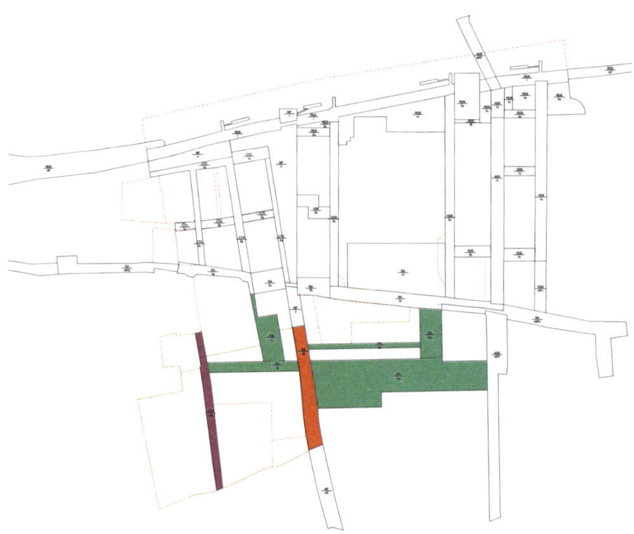

Phase 3

#305# **AMBITION 5**

CARBON FOOTPRINT MANAGEMENT

Materials for public spaces.

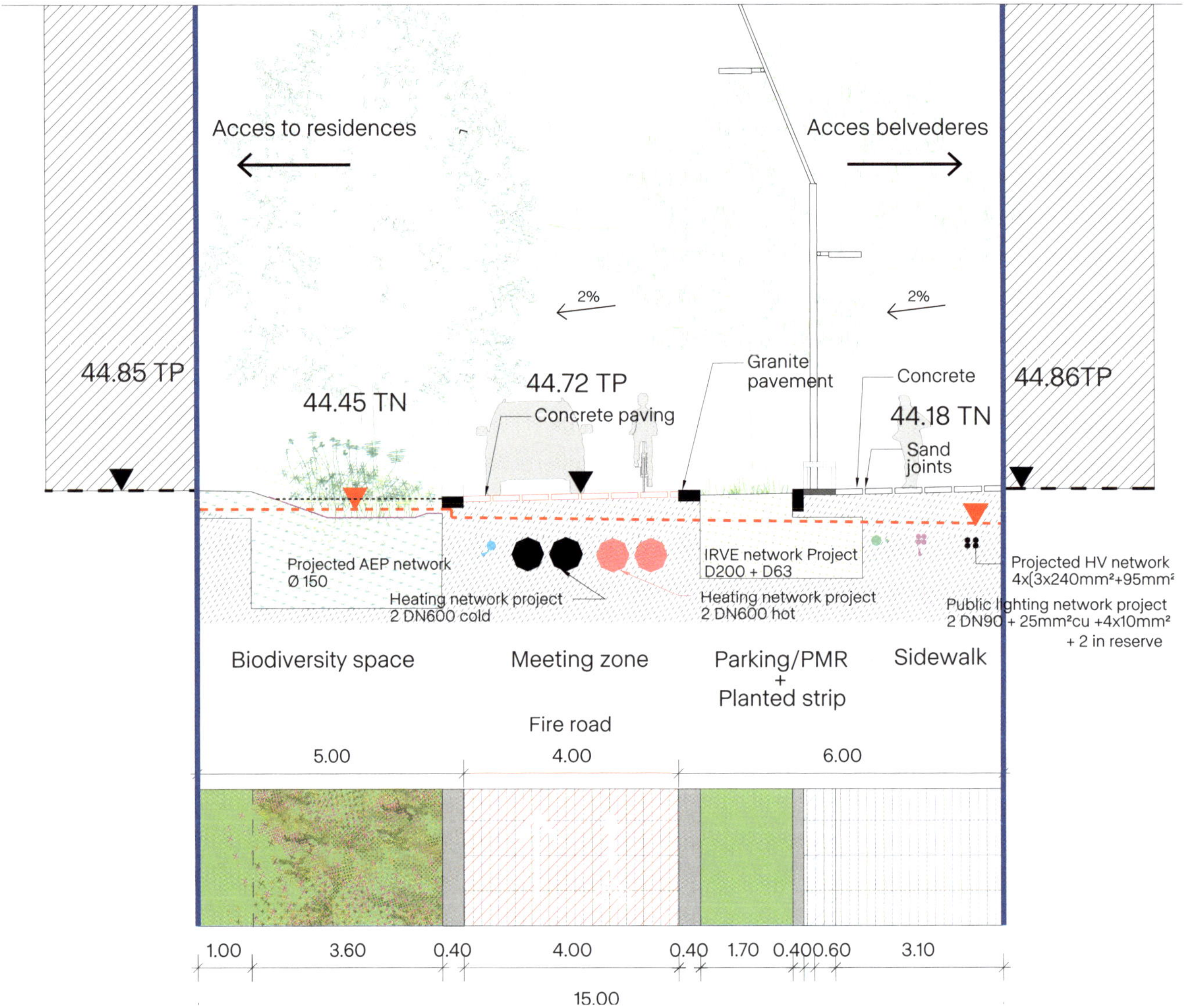

Acces to residences
Acces belvederes
2%
2%
44.85 TP
44.45 TN
44.72 TP
Concrete paving
Granite pavement
Concrete
44.18 TN
Sand joints
44.86TP
Projected AEP network
Ø 150
Heating network project
2 DN600 cold
IRVE network Project
D200 + D63
Heating network project
2 DN600 hot
Projected HV network
4x(3x240mm²+95mm²
Public lighting network project
2 DN90 + 25mm²cu +4x10mm²
+ 2 in reserve
Biodiversity space
Meeting zone
Parking/PMR
+
Planted strip
Sidewalk
Fire road
5.00
4.00
6.00
1.00
3.60
0.40
4.00
0.40
1.70
0.40
0.60
3.10
15.00

mineral

50%

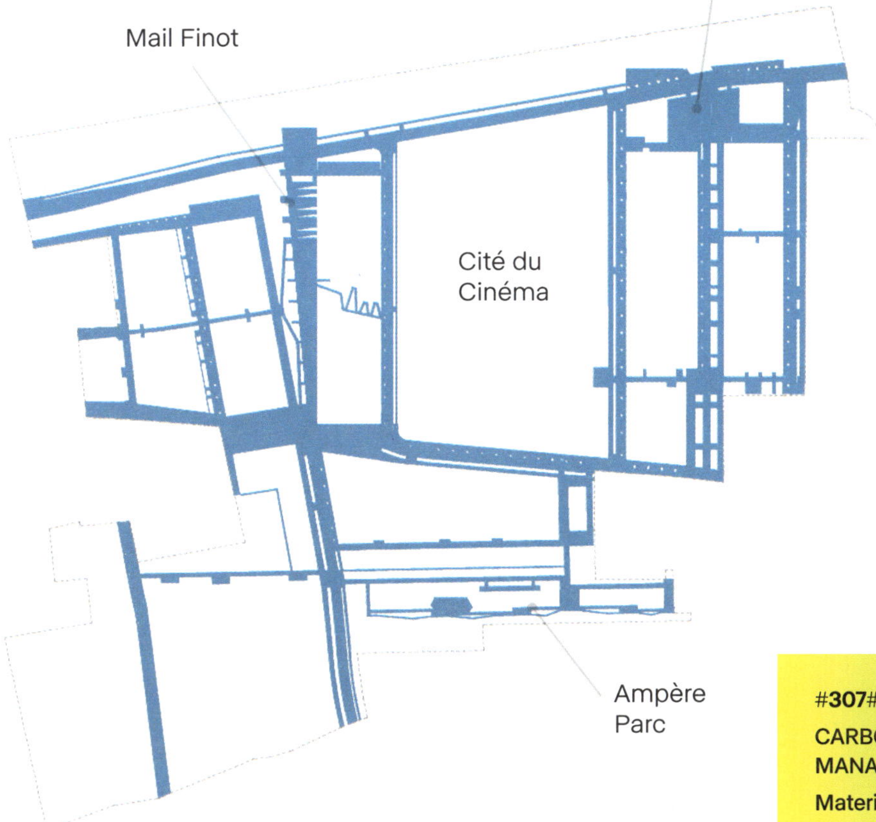

#307# AMBITION 5

CARBON FOOTPRINT MANAGEMENT

Materials for public spaces.

Mineral space = 8,5 ha

↓

CARBON BALANCE ?
about 8000 T CO_2 eq*

* Carbon footprint for roads and sidewalks only (i.e. excluding furniture, lighting, supports and planted areas).

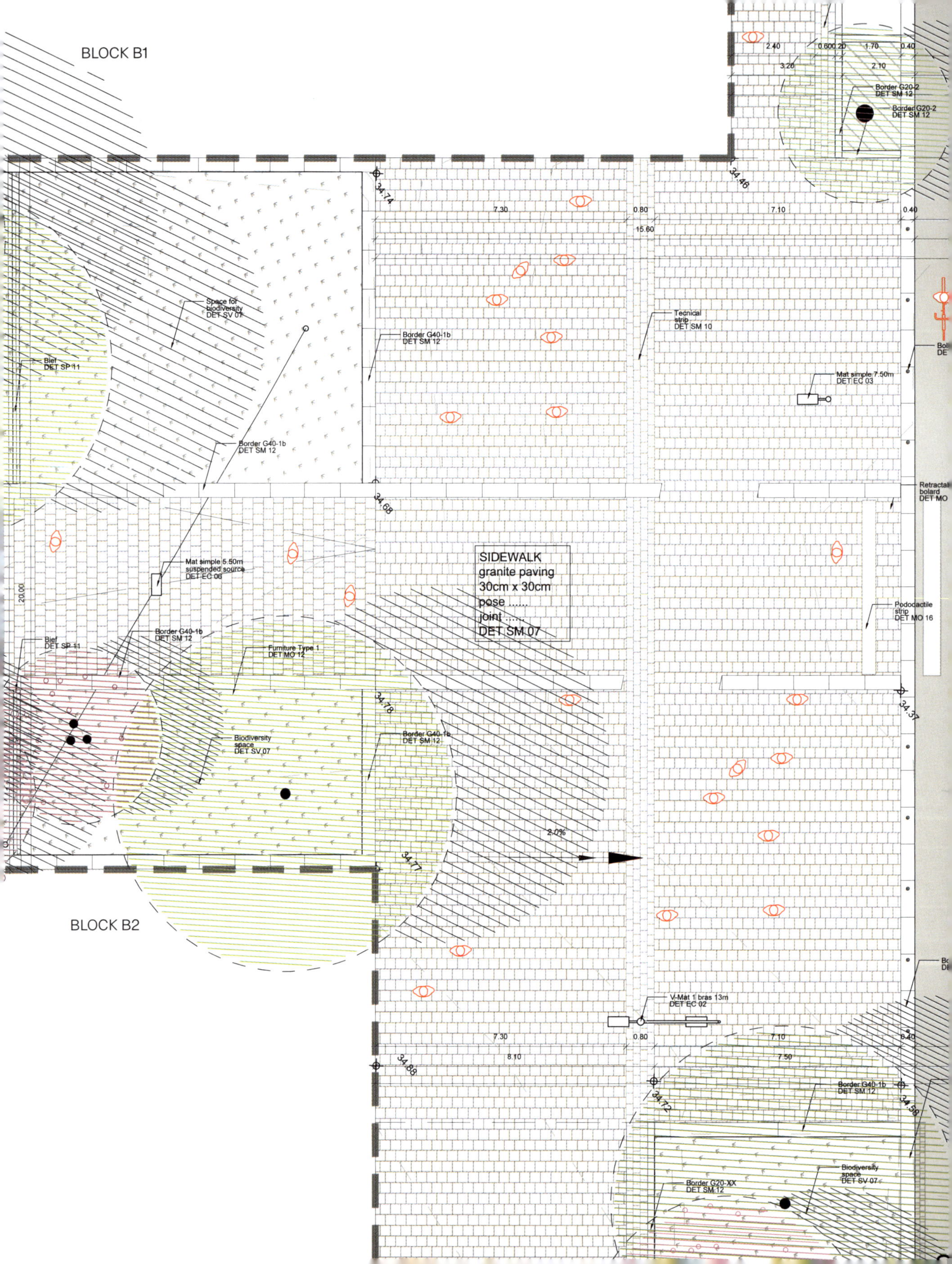
BLOCK B1
BLOCK B2
Space for biodiversity DET SV 07
Bief DET SP 11
Border G40-1b DET SM 12
Tecnical strip DET SM 10
Mat simple 7.50m DET EC 03
Border G20-2 DET SM 12
Retractable bolard DET MO
Mat simple 5.50m suspended source DET EC 06
SIDEWALK
granite paving
30cm x 30cm
pose ......
joint ......
DET SM 07
Furniture Type 1 DET MO 12
Biodiversity space DET SV 07
Podotactile strip DET MO 16
2.0%
V-Mat 1 bras 13m DET EC 02
Border G20-XX DET SM 12
7.30
0.80
15.60
7.10
0.40
8.10
7.50
20.00
34.74
34.46
34.68
34.18
34.77
34.88
34.72
34.37
34.58

#309# AMBITION 5

CARBON FOOTPRINT MANAGEMENT

Materials for public spaces.

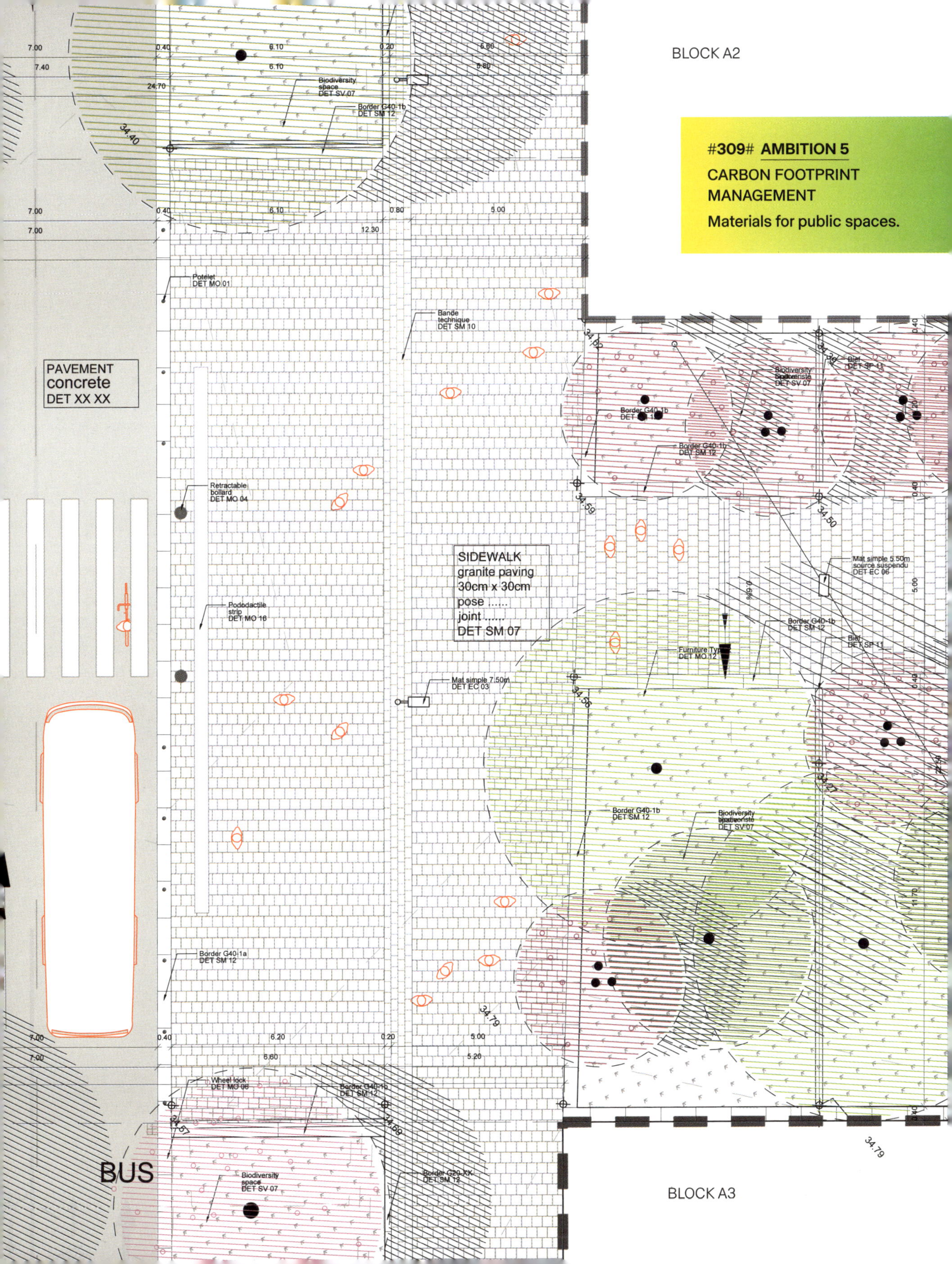

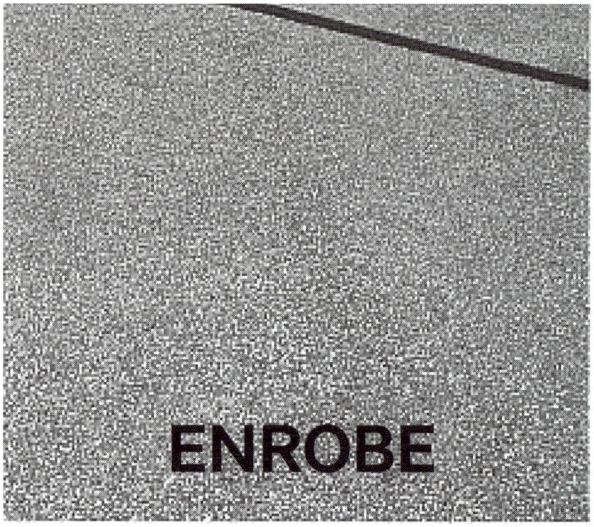
ENROBE

CONCRETE

GRANIT

FILLING
GRANIT

WOOD

FILLING
WOOD

#311# **AMBITION 5**

CARBON FOOTPRINT MANAGEMENT

Materials for public spaces.

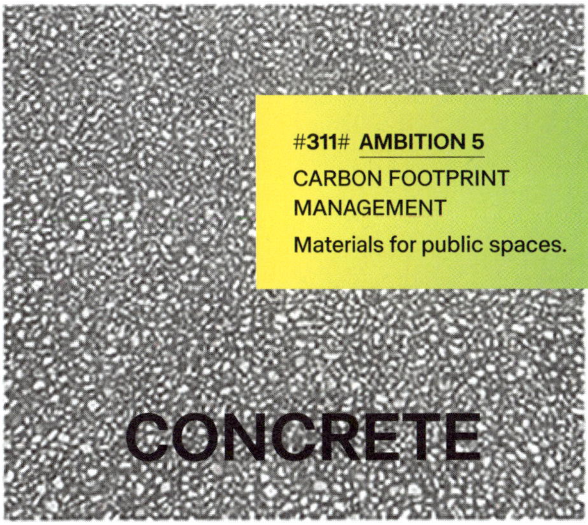

FILLING GRANIT

Partnership with the Bonneuil-sur-Marn site
Examples of reused public spaces :
-Extension of tramway T3
-Redevelopment of the Broussais Hospital District
-Place de la Bastille
-Reuilly barracks site
-Truillot garden

Lyon confluence

RECYCLED CONCRETE

100% recycled concrete aggregate concrete
Working with VICAT
Example of a public space in recycled concrete:
-Lyon Confluence

Lyon confluence

Lyon confluence

#313# **AMBITION 5**

CARBON FOOTPRINT MANAGEMENT

Materials for public spaces.

Porous paving stones

Place de la Bastille

Place du Panthéon

PARC DES DOCKS

MONT SAINT MICHEL

#315# **AMBITION 5**

CARBON FOOTPRINT MANAGEMENT

NANTES

LE BOIS

Granite pavers

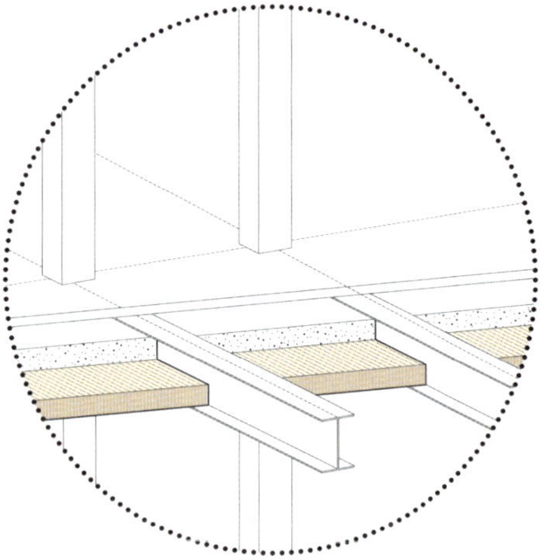

Hybrid floor module, wood and concrete structure (insulation).

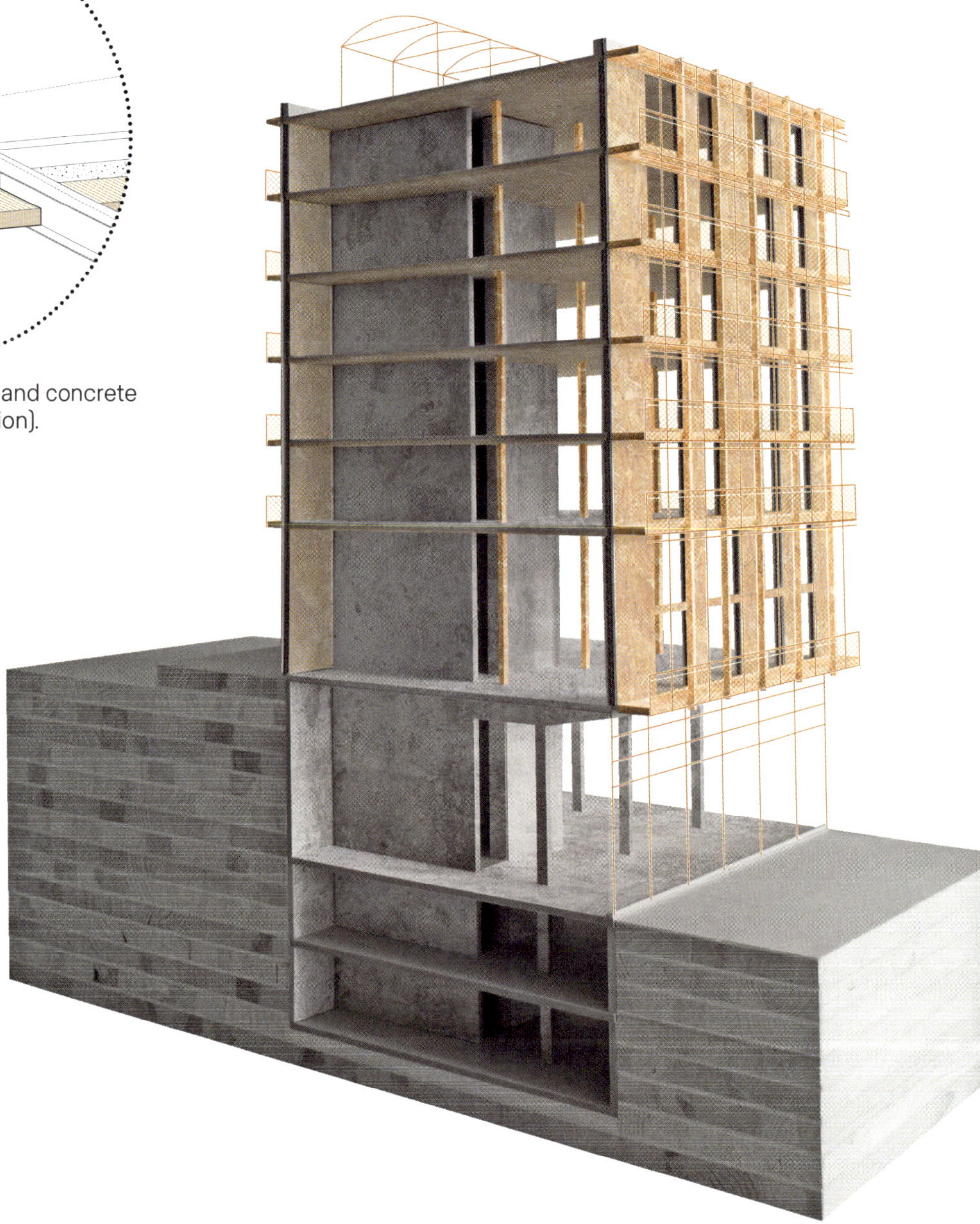

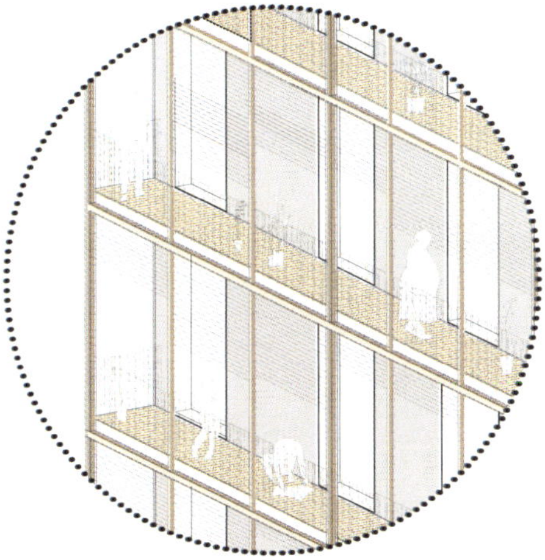

Double-skin balcony for thermal, light and spatial comfort

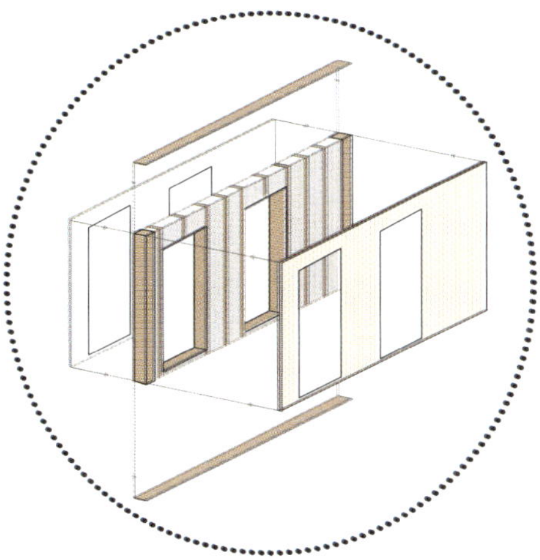

Façade module: prefabricated wood panels

#319# **AMBITION 5**

CARBON FOOTPRINT MANAGEMENT

Timber construction for an innovative neighbourhood. Construction principle.

A hybrid structure. An innovative concept adapted to a complex operational context.

The Olympic Village project in the heart of part of Greater Paris, on land that has already been built on, requires us to adapt the way we build cities. First and foremost, we must respect what already exists, the residents, the architecture, and the history of the area; we must work with a fragile, changing fabric. The time between now and 2024 is relatively short, and the correct phasing of the works is crucial.

Building in wood is the obvious choice, because the entire process involved meets the many innovative expectations of the various players involved:

– a clean, low-noise site

– the use of environmentally-friendly materials

– create a sustainable and flexible neighbourhood

– make it possible to construct a large number of buildings in a short space of time

– simplify the phasing of the works.

Ultimately, it's one more step towards building a post-Kyoto, post-Cop21 metropolis that's gentler and lighter metropolis.

Stage 1: concrete core

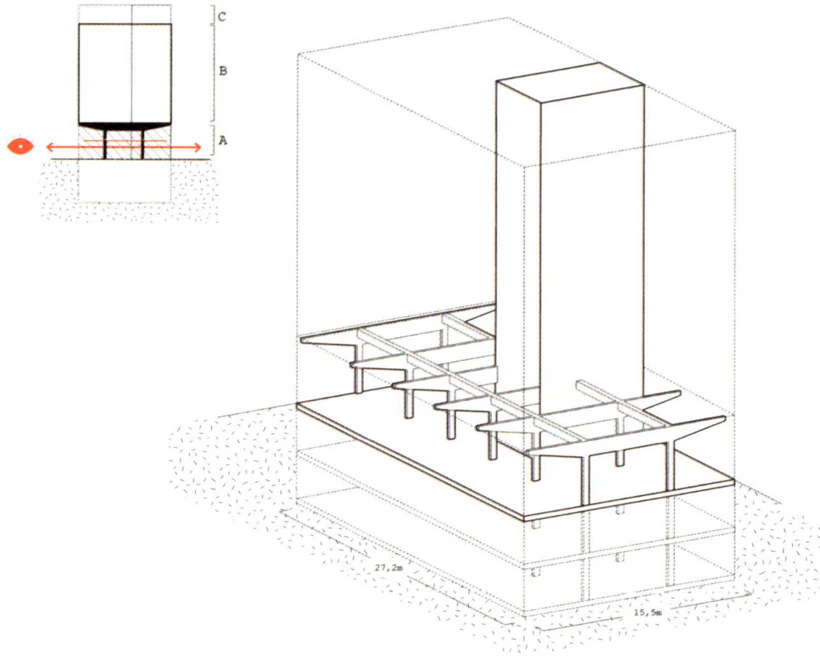

Stage 2: modules

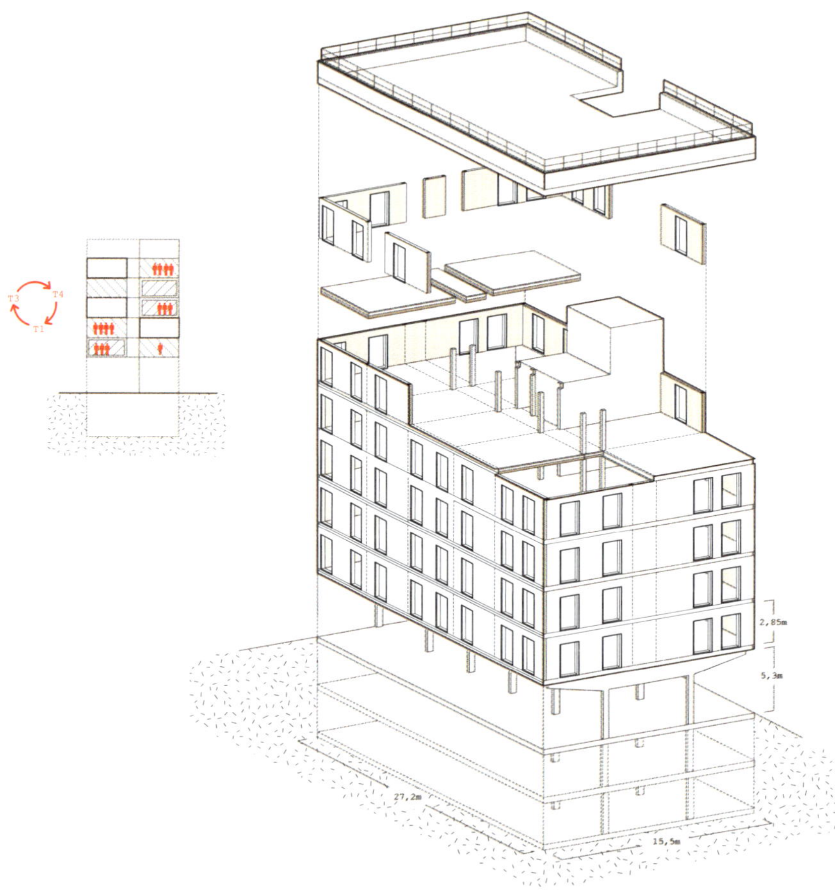

Hermann Kaufmann, LCT ONE, execution of concrete parts, primary structure

LIN, BGW, delivery of the facade

LIN, BGW, machining of wood/concrete floor sections

LIN, BGW, installation with light equipment

LIN, BGW, Prefabrication of wooden facades

Sidler materials, removal of pre-constructed floors

Stage 1: concrete core

The first stage consists of creating the concrete and structural part of the shell. This mainly involves the core of the building and the partitioned accesses. This part of the building will serve as the structure for the future removal of the floors and façade modules. During this "in situ" stage, construction of the timber or concrete/timber sections can begin. In a way, this saves time, as the construction of the building is optimised insofar as it is not dependent on the construction site itself, but on pre-fabrication and delivery.

Stage 2: modules

Both the floors and the façade are made up of modules pre-fabricated in the factory to plan, delivered and assembled on site.

Floor module
The floors have a hybrid composition: a layer of wood first, then concrete to ensure the best acoustic and thermal performance. Once pre-constructed, these modules are assembled on site to form the floor.

Facade module
These modules can be made entirely of wood, from the posts and beams to the insulation materials. These modules are also prefabricated and delivered to the site.

Concept and urban intentions - Floor details

HOUSING

OFFICES

HOUSING

Concrete floor HQE, qualitel housing

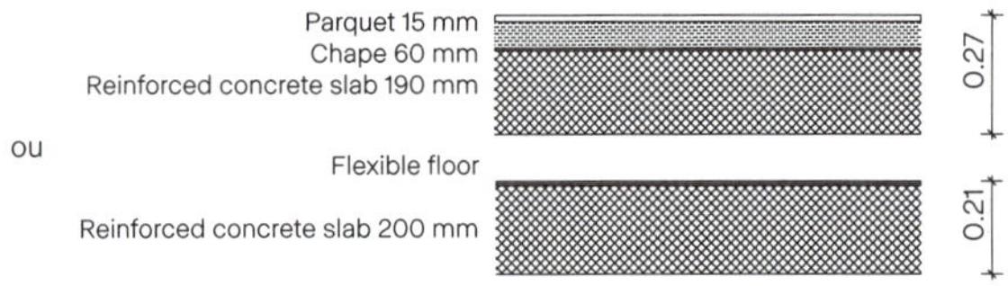

CLT type wooden floor

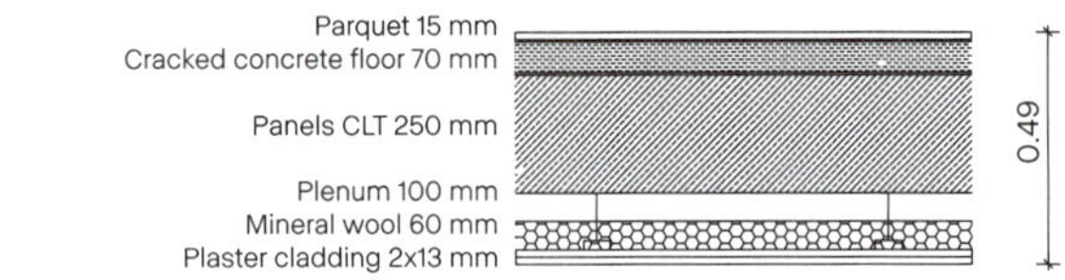

Wooden floor joisting

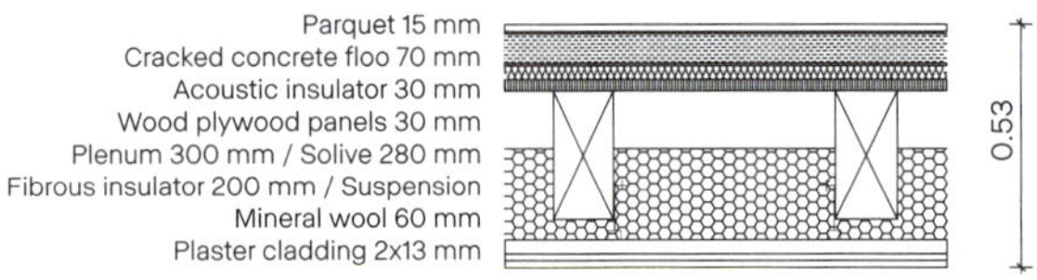

OFFICES

Concrete floor

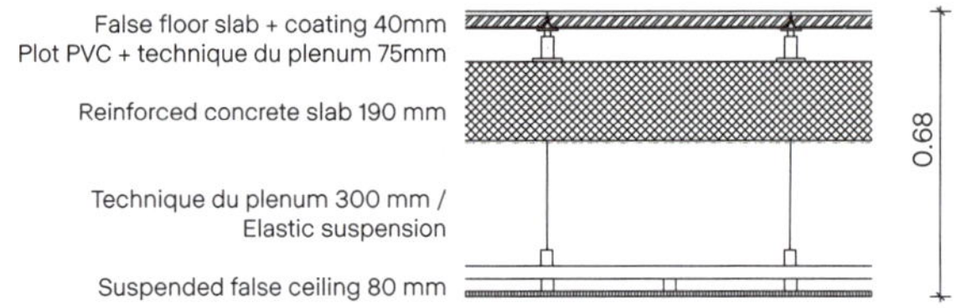

CLT type wooden floor

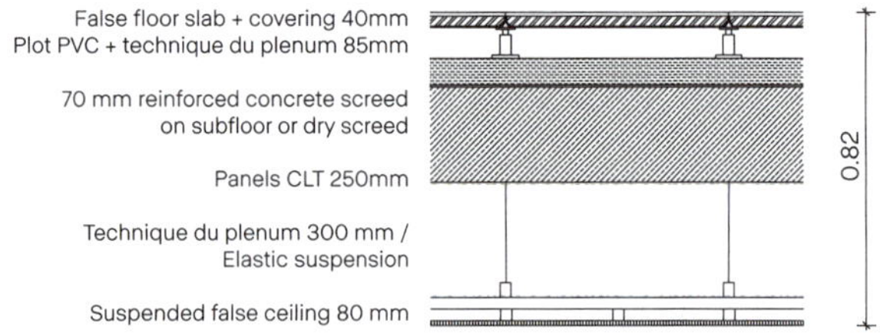

Wooden joist flooring

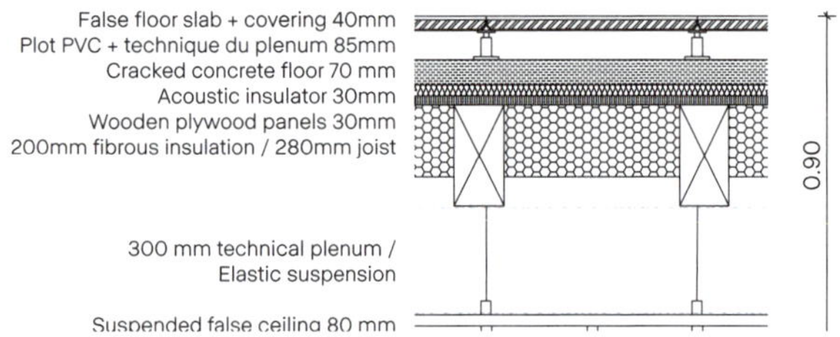

Urban concept and intentions - Constructibility

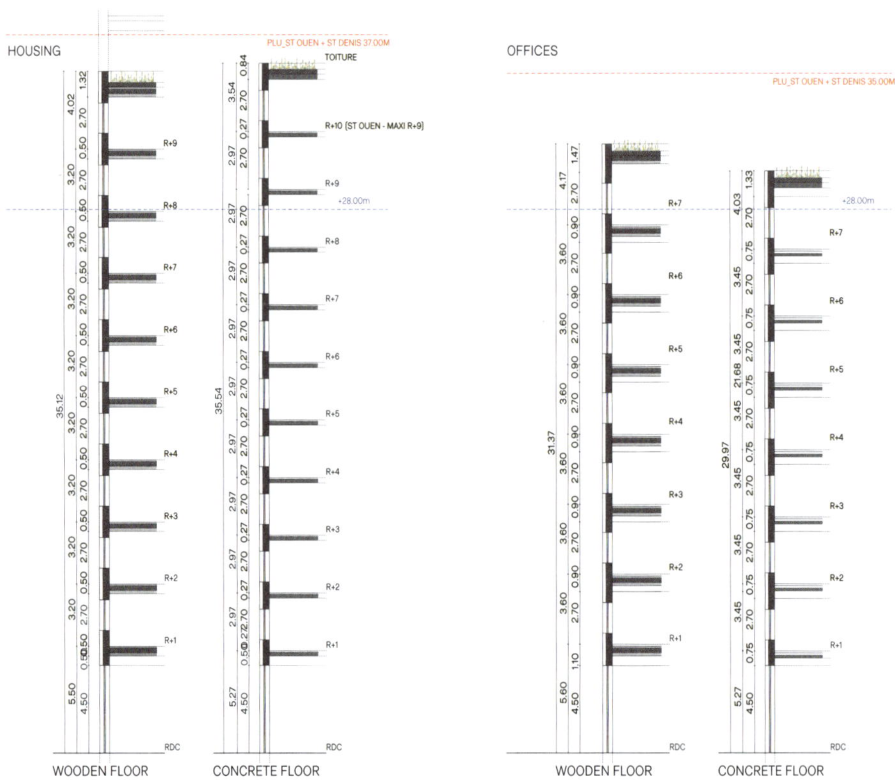

Calculation mode

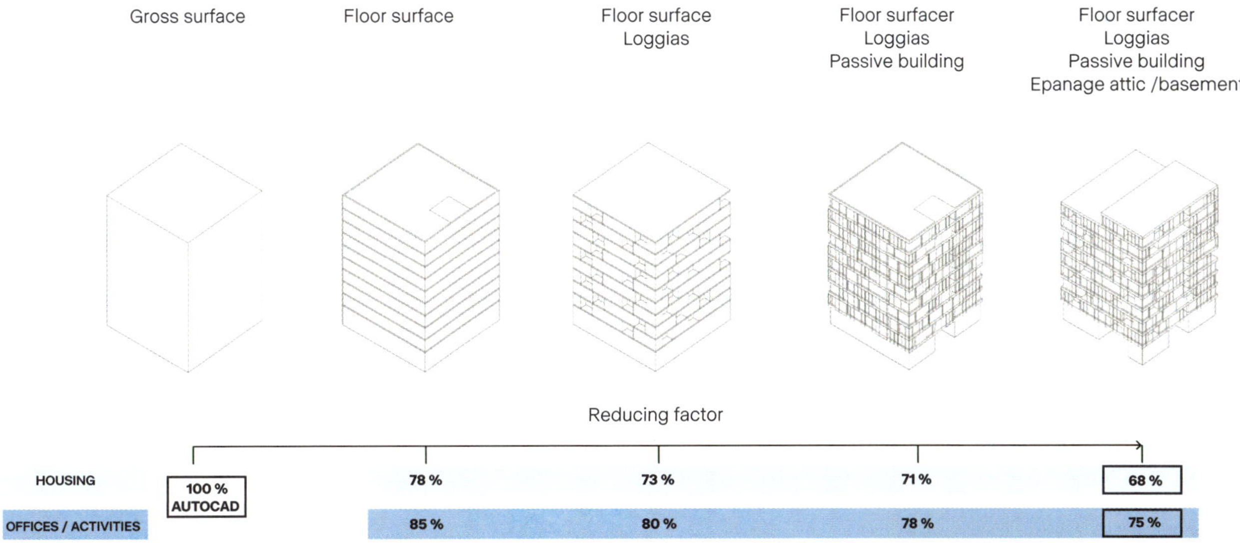

#323# AMBITION 5

CARBON FOOTPRINT MANAGEMENT

Wood construction for an innovative neighbourhood.

Typology focus

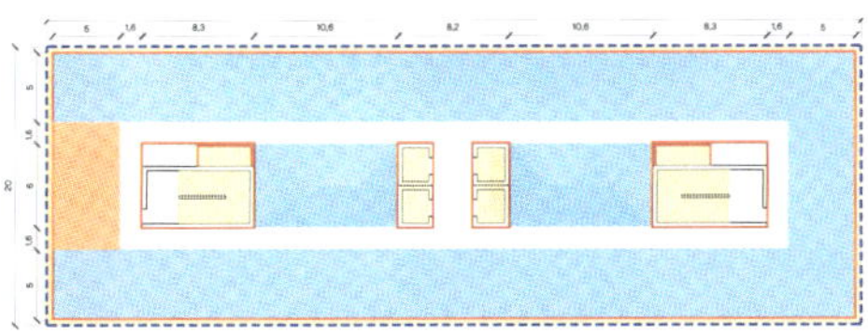

Offices - Maxwell

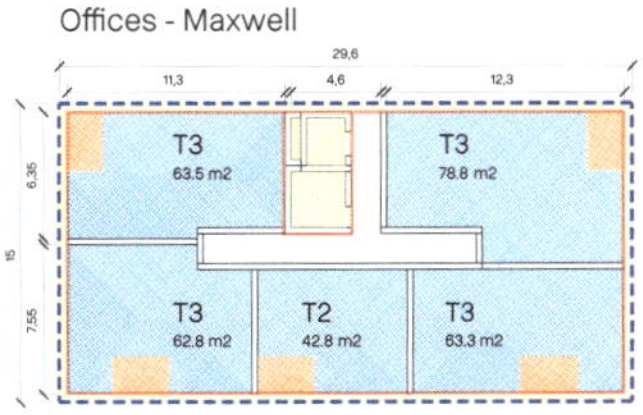

Housing - Les Grandes Maisons

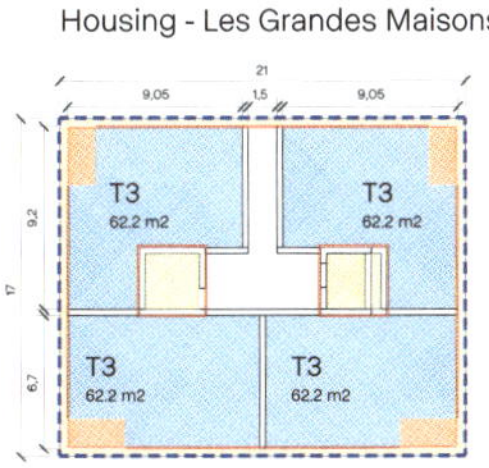

Housing - La Ligne

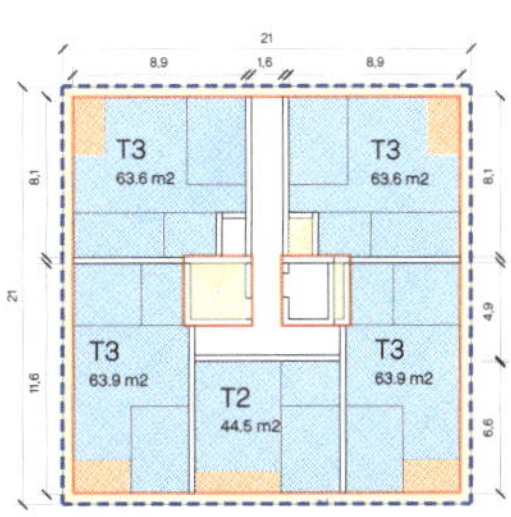

Housing - Les Quinconces

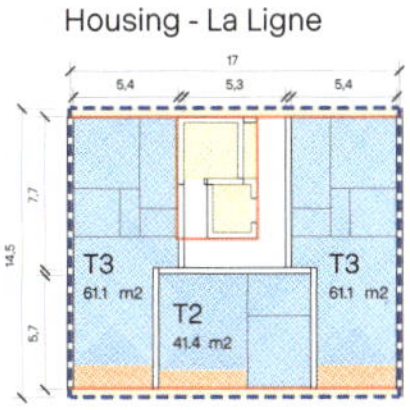

Housing - UniverSeine

Housing - Les Quinconces

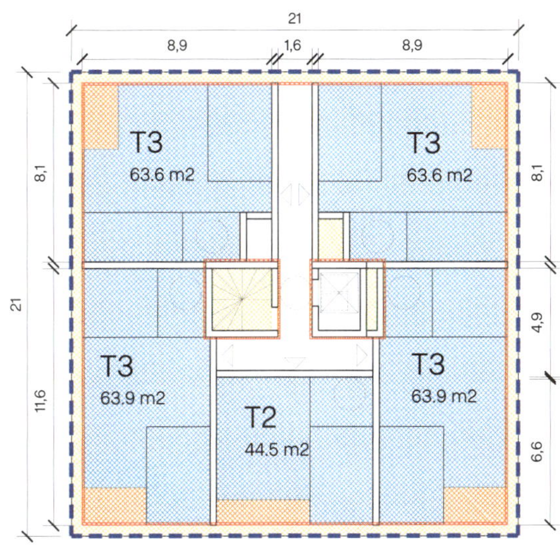

PLOT 21 x 21			
4 th FAMILY			
SURFACE	DEDUCTION	TOTAL	RATIO
SHOB	-	441.0	
SDP	91.4	349.6	0.79
BALCONIES	25.5	324.1	0.93
LIABILITIES/WOOD	10.8	313.4	0.97

DEMOLITION

AMBITION 6

ENERGY AND PRODUCTIVITY IN CITIES

The densification of a district over an area such as that of the Athletes' Village is necessarily accompanied by an adaptation of the energy infrastructures. These were not conceived as a dual project in the district's programming, relegating supply to a technical issue, but rather as a specific imaginary that would accompany the design of the site through the fictions, references and "what ifs" that have studded the centuries of industry on the site. What ifs" that have punctuated the site's centuries of industry. As a witness to the past and harbinger of the future, the Athletes' Village must to take full account of the physicality of the urban infrastructure infrastructure, a component of the project - numerous fictions and intervention drawings for localising and territorialising the site's energy production have thus studded the design, whether by transforming a park into a productive double or by modelling the Cité du Cinéma as a building-machine at the heart of the site's general production. Energy has gone from being a technical problem to an urban and social object at a time when we are becoming increasingly aware of the planet's energy limits.

Connected to Plaine Commune's heating and cooling networks, the Village des Athlètes further meshes the urban energy fabric, helping to balance the energy loop.

1960

2000

#327# **AMBITION 6**

ENERGY AND PRODUCTIVITY IN CITIES

Productivity and urban diversity

1960
From the crane path to concrete prefabrication.
Construction of the 4000,
La Courneuve, 1960

2000
Melting Powew , 2009
Photographer Stéphane Couturier

2025
High-performance buildings made of wood Wilson School of Design, Kwantlen Polytechnic University.

2025

Program plan - Existing

- **Existing condition**
- Housing
- Student accommodation
- Offices
- Commercial activity
- Industrial activity
- Cité du Cinéma
- Public equipment +Training
- Miscellaneous equipment

Program plan - Post-JO phase

#329# **AMBITION 6**

ENERGY AND PRODUCTIVITY IN CITIES
Productivity and urban mix

Program plan: existing - post-Olympic Games

- **Future programme**
- 1/5000e
- Residential
- Offices
- Sports facilities
- School facilities
- Student residence
- Hotel
- Urban agriculture
- Leisure

Program plan

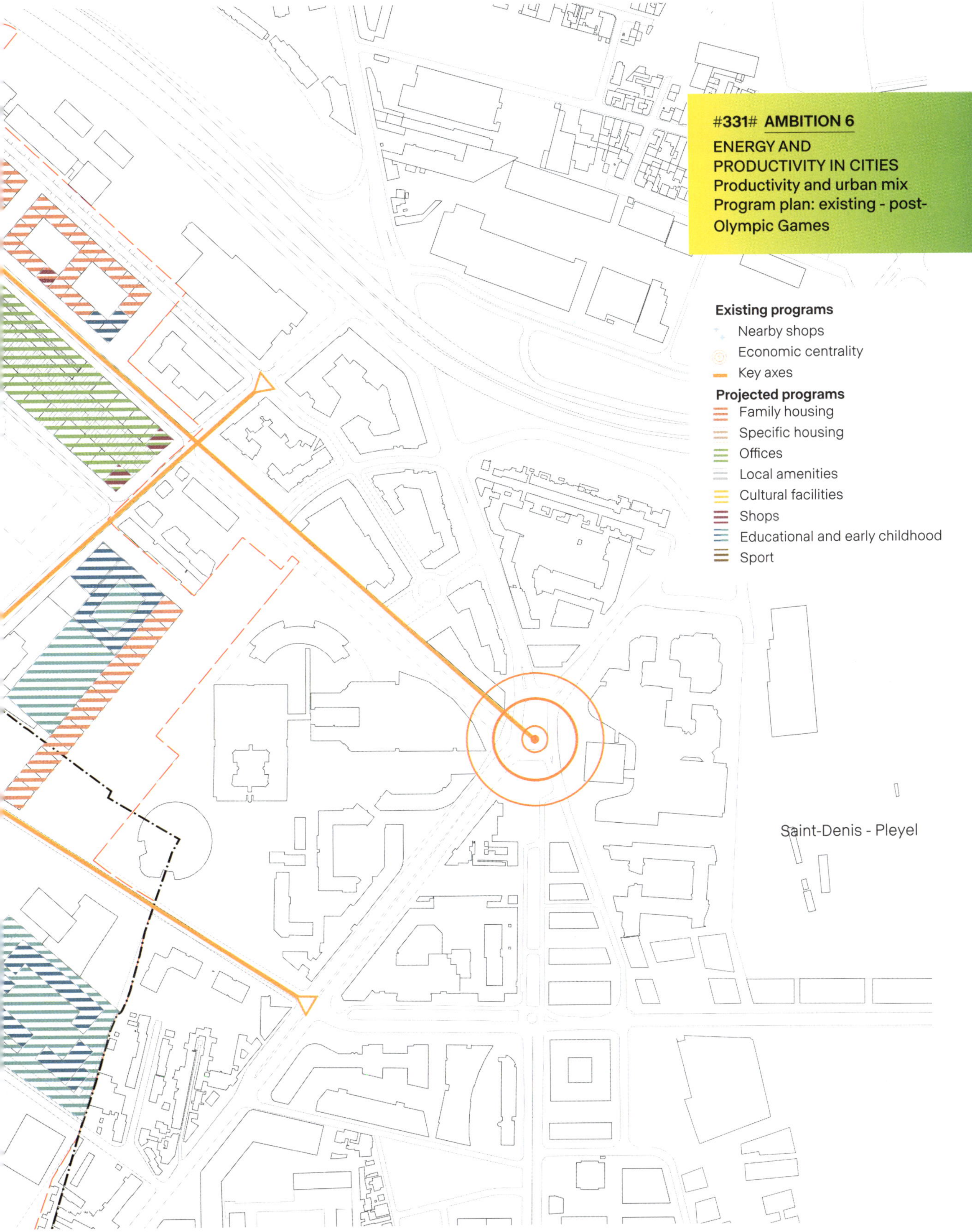
#331# AMBITION 6
ENERGY AND PRODUCTIVITY IN CITIES
Productivity and urban mix
Program plan: existing - post-Olympic Games
Existing programs
Nearby shops
Economic centrality
Key axes
Projected programs
Family housing
Specific housing
Offices
Local amenities
Cultural facilities
Shops
Educational and early childhood
Sport
Saint-Denis - Pleyel

Gennevilliers
Île Saint-Denis
Vieux Saint_Ouen

#333# **AMBITION 6**

ENERGY AND PRODUCTIVITY IN CITIES
Productivity and urban mix

Program plan: existing - post-Olympic Games

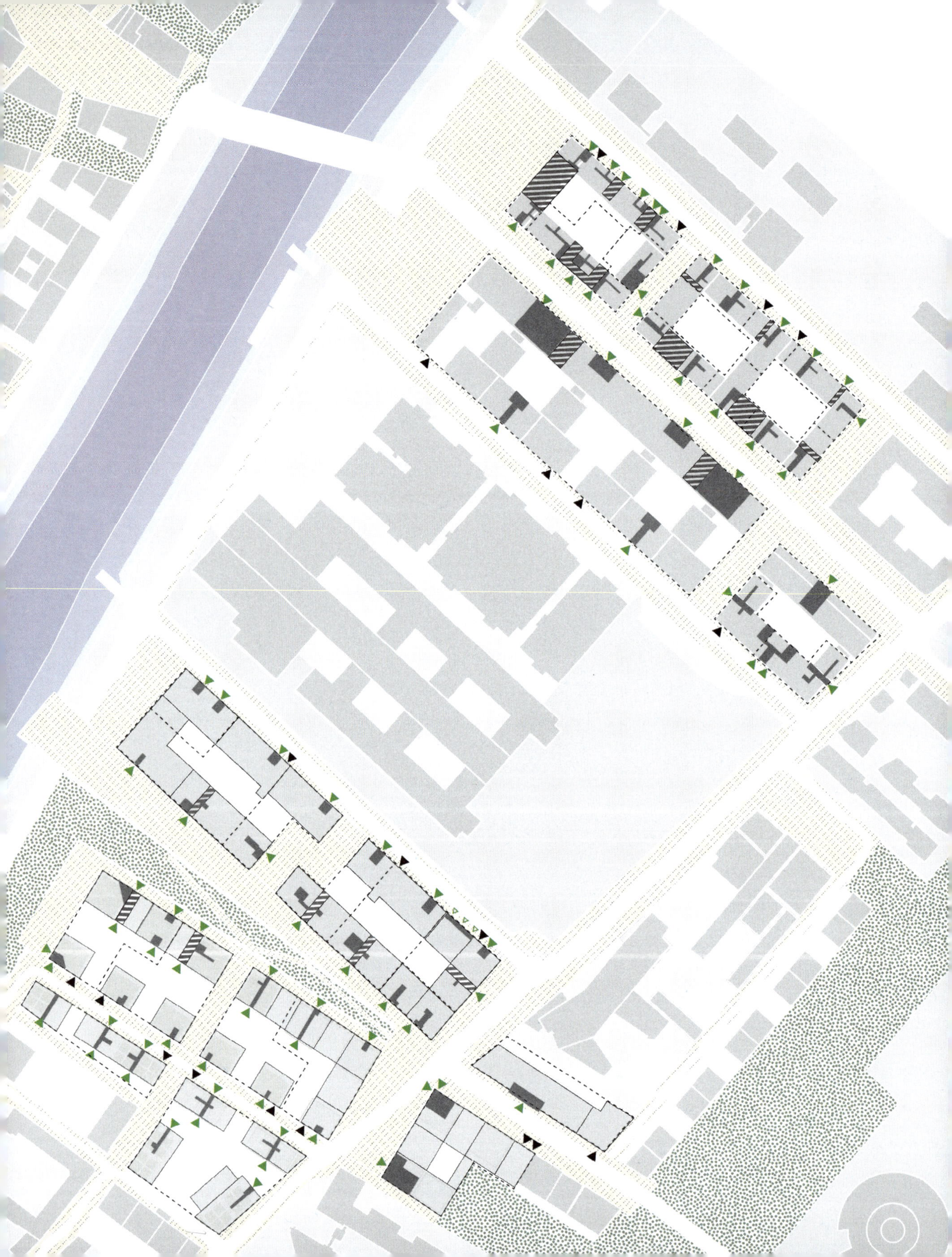

#335# **AMBITION 6**

ENERGY AND PRODUCTIVITY IN CITIES

Productivity and urban mix.

Access organisation & management units

▼ Pedestrian access
▼ Vehicle access

Acces halls
Access porches

- - - - Co-ownership limits

Accès équipement
en toiture

#337# AMBITION 6

ENERGY AND PRODUCTIVITY IN CITIES

Productivity and urban mix.

Dedicated premises at the basement
- Private activities, services and facilities
- Shops
- Restaurants
- Nurseries

Complementary activities (openness to be specified)
- Restaurant and RIE - Student residence and offices
- Cultural facilities - Media Museum - Vatting hall

Private functions
- Flats
- Halls and miscellaneous premises
- Car parks and access ramps

Summary plan - Coherent programming on a wider scale
(Offers December 2019)

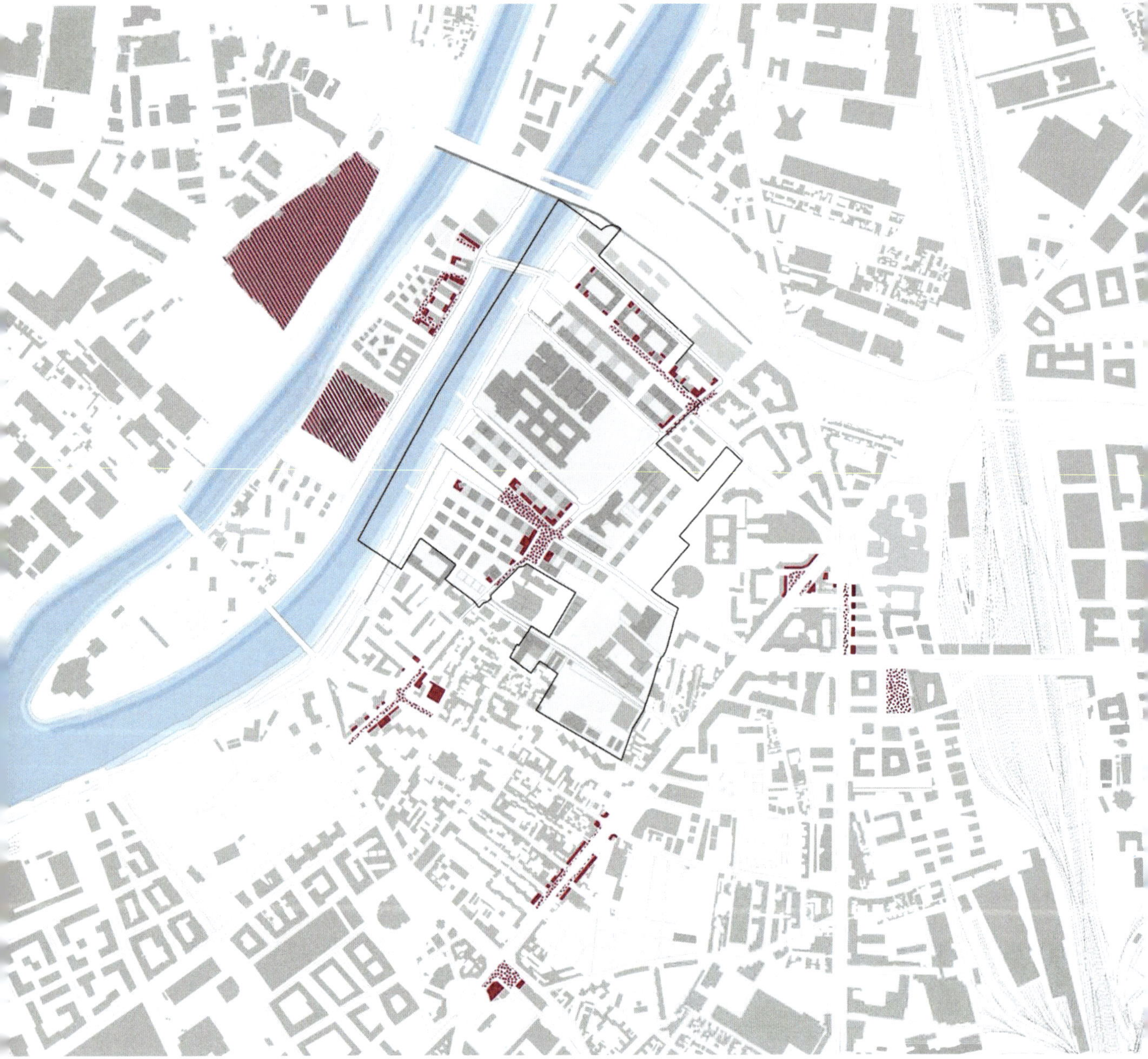

Summary plan - A coherent programme on a wider scale

#339# **AMBITION 6**

ENERGY AND PRODUCTIVITY IN CITIES

Productivity and urban mix

A programme of local shops contained around "living" centres (network of neighbourhood centres) that complement the existing ones (Vieux-Saint-Ouen in particular)

A programme of destinations

A diversified and structured offer contributing to the liveliness of public spaces.

Summary plan - Coherent programming on a wider scale
(Offers december 2019)

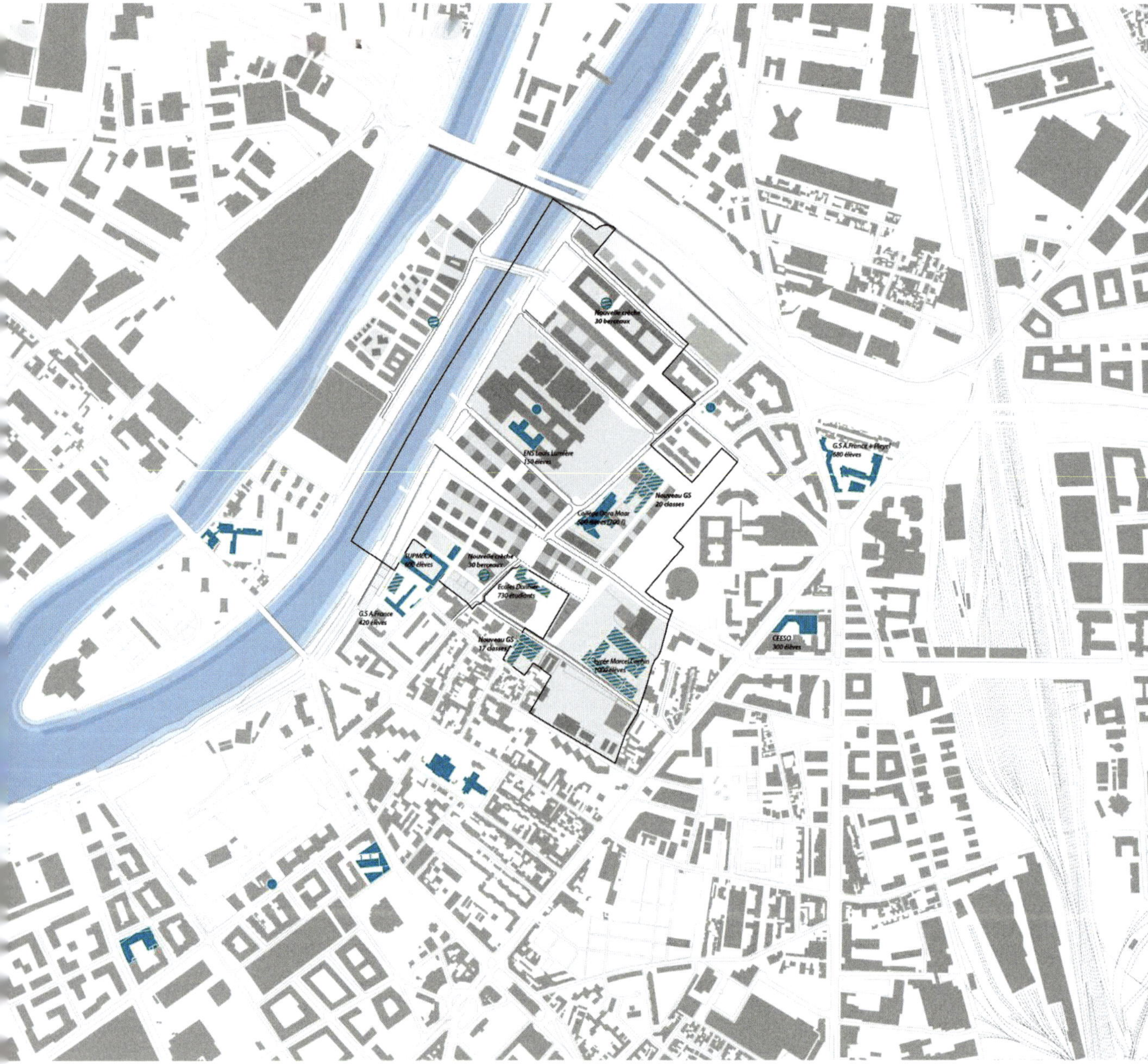

Summary plan - Ground floor entertainment (Offers December 2019)

#341# **AMBITION 6**

ENERGY AND PRODUCTIVITY IN CITIES

Productivity and urban mix

An extensive network of facilities for children, young people and education:

- **Early childhood**
- **Education (primary, lower and upper secondary)**
- **Higher education**

- Shops and restaurants
- Services
- Coworking
- Crafts/workshops
- Cultural facilities
- Public sports facilities
- Free sports area
- Sports "loop" circuit
- Creche: private/public
- Nursery/primary school
- Secondary school
- Higher education

Les Socles - Saint Denis - Sector A

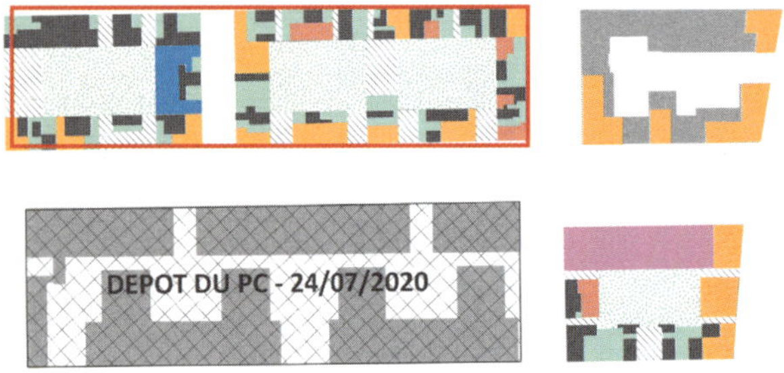

Programming ground floors
(According to the destinations and sub-destinations of the Urban Planning Code)

- Shops and services
- Public facilities and services
- Other secondary or tertiary sector activities

Porosities and animation in public spaces
(Organisation of residential functions on the ground floor)

- Porches and covered passageways
- Green city block hearts
- Residential functions contributing to urban vitality (hall, bicycle rooms, caretaker's lodge, communal areas)
- Housing in the ground floor
- Other residential uses

Les Socles - Saint Denis - Sector B

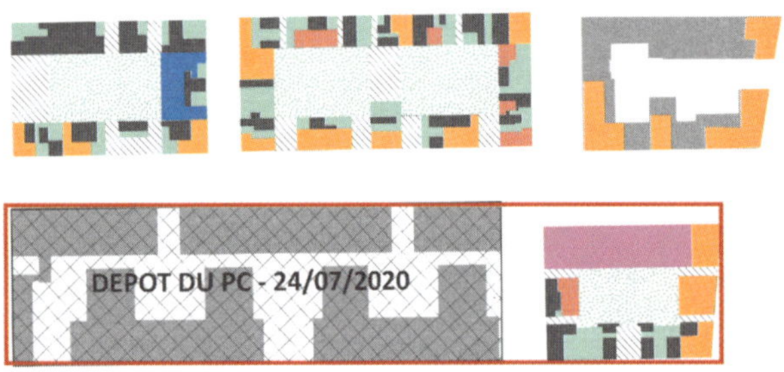

#343# **AMBITION 6**

ENERGY AND PRODUCTIVITY IN CITIES

Productivity and urban mix.

Les Socles - Saint Ouen - City block D

Les Socles - Saint Ouen - City block E

The banks of the Seine

The prows

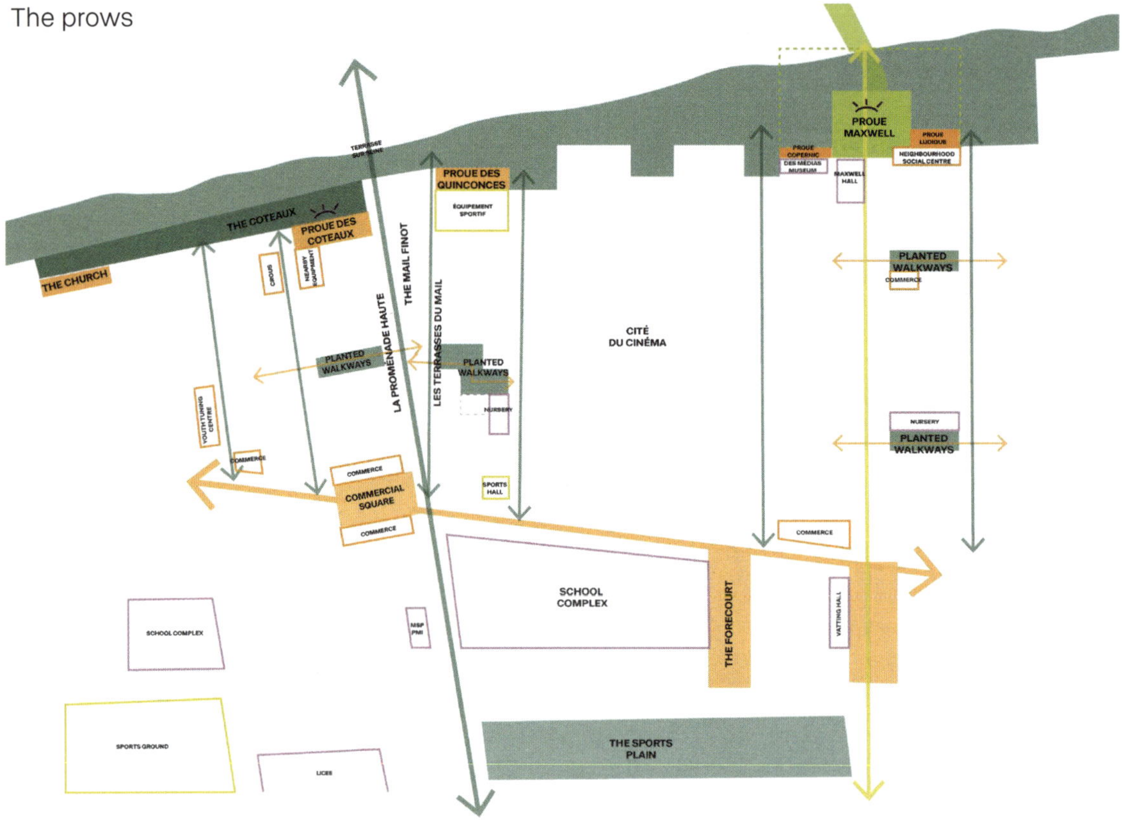

Place Ampère

Diagram of activities and entries

Ground floor programming
(In accordance with the uses and sub-uses set out in the French Code de l'Urbanisme)

- Retail and service activities
- Public facilities and services
- Other secondary or tertiary sector activities

Porosity and liveliness of public spaces
(Organisation of residential functions on the ground floor)

- Porosity and liveliness of public spaces
- Porches and covered passageways
- Green city blocks heart (lobby, bicycle rooms, caretaker's lodge, communal areas)
- Ground floor accommodation
- Other residential functions

Residential use

- Pedestrian access
- Vehicle access
- Access halls
- Vertical circulation
- Communal areas / RE reception halls
- Caretaker's lodge
- Ground floor accommodation
- Porches / Rifts
- Car parking
- Bicycle parking
- Co-ownership boundaries

Linear-active ground floors

Lieux de destination

Loisirs, sports et culture

Services et commerces de proximité

Polarities

Activating the banks of the Seine

Attractors / Fixed barges

Attractors / Barges

Local hubs

Open spaces

Pedestrian area / Finot Mall, Place Ampère

Public spaces dominated by plants Hillside and Ampère Park

Planted and landscaped private island cores

Condominiums, management units (Indicative layout)

#345# **AMBITION 6**

ENERGY AND PRODUCTIVITY IN CITIES

New central areas

During the consultation process, the teams were given an outline of how the ground floor programs would be organised.

It differentiates between three main types of programs:

- The destination areas, linked to the Seine, will strengthen the district's metropolitan influence by developing activities in the fields of sport, culture, and leisure.
- The areas dedicated to economic activities will help to maintain and develop urban diversity and productivity. Craftsmen and SMEs will be in premises that are adapted and adaptable to their different needs and changes.
- Two centres for local shops and services will meet the daily needs of residents and users, complementing the existing commercial centres in the area.

#347# **AMBITION 6**

ENERGY AND PRODUCTIVITY IN CITIES

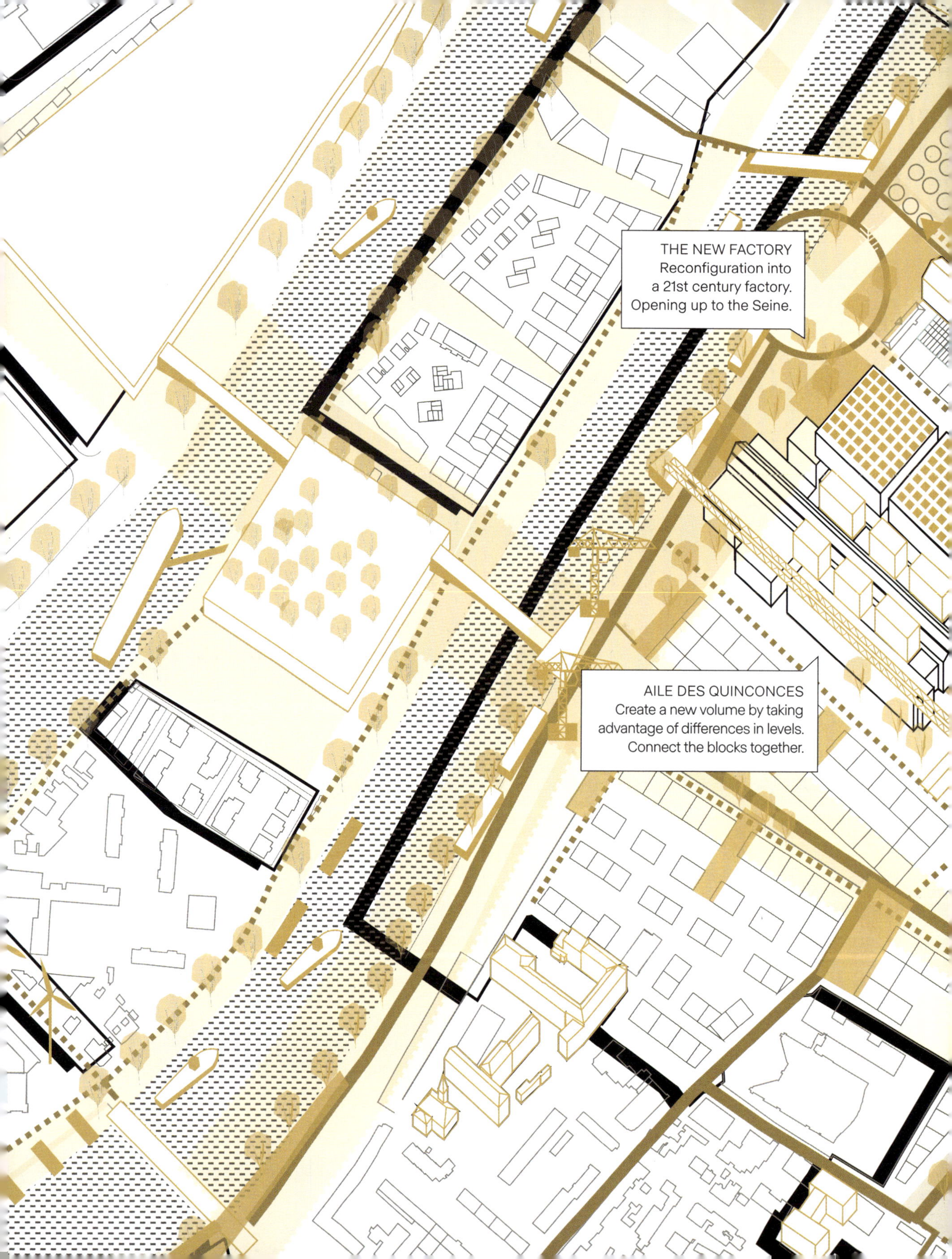
THE NEW FACTORY
Reconfiguration into
a 21st century factory.
Opening up to the Seine.
AILE DES QUINCONCES
Create a new volume by taking
advantage of differences in levels.
Connect the blocks together.

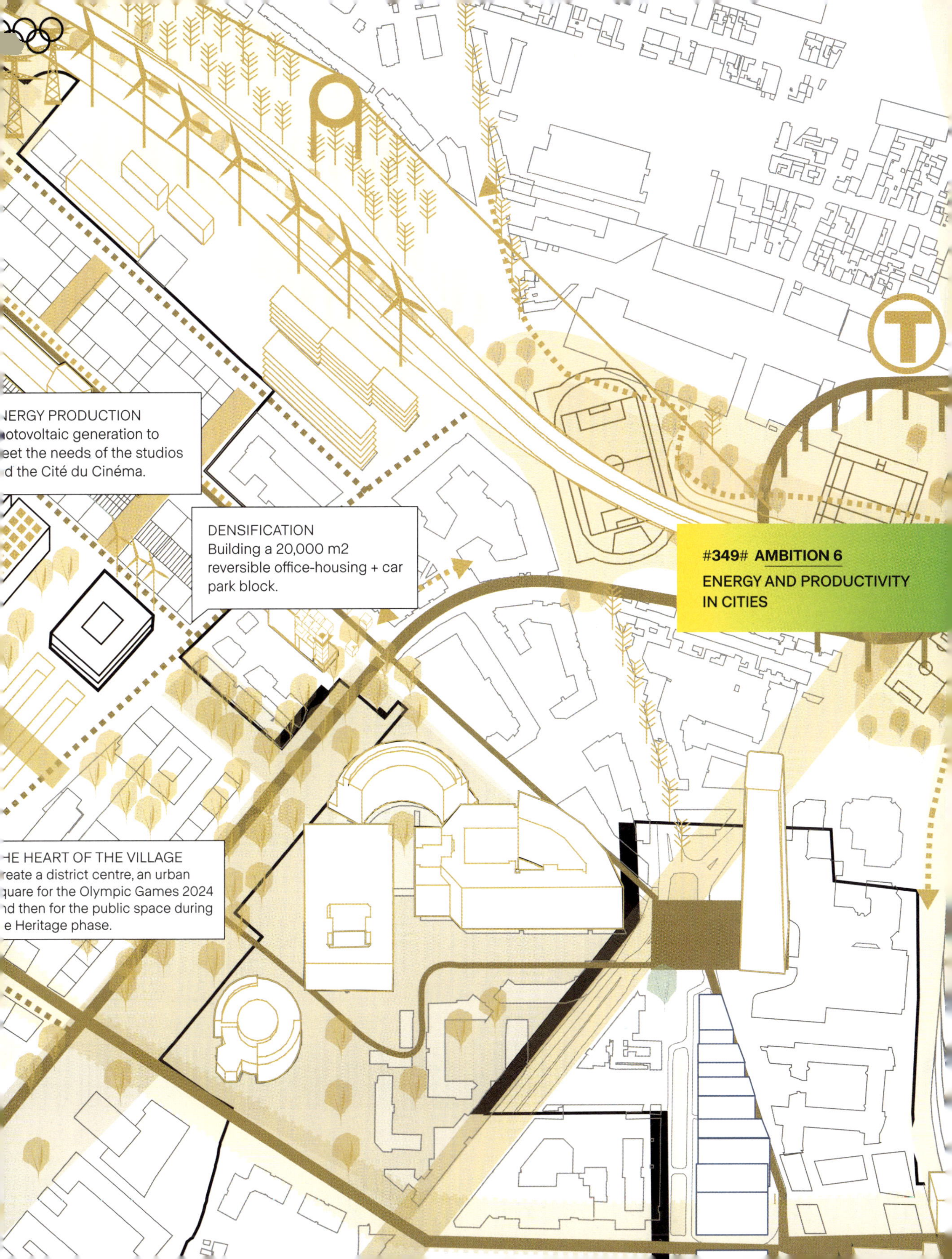

ERGY PRODUCTION
otovoltaic generation to
eet the needs of the studios
d the Cité du Cinéma.
DENSIFICATION
Building a 20,000 m2
reversible office-housing + car
park block.
HE HEART OF THE VILLAGE
reate a district centre, an urban
quare for the Olympic Games 2024
d then for the public space during
e Heritage phase.
T

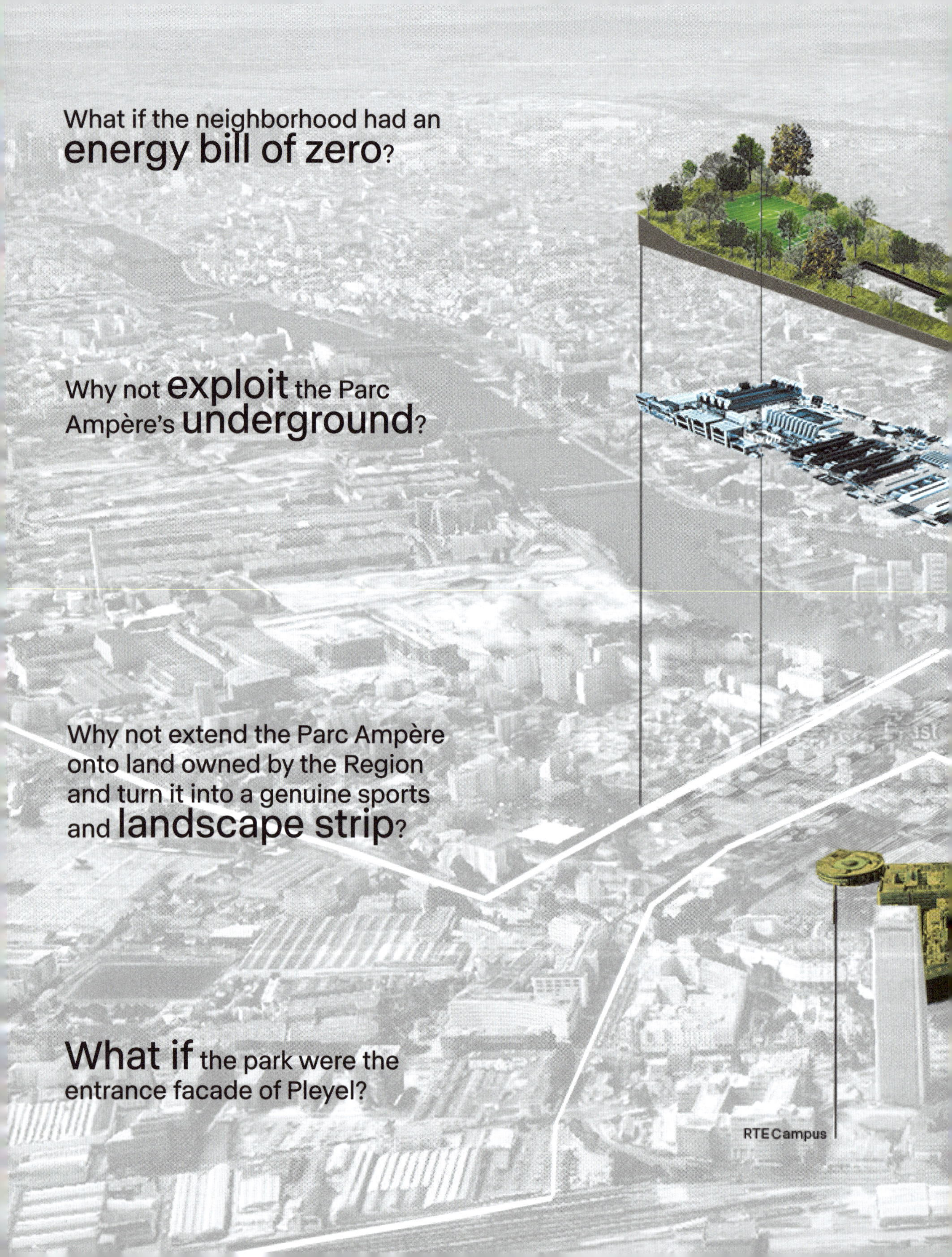
What if the neighborhood had an energy bill of zero?
Why not exploit the Parc Ampère's underground?
Why not extend the Parc Ampère onto land owned by the Region and turn it into a genuine sports and landscape strip?
What if the park were the entrance facade of Pleyel?
RTE Campus

Why not use the infrastructure of the sports complex: an indoor stadium, a swimming pool, an outdoor stadium, a rowing club and a bowling green during the Games?

#351# **AMBITION 6**

ENERGY AND PRODUCTIVITY IN CITIES

The Ampère Park and its double.

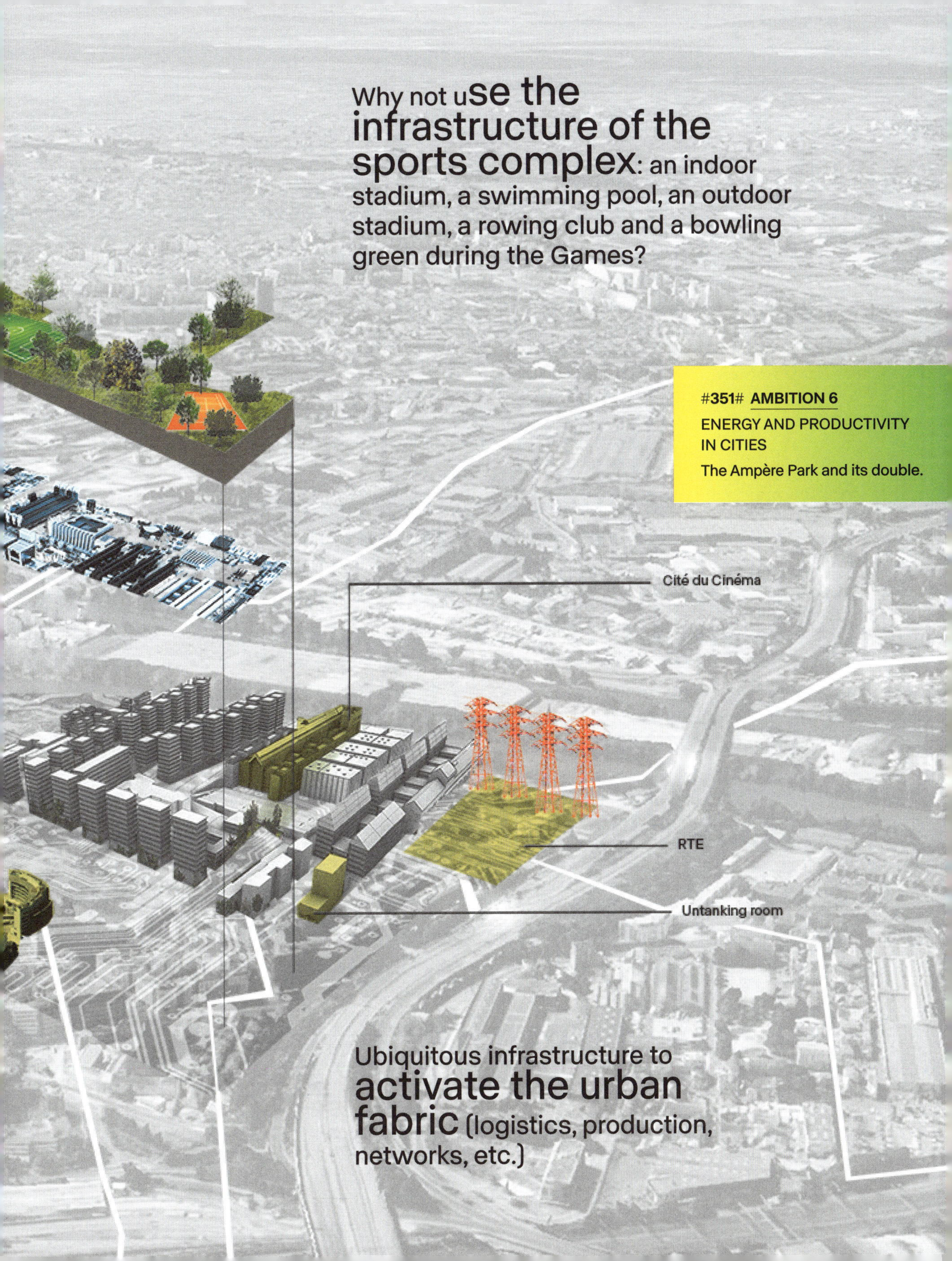

Ubiquitous infrastructure to activate the urban fabric (logistics, production, networks, etc.)

Why not imagine a bus station on two levels? a belvedere park as a legacy?

#353# **AMBITION 6**

ENERGY AND PRODUCTIVITY IN CITIES

The bus station and its double.

Why not imagine a multi-use park that is also a railway station, a hub for networks, a place for mobility, sport and facilities, an attractive location for the Pleyel hub?

How can we reinvest an industrial heritage? Can't we imagine a redevelopment of and around the Cité du Cinéma along the lines of London's Battersea Power Station?
Saint-Denis
Can we imagine a new form of 21st century factory to reinvest the old Saint Denis thermal power plant?
The Cité du Cinéma as a building-machine at the heart of the site's overall production?

#355# **AMBITION 6**

ENERGY AND PRODUCTIVITY IN CITIES

The Cité du Cinéma and its double.

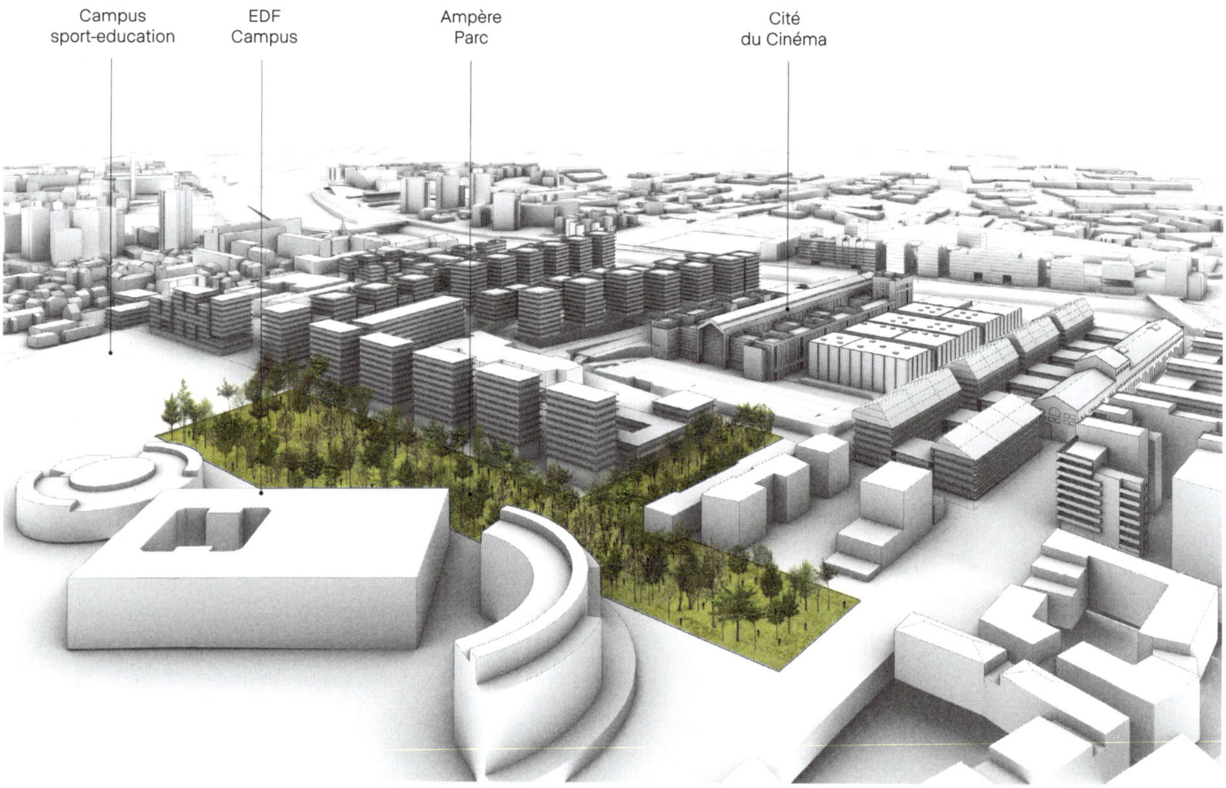
Campus
sport-education
EDF
Campus
Ampère
Parc
Cité
du Cinéma

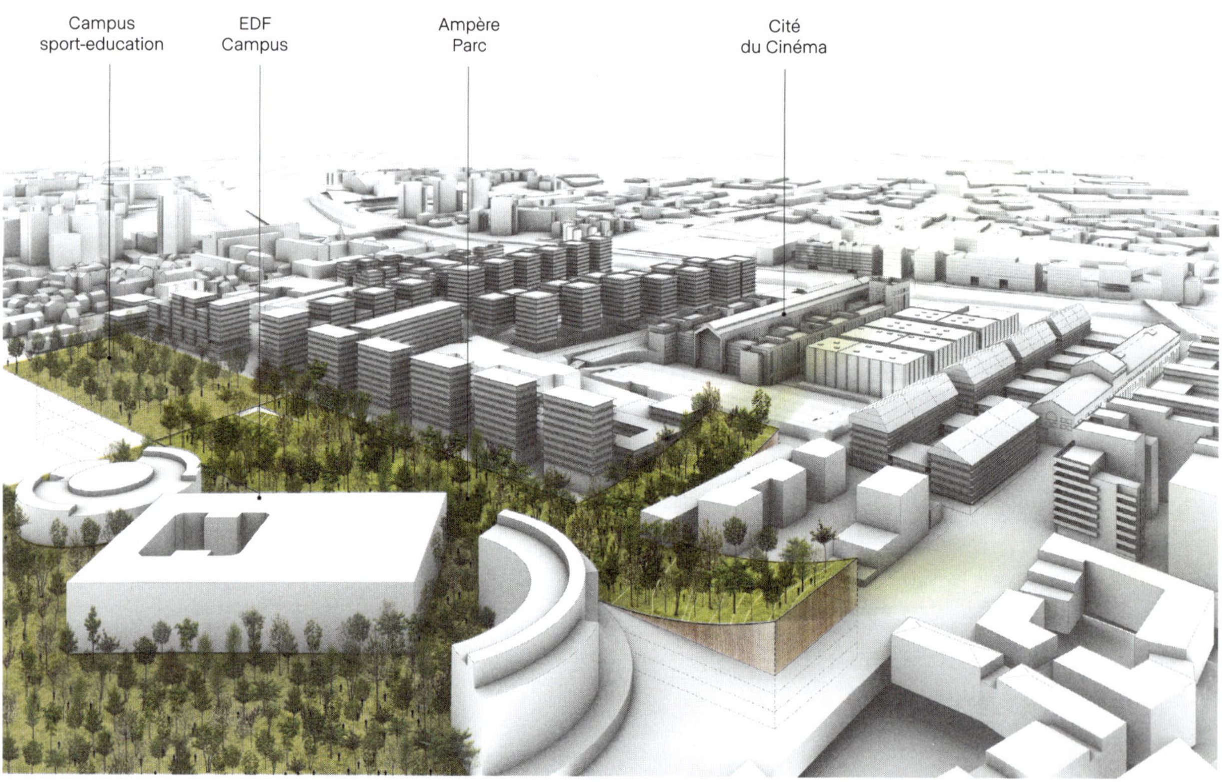
Campus
sport-education
EDF
Campus
Ampère
Parc
Cité
du Cinéma

PARC AMPERE
ILOT PRIVE

PARC AMPERE
ILOT PRIVE

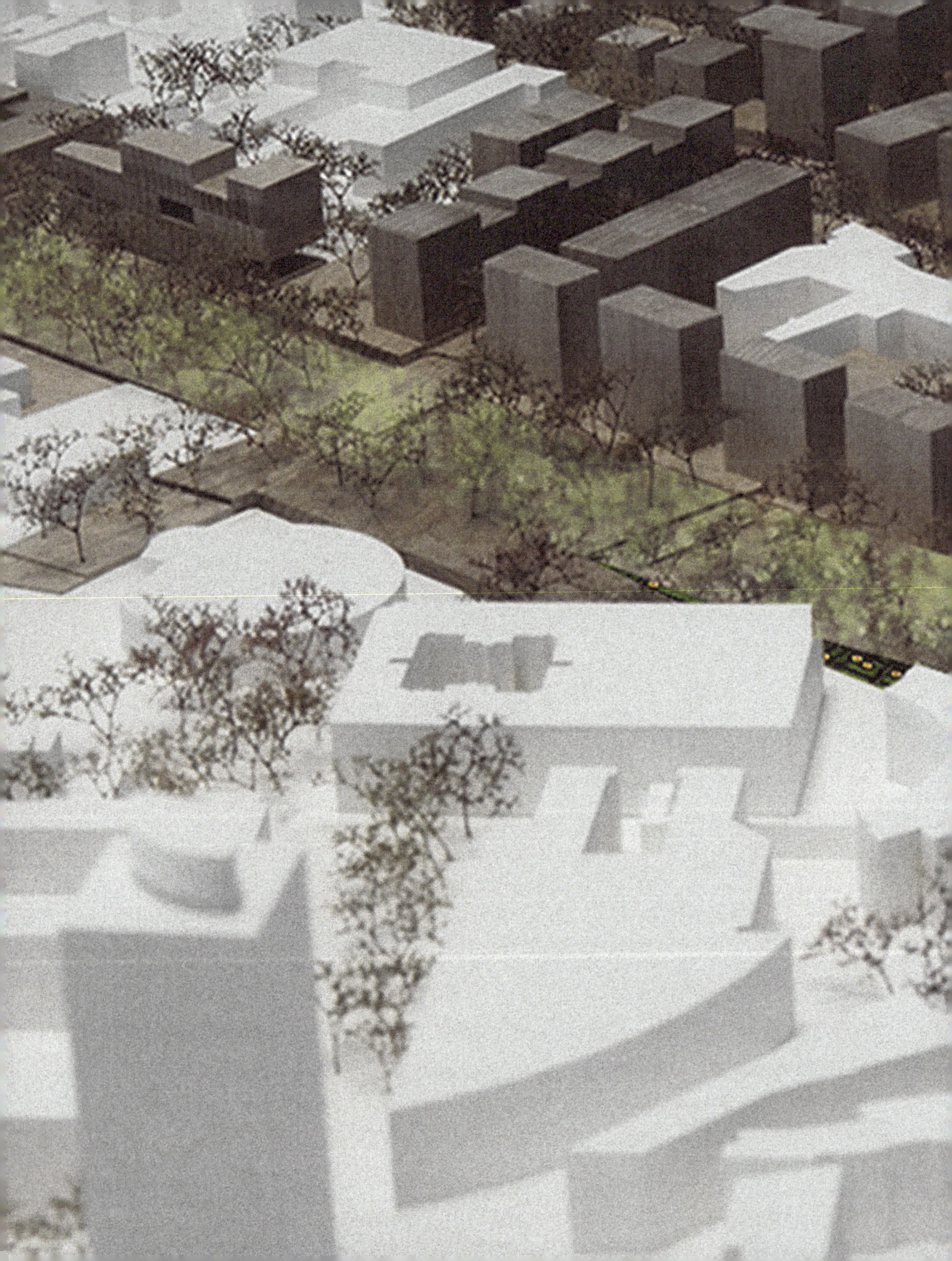

#359# **AMBITION 6**

ENERGY AND PRODUCTIVITY IN CITIES

AMBITION 7

ACCESSIBLE MOBILITY

The Pedestrian's Role in the City - one of the most important subjects concerning the perception of a neighborhood or a street. The evolution of mobility, and perhaps even more so the perception of it, particularly in a neighborhood built with a focus on sports, must be a strong marker for the design of a neighborhood in the 21st century. Near one of the future major metropolitan hubs of Greater Paris, the Village focuses its mobility strategy on the sharing of transportation modes and the reduction of car usage in the city: thus the Village anticipates and supports the decrease in the modal share of cars in the area. Despite being marked by a steep slope towards the Seine, the Village is entirely accessible to wheelchair users. Beyond a technical question about the slopes to be respected, its design aims to make it as inclusively accessible as possible. Robust design principles have therefore been implemented, starting with the clarity and readability of spaces. The streets are wide and clear, the urban plan easily readable for the user without becoming repetitive. The sidewalks are designed to leave 1.4m of width without obstacles and to treat the different urban functions they carry in bands: free circulation, biodiversity band, technical band for furniture and lighting, green band carrying the urban landscape, and the urban services band - bike and car parking, etc. From these simple design elements, the different typologies of streets on the site are assembled.

Village des athlètes 1924
09
15

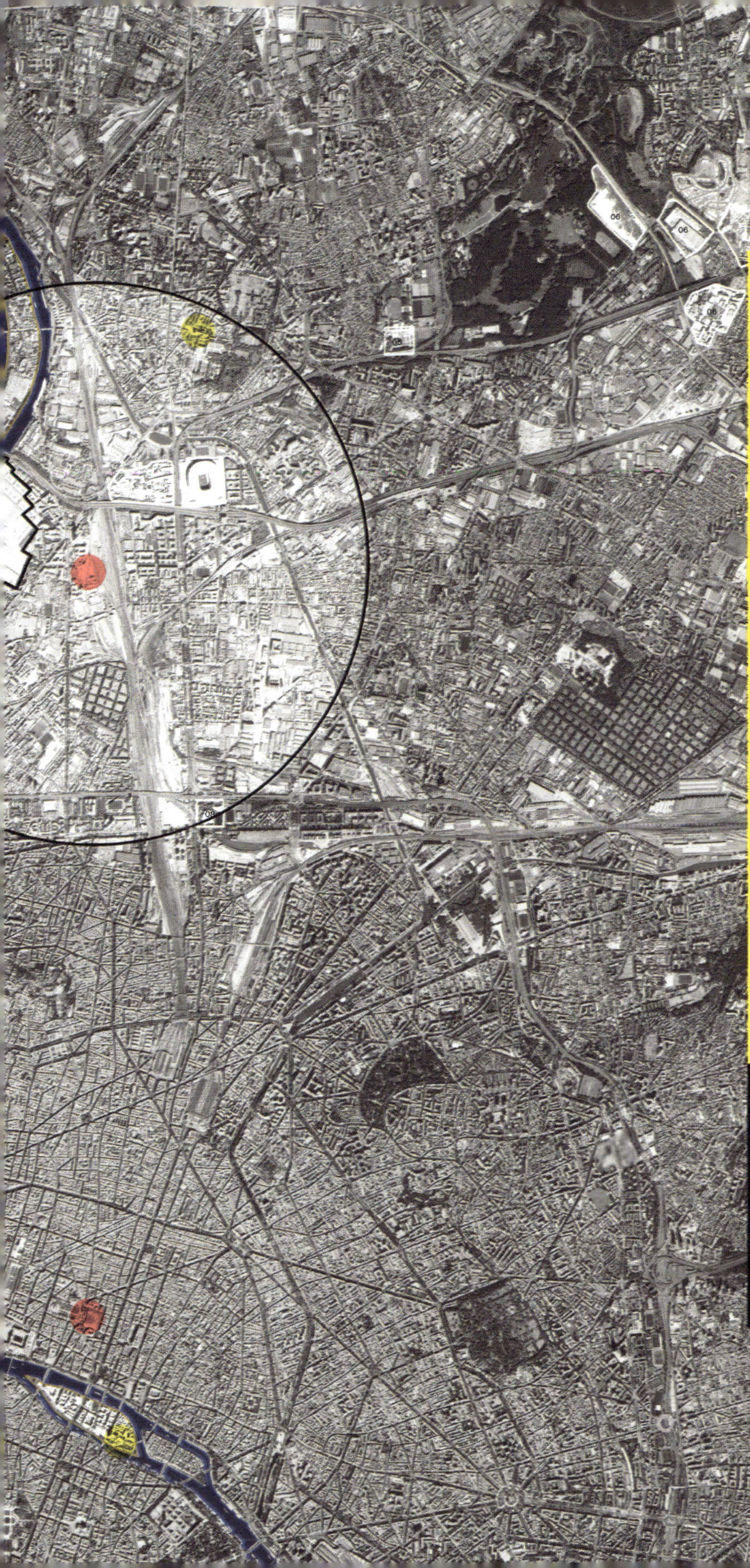

#363# **AMBITION 7**

ACCESSIBLE MOBILITY

In the heart of Paris

The Village covers fifty-one hectares of L'Ile-Saint-Denis, Saint-Denis and Saint-Ouen-sur-Seine, helping to strengthen the links between these communities and their residents. As in the heart of the capital, in Seine-Saint-Denis the population of this area has founded another heart, at the heart of the great heart of the "city-region".

Today, this area is one of the most dynamic in Greater Paris in terms of urban change. By 2050, it should have a robust, legible urban fabric, based on a "linking urbanism" that will make it one of the central points of a metropolitan geography.

The opening of Saint-Denis Pleyel, an emblematic station of the Grand Paris Express, will also play a decisive role in the area's transformation, reinforcing its status as a major hub of Greater Paris. Footfall at the future interchange will be comparable to that at Châtelet-Les-Halles.

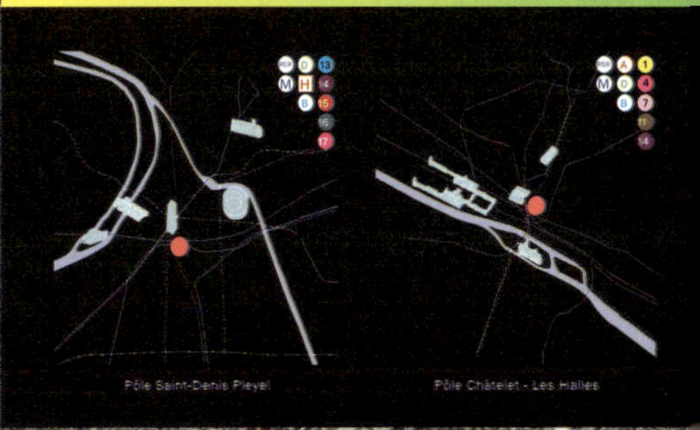

LES AGNETTES
LES GRÉSILLONS
COLOMBES
LA GARENNE COLOMBES
NANTERRE LA FOLIE
BOIS-COLOMBES
NANTERRE LA BOULE
RUEIL
15
BÉCON LES BRUYÈRES
PORTE DE CLICHY
14
LA DÉFENSE
RUEIL SURESNES MONT-VALÉRIEN
15
SAINT-CLOUD
PONT DE SÈVRES
ISSY RER
CHÂTILLON MONTROUGE
15
FORT D'ISSY VANVES CLAMART
BAGNEUX
SATORY
VERSAILLES CHANTIERS
18
VILLEJUIF INSTITUT G.-ROU
CHEVILLY TROIS-CO
SAINT-QUENTIN EST
ENVIRONS DE PARIS
CEA SAINT-AUBIN
ANTONYPÔLE
MASSY PALAISEAU
18
↓ ORSAY - GIF
↓ PALAISEAU

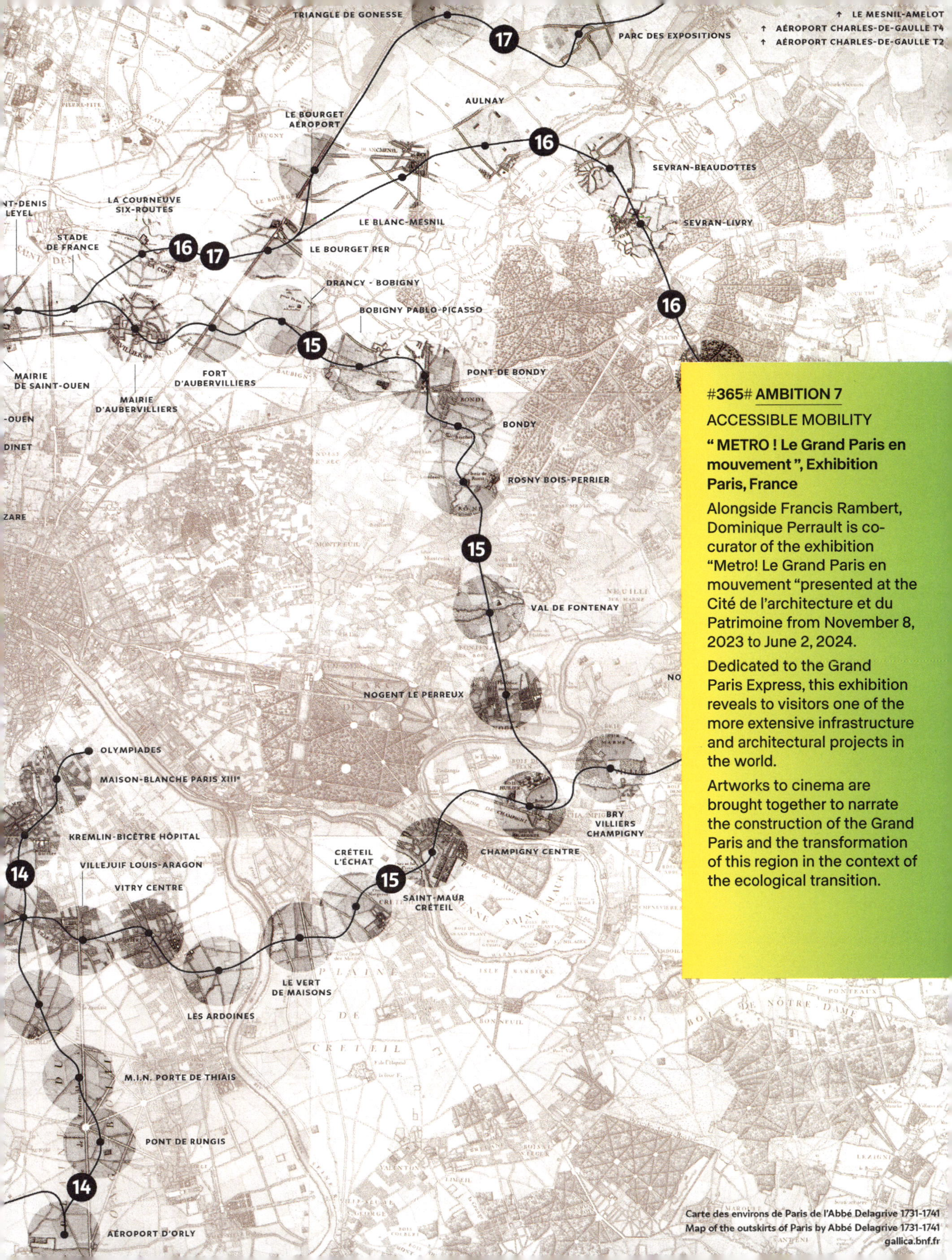

#365# **AMBITION 7**

ACCESSIBLE MOBILITY

" METRO ! Le Grand Paris en mouvement ", Exhibition Paris, France

Alongside Francis Rambert, Dominique Perrault is co-curator of the exhibition "Metro! Le Grand Paris en mouvement "presented at the Cité de l'architecture et du Patrimoine from November 8, 2023 to June 2, 2024.

Dedicated to the Grand Paris Express, this exhibition reveals to visitors one of the more extensive infrastructure and architectural projects in the world.

Artworks to cinema are brought together to narrate the construction of the Grand Paris and the transformation of this region in the context of the ecological transition.

Carte des environs de Paris de l'Abbé Delagrive 1731-1741
Map of the outskirts of Paris by Abbé Delagrive 1731-1741
gallica.bnf.fr

Percentage of households without a car

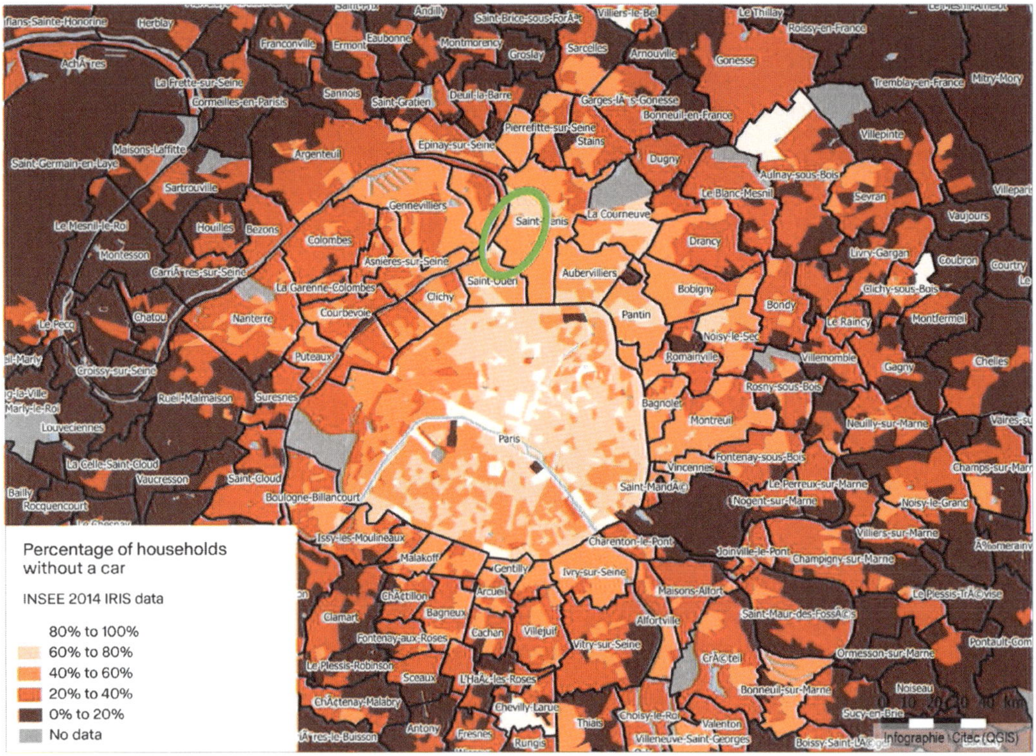

Average number of cars per household

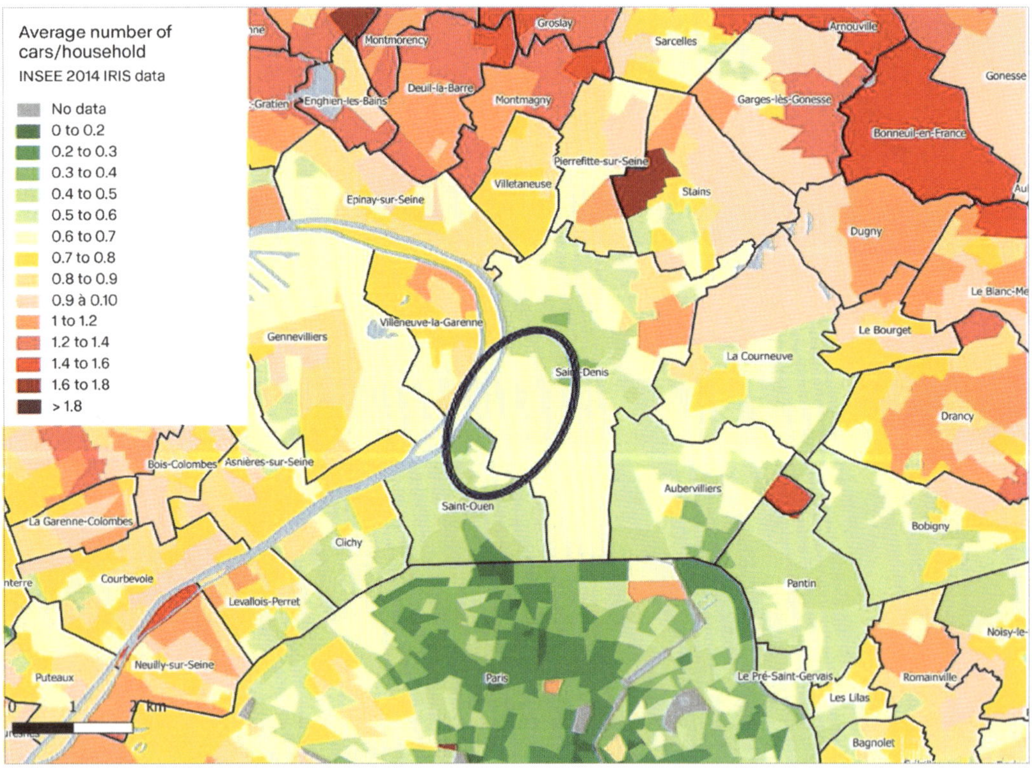

Current situation. Existing traffic 2018

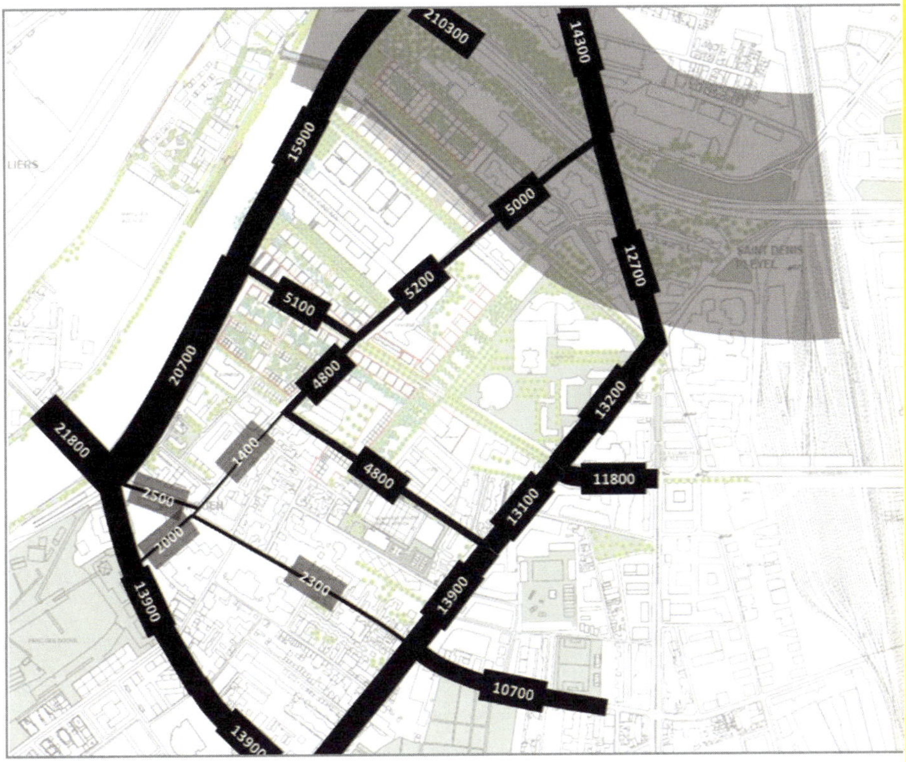

#367# AMBITION 7

ACCESSIBLE MOBILITY

Travel and mobility

Existing traffic in Average Annual

A86: around 200,000 vehicles/day

- RD1: between 16,000 and 20,000 vehicles/day

- Rue Ampère: around 5,000 vehicles/day

- Rue Nicolau: around 5,000 vehicles/day

- Rue Marcel Cachin: around 5,000 vehicles/day

Estimated current parking supply

- 90 on-street public parking spaces

- 740 private surface parking spaces for activities

- A significant number of additional underground spaces (over 300 spaces?)

Estimates of traffic generation for the timeframe of the project are based on the following assumptions modal share of individual motorised vehicles of 25%.

Current situation. Home-work. Saint Denis

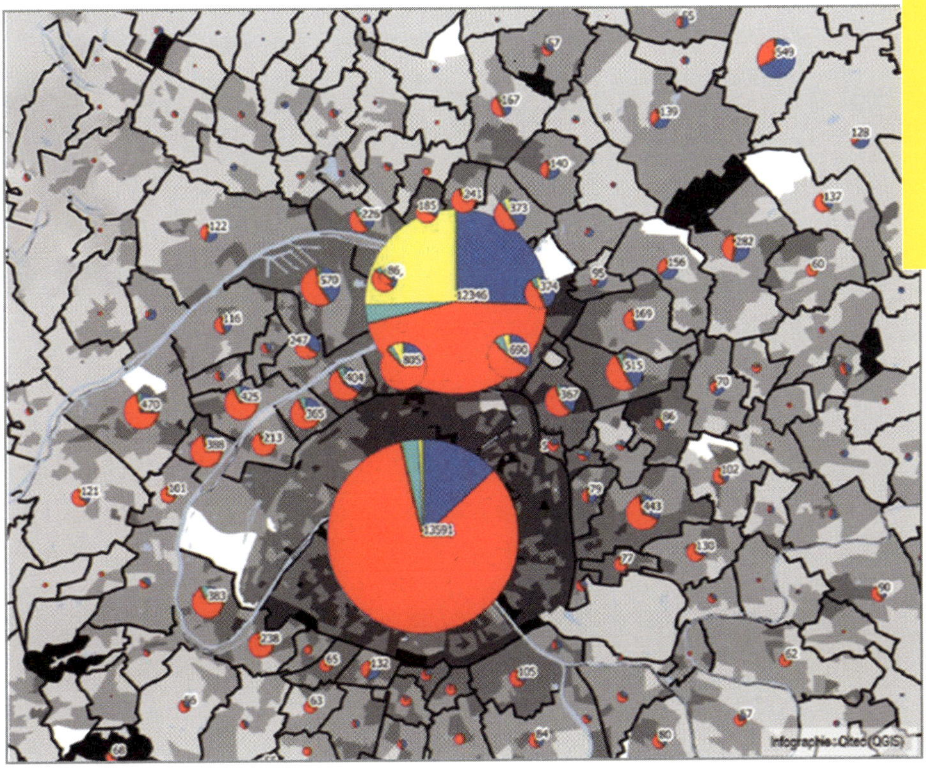

Modal share of home-to-work From Saint Denis

- Walking
- 2 wheels
- Public transport
- Car

Part des mènages

- 80& to 100%
- 60% to 80%
- 40% to60%
- 20% to 40%
- 0% to 20%
- No data

Individual motorized transport - Context-Franchises

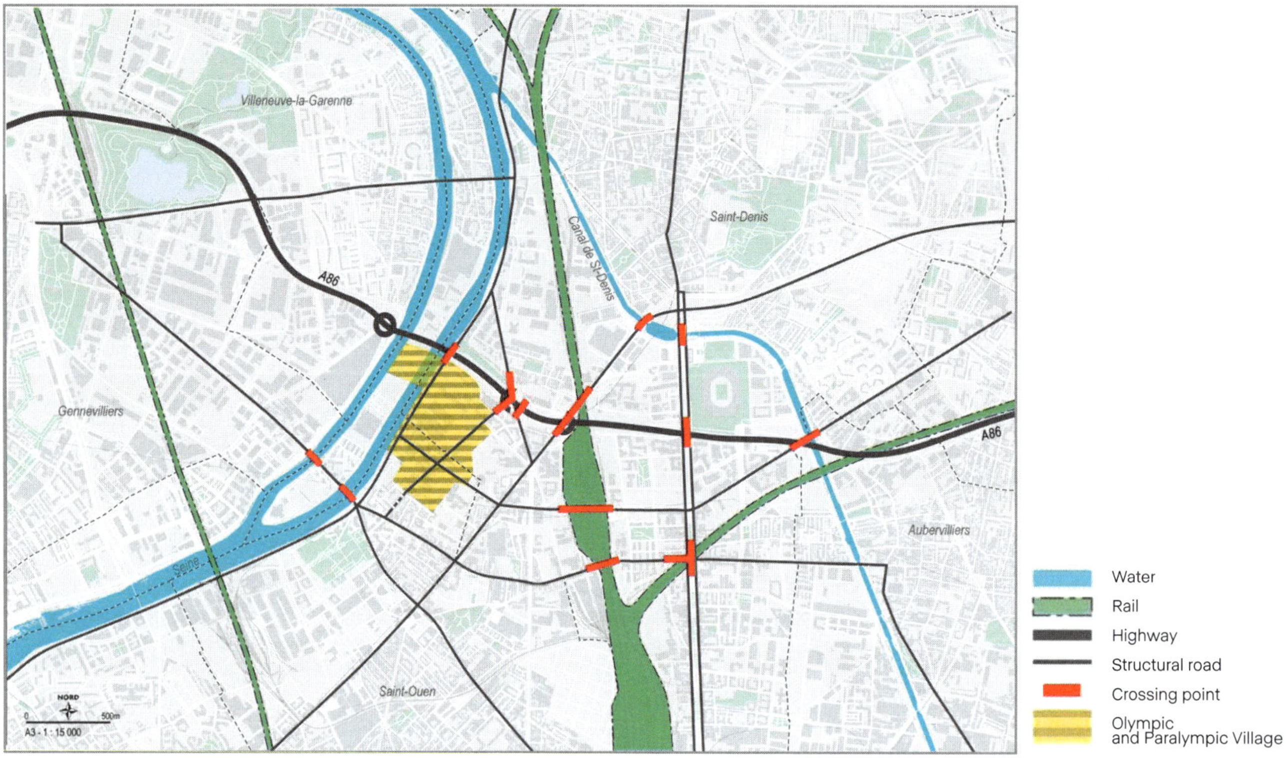

Motorized individual transport - Motorized accessibility

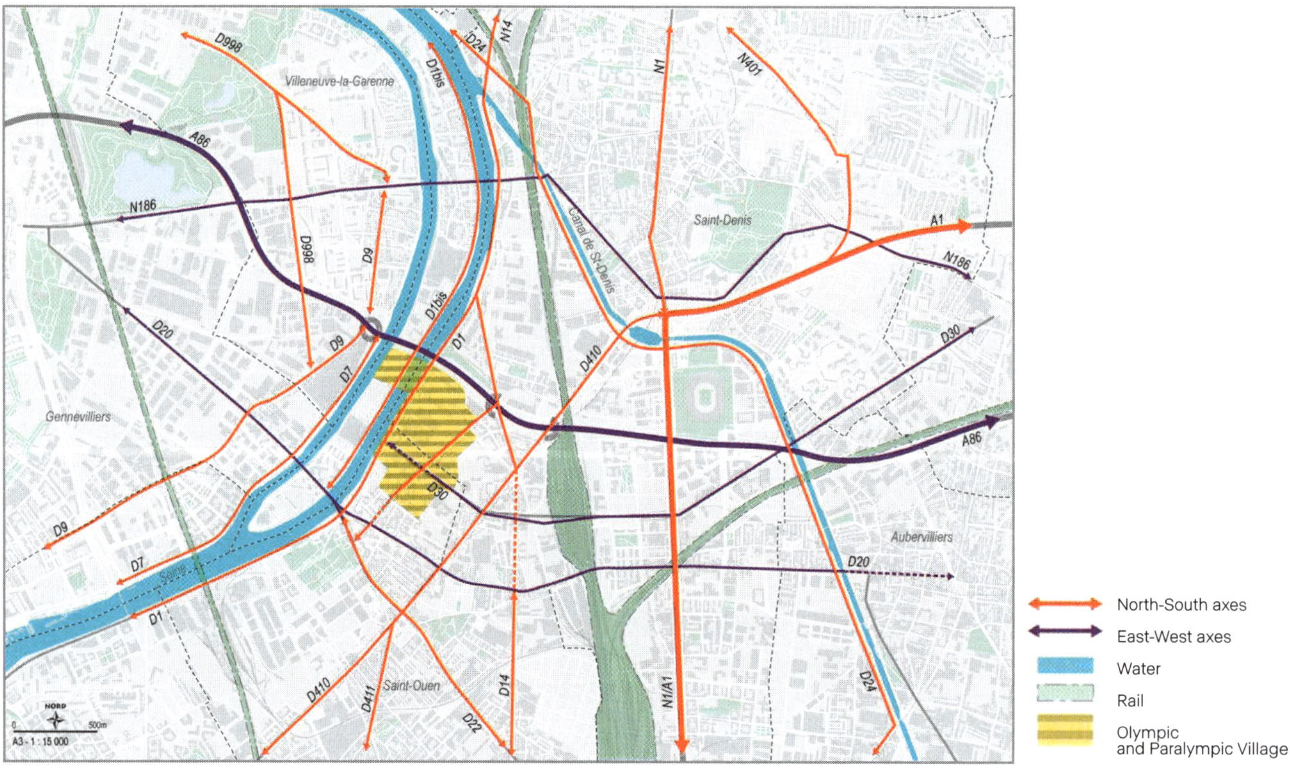

Individual motorized transport - Urban expressways -IDF

#369# **AMBITION 7**
ACCESSIBLE MOBILITY
Travel and mobility.

Traffic trends on Paris region's urban expressways and the Paris ring road (Base 100 in 2001)

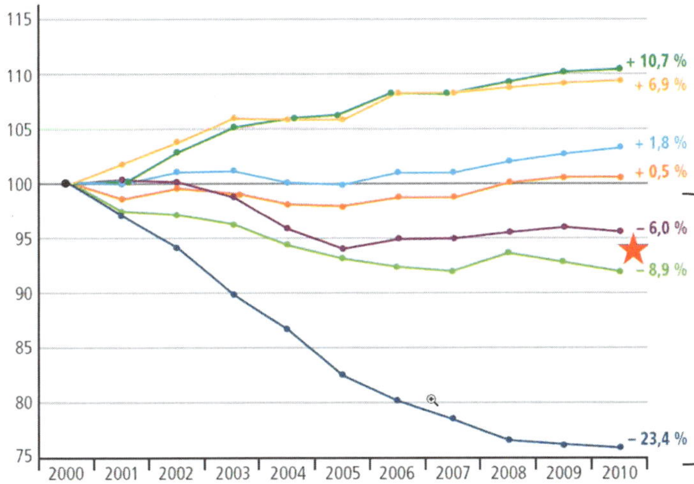

Area of intensified public transport supply (2018)

Area of intensification of public transport services (Grand Paris Express-2030)

Note: Vehicles x km from 6 a.m. to 8 p.m. on the VRU, vehicles x km per hour from 7 a.m. to 9 p.m., per km of roadway on the BP:
Source: DIRIF, SIRIUS 1 and 2 networks, City of Paris

Source: PDUIF

★ Olympic and Paralympic Village (between A86 and boulevard périhperique)

- Francilienne
- Boulevard périphérique
- Paris intra muros
- Radials (between A86 and BP)
- Radials (between A86 and Francilienne)
- All urban expressways

Individual motorized transport - Traffic plan - Horizon 2030

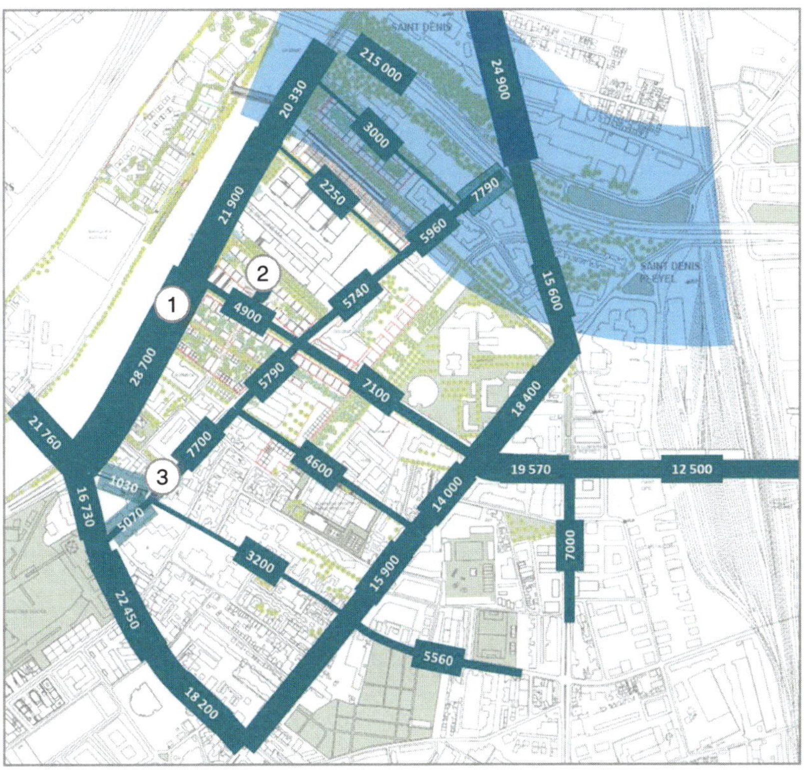

Traffic Horizon 2030

RD1 between 20,330 and 28,700v./d.
Rue Ampère ~5700 v./d.
Rue Nicolau ~5000 v./d.
Rue M.Cahin ~4600 v./d.

1. **Calming** of the RD1 2x1 lane, which still carries high levels of traffic.
2. **Question** the Finot bar between Ampère and RD1, and its definition as a structuring axis (cf.PLD), in light of low traffic levels.
3. **Impact** of two-way traffic on Rue de Saint-Denis (St Ouen)

T estimates by Citec. based on HPM and HPS model data

Existing public transport

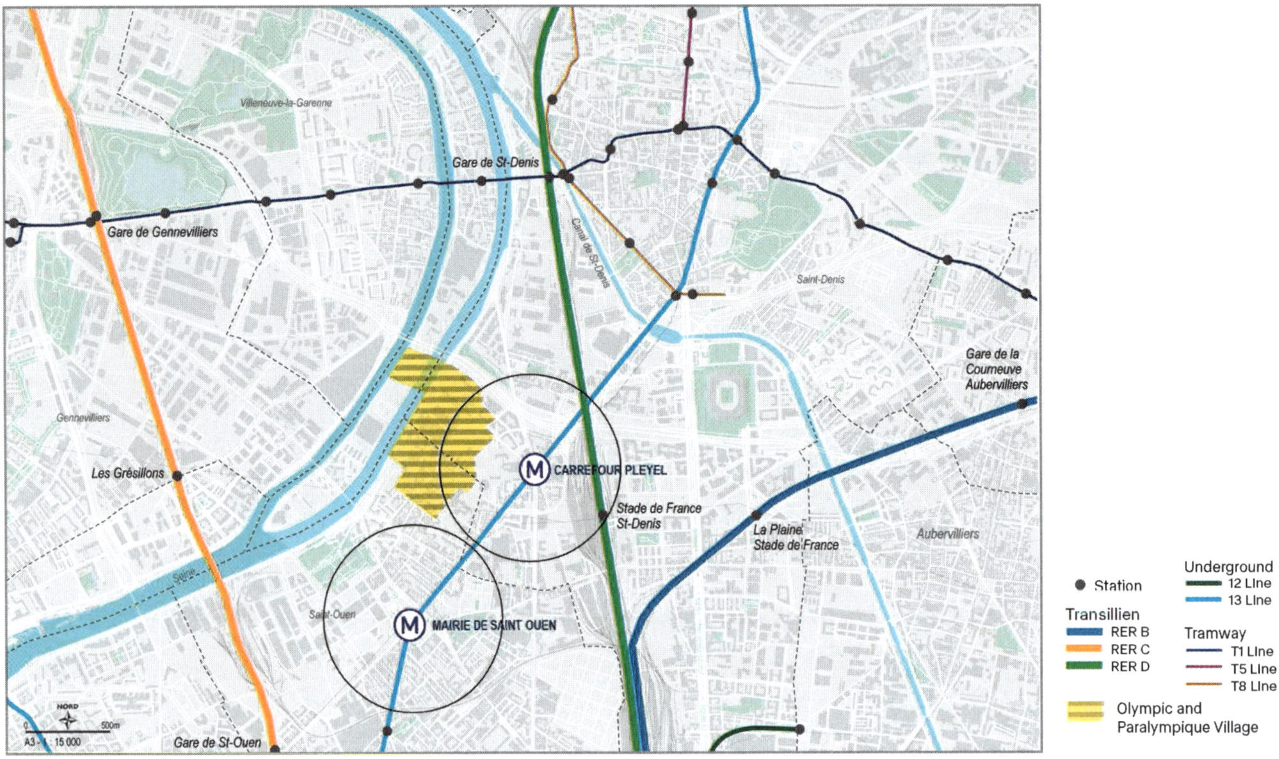

Future public transport

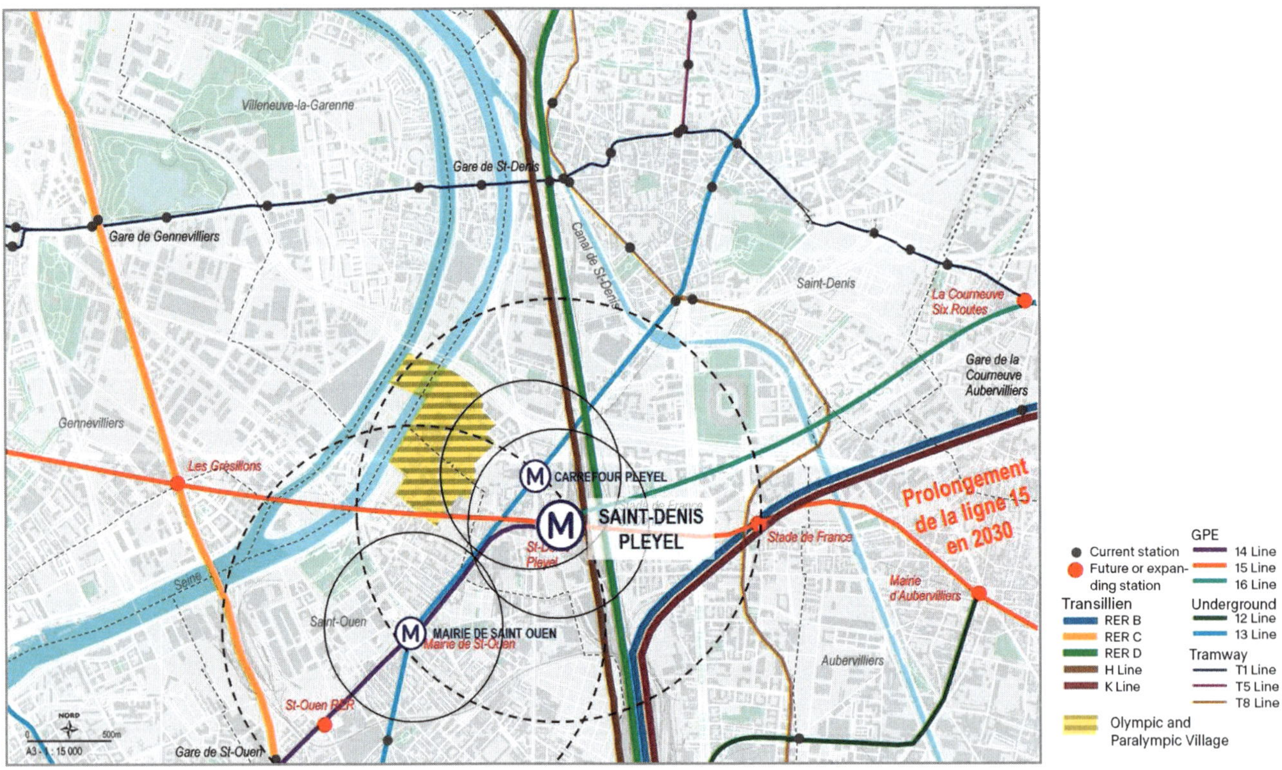

Public transport - Isochrones Pleyel station

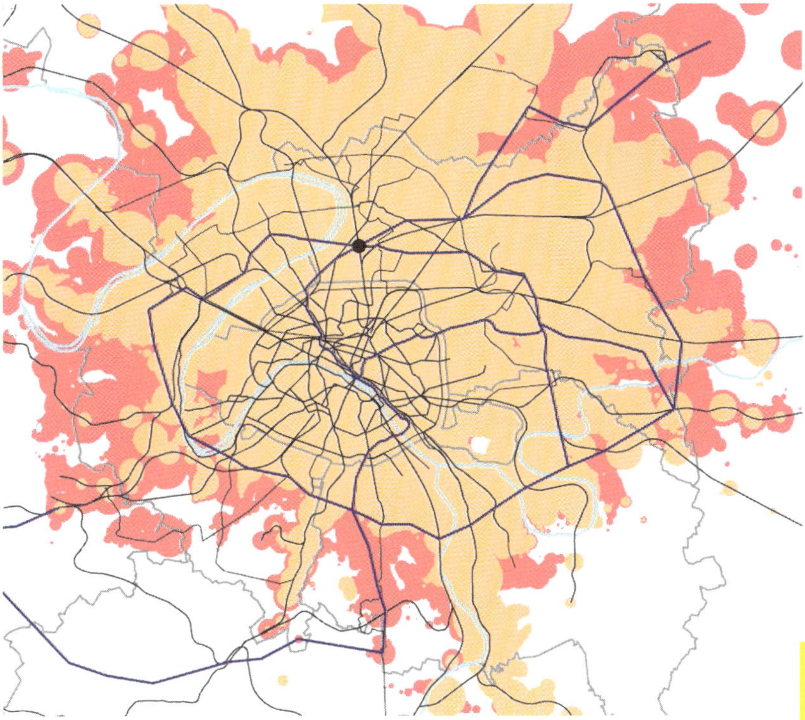

Accessibility areas of the metropolis by main public transport

- RGPE
- other transport networks (train, RER, metro, tramway)
- departure station

Area reachable in less than 45min. from departure station

- 2013
- horizon 2030

The calculation of these isochronous surfaces takes into account an end of journey on foot (5km/h). The isochrone is based on the main public transport station (RER, metro, streetcar or bus) closest to the future station. Projections of accessible jobs in 2030 take into account both improved accessibility and projected job growth.
Sources : DRIEA, SCEP 2013

2013-2030 accessibility trends from Saint-Denis Pleyel station for a a 45-minute journey by public transport :

Territory: +42%

Employment : +36%

Public transport - Saint-Denis Pleyel interchange

250 000 TRIPS
Per day

9 000 INHABITANTS
within a 1km radius of the station

22 000 JOBS
within a 1km radius of the station

27M
quay depth

FASTER JOURNEYS

Saint-Denis Pleyel → La Défense	13 min	versus 27 min today
Saint-Denis Pleyel → Orly Airport	40 min	compared with 1 h 04 today

CONNECTION(S) :

M 14 15 16 17 RER D

#371# AMBITION 7

ACCESSIBLE MOBILITY

Public transport
Existing public transport:

By the time the project is completed (2025), there will be a significant increase in the range of public transport services available, with the creation of the Grand Paris Express Saint-Denis Pleyel station interchange, which is set to become the leading station in Greater Paris in terms of passenger numbers. Its appeal will extend far beyond the 500 metre radius, to match that of an urban train station. With an attractive radius of 1,000 metres, the entire project area is covered.

With the development of the Saint-Denis Pleyel interchange and the construction of the pedestrian-bike-bus bridge to the Ile-de-Saint-Denis, the direct service available to the Village des Athlètes project area will increase significantly. Following the reconfiguration of existing bus routes and the development of new routes.

(Source: Ile-de-France Mobilités)

Public transport - Bus stop project

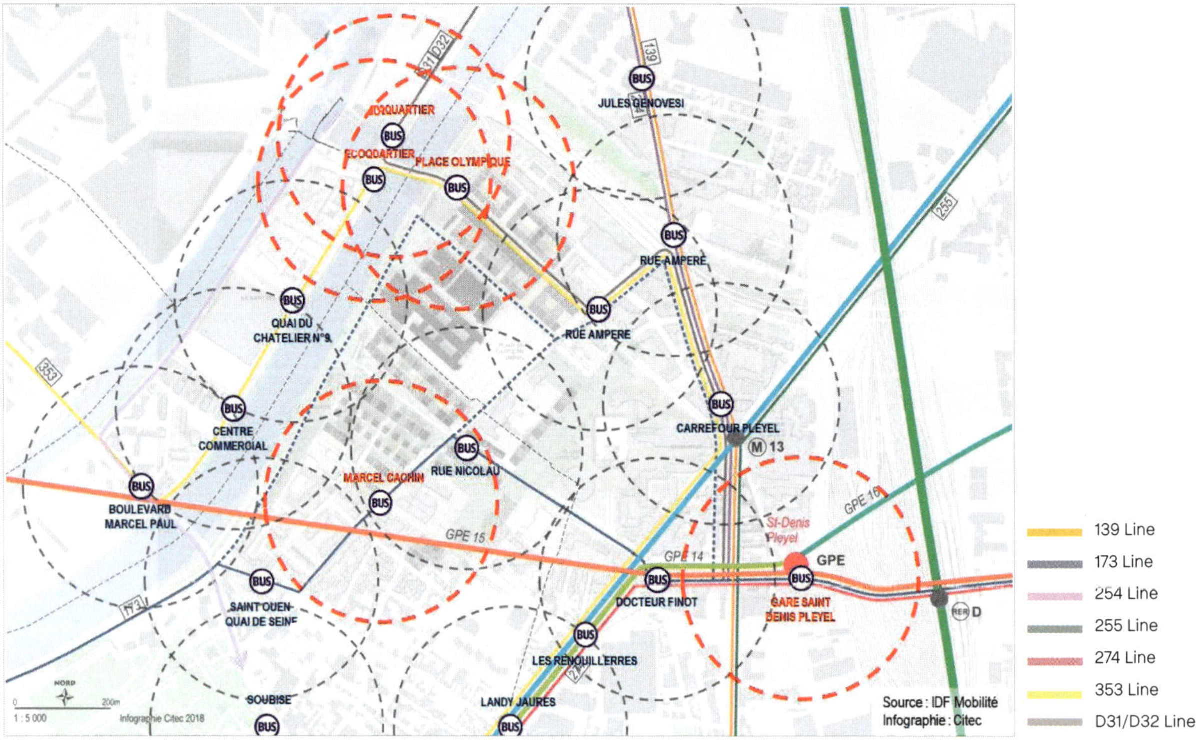

Public transport - Pedestrian metrics

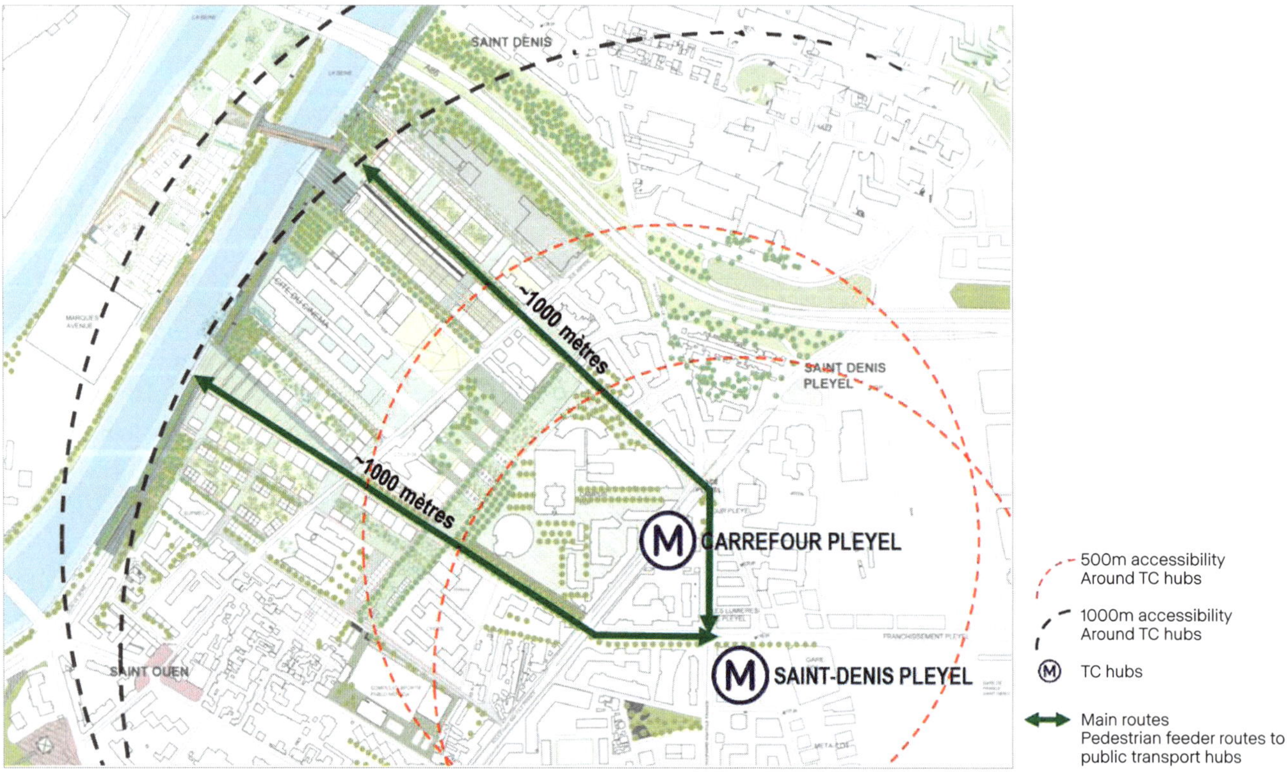

Public transport

Changes in road capacity according to changes in public transit supply

#373# AMBITION 7
ACCESSIBLE MOBILITY
Travel and mobility.

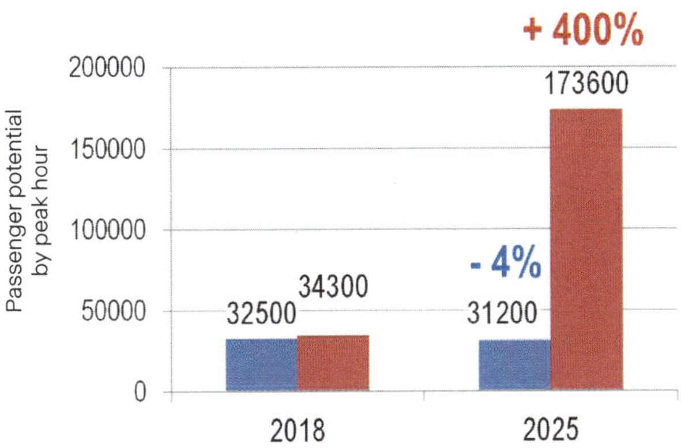

Sum of potential passengers on access roads to the site (existing and future situation).

Sum of potential passengers on metro and bus lines crossing the area (existing and future situation)

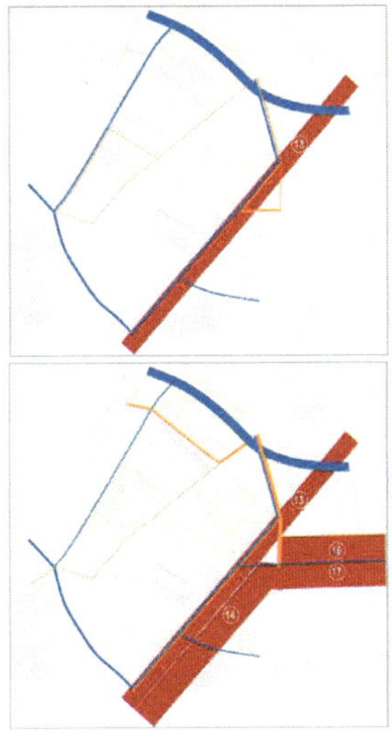

Access roads (in pers/h)

Buses passing through the area (passengers/h)

Subways near the area (passengers/h)

Public transport - Transport - RATP Plan

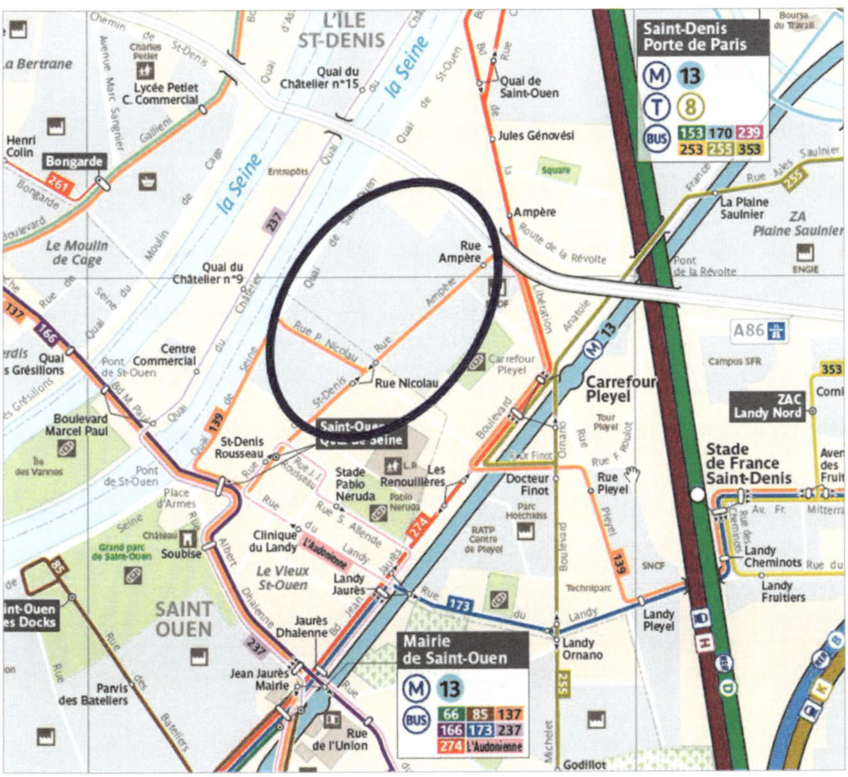

Parking - Modal shares - PDL Plaine commune

Distribution of modes of transport in plaine comune

	DÉPLACEMENTS INTERNES AU TERRITOIRE	DÉPLACEMENTS D'ÉCHANGE AVEC L'EXTÉRIEUR	ENSEMBLE DES DÉPLACEMENTS (HORS TRANSIT)
Marche	68 %	5,9 %	36,3 %
Vélo, deux-roues motorisés	1,8 %	3,9 %	2,9 %
Transports collectifs	12,8 %	50,1 %	31,8 %
Voiture	17,4 %	40,1 %	29 %

Source : PLD Plaine Commune

Modal shift in plaine comune, excluding transit

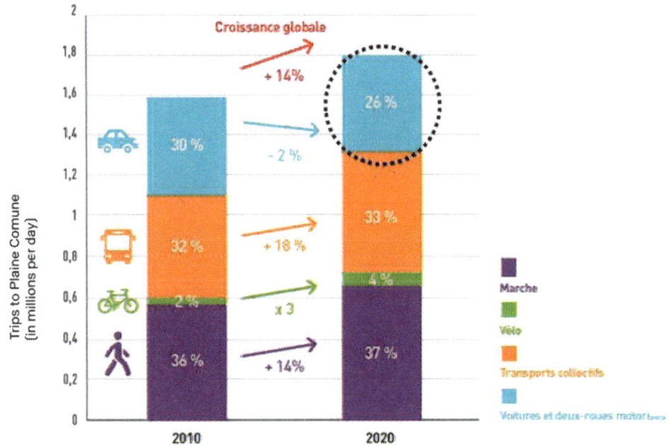

A target of 26% modal share for cars and two-wheelers motorized two-wheelers territory of Plaine Commune territory, which requiresto be more restrictive car use in neighborhoods with good public transportation.

Parking - Assumptions - Parking estimates

Parking

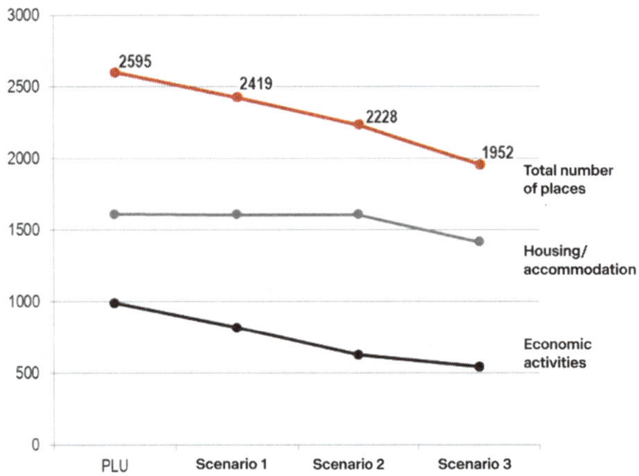

		PLU	Hyp 1	Hyp 2	Hyp 3
housing accession	pl/log	0.7	0.7	0.7	0.6
social housing	pl/log	0.5	0.5	0.5	0.4
hotel, social houses	chambre/pl	4	4	4	4
St-Denis offices	m2/pl	135	150	200	250
St-Ouen offices	m2/pl	150	150	200	250
activities	m2/pl	50	80	100	100

Modal share - France

Modal share of cars in major french conurbations based on EMD data

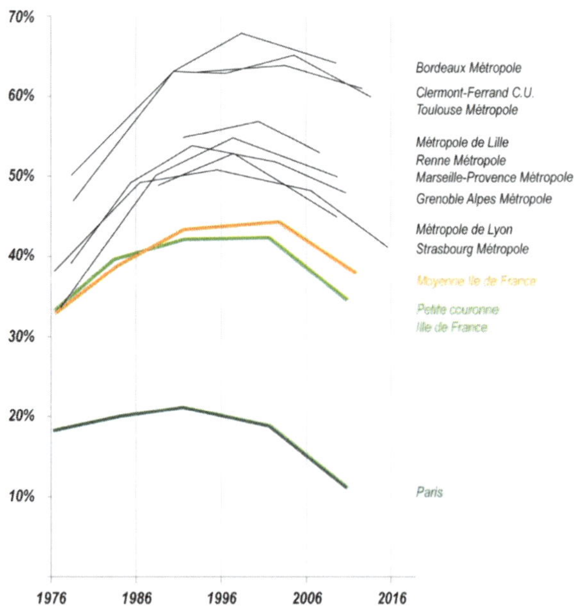

Road network scenario - Minimum accessibility

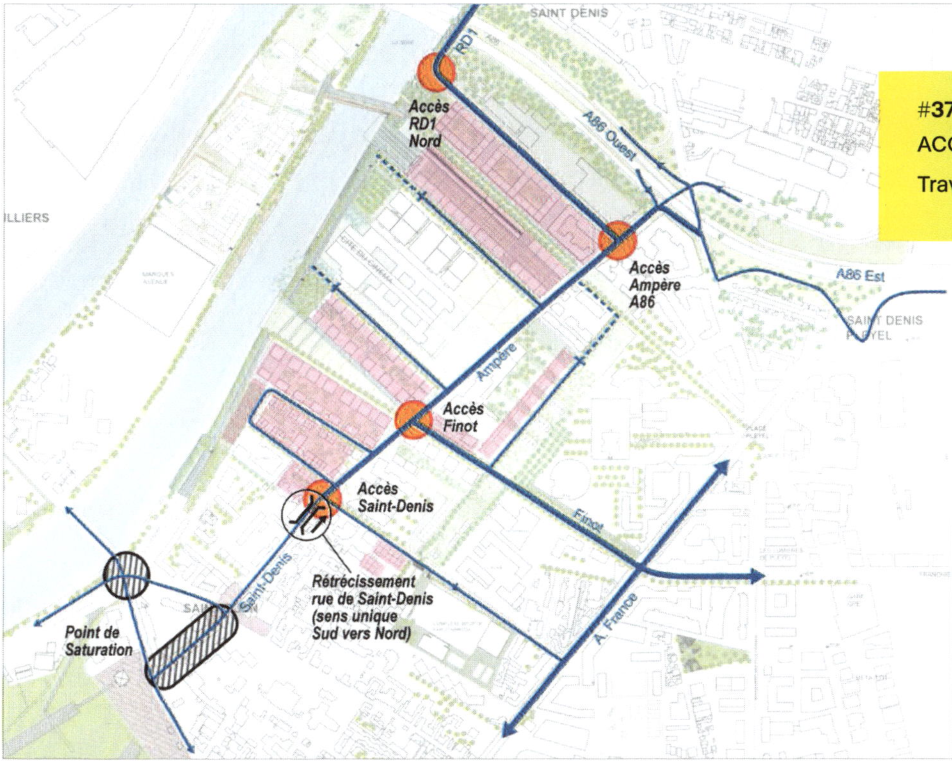

#375# **AMBITION 7**

ACCESSIBLE MOBILITY

Travel and mobility.

Road network scenario - Scenario 25 Hoppers

Active mobility - Active modes - Public spaces

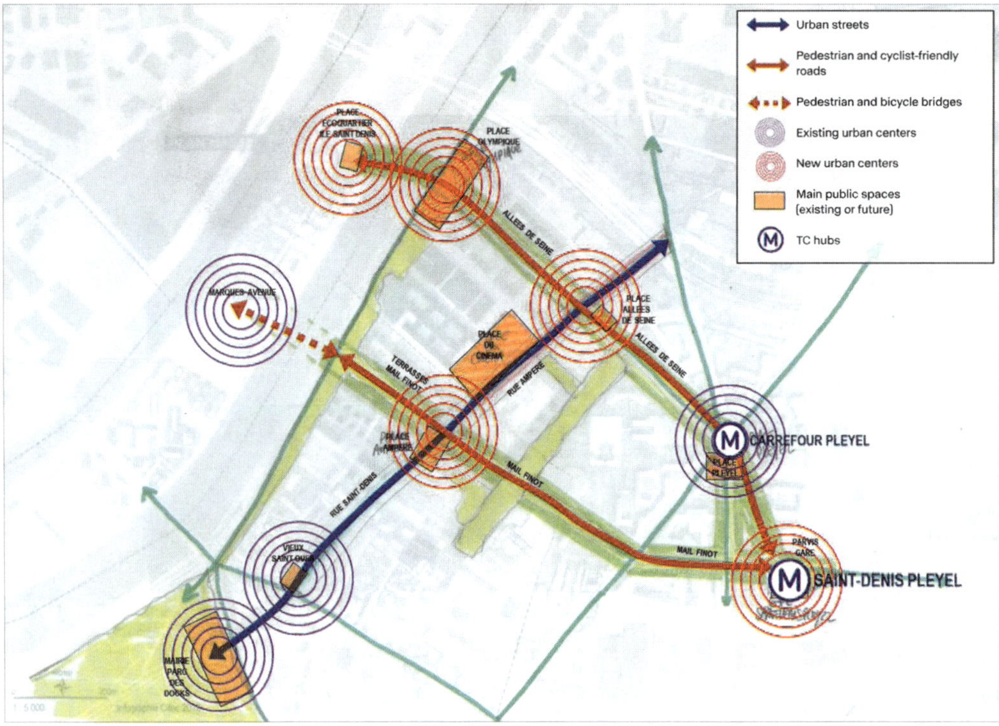

Active mobility - Active modes - Green public spaces

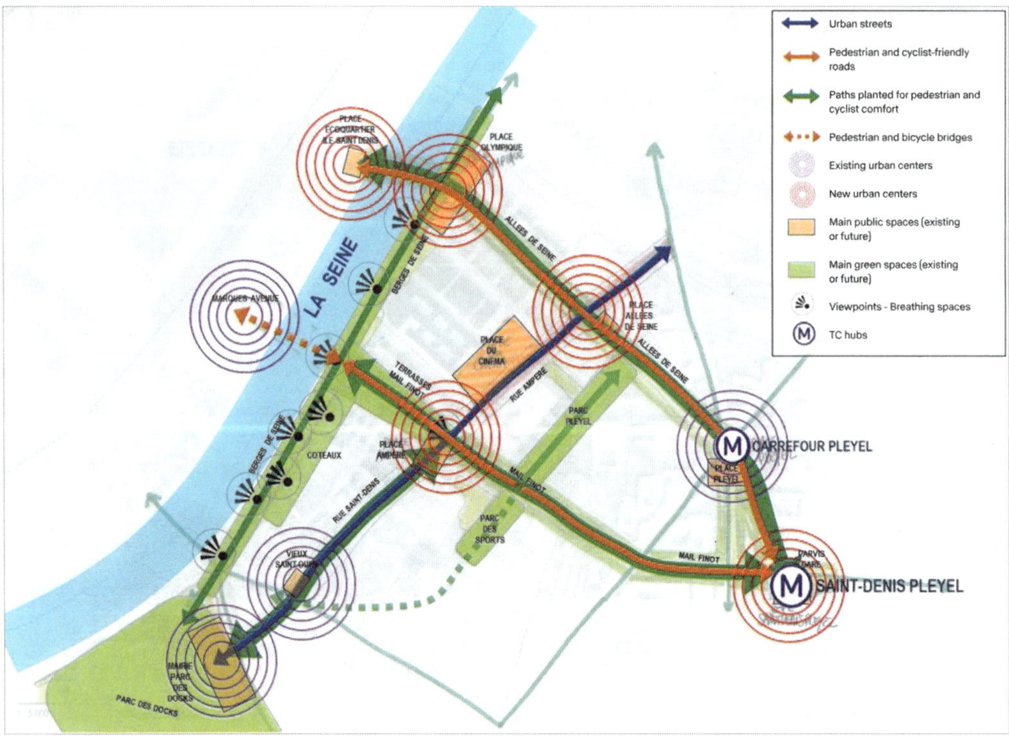

Active mobility - Cycle routes

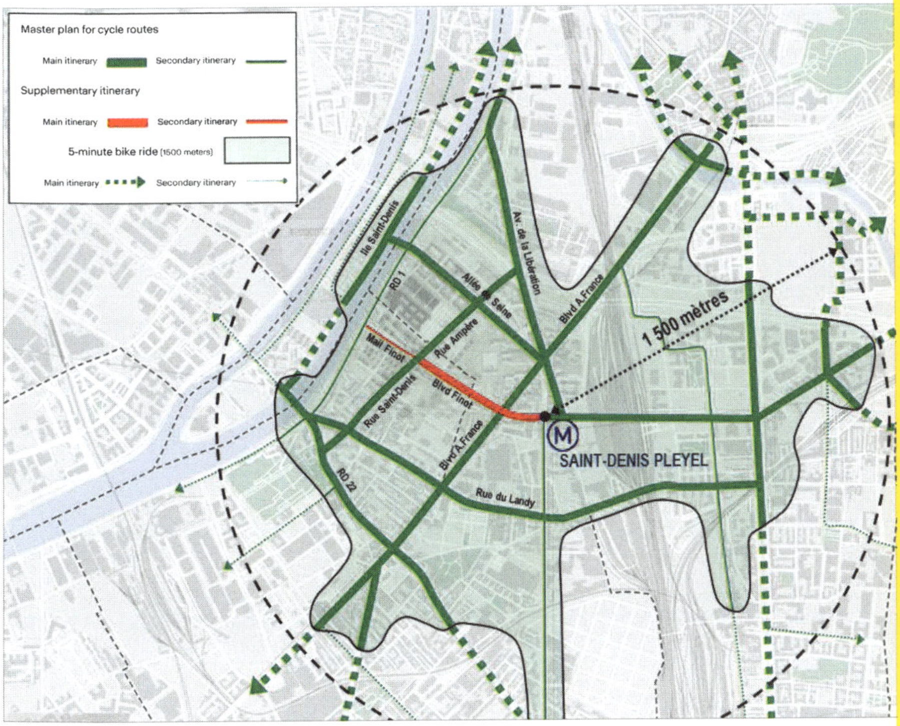

Active mobility - Active modes - Distance/Time

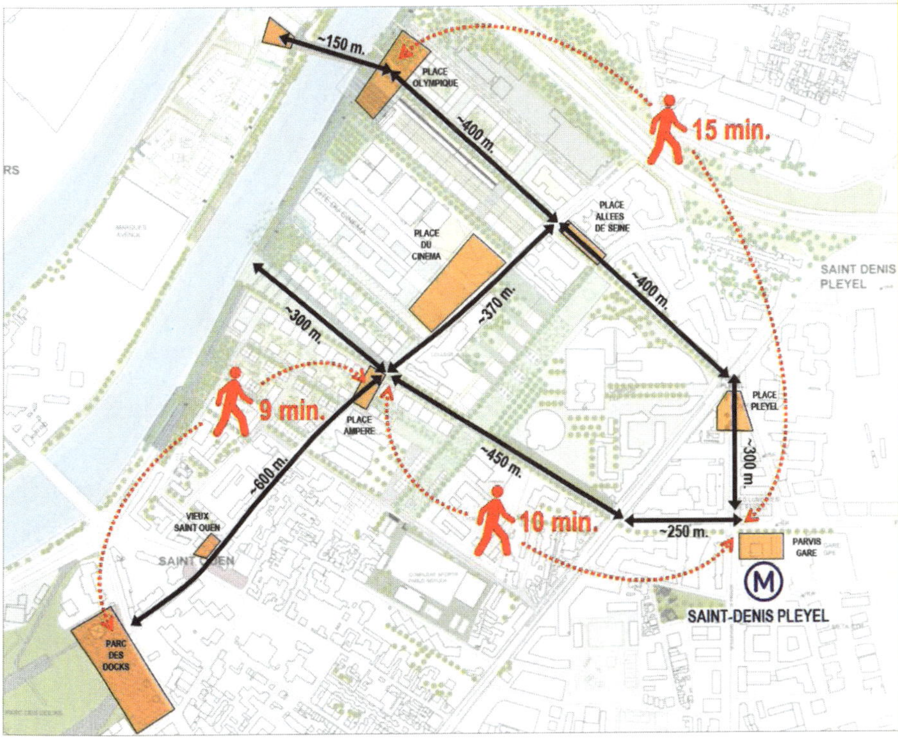

#377# AMBITION 7
ACCESSIBLE MOBILITY

15-minute city

Accessibility by bicycle: The conditions for travel by active modes, i.e. walking and cycling, are at the heart of the definition of the urban project.

All the roads have comfortable pavements and cycle facilities adapted to the different types of roads. The entire project is less than 5 minutes by bicycle from the Saint-Denis Pleyel interchange.

Cycling remains a strategic means of getting to and from inter-neighbourhood links and public transport services. The Master Plan for Cycle Facilities provides for a dense network of cycle routes within a radius of 1,500 metres around the Saint-Denis Pleyel interchange, allowing for a 5-minute cycle journey. Cyclists will also be able to return to the station over longer distances. To strengthen the network of cycle routes, a two-way cycle lane will be added in the extension of boulevard Finot, between boulevard Anatole France and rue Ampère.

A secondary cycle route will be added on the rue des Quinconces between the rue Ampère and the RD1, in connection with the development of the banks of the Seine. Cycle lanes are planned on rue Ampère, as well as a two-way cycle lane on rue Volta.

BIODIVERSITY AREA

#379# AMBITION 7
ACCESSIBLE MOBILITY
A city for all.

Mail Finot - Ramp perspectives

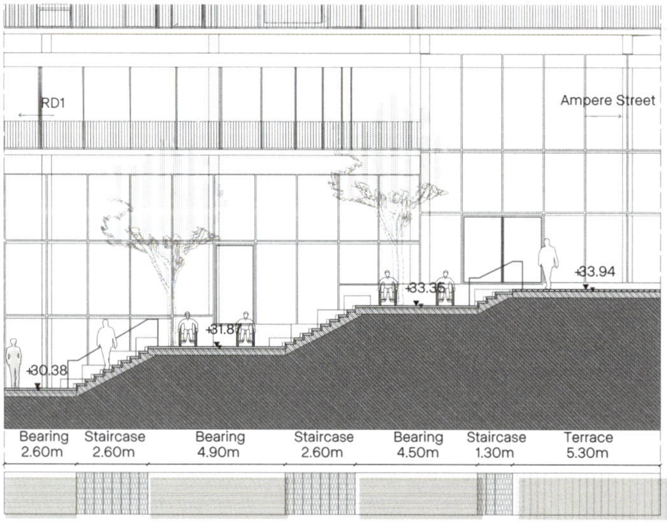

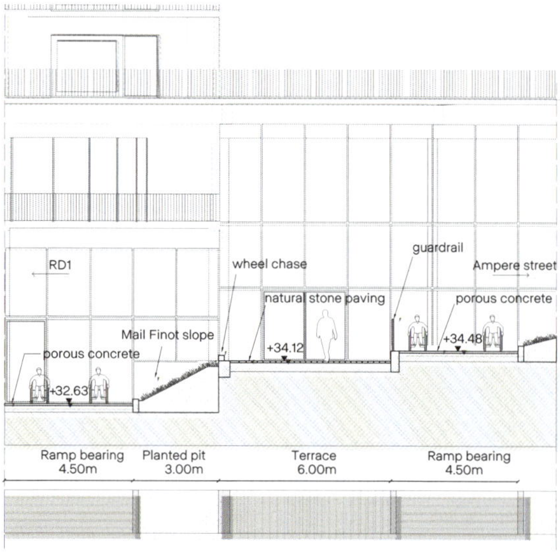

#381# **AMBITION 7**

ACCESSIBLE MOBILITY

Travel and mobility.

Ramps - details

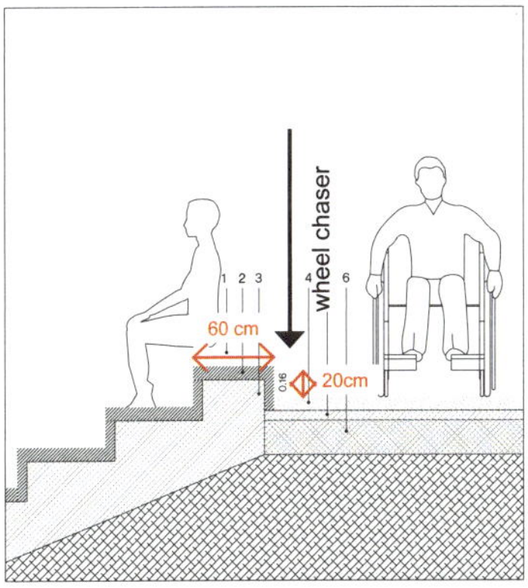

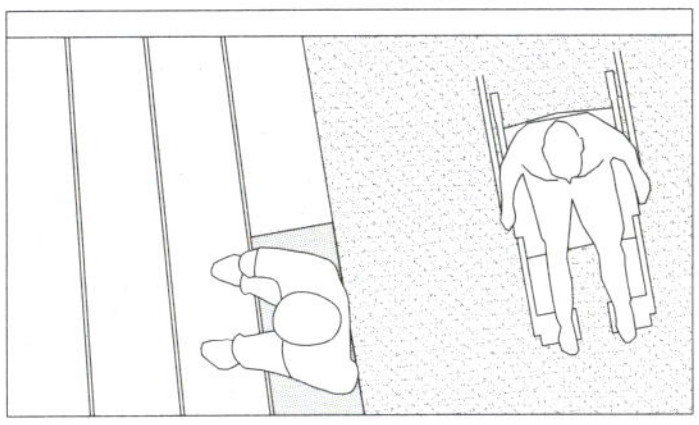

LEGEND DET SP 05.01

1 - Wooden seat, one-off element
2 - Finishing concrete steps
3 - Concrete stepped structure
4 - Porous concrete 8cm
5 - Base 4cm
6 - Ramp structure

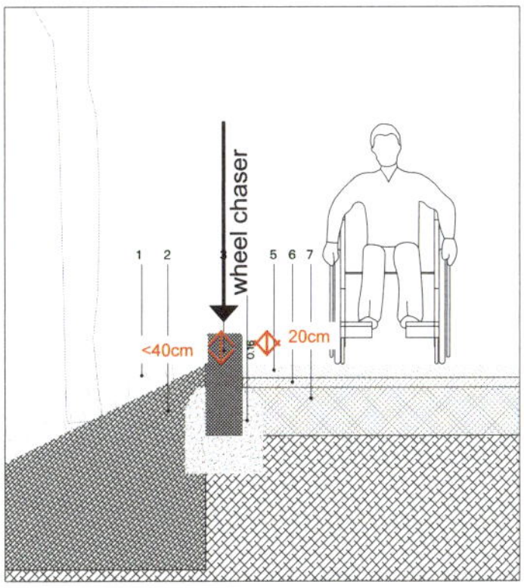

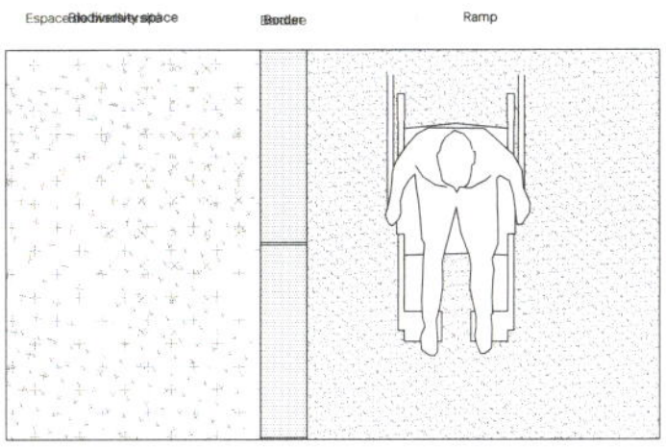

LEGEND DET SP 05.03

1 - Plantes area
2 - Top soil
3 - Border 20x50cm
4 - Border support
5 - Porous concrete 8cm
6 - Base 4cm
7 - Ramp structure

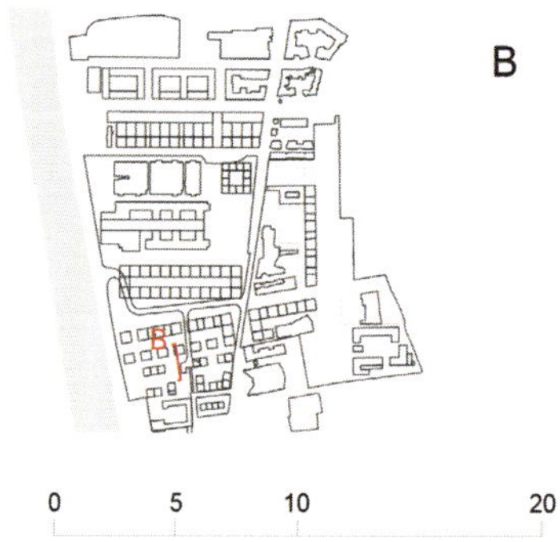

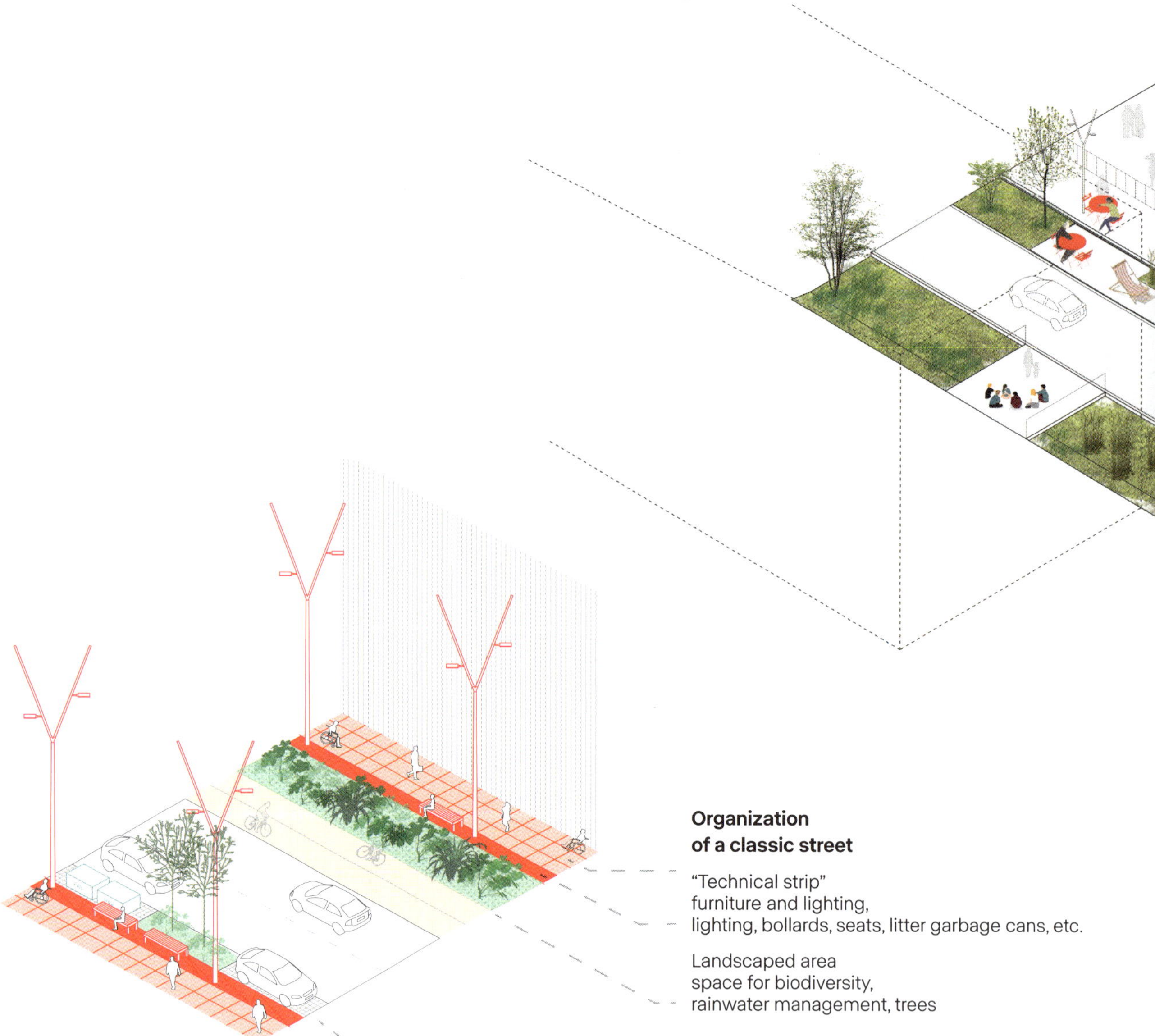

Organization of a classic street

"Technical strip"
furniture and lighting,
lighting, bollards, seats, litter garbage cans, etc.

Landscaped area
space for biodiversity,
rainwater management, trees

Service band
parking for cars, 2-wheelers and bicycles, recharging stations, recycling bins, etc.

#383# AMBITION 7

ACCESSIBLE MOBILITY

A city for all.

The hillside alleys.

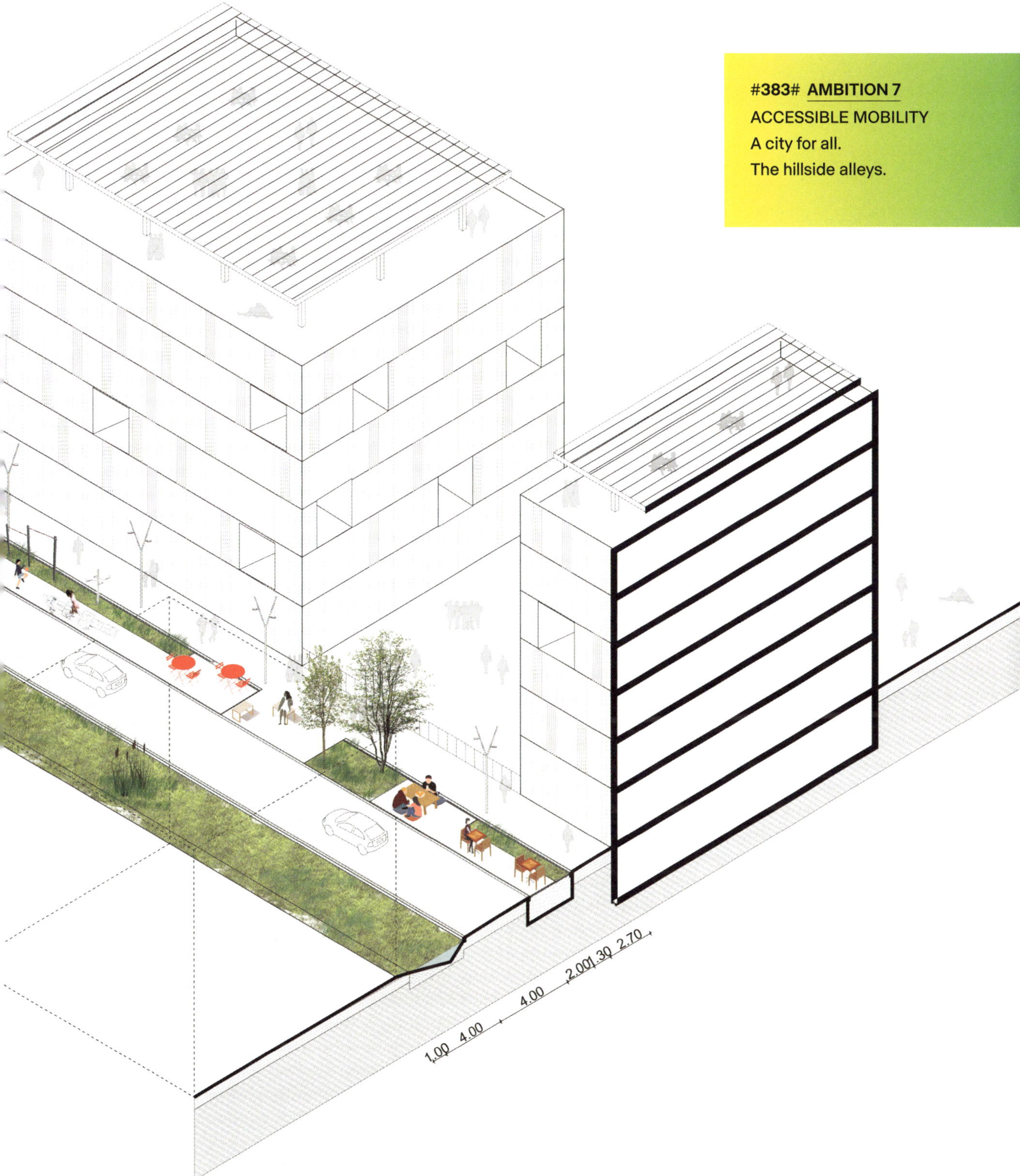

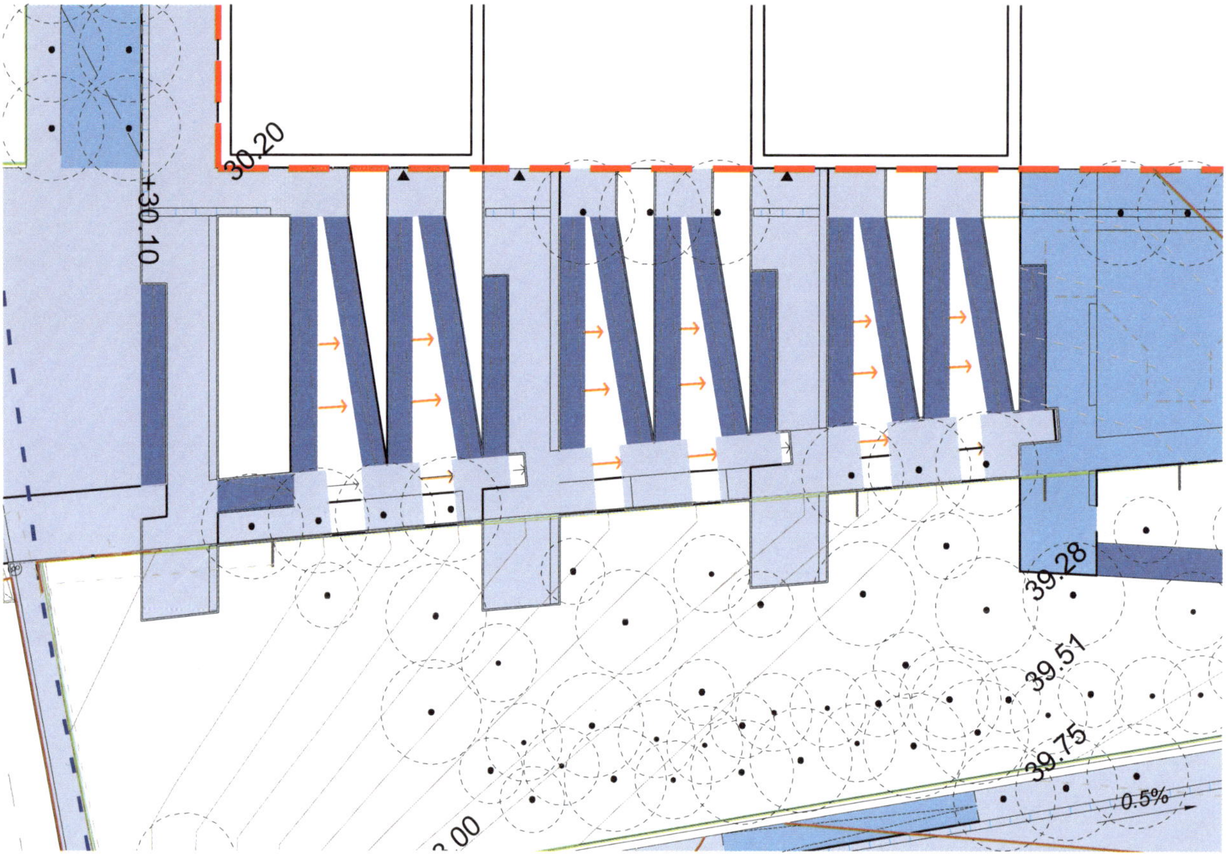
30.20
+30.10
39.28
39.51
39.75
0.5%

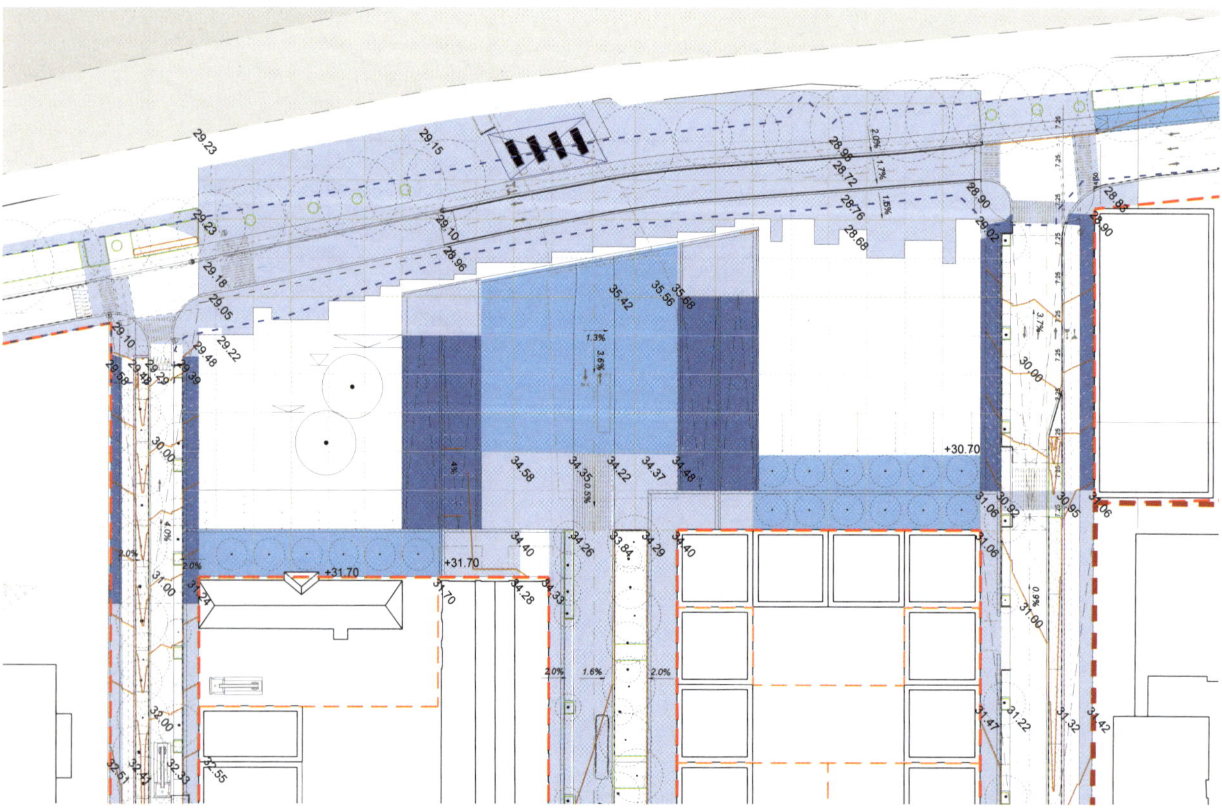
29.23
29.15
28.95
28.72
28.76
28.68
28.90
29.02
28.85
28.90
29.23
29.10
28.96
29.18
29.05
29.22
29.10
29.48
29.39
35.42
35.56
35.68
1.3%
3.6%
34.58
34.35
34.22
34.37
34.48
+30.70
31.06
30.92
30.95
31.06
30.00
34.40
34.26
33.84
34.29
34.40
+31.70
+31.70
31.70
34.28
34.33
31.08
31.00
31.00
2.0%
1.6%
2.0%
32.00
32.51
32.41
32.33
32.55
31.47
31.22
31.32
31.42

Active mobility - Cycling routes

#385# AMBITION 7

ACCESSIBLE MOBILITY

A city for all.
The alleys at the top of the hill.

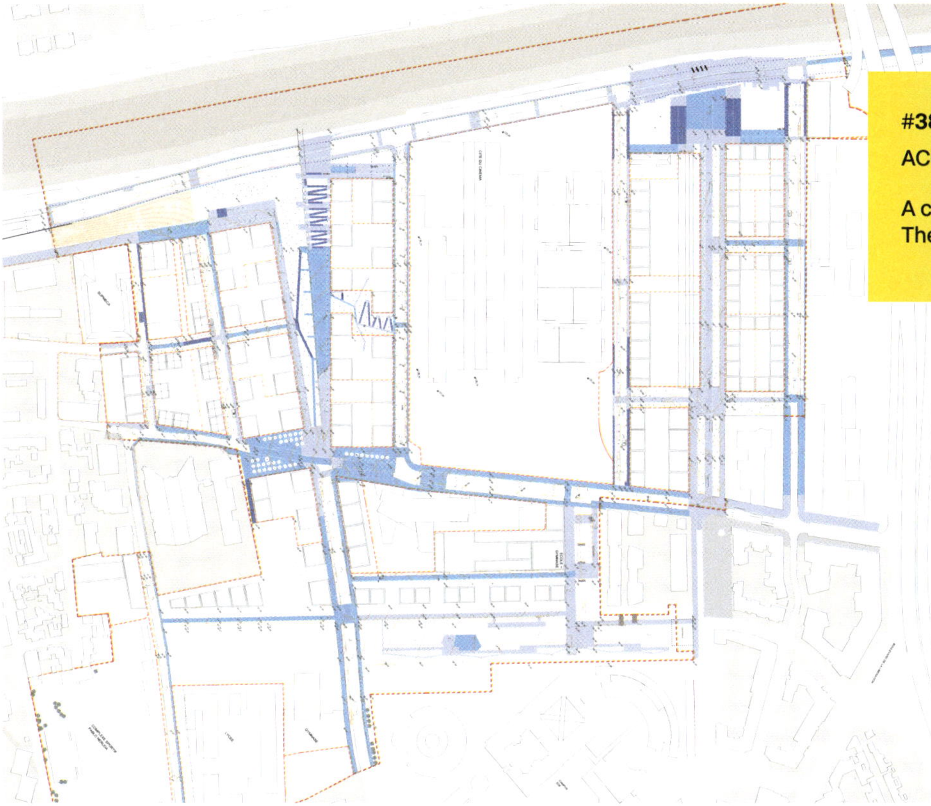

Accessibility

- Slope %
- Slope between 2% and 3%
- Slope less than 1%.

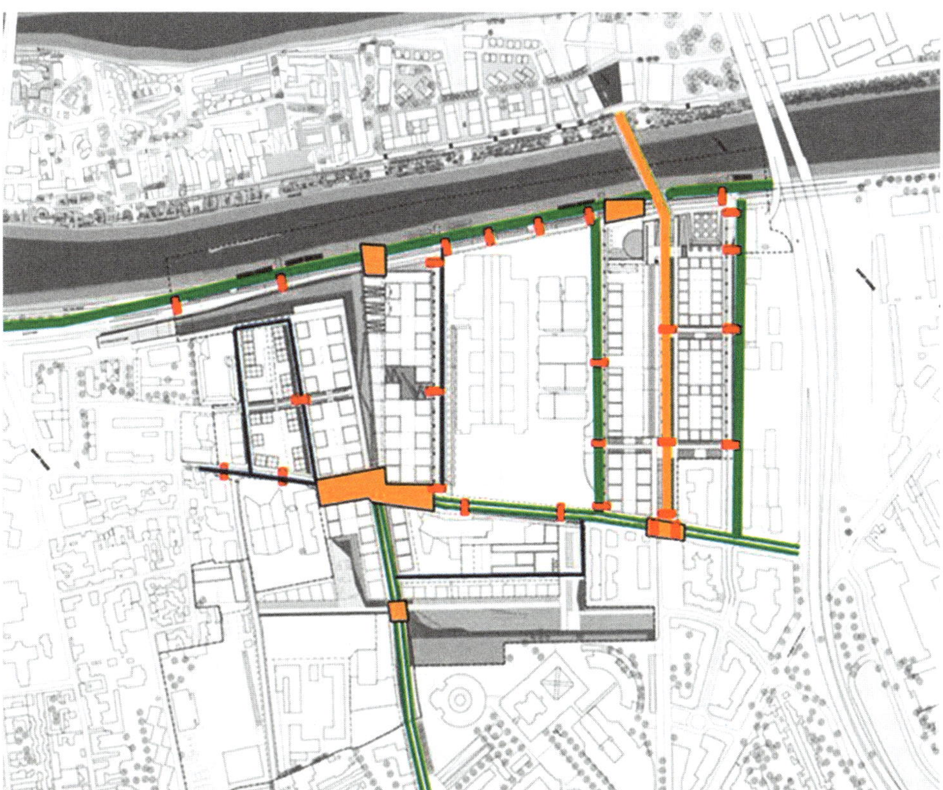

- Two-way cycle path
- Bilateral bike lanes

#387# AMBITION 7

ACCESSIBLE MOBILITY

A city for all
Olympic mobility.

TERRASSE
PLEYEL EN SEINE

#389# **AMBITION 7**

ACCESSIBLE MOBILITY

A city for all
Olympic mobility.

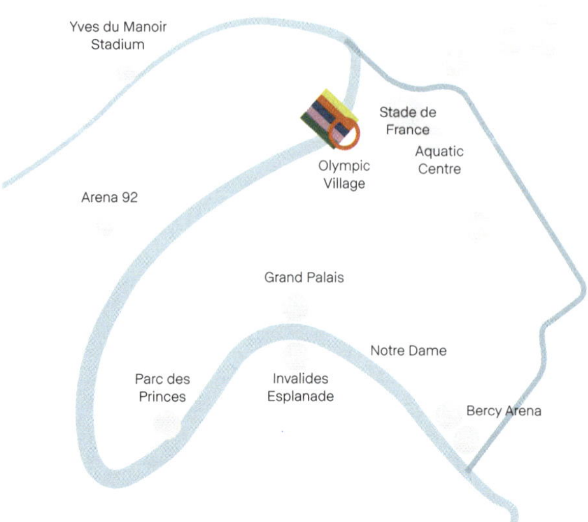
Yves du Manoir
Stadium
Stade de
France
Aquatic
Centre
Olympic
Village
Arena 92
Grand Palais
Notre Dame
Parc des
Princes
Invalides
Esplanade
Bercy Arena

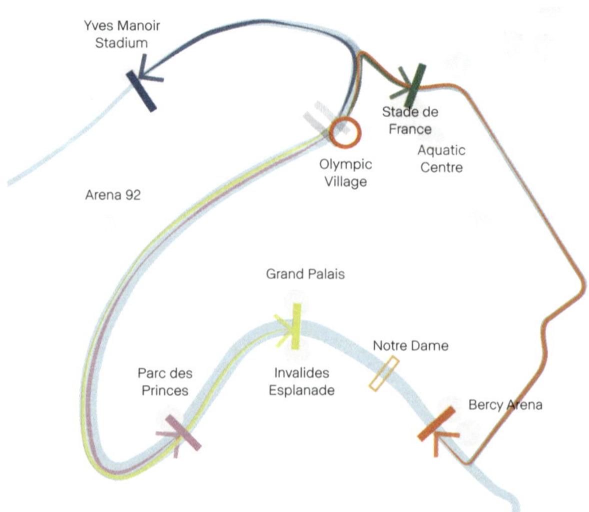
Yves Manoir
Stadium
Stade de
France
Aquatic
Centre
Olympic
Village
Arena 92
Grand Palais
Notre Dame
Parc des
Princes
Invalides
Esplanade
Bercy Arena

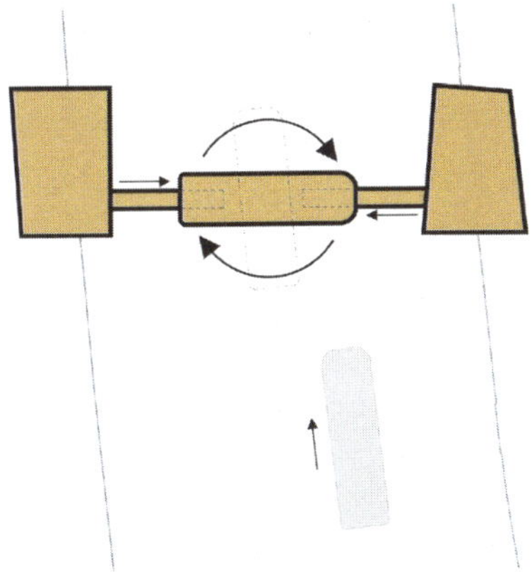

#391# **AMBITION 7**

ACCESSIBLE MOBILITY

A city for all
Olympic mobility.

The bridge boats
Imagine a floating, itinerant project house: During the construction period, the project house could be set up on the Seine opposite Notre-Dame on the Ile de la Cité, for example. The barge can be deployed as a bridge to link the two banks.

The barge is designed as a modular platform to accommodate the project house, transport passengers, generate energy, treat, and store water, collect waste, and so on. It is the floating showcase for the future district.

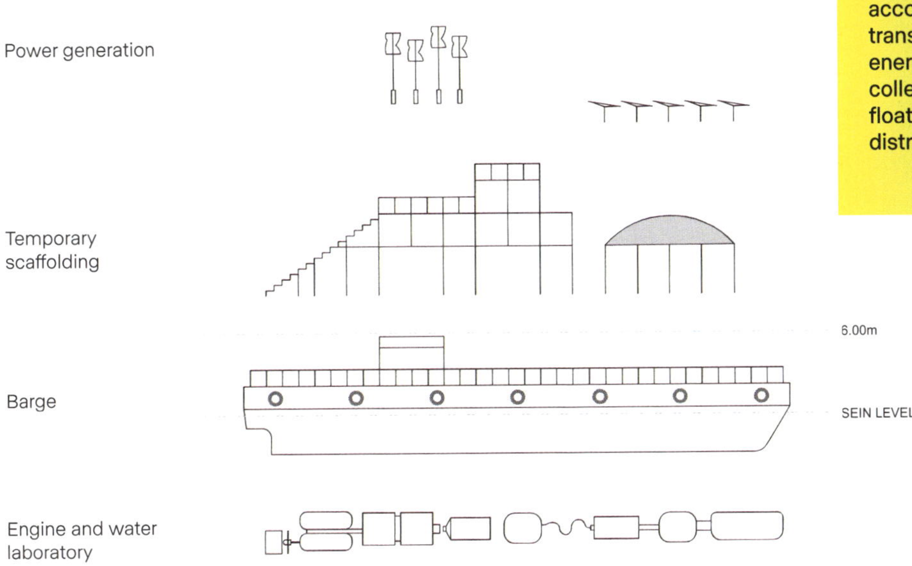

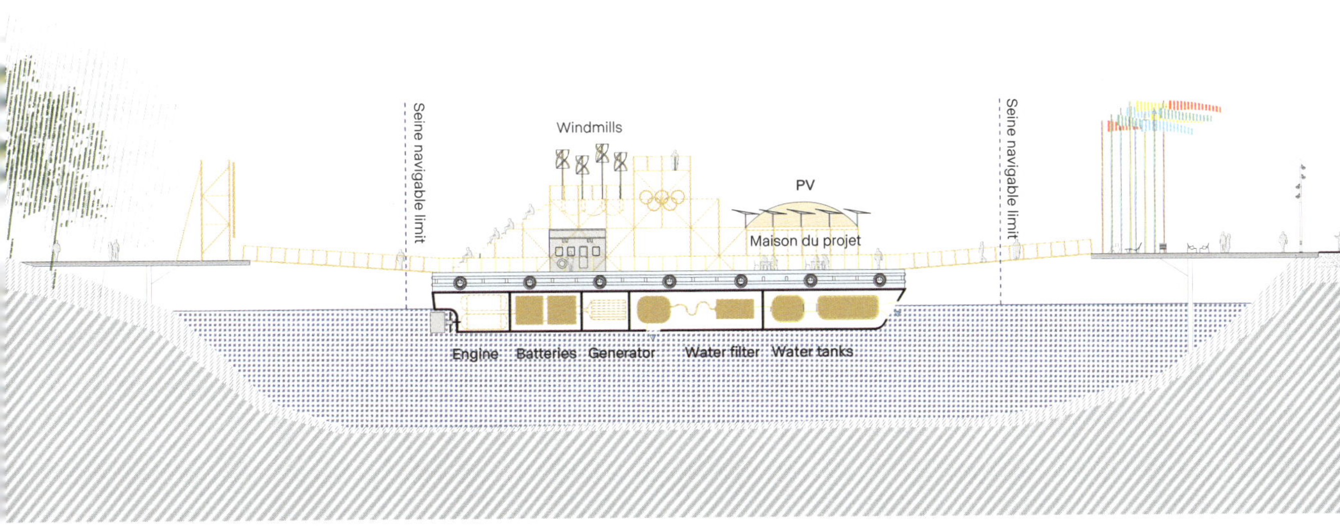

What if there was a cable network connecting the Stadium, the Isle of Vannes and the Village?
Parc des Chanteraines
Gennevilliers
TO
Village Olympique
Île Saint Denis
TO
TO
How can we turn this constraint into a vector for social cohesion?

#393# **AMBITION 7**

ACCESSIBLE MOBILITY

A city for all - Olympic mobility.
The A86 and its double

#395# **AMBITION 7**

ACCESSIBLE MOBILITY

A city for all - Olympic mobility.

Parking lots and their doubles.

#397#

AMBITION 8

WATER AND SOIL

What would the Athletes' Village be without the Seine?

As a major element in the design process, the relationship with the Seine is dealt with through architecture, urban planning and urban programming, but also - and perhaps above all - through the physical relationship with the river. Water in the city is a subject that has accompanied developments in urban planning from the very beginning, from its control to direct its flow and floods to its banishment and relegation to the sewer and relegated to sewers and layered plumbing networks.

Connecting with the land means reopening the ground to allow rain to infiltrate and reach the watercourse: a system of basins, ditches and diversion bays is set up to support and restore the water's gravitational movement towards the river.

This first hydric act, facilitated by the design of the streets, is a piece that takes its place in the entire imaginary of the river in the city: that of the barges and their use as a historic transport network, echoing the ambitious opening ceremony of the Olympic Games, but also that of bathing and crossings. The whole project revolves around water, demonstrating that far from the hygienic fears of our forebears, water in the city is a breath of fresh air.

ILE DE VANNES
GUINGUETTE

#399# AMBITION 8

WATER AND SOIL

The tip of the island: reaching the village by river.

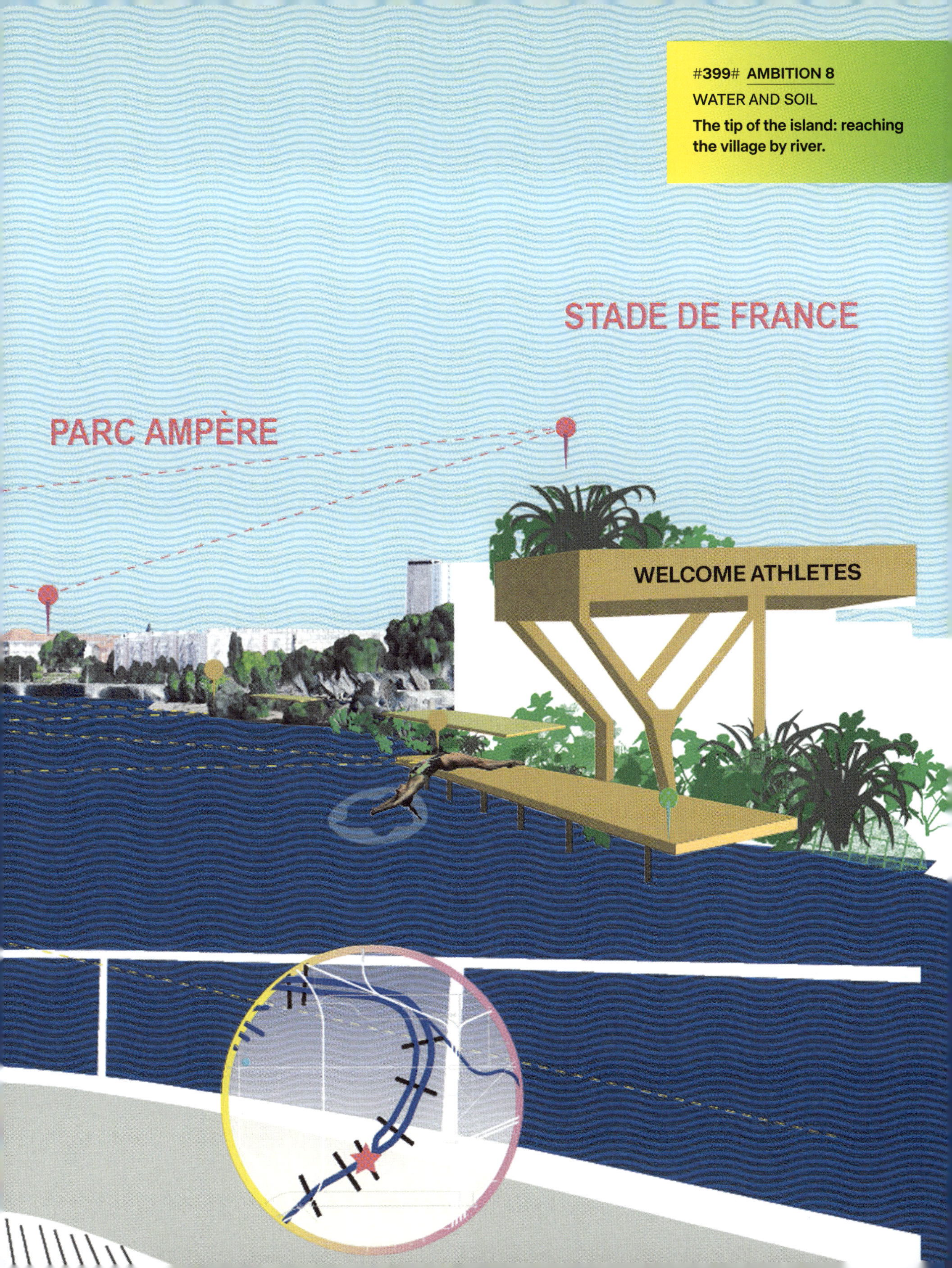

#401# AMBITION 8

WATER AND SOIL

The Seine, one river

The Athletes' Village is set on either side of a major river, deeply linked to the image of Paris and Greater Paris. Winding its way through the metropolis, the Seine borders the municipalities of Saint-Ouen-sur-Seine, Saint-Denis, L'Ile-Saint-Denis and Gennevilliers.

This first-rate landscape component is a precious asset for the lives of the area's athletes and future residents. It is a major asset, as are the gently sloping topography and distant views.

#403# **AMBITION 8**

WATER AND SOIL

The Seine: from island to island

The Seine establishes a physical and imaginary link between the Ile de la Cité, the historic heart of Paris, and the Ile-Saint-Denis. Because of the waterfront location of the Athletes' Village and the choice to hold the opening ceremony of the Games on the Seine, these two islands will be linked by the importance that will be given to the river throughout the Olympic event and, in the longer term, by the reclamation of their banks.

ECOQUARTIER FLUVIAL
ILE DES VANNES
OLYMPIC PLACE
CITÉ DU CINÉMA

#405# AMBITION 8
WATER AND SOIL
Study model. Integration into the surrounding area.

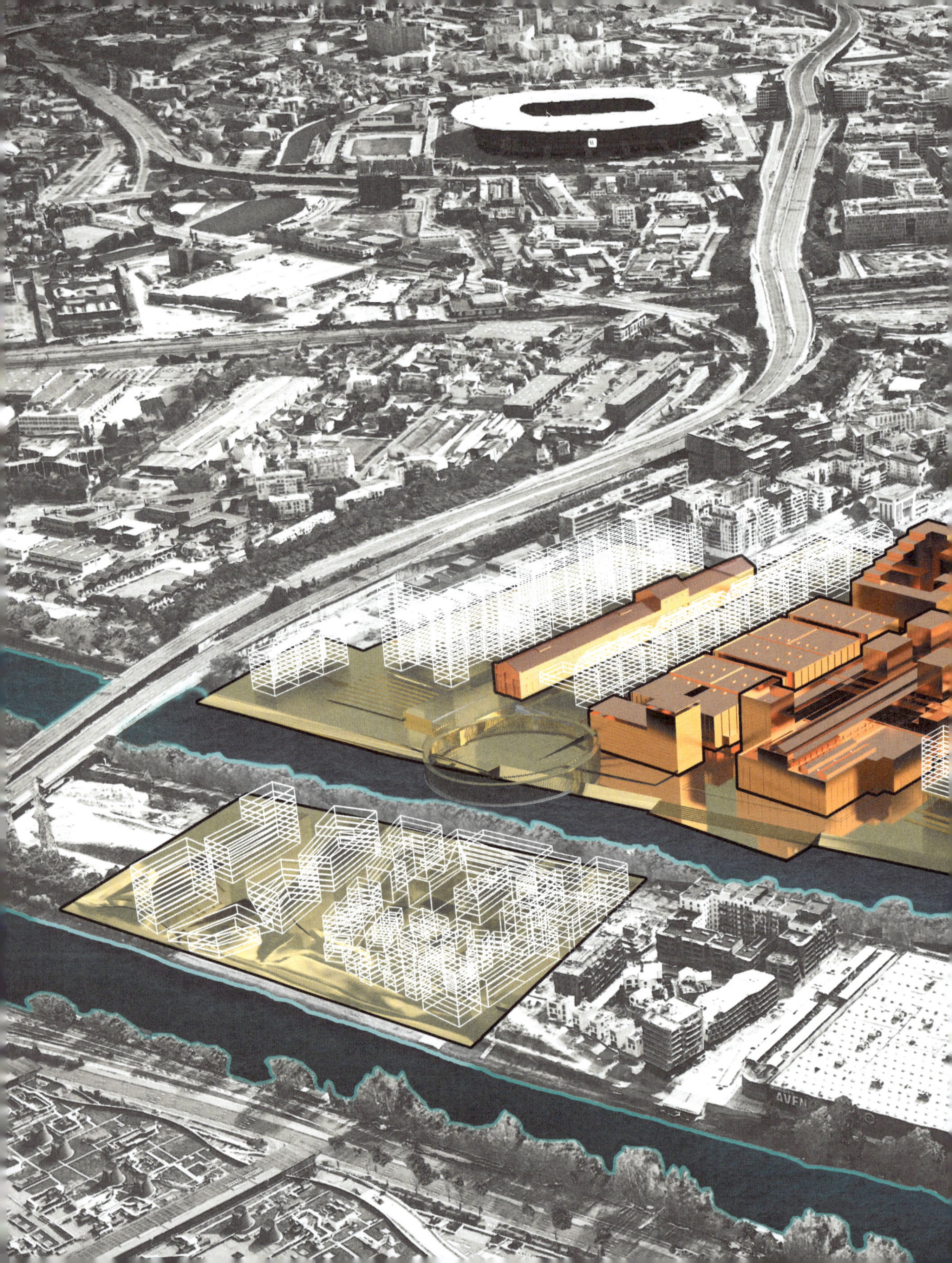

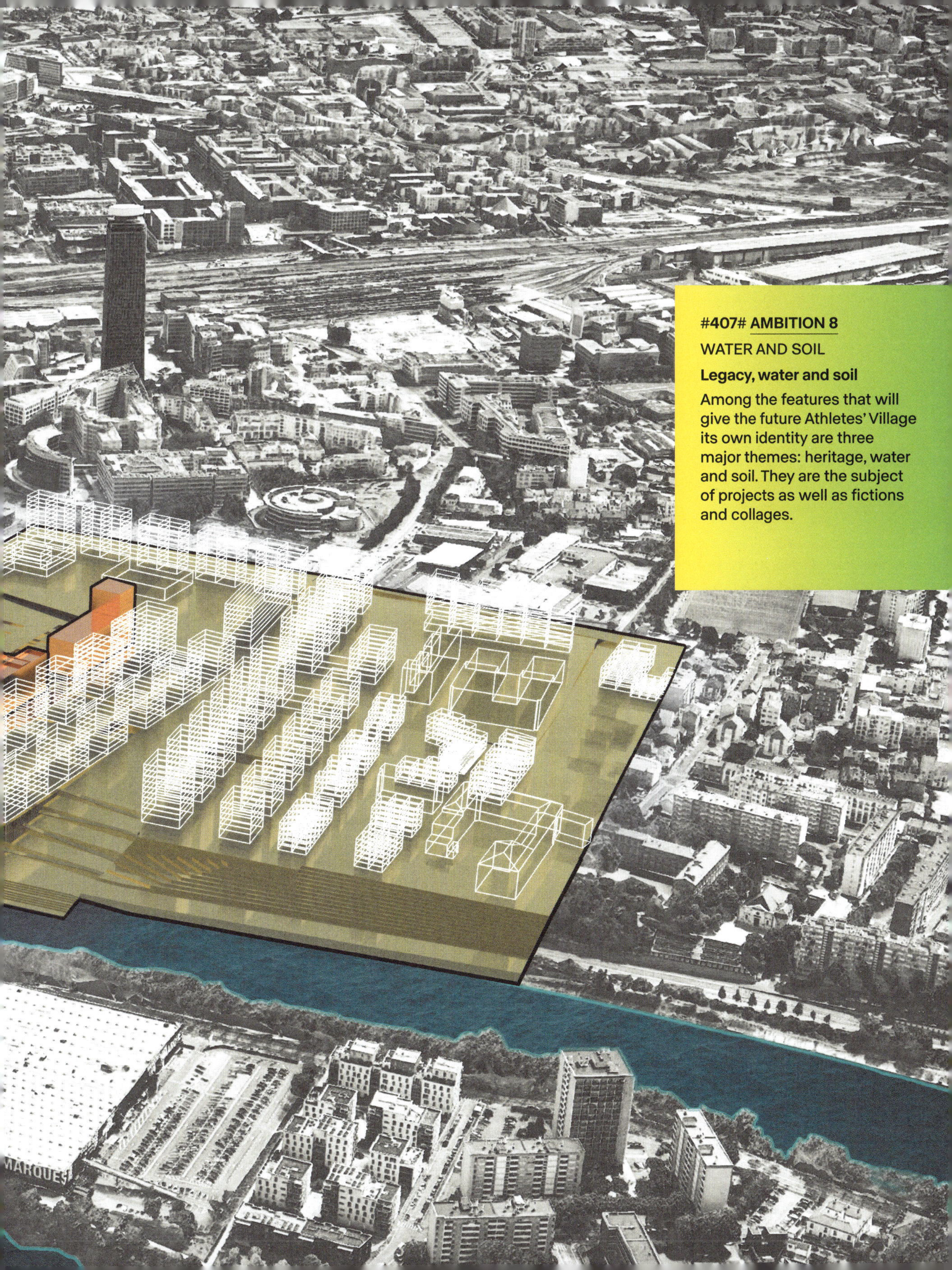

#407# **AMBITION 8**

WATER AND SOIL

Legacy, water and soil

Among the features that will give the future Athletes' Village its own identity are three major themes: heritage, water and soil. They are the subject of projects as well as fictions and collages.

la guinguette olympique

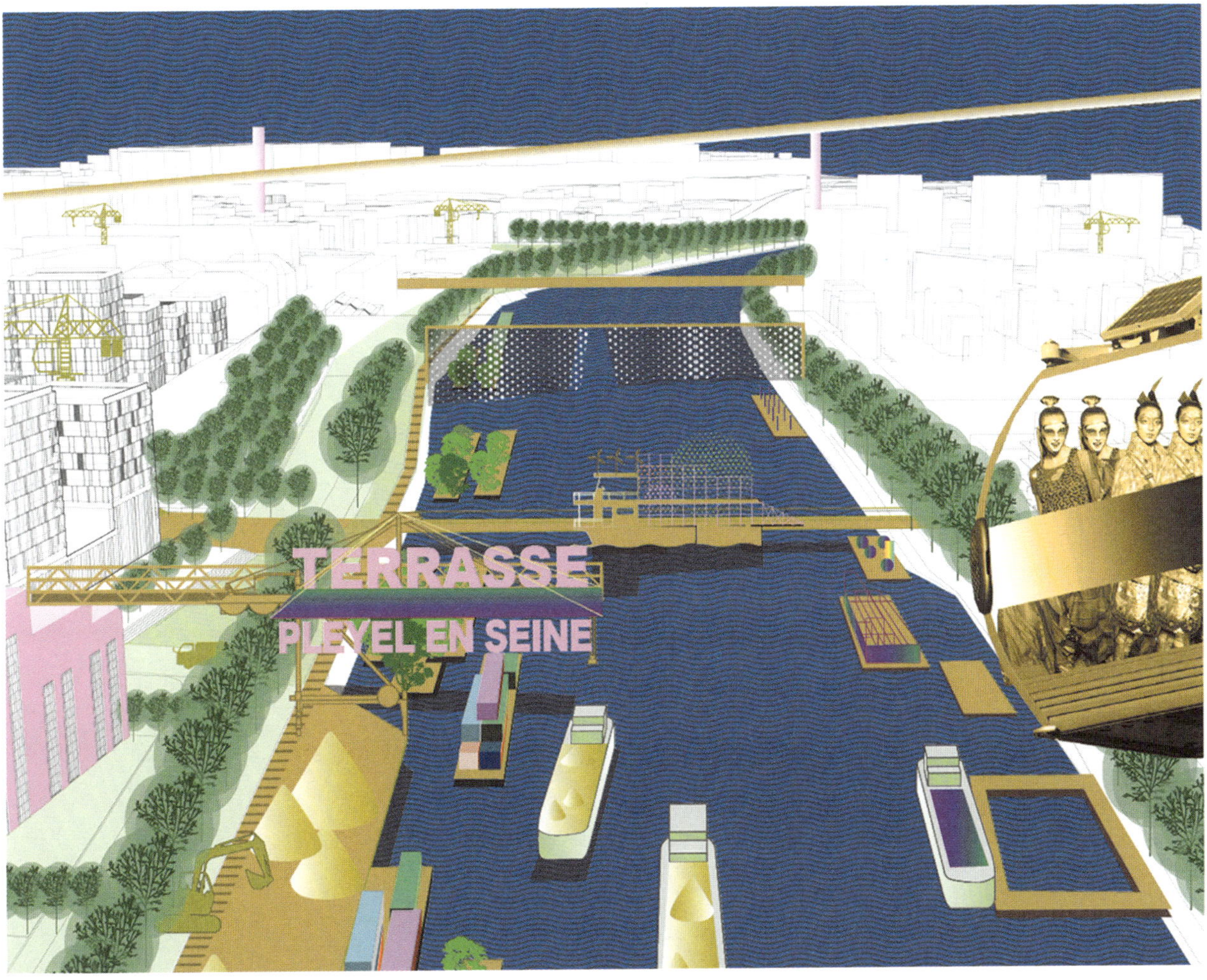
TERRASSE
PLEYEL EN SEINE

M3

#411# **AMBITION 8**

WATER AND SOIL

The Seine.

PARIS
Paris 2024

#413# **AMBITION 8**

WATER AND SOIL

The Seine.

The Athletes' Experience.
The Olympic Village
Square and Les Berges.

#415# **AMBITION 8**

WATER AND SOIL

The olympic Seine.

#417# AMBITION 8

WATER AND SOIL

The Seine.

Athletes' Place.
View from Ile-Saint-Denis.

#419# **AMBITION 8**

WATER AND SOIL

The neighbourhood in heritage phase.

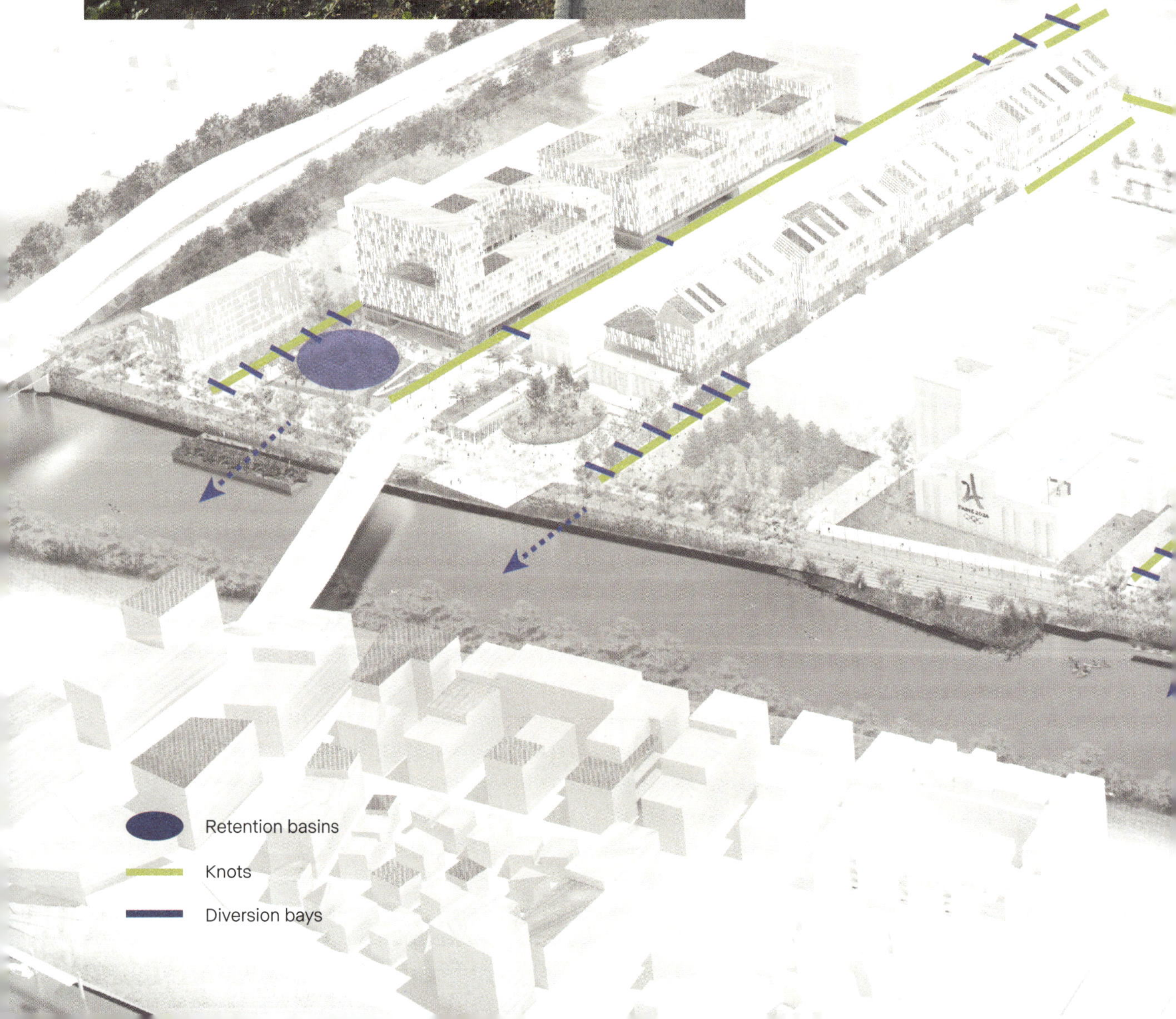
Retention basins
Knots
Diversion bays

#421# **AMBITION 8**

WATER AND SOIL

Rainwater Management

Virtuous water management. A district that reconnects with the Seine.

A site that slopes naturally to the Seine

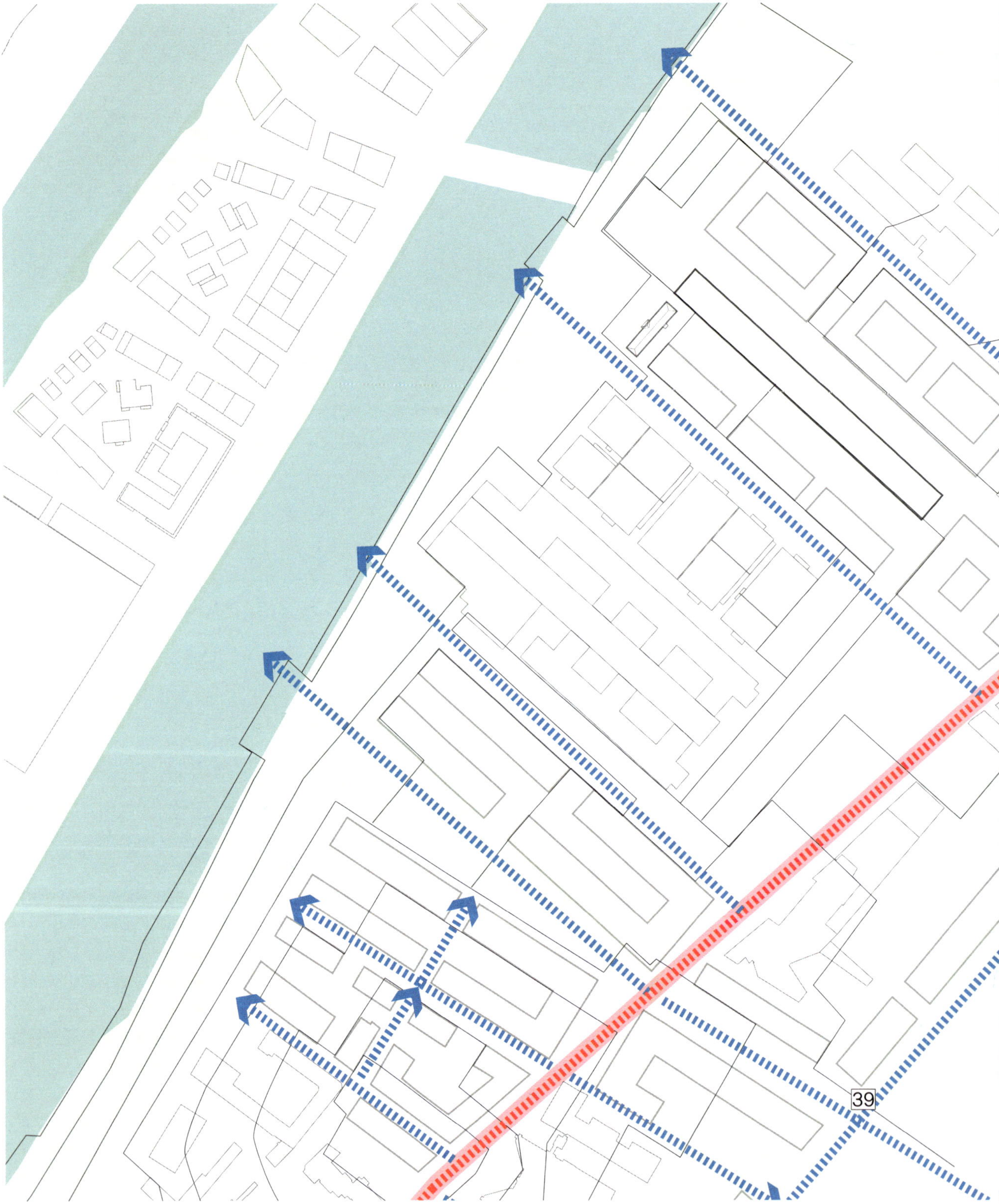

#545# **AMBITION 8**

WATER AND SOIL

Public spaces sloping down to the Seine - a site that slopes naturally down to the Seine.

The levelling of the neighbourhood accentuates and enhances the topography of the site sloping down towards the Seine. The grading of the public spaces follows the natural flow of water.

Rue Saint-Denis/ Ampère represents the ridgeline of the district.

– High Line, United States
– CBS Campuslans, Marianne Levinsen, Copenhagen
– Marina Park, Batlle I Roig, Barcelona

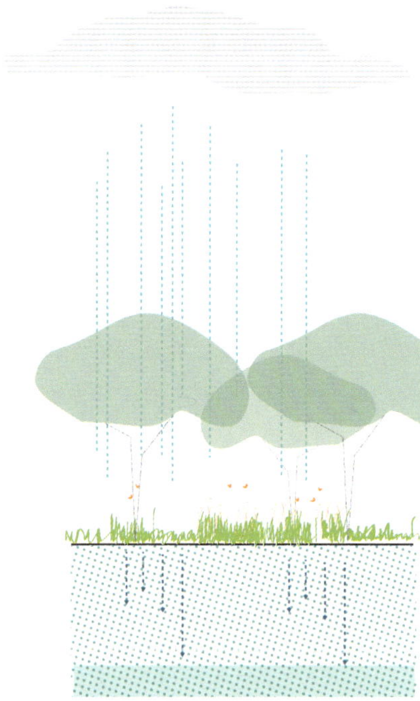

Public spaces sloping down to the Seine
The water cycle: gravity-based management of rainwater.

Fine grading of public and private spaces allows for gravity-fed rainwater management.
This choice makes it easy and intuitive to channel water towards the Seine, and reinforces the district's ambition for resilience. A number of landscaping tools have been put in place to make the water's path through the public space visible and obvious.
A non-drinking water supply system is planned at the low point of the Parc des Sports.

Tree-lined valley Intermediate permeable garden
Private rainwater collection Discharge of excess private wastewater
Exceptional discharge into the Seine
AENP Supply to non-drinking water network

Inducing evapo-transpiration

In summer, the same levelling of the public spaces means that water can be channelled to water the green spaces and cool the mineral areas.

From the non-potable water network, which is also supplied by the park, the water for watering is distributed to the public spaces from rue Saint-Denis/Ampère, the crest line of the neighbourhood.

#425# **AMBITION 8**
WATER AND SOIL
Rainwater Management.

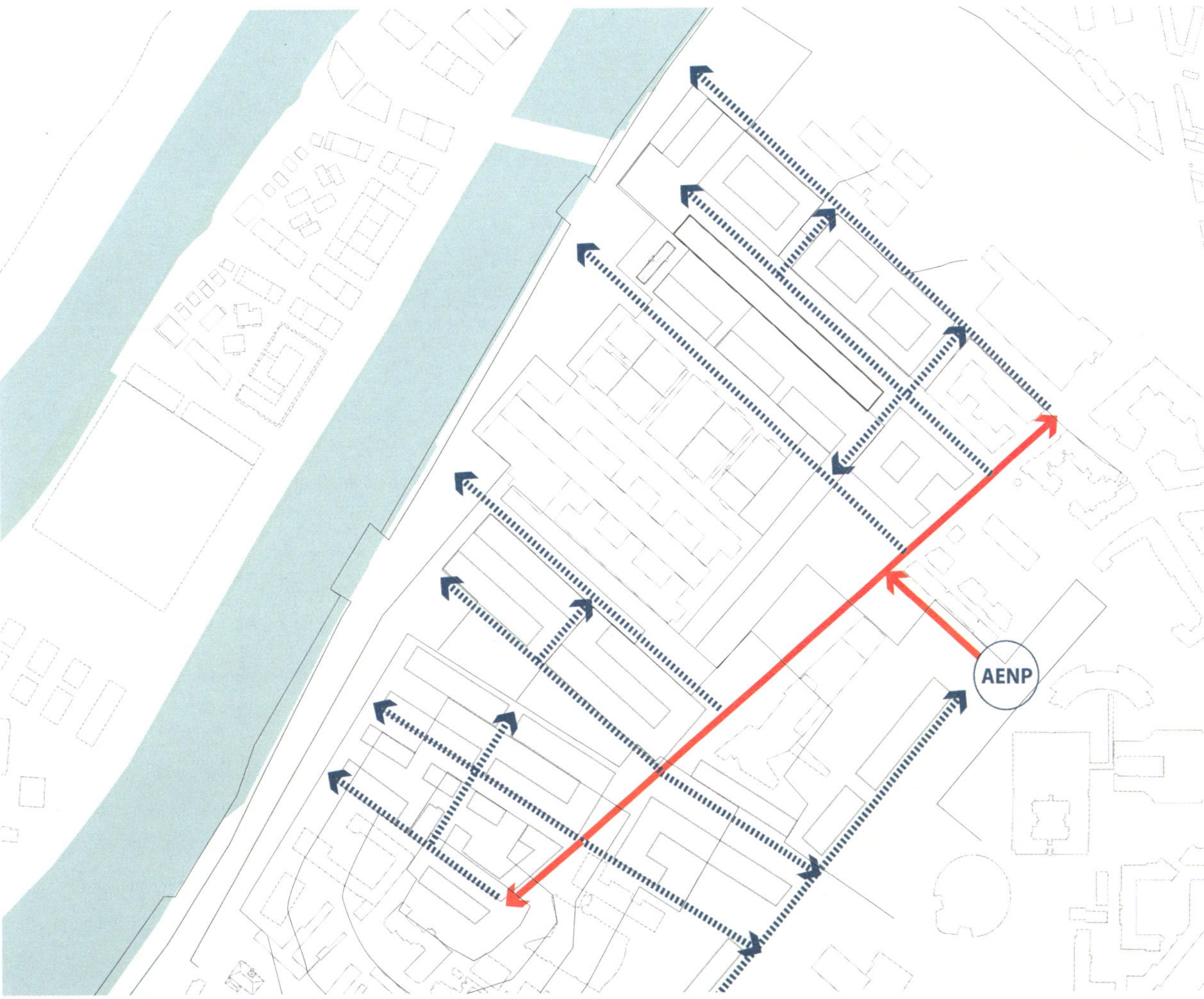

The water cycle

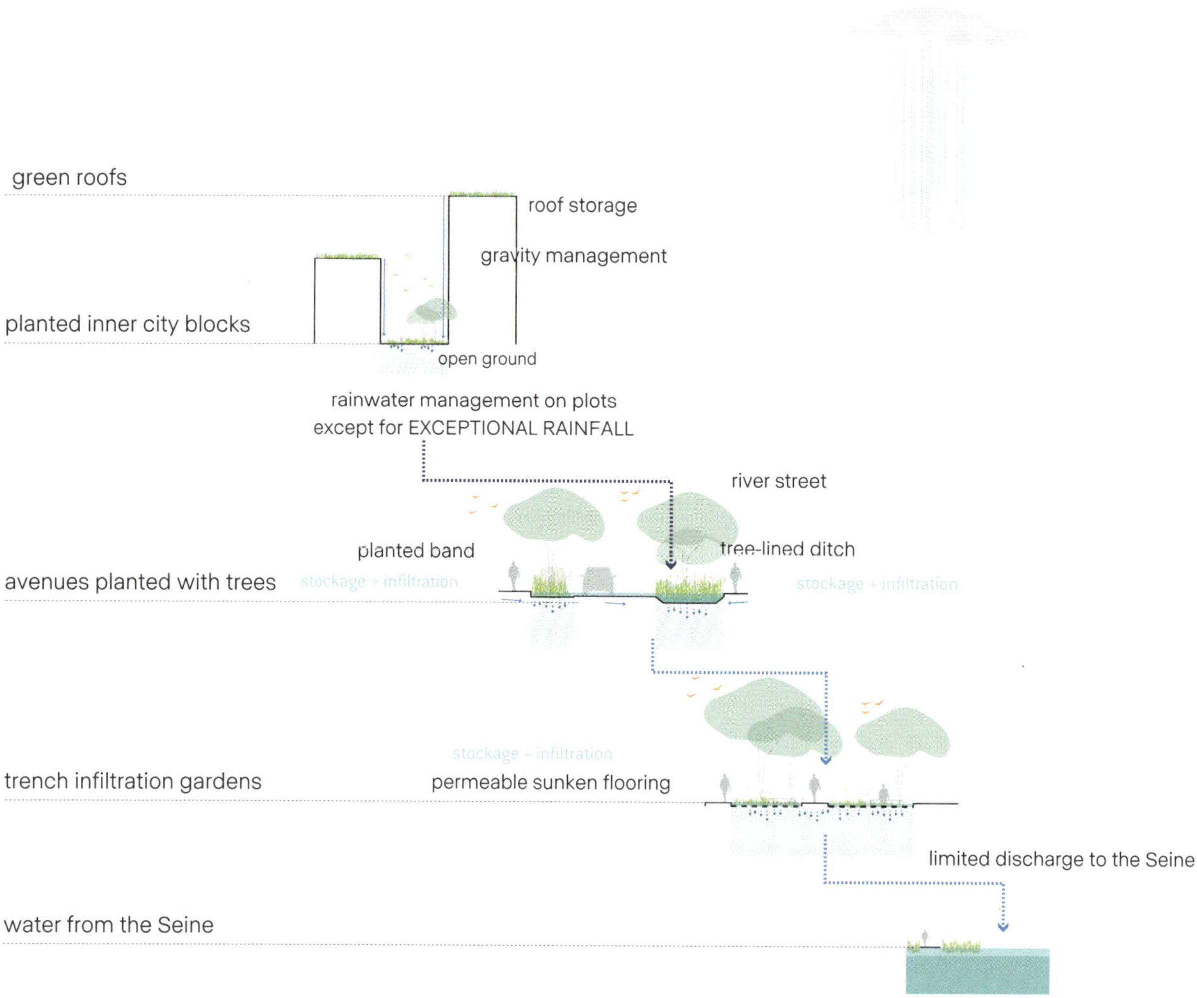

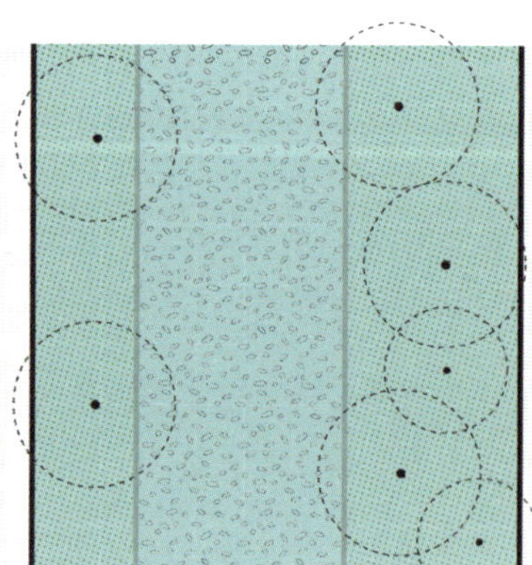

#427# **AMBITION 8**

WATER AND SOIL

Rainwater Management.

The water cycle - Gravity-based rainwater management

The water path: from the roofs, to the valleys and "river" streets, to the sunken gardens,

Finally, it crosses the RD1 and is exceptionally discharged into the Seine.

The river street with its tree-lined valleys for the retention and infiltration of rainwater.

The principle adopted in the design of the roads is to minimise impermeable surfaces in favour of permeable infiltration and storage surfaces.

Fresh linear tree gardens slope down to the Seine, collecting and infiltrating rainwater from the mineral pavements. Rainwater is managed entirely on the surface when the urban and infrastructural context allows for permeable hollow spaces.

Slopes in excess of 2% require channels to be laid out in the ditches to maximise their capacity in terms of water volume. Floodable streets channel rainwater towards the Seine.

We have agreed to temporarily flood the pavements in order to minimise the impact of storm rainfall on the whole area and to allow the entire Village to return to normal conditions relatively quickly.

Only the pavements, which are higher than the road level, remain dry to keep the water away from the feet of the buildings and ensure pedestrian access to the area. This principle reinforces the resilience sought in the design of the public spaces.

Public spaces leading down to the Seine - Le Mail Finot

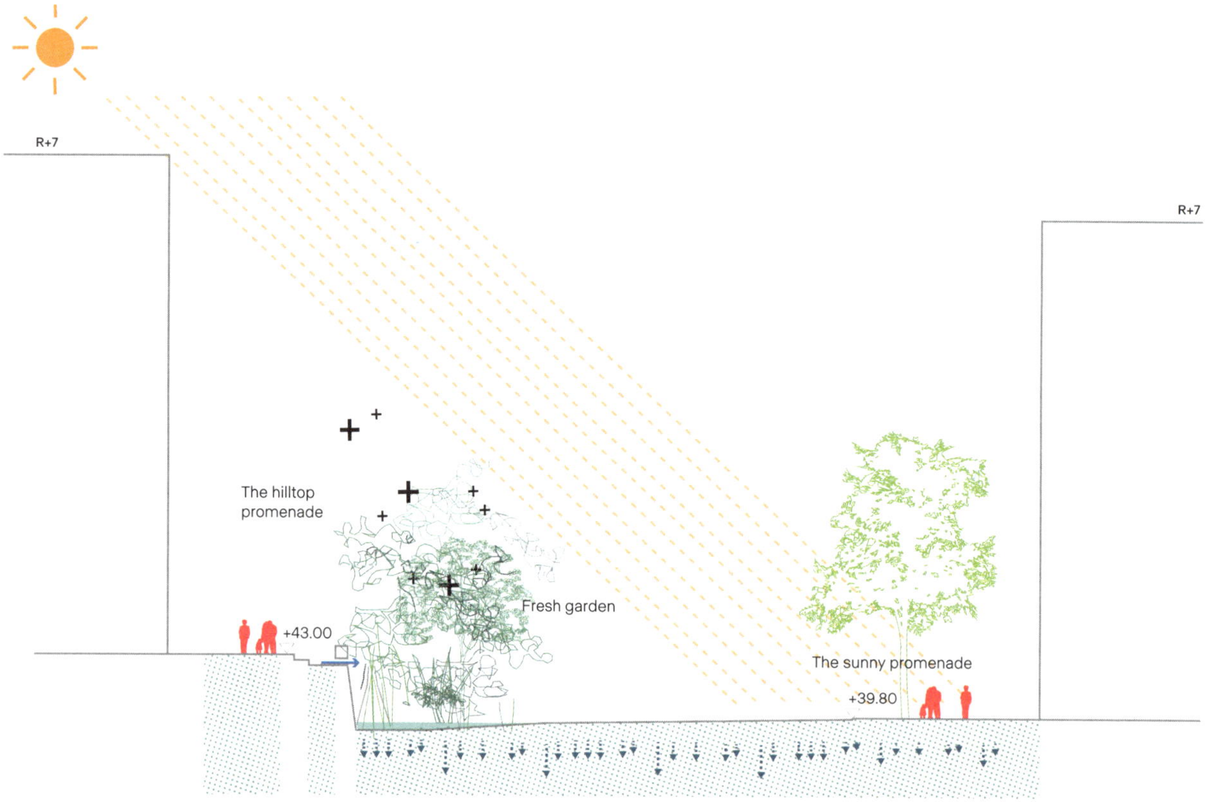

Public spaces leading down to the Seine - From Coteau to Seine

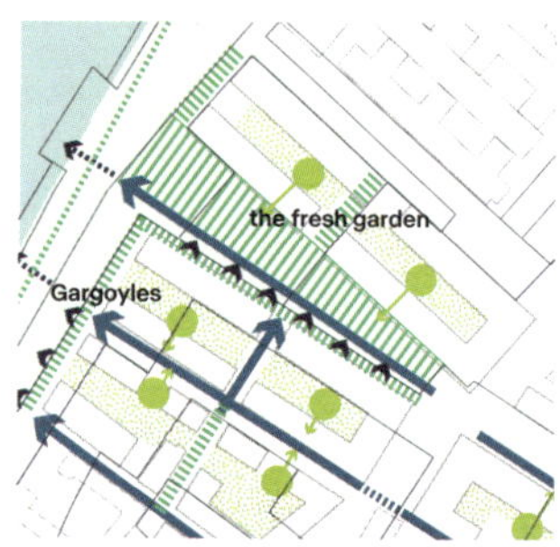

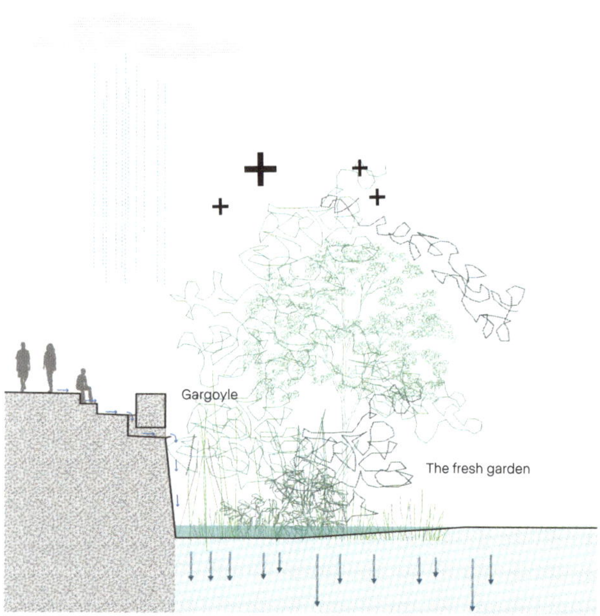

Ten-year rainfall storage

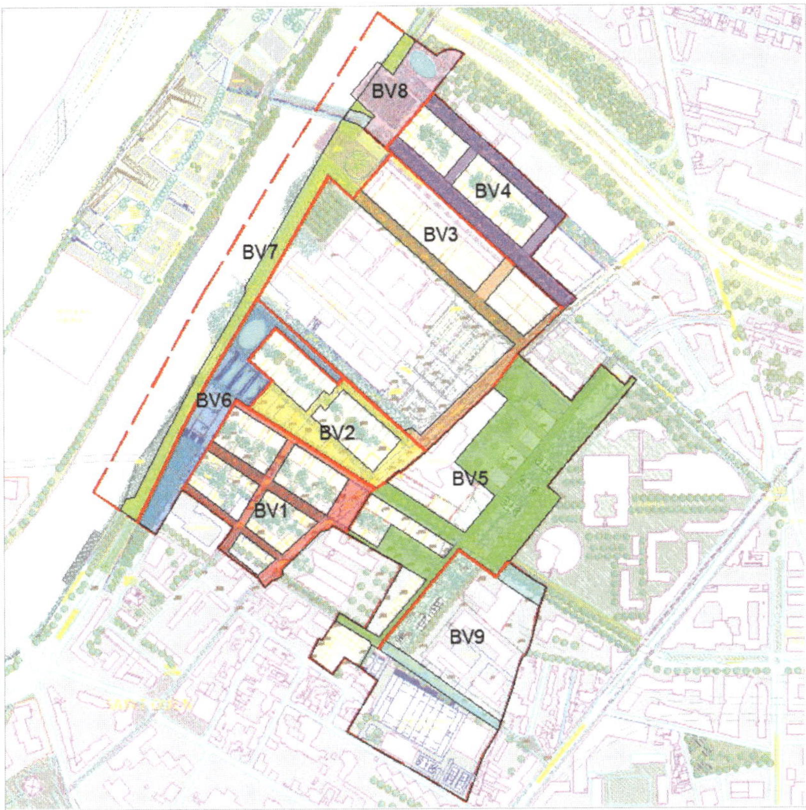

Longitudinal profile of ditches

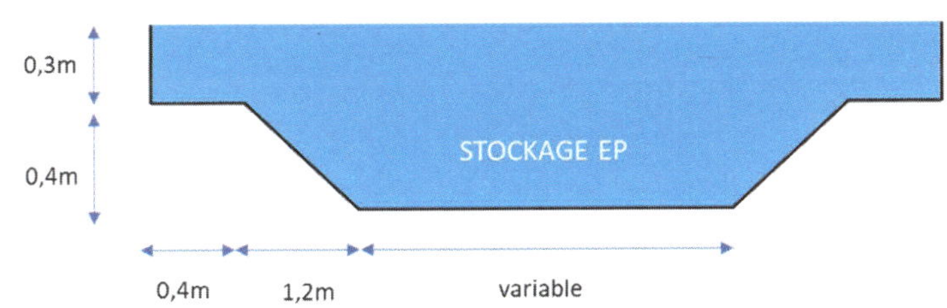

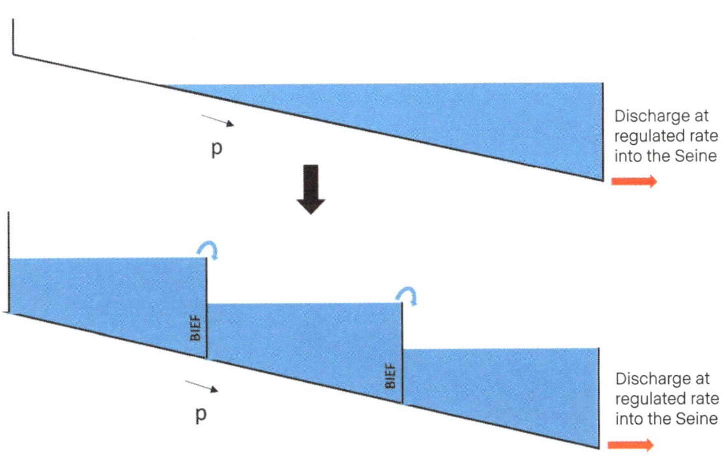

#429# AMBITION 8

WATER AND SOIL

Rainwater Management.

The Finot Mall

The hydraulic link between the rainwater coming from the top of the hillside and the Mail Finot is designed in this way: the water is collected at the edge of the high promenade and then discharged into the cool garden of the mall at the foot of the wall through a siphonic drainage system.

From the hillside to the Seine

The rainwater that runs down from the upper promenade of the hillside to the Mail Finot Mall is enhanced by a siphonic drainage system. A cool, shaded garden collects and infiltrates the rainwater at the foot of the hillside retaining wall. In summer, this garden acts as a real vector of coolness in the neighbourhood.

Storage for ten-year rainfall

The main storage structures are designed for ten-year rainfall. The aim is to manage rainwater as far upstream as possible in order to make the most of the project's storage opportunities. This avoids the creation of overly large structures downstream of the project, especially as the presence of surface water strongly restricts storage along the banks of the Seine. The catchment areas are therefore studied from upstream to downstream.

Implementation - The proposed implementation of temporary flooding zones

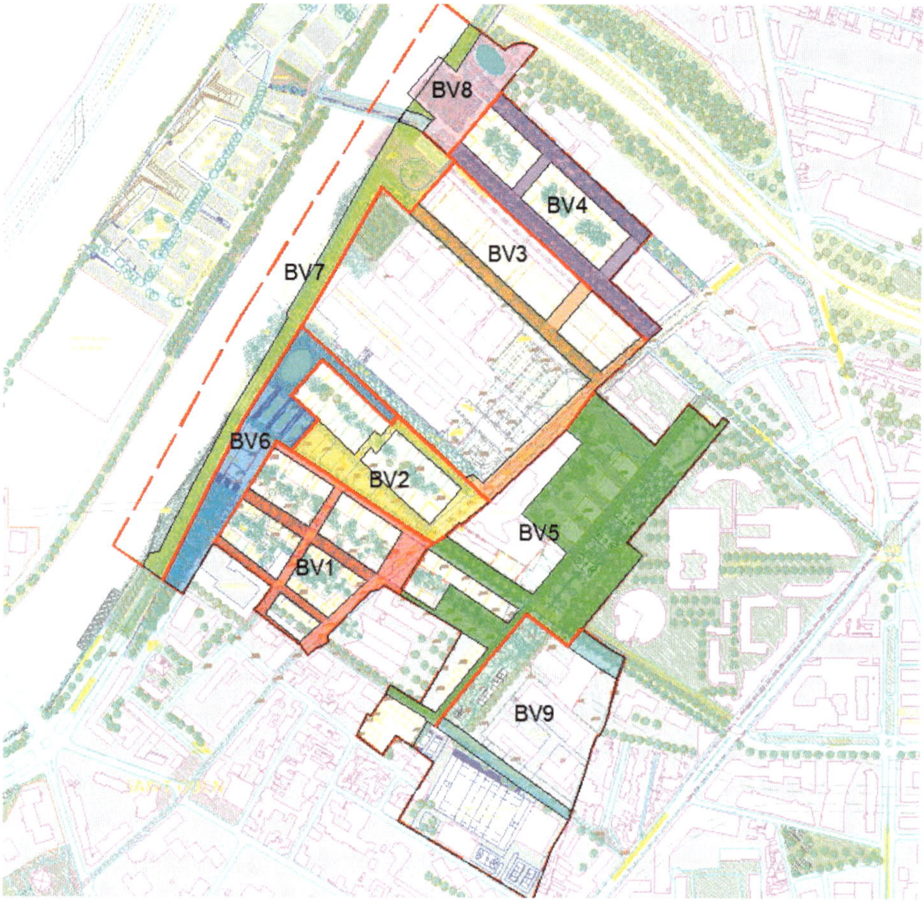

Dimensioning linear storage spaces

	Linear	Width
ESL 1	165 ml	2,5 m
ESL 2	185 ml	4,0 m
ESL 3	130 ml	4,0 m
ESL 4	170 ml	5,4 m
ESL 5	310 ml	4,0 m
ESL 6	330 ml	4,0 m
ESL 7	85 ml	4,0 m
ESL 8	130 ml	4,0 m
ESL 9	90 ml	4,0 m
ESL 10	480 ml	5,0 m

Dimensioning temporary flood zones

	Volume	Surface
BV6	420 m3	1 400 m2
BV8	255 m3	850 m2

Catchment areas 1 - 2 - 3 - 4 - 5

Rainwater from catchment areas 1 - 2 - 3 - 4 - 5 will be managed through the creation of linear which will both store and convey rainwater.

Cross-section

The profile of the linear storage areas must meet a number of requirements:

– Optimising the volume stored for a given width

– Compliance with regulations on falls: maximum height along areas accessible to the public ≤ 40cm

– Slope stability: as a first approach, the maximum slope is defined as 1/3.

The proposed cross-section at the level of the most constrained roads incorporates an intermediate level 40 cm wide along the public spaces, which allows the profile to be deepened in its central part, and therefore optimise storage capacity. The theoretical technical section is shown below.

Layout of linear storage areas Rainwater management

As illustrated in the figure, rainwater from the catchment areas is collected in linear storage areas (LSAs) as follows:

-BV1: ESL 1 + ESL 2 + ESL 3

-BV2: ESL 4

-BV3: ESL 5

-BV4: ESL 6

-BV5: ESL 7 + ESL 8 + ESL 9 + ESL 10

The linear storage areas for the ten-year rainfall have been sized accordingly:

Catchment areas 6 and 8 will be managed by creating temporary flooding zones in public spaces, which will act as a buffer before the discharge of a regulated flow into the Seine. Given the high authorised discharge rate (10L/s/Ha), the emptying time for a ten-year rainfall is around 7 hours. This principle is therefore entirely acceptable, provided that pedestrian traffic and paths are maintained.

Sizing

The height of water retained for these temporary flooding zones is 30cm, which complies well with the regulations on waterfalls (maximum height along spaces accessible to the public ≤ 40cm).

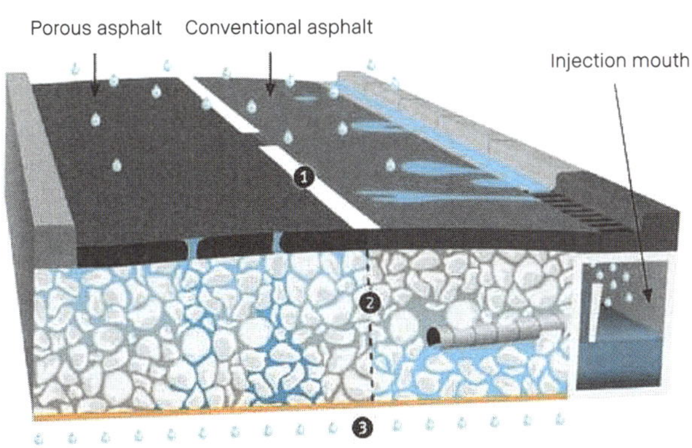

Linear storage spaces.
Example: Typical profile of a linear storage structure

PRIVATE LIMIT
PUBLIC LIMIT
Um
ELM CHAMPETRE
Ulmus minor
Cb
COMMON CHARM
Carpinus betulus
APARTMENT
+42.46
+42.31
NPHE
Fire road
Green space
1.10
4.00

#433# **AMBITION 8**

WATER AND SOIL

Rainwater management.

Areas of temporary flooding

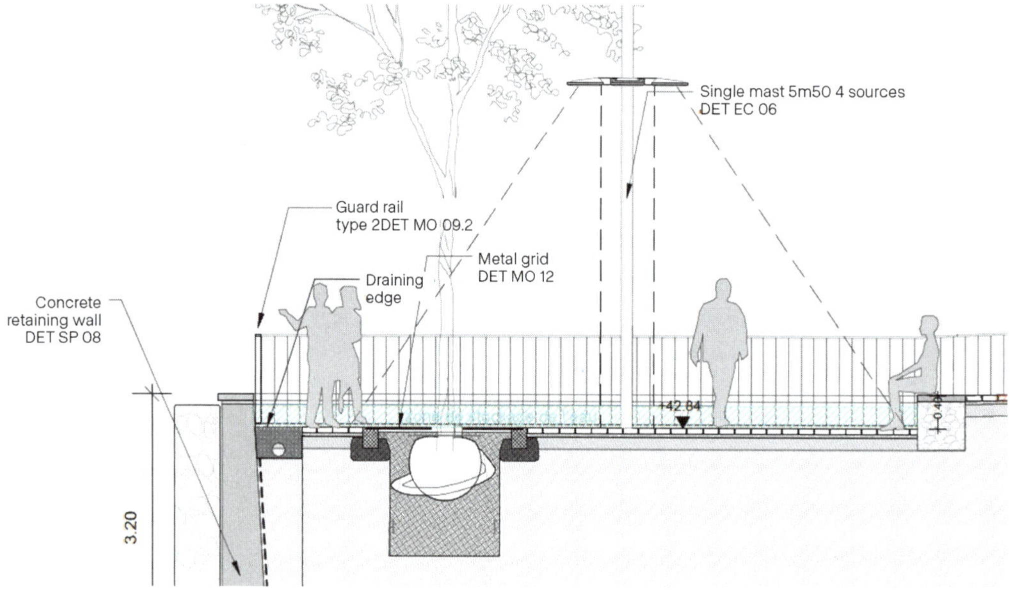

Linear storage spaces

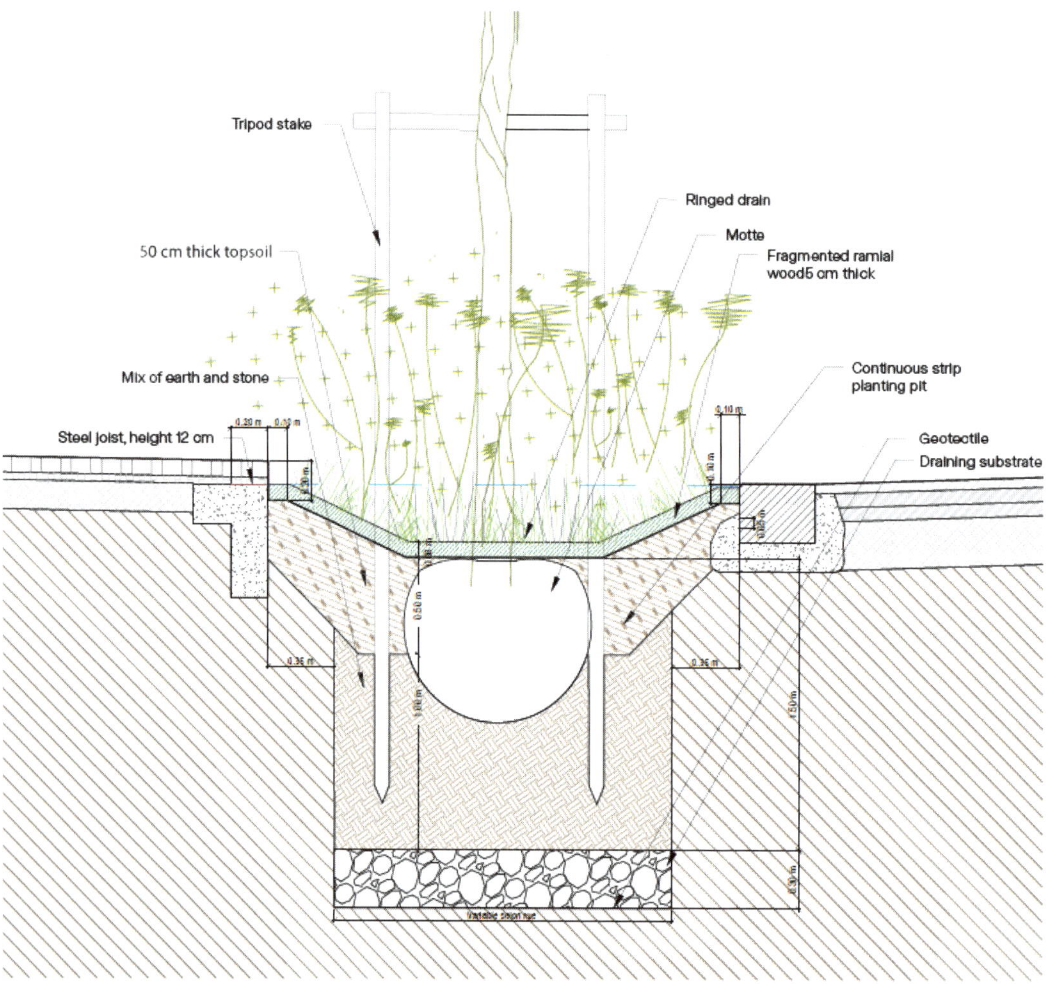

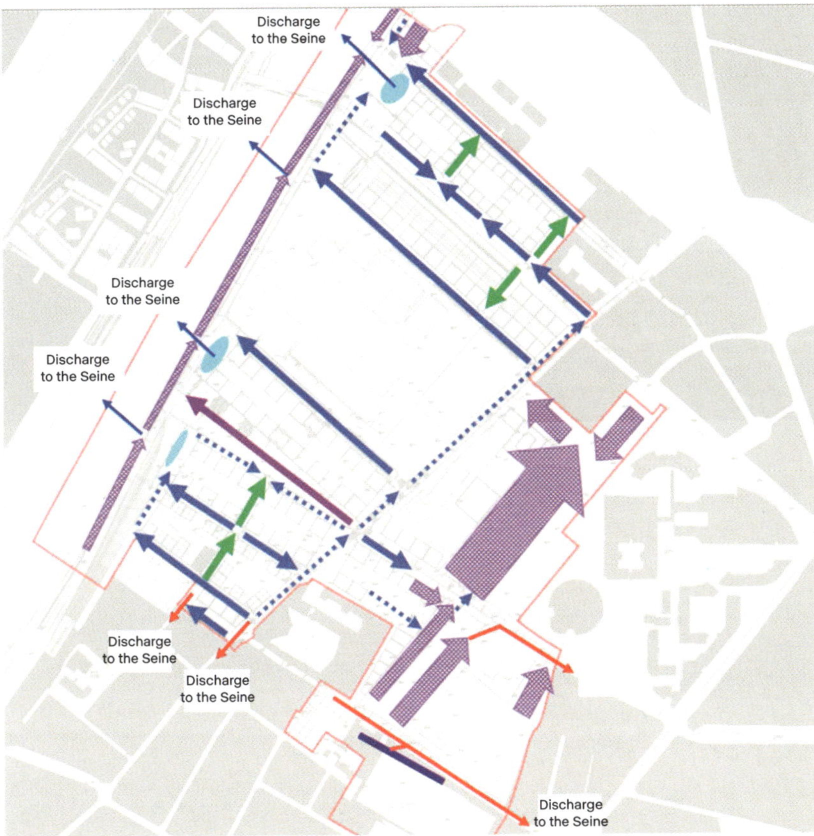

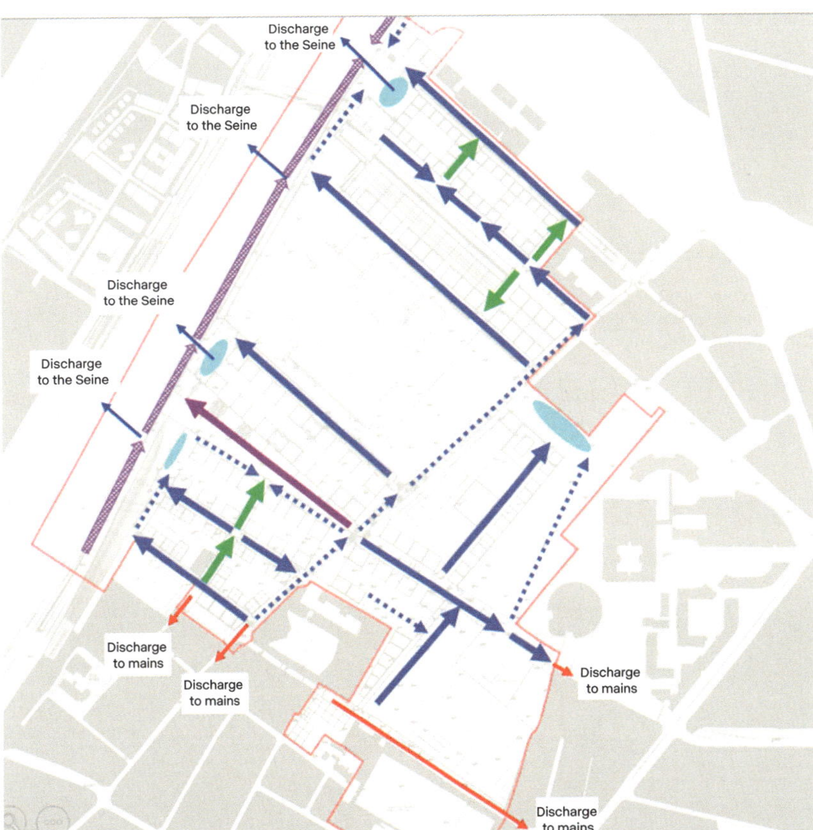

#435# **AMBITION 8**

WATER AND SOIL

Rainwater management.

TEMPORARY FLOOD ZONES

Left: Cross-section of temporary flood zone on the Coteaux

RESERVOIR PAVEMENTS

Right: Reservoir pavement operating principle

- Linear storage space
- Sealed linear storage space
- Sunken gardens
- Reservoir pavements
- Underground storage
- Surface run-off
- Temporary flood zone
- Discharge to the Seine
- Discharge to existing network (conservation of current operation)

#437# **AMBITION 8**

WATER AND SOIL

Rainwater management

SUMMARY SANITATION PLAN

- " Zero discharge of water into the network" objective
- Differentiated operation depending on the rainfall event.
- Gravity-fed, open-air stormwater management
- Permeable pavements
- Reversible operation during hot spells

Villeneuve
la Garenne
St. Ouen
St. Ouen
Mon de la Cage
Canal
Maillot
Porte
Clichy
la
Garenne
ROUTE
de
Mon de Seine

Saint-Ouen illustré
REPUBLIQUE FRANÇAISE
5c
POSTES

17. Saint-Ouen. — L'Eglise et le Château

#439# **AMBITION 8**

WATER AND SOIL

The area has a long industrial history focused on energy production. It was home to fuel depots, thermal power stations power stations, transformer stations and goods warehouses.

The development of industry radically changed the face of the site, which has inherited the scale and urban morphology of this period.

At this time, the Seine also had an industrial function. It was the main logistical axis, and the riverbanks were remodeled to accommodate loading cranes and barge moorings.

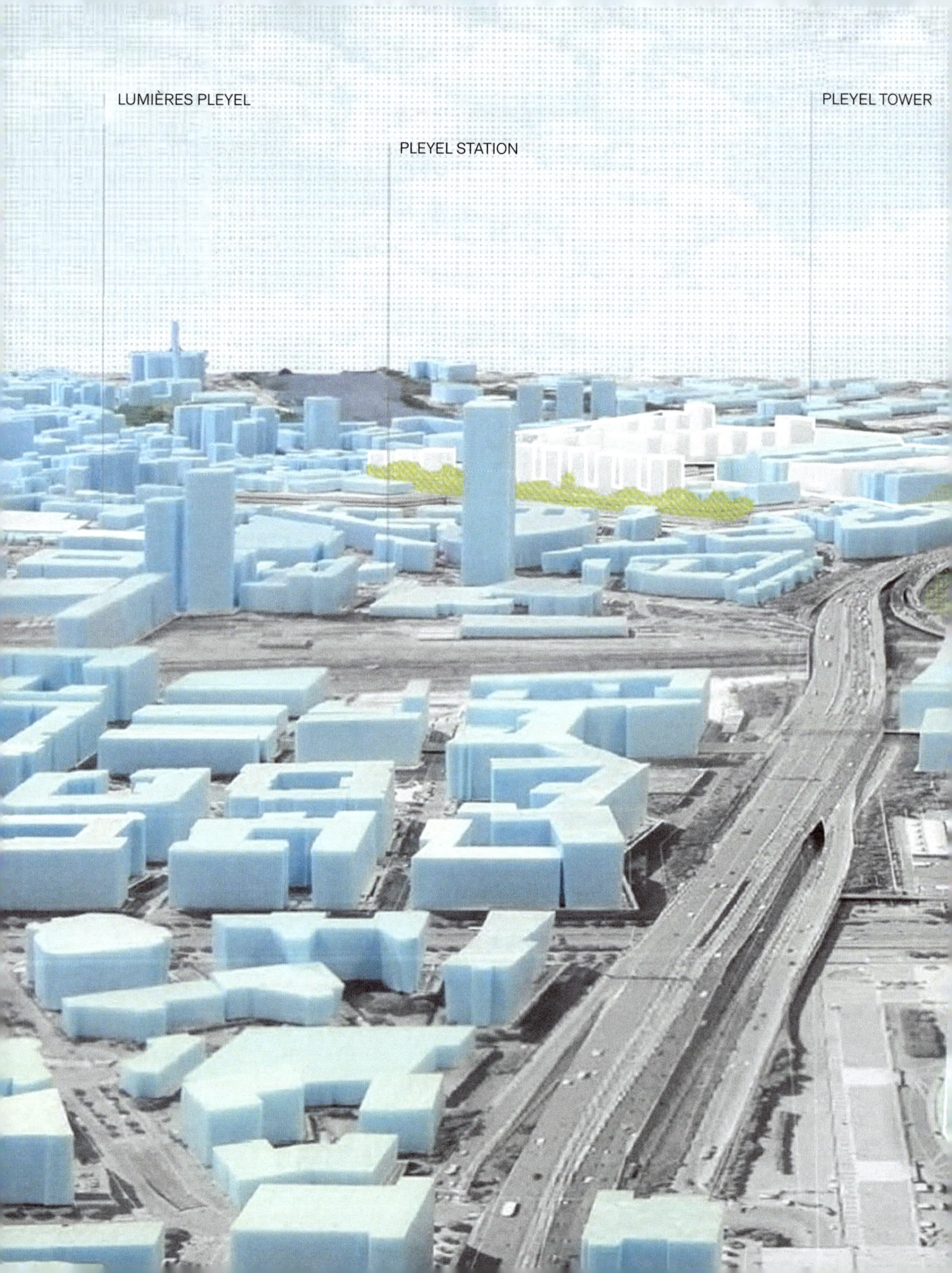
LUMIÈRES PLEYEL
PLEYEL STATION
PLEYEL TOWER

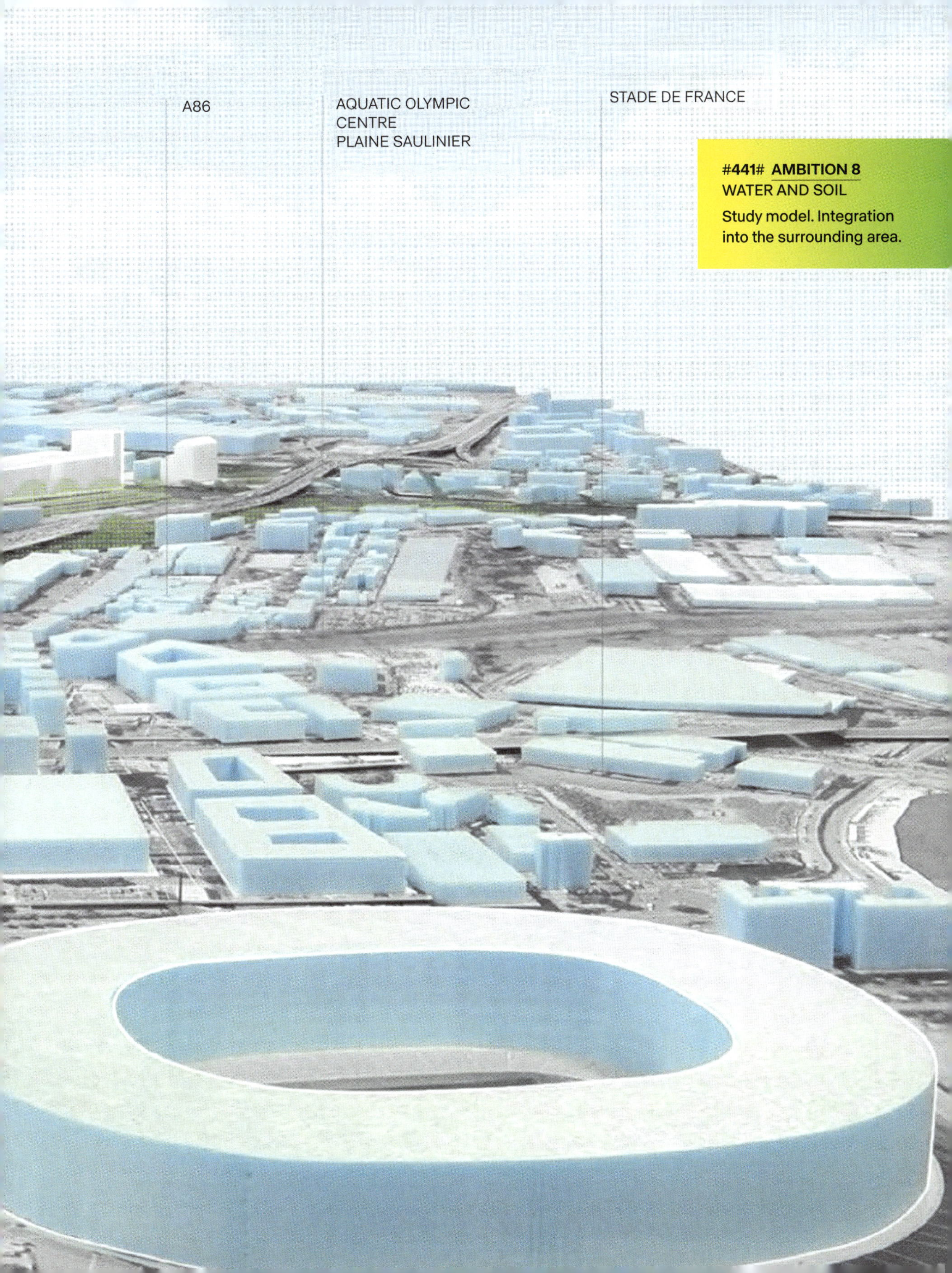

#441# AMBITION 8
WATER AND SOIL
Study model. Integration into the surrounding area.

#443# **AMBITION 8**
WATER AND SOIL

Tomorrow's Site
2019 Masterplan

The Athletes' Village is anchored in a singular geography, marked by the banks of the Seine and wooded hillsides, right next to the church of Vieux Saint-Ouen. Between these two levels, gently sloping public spaces open the district to the river, providing access to the water and offering views of the wider landscape.

The construction of a Village from scratch, but a mixed neighbourhood whose soul was already present.

In fact, this district would have been like others if what was "already there" had not been exceptional: the river, to which the old site turned its back, whereas the roads of the future district would converge in its direction; the natural resources of the area; or the Cité du Cinéma and Maxwell Hall.

#445# AMBITION 8

WATER AND SOIL

Athletes' Square

Opening onto the Seine.

#447# **AMBITION 8**
WATER AND SOIL

Tomorrow's Site.
2021 Masterplan.

Masterplan 2021

#451# **AMBITION 8**

WATER AND SOIL

Athletes' Square
Opening onto the Seine.

#453# **AMBITION 8**

WATER AND SOIL

Mail Finot

Opening onto the Seine.

2024
OLYMPIC AND PARALYMPIC GAMES
15,600 Athletes and their accompanying team members

2025
8000 Inhabitants aprox.

ILE-SAINT-DENIS: (ZAC Fluvial Ecoquartier)
320 homes (including 30% social housing)
130 student accommodation units and 1 hotel
10,200m2 of office space
4,000m2 of activities and services
1300m2 of local shops

SAINT OUEN + SAINT-DENIS: (ZAC Athletes' Village)
1,900 homes (including 25% to 40% social housing depending on the municipality)
750 special housing units and 1 hotel
117,000m2 of activities, offices and services
2000m2 of local shops

#455# **AMBITION 8**

WATER AND SOIL

2026 - Time 03

"Heritage" district.

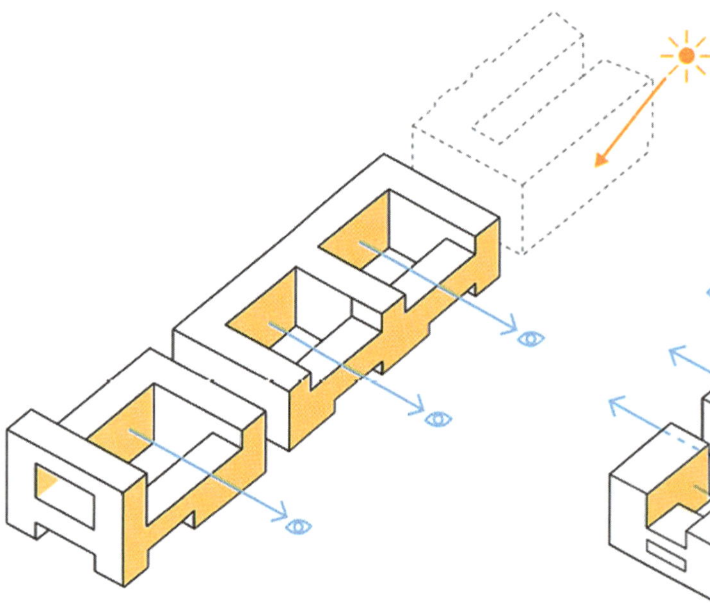

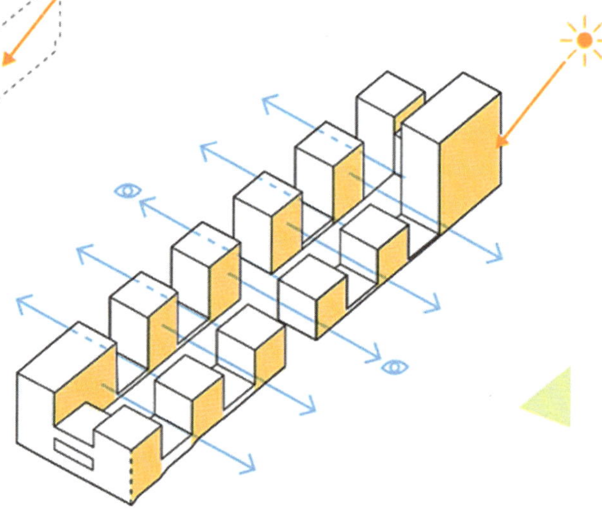

#457# **AMBITION 8**

WATER AND SOIL

A Compact and Sustainable Morphology

Sunlight and views.

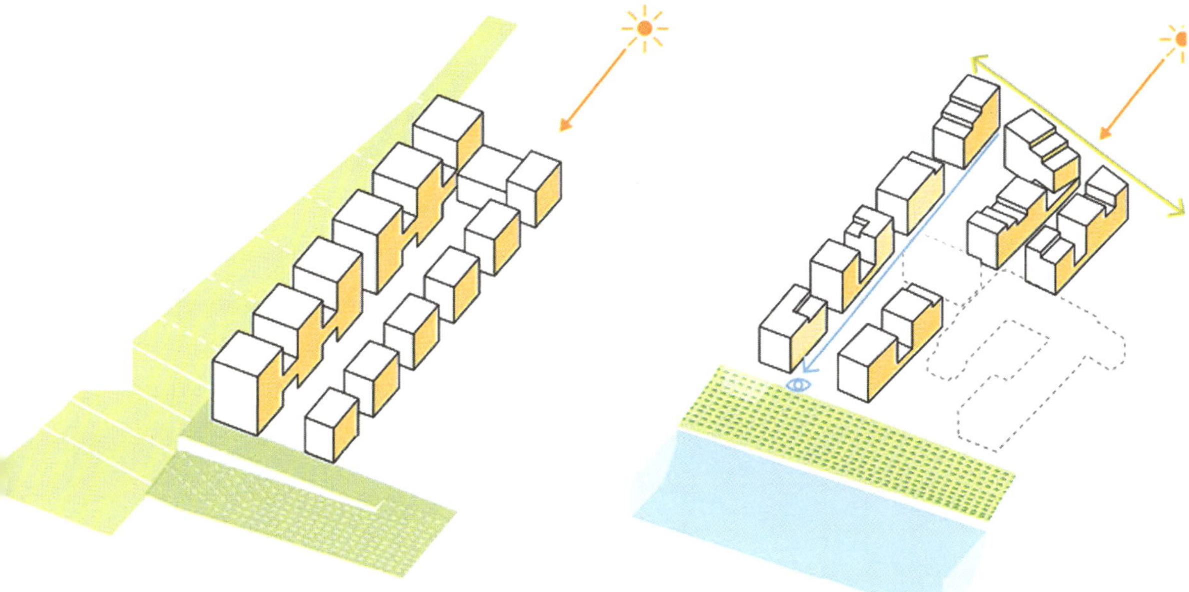

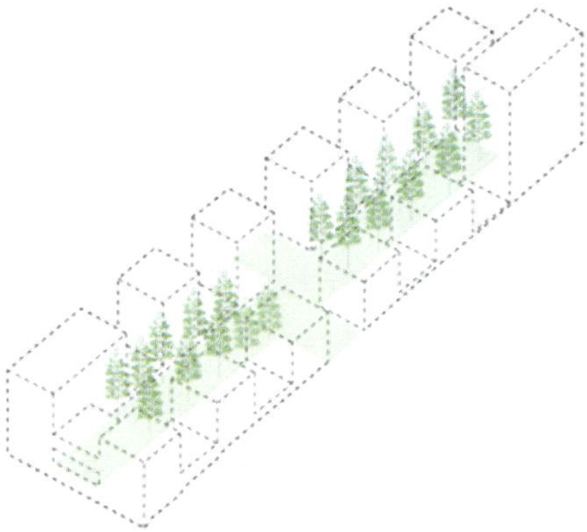

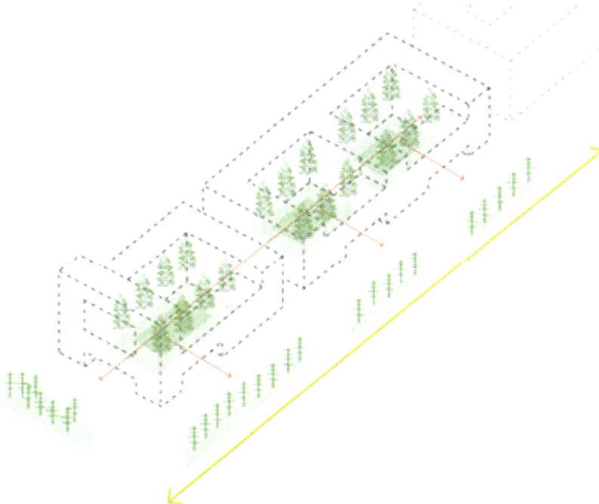

#459# **AMBITION 8**

WATER AND SOIL

Core Areas Open to the Seine

Openness and transparency

A block interior organized on a simple framework and oriented towards the Seine. The quiet and semi-private garden courtyards prioritize gardens and private terraces.

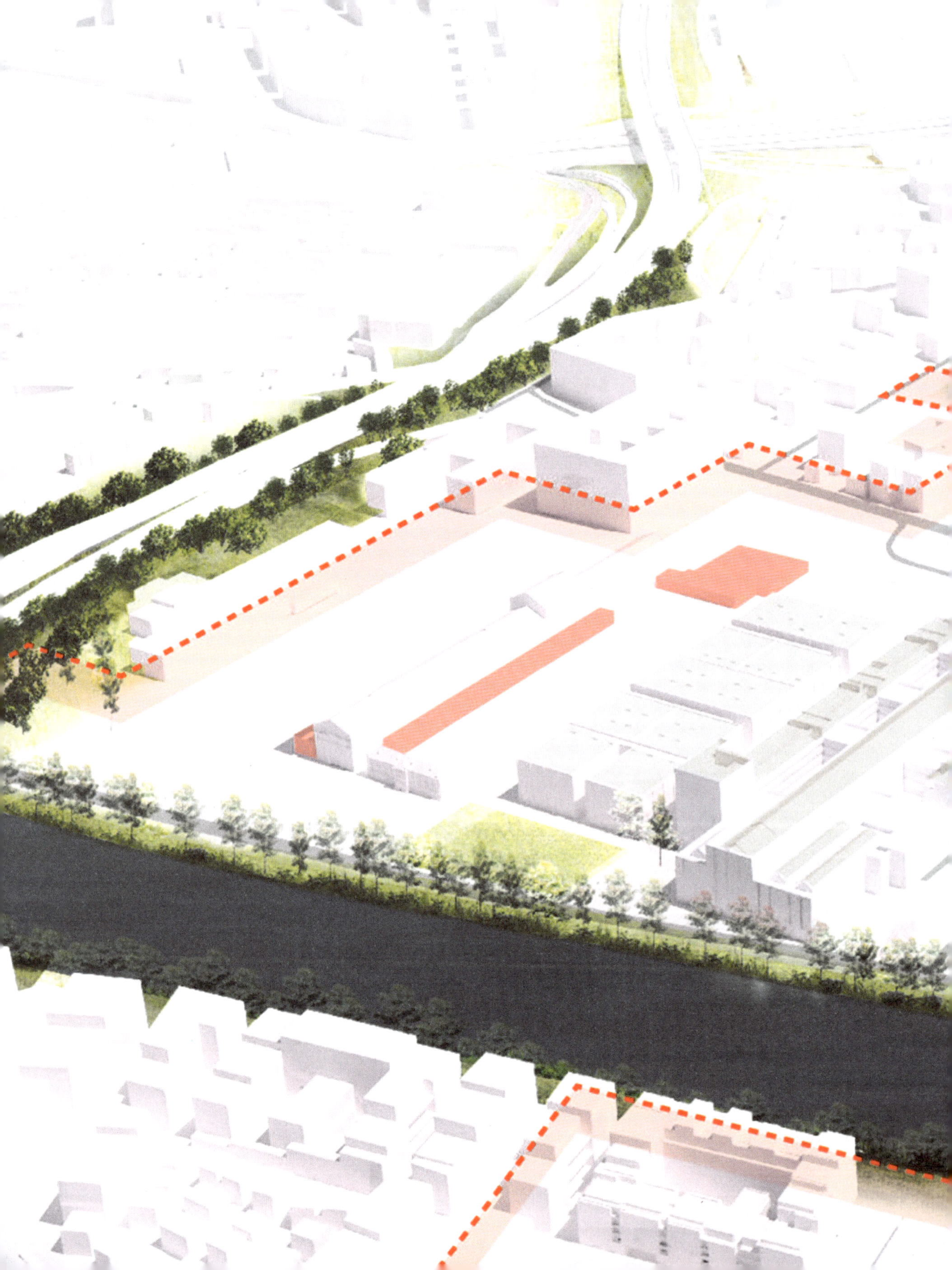

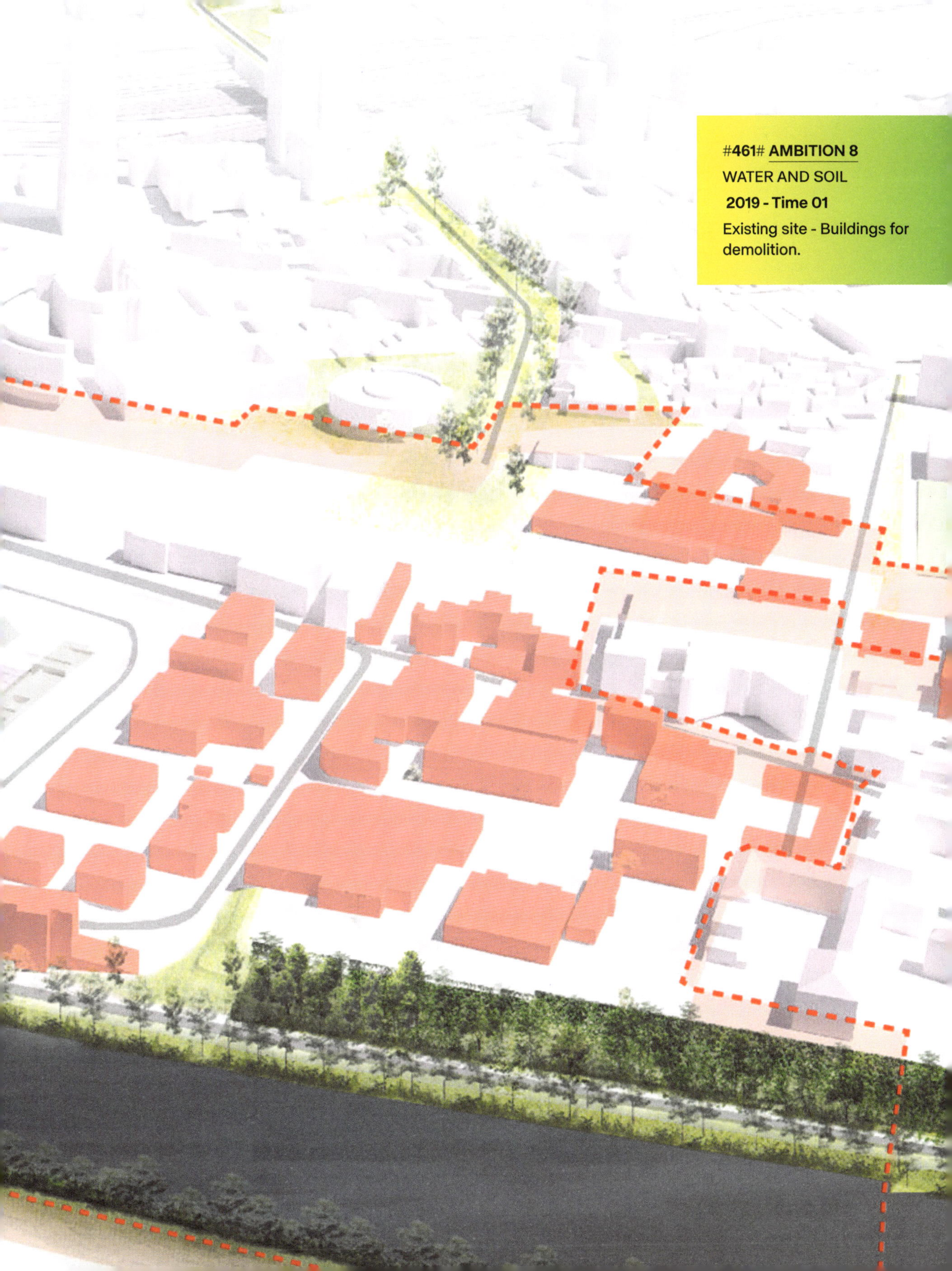

#461# **AMBITION 8**

WATER AND SOIL

2019 - Time 01

Existing site - Buildings for demolition.

#463# <u>AMBITION 8</u>

WATER AND SOIL

2024 - Temps 02

During the Olympics and Paralympics.

PARIS
PARIS

#465# **AMBITION 8**

WATER AND SOIL

2024 - Time 02

During the Olympics and Paralympics.

PARIS
PARIS
PARIS
Les Saveurs du Monde
World Flavors
TEAM
SOUTH AFRICA

#467# **AMBITION 8**

WATER AND SOIL

2024 - Time 02

During the Olympics and Paralympics.

ESPAÑA

#469# **AMBITION 8**

WATER AND SOIL

2024 - Time 02

During the Olympics and Paralympics.

PARIS

#471# **AMBITION 8**

WATER AND SOIL

2024 - Time 02

During the Olympics and Paralympics.

Urban Forms

Quality of use is considered at all scales (buildings, blocks, public spaces) to define a district that is both unified in its image and contrasted in its uses.

The master plan includes a detailed study of the dimensions of each building element, its relationship to public space, its capacity for programmatic adaptability during the Olympic phase and its reversibility during the legacy phase. Each building block develops its own identity, playing a specific role in a coherent, clear urban scenario.

#473# AMBITION 8

WATER AND SOIL

2024 - Time 02

Heritage Phase.

#475# AMBITION 8

WATER AND SOIL

2024 - Time 02

Heritage Phase.

#477# **AMBITION 8**

WATER AND SOIL

2024 - Time 02

Heritage Phase.

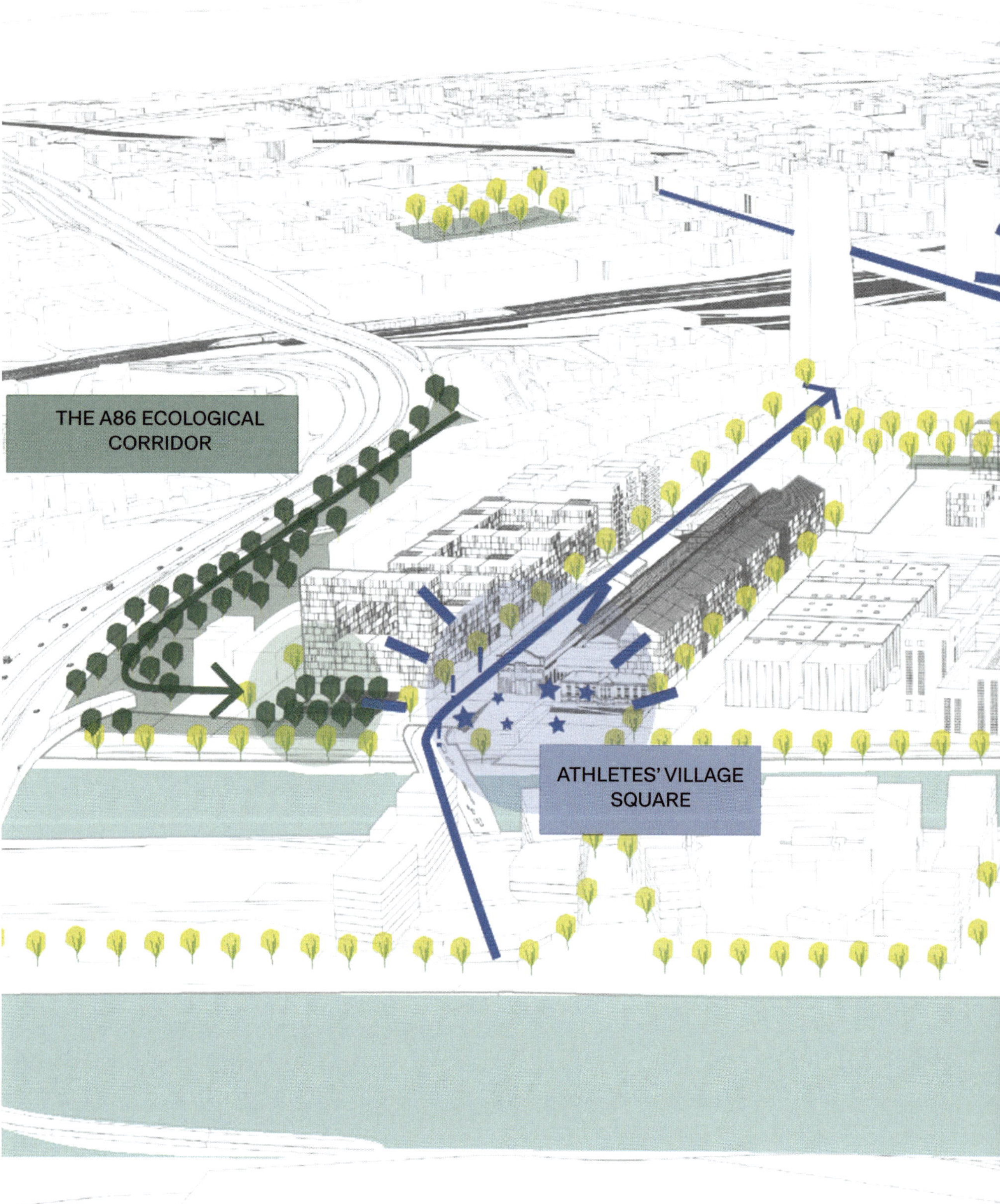
THE A86 ECOLOGICAL CORRIDOR
ATHLETES' VILLAGE SQUARE

#479# **AMBITION 8**

WATER AND SOIL

Creating Identity Areas Urban Logic.

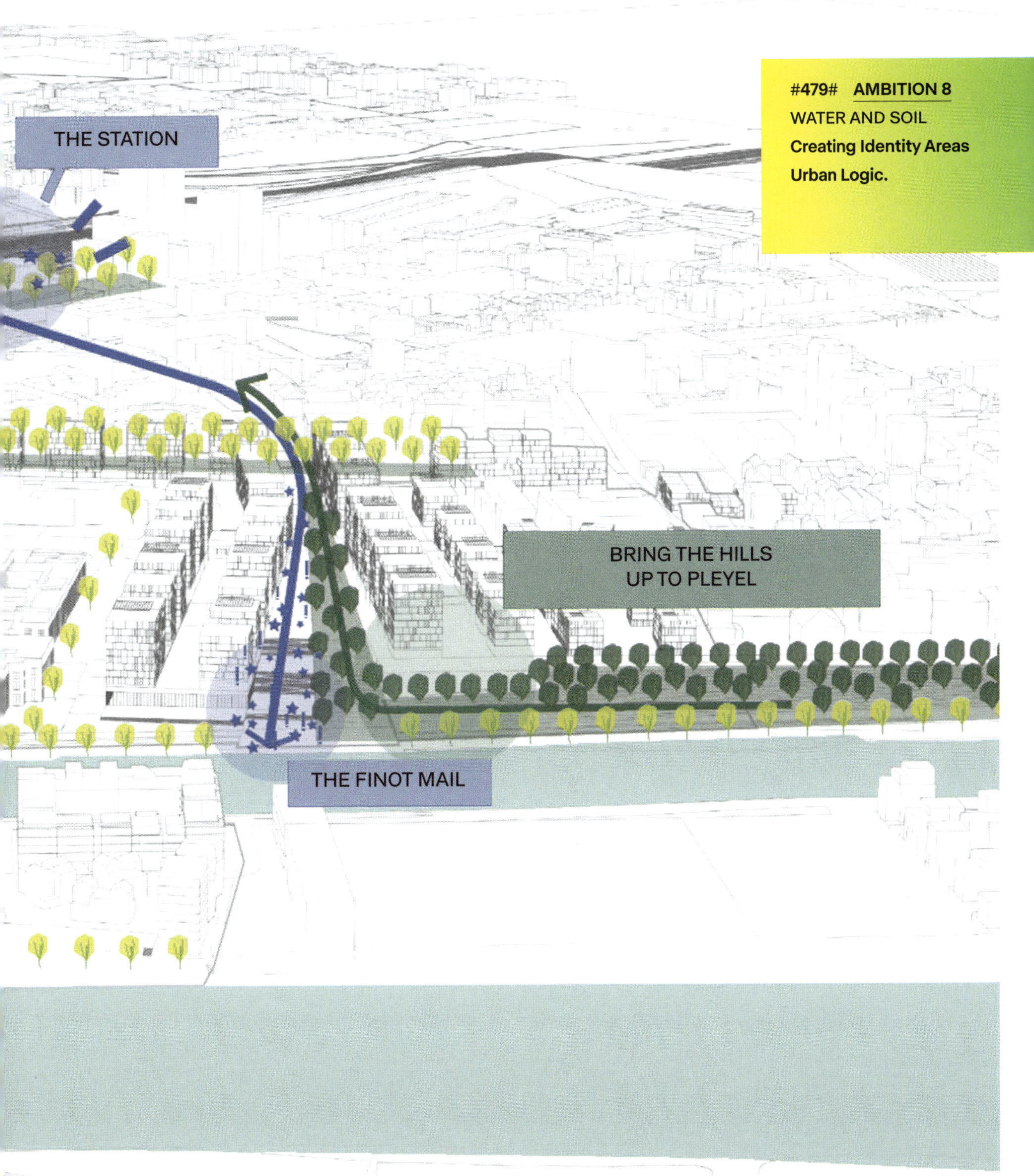

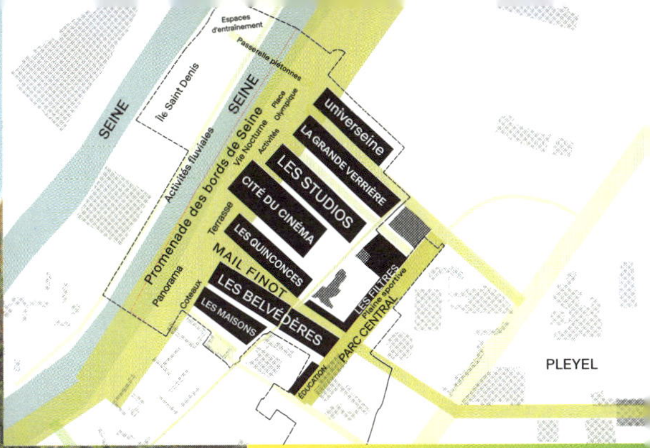

#481# **AMBITION 8**

WATER AND SOIL

Mail Finot

From Pleyel to the Seine - Metropolitan Public Spaces

The grid of public spaces is the structuring element of the village's urban project. It will form the backbone of this new district and help to give it its identity. It will also ensure that it is "linked" with neighbouring districts (the southern district of Ile-Saint-Denis, Vieux-Saint-Ouen, Pleyel).

SOCIAL SPORT CLUB

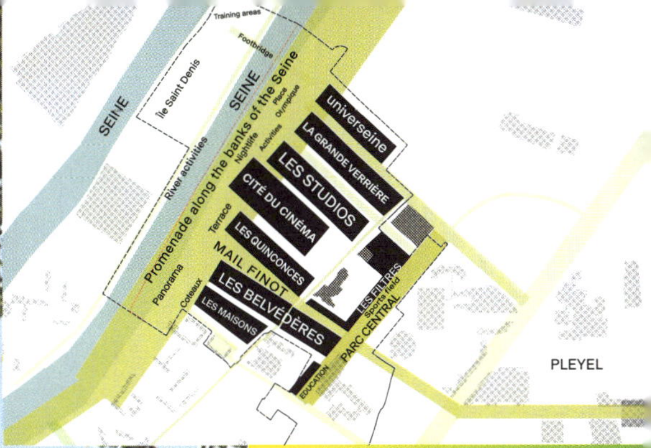

#483# **AMBITION 8**

WATER AND SOIL

Mail Finot

The major perpendiculars to the Seine, major links between Pleyel and the river:

– The Mail Finot, giving a clear view of the Seine / Finot axis.

– Pleyel / Saint-Denis, L'allée de Seine, as an extension of the future pedestrian bridge over the Seine, a key link between the Universeine district, the river eco-district and the Pleyel hub.

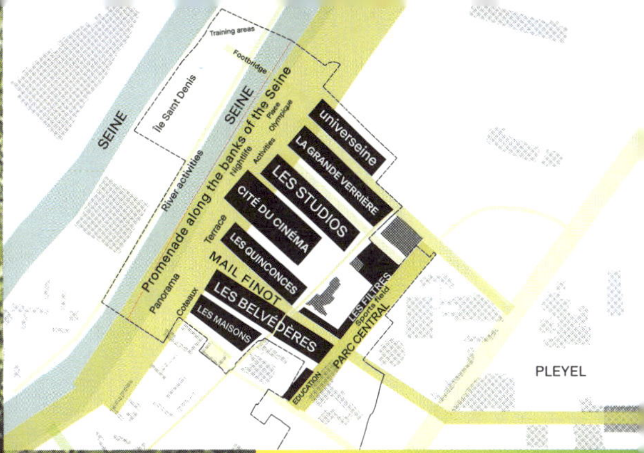

#485# **AMBITION 8**

WATER AND SOIL

Allée de Seine

From Pleyel to the Seine.

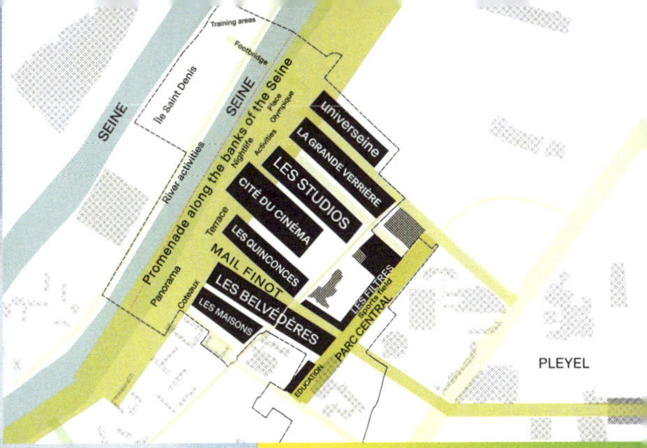

#487# **AMBITION 8**

WATER AND SOIL

Allée de Seine

From Ile-Saint-Denis and the footbridge to Pleyel.

AMBITION 9

BIODIVERSITY IN URBAN AREAS

Sustainability issues have been included in the roadmap at two levels: the reversibility of the Village as a mixed-use neighbourhood and eco-urbanity, with three objectives: biodiversity, climate resilience and decarbonisation. The ambition of the Greater Paris metropolitan area is to extend the model of certified High Environmental Quality neighbourhoods.

The planting and afforestation program for the Village's public spaces, drawn from the inert wasteland, aims to promote a habitat conducive to flora and fauna, by ensuring the continuity of biotopes in the urban environment through herbaceous, shrubby and arborescent plant strata.In addition to the greenways of the Mail Finot and the Allée de Seine, the Deux Rives park and the Mail Ampère park - the extent of which has yet to be defined to ensure that it remains faithful to the projections of the November 2019 Development Guide Plan and is not cut down by new buildings - each central block is generously planted with open-air vegetation. Residents have access to these areas via ground-floor passageways.Visible from the street, these gardens offer a variety of views of the great river and urban landscape, amplifying the feeling of spatial fluidity. An ecologist has been assigned to each block team to work on biodiversity. In this way, the Village offers a model of ecological thinking applied to development, where greening programmes are so often nothing more than elements of language and ersatz thinking from which no landscape emerges. New, highly innovative projects, however, resulting from collaborations between botanists, architects and urban planners, reflect the rise of ecological urbanity and a paradigm shift in the design of sustainable projects, right up to "Regenerative Design" aimed at the co-evolution of urban and natural systems in partnership.

We can expect the city to be redefined as a natural environment in the sense of an urban ecosystem (naturalized as the first "living environment" in our civilization), generating biotopes to create permeability between rural spaces and urban districts.From the squares and parks of the Paris of Baron Haussmann and the engineer Alphand to the garden cities of the Seine department and the Prost development plan (1934), the policy of planting and landscaping in urban planning is an eco-urbanity of well-being and health.

Climate trajectory modelling requires us to combat heat islands. The location of the Olympic Village facing the Seine is enviable, and the planting of vegetation is an important health issue.More than Paris, it is the inner suburbs that will be most affected by rising temperatures, due to the lack of vegetation cover to moderate them through evapotranspiration, as a result of the massive artificialisation of land and the widespread use of concrete.The difference can be between one and eight degrees. With 87% of its surface area urbanised, the city threatens to become a furnace. The planting of open spaces in the Olympic Village, with its high biodiversity coefficient, will help to moderate the effects of heat and purify the air. 1.4 million people in the Greater Paris region are exposed to levels of contamination that exceed regulatory standards. Trees provide benefits. They are of public benefit. Reflection on the regulation of microclimates is encouraging the creation of green roofs, which can regulate the temperature inside buildings. The albedo of plants is generally higher than that of materials.

Chanteraines Park
Project perimeter
Docks Park
Pierre Lagravère Park
Robinson Park
Ile de la Jatte Park
Lebaudy Park
Sports Fields
Champs Élysées Garden
Chateau Park
Tuilleries Garden
Invalides Esplanade
Tour Eiffel Garden
Champs de Mars
National Domain of Saint Cloude
André Citroën Park
Trapeze Park
Nautical Park Ile Monsieur
Ile Saint-Germain Park
Garden of the Ile Seguin

#493# **AMBITION 9**

BIODIVERSITY IN URBAN AREAS

Reconnecting with the Seine. Metropolitan Landscapes.

Natura 2000
RNRU Berges de Seine
Butte Pinson regional estate
Départemental park Ile-St-Denis
Chanteraines Park
Sévines Park
St-Ouen Great Park
Railway line

#495# **AMBITION 9**

BIODIVERSITY IN URBAN AREAS

Ecological continuities

The Seine: the city's ecological artery.

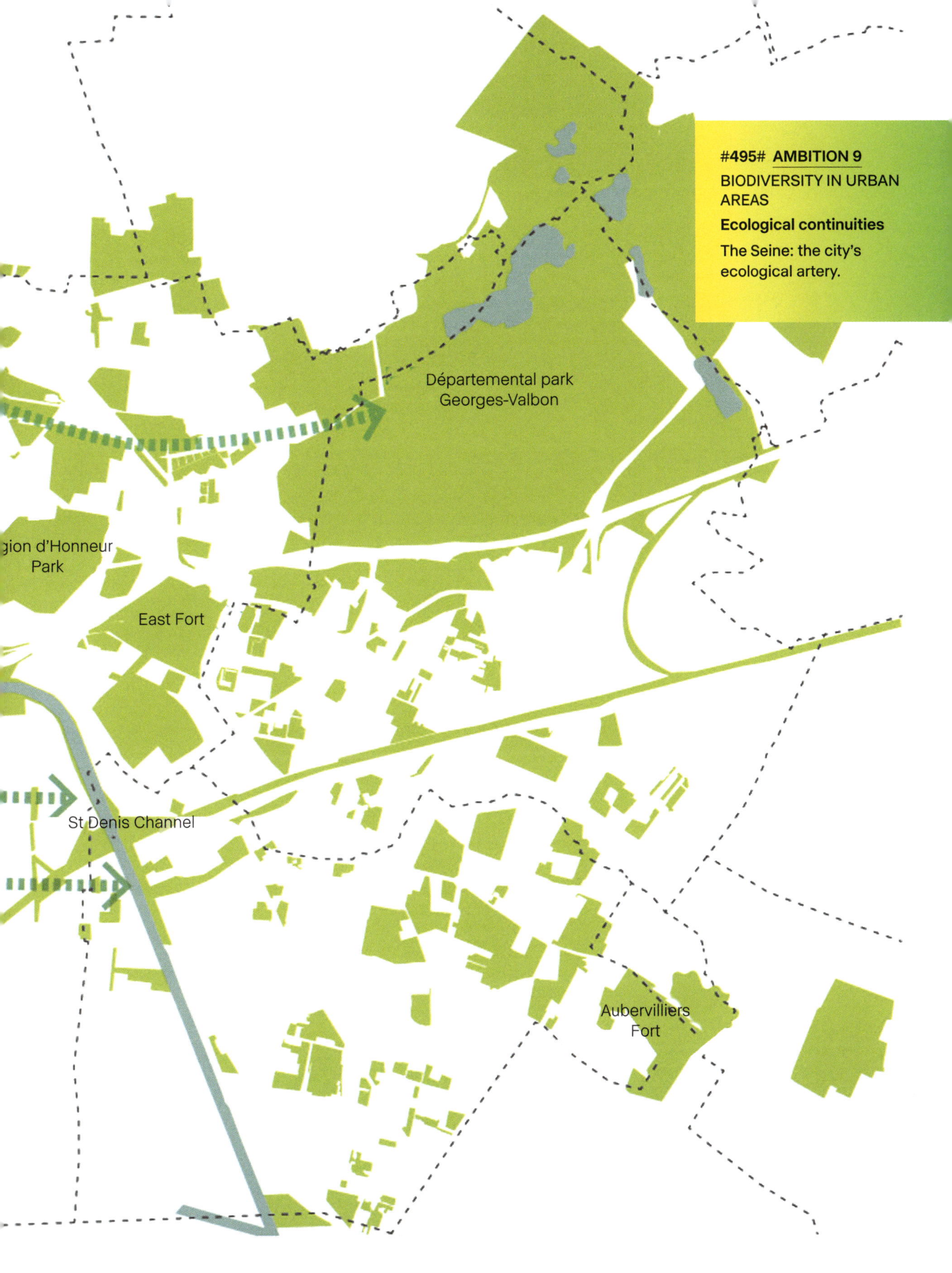

Les Rives park
Mail Finot
Allées de Quartier
Ile Saint-Denis
Vieux Saint-Ouen
Grand parc de Docks

#497# **AMBITION 9**
BIODIVERSITY IN URBAN AREAS

The great landscape of the district

Going up the Seine - nature in the city.

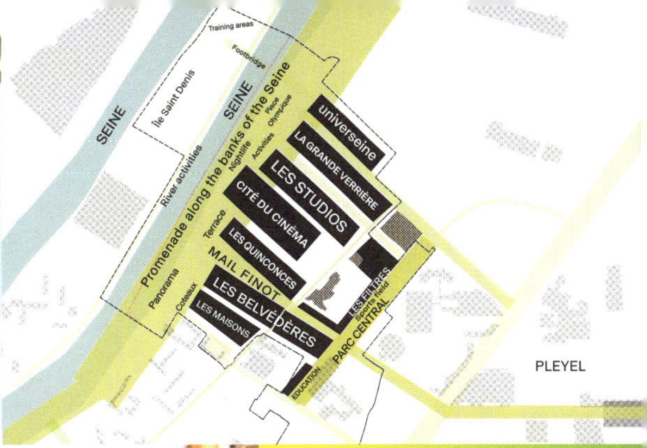

#499# AMBITION 9

BIODIVERSITY IN URBAN AREAS

Banks of the Seine

Upgrading the departmental road

A linear park 860 m long and 4.3 hectares in size: the banks of the Seine are part of a territorial scale. Beyond the district, the Grand Parc des Rives should extend as far as the Parc des Docks to the south and as far as the confluence of the Canal St-Denis and the Seine.

The riverside project will also see the RD1 upgraded to an urban boulevard (closed during the Olympic phase) and the plane tree line along it enhanced.

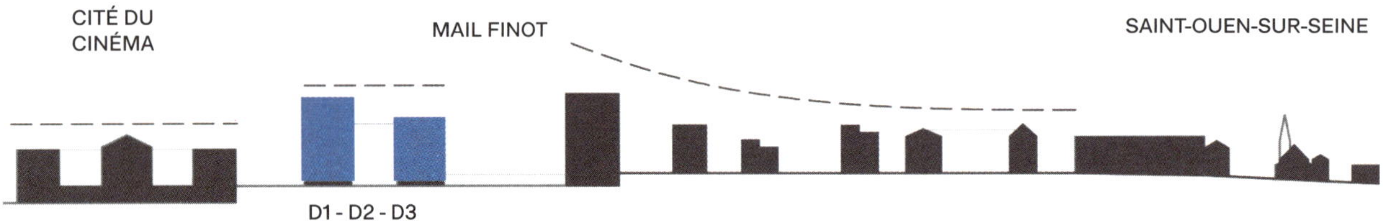
CITÉ DU CINÉMA
MAIL FINOT
SAINT-OUEN-SUR-SEINE
D1 - D2 - D3

Mail Finot
+29 ngf
Walk-through city block
Ampere street
+39 ngf
Saint Denis street

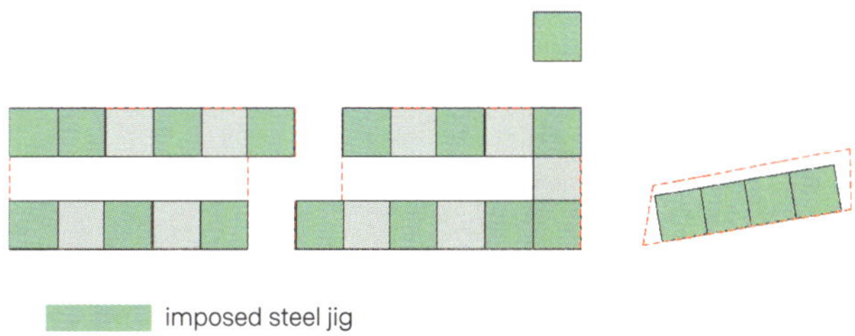

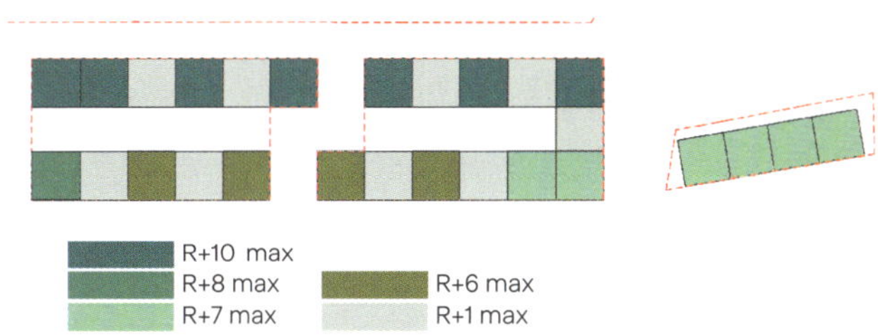

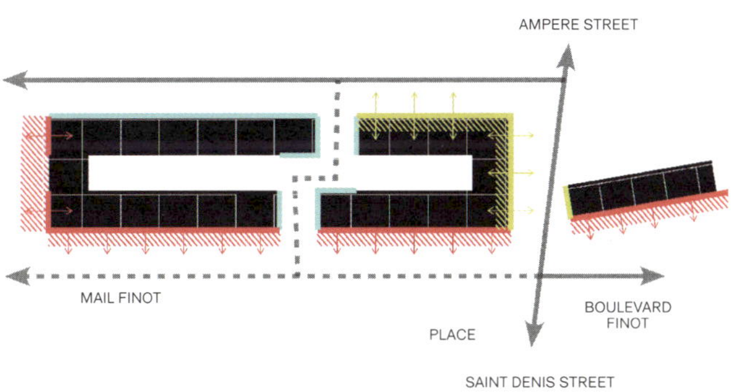

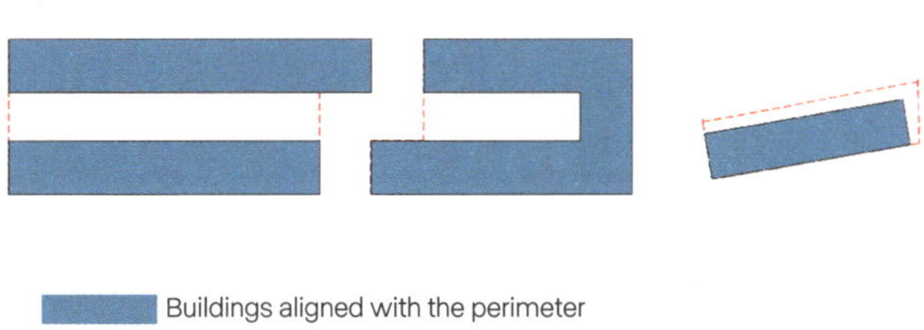

#501# AMBITION 9

BIODIVERSITY IN URBAN AREAS

Scores - Lot sheets

CHARACTERISTICS OF THE SECTOR
URBAN AND LANDSCAPE REQUIREMENTS

STEEL JIGS
Capable volumes vary according to their position in the chosen morphology. There are two distinct templates: the first is based on a 21m square plan and the second on a 21x42m parallelepiped volume. These clear, pure volumetrics are intended to give rise to a homogeneous urban piece on the scale of the district, giving it a large-scale identity.

HEIGHTS
For bioclimatic reasons, heights vary according to location. On the Mail Finot side, the buildings are lower to form an R+6 frontage (and occasionally R+7/8 on the bow and stern) to allow good sunlight into the interior landscape. This height is a maximum. The opposite façade, along the Cité du Cinéma, is based on an R+9/R+10 up to the limits of the PLU. In-between volumes may not exceed the ground floor line, as these are sometimes two storeys high, particularly near the Seine, due to the slope of the land. The office building is punctuated by a differentiated floor plan, allowing the college courtyard to be bathed in sunlight.

RELATIONSHIP WITH PUBLIC SPACE
The only road open to motor traffic is located along the Cité du Cinéma. It contains the car park entrances for each of the condominiums. The pedestrian nature of the Finot Mall prevents any car park ramps from being built along this route. Occasional access may be provided on the rue Ampère side, provided this does not disrupt traffic. Access to the dwellings is via walk-through lobbies, which are largely open and glazed between the street and the heart of the landscaped block. The levelling of the landscape at the heart of the urban area should encourage visual and physical links between the two built-up areas.

ALIGNMENTS
Throughout the sector, the buildings are aligned with the boundaries of the plots to "hold" the street and mark the continuity towards the Seine. These "clear" lines are fixed. An empty strip of land forms a continuous planted heart of the block, stretching all the way to the slopes. The alignments define the structure of the road network and public spaces. Building D3 must respect the alignment along Boulevard Finot Extended and mark the corner with Rue Saint Denis. This block forms one of the façades of the square located further south - thickening the rue de Saint-Denis.

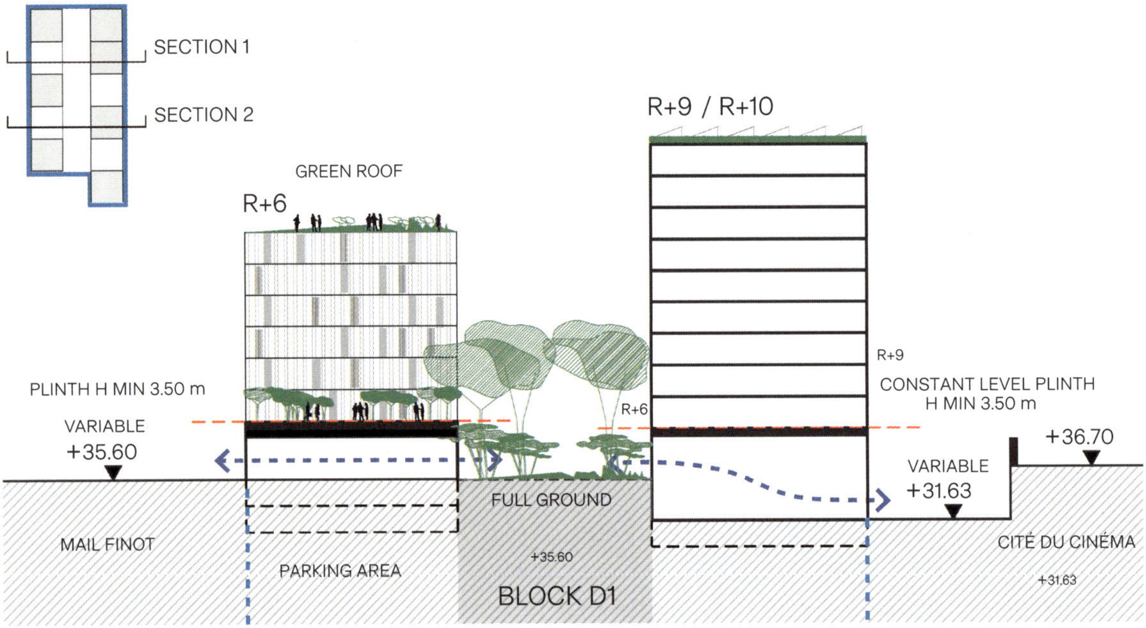

Section 1 - Principle (approximate heights)

TRANSPARENCY TOWARDS THE HEART OF THE BLOCK

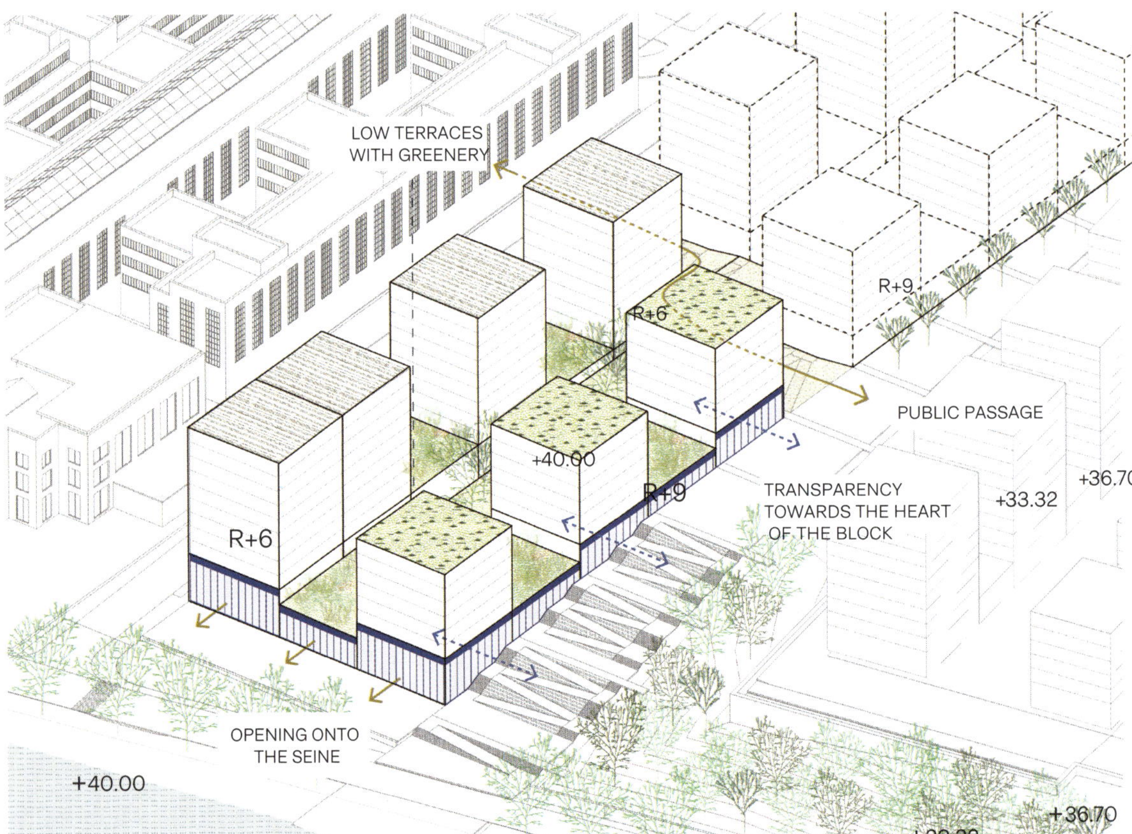

#503# AMBITION 9

BIODIVERSITY IN URBAN AREAS

Block D1. The heart of the block.

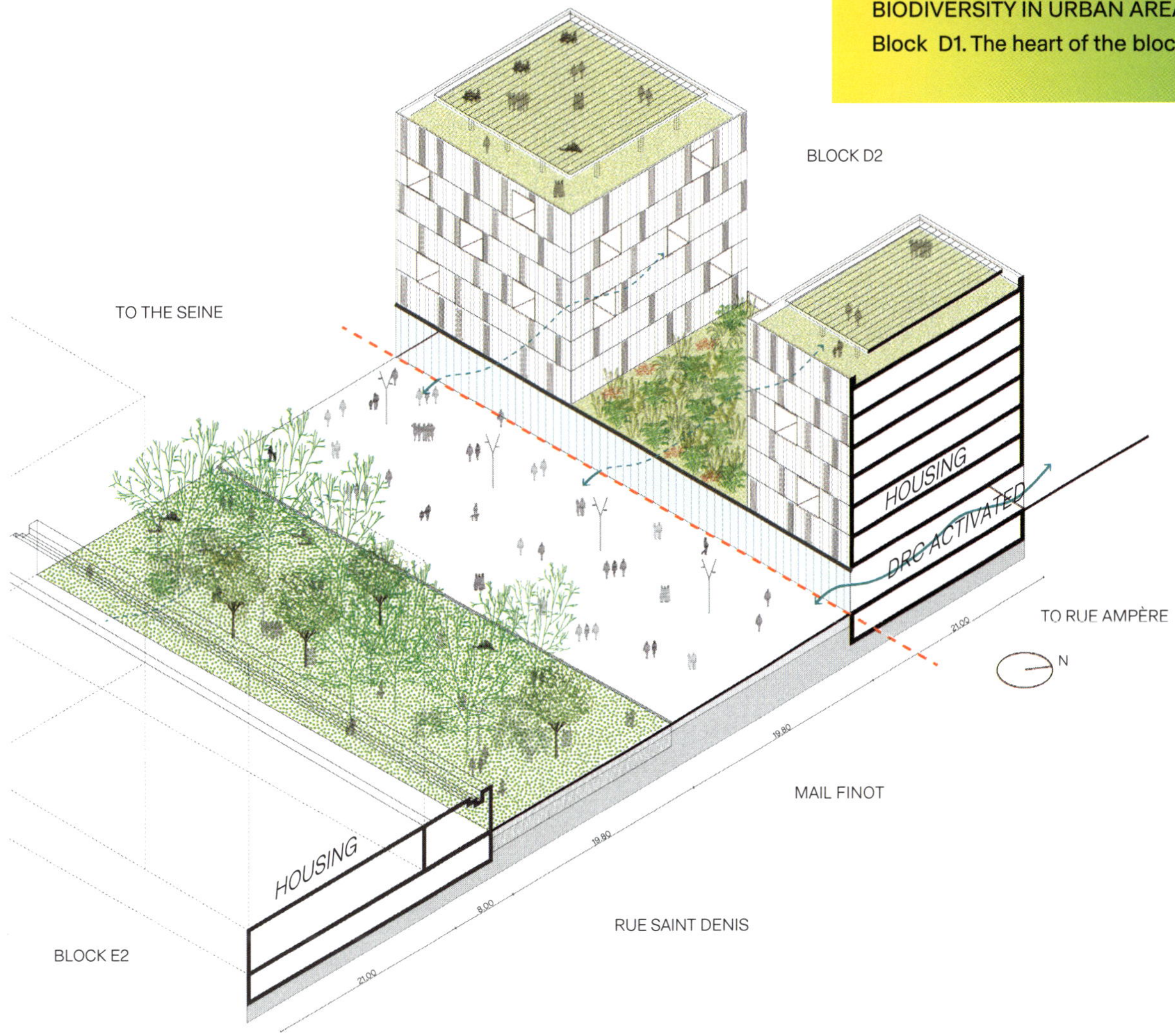

Axonometric section of Finot Mail in block D2

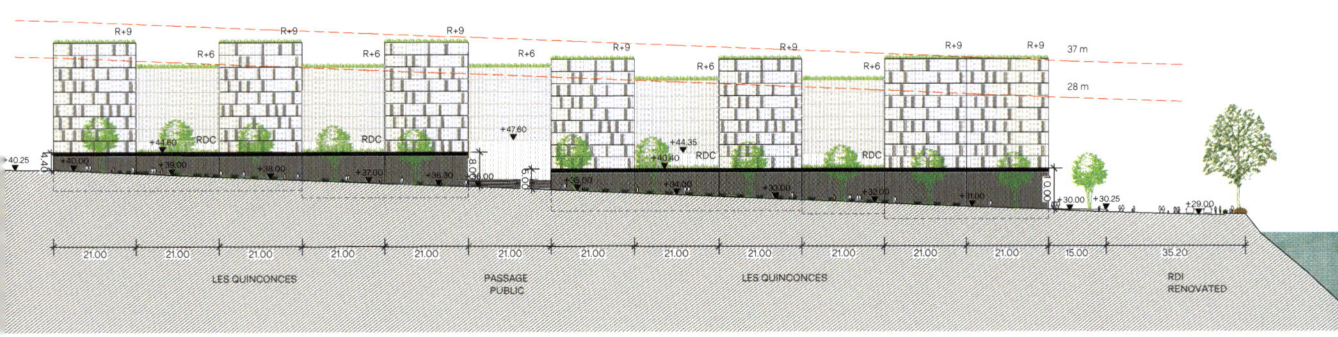

Longitudinal section of the street running alongside the Cité du Cinéma

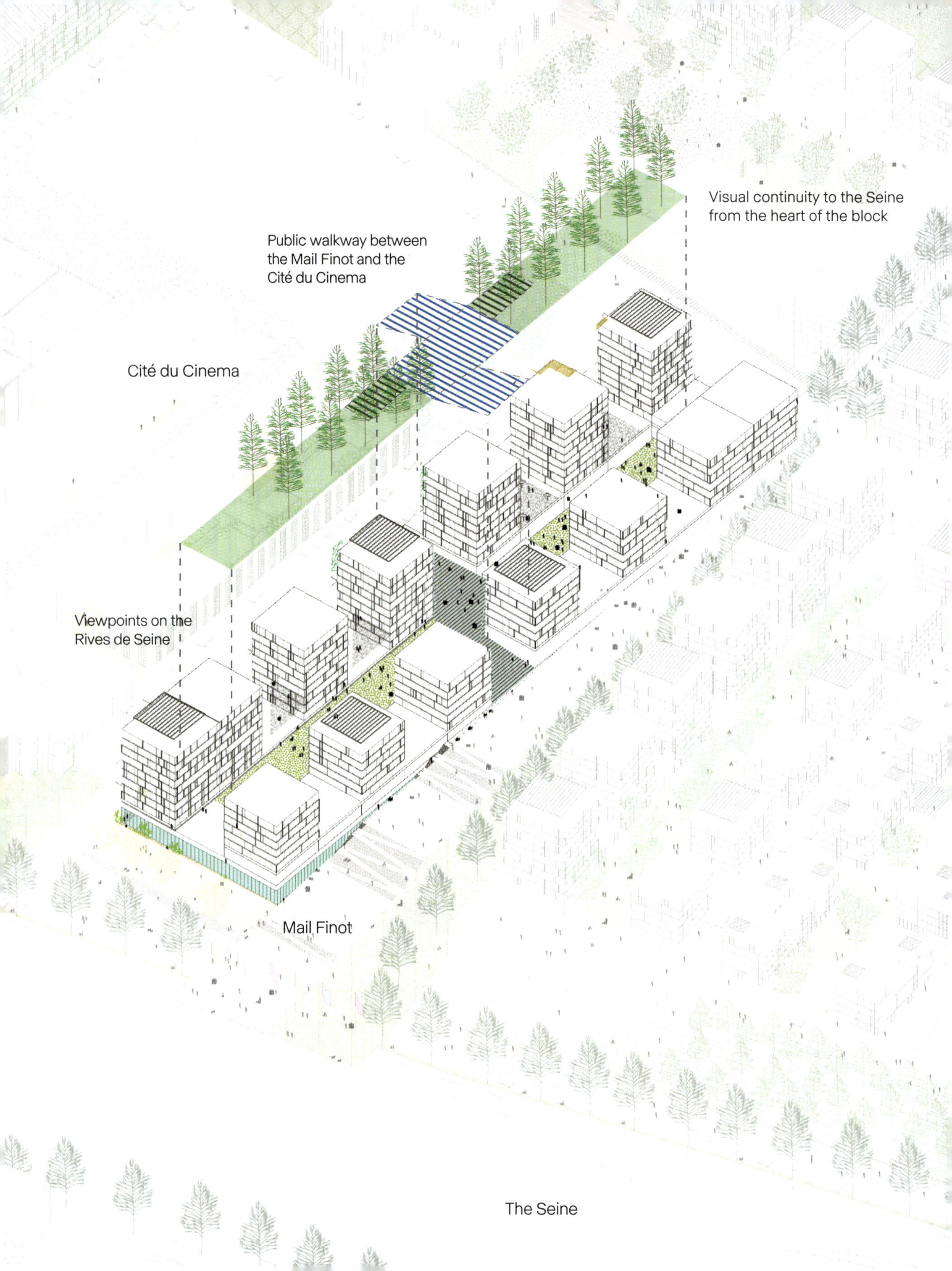

Visual continuity to the Seine from the heart of the block
Public walkway between the Mail Finot and the Cité du Cinema
Cité du Cinema
Viewpoints on the Rives de Seine
Mail Finot
The Seine

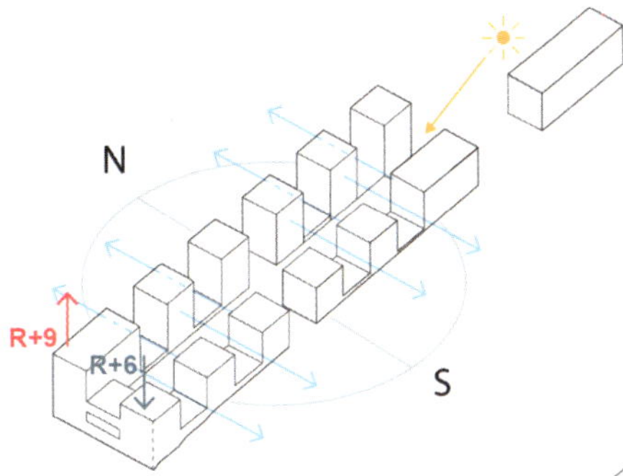

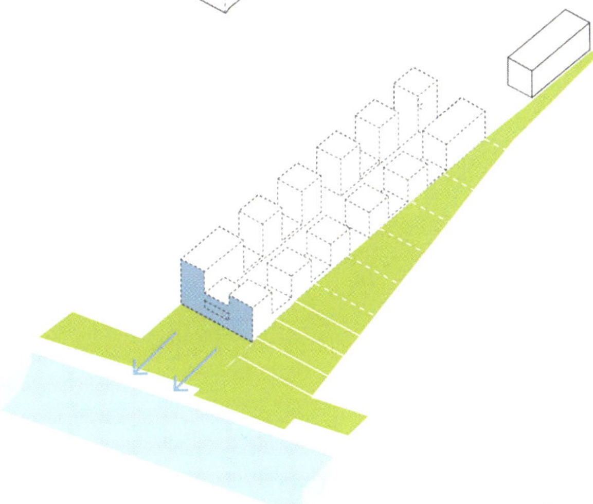

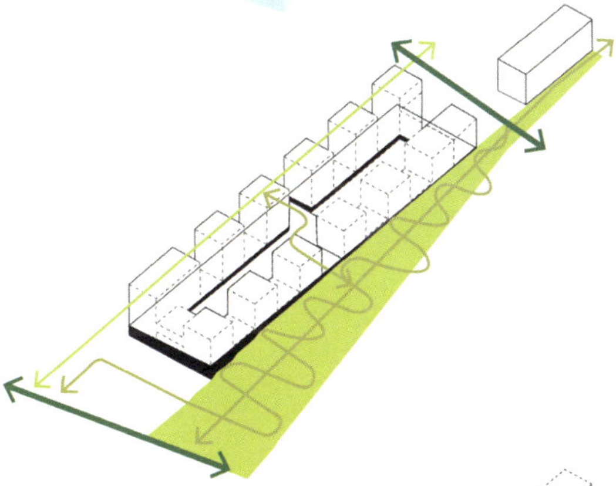

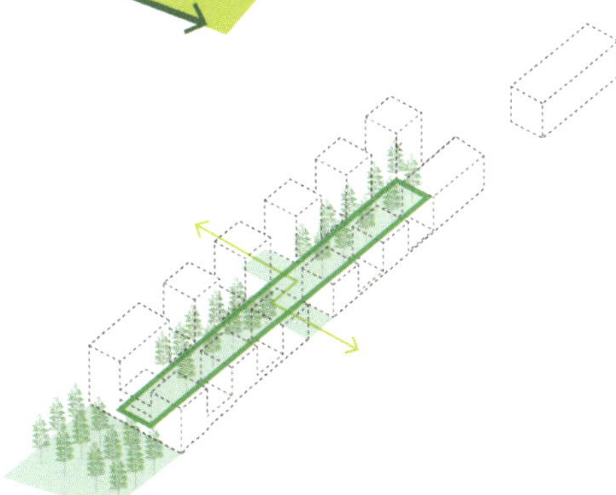

#505# **AMBITION 9**

BIODIVERSITY IN URBAN AREAS
Scores - Lot sheets

BIOCLIMATISM, SUNLIGHT AND VIEWS

Two factors underpin the bioclimatic nature of the Quinconces urban development. The two building lines are asymmetrical, with the higher part to the north and the lower part to the south. Secondly, the Quinconces morphology allows the dwellings to be more open to views and sunlight, as well as improving the natural ventilation of the inner courtyards. The verticality of the buildings allows the prevailing winds to pass through and refresh the landscaped inner blocks.

THE PROW

The urban form follows the topography from the rue de Saint Denis to the RD1. The sequence of buildings reveals a distinctive bow marked by a large base volume. The clearings facing the Seine provide a physical link between the slopes of Saint-Ouen-sur-Seine and the landscaped banks of the Seine. The architecture of this bow should highlight the building frontage facing the river and, above all, anchor this urban element in the geography of the Seine Valley.

WATERLINE, THE GROUND FLOOR

Two continuous lines form a base along the Mall Finot and turn around along the street opposite the Cité du Cinéma. Each horizontal line creates a unified base that expands downwards, following the slope and topography of the terraces on the site. This volume stands out from the architecture of the upper floors to integrate the activities and facilities associated with life in the district. This attention to detail enhances the perspective towards the Seine, echoing the base of the "Belvederes".

HEART OF THE DISTRICT

The landscape in the centre of the area should be visible from the public spaces. The continuity of the base must be able to offer occasional porosities, allowing the relationships between communal, private, and public areas to be understood. The topography will act as a revealing element here, and will need to adapt to the gradients on either side of the "ship".

Tree strata

Carpinus betulus

Prunus avium

Franixus excelsior

Quercus robur

Dryopteris filix max

Pteridium aquailinum

Calluna vulgaris

Astrantia major

Castanea sativa

Amelanchier lamarckii

Cornus mas

Shrub strata

Viburnum lantana

Lingustrum vulgare

Spirea x cinerea

Rosa canina

Herbaceous strata

Archillea millefolium

Allium ursinum

Anemone coronaria
"The Bridge"

Aruncus dioicus

Filipendula ulmaria

Galium odoratum

Campanula latifolia

Geranium pratense

Iris sibirica

Carex pendula

Melica uniflora

Molinia caerulea

Festua pratensis

Calamagrostis arundinacea

Briza media

Deschampsia cespitosa

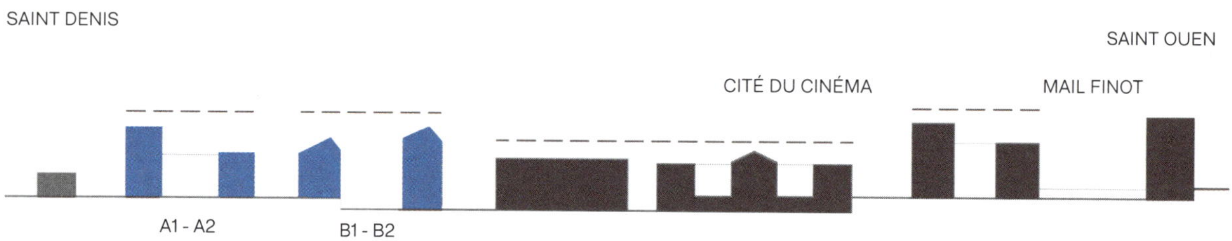
SAINT DENIS
SAINT OUEN
CITÉ DU CINÉMA
MAIL FINOT
A1 - A2
B1 - B2

THE SEINE
A86
+29 ngf
Seine Allée
Rue Ampère
PLEYEL
PARK

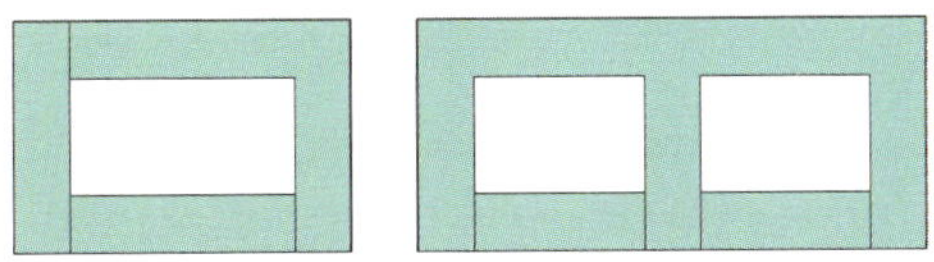

imposed steel jig

Prow - Emergence principle - R+14/ R+15
High lines - R+9/R+10
Intermediate lines - R+7

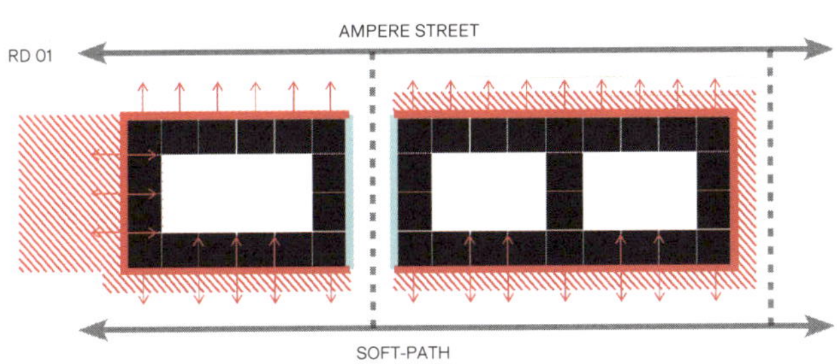

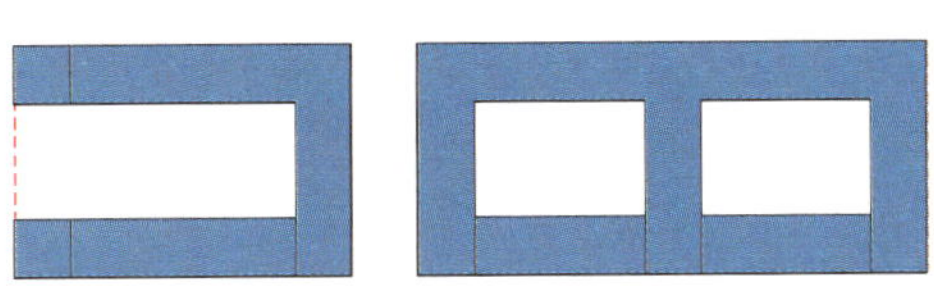

Principle of facade layout within the perimeter

#509# AMBITION 9

BIODIVERSITY IN URBAN AREAS
Scores - Lot sheets

STEEL JIG
The envelope defines a very clear relationship between the built spaces and the heart of the blocks. The 15-metre-wide construction templates allow for the integration of large outdoor spaces and through-planning flats. The aim is to create a compact, dense, continuous urban component to the existing block. At the head of this "ship", a remarkable volume marks the prow of the project.

HEIGHTS
The heights vary to provide the best possible sunlight for the homes and the heart of the block, while respecting the 37m limit set out in the PLU. The buildings are taller on the Rue Volta side and on the cross facades. A second line along the dual carriageway is marked by a varied building scale, from R+7 to R+10. Occasional overruns to R+11 may be made along Rue Volta if they help to diversify the urban frontage. The height of the facade overlooking the Seine is the highest point of the urban development.

RELATIONSHIP TO PUBLIC SPACE
Access to the dwellings is via through lobbies, which are largely open and glazed between the street and the heart of the block. Access to the car parks is via rue Volta. The project is designed to encourage visual links between public and private spaces. These openings, which are planned for each block, should provide generous visual openings for pedestrians on the ground floor.

ALIGNMENTS
Throughout the sector, the buildings are set at the boundaries of the plots to highlight the street and the continuity towards the Seine. These clear lines are fixed but flexible within the plot. The thickness of the buildings should make it possible to create walk-through flats from T3 upwards and create a continuous empty strip at the heart of the block, giving the courtyards a simple, strong geometry.

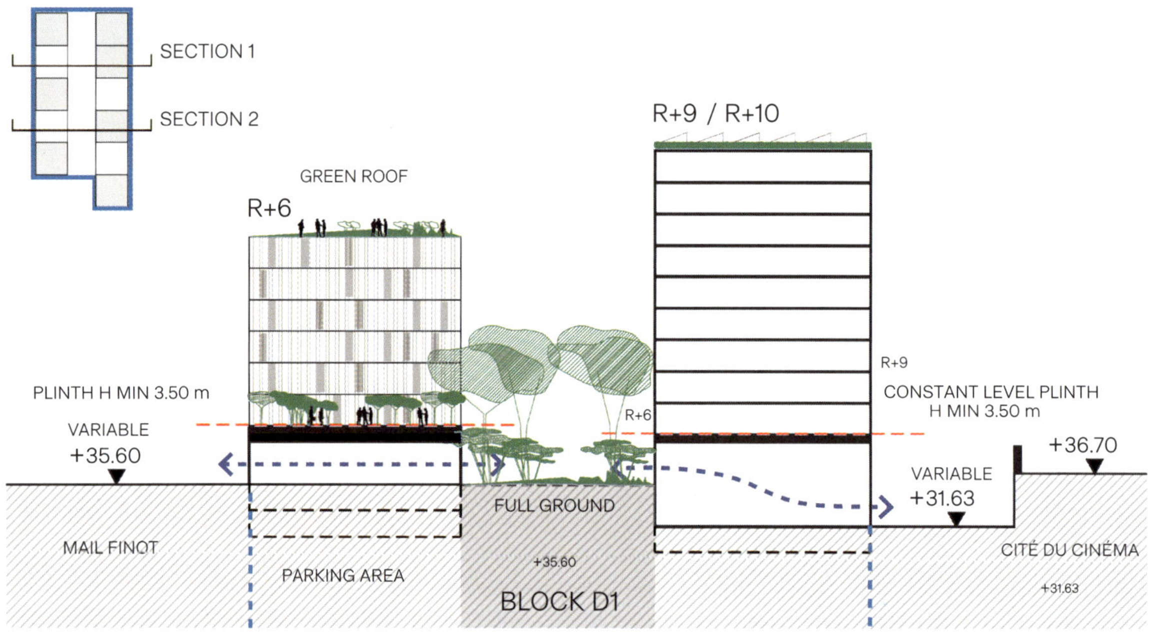

Section 1

← – → Transparence towards the heart of the block

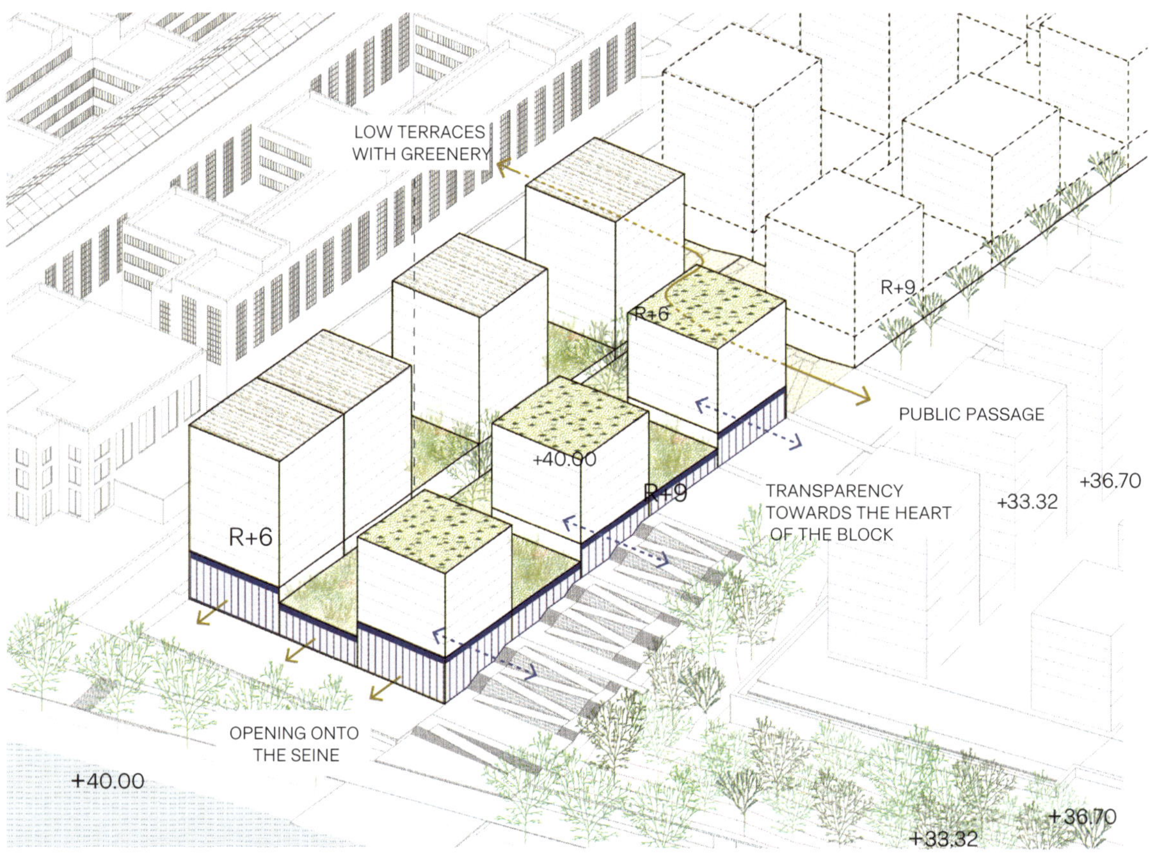

#511# AMBITION 9

BIODIVERSITY IN URBAN AREAS

Block D1. The heart of the block.

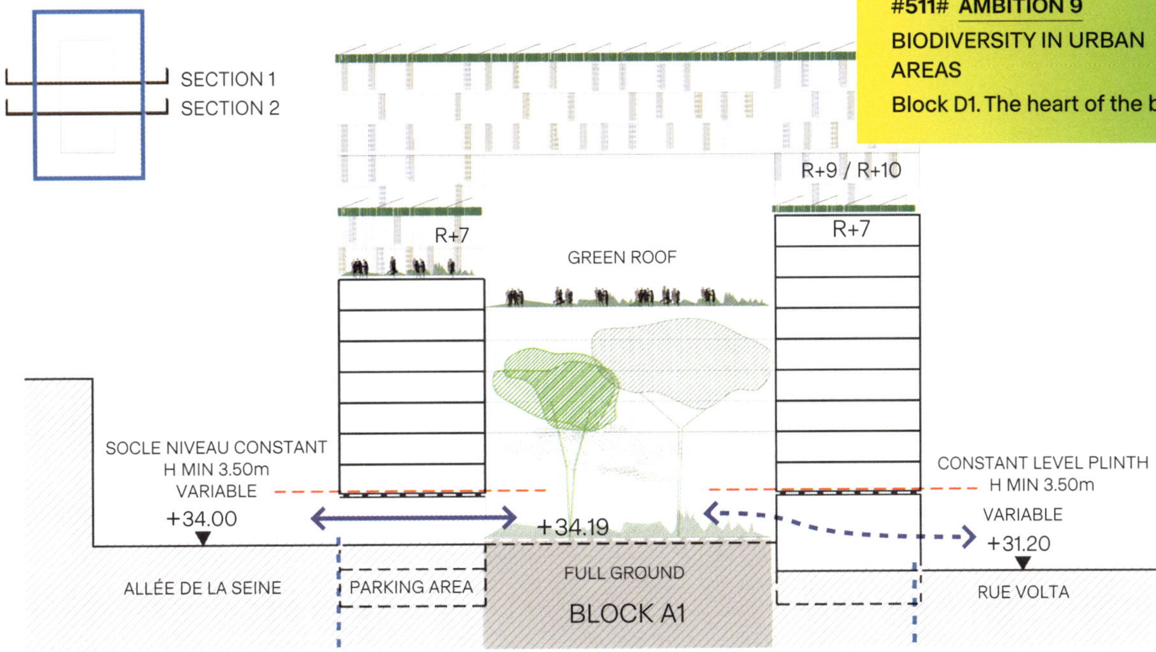

Coupe 1

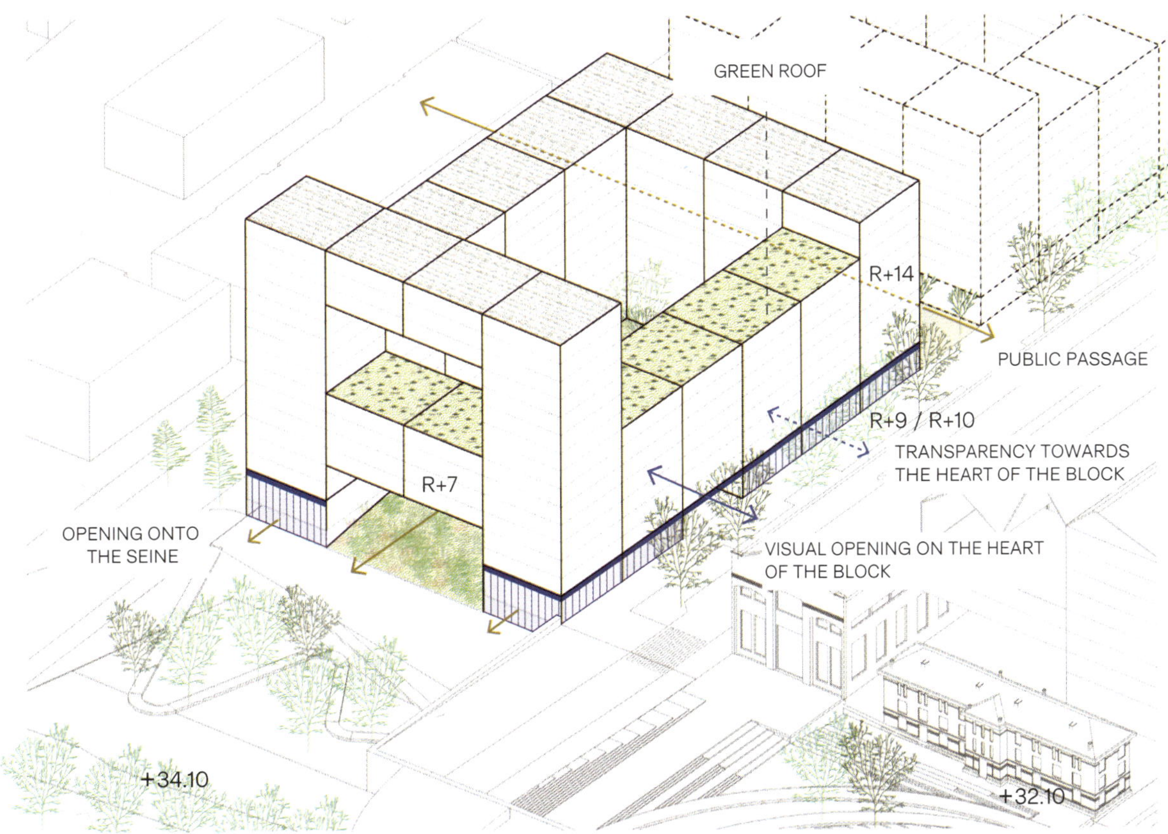

Axonométrie

Visual continuity
down to the Sein
from the heart of
the block
Public passage
Rives de Seine
Park
Amphitheatre
of greenery
Olympic
Village

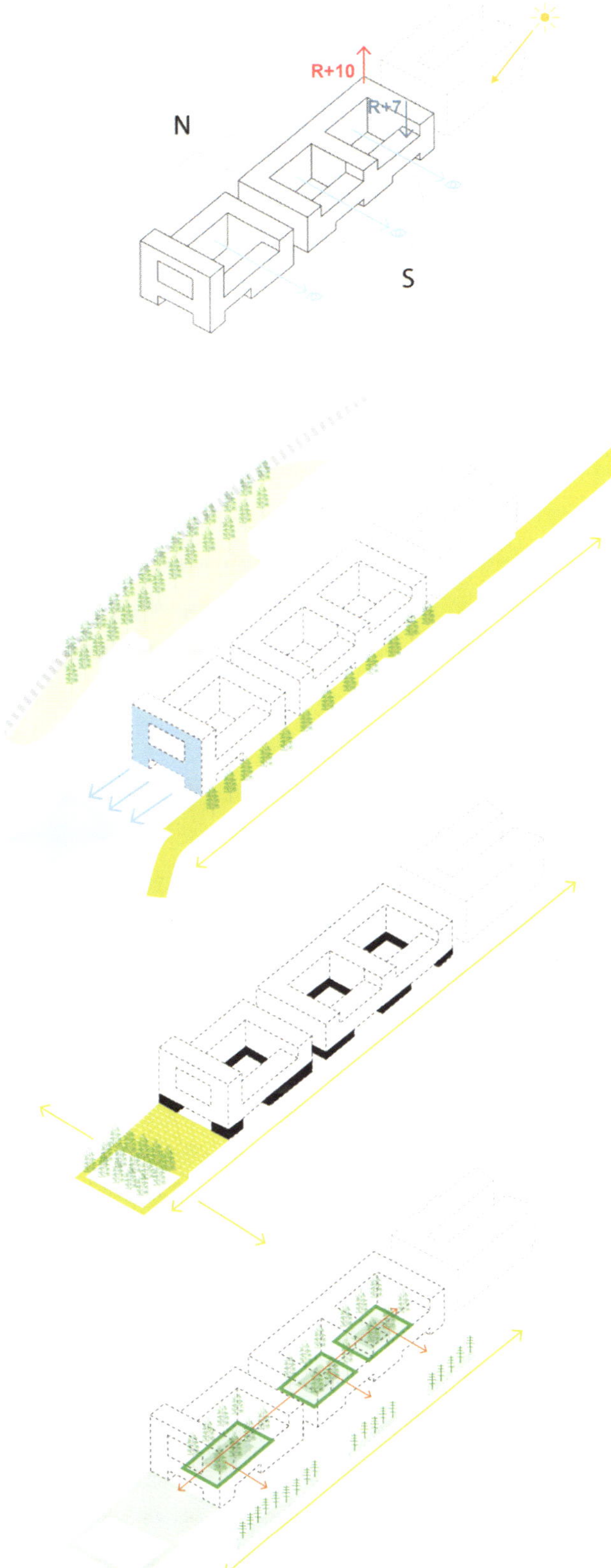

#513# **AMBITION 9**

BIODIVERSITY IN URBAN AREAS

Scores - Lot sheets

CLIMATE, SUNLIGHT, AND VIEWS

The morphology of the block is asymmetrical between its northern and southern parts. Two lines of different heights mark the plot, with lower buildings to the south to promote sunlight for the flats and open views towards the Seine for as many people as possible. Porosities on the ground floor ensure that the heart of the block is naturally ventilated.

THE PROW

The massing of the bow of the building is intended to mark the place of the Olympic and Paralympic Village within the Saint-Denis area. Visible from the Seine and the A86 motorway, the bow is designed as a landmark building, an emergence linked to the Pleyel Tower in the distance. It gives a glimpse of the landscape at the heart of the block. As in the other sectors, this emergence is intended to create a varied, terraced façade overlooking the Seine, a characteristic feature in dialogue with the large scale of the Seine valley.

WATERLINE, THE GROUND FLOOR

A line forms a continuous base around each block. This horizontal volume must stand out from the architecture of the upper volumes and turn around to face each public space. This volume must allow for the integration of services and facilities, as well as the lobbies and communal areas of the dwellings. To ensure permeability, the very large porches should provide a rhythm between the programs, openings, and entrances. The pedestals along the Allée de Seine should offer functions that will liven up the public space.

HEART OF THE DISTRICT

The central void in the heart of the blocks should allow for the creation of large-scale green spaces, designed as a succession of courtyards. Preserving a significant proportion of the land should be kept as open space, so that these unique landscapes can be developed and enjoyed by all residents.

Herbaceous strata

Anemone sylverstris

Linaria purpurea

Geranium macrorrhizum

Saponaria officinalis

Dryopteris filix max

Pteridium aquailinum

Calluna vulgaris

Astrantia major

Origanum vulgare

Geranium nodosum

Geranium robertianum

Epilobium hirsutum

Lythrum salicaria

Molinia caerulea

Deschampsia cespitosa

Epilobium angustifolium

Tree strata

Quercus robur

Quercus pubescens

Prunus avium

Sorbus torminalis

Betula pubescens

Betula pendula

Pyrus communis "Beech Hill"

Buxus sempervirens

Rosa pimpinellifolia

Viburnum opulus

Viburnum tinus

#515# **AMBITION 9**

BIODIVERSITY IN URBAN AREAS

Block A1

LANDSCAPE AND BIODIVERSITY

As a rule, preference should be given to planting large trees that open up views across the inner blocks towards the landscape along the banks of the Seine. The proposed plant palette should be consistent with that of the public spaces (the Plateau Jardin).

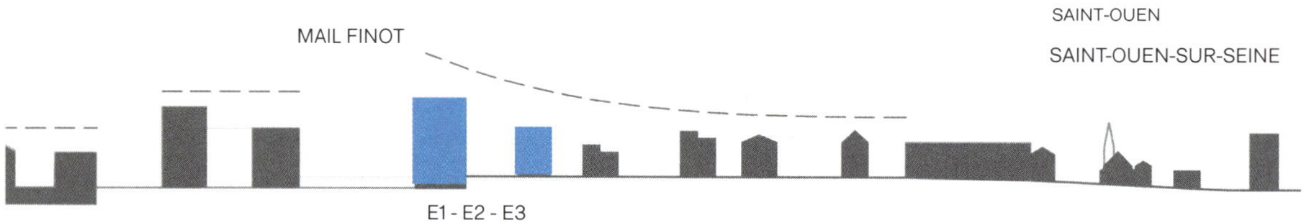
MAIL FINOT
SAINT-OUEN
SAINT-OUEN-SUR-SEINE
E1 - E2 - E3

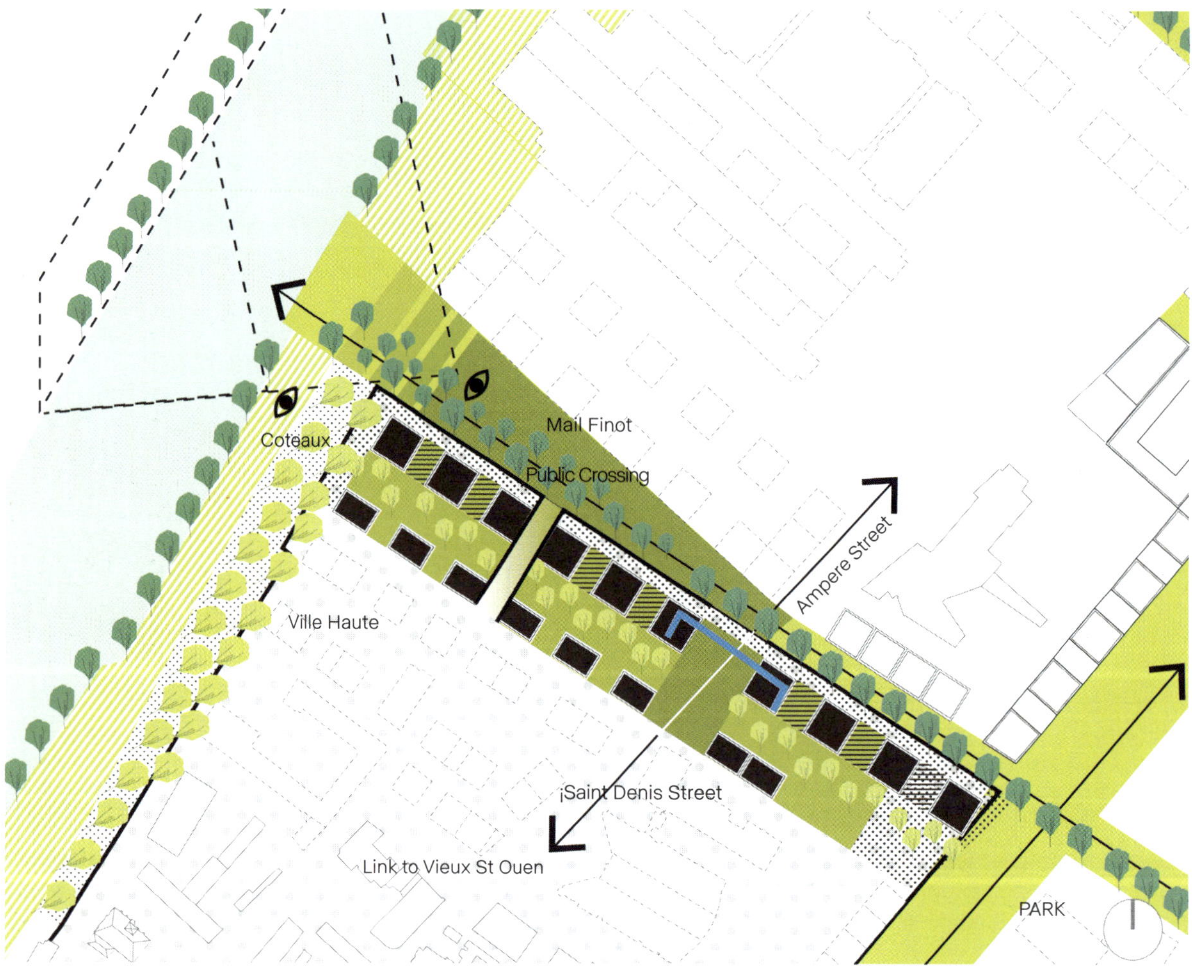
Mail Finot
Coteaux
Public Crossing
Ampere Street
Ville Haute
¡Saint Denis Street
Link to Vieux St Ouen
PARK

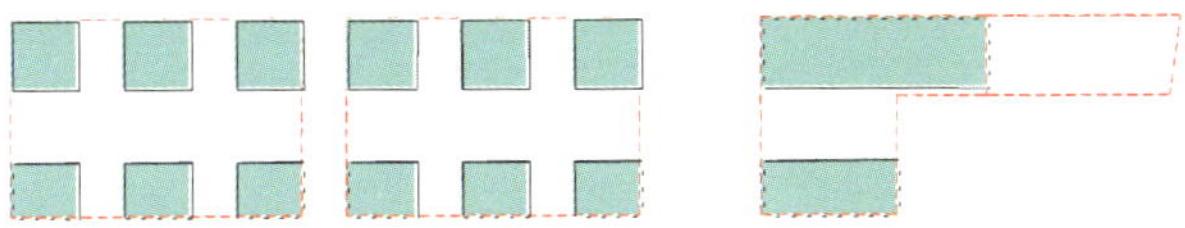

imposed steel jig

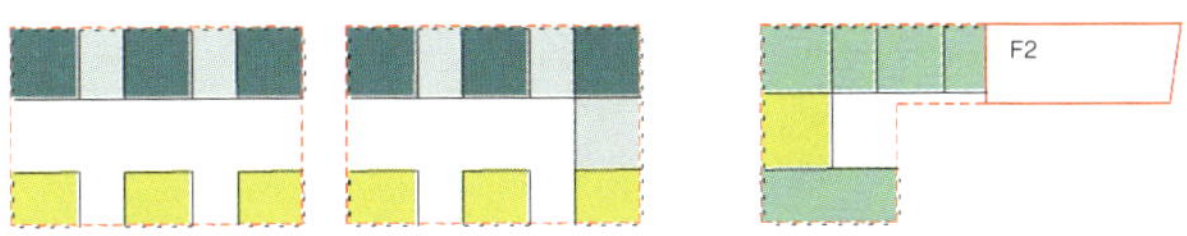

R+10 max
R+7 max and occasionally R+8
R+5 max and occasionally R+6 attics
R+1 max

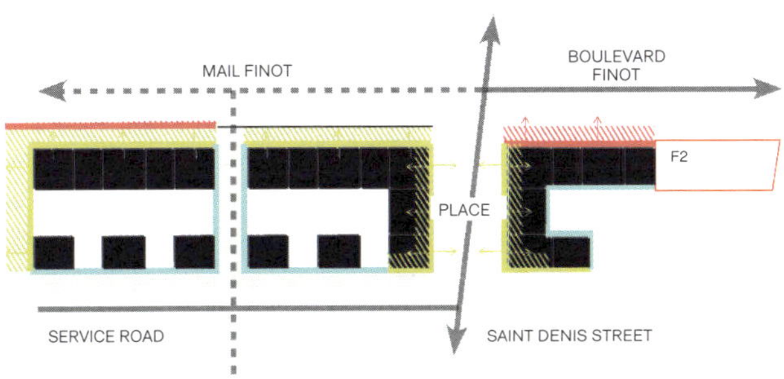

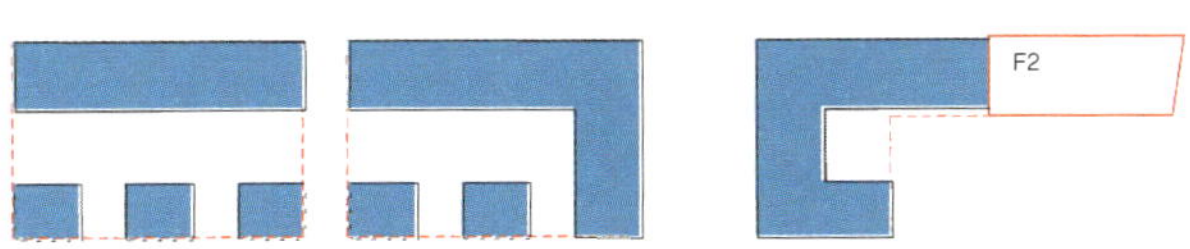

Facades in strict alignment with the perimeter

#517# AMBITION 9

BIODIVERSITY IN URBAN AREAS

Scores - Lot sheets

STEEL JIGS
The simple volumes are divided into two height lines. One line forms the silhouette of the Mail Finot, while the second line forms the link to Saint-Ouen- sur-Seine and the "Villas" through lower buildings. Beyond the square, towards the Park and the Pleyel district, the template marks the entrance to the site.

HEIGHTS
For bioclimatic reasons, heights vary according to location. On the Mail Finot side, the buildings are taller, forming an R+10 façade right up to the limits of the PLU, based on a 21m square plan. The second, parallel line of buildings has a maximum height of R+5 (R+6 in some cases with an attic) and develops with a 17x21m footprint.

RELATIONSHIP TO PUBLIC SPACE
The project must encourage visual porosity between public and private spaces. Access to the dwellings is via walk-through lobbies, which are largely open and glazed between the street and the interior landscape of the urban room.
Each access is distributed along the feeder roads to encourage retail outlets on the square. The car parks are connected only to the car service loop and are integrated into the volume of the buildings.

ALIGNMENTS
Throughout the sector, the buildings are aligned with the boundaries of the plots to "hold" the street and mark the continuity towards the Seine. These "clear" lines are fixed. An empty strip of land forms a continuous planted heart of the block, stretching all the way to the slopes. The alignments define the structure of the road network and public spaces.

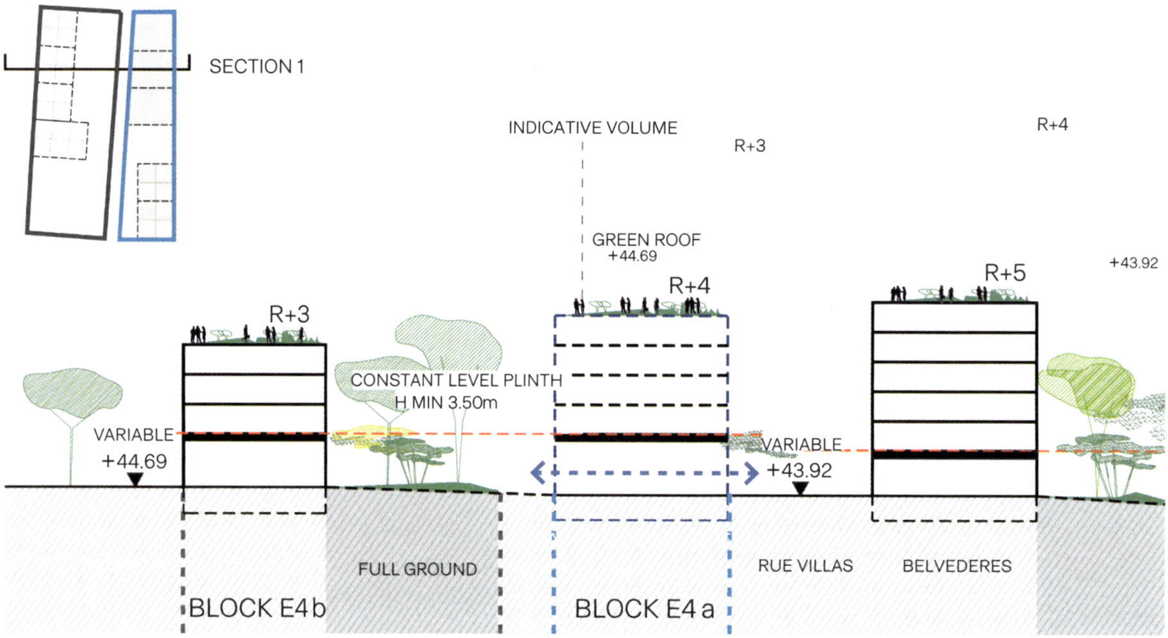

Section 1

Transparence towards the heart of the block

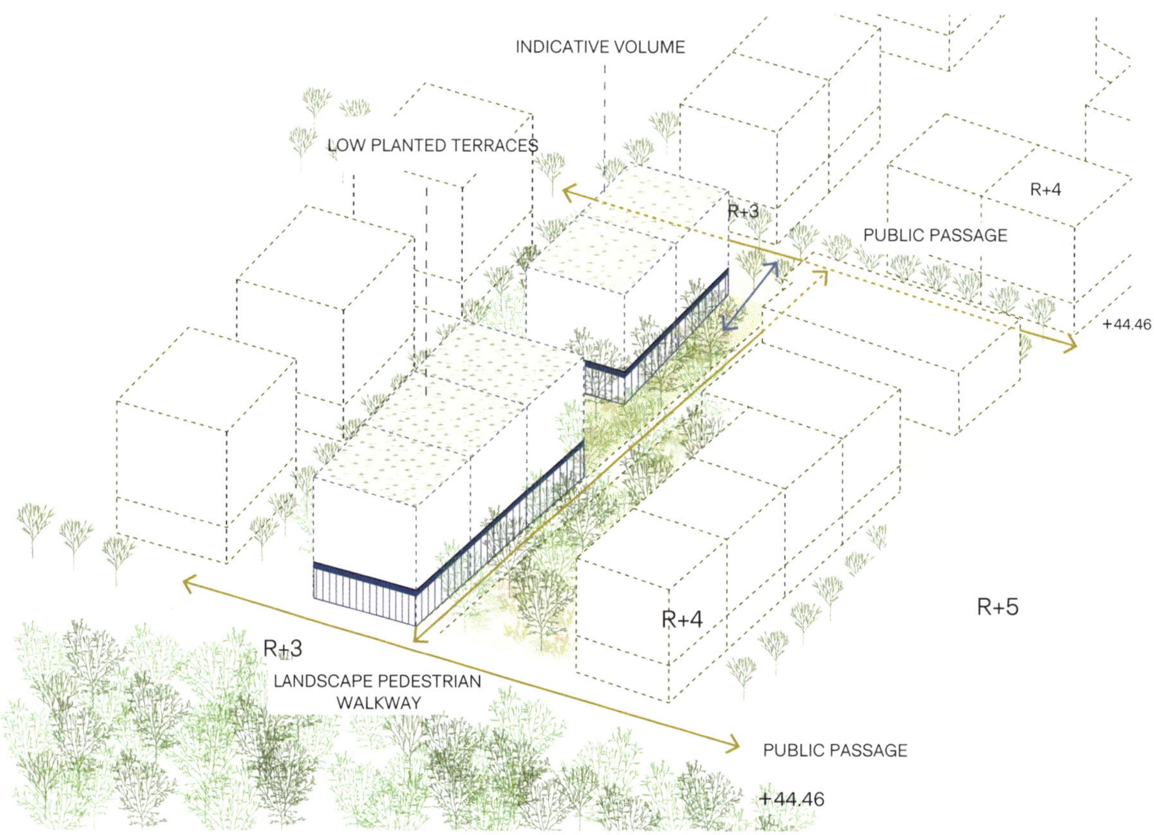

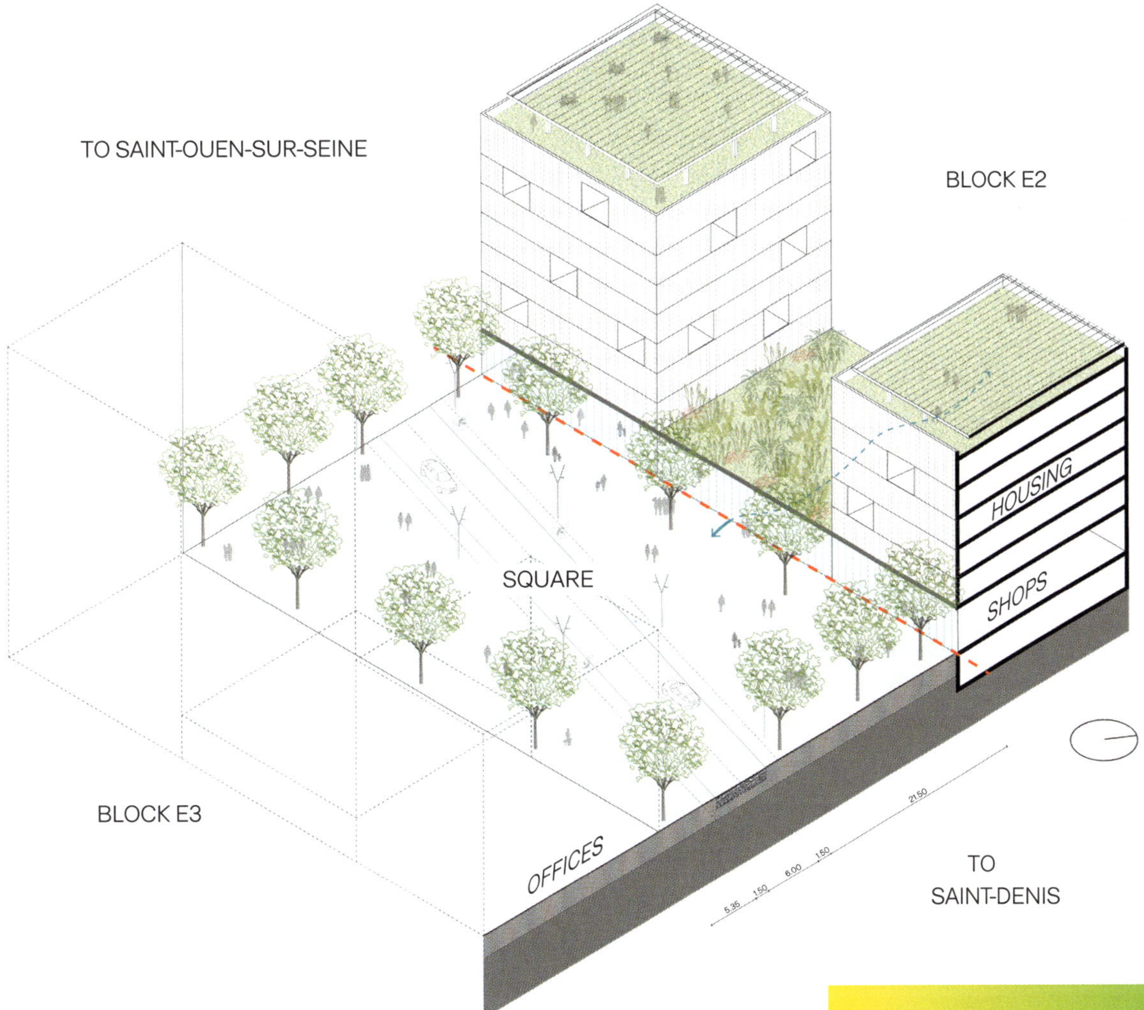

Axonometric section of the square between blocks E2 and E3

#519# AMBITION 9

BIODIVERSITY IN URBAN AREAS

Block E4A. The heart of the blocks.

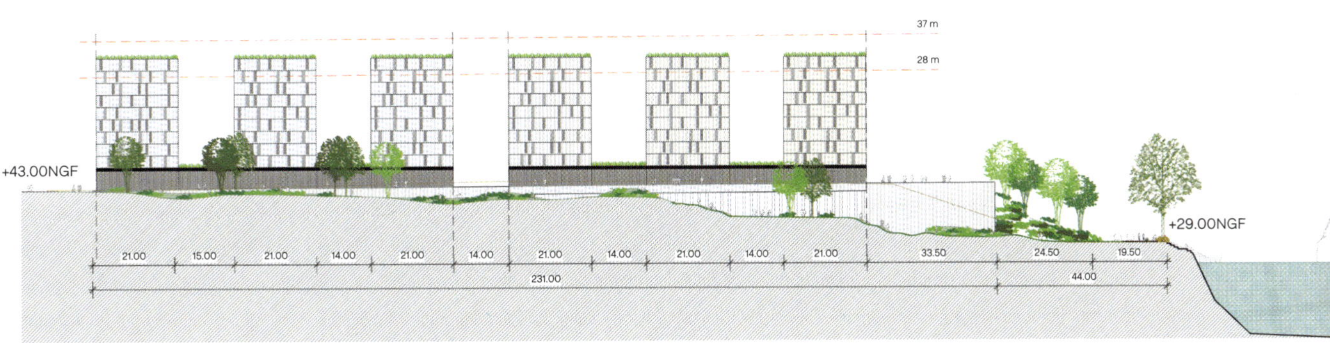

Longitudinal section of the Finot Mall, looking towards the Seine

Passage between Mail Finot
and Les Grandes Maisons
Visual continuity to
the Seine from the
heart of the block
Mail Finot
To Vieux
Saint Ouen
Views of the hillsides
and the Seine

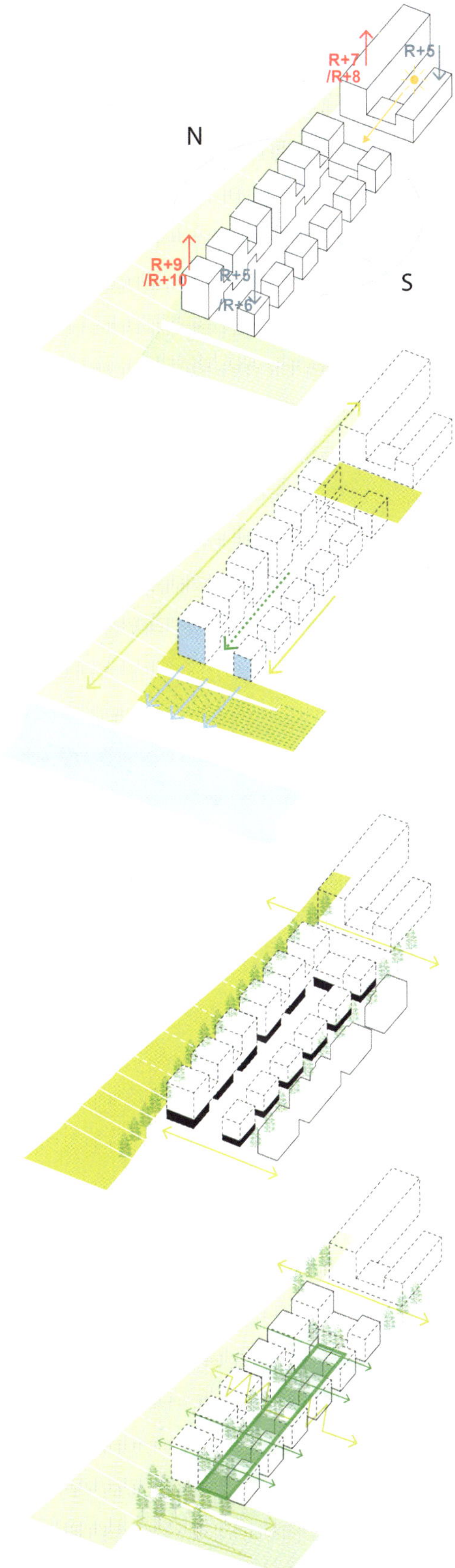

#521# **AMBITION 9**

BIODIVERSITY IN URBAN AREAS

Scores - Lot sheets

BIO-CLIMATISM, SUNLIGHT AND VIEWS
The urban morphology is based on the bioclimatic design of the Belvédères urban area, characterised by an asymmetrical shape between its northern and southern parts. Two different height lines mark the "ship" to encourage sunlight into the flats and open up the views. The aim is also to provide occasional cast shadows on the Finot mall to avoid the heat island effect in summer. The porous ground floor and vertical massing ensure that the heart of the block is naturally ventilated.

THE PROW
This bow is special in that it forms the pivot between two major public spaces: the Mail Finot and the promenade along the slopes of Saint Ouen. Topography plays a major role, as does nature. The continuity of the buildings must allow the emergence of a river front that is characteristic of the town of Saint-Ouen-sur-Seine.

WATERLINE, THE GROUND FLOOR
A continuous line forms a base along the Mall Finot, providing a balcony over the Mall and encouraging connections between the interior and exterior. This horizontal volume should stand out from the architecture of the upper volumes and look back onto the square associated with rue Saint-Denis.

DESIGN
The future presence of the Grand Paris Express structures (spine and tunnel) must be taken into account by the operators. Technical recommendations must be incorporated into the project.

HEAR OF THE DISTRICT
The landscaped central void must provide a continuous opening onto the Seine and be designed to be visible from the public space. The sequence of buildings along the service road to the south should create a rhythm between the buildings and the planted areas, extending the landscape of the blocks towards the street.

Herbaceous strata

Anemone sylverstris

Linaria purpurea

Geranium macrorrhizum

Saponaria officinalis

Dryopteris filix max

Pteridium aquailinum

Calluna vulgaris

Astrantia major

Lythrum salicaria

Molinia caerulea

Deschampsia cespitosa

Epilobium angustifolium

Tree strata

Catsanea sativa

Prunus avium

Betula pubescens

Sorbus domestica

Prunus mahaleb

Mauls x perpetu “Evereste”

Tilia cordata “Winter orange”

#523# **AMBITION 9**

BIODIVERSITY IN URBAN AREAS
Block E5

Generally, preference should be given to planting large trees that open views across the inner blocks towards the landscape along the banks of the Seine.

The proposed plant palette should be consistent with that of the public spaces (the limestone plateau).

A86
SAINT DENIS
AMPERE STREET
CENTRAL PARK
SOFT WAY
CITÉ DU CINÉMA
OLYMPIC
SQUARE
PASSERELLE
THE SEINE
ÎLE
SAINT DENIS

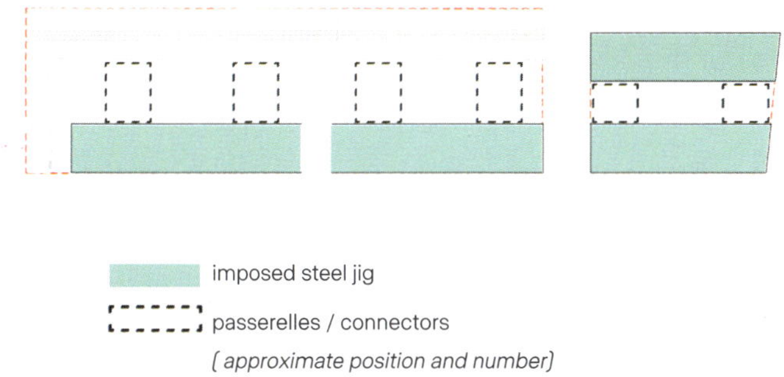

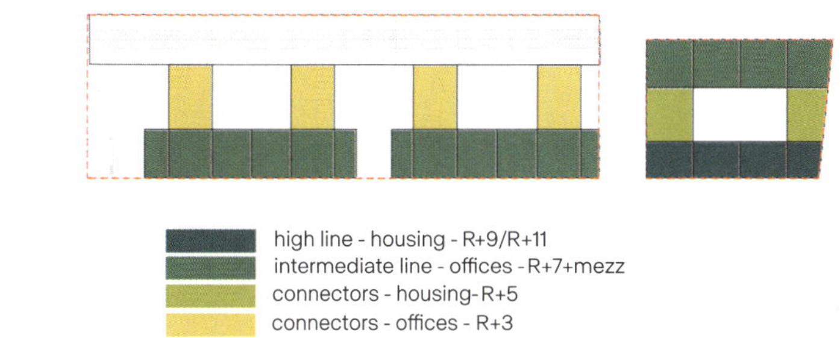

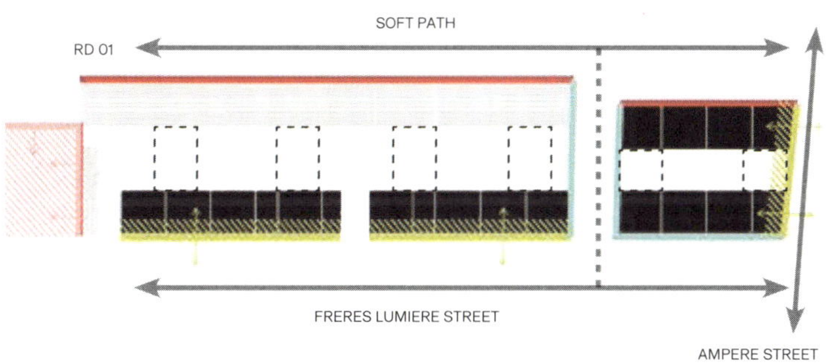

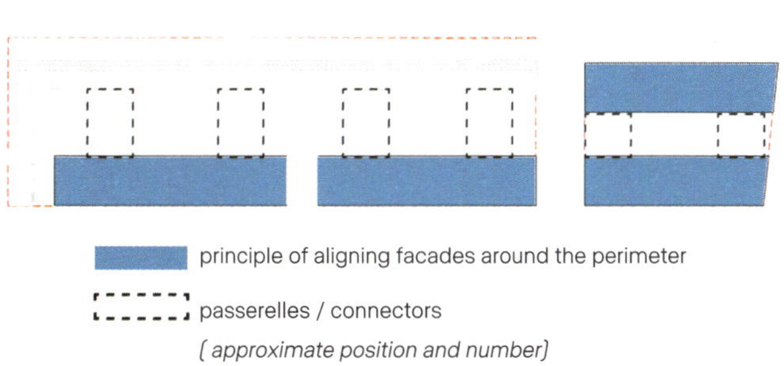

#525# AMBITION 9

BIODIVERSITY IN URBAN AREAS
Scores - Lot sheets

STEEL JIGS

The defined envelopes allow the projection of a tertiary complex. Maxwell Hall is integrated into the design to create a unified whole. The building gauges are 20m wide, arranged along the rue des Frères Lumière, with gaps between buildings of no less than 10m.

HEIGHTS

The height of office buildings is limited to R+7. Mezzanines or occasional overhangs may be added if they help to break up the skyline. Residential units may reach 11, 10 and 12 storeys (R+11) on occasion, with the same objective of asserting the skyline. The height of the "footbridges" or "connectors" must take into account the volume and limits of the Maxwell Hall roof. Those of block B2 will preserve an open and generous central garden.

RELATIONSHIP TO PUBLIC SPACE

Block B2 is linked to Maxwell Hall and will be pedestrianised via the soft lane linked to the Hall. Logistical and car park access will be via Rue des Frères Lumière to the south. A public pedestrian walkway between the blocks will provide cross-connections. The Copernicus building is part of the perimeter of the block, and special attention will be needed to integrate it with the rest of the development. The Copernicus pavilion will mark the urban façade of the Place Olympique.

ALIGNMENTS

The buildings are aligned with the boundaries of the plots to form the frontages of Rue Ampères and Rue Frères Lumière. The internal alignments should highlight the continuity towards the Seine by means of a continuous common void. the Seine through a continuous common void. The façade of Maxwell Hall should be visible and enhanced from Rue Ampère.

Block B1 - The heart of the blocks

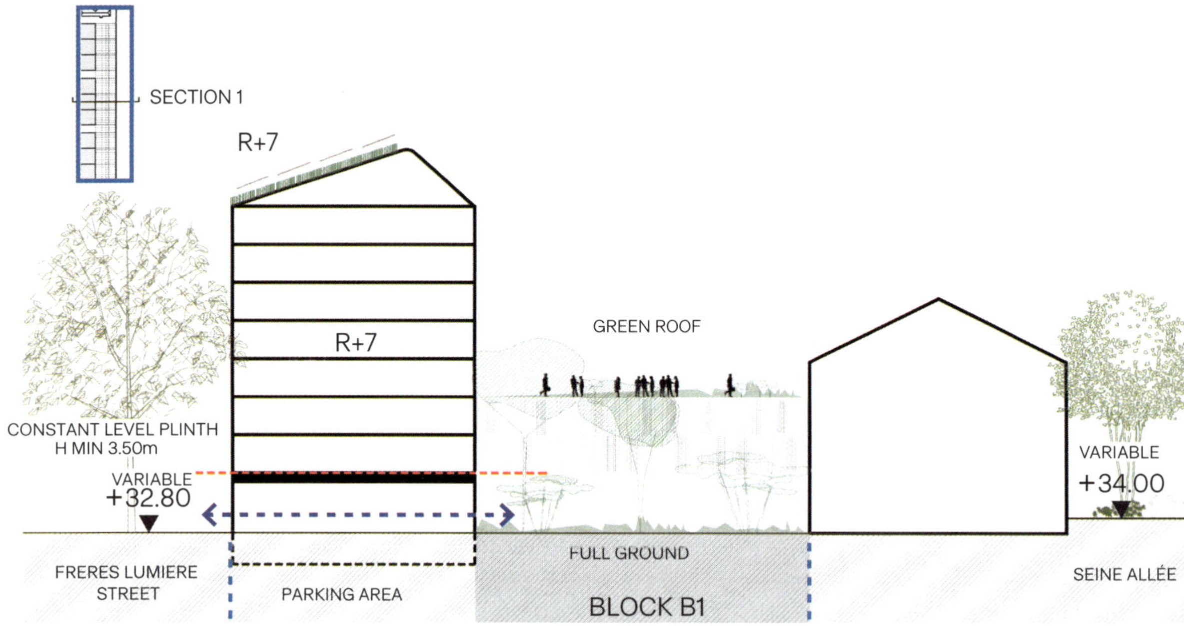

Section 1

← – → Transparence towards the heart of the block

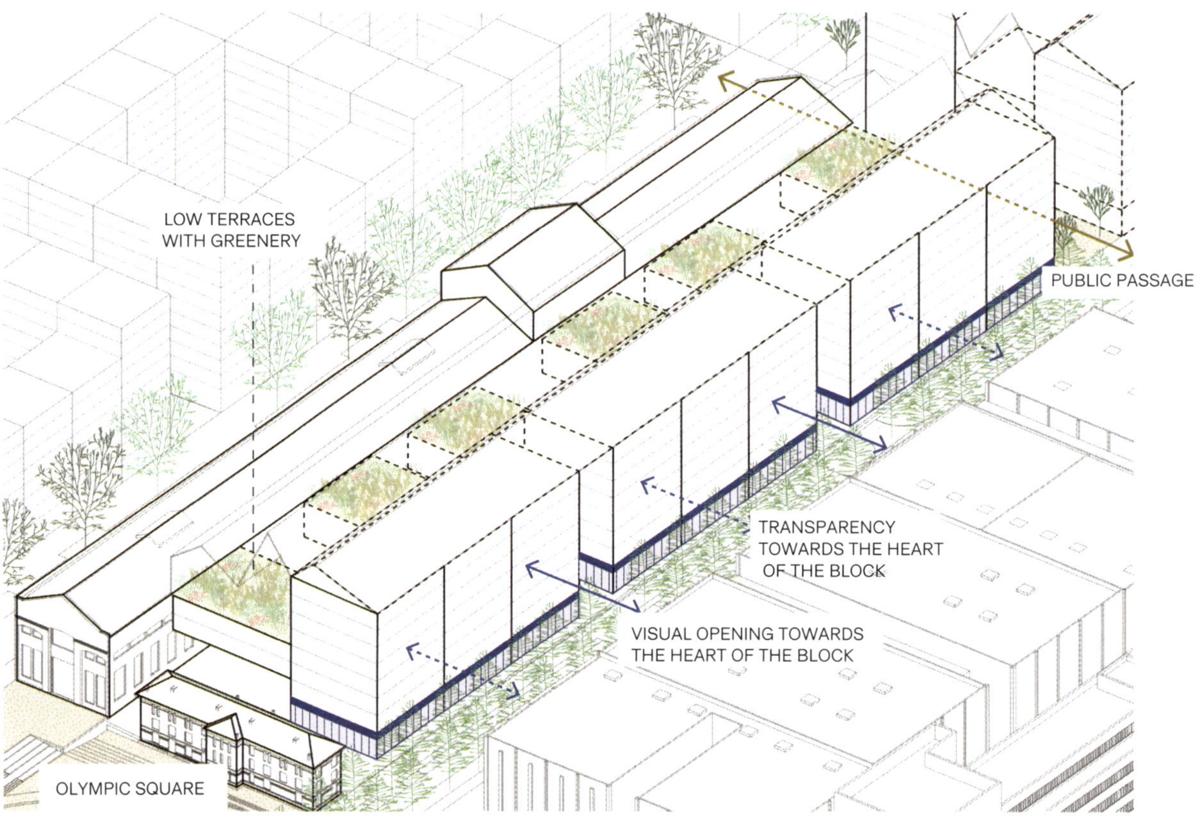

#527# AMBITION 9

BIODIVERSITY IN URBAN AREAS

Block B1. The heart of the blocks

HERITAGE
The sector includes two remarkable buildings to be preserved within B1. These are the Maxwell Hall and the Copernicus building. Dating from the time when the site was occupied by a thermal power plant, these two buildings will be incorporated into the architectural project in order to enhance them and adapt them to their new functions. The aim is to give them a new lease of life while ensuring that they are protected.

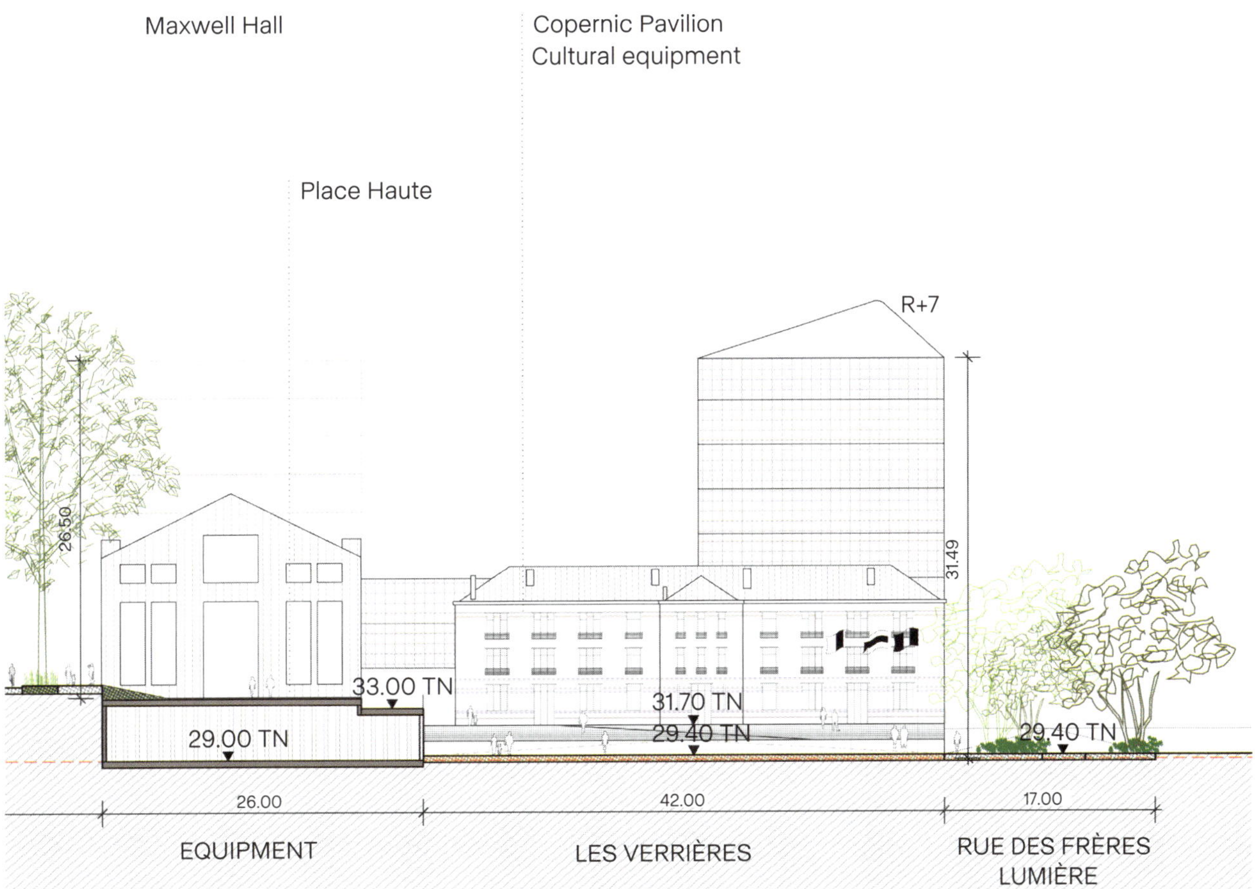

BlockB2 - The heart of the blocks

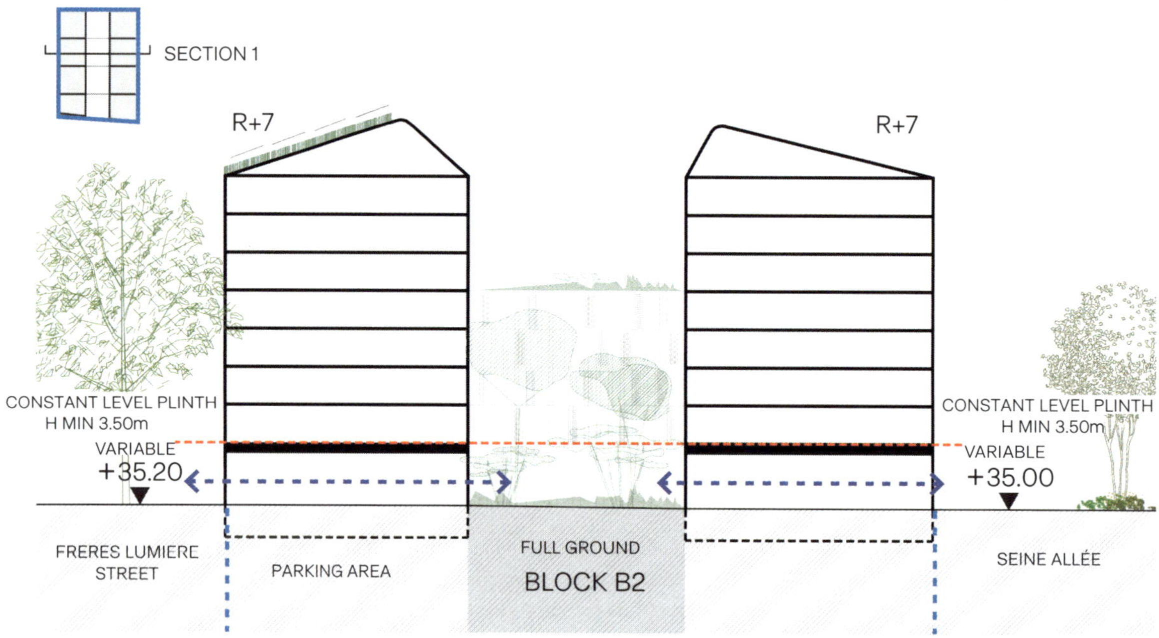

Section 1

← – → Transparence towards the heart of the block

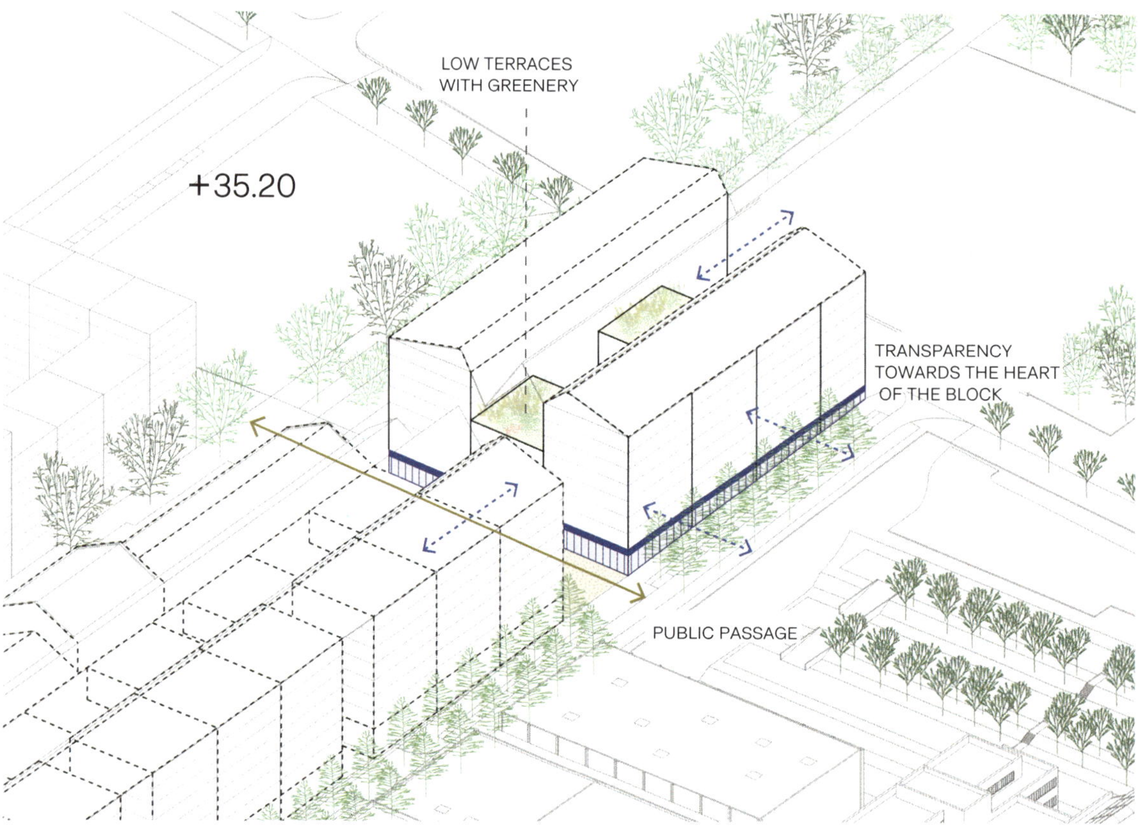

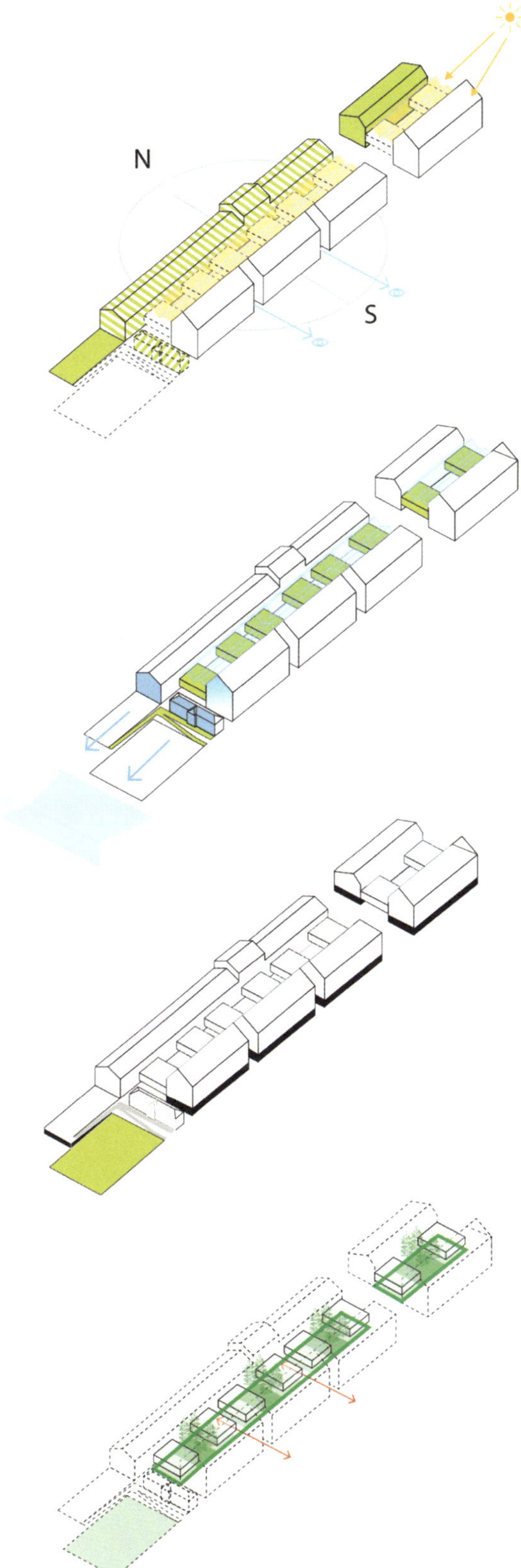

#529# **AMBITION 9**

BIODIVERSITY IN URBAN AREAS

Scores - Lot sheets

CLIMATE, SUNLIGHT AND VIEWS
The volumes and layout of the buildings will be designed to ensure optimum sunlight for the heart of the block and for the interior spaces. Porches and openings to the planted core area will enhance the natural ventilation of all the blocks. The landscaping of the heart of the block and the terraces will help to enhance biodiversity and will be adapted to the uses of future occupants.

THE PROW
For this block, the Copernicus Pavilion is at the head of the scheme, forming an ensemble associated with the Place Olympique. The silhouette of the facade overlooking the Seine is designed to match the massing of the existing building. The new building underlines the uniqueness of Place Olympique. The main feature of the bow is its association with the existing heritage.

WATERLINE, THE GROUND FLOOR
A line forms a continuous base around block B2. This horizontal volume must stand out from the architecture of the upper volumes and turn over onto each public space in connection with the base of Maxwell Hall. This volume must incorporate the services and access lobbies to the offices. For block B1, a horizontal line marks the base of the buildings until it turns around at the front of the Copernicus Pavilion. The plinths along Rue Ampère and the allée de Seine should offer functions that will liven up the public space.

HEART OF THE DISTRICT
The central void should allow the creation of a continuous heart of the block between the two blocks B1 and B2. Ecological continuity will be encouraged. The “connectors” perpendicular to the Hall are marked by a great deal of transparency and will aim for a certain lightness. These singular volumes should make it possible to integrate shared office spaces and combine green spaces to offer a renewed tertiary offering. The treatment of the central areas of the site also marks the link between the project and Maxwell Hall.

Herbaceous strata

Anemone sylverstris

Linaria purpurea

Geranium macrorrhizum

Saponaria officinalis

Dryopteris filix max

Pteridium aquailinum

Calluna vulgaris

Astrantia major

Origanum vulgare

Geranium nodosum

Geranium robertianum

Epilobium hirsutum

Lythrum salicaria

Molinia caerulea

Deschampsia cespitosa

Epilobium angustifolium

Tree strata

Quercus robur

Quercus pubescens

Prunus avium

Sorbus torminalis

Betula pubescens

Betula pendula

Pyrus communis “Beech Hill”

Buxus sempervirens

Rosa pimpinellifolia

Viburnum opulus

Viburnum tinus

#531# AMBITION 9

BIODIVERSITY IN URBAN AREAS

BLOCK B2

LANDSCAPE AND BIODIVERSITY

Generally, preference should be given to planting large trees that open views across the inner blocks towards the landscape along the banks of the Seine. The proposed plant palette should be consistent with that of the public spaces (the Plateau Jardin).

AMBITION 10

SPORT IN THE CITY

The post-Olympic legacy will be quite substantial: new neighbourhoods, swimming pools, schools, the Arena, housing, parks, and so on. The new footbridges in Saint-Denis and Ile Saint-Denis will help to reconnect these areas. However, with the exception of the banks of the Saint-Denis canal, redeveloped by Plaine Commune, the legacy will remain essentially confined to the strict perimeter of the Olympic structures. The sites are there, but the links between them are missing.

The use of sports facilities is becoming a design tool in its own right, affirming the place of soft modes and pedestrians and pedestrians in a public space often designed for motorised vehicles. The sports loop is presented as an essential link, free from projects and constraints. Its dimensions and shapes are variable, and its installation costs are minimal. It unifies areas through a specific treatment of public spaces and common furniture, linking emblematic places in a different way.

Sport is at the heart of the urban reflections surrounding the Athletes' Village. The Sport paths are a central element, the result of in-depth studies carried out by our agency.

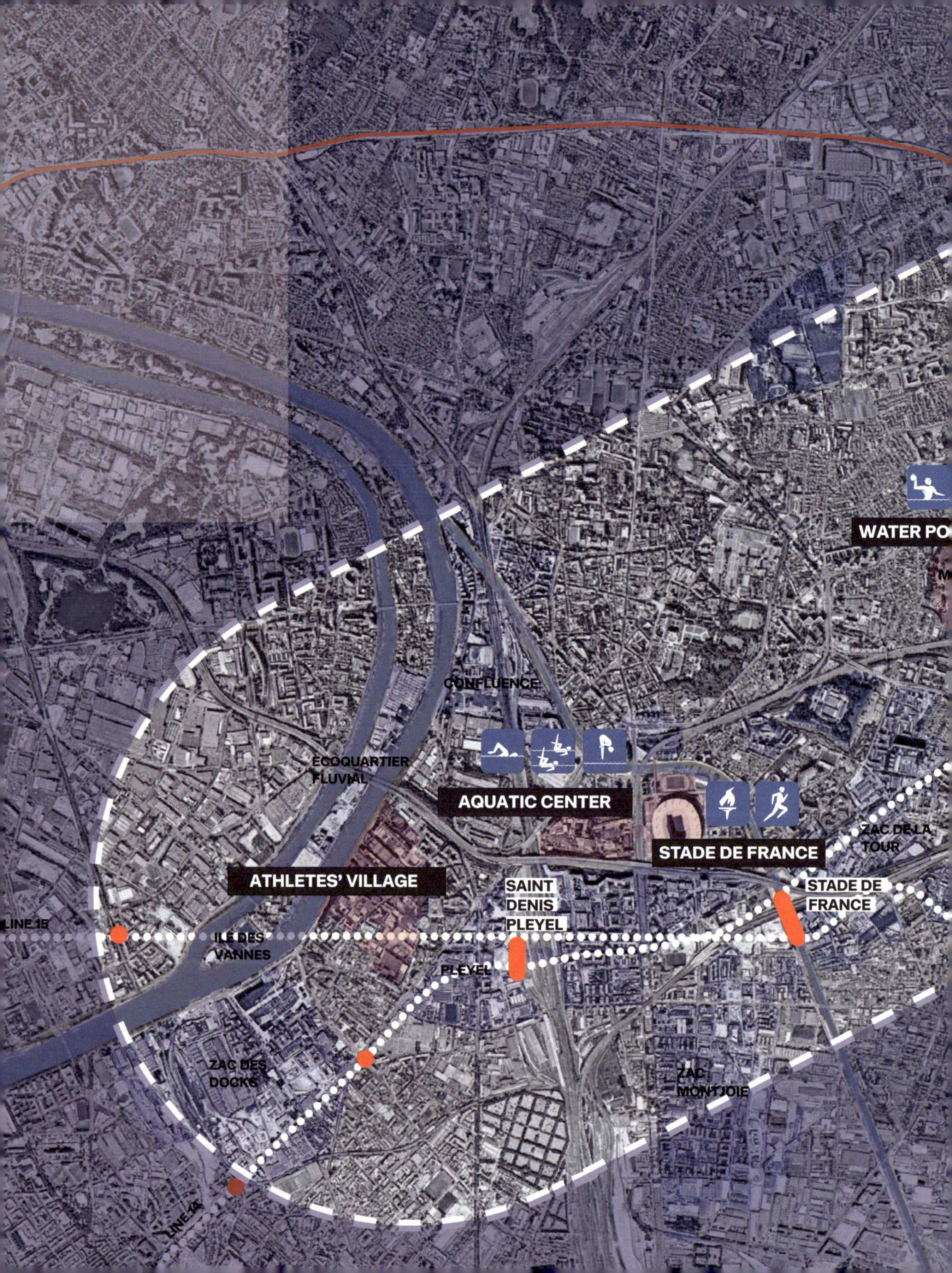
WATER PO
CONFLUENCE
ECOQUARTIER FLUVIAL
AQUATIC CENTER
STADE DE FRANCE
ZAC DE LA TOUR
ATHLETES' VILLAGE
SAINT DENIS PLEYEL
STADE DE FRANCE
LINE 15
ILE DES VANNES
PLEYEL
ZAC DES DOCKS
ZAC MONTJOIE
LINE 14

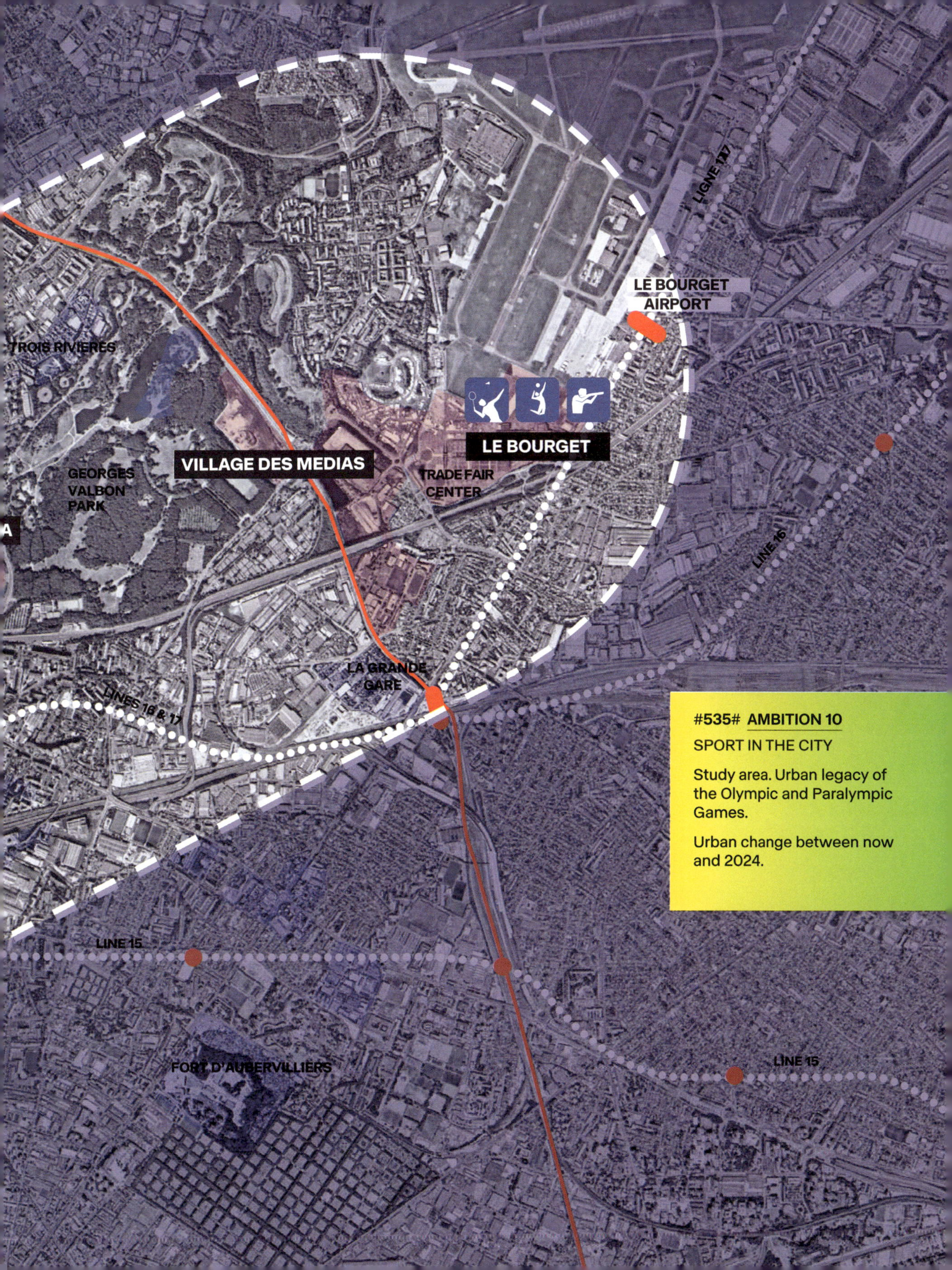

#535# AMBITION 10

SPORT IN THE CITY

Study area. Urban legacy of the Olympic and Paralympic Games.

Urban change between now and 2024.

1 UN NOUVEAU QUARTIER DE VILLE

LE VILLAGE DES ATHLÈTES

Après l'Olympiade, le Village des athlètes deviendra un tout nouveau quartier de ville pour Saint-Denis, Saint-Ouen-sur-Seine et L'Île-Saint-Denis. Les logements des athlètes seront transformés en 2 220 logements familiaux et 980 logements pour étudiants ou personnes âgées. 114 000 m² seront reconvertis en locaux d'activités, bureaux et commerces. Pour répondre aux besoins des habitants, de nouveaux équipements verront le jour : deux crèches, deux groupes scolaires, un lycée rénové, une centrale de mobilité... et pour se détendre, 7 hectares d'espaces verts sortiront de terre ainsi qu'une base nautique, une cité des arts et de nouveaux équipements sportifs. Tout cela dans un environnement plus calme avec l'aménagement des quais de Seine, la création d'un mur anti-bruit le long de la partie sud de l'A86 et l'enfouissement de lignes à haute tension.

2 LE CENTRE AQUATIQUE OLYMPIQUE

LE QUARTIER PLAINE SAULNIER

Un tout nouveau quartier, Plaine Saulnier, verra le jour autour du Centre aquatique olympique. Directement relié au Stade de France par une passerelle piétonne de 18 mètres, il comprendra environ 500 logements, des bureaux et activités, des commerces et services, des équipements publics dont un groupe scolaire et une crèche ainsi qu'un parc d'un hectare et plusieurs places et placettes. Après les Jeux, le Centre aquatique accueillera, dans ses deux bassins de natation et de plongeon de 50 m et de 25 m, tant le grand public et les scolaires que les compétitions nationales et internationales. Autour se développera un véritable pôle sportif : espace aqualudique (aquakids, parcours découvertes, bébés nageurs...), espace fitness, mur d'escalade, terrains de padel-tennis, football à cinq, basket-ball à trois, un skate parc et un lieu de restauration.

© VenhoevenCS & Atelier 234

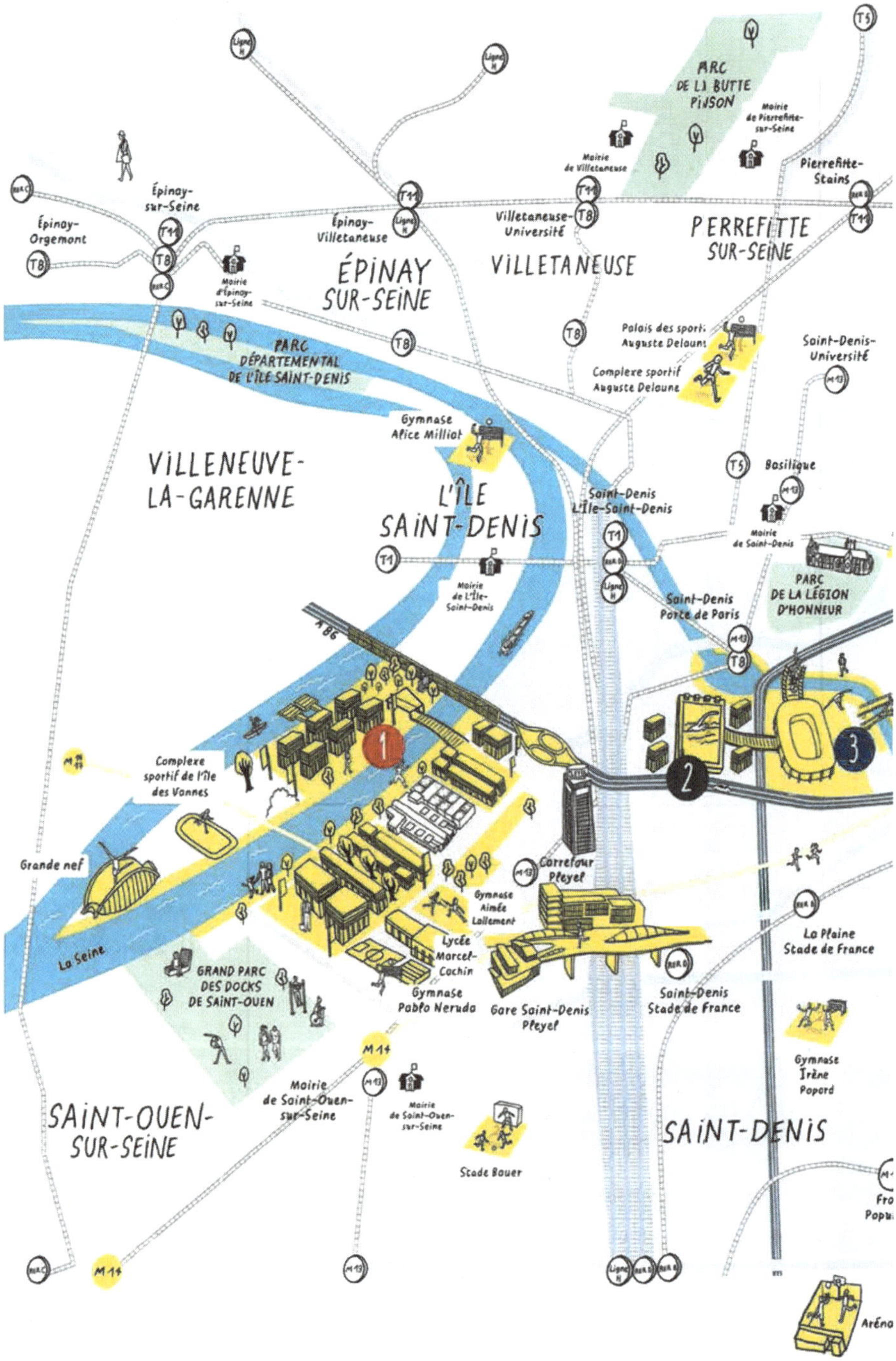

3 LE STADE DE FRANCE

© Luxigon/Paris 2024

Le Stade de France sera rénové pour améliorer le confort des athlètes et des spectateurs et son accessibilité pour les personnes à mobilité réduite. Ses abords et les espaces publics seront aussi réaménagés pour faciliter les accès en transports en commun. Il sera davantage connecté aux autres quartiers grâce à la création d'une passerelle au-dessus de l'autoroute A1 le reliant au Centre aquatique olympique et à la rénovation du pont tournant et des passerelles menant au centre-ville et au quartier Franc-Moisin.

4 LE CANAL SAINT-DENIS

© Raphaël Fournier

Pour les Jeux, l'aménagement en cours des berges du canal Saint-Denis sera accéléré. Objectifs : proposer un lieu de promenade agréable de jour comme de nuit sur les deux rives du canal et faciliter le passage d'une rive à l'autre pour les piétons et les vélos. Ainsi, une nouvelle passerelle sera créée au niveau du centre commercial Le Millénaire à Aubervilliers et le pont tournant ainsi que les passerelles menant au centre-ville et au quartier Franc-Moisin au niveau du Stade de France seront rénovées. Verront également le jour de nouveaux espaces de détente, de rencontres et de nouvelles pistes cyclables continues et qualitatives. Objectif également après les Jeux, développer les fêtes au bord du canal, les activités sur l'eau et pourquoi pas la baignade.

VOTRE TERRITOIRE APRÈS 2024 !

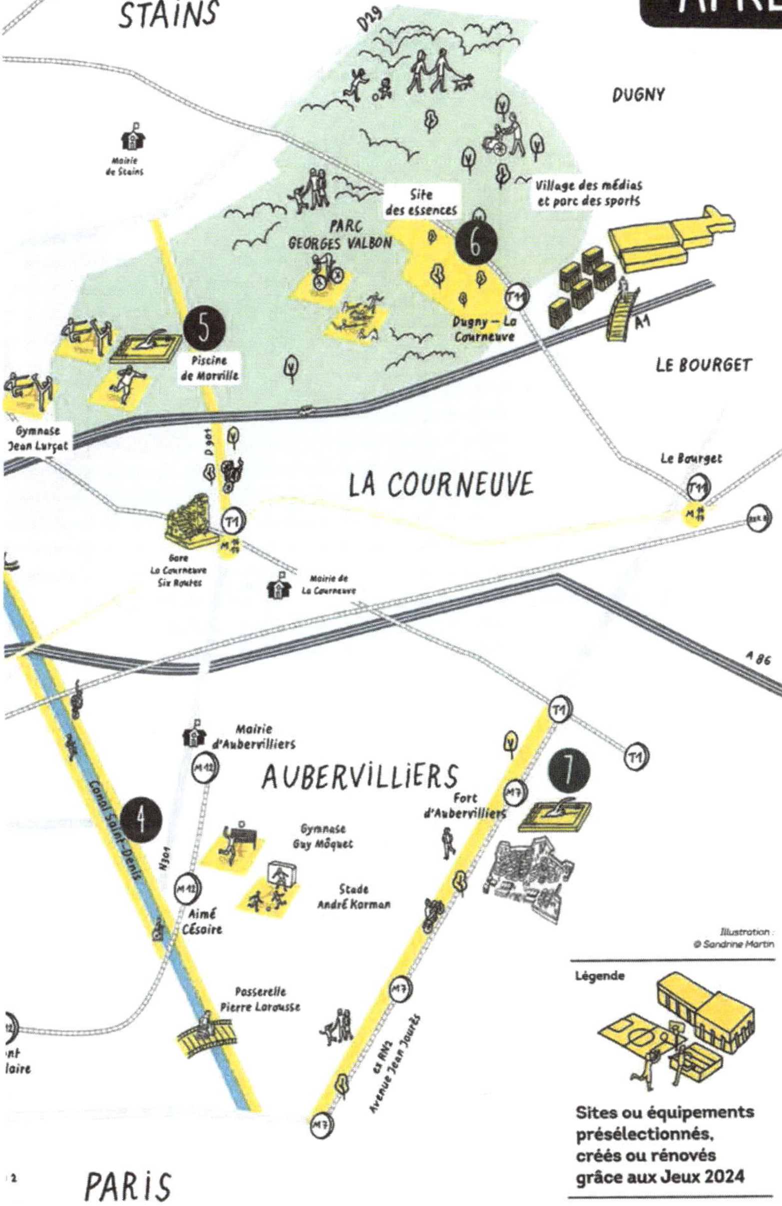

6 LE SITE DES ESSENCES DANS LE CLUSTER DES MÉDIAS

Ce terrain, situé à La Courneuve, accueillera les compétitions de tir pendant les Jeux. Entièrement dépollué, il deviendra ensuite une extension de 13 hectares du parc départemental Georges Valbon avec des espaces forestiers ouverts à la promenade et d'autres dédiés à la protection de la faune et à la sensibilisation des visiteurs. Ce site prend place dans un projet d'aménagement plus vaste qui verra naître un nouveau quartier de ville à Dugny et au Bourget.

© TVK - OLM - UrbanEco Igrec Pro Développement

7 LE CENTRE AQUATIQUE DU FORT D'AUBERVILLIERS

Avant et pendant les Jeux, ce centre aquatique servira de site d'entraînement pour les équipes nationales. Après les Jeux, il accueillera scolaires, grand public et associations. Il sera composé d'un bassin olympique de 8 lignes d'eau, d'un bassin polyvalent ainsi que d'un secteur de loisirs avec saunas extérieurs, plages intérieures et extérieures, solarium végétal, espaces de remise en forme et espace de restauration.

Ce centre aquatique sera au cœur du nouveau quartier du Fort d'Aubervilliers : 1 800 logements, activités, commerces, équipements (1 groupe scolaire et 1 crèche), 7 ha de jardins familiaux, plus de 8 ha d'espaces verts et un pôle de transports (ligne 7, ligne 15 du Grand Paris Express dès 2030 et 7 lignes de bus).

5 LE PARC DES SPORTS DE MARVILLE

Pour les Jeux, ce site d'une superficie de 33 hectares situé à cheval sur les communes de Saint-Denis et La Courneuve sera entièrement rénové puis ouvert aux habitants. Un centre aquatique sera construit avec un espace intérieur et un espace extérieur. L'espace couvert accueillera un bassin sportif de 33 m, trois petits bassins annexes et un espace de bien-être (balnéo et fitness). L'espace extérieur comprendra un bassin nordique de 25 m ouvert toute l'année et des espaces d'agréments ouverts lors de la saison estivale (bassin et plage), ainsi qu'un petit snack. Les différents sites d'entraînement redeviendront gymnases et salle de sport juste après les Jeux sans aucun délai d'adaptation. L'ancienne piscine sera conservée.

© Ph. Guignard

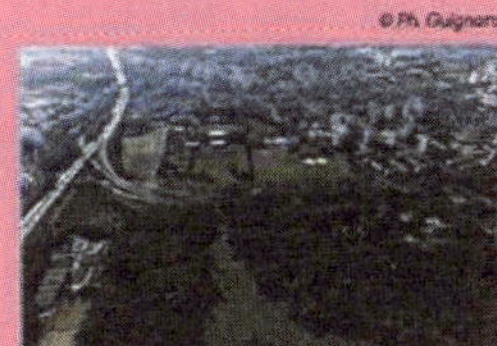

#537# AMBITION 10

HERITAGE PHASE.

The sports loop - Metropolitan links and soft mobility

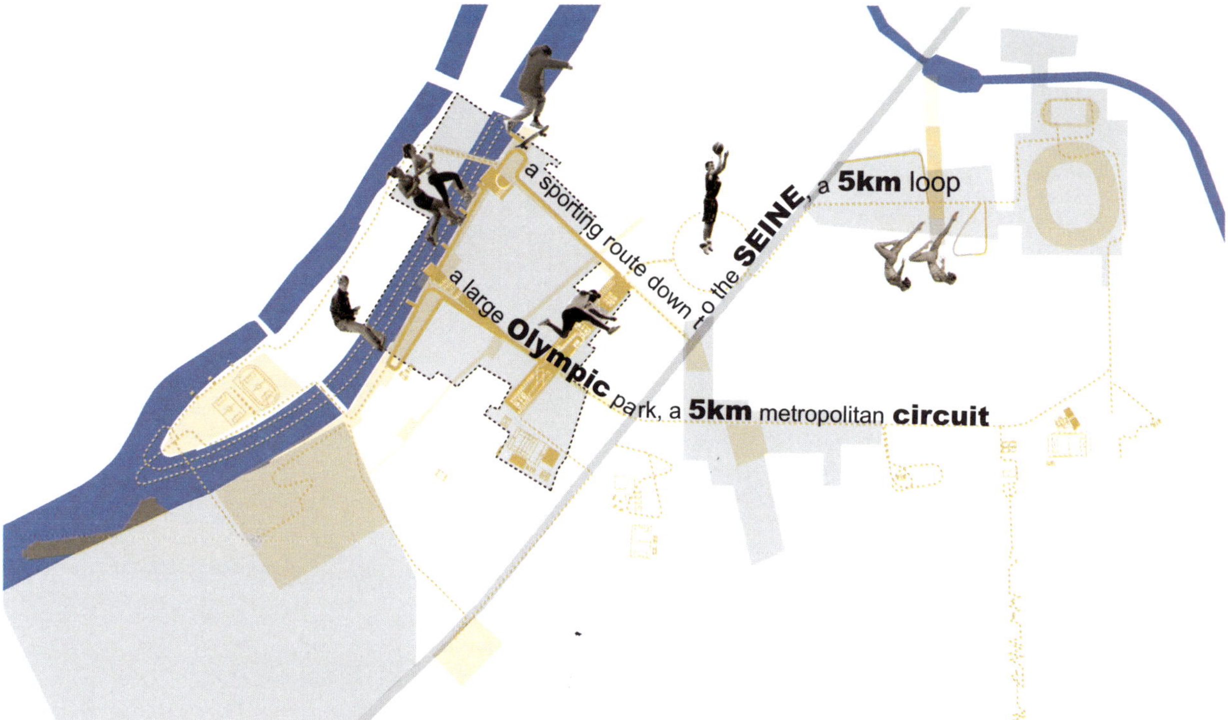

New metropolitan public spaces
The leisure and sports network
Cycle loops

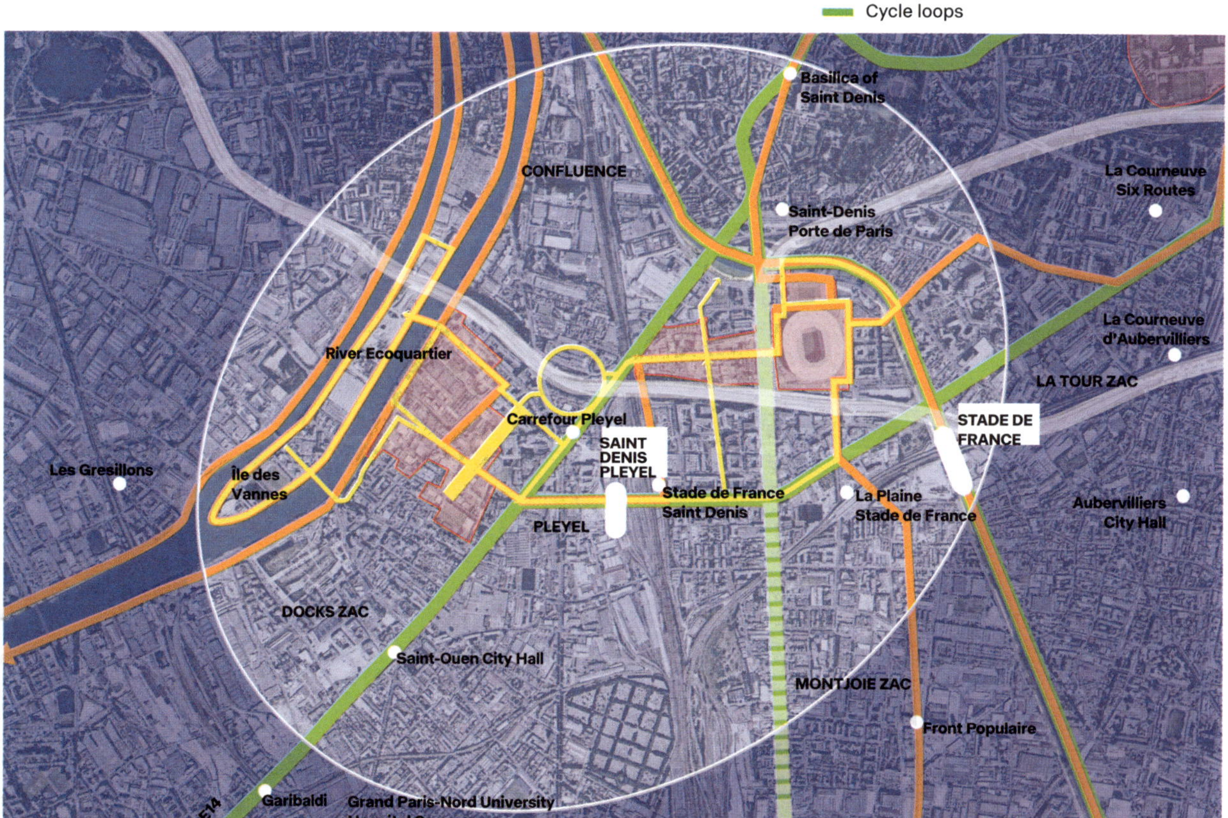

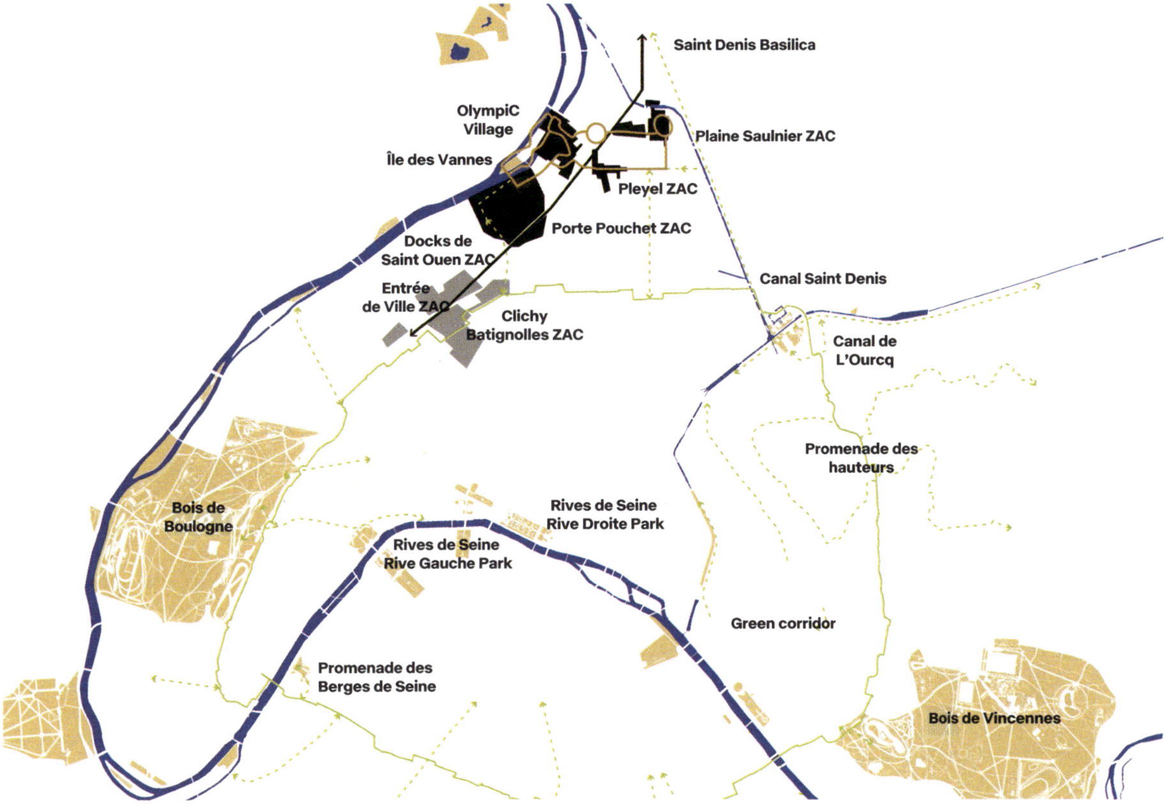

#539# **AMBITION 10**

SPORT IN THE CITY

Sport Paths

What place for sport in urban planning?

The sport paths represents an additional layer of mobility between the current heart of the Metropolis, Paris, and the future nerve centre that will be Carrefour Pleyel and the surrounding area.

In early 2019, the APUR identified a sports loop that had already been set up along the Green Belt route around Paris. Applications such as Strava demonstrate the importance of sporting uses in public space, and how these two elements can interact without territorial constraints.On a wider scale, public spaces could form part of a metropolitan sports trail linked to the arrival of the Olympic and Paralympic Games in Plaine Commune. The Athletes' Village, Parc des Docks, Ile-des-Vannes, the Stade de France and the Olympic Aquatic Centre would be connected by a large path, the details of which have yet to be worked out.

Every inhabitant of the area would have access to a public sports trail or facility within five minutes of their home. In line with the ambitions of the City of Paris to create a continuous sports walkway along the 40km length of the green belt (APUR study "Parcours sportifs de la ceinture verte", 2019), the pathway would link the major sports venues, Paris and its suburbs.

Sports facilities - Avenue du Président Wilson (cycling facilities, sports areas)

Rue Camille Moke (cycle paths and heritage)

Views - Pointe de l'Ile des Vannes (lookout point over Greater Paris)

Vegetation - Avenue du stade de France (vegetation and dimensions)

Existing + project - Major operations to be connected

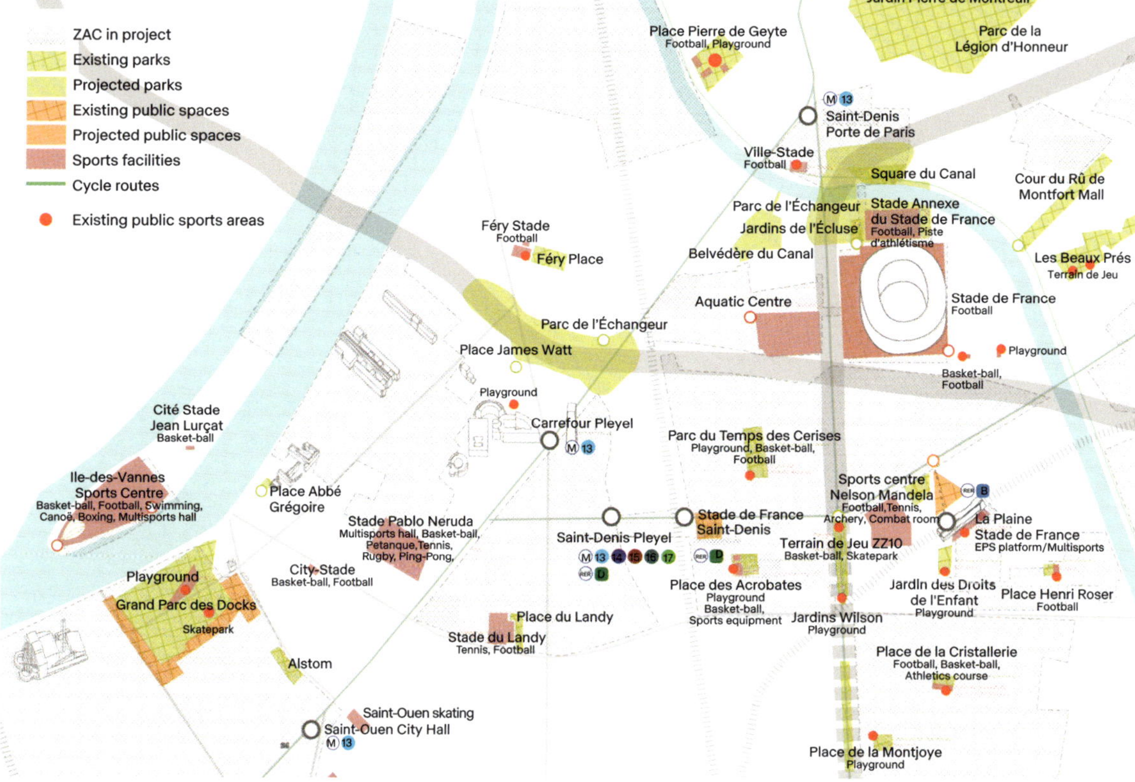

Station definitions

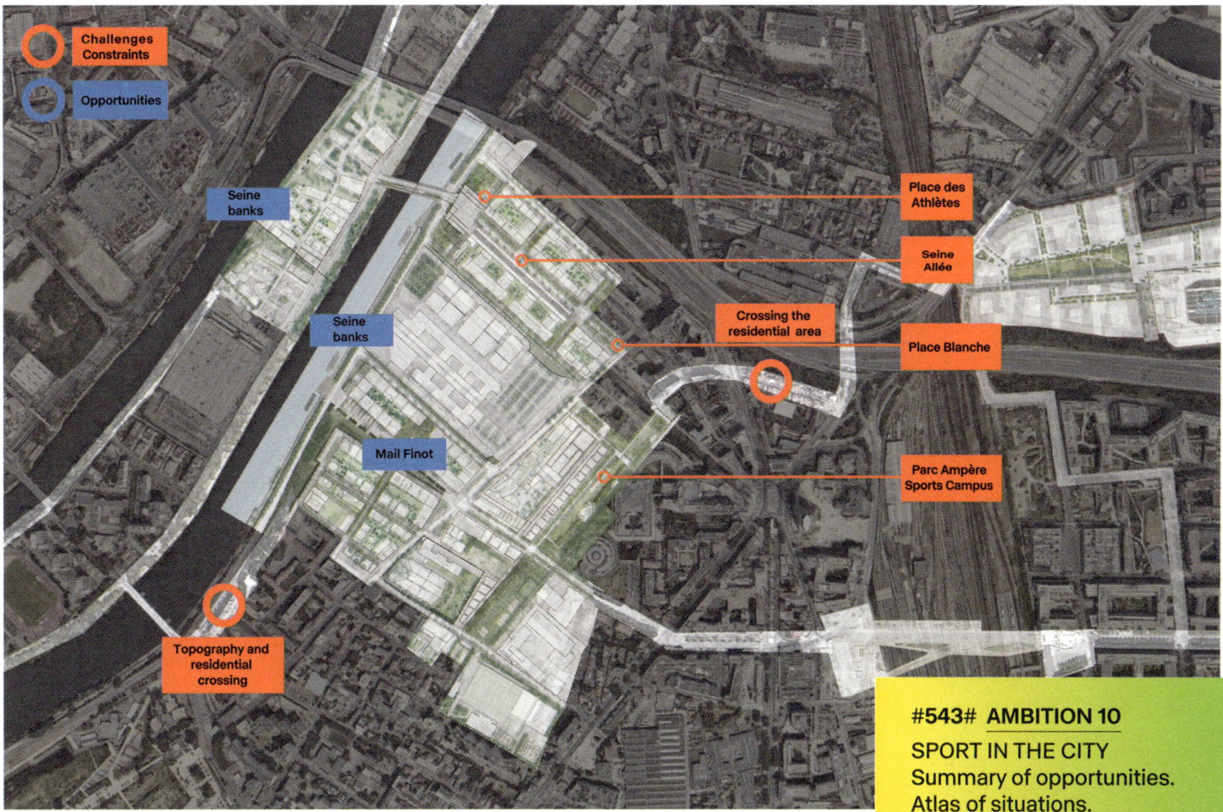

#543# AMBITION 10

SPORT IN THE CITY
Summary of opportunities.
Atlas of situations.

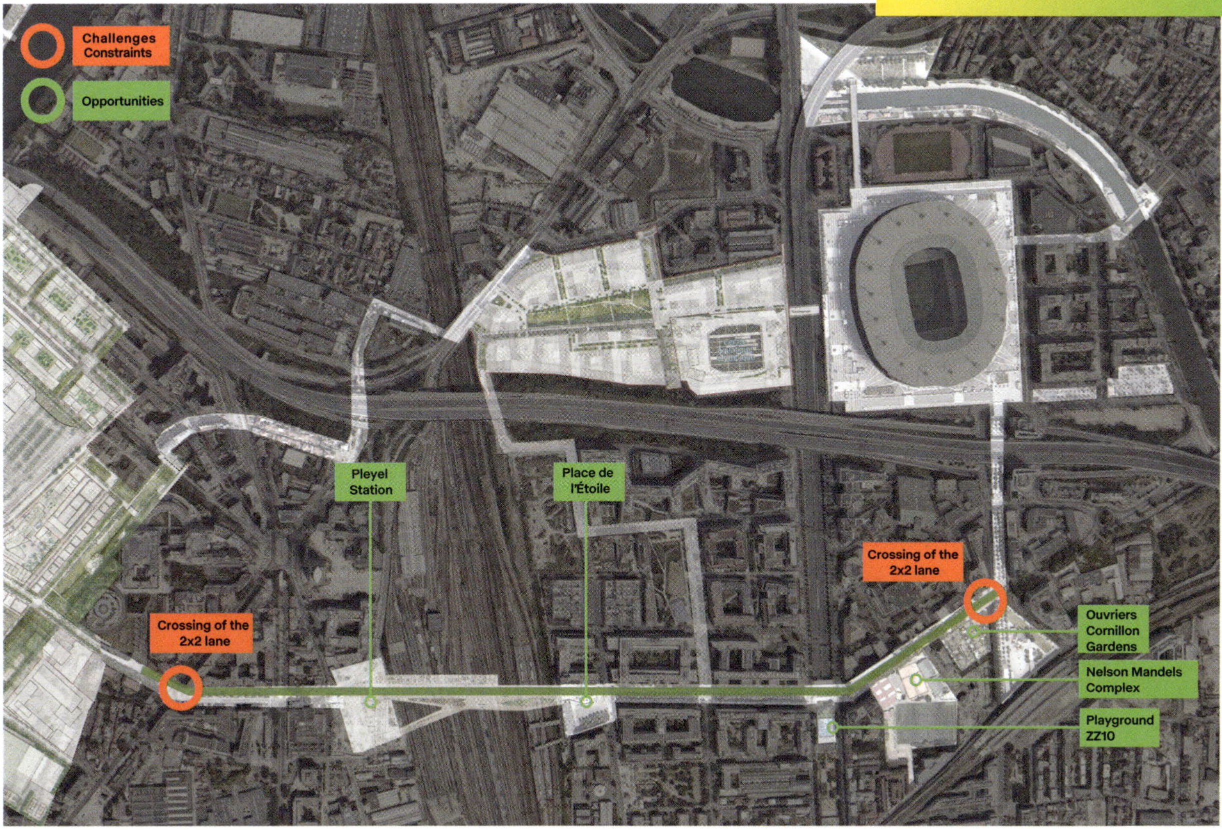

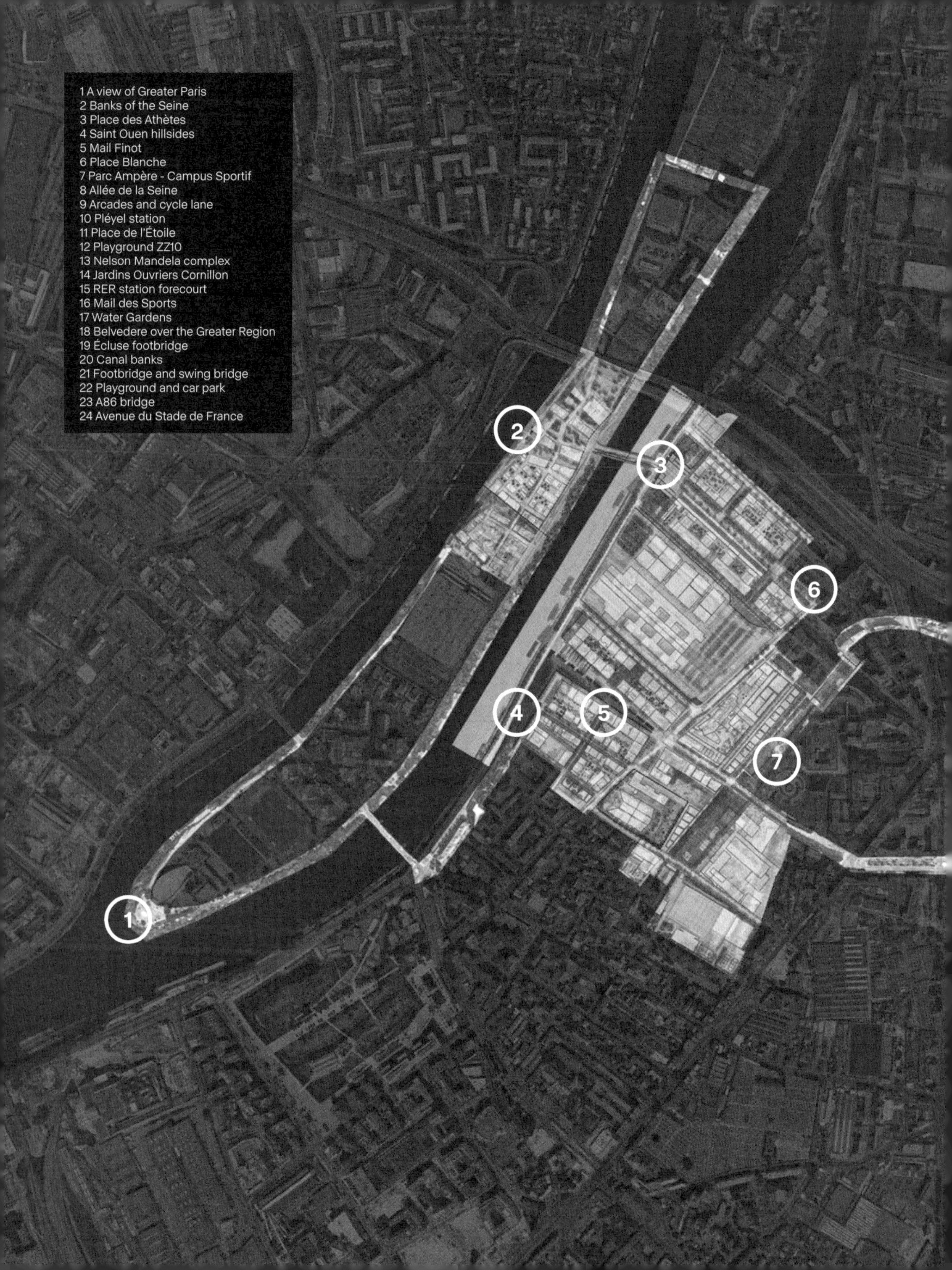
1 A view of Greater Paris
2 Banks of the Seine
3 Place des Athètes
4 Saint Ouen hillsides
5 Mail Finot
6 Place Blanche
7 Parc Ampère - Campus Sportif
8 Allée de la Seine
9 Arcades and cycle lane
10 Pléyel station
11 Place de l'Étoile
12 Playground ZZ10
13 Nelson Mandela complex
14 Jardins Ouvriers Cornillon
15 RER station forecourt
16 Mail des Sports
17 Water Gardens
18 Belvedere over the Greater Region
19 Écluse footbridge
20 Canal banks
21 Footbridge and swing bridge
22 Playground and car park
23 A86 bridge
24 Avenue du Stade de France
2
3
6
4
5
7
1

#545# AMBITION 10

SPORT IN THE CITY

Summary of opportunities.
Atlas of situations.

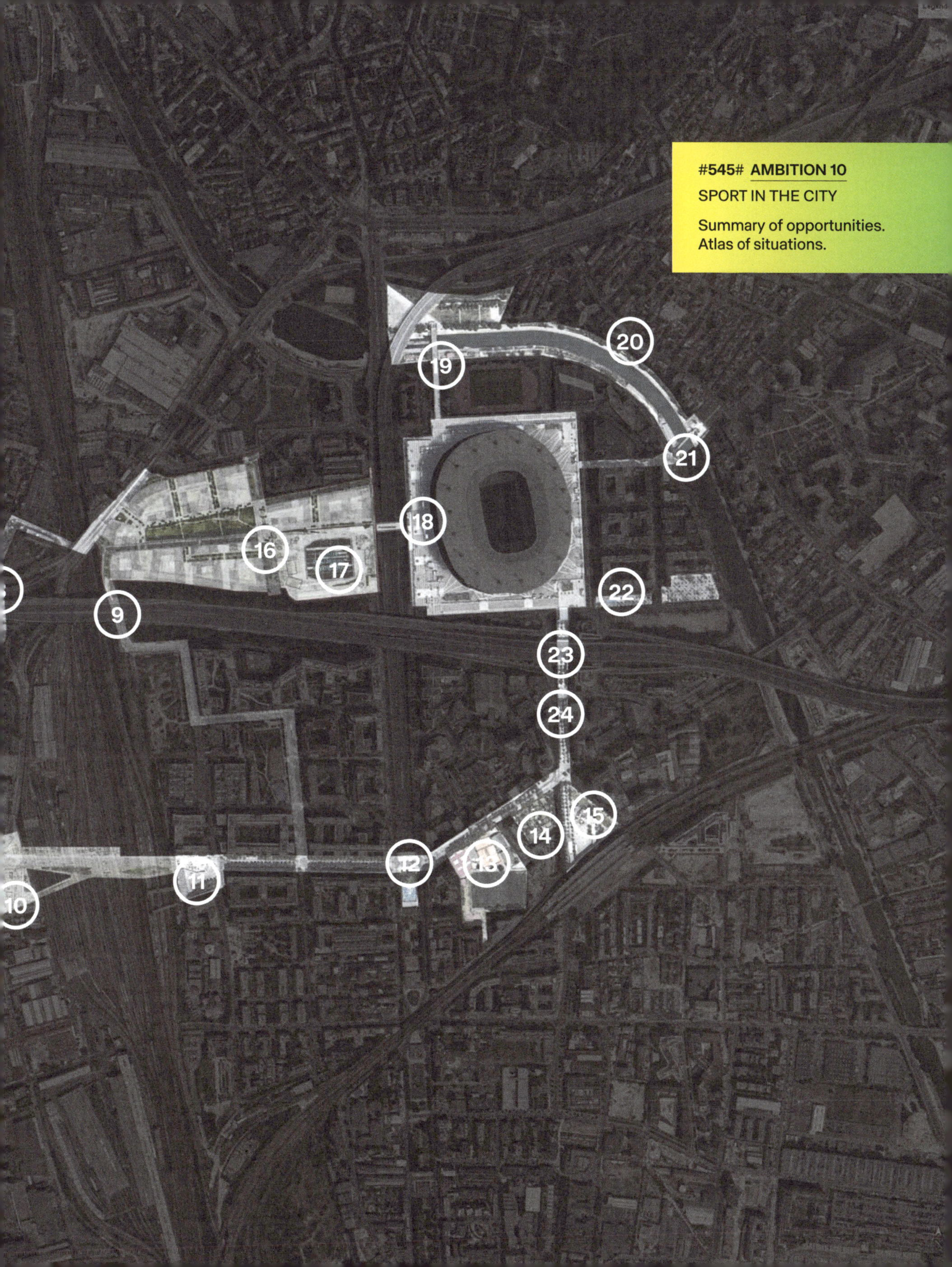

Existing + planned parks
Planned parks
Existing + planned public spaces
Existing + planned sports facilities
Cycle loops
Sports loop
Place de la Batelière
Athletes' square
Stade Féry
Seine Allée
Mail Finot
Square James Wa
City-Stadium Jean Lurçat
City-Stadium
Square Abbé Grégoire
Sports Centre Ile des-Vannes
Parvis
Pablo Neruda Stadium
City-Stadium
Grand Parc des Docks
Square du
Landy Stadium
Alstom
Patinoire de Saint-Ouen
Mairie de Saint-Ouen
M 13

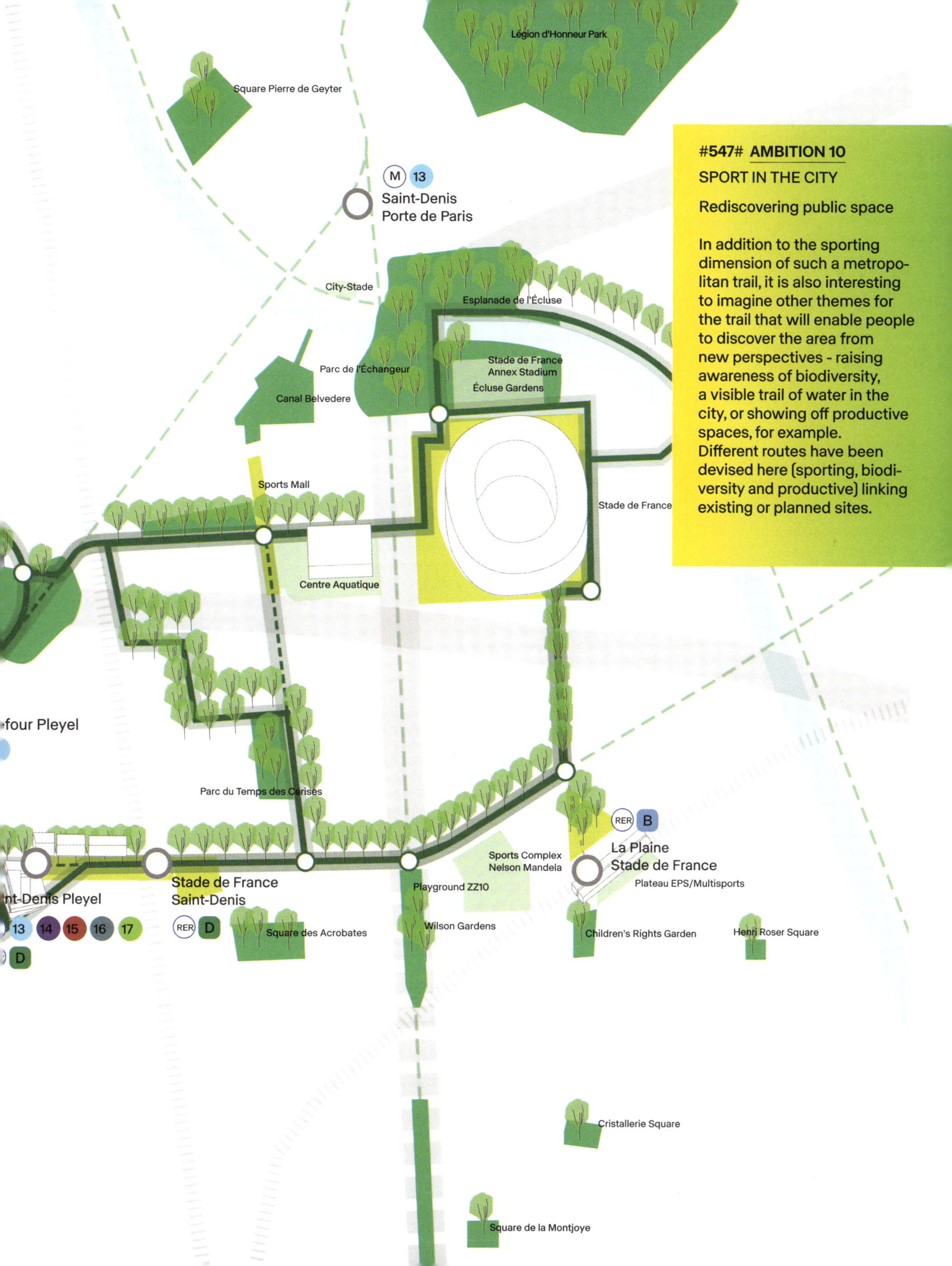

#547# AMBITION 10

SPORT IN THE CITY

Rediscovering public space

In addition to the sporting dimension of such a metropolitan trail, it is also interesting to imagine other themes for the trail that will enable people to discover the area from new perspectives - raising awareness of biodiversity, a visible trail of water in the city, or showing off productive spaces, for example. Different routes have been devised here (sporting, biodiversity and productive) linking existing or planned sites.

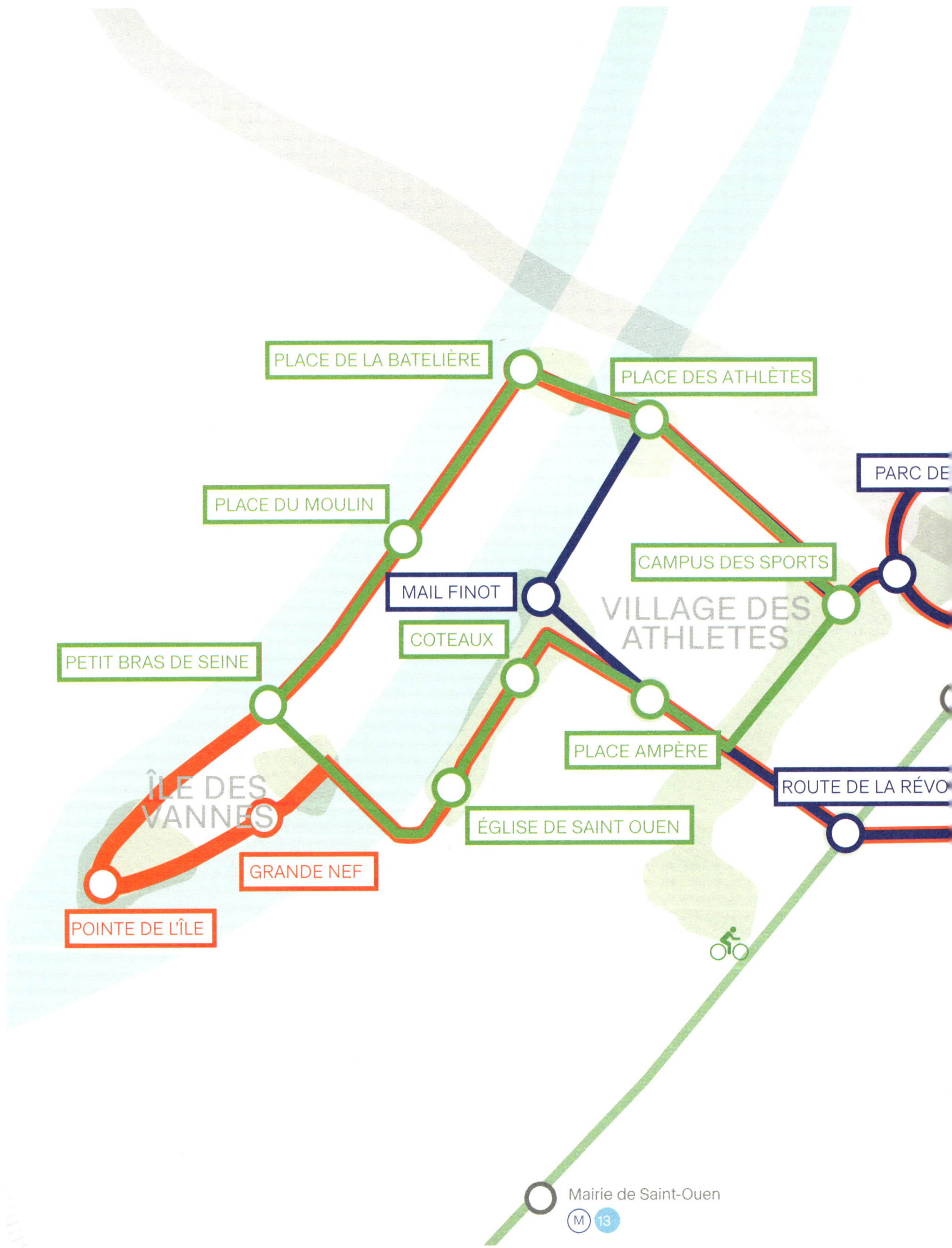

PLACE DE LA BATELIÈRE
PLACE DES ATHLÈTES
PARC DE
PLACE DU MOULIN
CAMPUS DES SPORTS
MAIL FINOT
VILLAGE DES ATHLETES
COTEAUX
PETIT BRAS DE SEINE
PLACE AMPÈRE
ROUTE DE LA RÉVO
ÎLE DES VANNES
ÉGLISE DE SAINT OUEN
GRANDE NEF
POINTE DE L'ÎLE
Mairie de Saint-Ouen
M 13

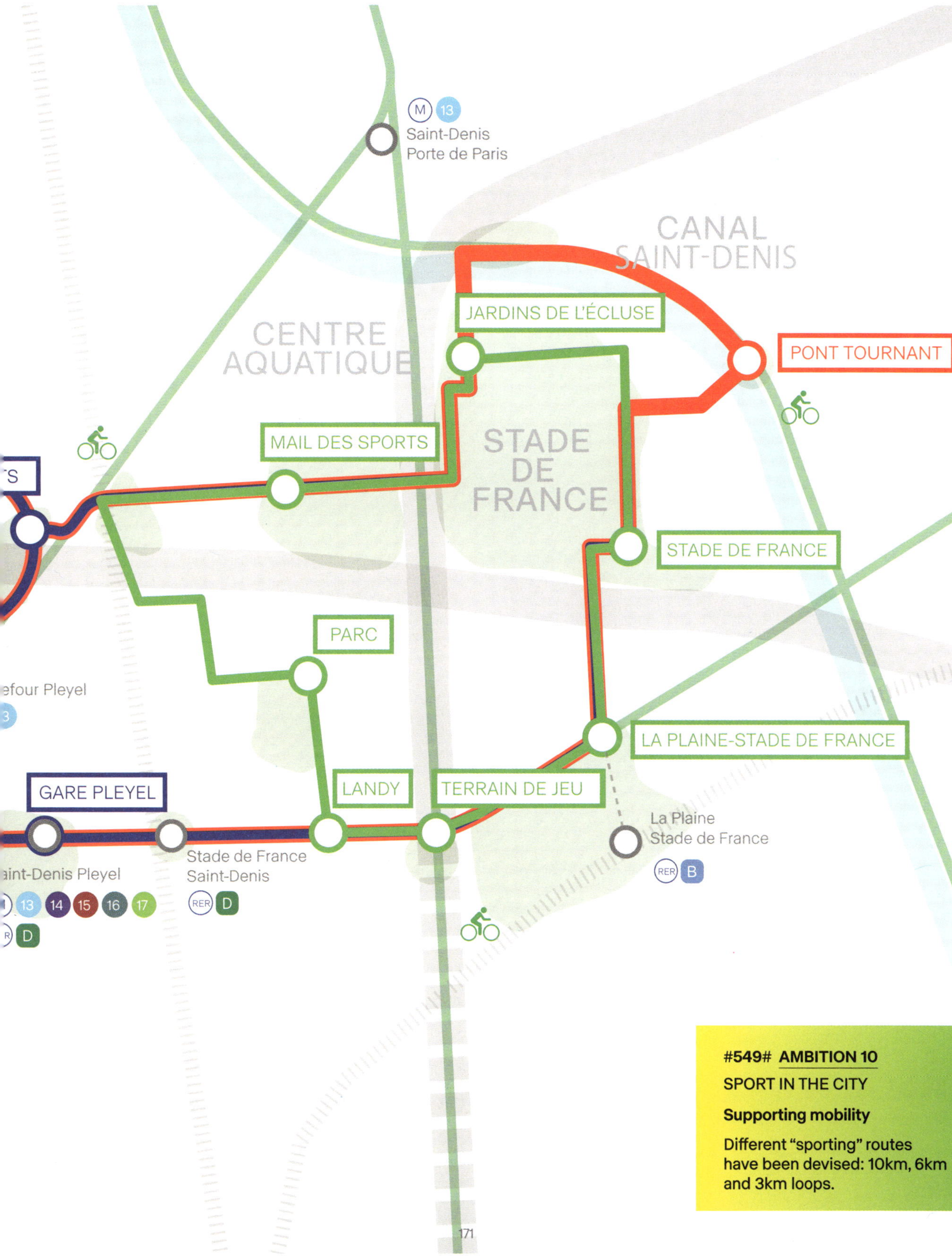

#549# **AMBITION 10**

SPORT IN THE CITY

Supporting mobility

Different "sporting" routes have been devised: 10km, 6km and 3km loops.

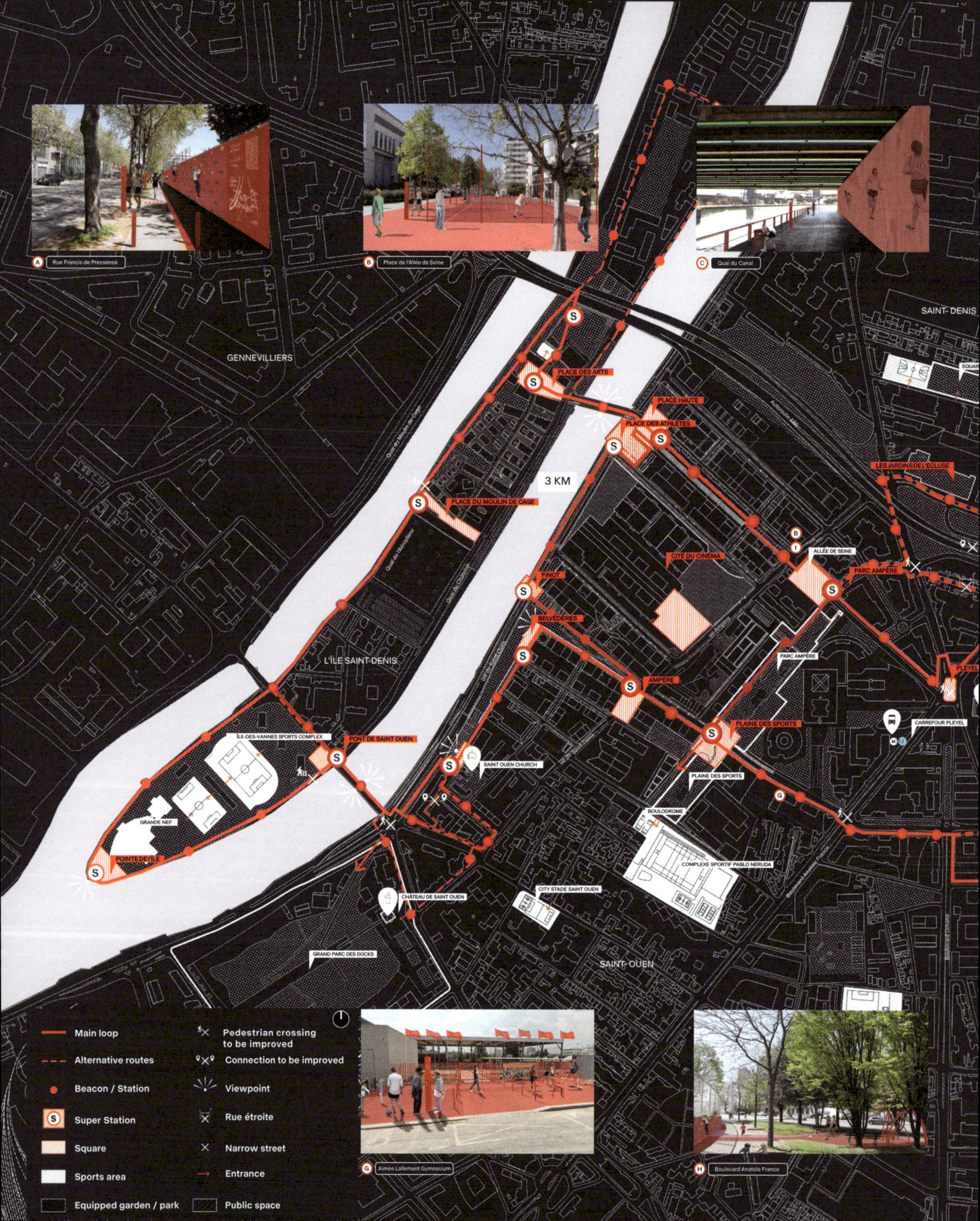

A Rue Francis de Pressensé
B Place de l'Allée de Seine
C Quai du Canal
SAINT-DENIS
GENNEVILLIERS
PLACE DES ARTS
PLACE HAUTE
PLACE DES ATHLÈTES
LES JARDINS DE L'ÉCLUSE
3 KM
PLACE DU MOULIN DE CAGE
CITÉ DU CINÉMA
ALLÉE DE SEINE
PARC AMPÈRE
FINOT
BELVÉDÈRES
L'ÎLE SAINT-DENIS
PARC AMPÈRE
PLEYEL
AMPÈRE
PLAINE DES SPORTS
CARREFOUR PLEYEL
ÎLE-DES-VANNES SPORTS COMPLEX
PONT DE SAINT OUEN
SAINT OUEN CHURCH
PLAINE DES SPORTS
GRANDE NEF
POINTE DE L'ÎLE
BOULODROME
COMPLEXE SPORTIF PABLO NERUDA
CHÂTEAU DE SAINT OUEN
CITY STADE SAINT OUEN
GRAND PARC DES DOCKS
SAINT-OUEN
Main loop
Alternative routes
Beacon / Station
Super Station
Square
Sports area
Equipped garden / park
Pedestrian crossing to be improved
Connection to be improved
Viewpoint
Rue étroite
Narrow street
Entrance
Public space
G Aimée Lallement Gymnasium
H Boulevard Anatole France

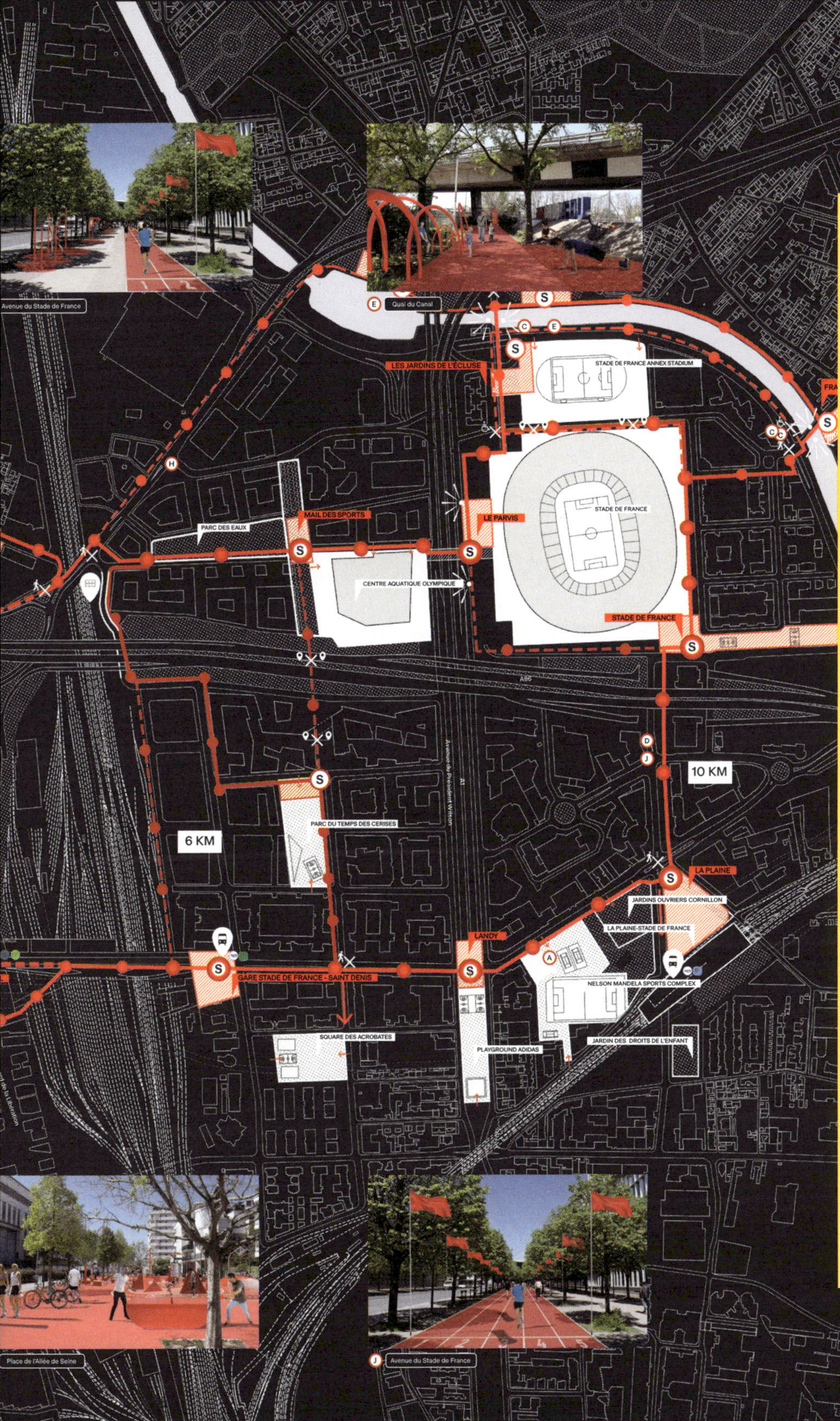

#551# AMBITION 10

SPORT IN THE CITY

The sporting dimension, benefiting the inhabitants of Greater Paris, must leave an enduring mark of the Olympic event, both through new local facilities and within public spaces. The agency has developed the concept of a sports trail as one of the narratives that contributed to the design of the Athletes' Village, aiming to make it a part of the Games' legacy for the benefit of Greater Paris residents.

Originally conceived for the Seine-Saint-Denis area, the sports path has been expanded here as a narrative, echoing the history of the river and its banks, bridging distances in both time and space. The concept is also under examination in Berlin, at the Senate's request, focusing on the Velodrome and the Olympic Swimming Pool. Additionally, it is being explored in Le Mans, centered around the 24-hour race circuit, where the path connects various venues including the circuit, racecourse, stadiums, sports fields, and golf course into a cohesive whole.

Programme and usage - The beacon

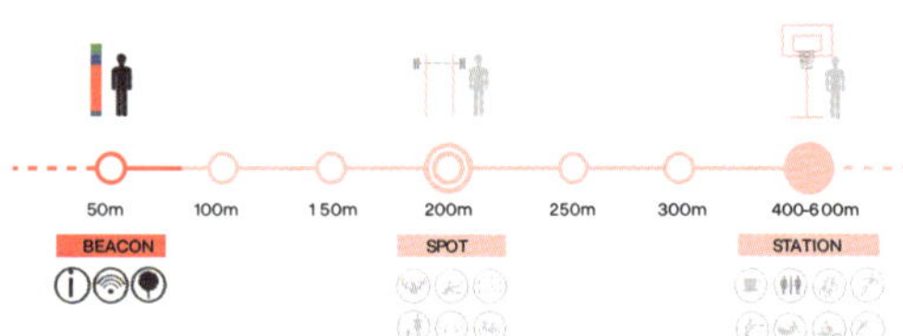

Visual identity

Wifi zone

Signposting

PRACTICAL INFORMATION

FRESHNESS ZONE

Landmark

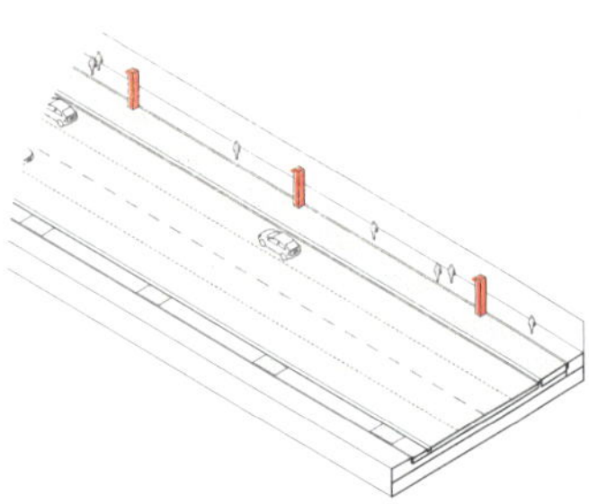

BEACON

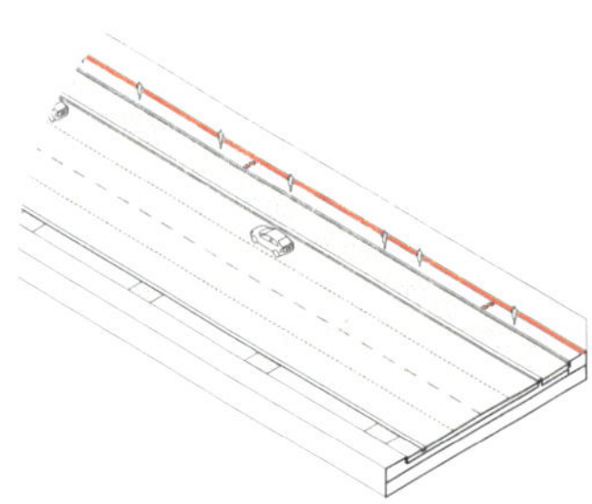

FLOOR LINE

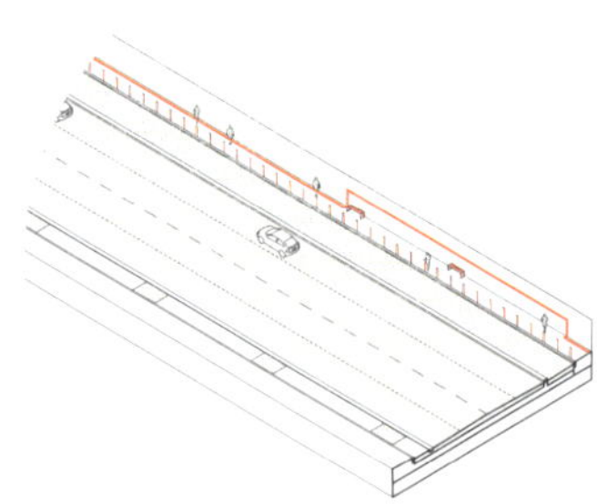

EXISTING URBAN EQUIPMENT

#553# AMBITION 10

SPORT IN THE CITY

Programme and use.

Programme and usage- The spot

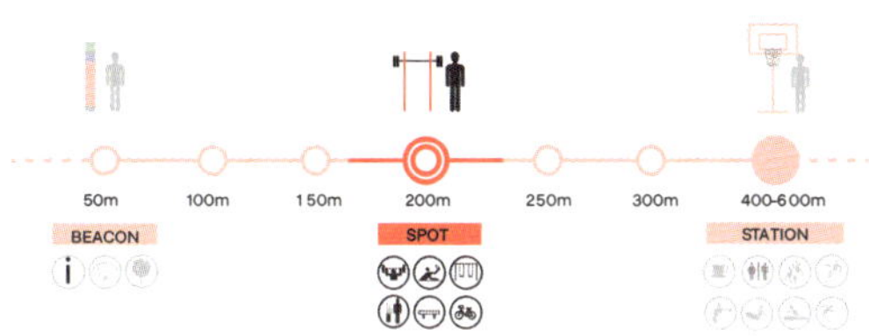

Visual identity

MULTI-USE FURNITURE

Drinking fountain

Wifi zone

Freshness zone

Practical information

UNIVERSAL ACCESSIBILITY

Bike station

Signposting

URBAN FITNESS TRAIL

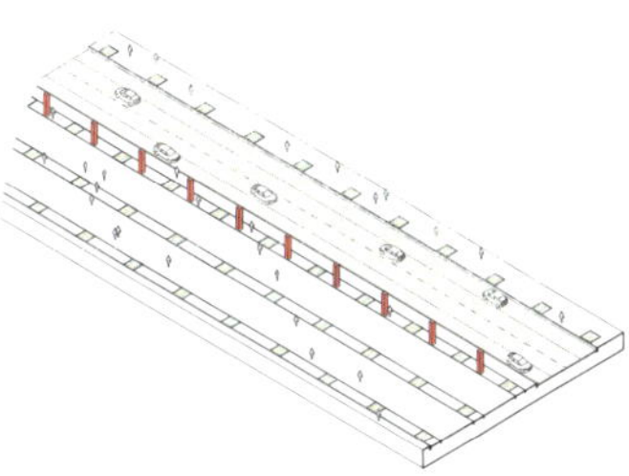

BEACON AND EXISTING FURNITURE

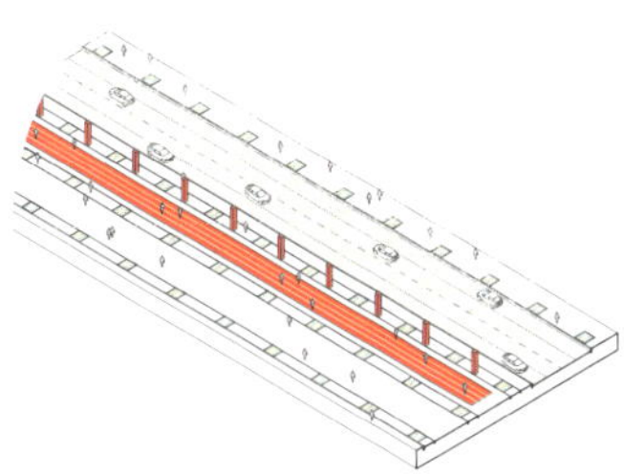

ACTIVITY AREA

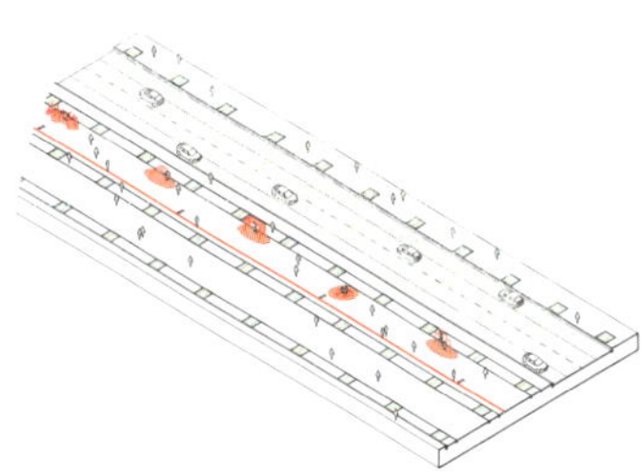

ONE-OFF SPORTS FACILITIES

Programme and usage - The station

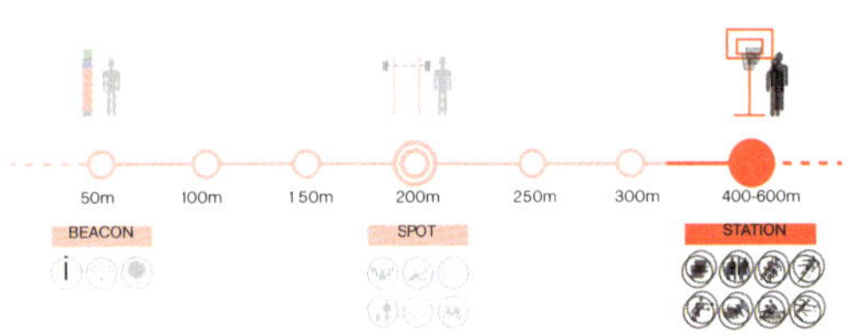

Visual identity

URBAN HEALTH TRAIL

Drinking fountain

Wifi zone

PLACE OF SERVICES

Practical information

Freshness zone

UNIVERSAL ACCESSIBILITY

Underground staiom

URBAN FITNESS TRAIL

Bike station

Signposting

MULTI-USE FURNITURE

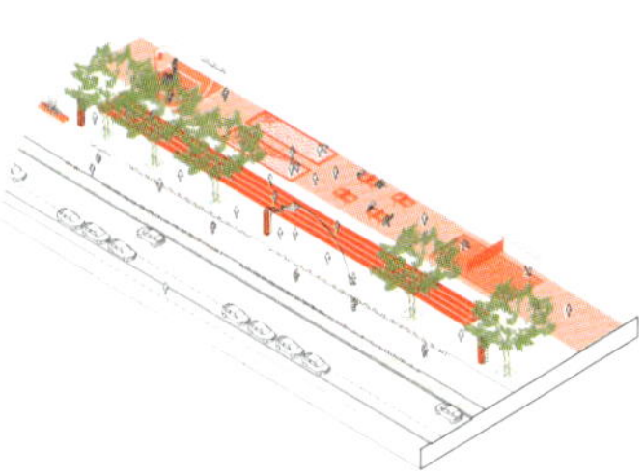

MULTI-USE FURNITURE

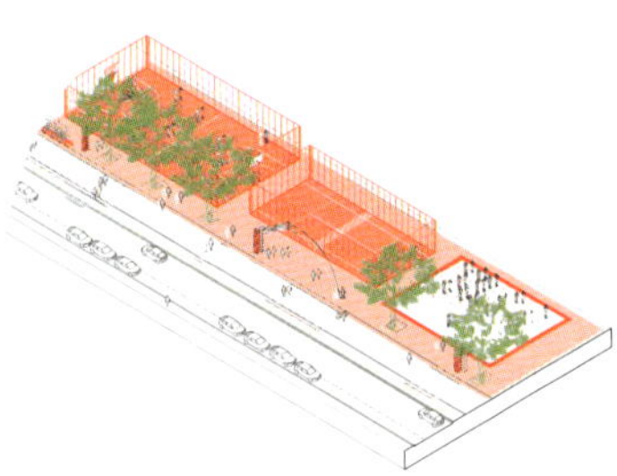

URBAN SPORTS GROUND

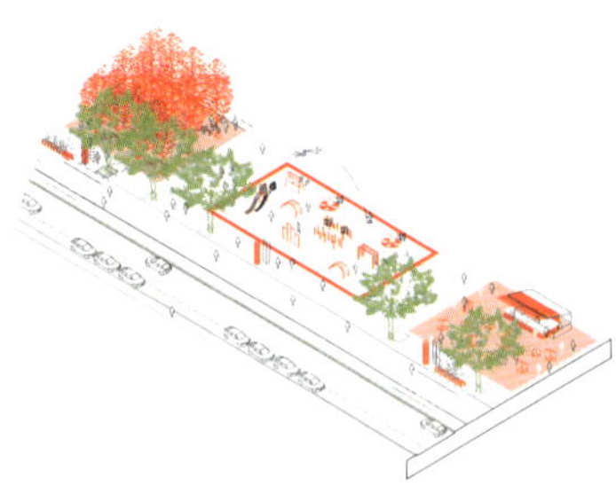

PLACE OF SERVICES

#555# AMBITION 10

SPORT IN THE CITY

Programme and use.

Continuity of vegetation and convivial spaces

Fontains

Signage and art installations

Sports furniture

Playful furniture

Meeting places

Sports loop - Focus on the main public spaces

Composition of the sports loop

- Clean signage
- Consistent furniture
- Ground treatment
- Quality and coherent leisure facilities
- Spaces for specific activities
- Multi-strata plant continuity

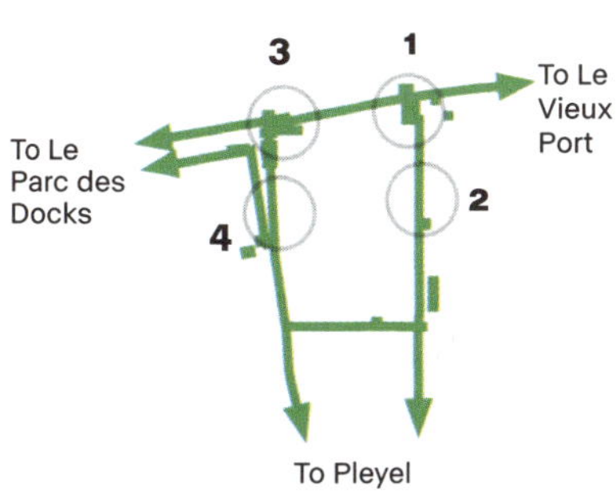

Olympic terrace

1

Finot terrace

3

Allée de Seine

2

Mail Finot

4

A sporting territory - A wide range of programmes

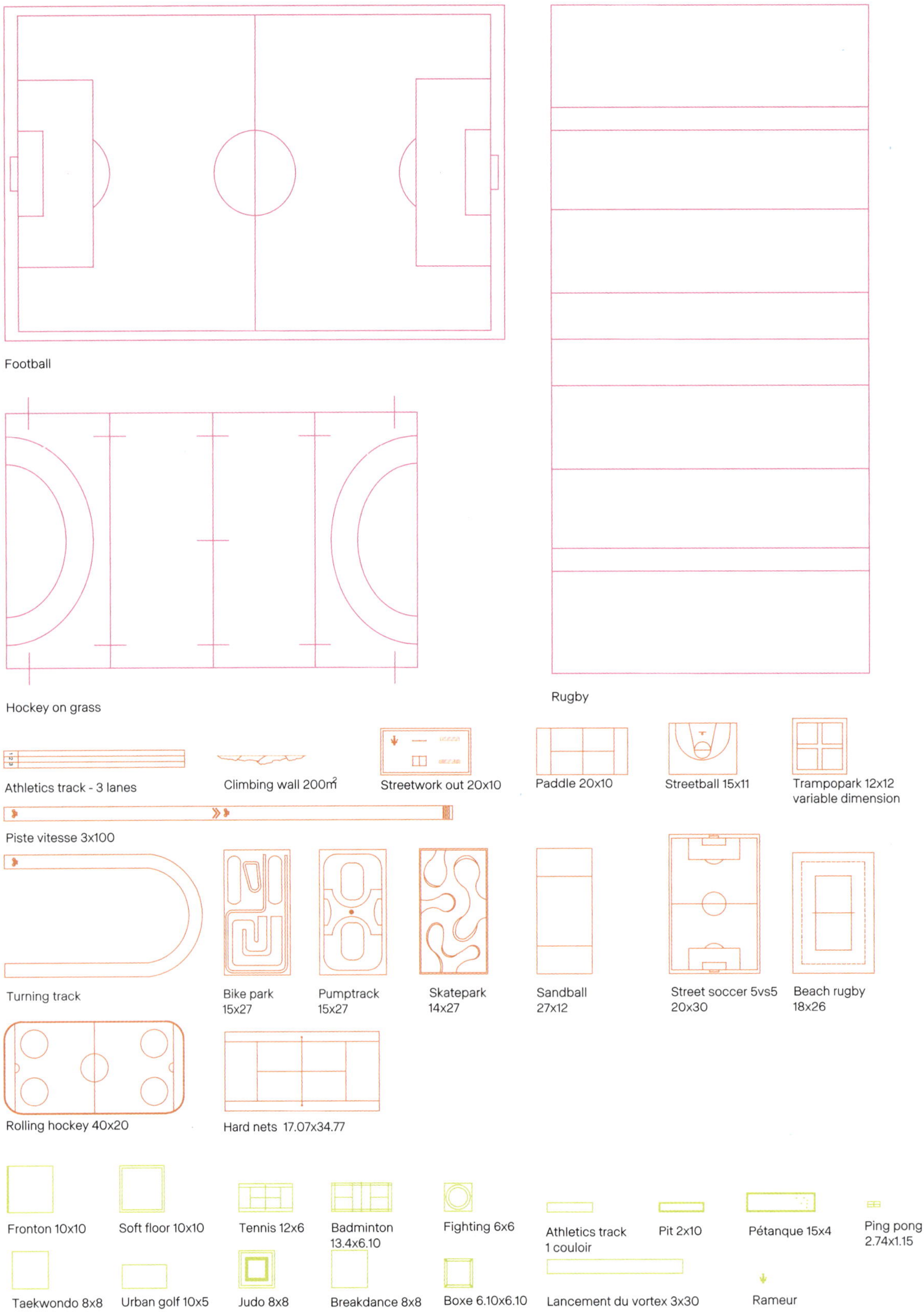

#557# AMBITION 10

SPORT IN THE CITY

What will be the legacy of the 2024 Olympic Games?

A place of sport and leisure for local residents, but also a destination? How can we make it a spotlight, an attractive and innovative destination?

Can we imagine Olympic and Paralympic sports being played in public spaces?

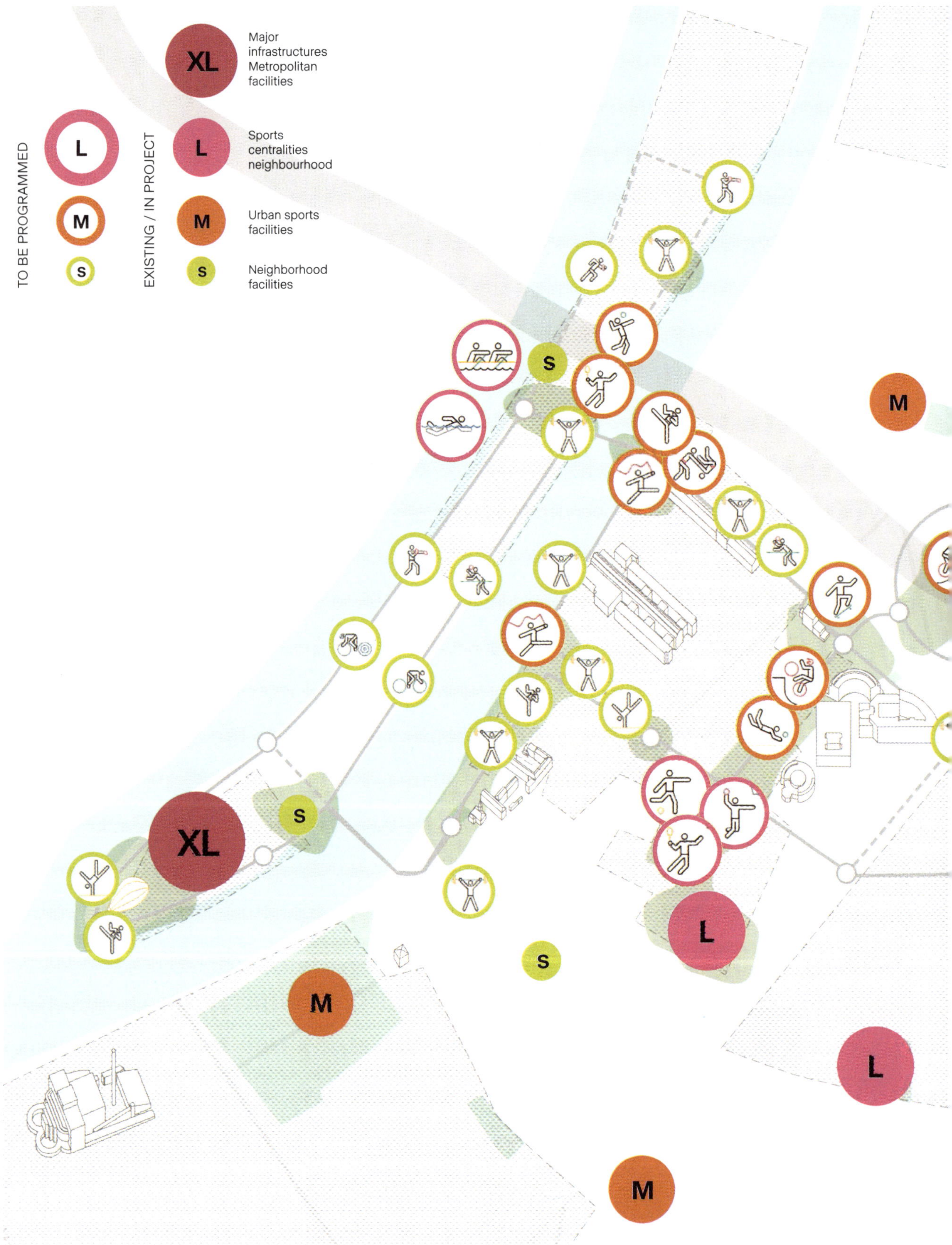
TO BE PROGRAMMED
EXISTING / IN PROJECT
XL
Major infrastructures Metropolitan facilities
L
Sports centralities neighbourhood
M
Urban sports facilities
S
Neighborhood facilities

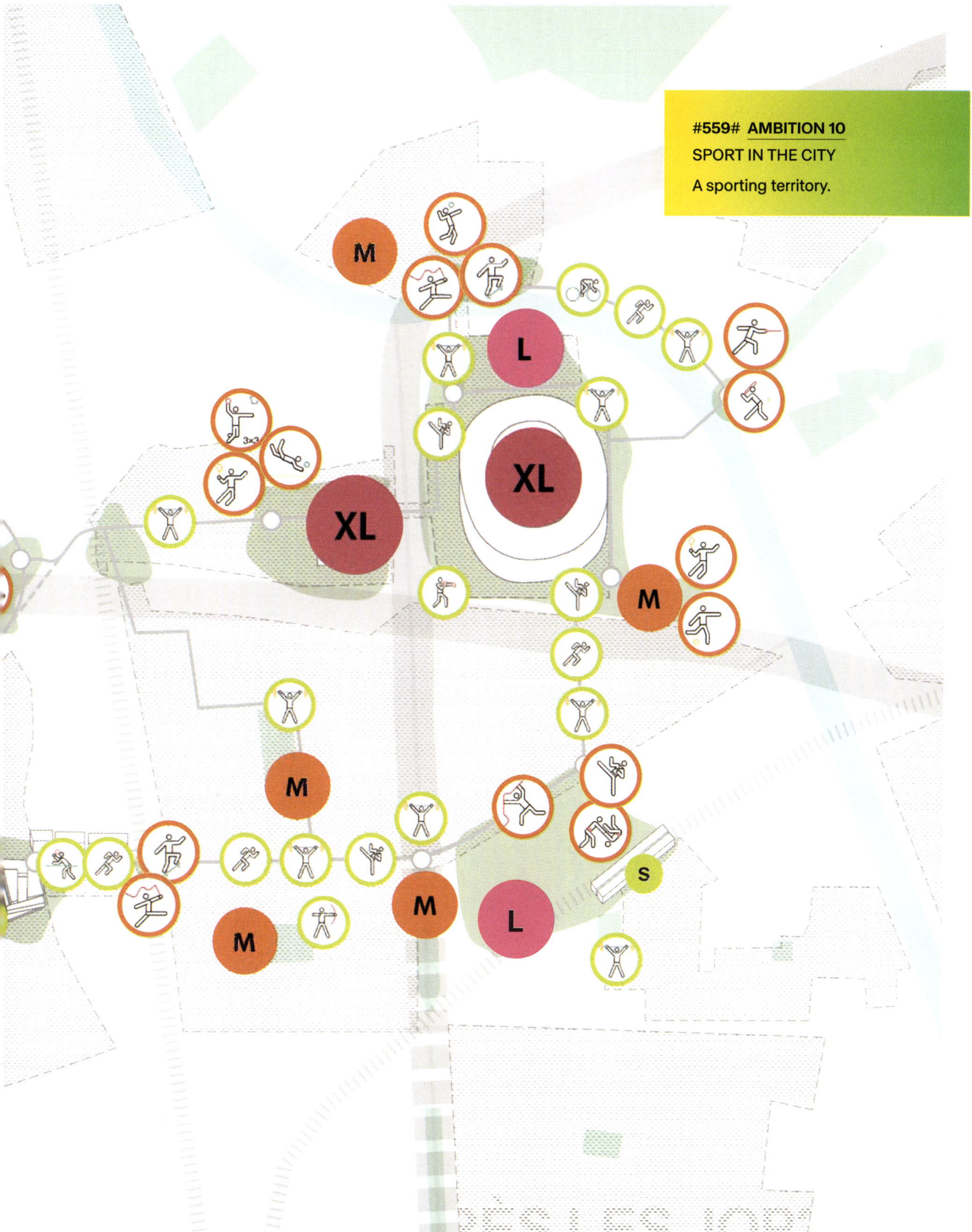
#559# AMBITION 10
SPORT IN THE CITY
A sporting territory.
M
L
XL
XL
M
M
M
M
L
S
3x3

#561# AMBITION 10

SPORT IN THE CITY

Velodrome and Olympic Swimming Pool, Berlin, Germany

The concept as antecedent.

1 KM
0,5 KM

#563# **AMBITION 10**

SPORT IN THE CITY

Velodrome and Olympic Swimming Pool, Berlin, Germany

International competition, winning project 1992, completion of velodrome November 1997/pool November 1999.

This project is linked to the reunification of the two Germanies and the candidacy of Berlin, a city on the verge of becoming the capital, for the 2000 Olympic Games. The chosen site lies at the intersection of networks and urban fabrics. To bring these systems together, the two buildings that would house the velodrome and the Olympic swimming pool disappeared. With the question of form out of the way, the project was able to address other concerns. The urban idea is to create a green space on a large scale, and within this green space, to erect buildings.

In Berlin, there is a potential for mixing nature and architecture. And this mixture is a form of work that we can develop in the city. The idea was to create an orchard. In other words, to plant apple trees. When you approach this orchard, you discover two tables, embedded in the ground, projecting out about a metre high... One round, the other rectangular, covered in a metallic fabric that vibrates in the sunlight and looks more like a water feature than a building.

OBSERVATOIRE
EINSTEIN PARK
ANTON-SAEFK OW PARK
VOLKSPARK PRENZLAUER
VELODROME
HEALTHLY AND SPORT PARK
OLYMPIC POOL
U
HAUSBURGPARK
FENNPFUHLPARK
BLANKENSTEINPARK
STADTPARK
FORCKENBECKPLATZ

#565# AMBITION 10

SPORT IN THE CITY

Velodrome and Olympic Swimming Pool, Berlin, Germany.

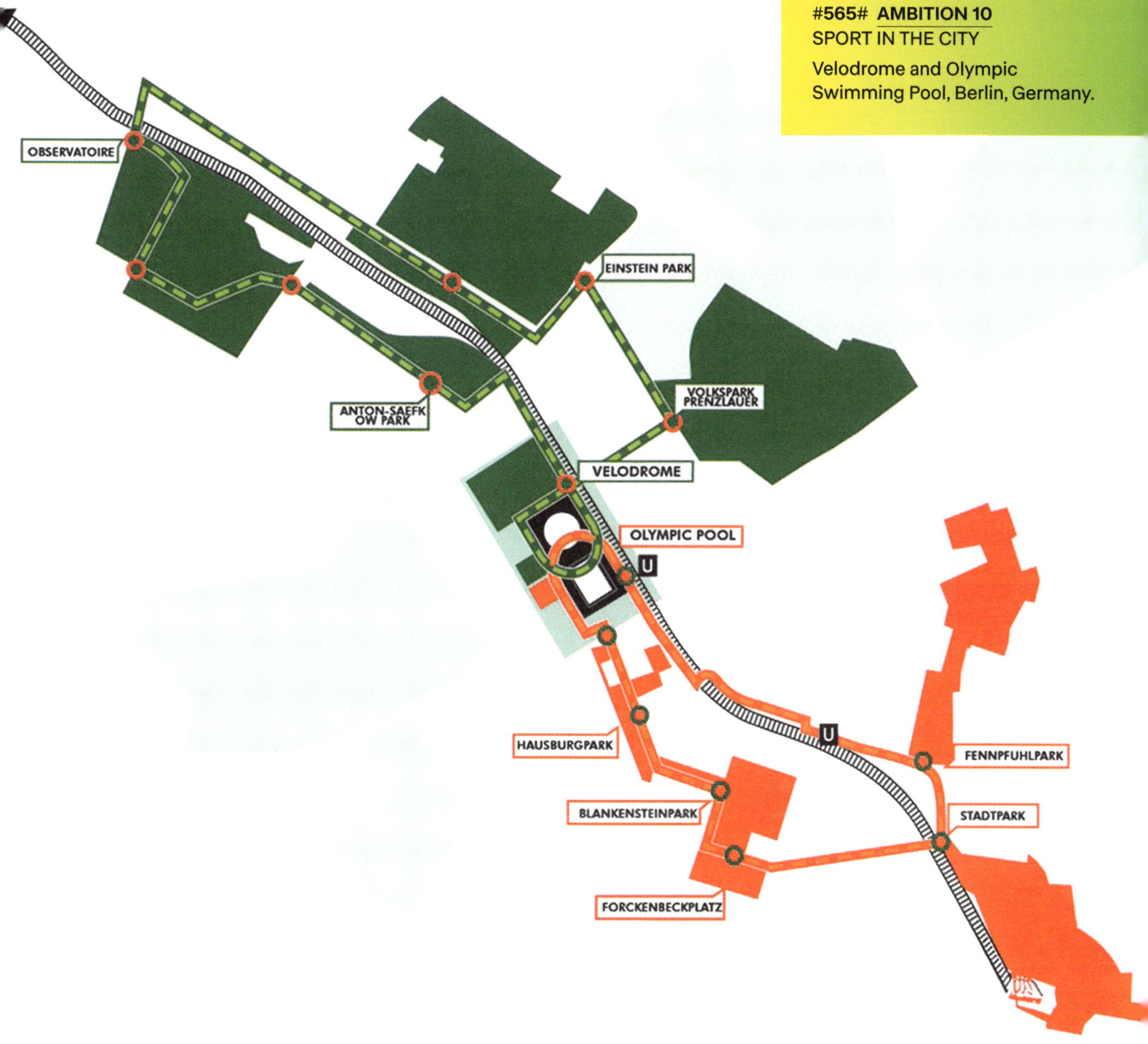

#567#

AMBITION 11

URBAN FURNITURE AND LIGHTING 2050

Gaëlle Lauriot-Provost's approach to designing public spaces is inseparable from her work on the atmospheres that give them their personality. At the start of her assignment, she planned to develop all the street furniture, including public lighting. As far as the furniture is concerned, the company has developed a complete range of objects that meet all the needs of the city - benches, bus shelters, chairs, tables, armchairs, masts of various sizes - as well as all the environmental and technological requirements. Large umbrellas, for example, not only had to provide protection from the sun, but also had to be connectable, allowing loudspeakers to be hooked up, and so on.

The public lighting was designed like the lighting in a house. Large areas, such as the main thoroughfares, benefit from powerful lighting thanks to tall masts, while the smaller streets are lit by installations reminiscent of village garlands, creating an impression that is both warm and reassuring. In the end, the local authority opted for other options than these, choosing existing furniture. Nonetheless, this important work provided food for thought for the Village des Athlètes urban design team, and forms part of its legacy.

#569# AMBITION 11

URBAN FURNITURE AND LIGHTING 2050

View of the Village.

Peter Doig, Milky way, 1990

#571# **AMBITION 11**

URBAN FURNITURE AND LIGHTING 2050

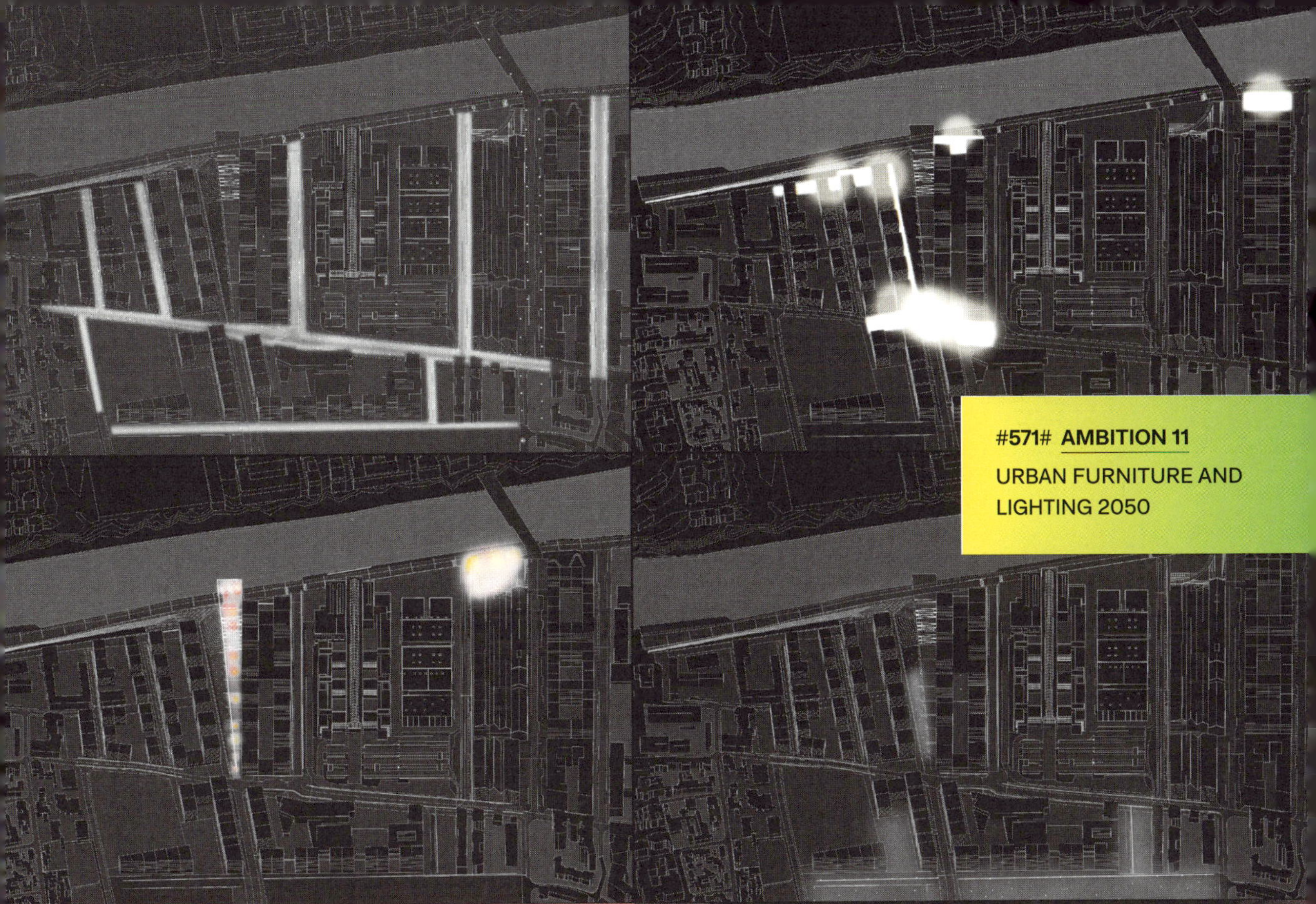

Robert Delaunay, Landscape nocturnal, 1906-1907

Paul Klee, Diana 1931

#573# **AMBITION 11**

URBAN FURNITURE AND LIGHTING 2050

Lighting plan.

Lighting plan - Typology

1
THE FINOT MALL AND THE OLYMPIC SQUARE : FLAGSHIP SPACES, ANTICIPATED USES FOR EVENTS

2
FROM THE SEINE TO PLEYEL : THE MAIN ROUTES

3
LES BERGES DE SEINE: A METROPOLITAN DISPLAY

4
THE RESIDENTIAL NEIGHBOURHOOD: LOCAL LIGHTING

5
THE BOWS AND SQUARES : FAVOURITE PLACES FOR RESIDENTS

6
LES VENELLES: FRIENDLY CROSSINGS

7
BIODIVERSITY AREAS: A BLACK SCREEN

#575# AMBITION 11

URBAN FURNITURE AND LIGHTING 2050.

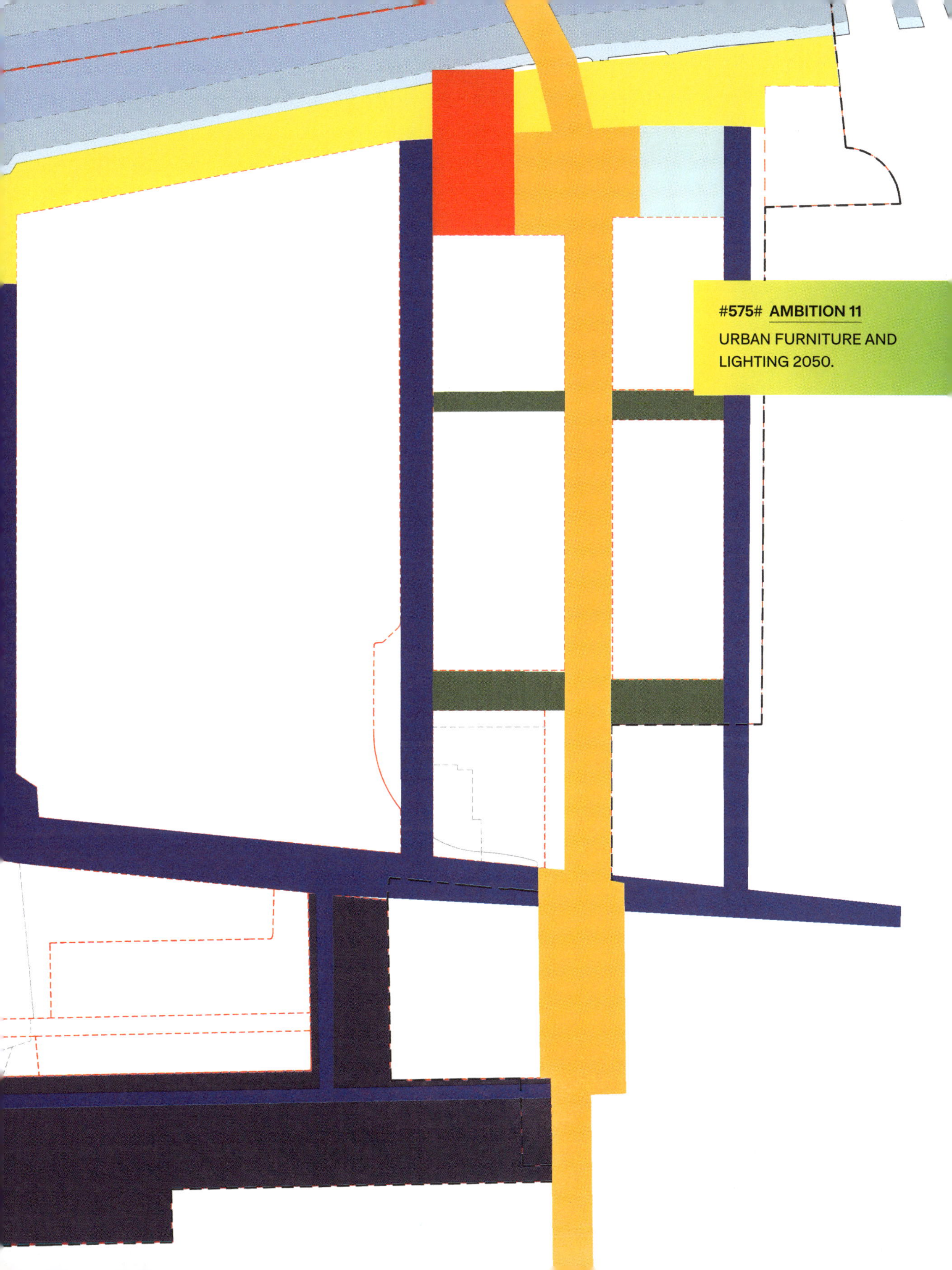

Mail Finot section

Mail Finot and Place Olympique lighting plan

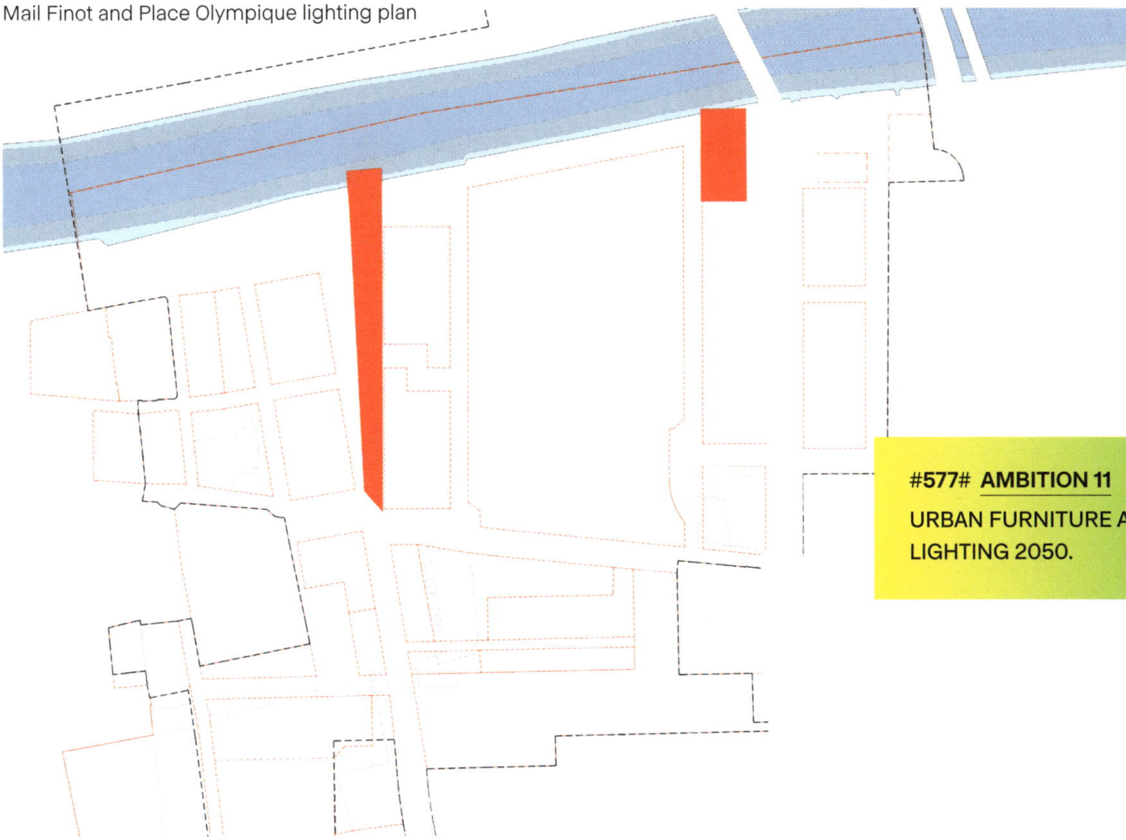

#577# **AMBITION 11**

URBAN FURNITURE AND LIGHTING 2050.

Axonometry Mail Finot

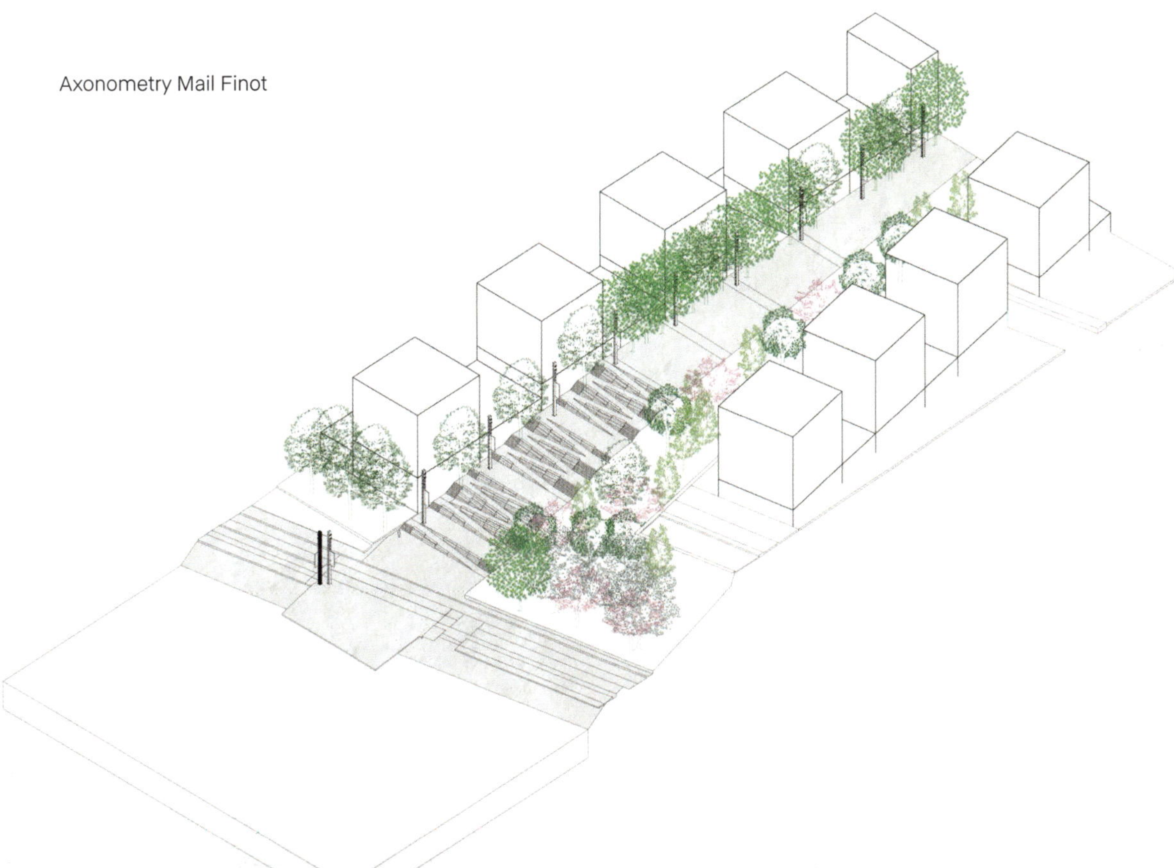

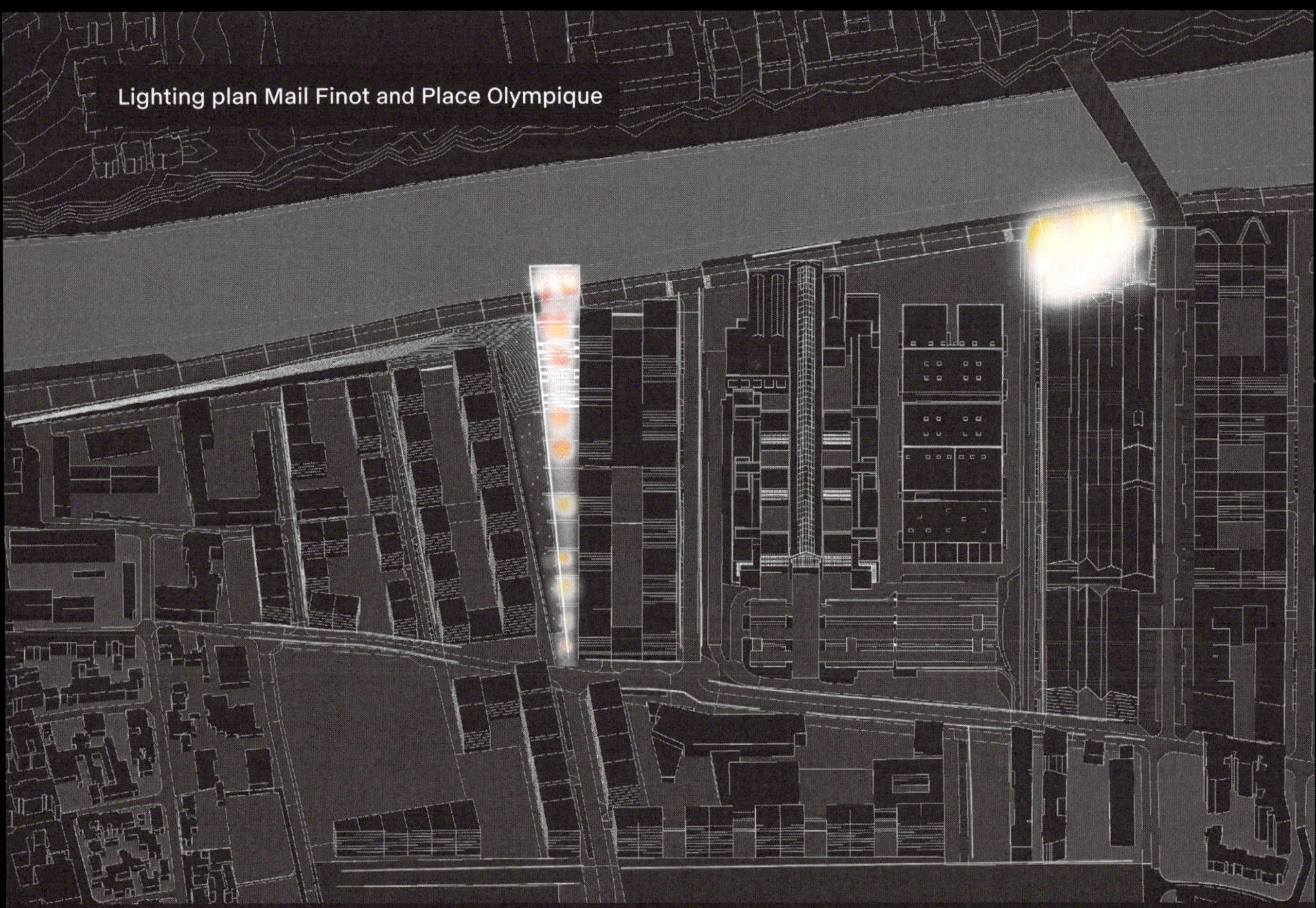
Lighting plan Mail Finot and Place Olympique

Lighting study Mail Finot (ingérop)

Overview of results - Place

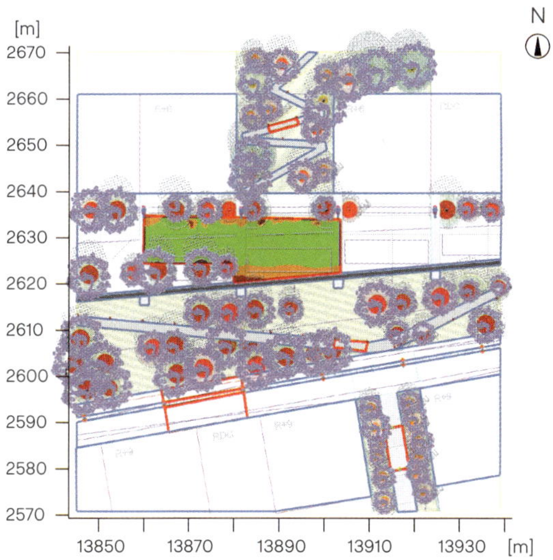

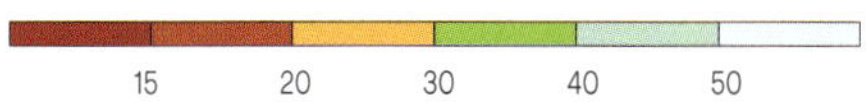

General information		
Calculation algorithm used		average indirect share
Height of assessment surface		0.25 m
Maintenance factor		0.80
Luminous flux from all lamps The quantity of luminous flux differs from the photometric data		144519.7 lm (57.68% gradé)
Overall puissance		3330 W
Overall puissance per surface area (9765.51 m²)		0.34 W/m²
Lighting		
Lighting medium	Em	35.2 lx
Minimal lighting	Emin	11.6 lx
Maxima lighting	Emax	45.3 lx
Uniformity Uo	Emin/Em	1:3.03 (0.33)
Uniformity Ud	Emin/Emax	1:3.9 (0.26)

TypeAff.	Brand	
1 12	selux	
	N° order	: SX 936 11-9
	Luminaire name	: Avanza 450
	Lamps	: 1 x LED 25 W / 3000 lm

Outdoor summary Mail Finot

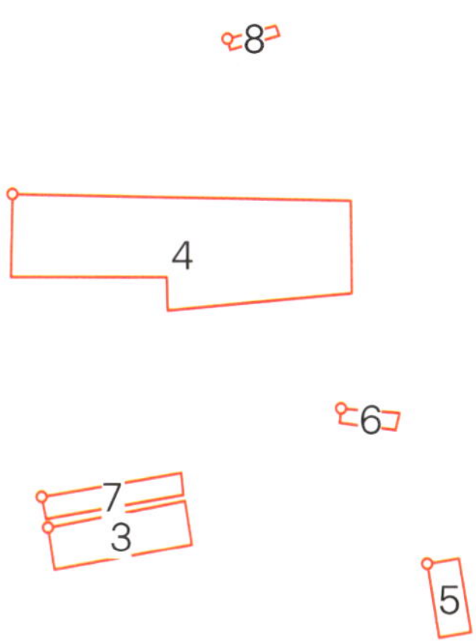

General information

Calculation algorithm used	part indirecte moyenne
Maintenance factor	0.80

Measuring surfaces

3 Sidewalk 1

Lighting — Calculation grid: 5.66m x 17.47m (8 x 26 Points), Hauteur = 0.20m

	Ē m	Emin	Uo	Ud
	19.1 lx	10.2 lx	0.53	0.24
P1	>= 15.0 lx	>= 3.00 lx		

4 Place

Lighting — Calculation grid: 13.81m x 42.73m (11 x 34 Points), Hauteur = 0.25m

	Ē m	Emin	Uo	Ud
	35 lx	11.6 lx	0.33	0.26
P1	>= 15.0 lx	>= 3.00 lx		

5 Passage

Lighting — Calculation grid: 4.16m x 9.1m (8 x 17 Points), Hauteur = 0.25m

	Ē m	Emin	Uo	Ud
	24 lx	20 lx	0.83	0.71
P3	>= 7.50 lx	>= 1.50 lx		

6 Path

Lighting — Calculation grid: 2.06m x 7.24m (6 x 22 Points), Hauteur = 0.15m

	Ē m	Emin	Uo	Ud
	27 lx	7.46 lx	0.27	0.04
P3	>= 7.50 lx	>= 1.50 lx		

7 Sidewalk 2

Lighting — Calculation grid: 2.94m x 17.69m (7 x 42 Points), Hauteur = 0.15m

	Ē m	Emin	Uo	Ud
	22 lx	10.5 lx	0.47	0.22
P1	>= 15.0 lx	>= 3.00 lx		

Lighting plan from the Seine to Pleyel

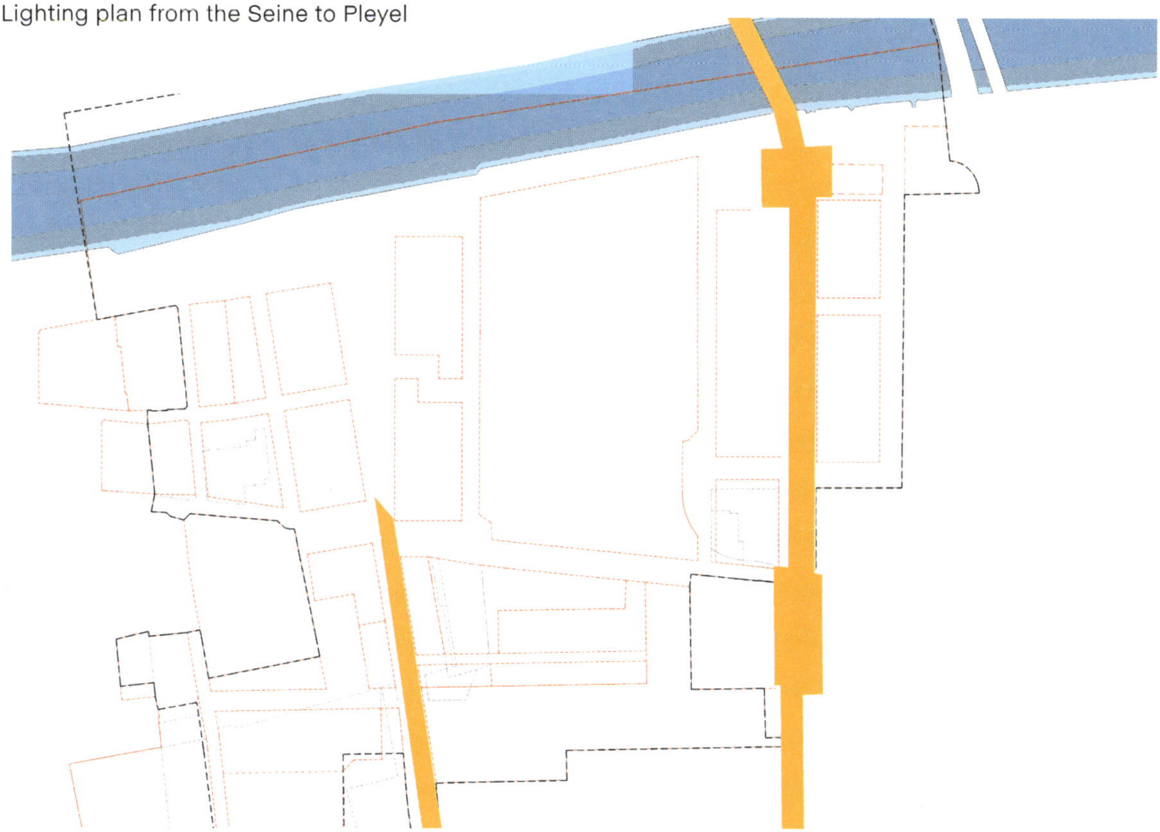

Axonometry Allée Seine

#581# AMBITION 11

URBAN FURNITURE AND LIGHTING 2050.

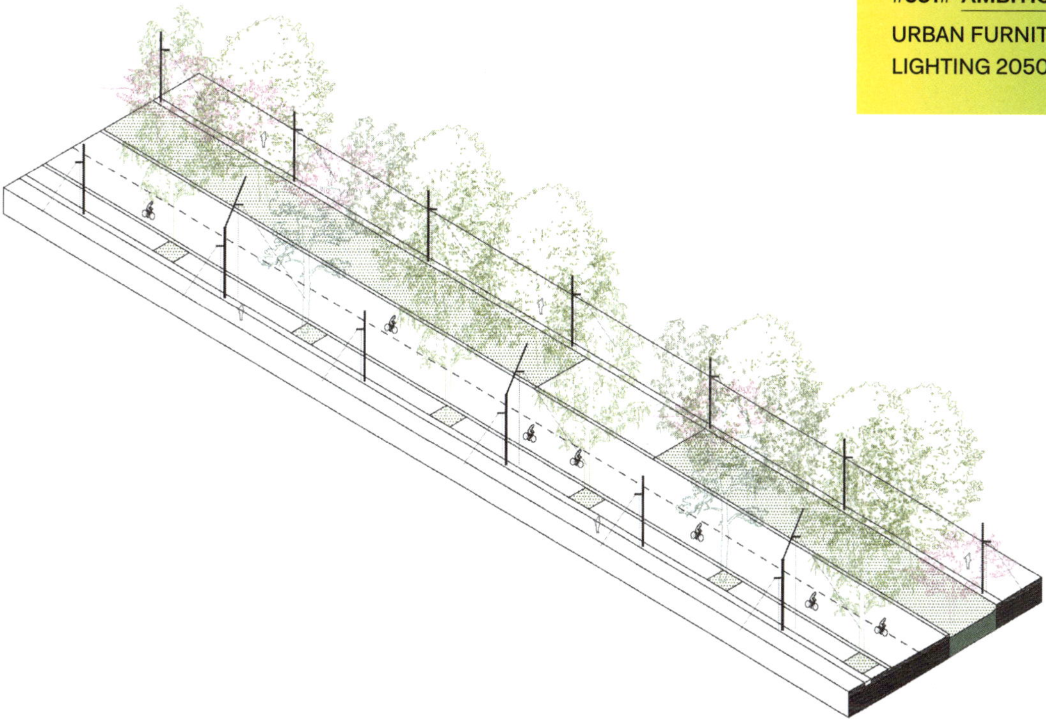

Berges de Seine elevation

Berges de Seine lighting plan

Axonometry of RD1 and hillsides

#583# AMBITION 11

URBAN FURNITURE AND LIGHTING 2050.

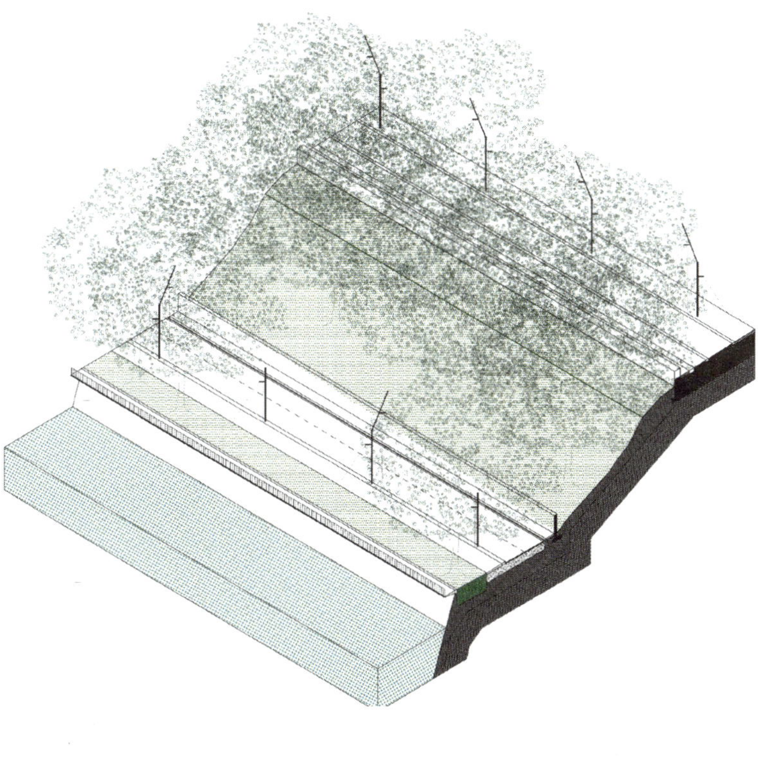

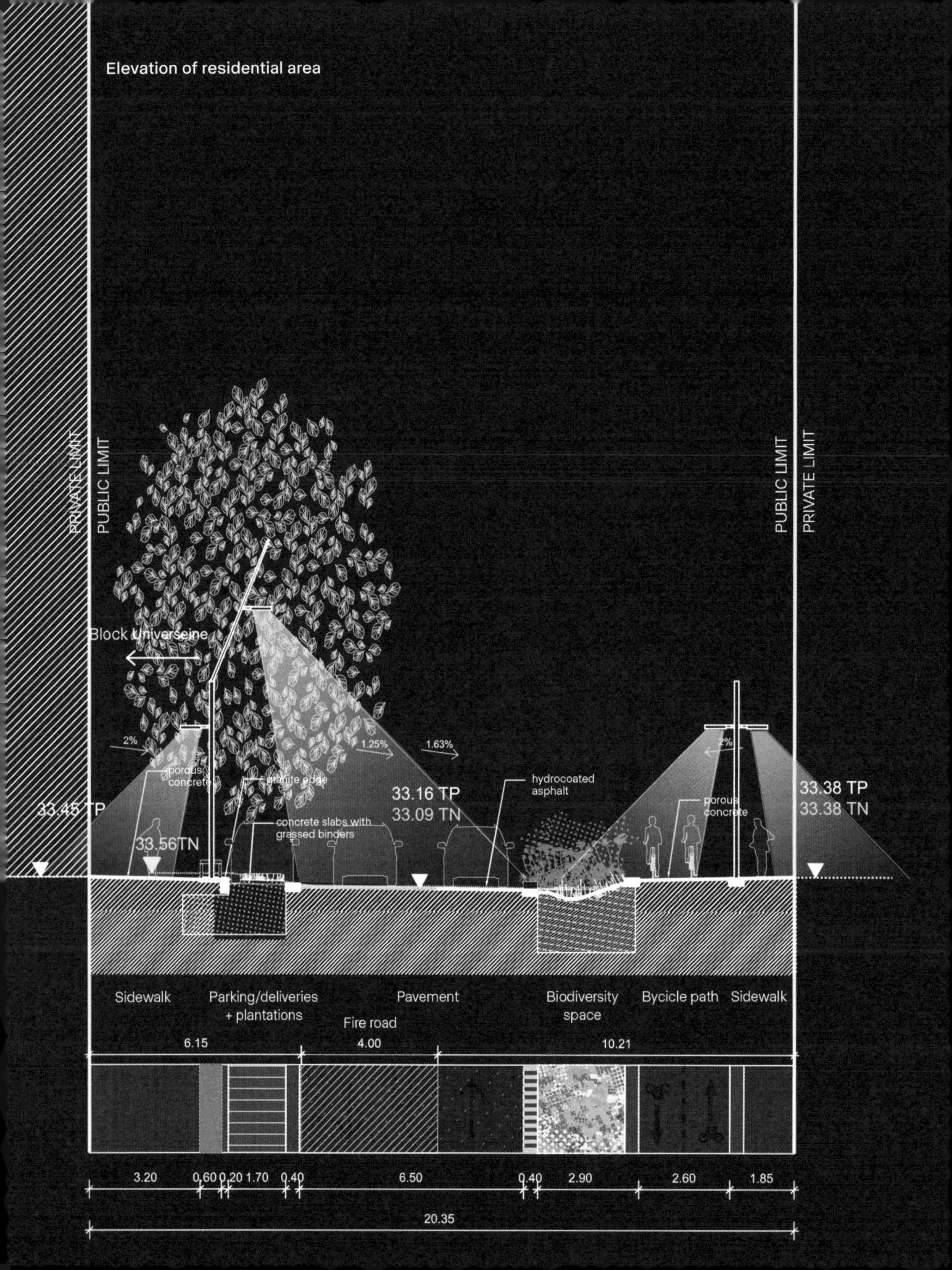

Elevation of residential area
PRIVATE LIMIT
PUBLIC LIMIT
PUBLIC LIMIT
PRIVATE LIMIT
Block Universeine
2%
porous concrete
granite edge
1.25%
1.63%
hydrocoated asphalt
2%
porous concrete
33.45 TP
33.56TN
concrete slabs with grassed binders
33.16 TP
33.09 TN
33.38 TP
33.38 TN
Sidewalk
Parking/deliveries + plantations
Pavement
Fire road
Biodiversity space
Bycicle path
Sidewalk
6.15
4.00
10.21
3.20
0.60
0.20
1.70
0.40
6.50
0.40
2.90
2.60
1.85
20.35

Elevation of residential area

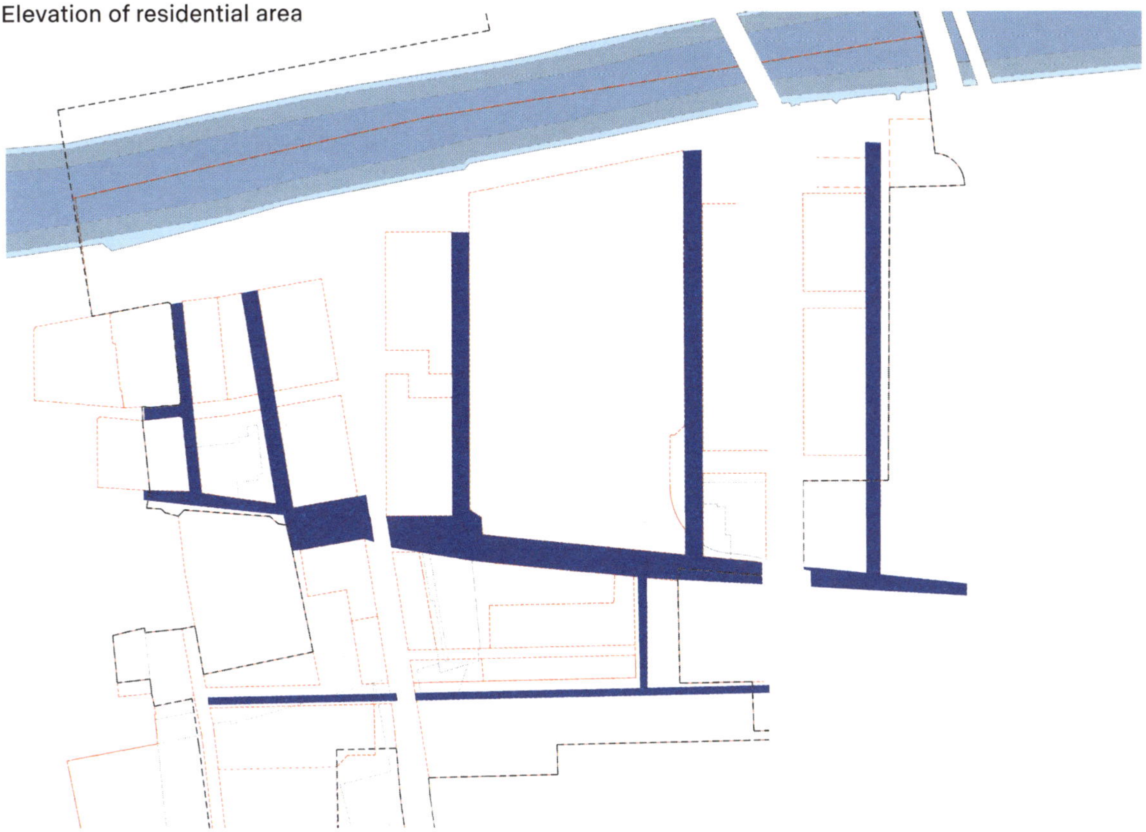

Axonometry rue des Quinconces

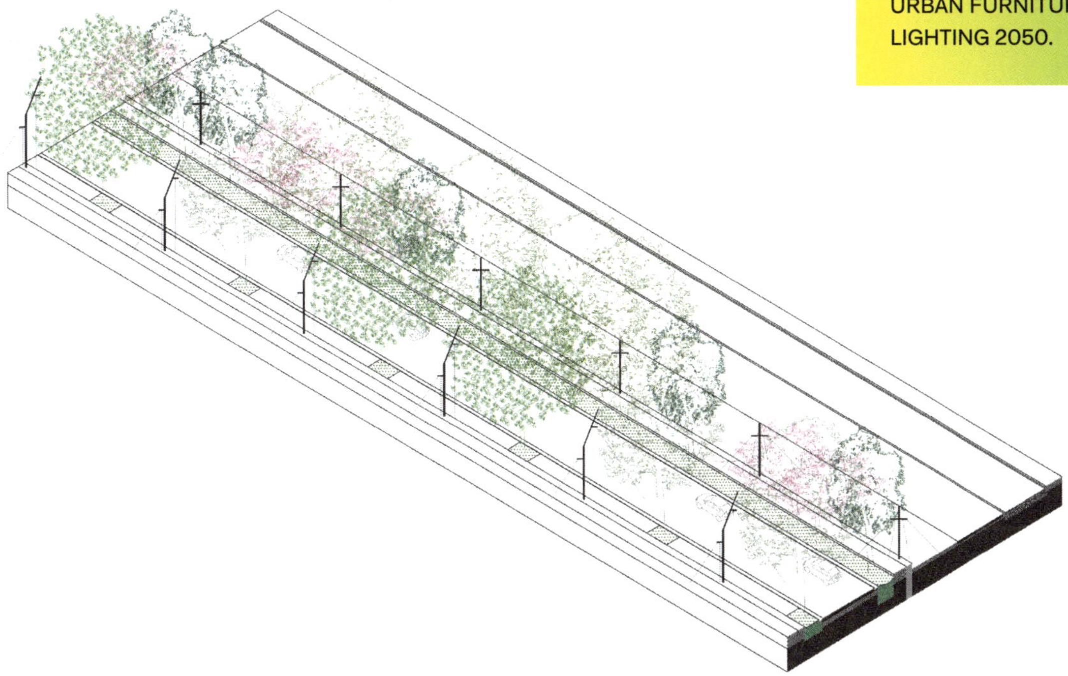

#585# AMBITION 11

URBAN FURNITURE AND LIGHTING 2050.

Elevation of bows and squares

Bow and square lighting plan

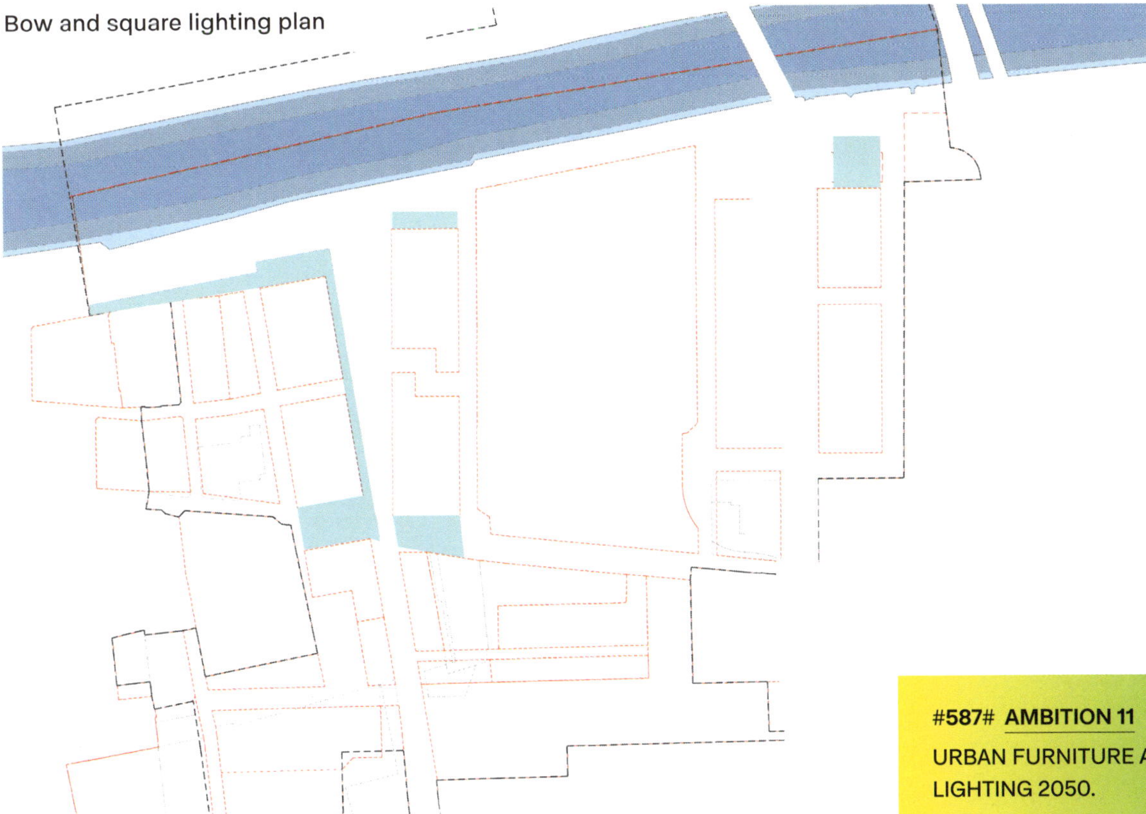

#587# AMBITION 11

URBAN FURNITURE AND LIGHTING 2050.

Axonometry terrace

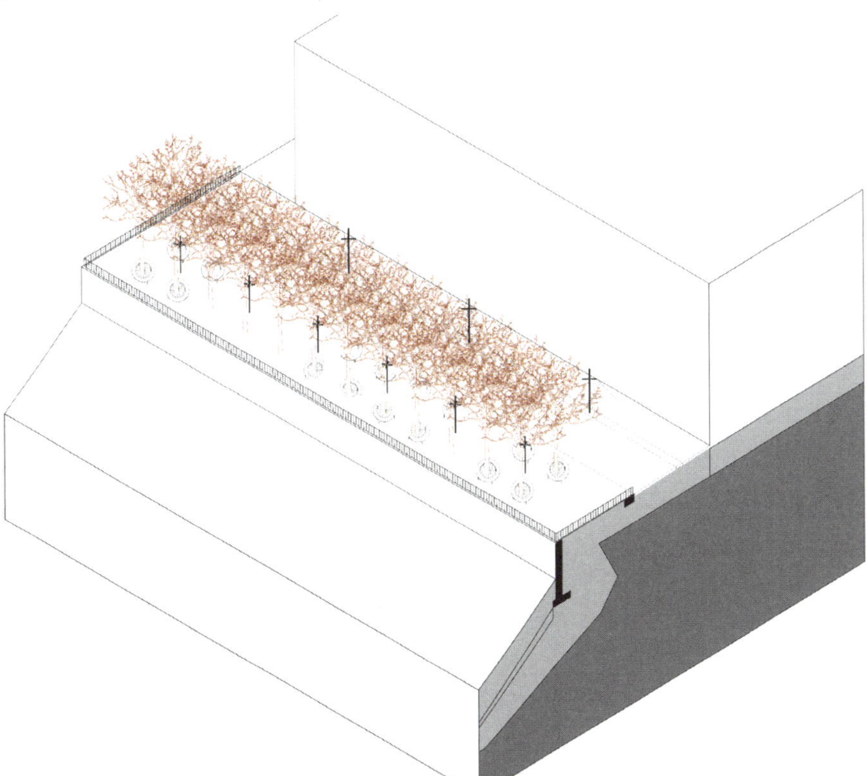

Elevation of alleyways

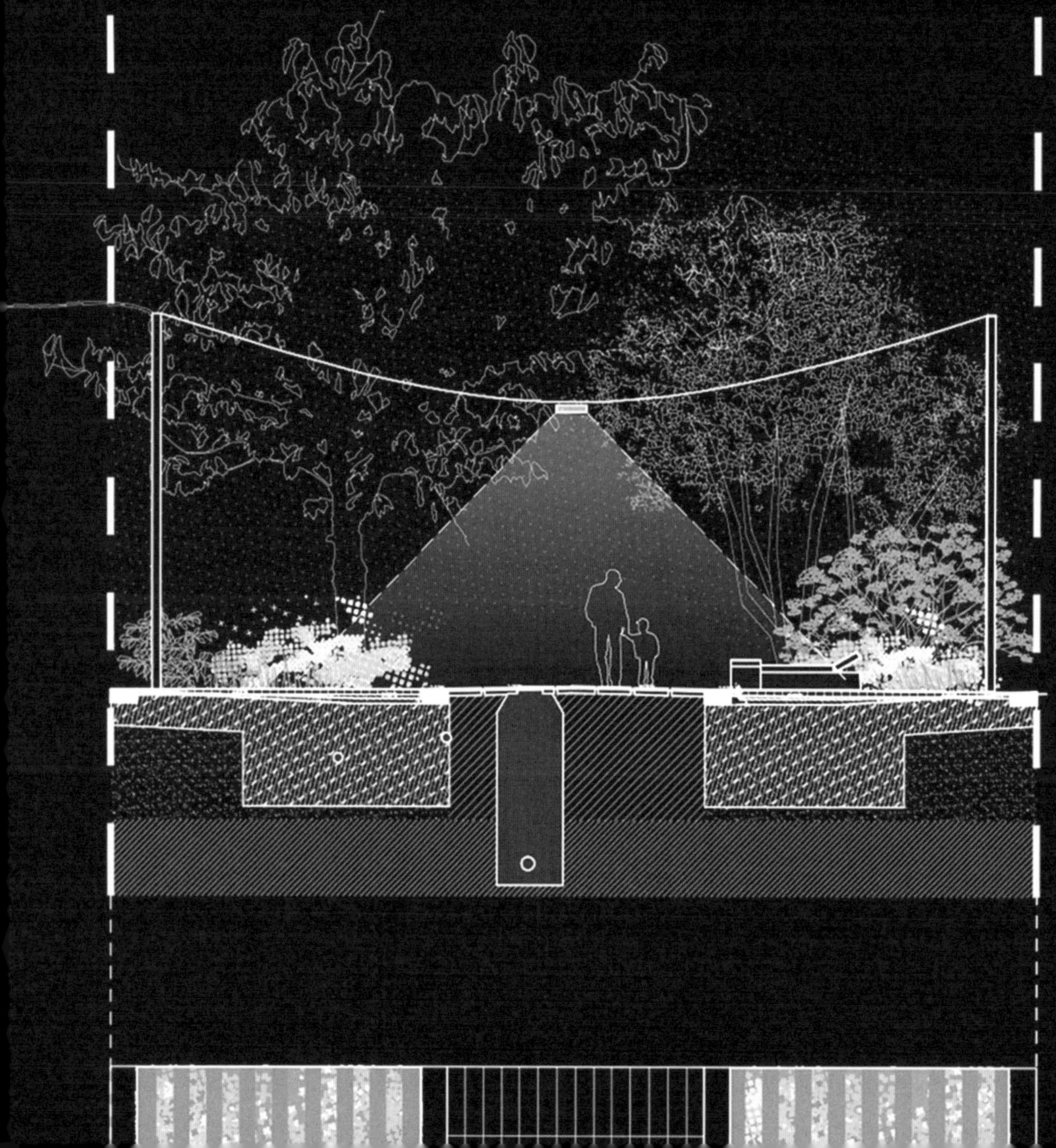

Lighting plan for alleyways

Axonometry rue des Villas

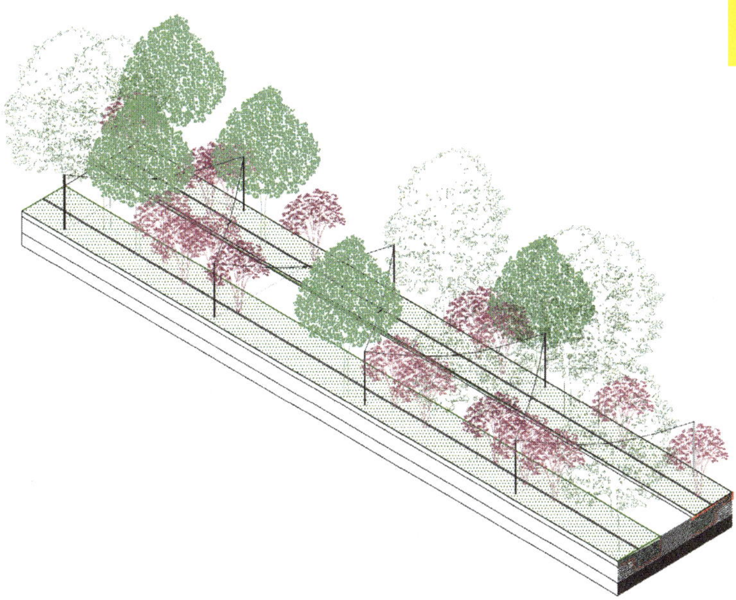

#589# AMBITION 11

URBAN FURNITURE AND LIGHTING 2050.

Elevation of biodiversity areas

Lighting plan for biodiversity areas

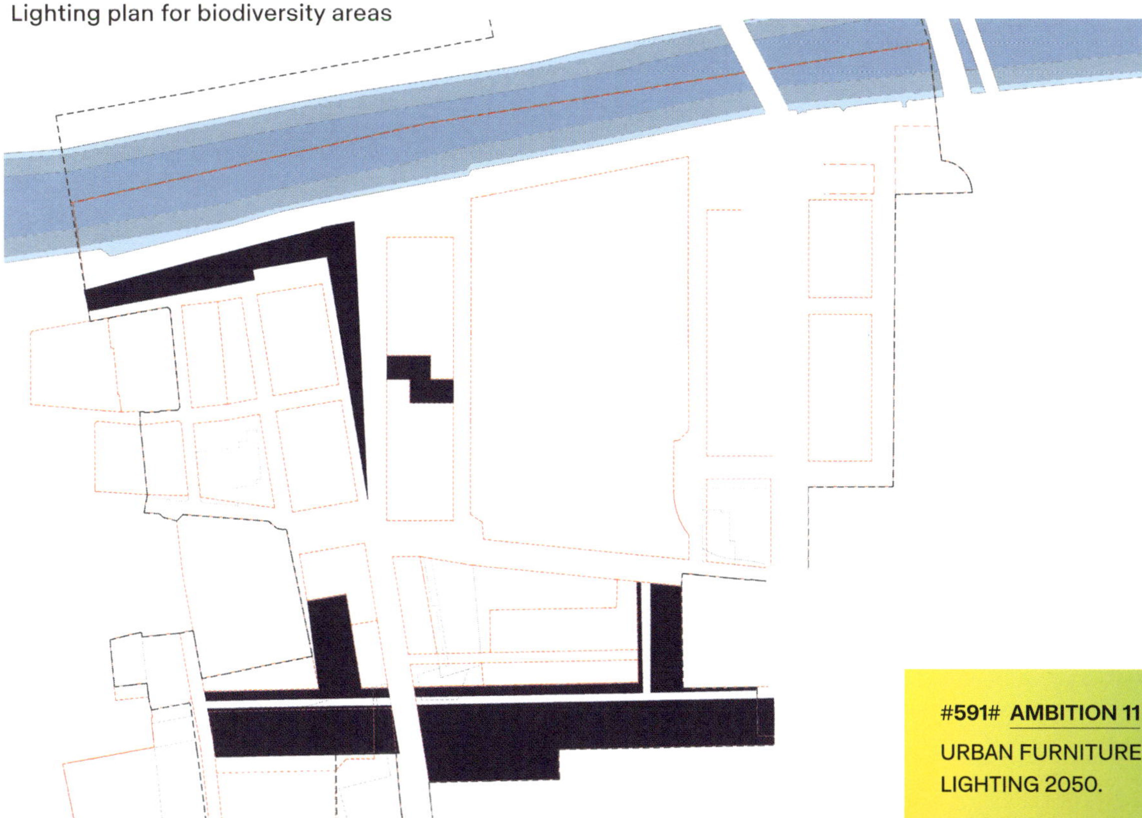

#591# **AMBITION 11**

URBAN FURNITURE AND LIGHTING 2050.

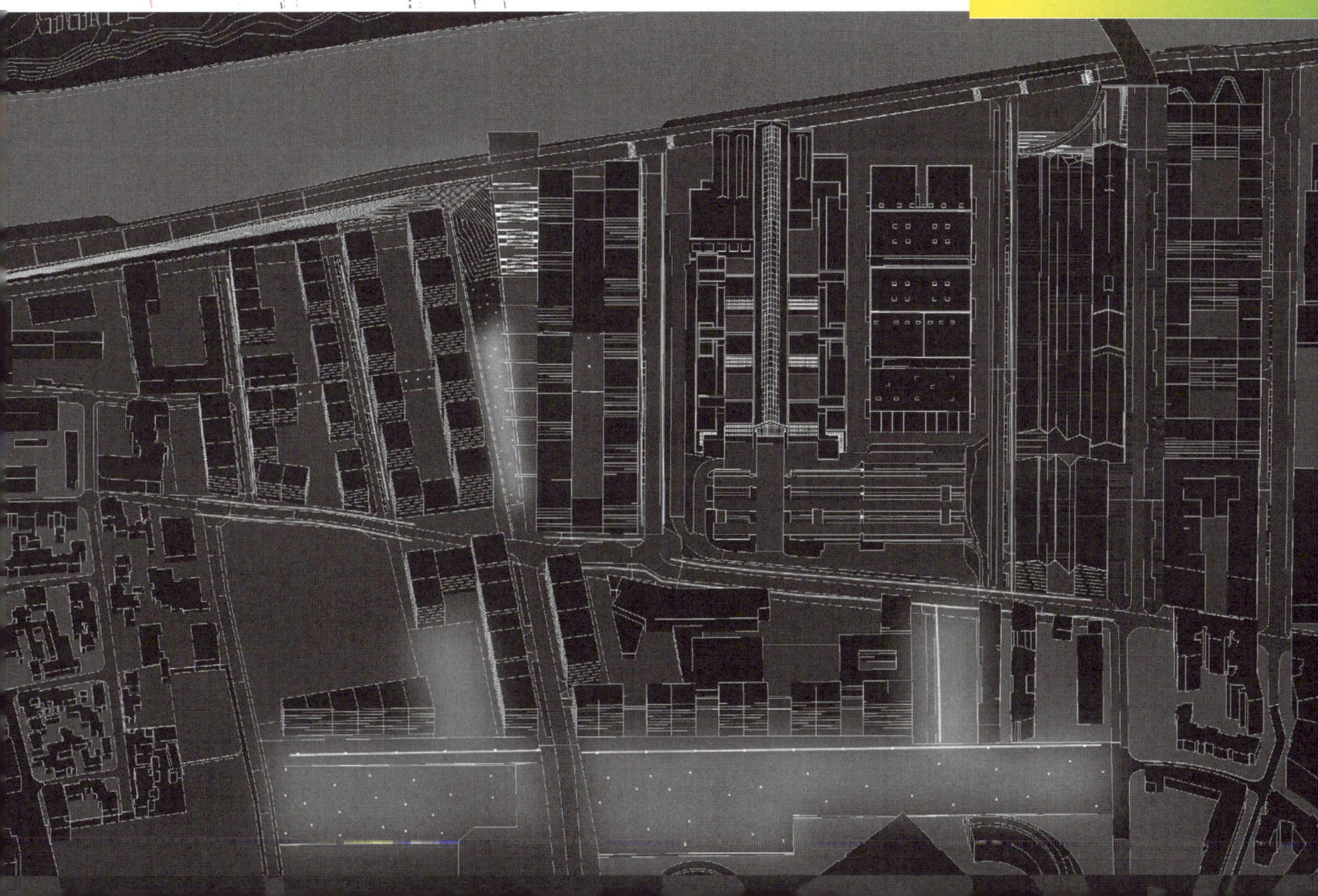

Elevation
Detachment systems

#593# AMBITION 11

URBAN FURNITURE AND LIGHTING 2050.

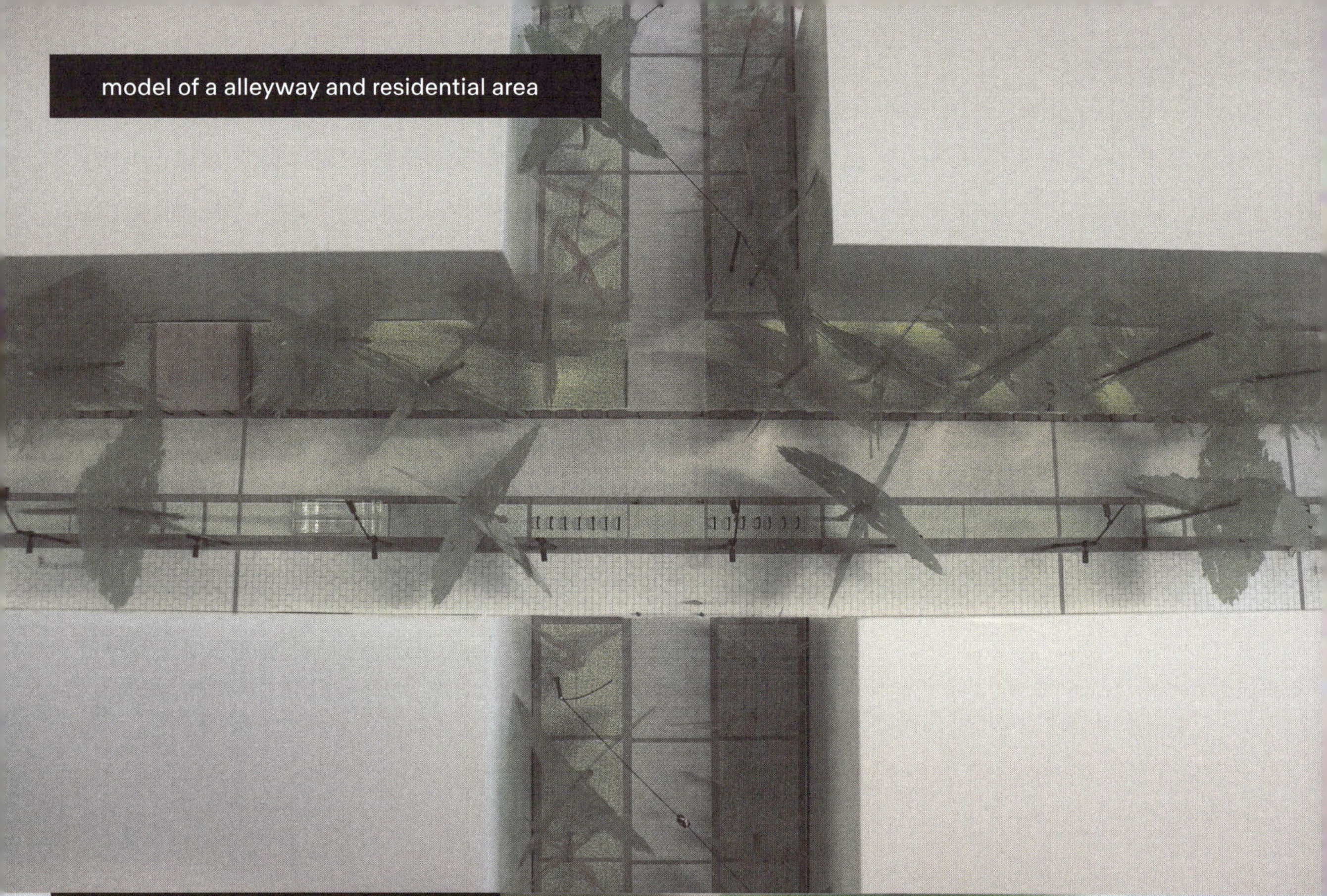

model of a alleyway and residential area

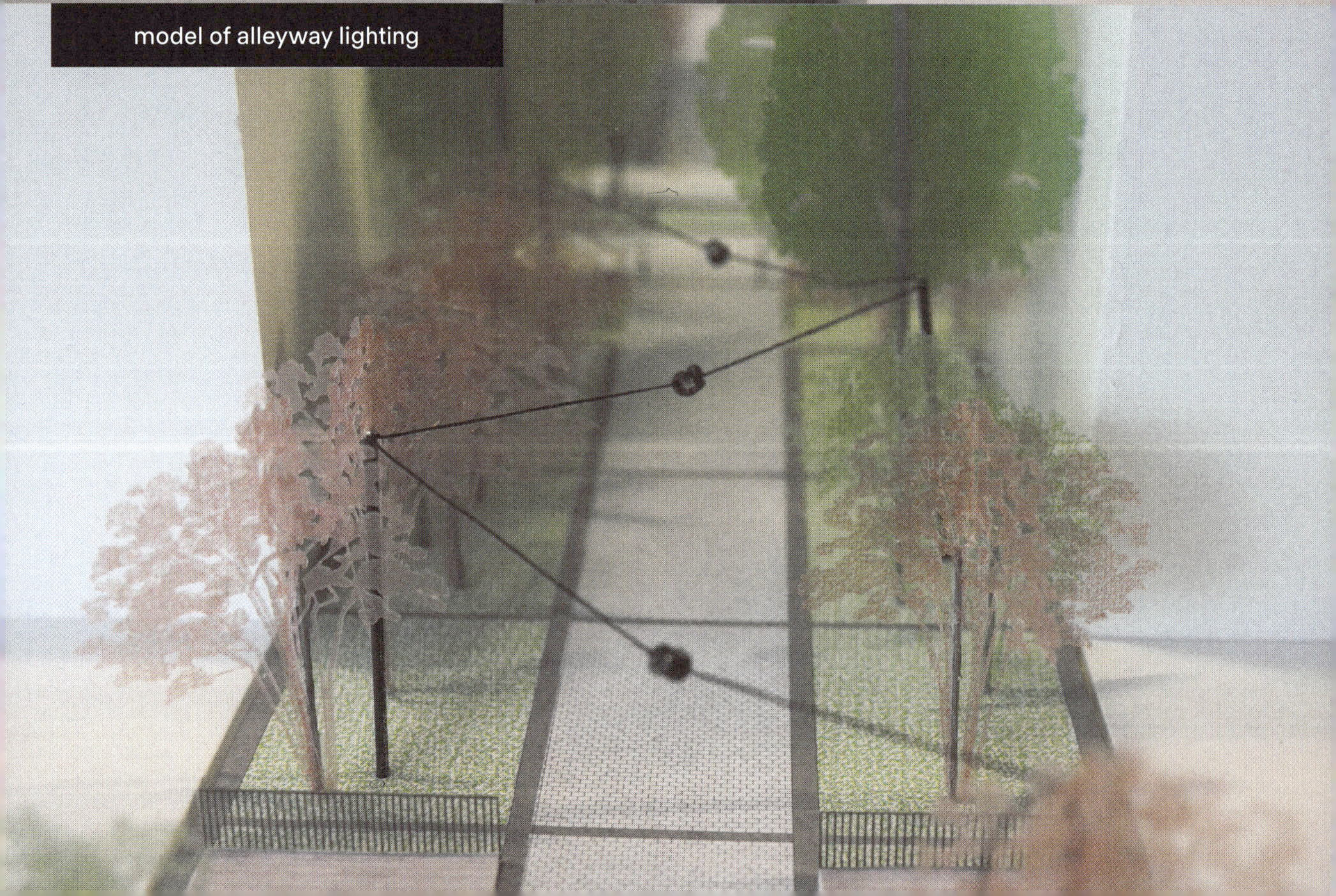

model of alleyway lighting

model of Mail Finot

#595# **AMBITION 11**

URBAN FURNITURE AND LIGHTING 2050.

Rendering image of the luminaires

#597# **AMBITION 11**

URBAN FURNITURE AND LIGHTING 2050.

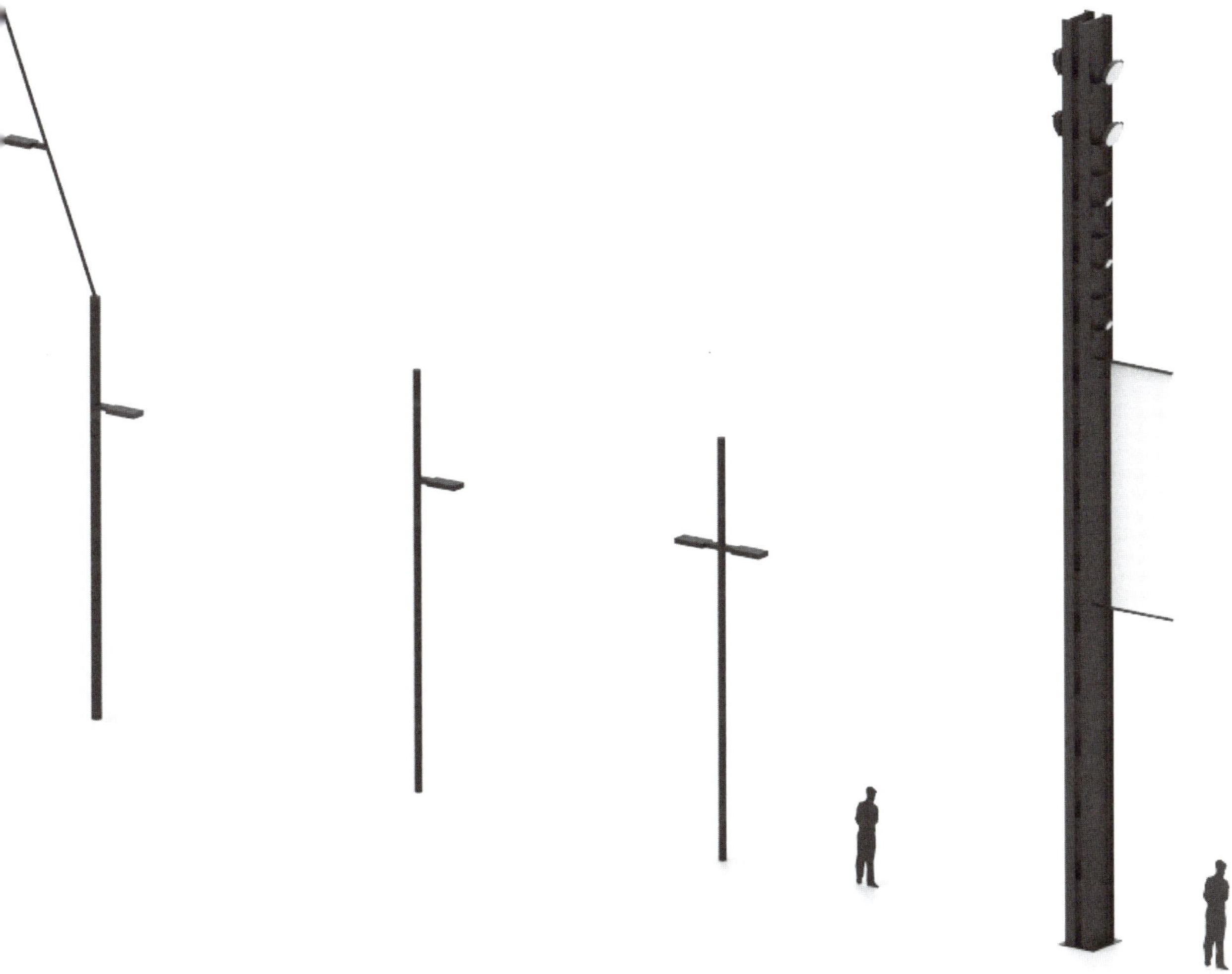

Photo-model of the luminaires

Elevation drawing of luminaires

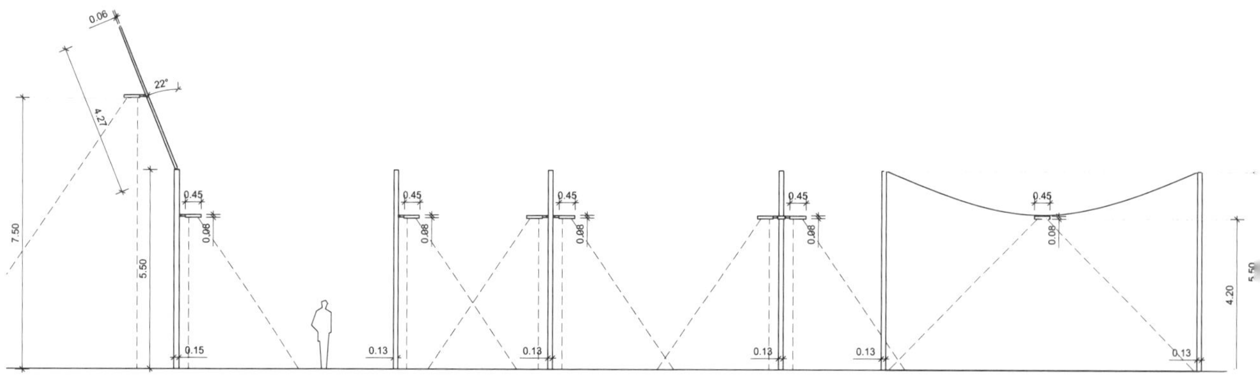

#599# AMBITION 11

URBAN FURNITURE AND LIGHTING 2050.

Louis Toffoli, Quai in Ivry, 1951

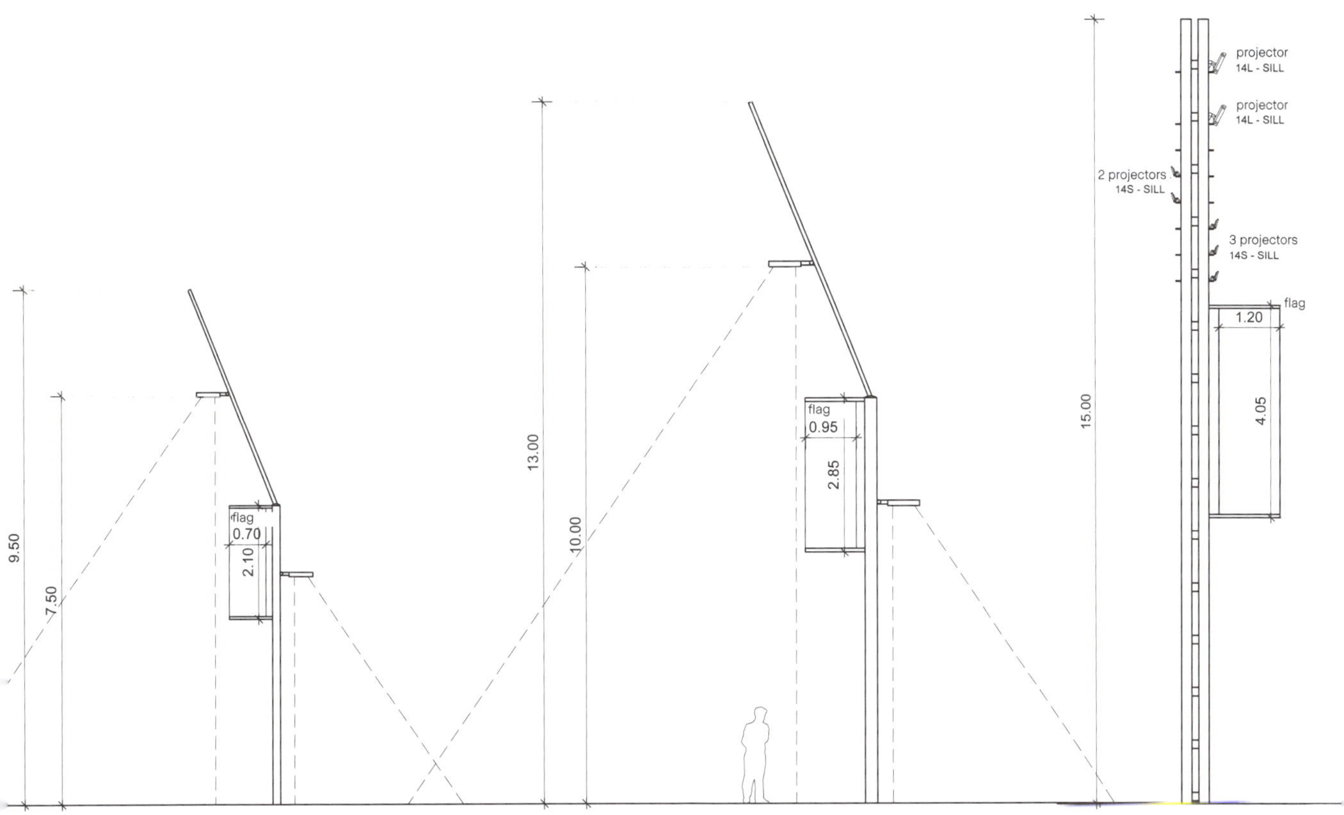

LARGE 15 M MAST

7 SPRINGS (FROM 6 TO 14M)

Mat bipode en acier
Sablage et peinture liquide multicouches antirouille
RAL noir
Structure IPE et HEB standarts

1- IPE 600mm x 220mm
2- IPE 600mm x 220mm
3- Gap of 125 mm between the footings of the 2 IPEs
4- L-shaped fixing plate
5- 2 HEB 160 between the 2 IPEs
6- SILL 14L LED spotlight
7- SILL 14L projector LED source
8- Removable flag holder
9- Microperforated canvas flag
10- Exit hatch with closure
11- Fairground light integrated into the electrical box
12- Mast extension below ground level
13- Fixing plate
14- Concrete base

Off-lot
Lot concerned

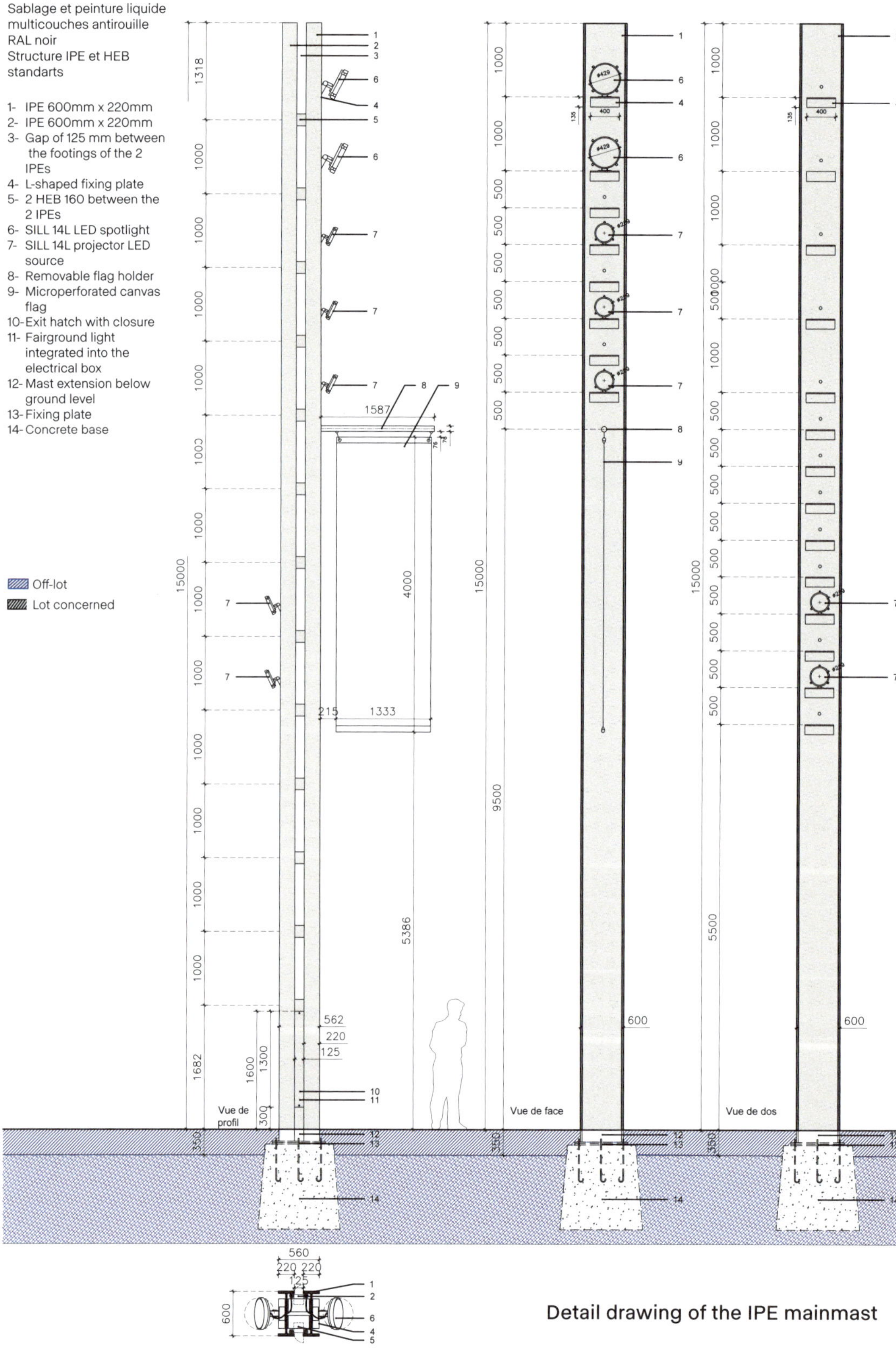

Detail drawing of the IPE mainmast

LARGE 15 M IPEMAST

7 SPRINGS (FROM 6 TO 14M)

1- IPE 600mm x 220mm
2- IPE 600mm x 220mm
3- Gap of 125 mm between the footings of the 2 IPEs
4- L-shaped fixing plate
5- 2 HEB 160 between the 2 IPEs
6- 14L spotlight from SILL
7- 14L spotlight from SILL
8- 60mm diameter metal tube for cable routing
9- Hole in each board for power supply pass-through
10- Access hatch with tamper-proof closure
11- Fairground light integrated into the electrical box

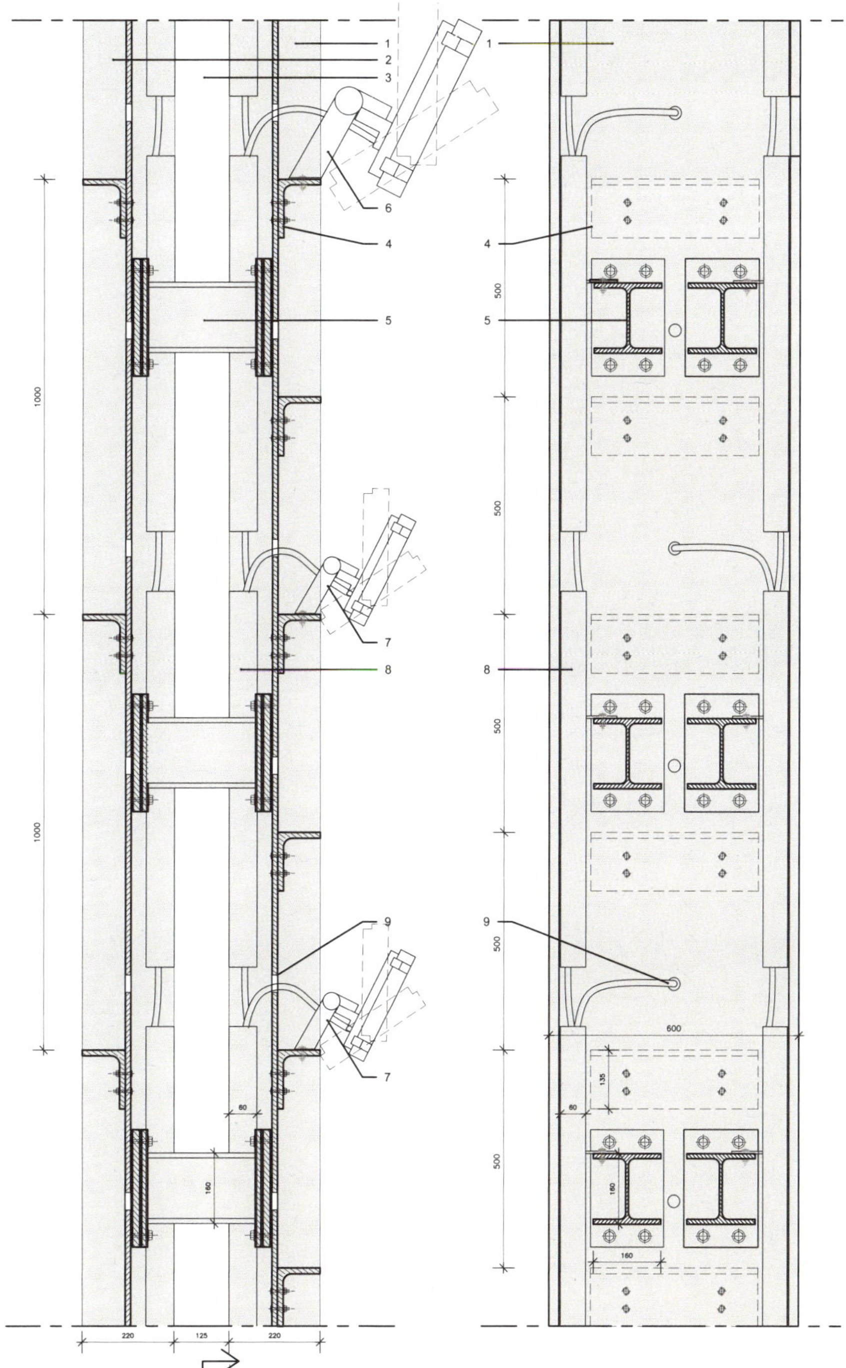

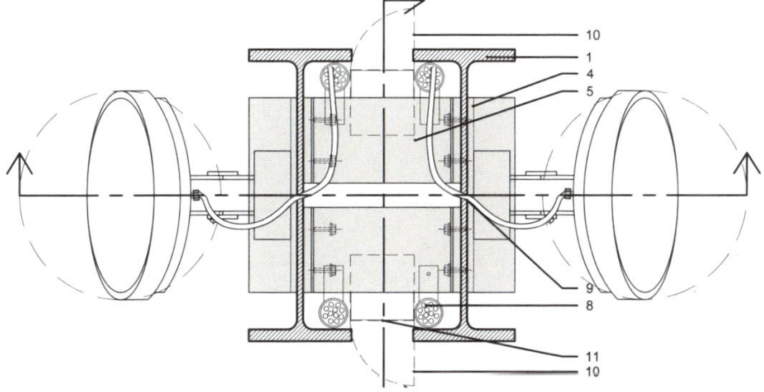

Plan of the Place Haute Panoramique

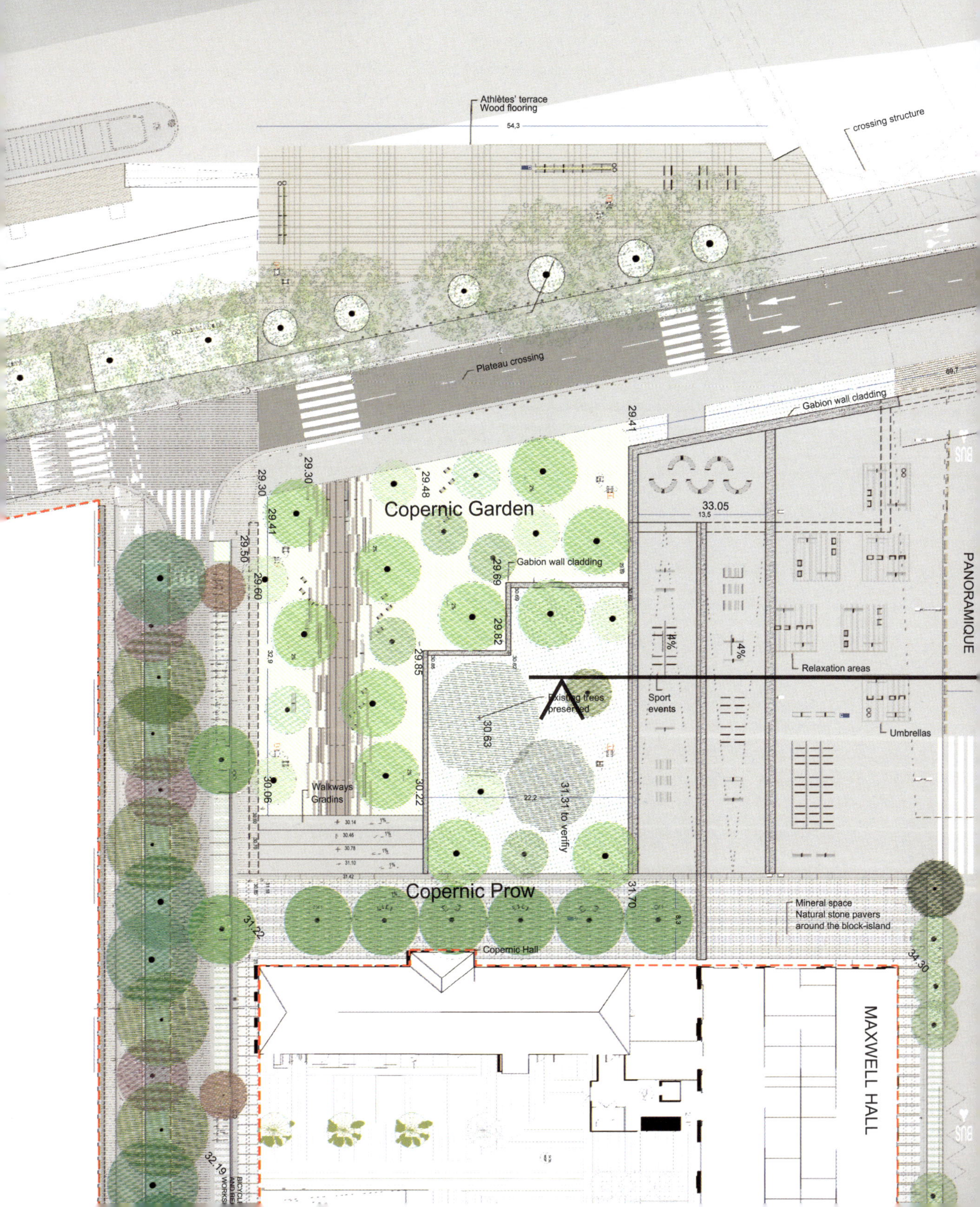

#603# AMBITION 11

URBAN FURNITURE AND LIGHTING 2050.

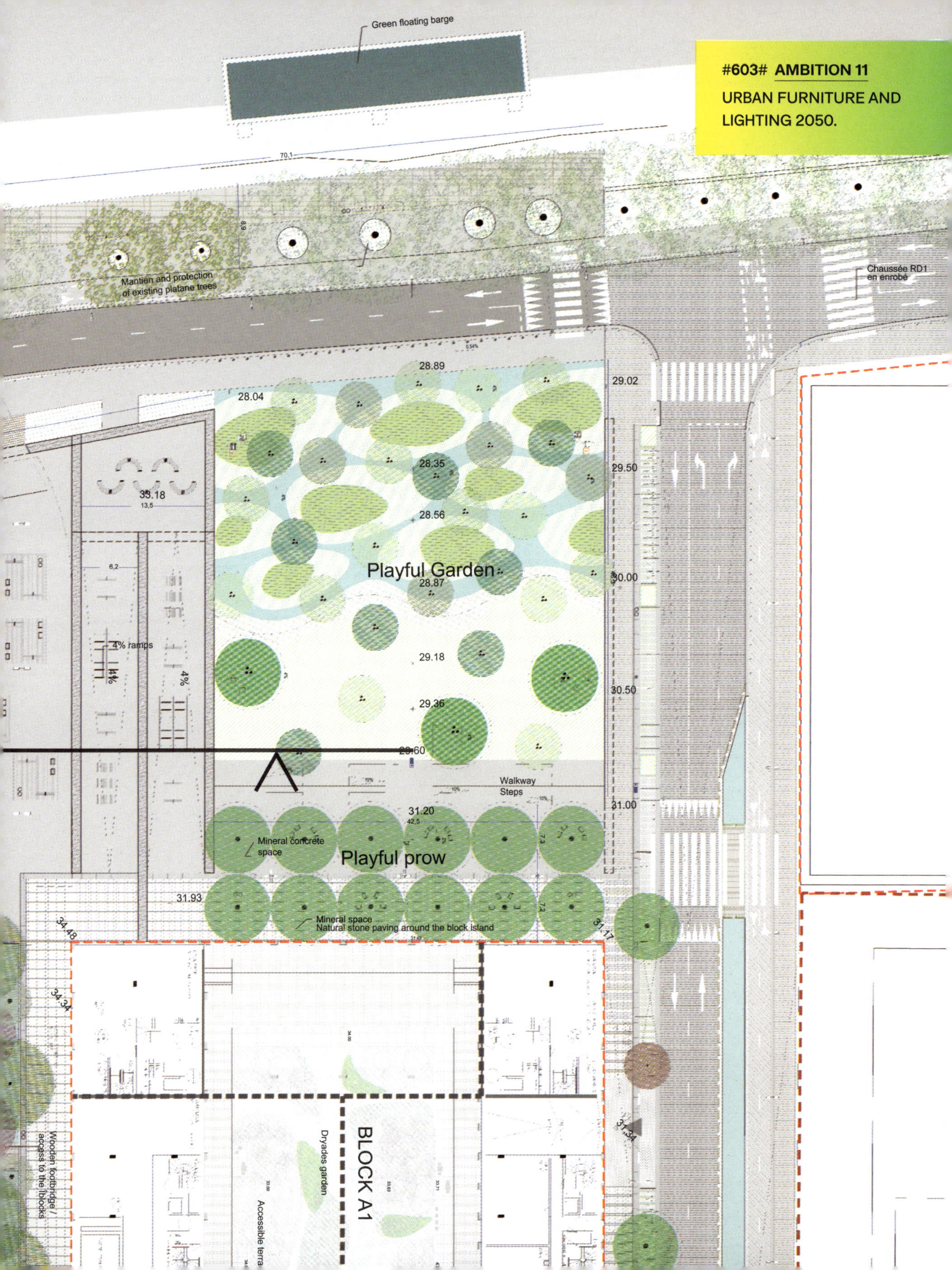

Elevation section of the Place Haute Panoramique

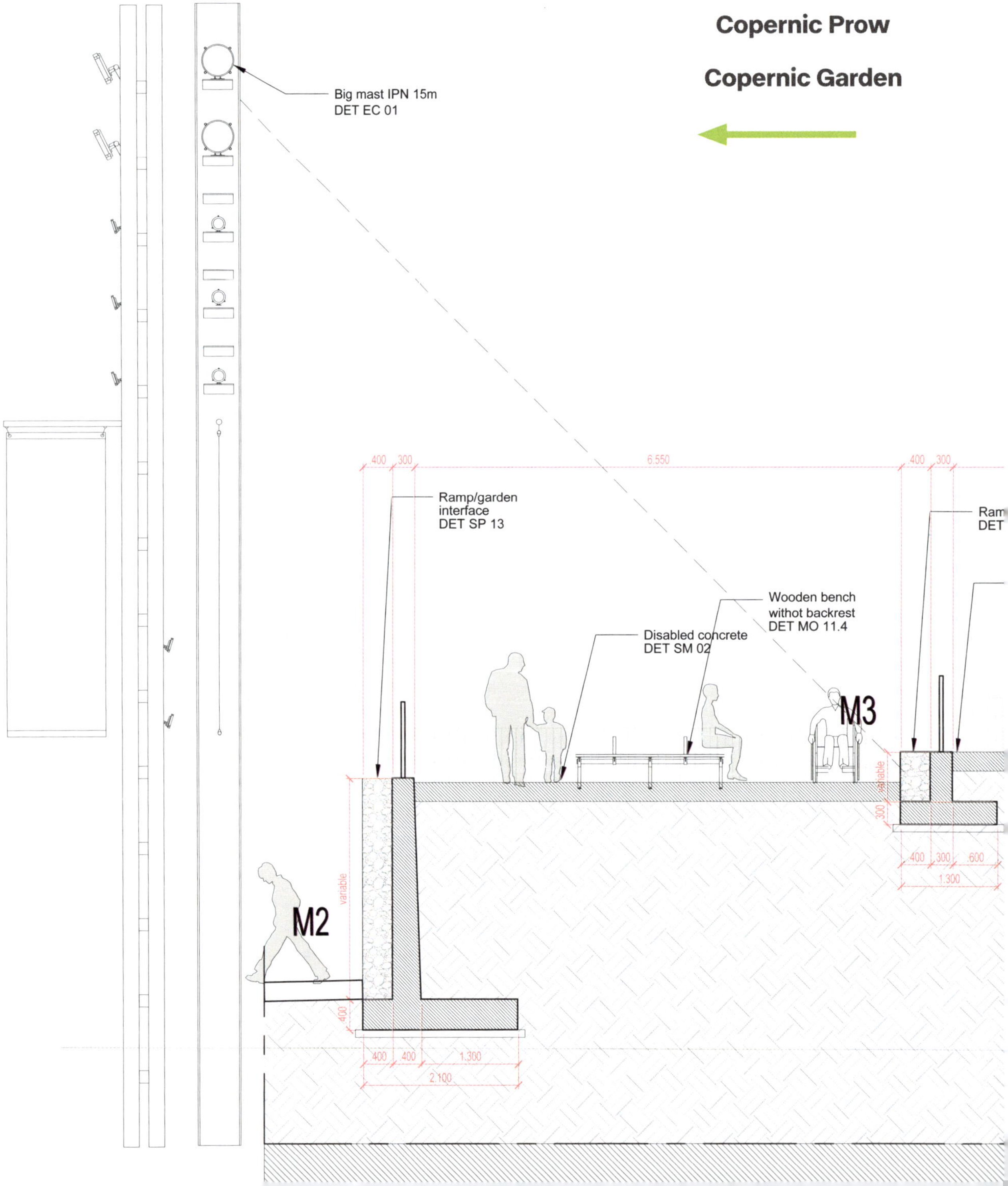

#605# **AMBITION 11**

URBAN FURNITURE AND LIGHTING 2050.

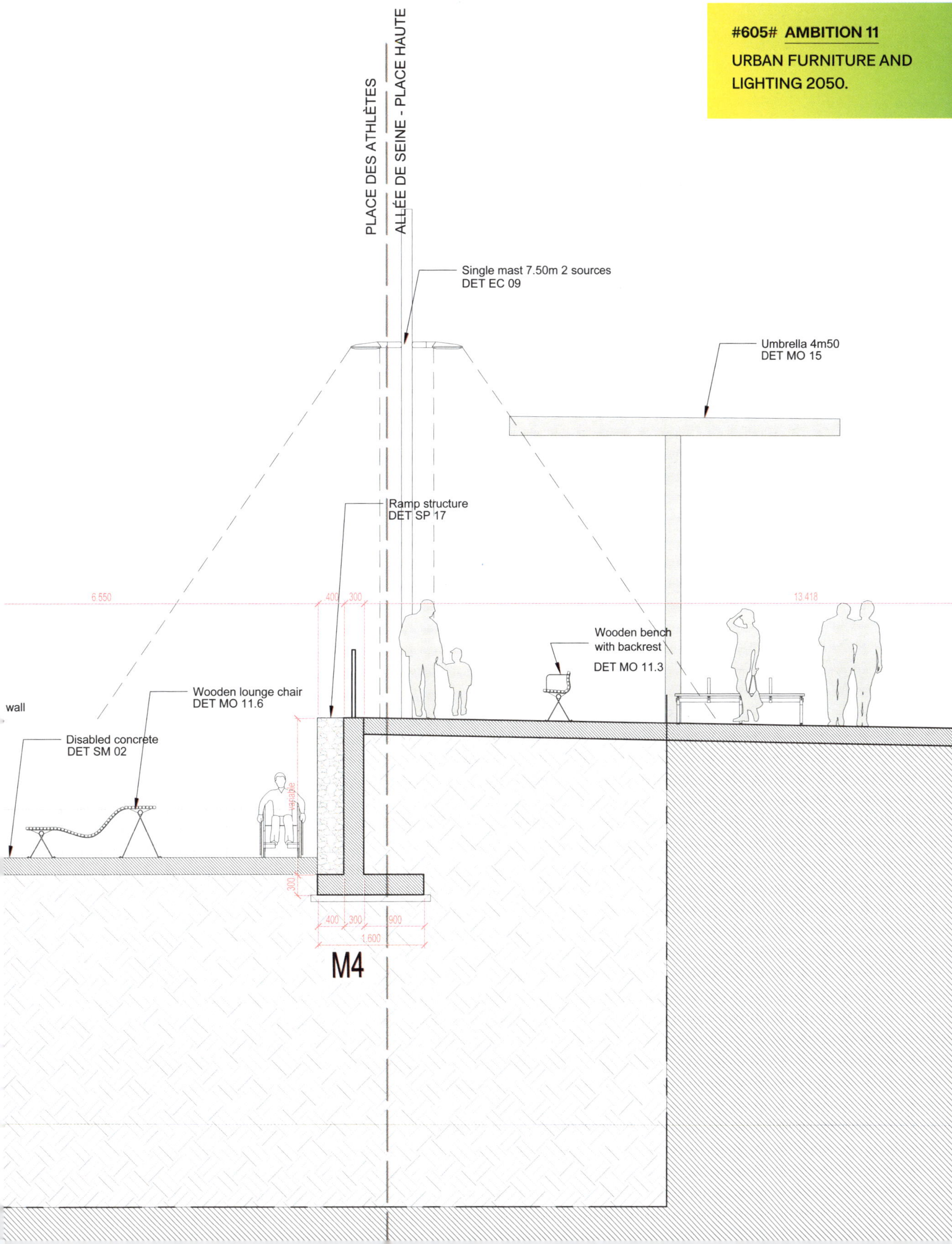

Elevation section of the Place Haute Panoramique

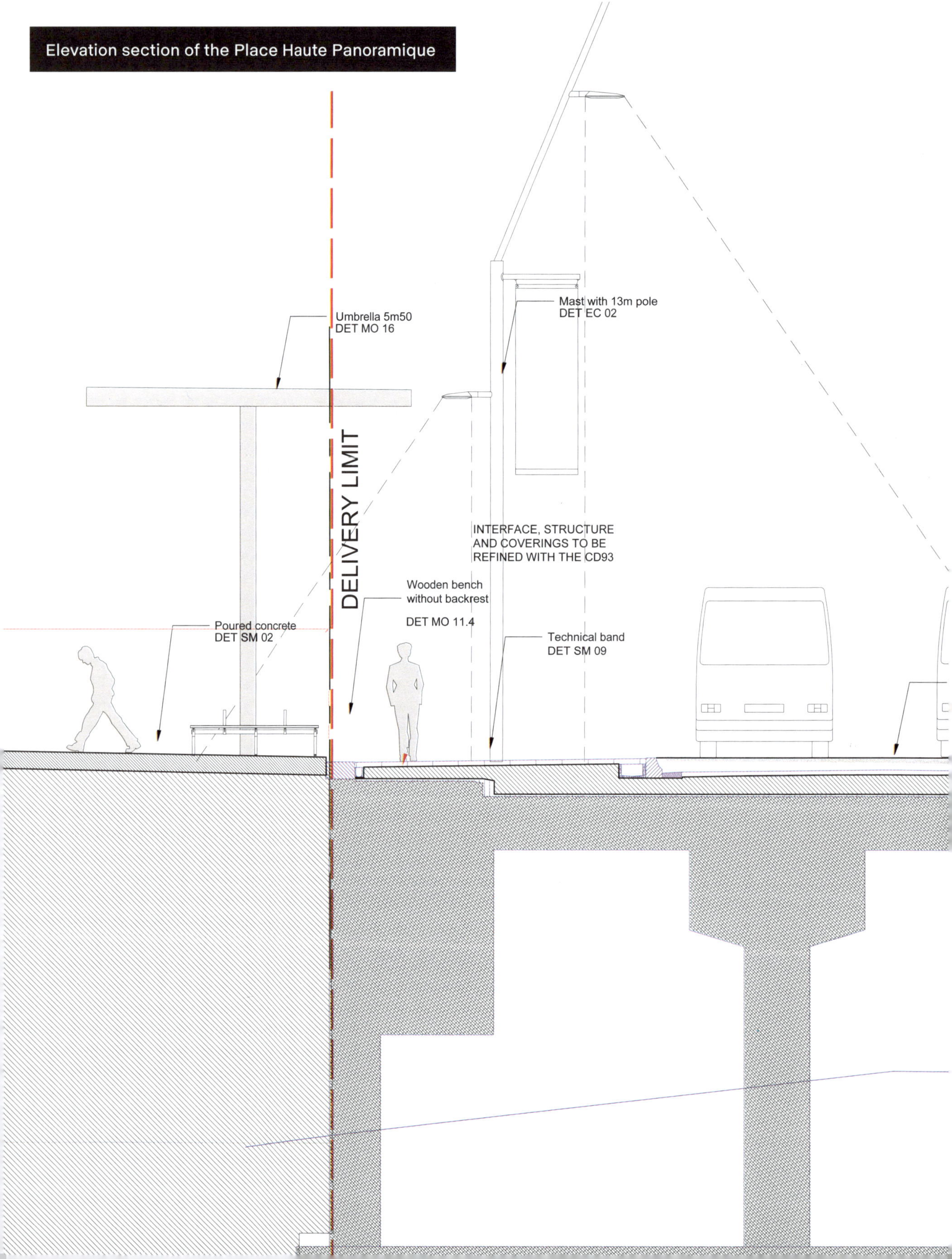

#607# AMBITION 11

URBAN FURNITURE AND LIGHTING 2050.

Place Panoramique

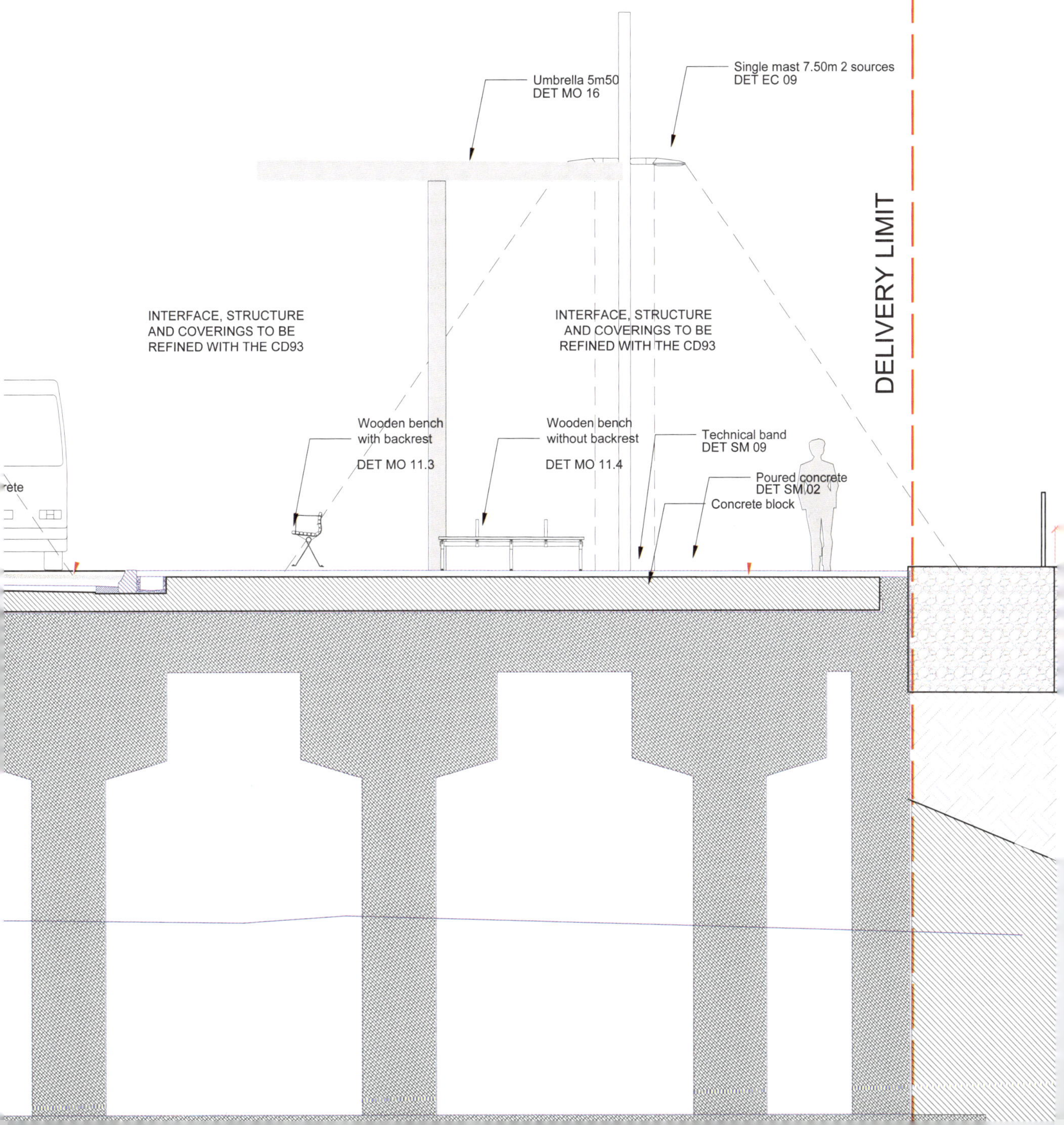

Elevation section of the Place Haute Panoramique

Playful prow

Playful garden

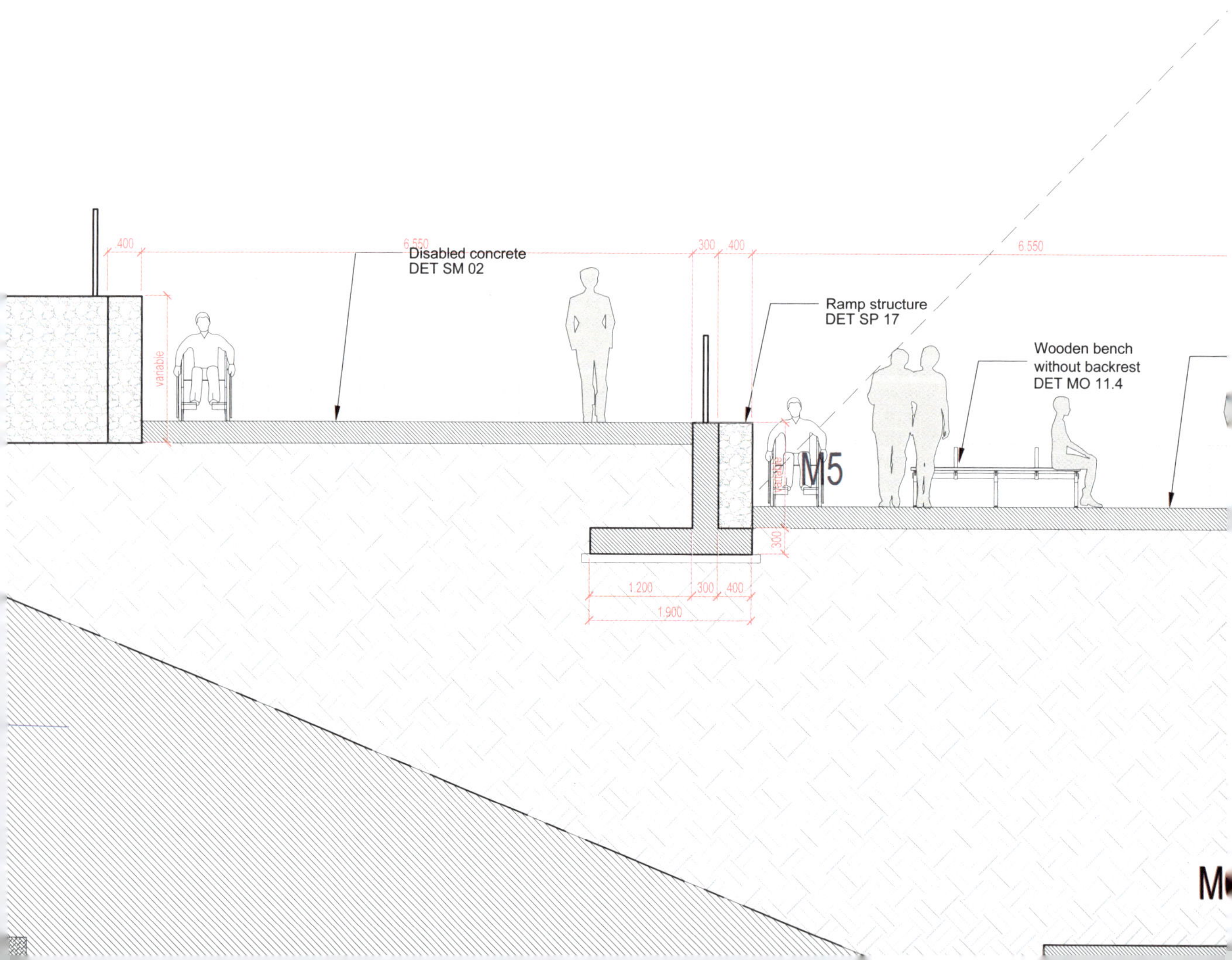

#609# AMBITION 11

URBAN FURNITURE AND LIGHTING 2050.

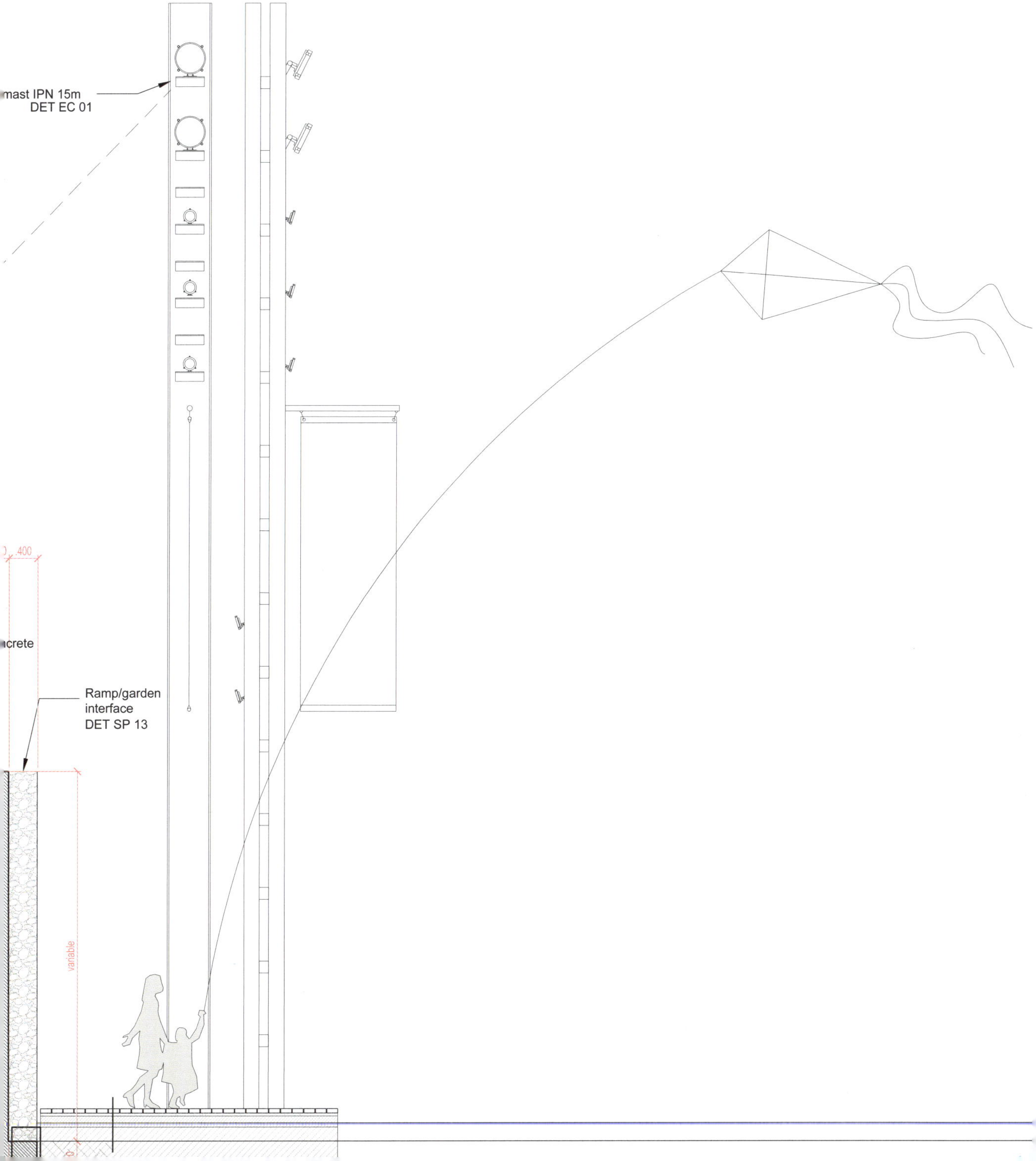

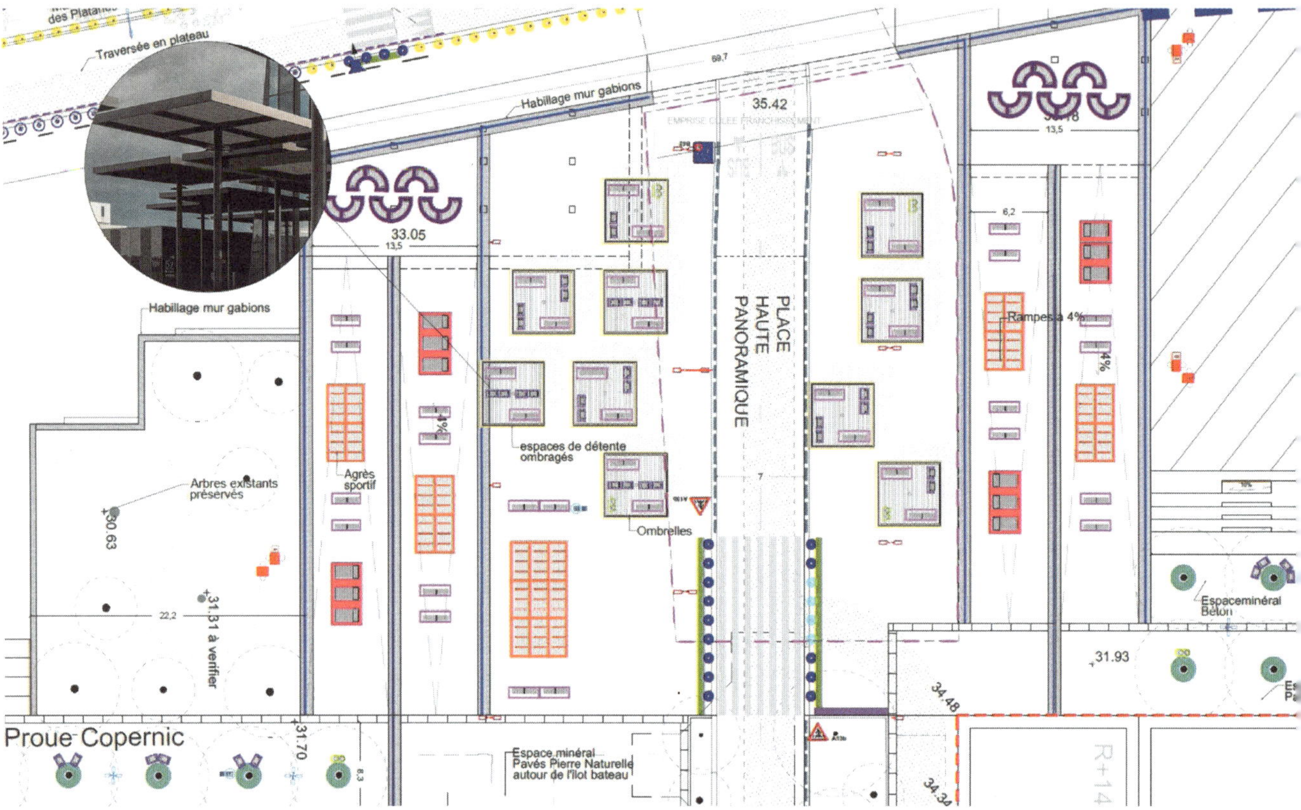
Traversée en plateau
Habillage mur gabions
35.42
33.05
PLACE HAUTE PANORAMIQUE
Habillage mur gabions
Rampes à 4%
espaces de détente ombragés
Agrès sportif
Arbres existants préservés
30.63
Ombrelles
31.31 à vérifier
Espaceminéral Béton
31.93
34.48
Proue Copernic
31.70
Espace minéral Pavés Pierre Naturelle autour de l'îlot bateau
R+14

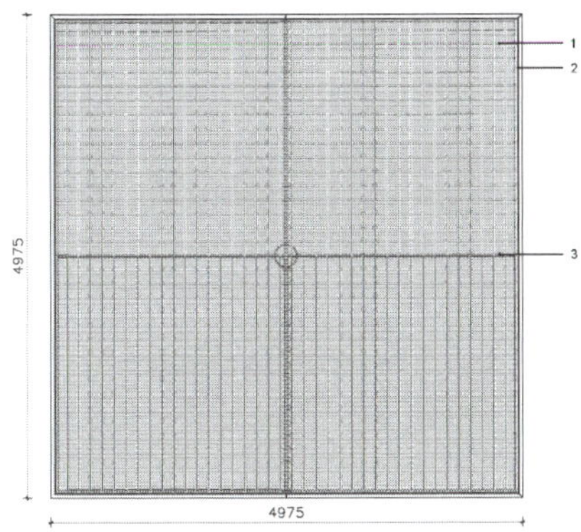

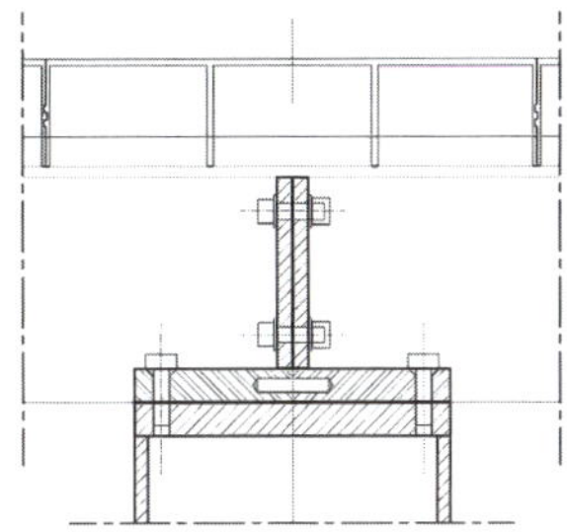

Detail: Cross-section of the junction between mast and umbrella frames

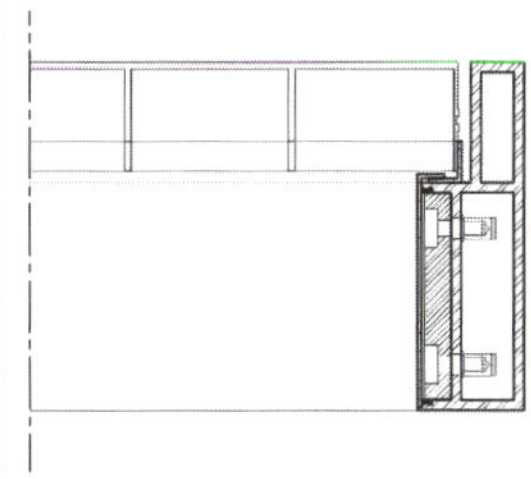

Detail: Section of edge profile

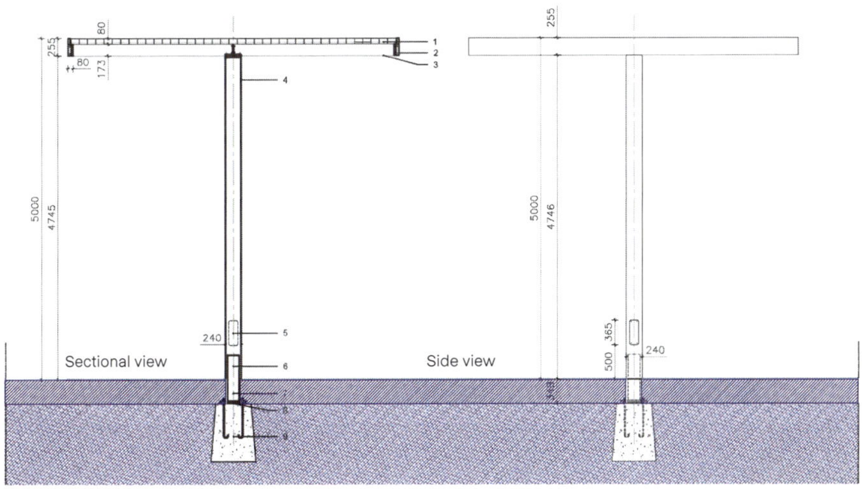

Off lot

Lot concerned

Cross-section of the roof profiles

Close-up of the perforation in the roof

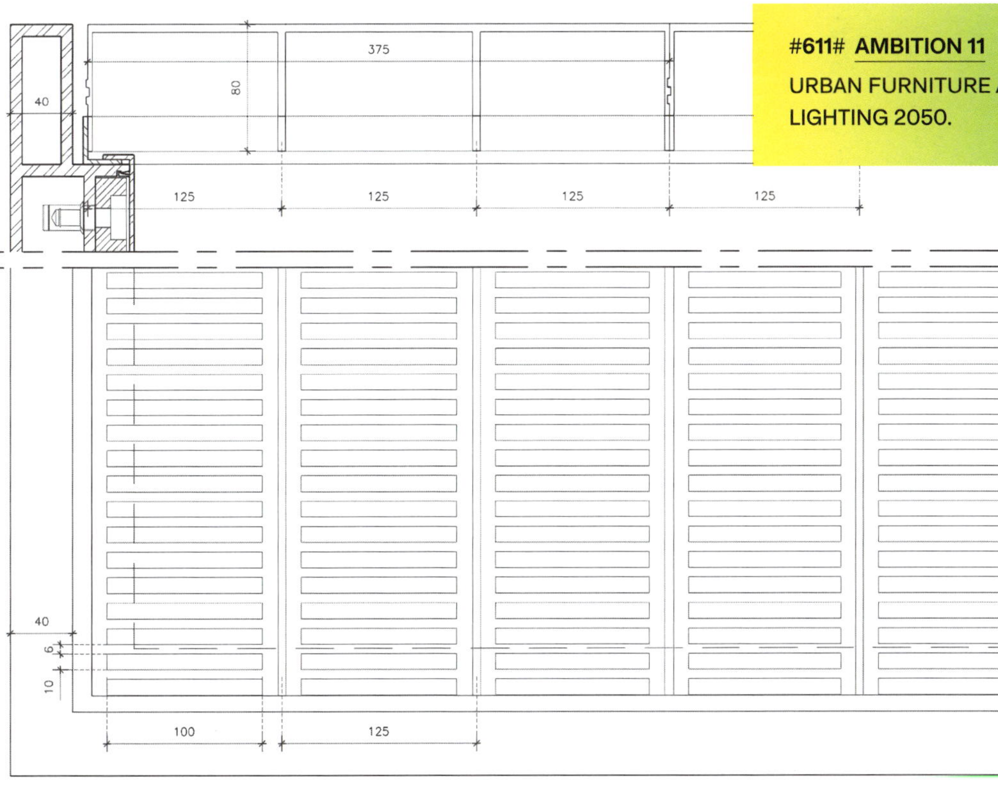

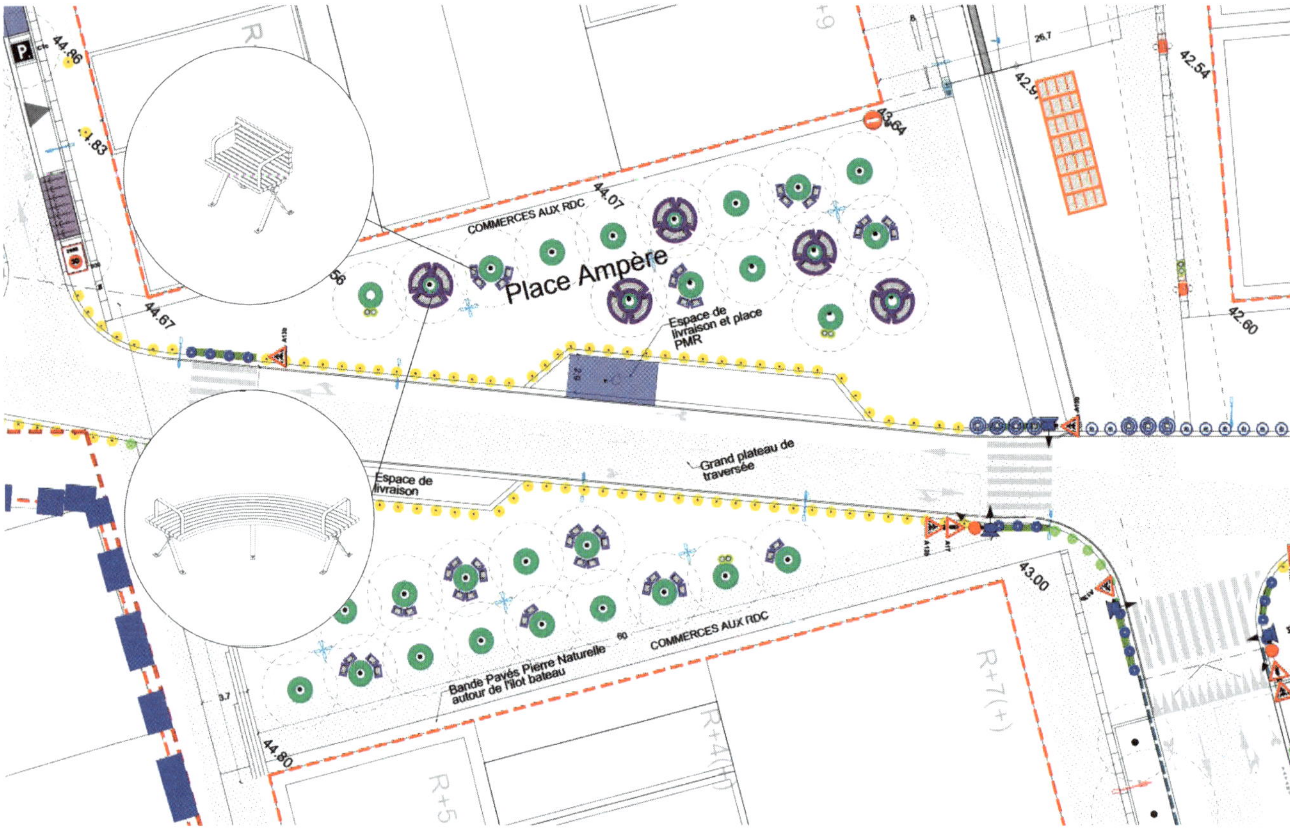

Place Ampère
COMMERCES AUX RDC
Espace de livraison et place PMR
Grand plateau de traversée
Espace de livraison
Bande Pavés Pierre Naturelle autour de l'ilot bateau
COMMERCES AUX RDC

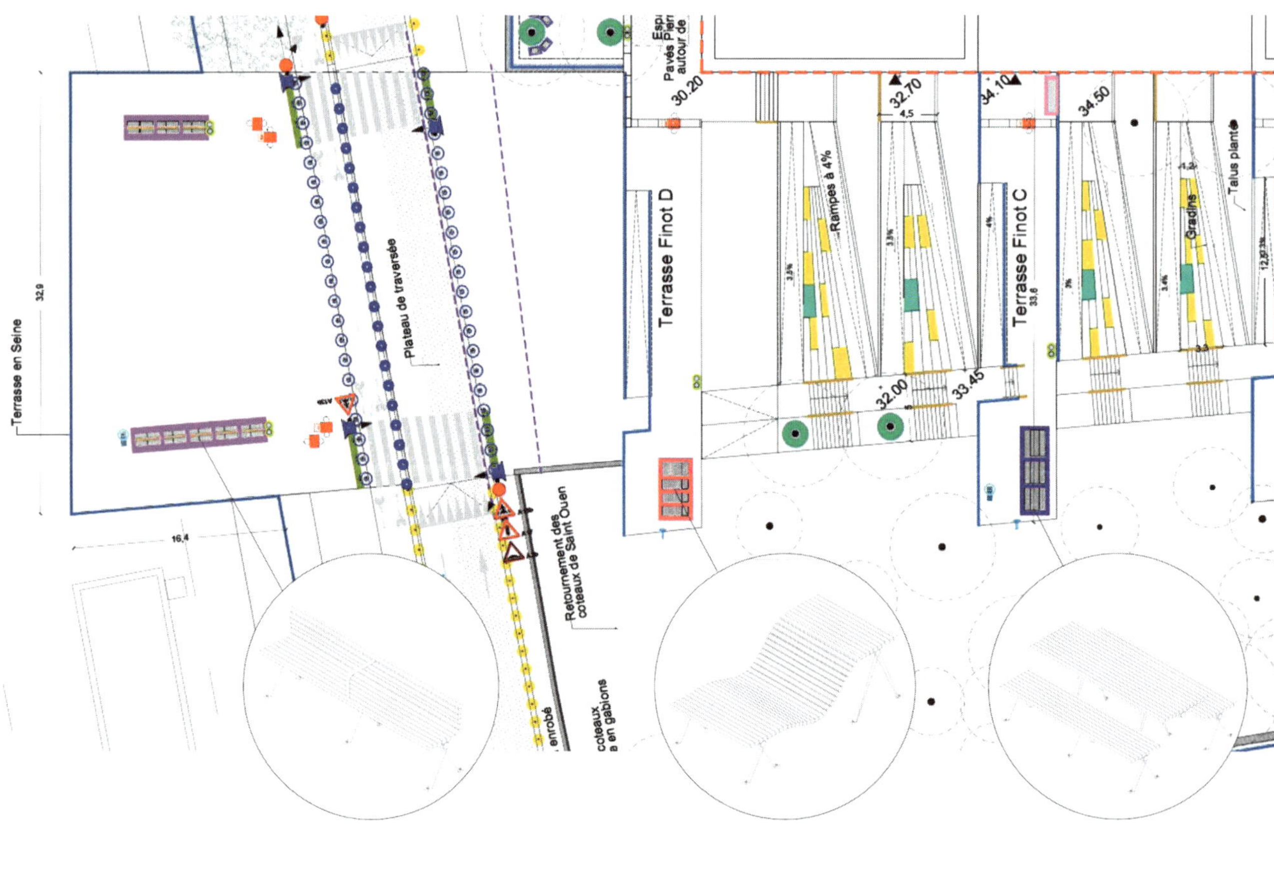

Terrasse en Seine
Plateau de traversée
Retournement des coteaux de Saint Ouen
Terrasse Finot D
Rampes à 4%
Terrasse Finot C
Gradins
Talus planté

#613# AMBITION 11

URBAN FURNITURE AND LIGHTING 2050.

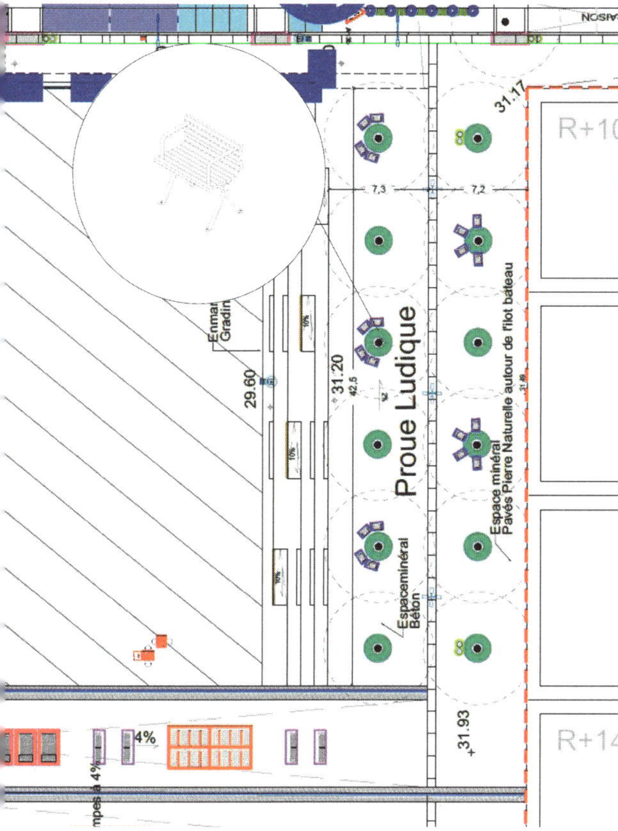

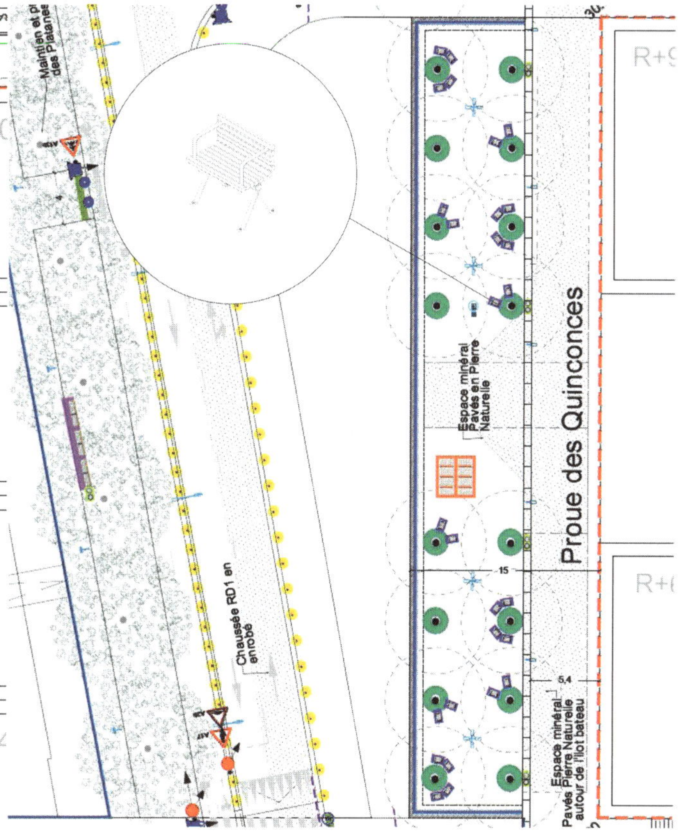

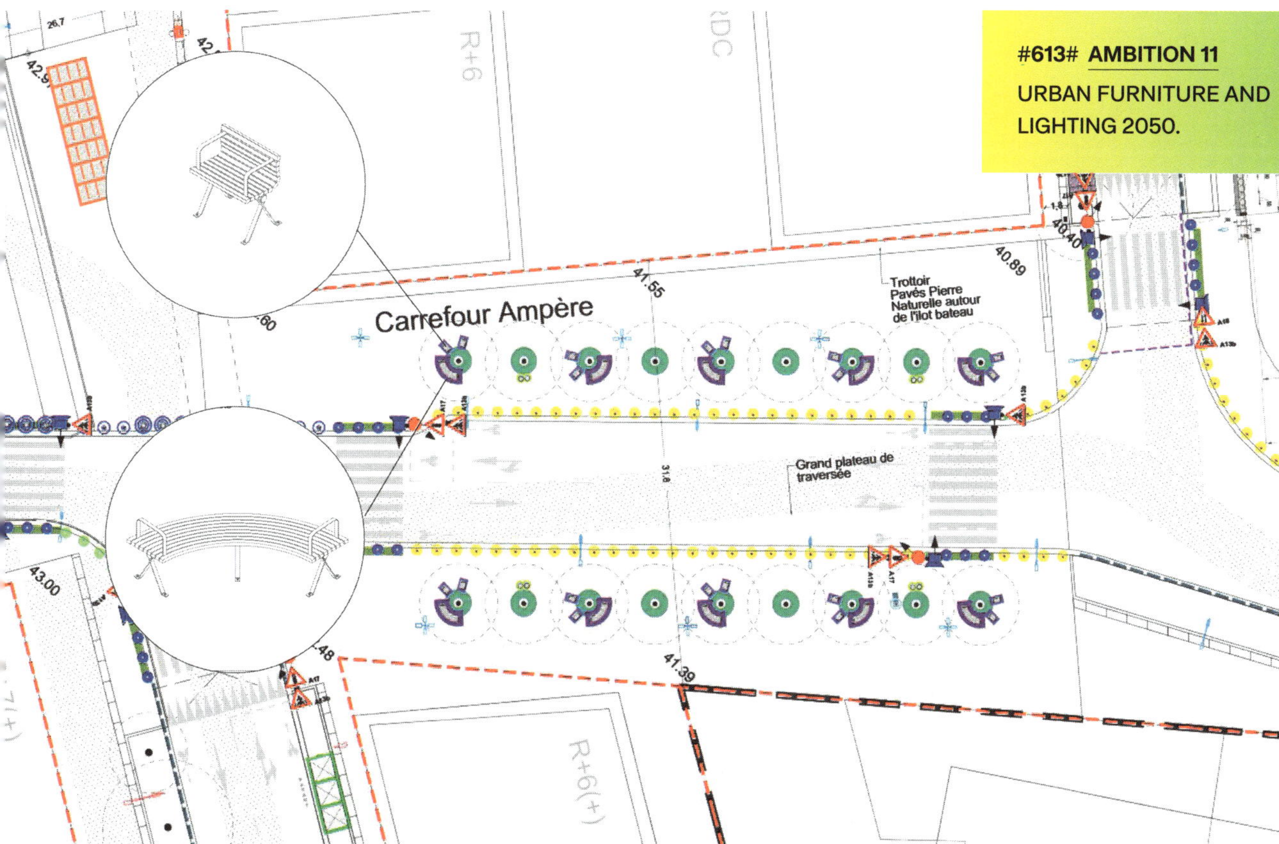

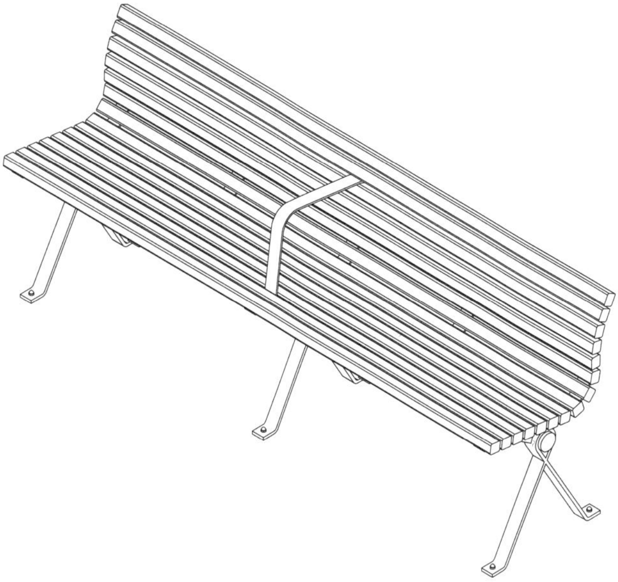

DET MO 11.2
WOODEN BENCH WITH BACKREST AND ARMREST

DET MO 11.3
WOODEN ARMCHAIR WITH ARMREST

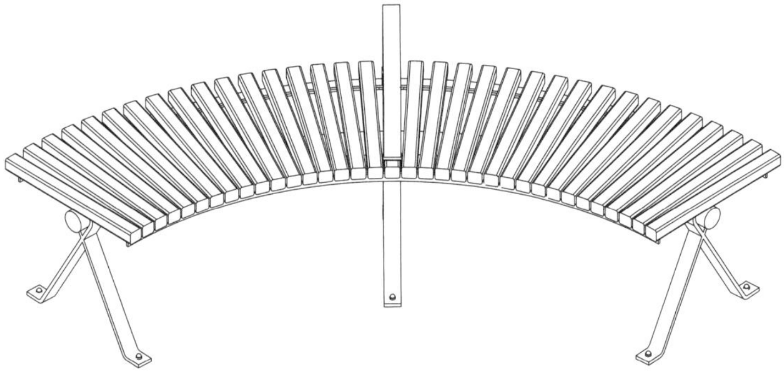

DET MO 11.5
CIRCULAR WOODEN BENCH WITHOUT BACKREST WITH ARMREST

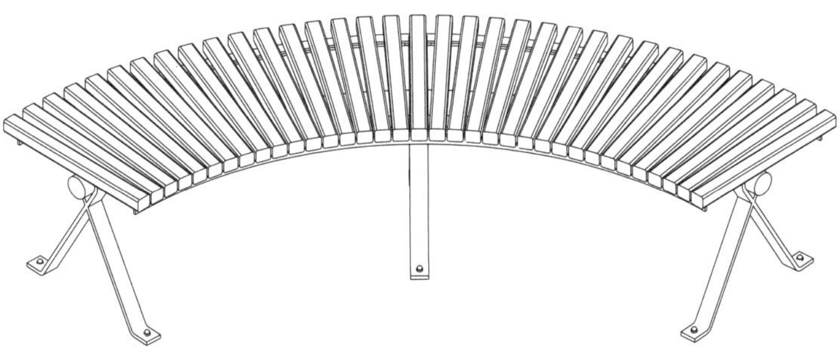

DET MO 11.5bis
CIRCULAR WOODEN BENCH WITHOUT BACKREST OR ARMRESTS

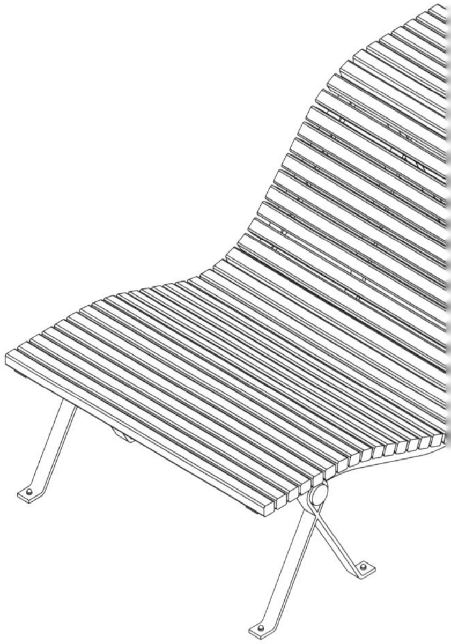

DET MO 11.6
WOODEN CHAISE LONGUE

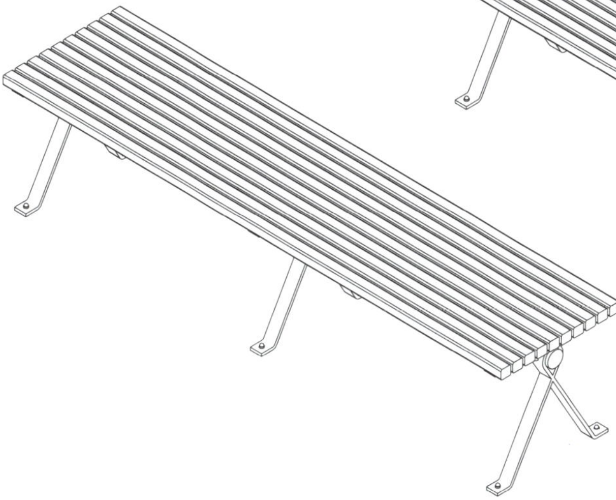

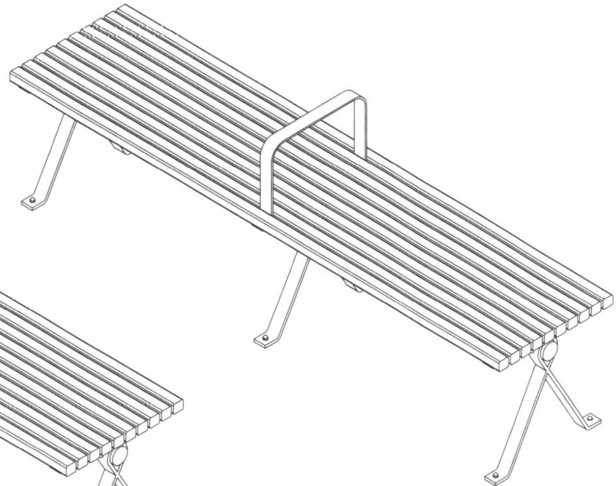

DET MO 11.4
BACKLESS WOODEN BENCH WITH ARMREST

DET MO 11.4 bis
BACKLESS WOODEN BENCH WITH ARMREST

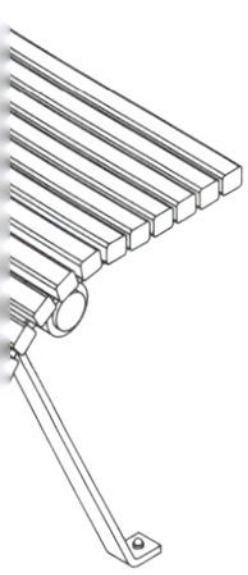

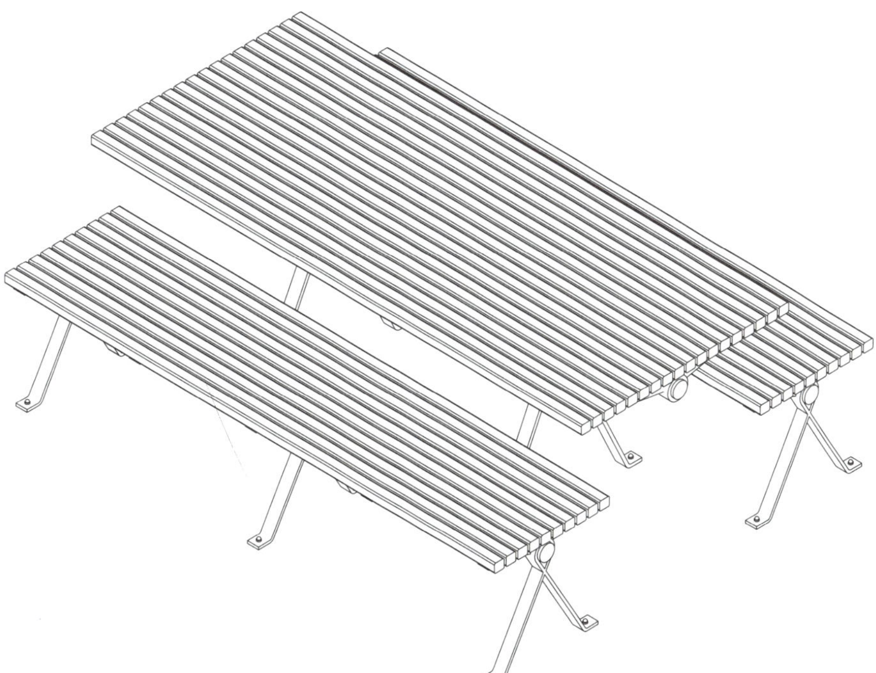

DET MO 11.7
WOODEN TABLE AND BENCHES

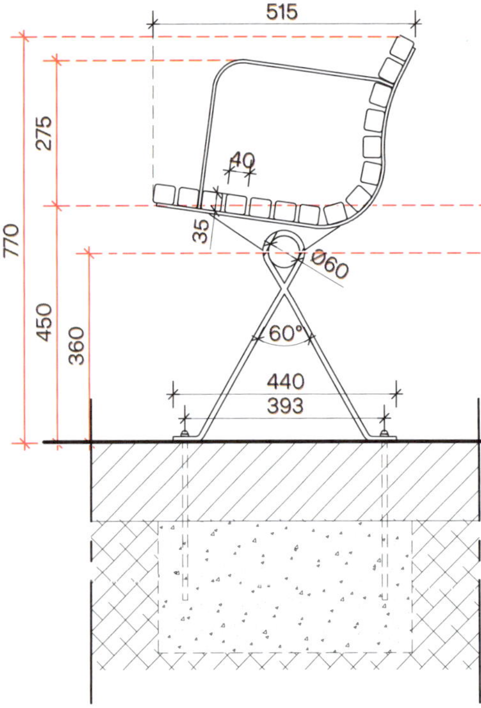

WOODEN BENCH WITH BACKREST
AND BACKREST SHELF

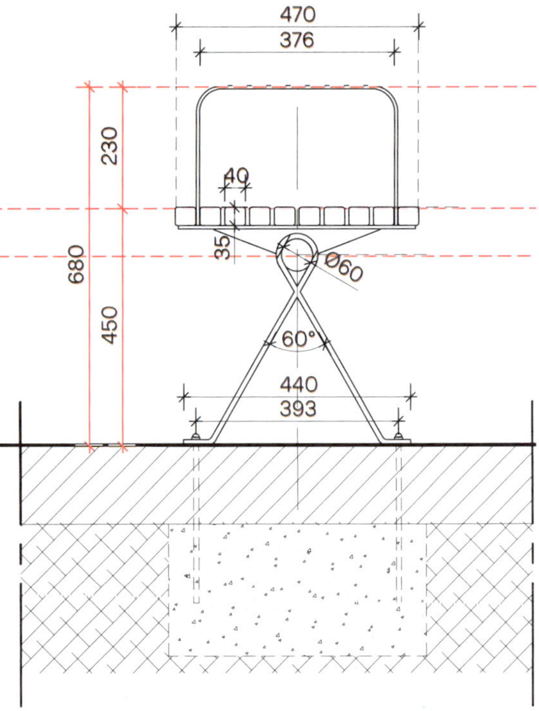

WOODEN BENCH WITH OUTOUT BACKREST
AND BACKREST SHELF

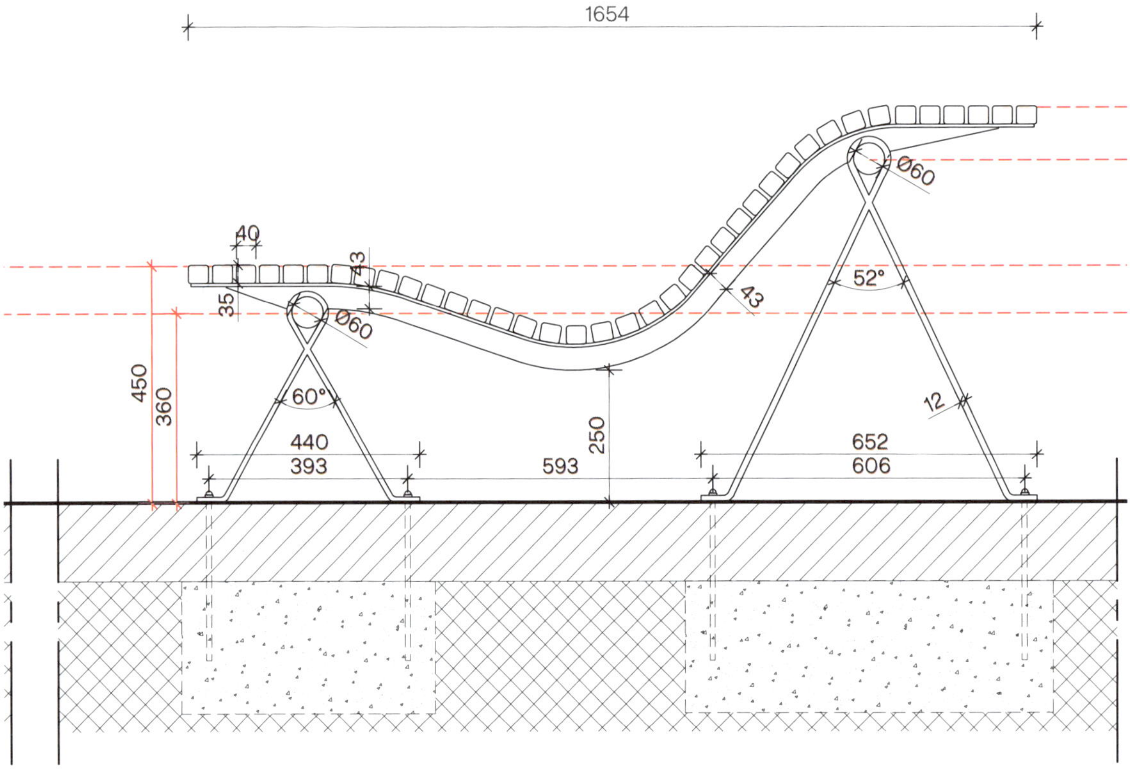

WOODEN CHAISE LONGUE

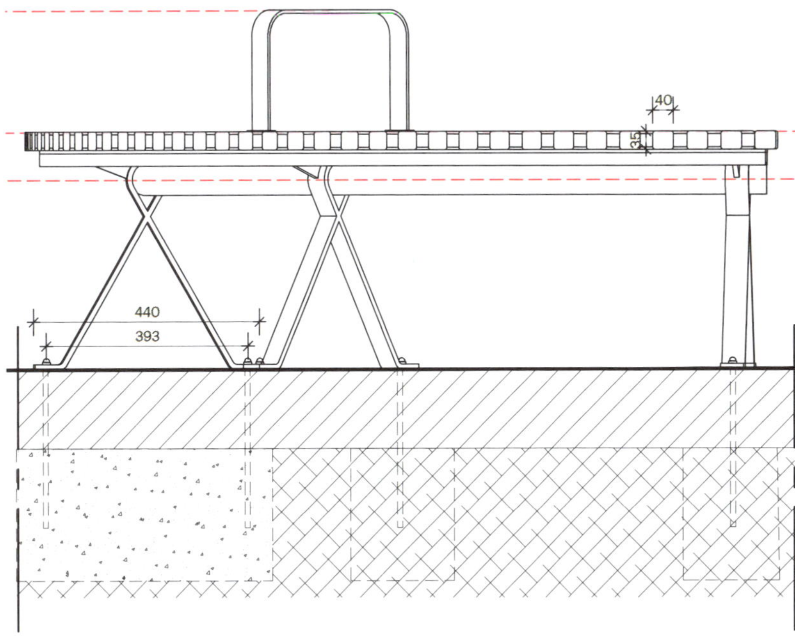

CIRCULAR WOODEN BENCH WITHOUT BACKREST WITH ARMREST

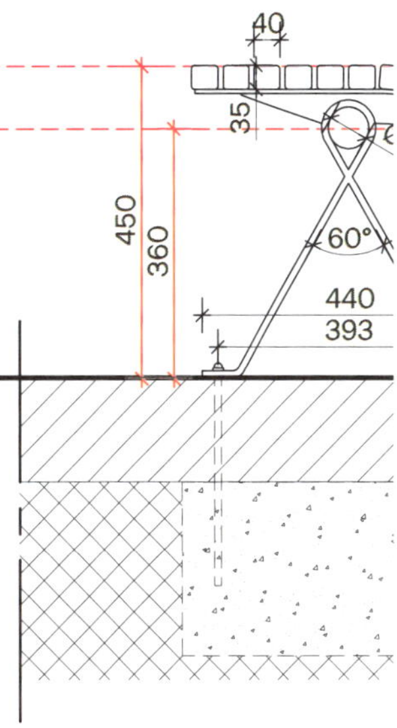

WOODEN CHAISE LONGUE

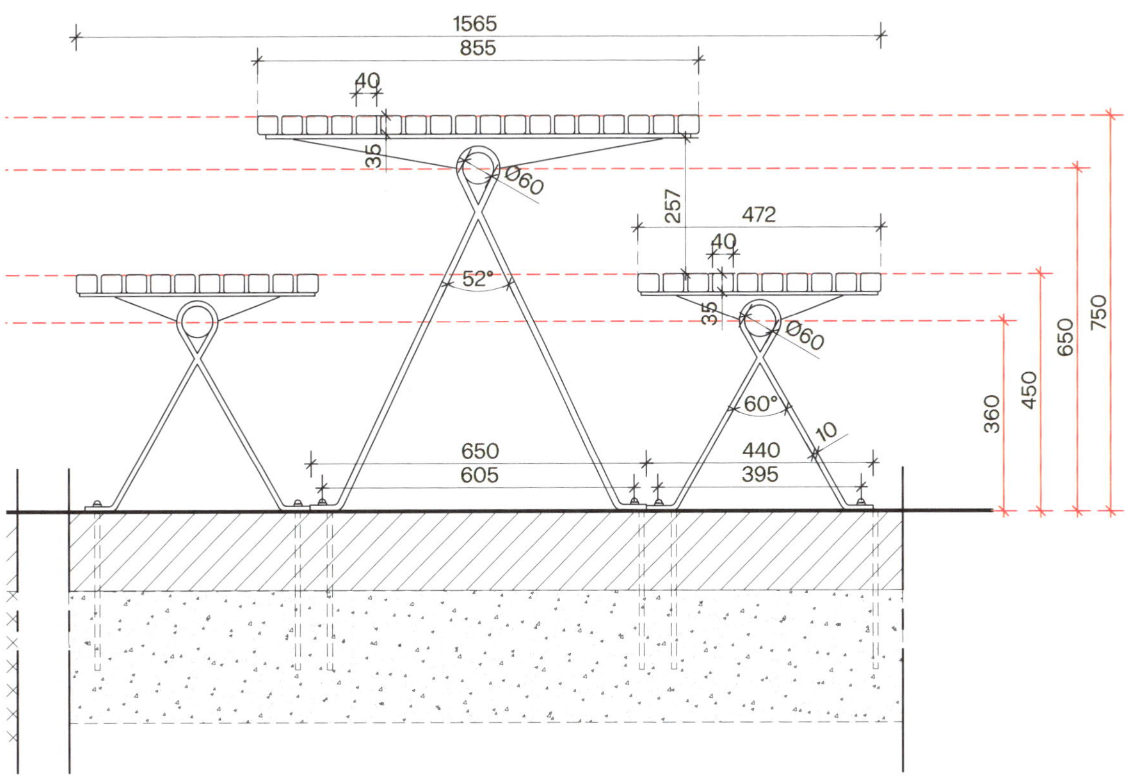

WOODEN TABLE AND BENCH

Bench elevation

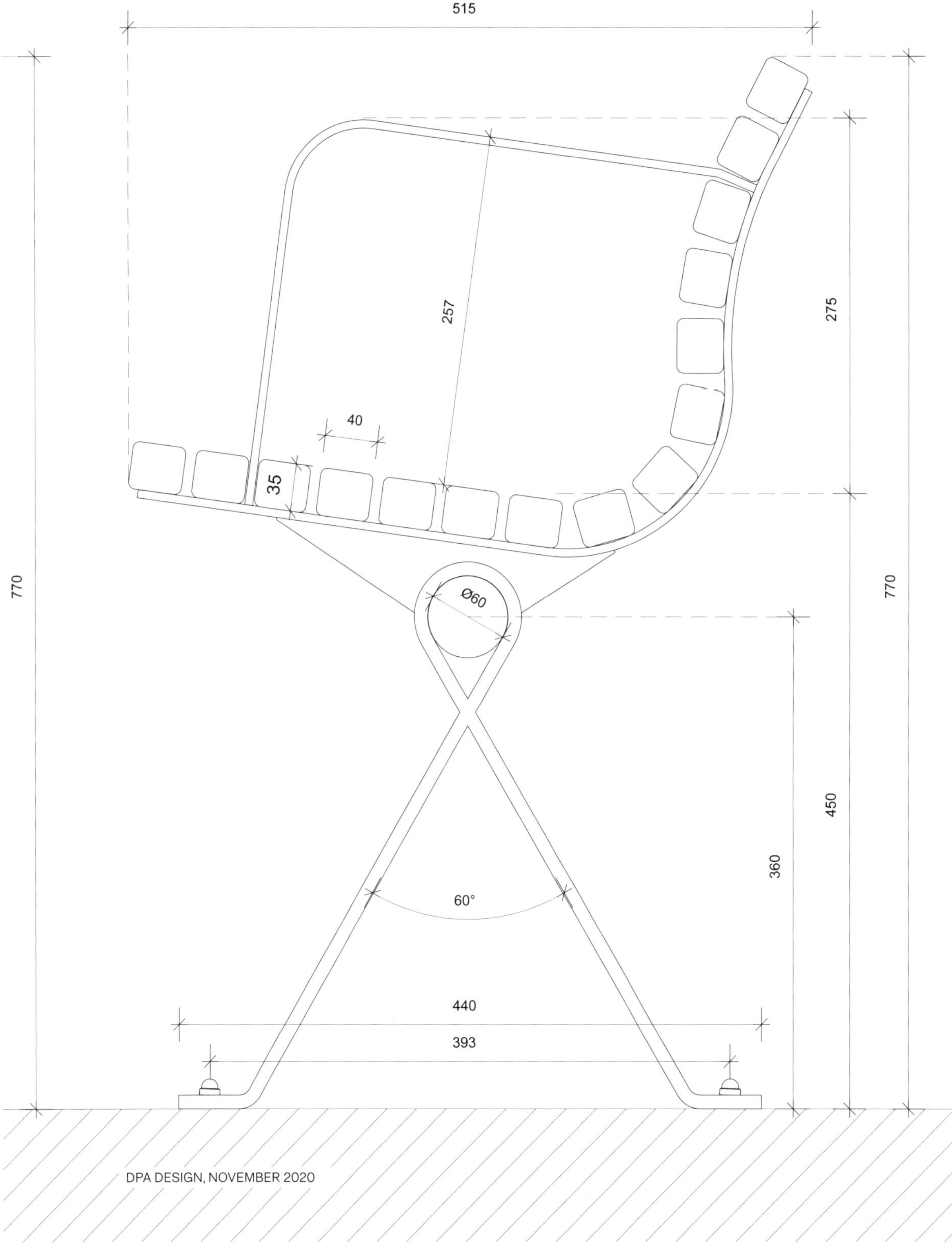

DPA DESIGN, NOVEMBER 2020

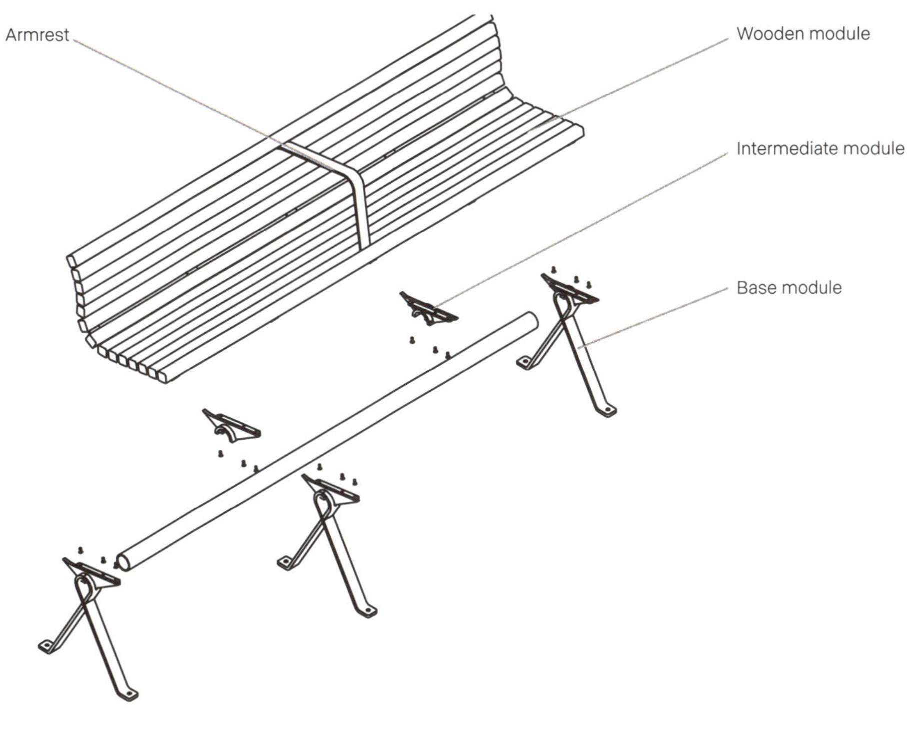
Armrest
Wooden module
Intermediate module
Base module

HALLE MAXWELL
CITE DU CINEMA

#621#

AMBITION 12

CHORAL ARCHITECTURE

Sisyphus and Planning.

For collaborative and collective intelligence, and unshackled urbanism.

There is a whole world between *Urban design* – the generation of a metropolitan district – and *Urban planning* – the programmatic and planned vision of a territory. In this sense, as a model, the Village is symptomatic of the deficiencies plaguing public development, whose lessons extend to the Grand Paris project and to the culture of the state as such. The sprit animating planning in France has indeed become shrunken and impoverished, sliding backwards from its illustrious past.

Are the state and its institutional relays equal to the heritage to which they are committed and whose lip service rhythms every speech? More than skepticism, what prevails is an acknowledgement of non fulfilment – at best – or of systemic encumbrance – at worst. Though we must allow ourselves to become despondent about the future.

Public development policy is a poor rival to the performance achieved by the Olympic Village in terms foresight and vision (of its metropolitan future). Whereas reversibility is the crux of the project, public authorities are disengaging while wishing all the best to the Village. Agility is also unequally distributed. The project management and the teams of architects have succeeded a tour de force by integrating a new, souple, and spacious urban entity, straddling a dense intermunicipal fabric, but the state has great difficulty measuring the territory it intends to develop. Victim of its contradictions, oxymorons, deals, renouncements, inertias and impossibilities, it has failed itself. Something is out of whack.

Although having managed to remarkably fulfil its objectives, time is running out. SOLIDEO is slated to disappear in 2026, the moment that the mutation of the interior spaces of the Village will be are completed and the first inhabitants will begin taking possession of their apartments, shops and offices. Admittedly, its road map will have been respected, with undeniably efficient accounting, but will its mission have been truly and completely fulfilled? The future of the Village, we must reiterate, lies beyond it.

The dimensions of a metropolis, of twelve million inhabitants, including Paris, encumber the efficiency of a single planning process. But a series of unified entities, conceived on the scale of each "center" of the metropolis, each adapted to a geographic area, its population, its socioeconomic profile, its cultural facilities and its specific development challenges, would allow for fine-tuned work, sustained over time. SOLIDEO could conceivably prolong its action by a few years to be able intervene at a crucial step in the growth of the metropolis, here in the launch of a future district. Yet, it must be dissolved and abandon the ramp. Que sera sera. Here, the state is failing to meet its obligations.

I proposed, in vain, that urbanist working groups of substitution be set up for this purpose. However, I had the example of this one, which I had taken the initiative to create upstream of the Village constructions site, between 2018 and 2020. It included the different architecture teams involved – distributed in turn among thematic and technical sub working groups, tasked with assembling and coordinating the programs. It demonstrated the virtue of collaborative intelligence, at the service of a comprehensive vision. Regular exchanges took place with the developers, construction companies, SOLIDEO, the services of Plaine-Commune, the elected officials of Saint-Denis, Saint-Ouen and the Ile-Saint-Denis, the department, the COJO and the numerous public and private stakeholders that gravitated around the shared project of building an Olympic Village and its metropolitan implementations. This urbanism and architecture working group entered the domain of heritage through the methodology of action it proposed. Alas, the inertia of the public authorities and their self-blocking impediments made impossible such a structure for dialogue, capable of supporting work on planning – whose existence we are still seeking, like Diogenes, searching with his lantern.

The Atelier International du Grand Paris, created in 2010, whose second scientific council I joined, was also an admirable undertaking for challenging projects, for thinking, for collaborations and communication, in the logic of transversality of knowledge and disciplines. A unique space of experimentation, which, here again, fizzled out. The teams offered to apply their proposals on "test territories" to evaluate and discuss their effectiveness. All for naught. The only acknowledgement of the work these teams accomplished was a minimalist exhibition on the last floor of the Palais de Tokyo and a special issue of Urbanisme magazine, for a specialized readership. An intellectual waste of time and effort. The state and the municipalities were proudly disinterested in the AIGP, even forgetting it existed (and its financing even more so). Despite its expertise, it was regarded with distain and no request for an urban strategy with a view to the Olympic Games was forthcoming. End of chapter.

We lack a zone for meeting and sharing between clients and designers, of which the "Fabrique de la Ville" (Factory of the City), created by Jean-Louis Subileau and Guillaume Hebert, is a remarkable example. This team advocates a method for action blending policy and urbanism, culture and economy to move the city forward and to harmonize the aspirations of society and its citizens. In 2018, my firm mandated them to conduct an urban and programmatic study for the conception of the Village and its continued success after the Games. The work was carried out in an extended partnership framework, marshalling elected officials, associated operators and candidates with project proposals. This was integrated into the commission because the Plaine Commune was worried about the arrival on its territory of such an unusual village and district of this scale,

The director of the 2021 Seoul Third Biennale of architecture and urbanism, I placed the event at a "Crossroads," the one of our collective histories and knowledge. Designed to present the knowhow of 200 international teams in the field of architecture and urbanism to visitors and to cities. Organized by theme and sector of action, it was another example of collaborative intelligence exceeding itself through collective intelligence.

Everything depends on the way a project is brought forward. However, in the case of the Olympic Village and in matters of planning, the state is a self-hindering actor, failing in flexibility and in depth of view. One might even wish for it to be reversible, like the Village. May it regain control of itself.

The concept of self-mutation implemented on the Olympic site is fruitful and economical. The period lends itself to this, yet the public developer does not intelligently assume its strategic interest.

The institutional and partnership environment of the Athletes' Village reveals a lack of ability to carry out long-term projects and of a programmatic understanding of the territory. Tunnel or silo vision, call it what you like, ends up with poorly integrated projects, sometimes juxtaposed or entrusted to a misguided logic of "Live and Become." In addition to the services of the state, paradoxically, elected officials seem to refuse planning, each one positioned at a distance, sometimes even resisting the idea. The reasons for this are complex. But the metropolis suffers from unravelling public action. We do not have to look as far as the Grand Paris Express to encounter this lack of vision. The creation of new subway lines is, strictly speaking, more of an infrastructure program than one of urban planning. The districts springing up around stations are a revealing example. Simply defining their perimeter at a radius of 800 meters cannot conceivably be called a development strategy. Here again, planning is the invisible man at the table.

We lack a genuine plan for surveying and analyzing the north side of the capital, precisely where the Athletes' Village stands, and more broadly on the "Plaine de France," whose scope encompasses the suburbs of the east side of Val-d'Oise. The Games cannot compensate for the shortcomings of territorial development nor accelerate what has simply been poorly thought out.

VILLAGE
OLYMPIQUE
PARALYMPIQUE
PARIS 2024
MISSION
ÎLE DE LA CITÉ
LE CŒUR DU
CŒUR

#625# **AMBITION 12**

CHORAL ARCHITECTURE

Agency exhibition and tours.

#627# AMBITION 12

CHORAL ARCHITECTURE

Agency exhibition and tours.

#629# **AMBITION 12**

CHORAL ARCHITECTURE

Village workshops.
Working meetings;

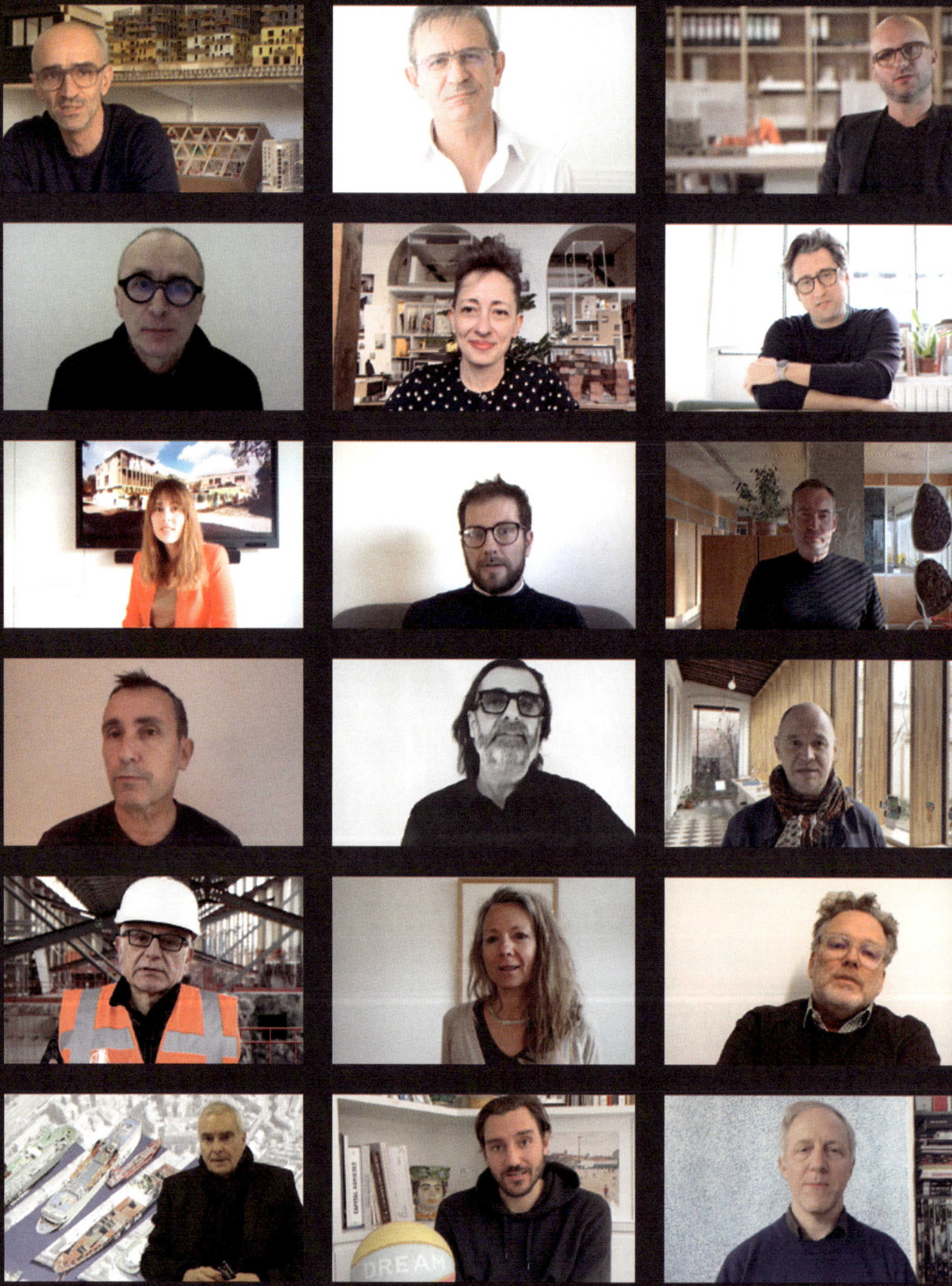
DREAM

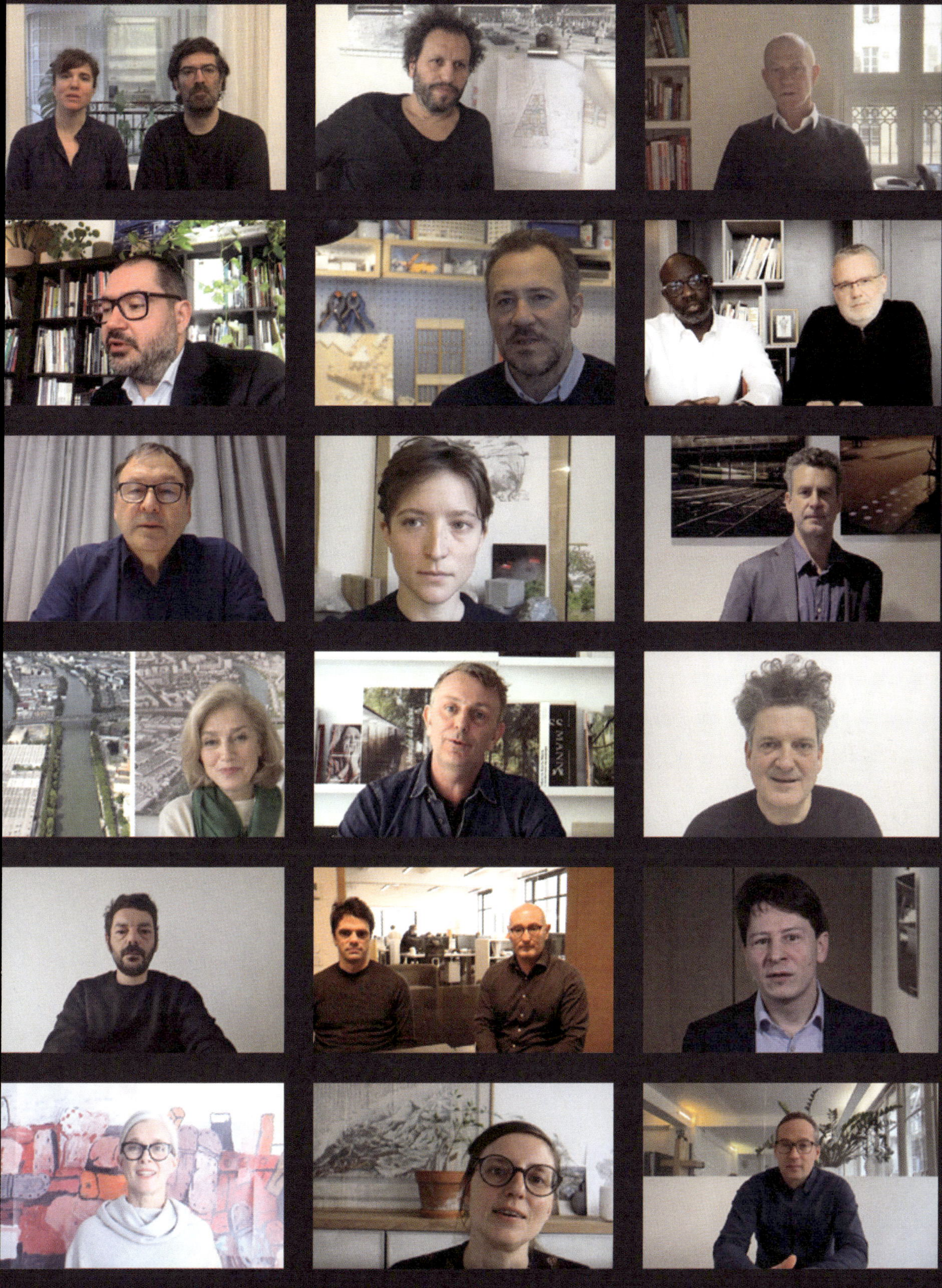

UAPS
BRENAC GONZALEZ
Lambert Lenack
Atelier Martel
KOZ
SUPMECA
ATELIER GEORGES
TN+
UAPS
UAPS
PASCAL GONTIER
SOA
KOZ
UAPS
BARRAULT PRESSACCO
ATELIER GEORGES
ATELIER GEORGES
NP2F
ATELIER GEORGES
BRENAC GONZALES
TN+
COBE
POST OFFICE
NP2F
DREAM
ECDM

#633# AMBITION 12

CHORAL ARCHITECTURE

The Village brings together more than 30 architects. How do you bring architects together on the scale of the ZAC?

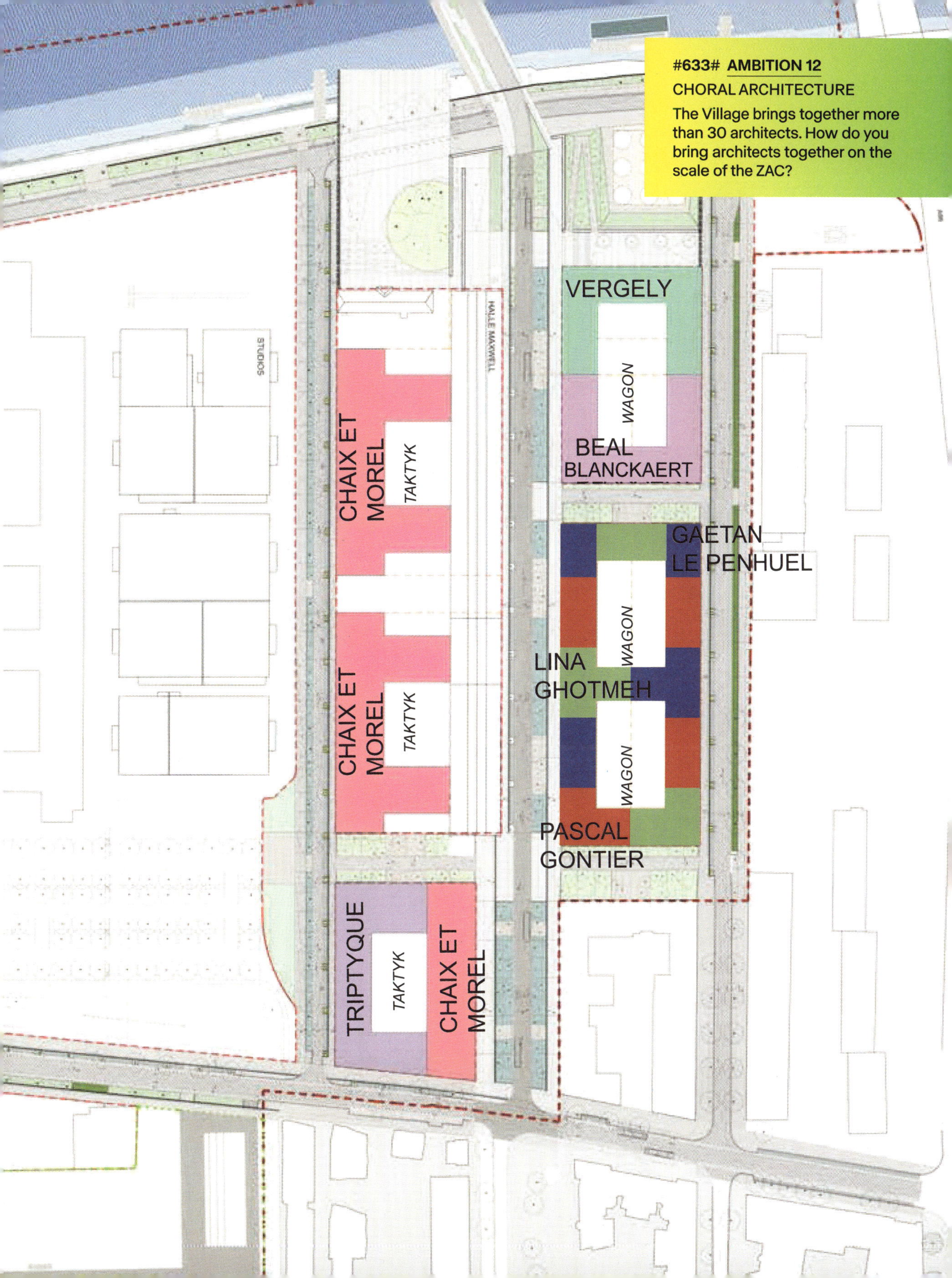

Block A
Cord: C. Vergely

Block B
Cord: Chaix&Morel

Block D
Cord: UAPS

Block E
Cord: COBE

Block E
Cord: KOZ + SUPMECA

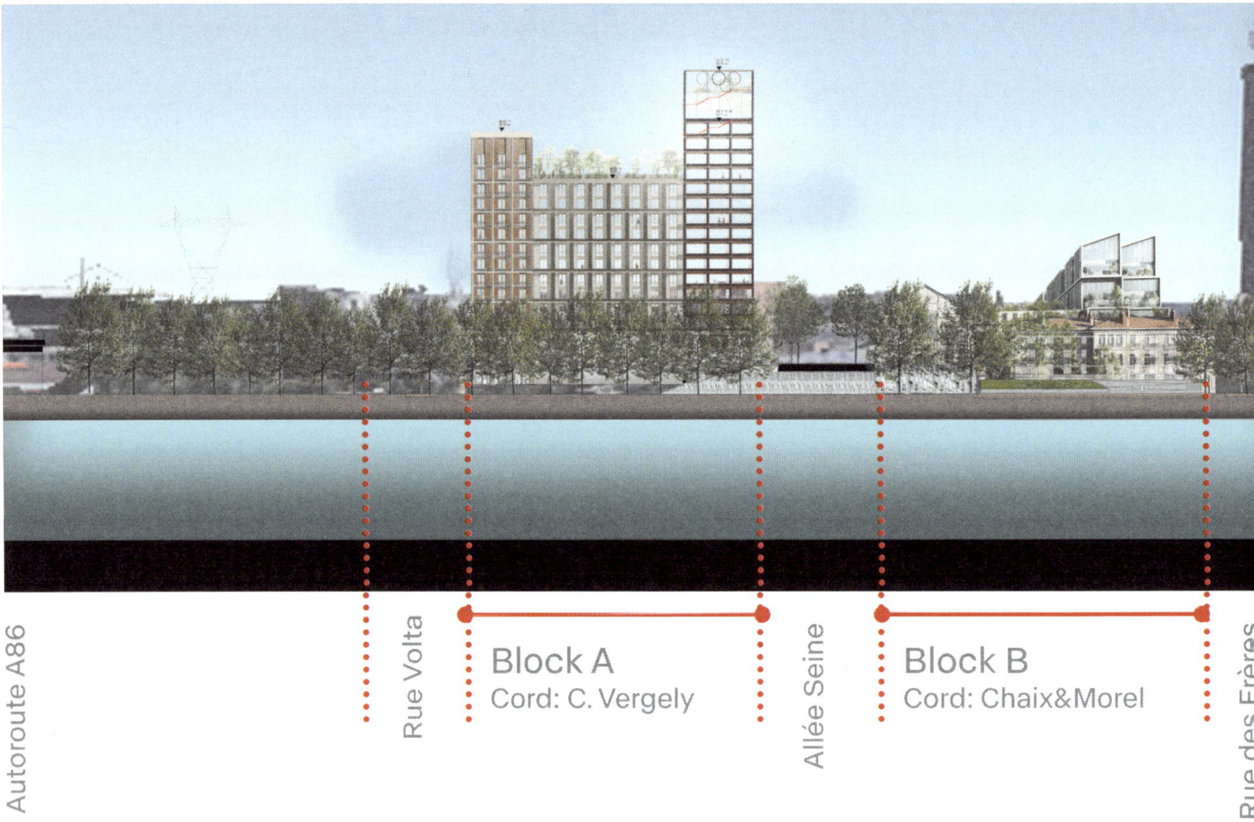
Autoroute A86
Rue Volta
Block A
Cord: C. Vergely
Allée Seine
Block B
Cord: Chaix&Morel

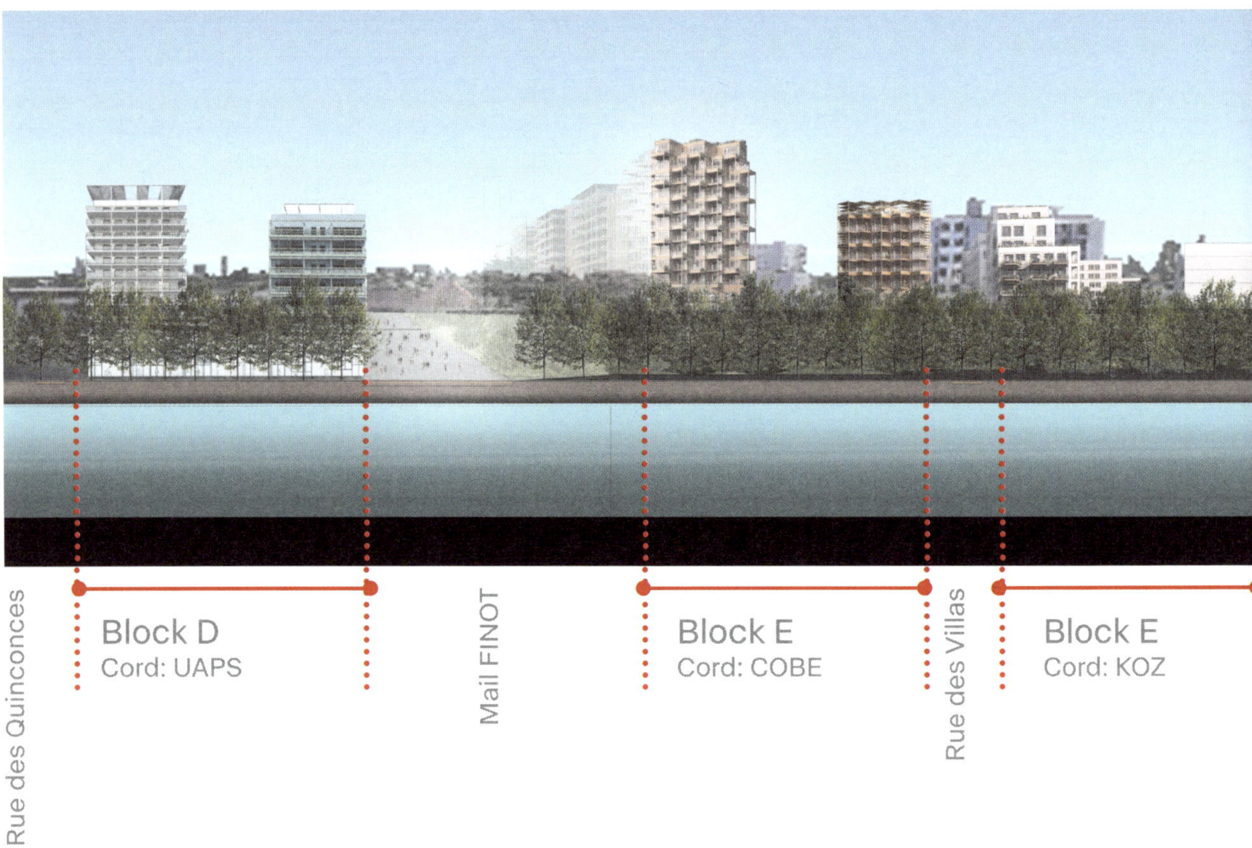
Rue des Quinconces
Block D
Cord: UAPS
Mail FINOT
Block E
Cord: COBE
Rue des Villas
Block E
Cord: KOZ

Cité du Cinéma

SUPMECA

Vieux Saint-Ouen

Église Saint-Ouen Le Vieux

#637# **AMBITION 12**

CHORAL ARCHITECTURE

Saint-Denis, Elevations Place Ampère.

South detail.

Sector A - COURS

Sector B - Maxwell Hall

Sector D - Quinconces

Sector E - Belvédère

Sector C - Cité du Cinéma

#639# AMBITION 12

CHORAL ARCHITECTURE

Village workshops
Prow combination.

Sector E - Villas

#641# AMBITION 12

CHORAL ARCHITECTURE

Urban cohesion
Aerial view of Saint-Ouen.

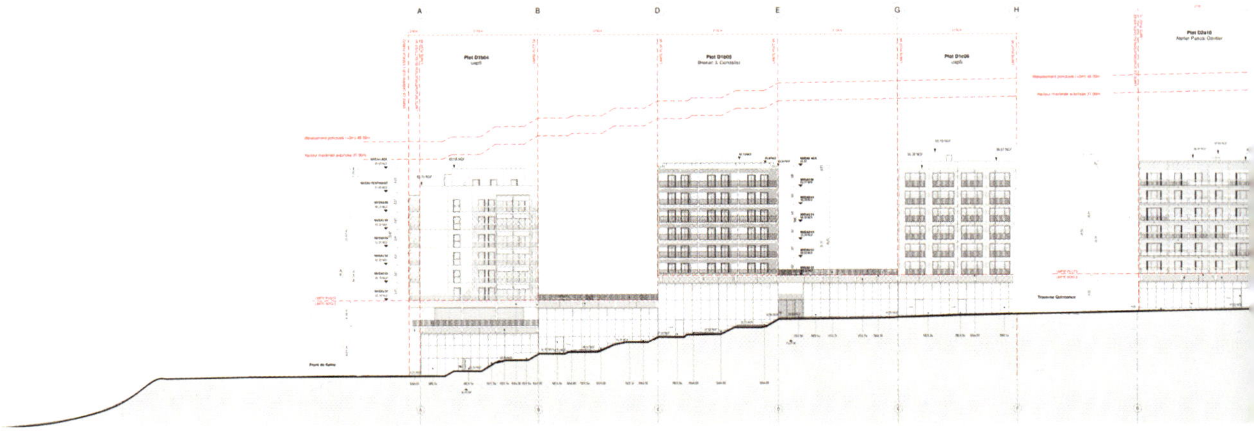

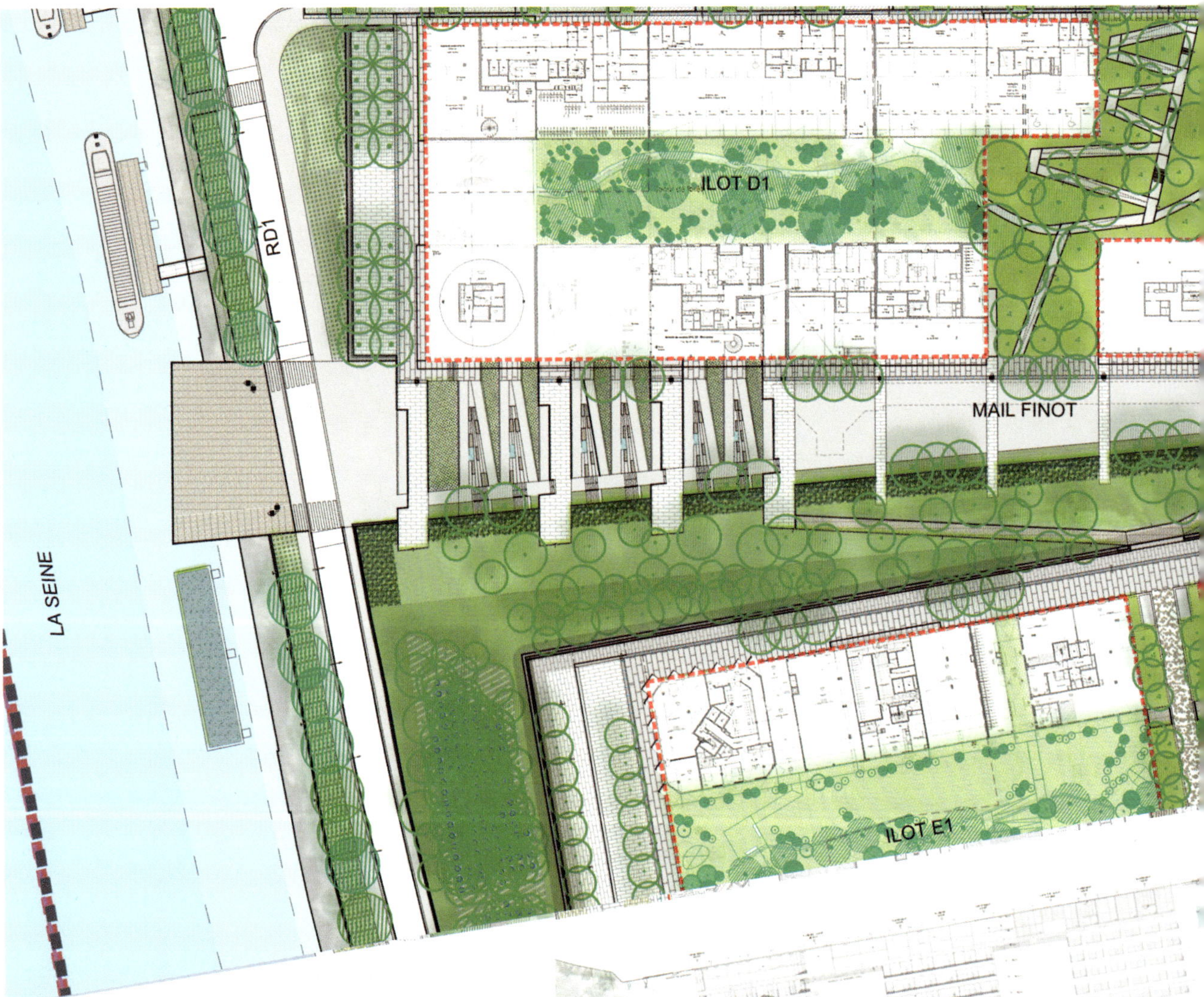

LA SEINE
RD1
ILOT D1
MAIL FINOT
ILOT E1

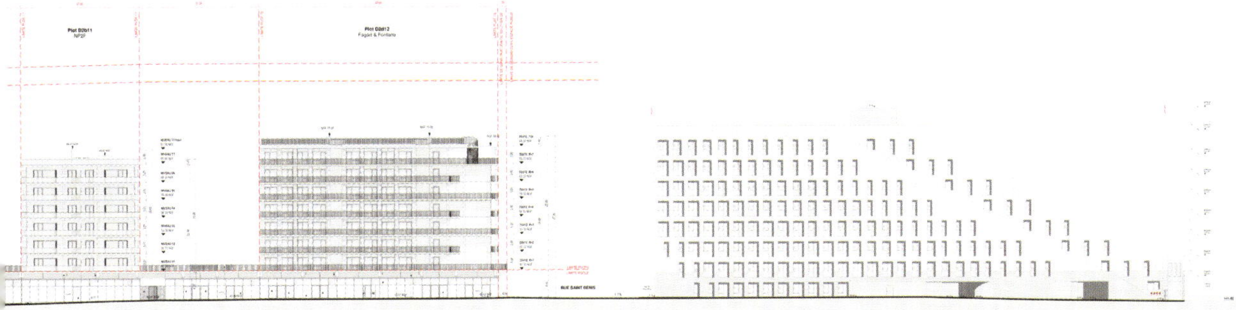

#643# AMBITION 12

CHORAL ARCHITECTURE

Urban cohesion
Mail Finot elevations.

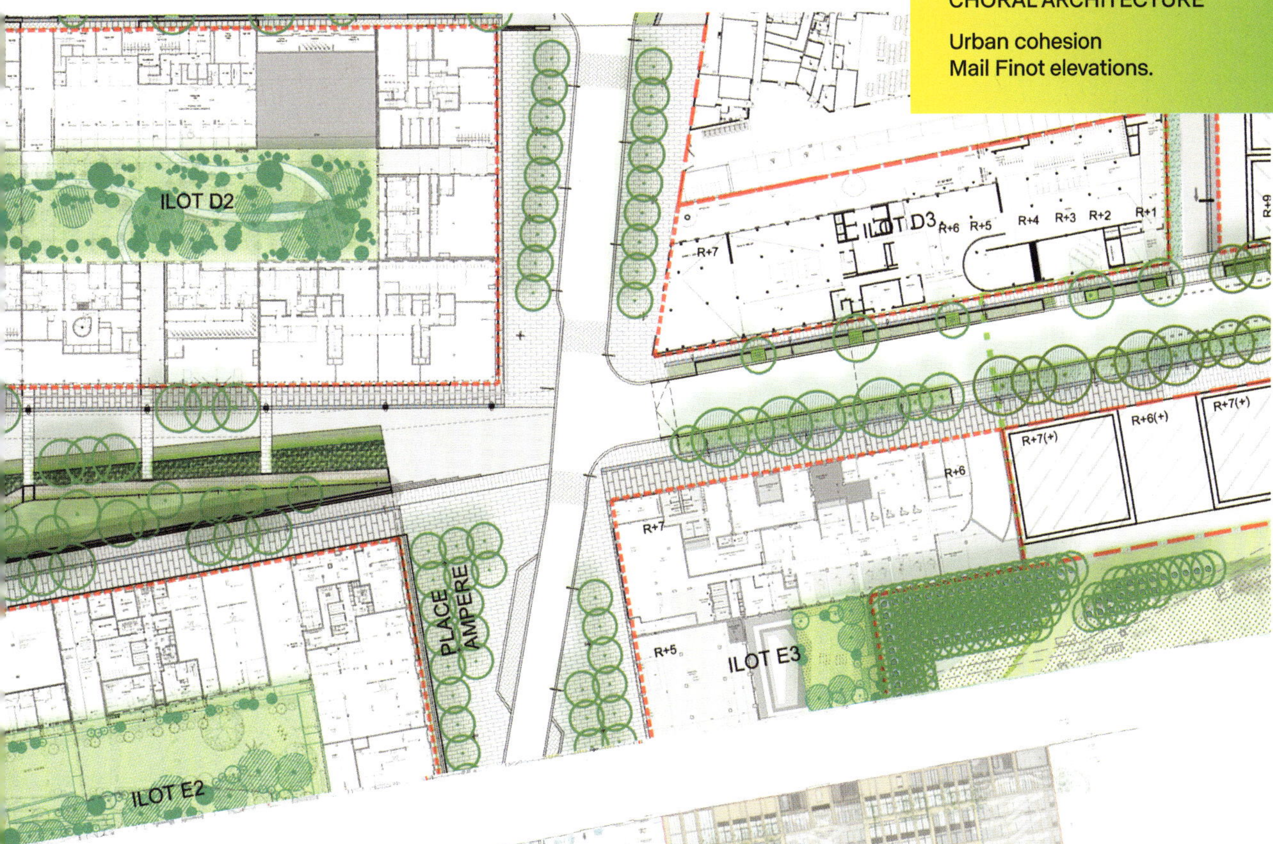

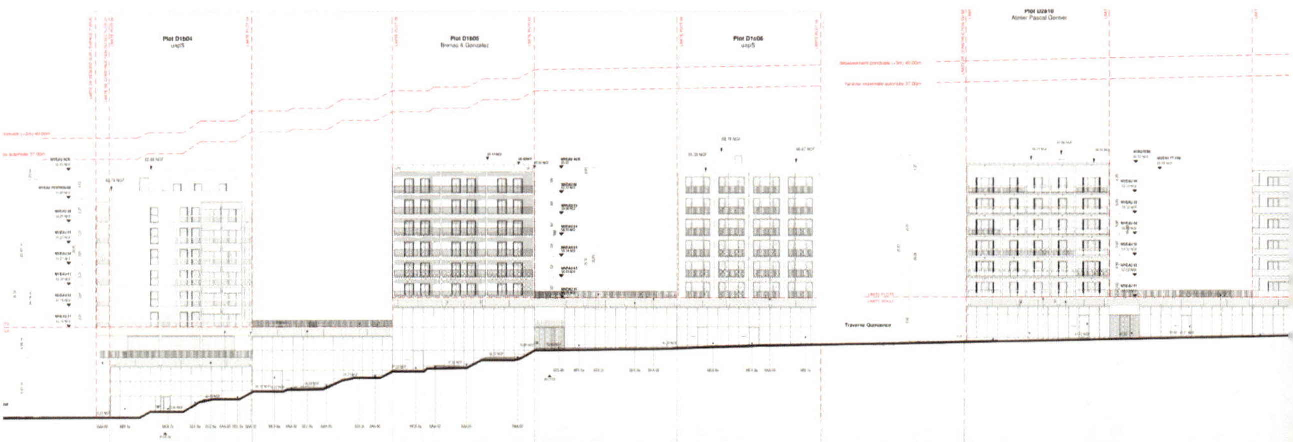
Plot D1b04
uapS
Plot D1b05
Brenac & Gonzalez
Plot D1c06
uapS
Atelier Pascal Gontier
Traverse Quinsance

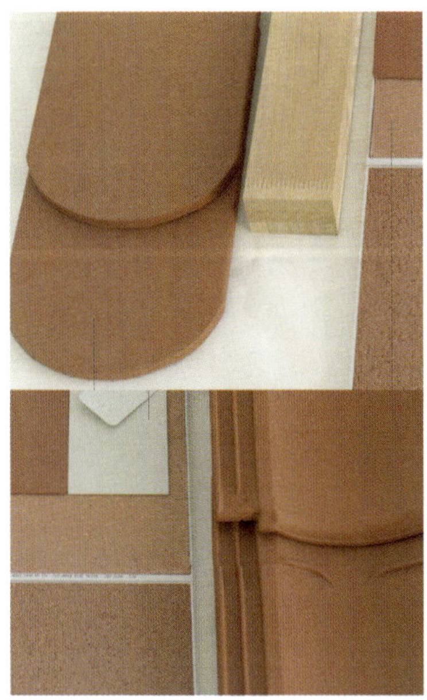

#645# AMBITION 12

CHORAL ARCHITECTURE

Urban cohesion
Mail Finot, Elevations - details.

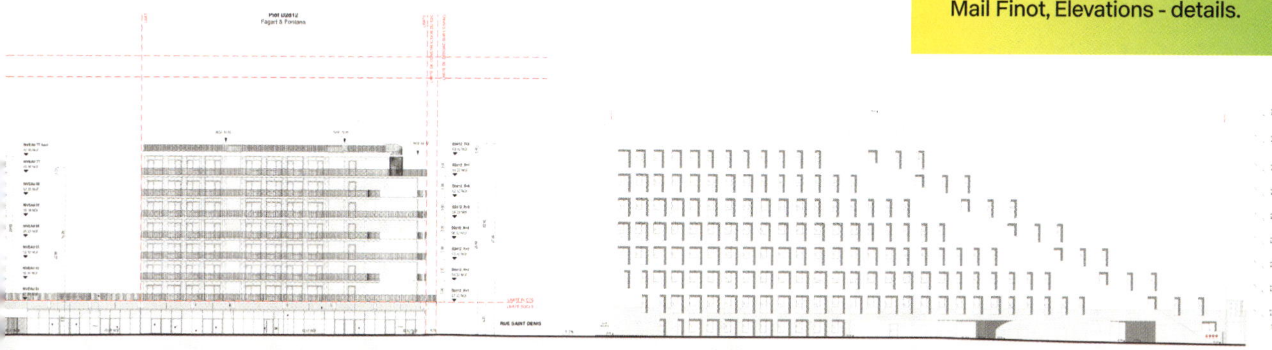

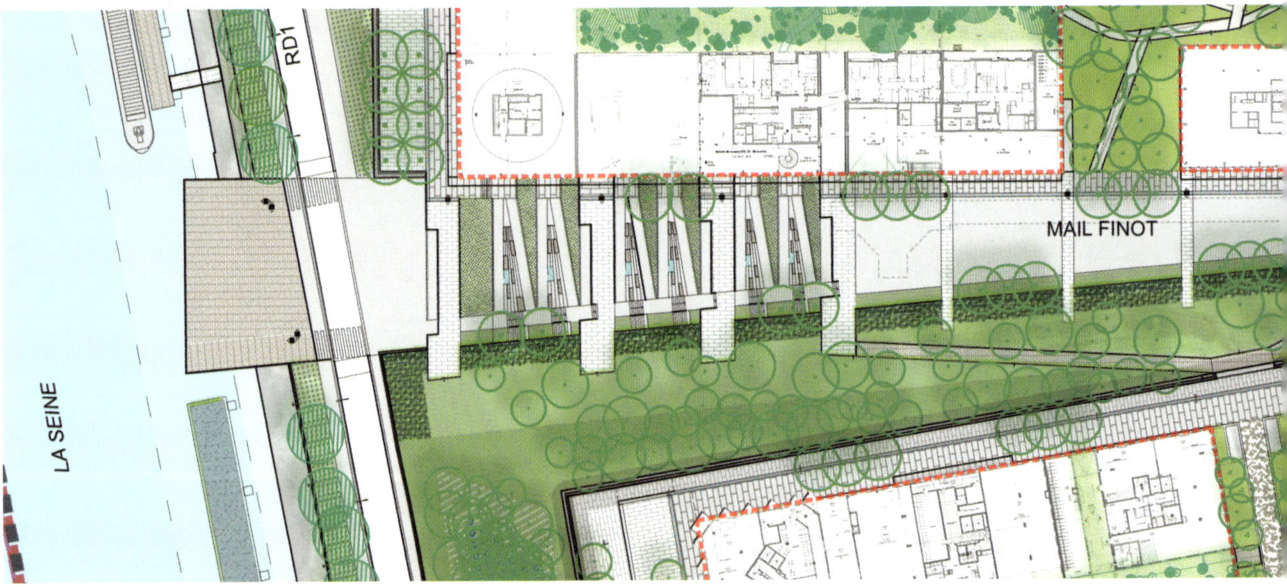
RD1
MAIL FINOT
LA SEINE

#647# AMBITION 12

CHORAL ARCHITECTURE

Urban cohesion
Mail Finot. Facade details.

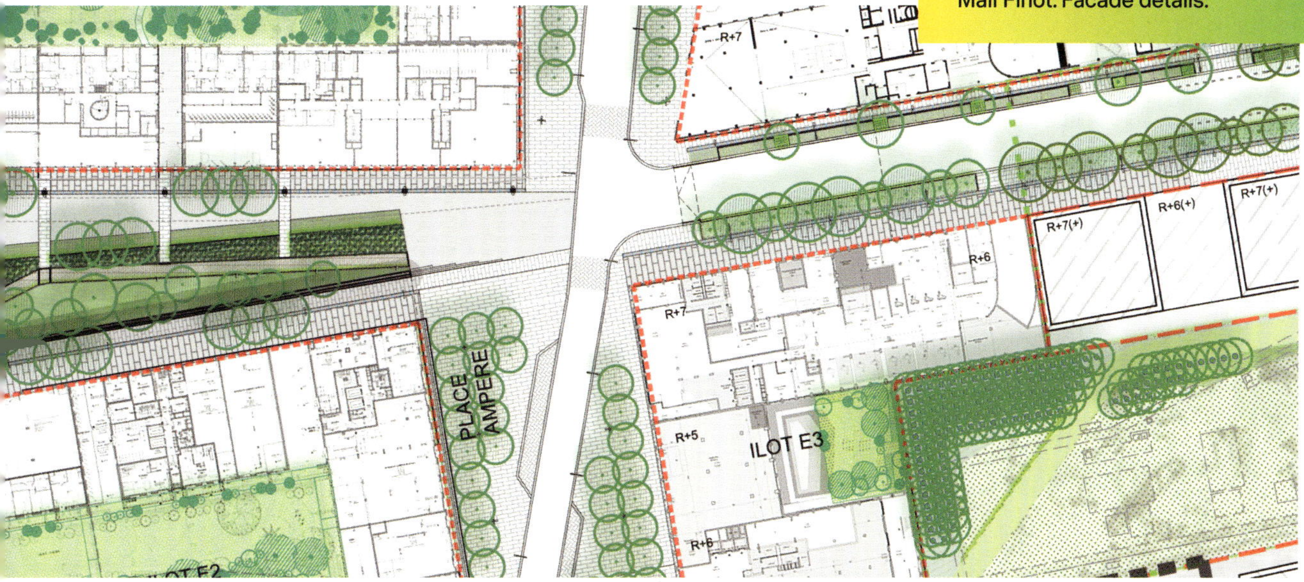

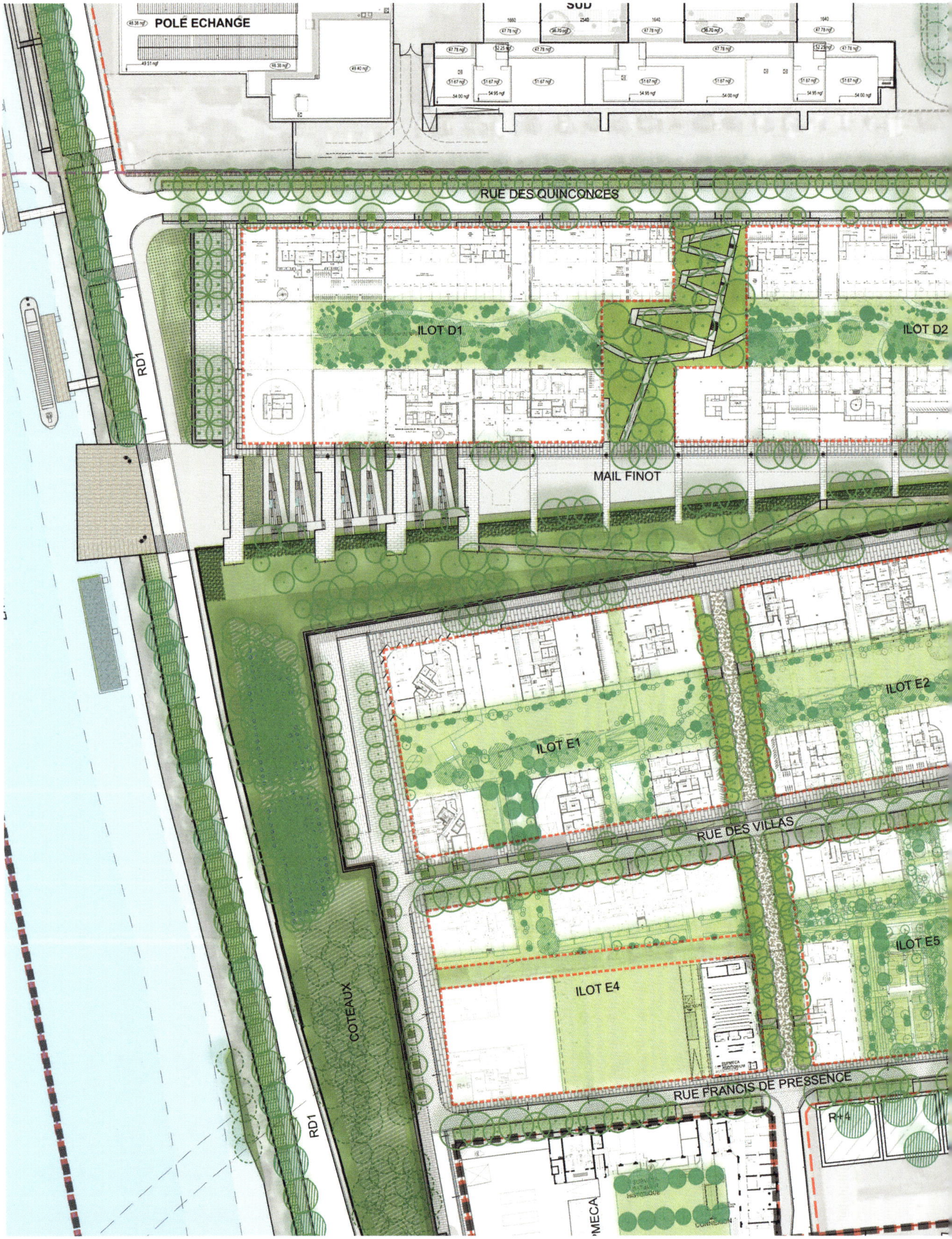
POLE ECHANGE
SUD
RUE DES QUINCONCES
ILOT D1
ILOT D2
RD1
MAIL FINOT
ILOT E2
ILOT E1
RUE DES VILLAS
ILOT E5
ILOT E4
COTEAUX
RUE FRANCIS DE PRESSENCE
R+4
RD1
MECA

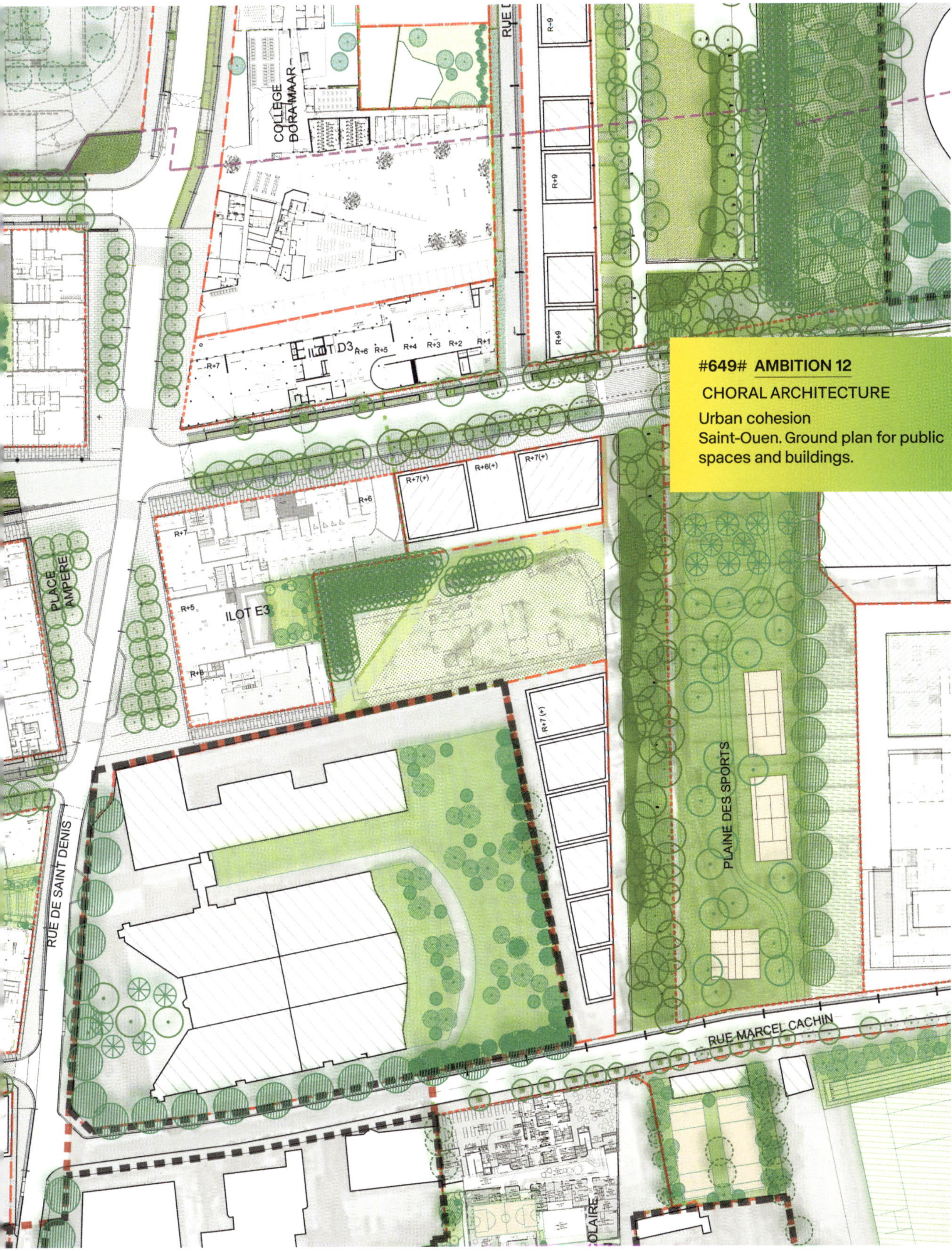

#649# AMBITION 12

CHORAL ARCHITECTURE

Urban cohesion
Saint-Ouen. Ground plan for public spaces and buildings.

E28-2

#651# AMBITION 12

CHORAL ARCHITECTURE

Urban cohesion
Mail Finot. Sector E.
Elevations - details.

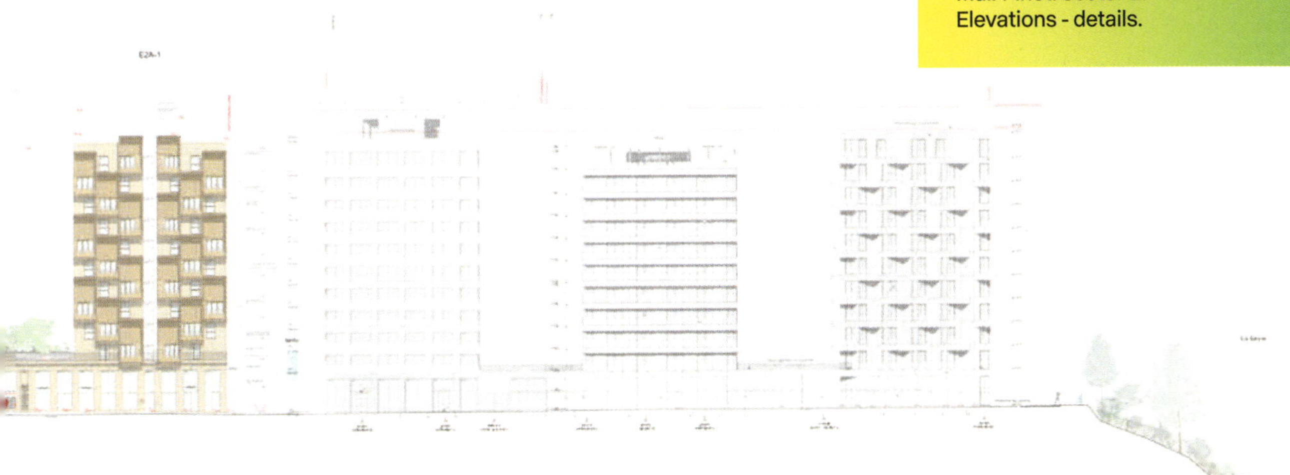

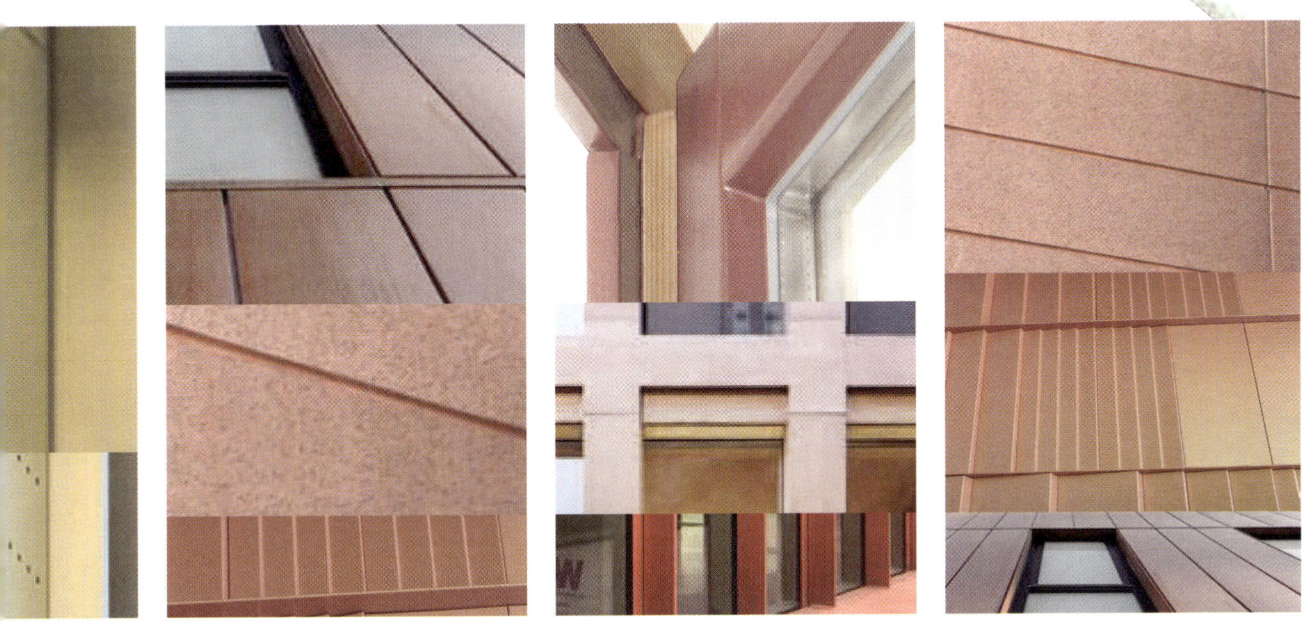

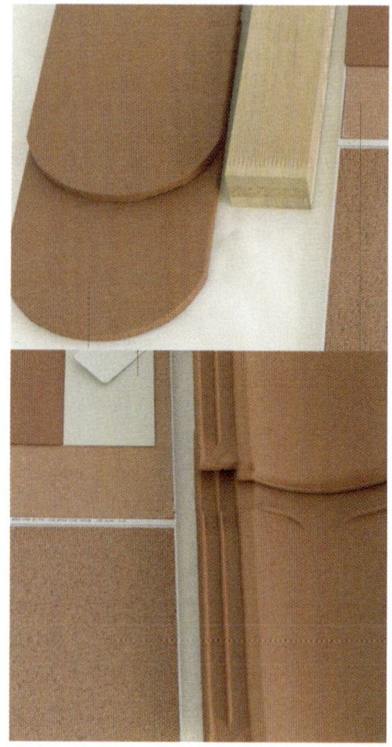

#653# **AMBITION 12**

CHORAL ARCHITECTURE

Urban cohesion
Mail Finot, Sector E
Façade details.

Pedestals - Saint Ouen - Mail Finot

#655# AMBITION 12

CHORAL ARCHITECTURE

Urban cohesion
Saint Ouen - Mail Finot
Pedestals.

#657# **AMBITION 12**

CHORAL ARCHITECTURE

Urban cohesion
Aerial view of Saint-Denis.

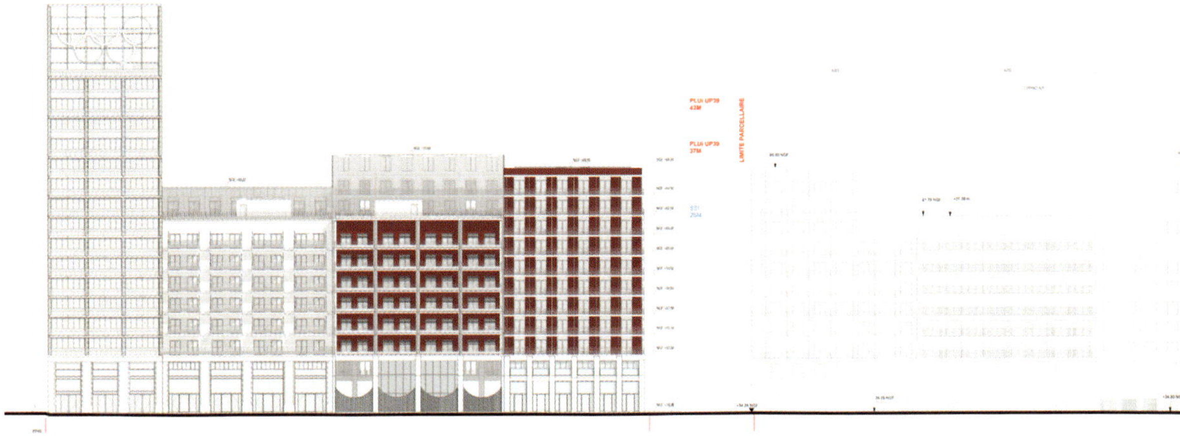

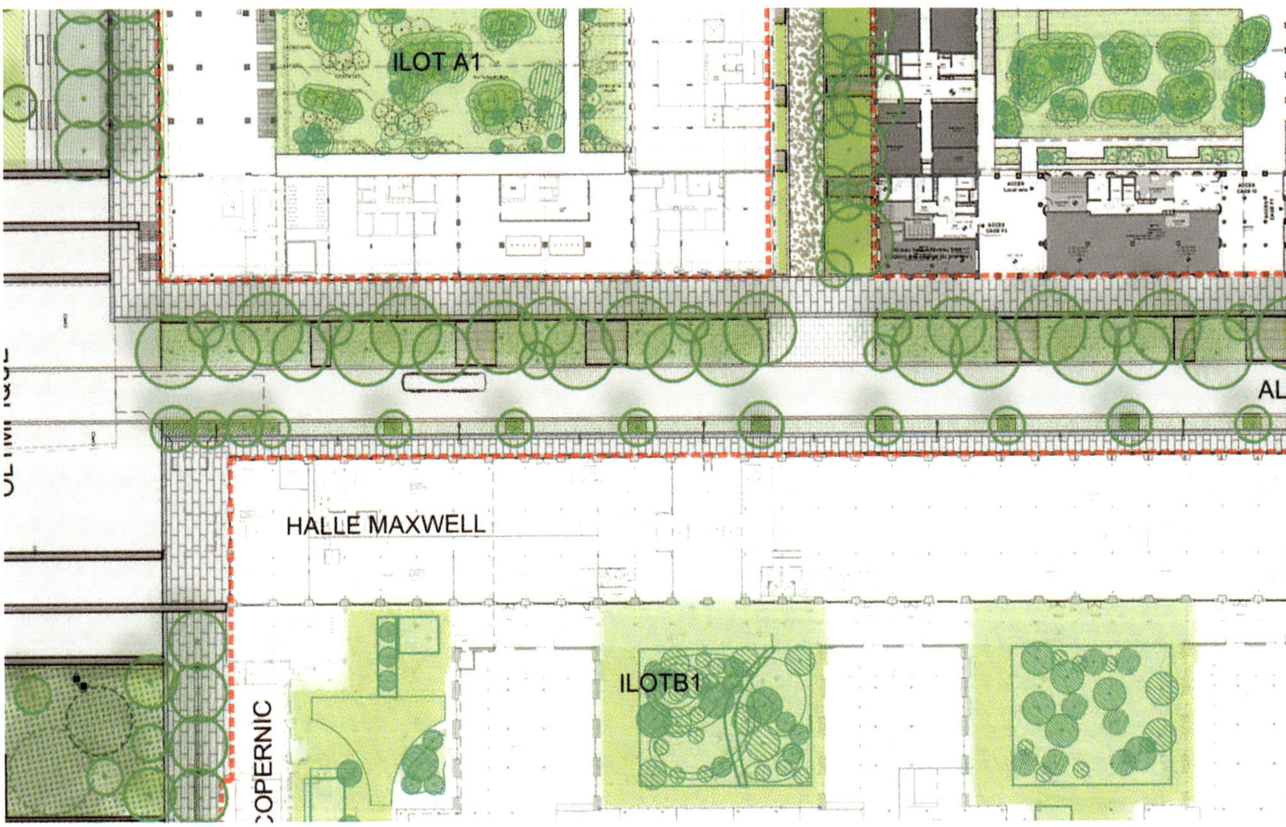
ILOT A1
HALLE MAXWELL
ILOTB1
COPERNIC

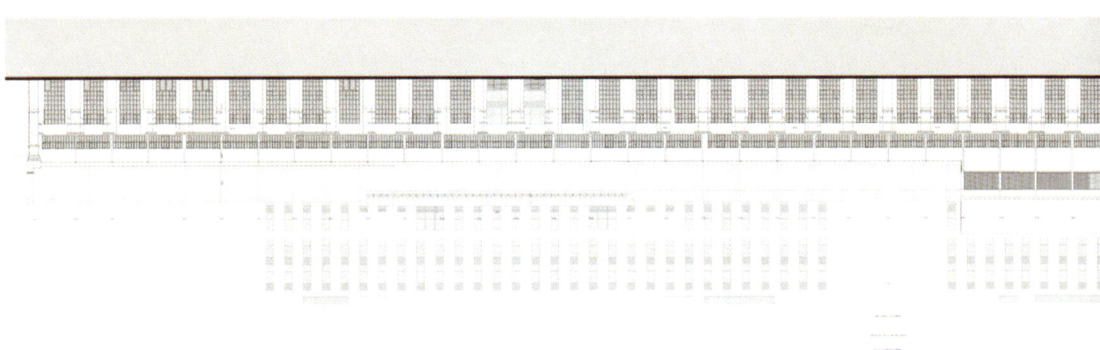

#659# AMBITION 12

CHORAL ARCHITECTURE

Urban cohesion
Saint Denis. Allée Seine. Elevations.

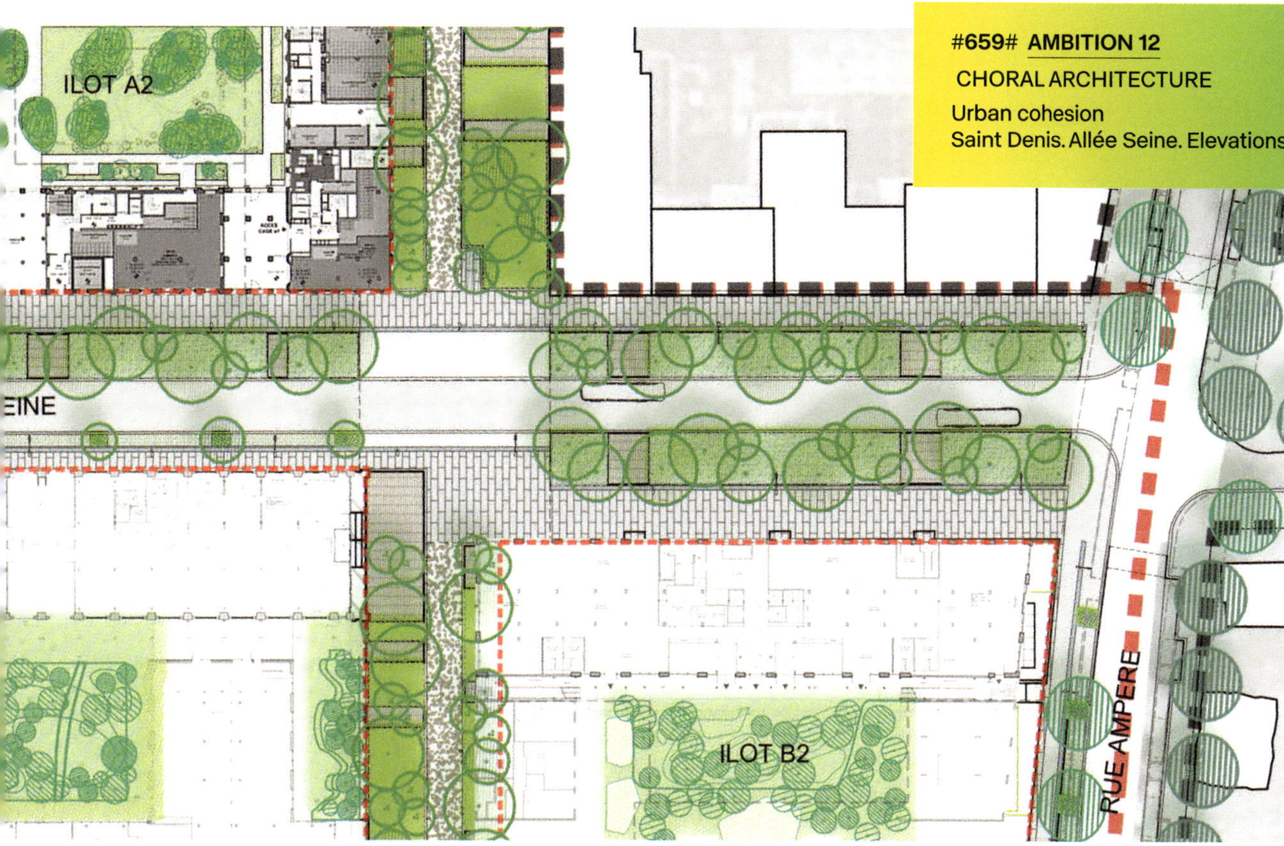

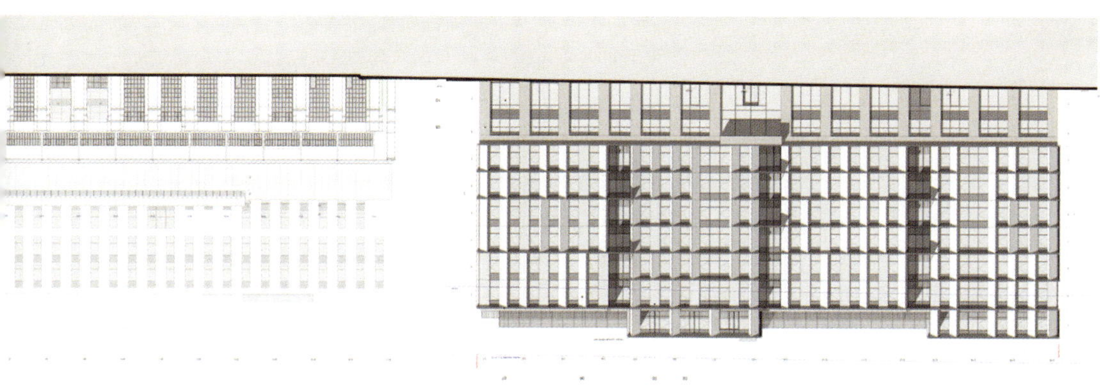

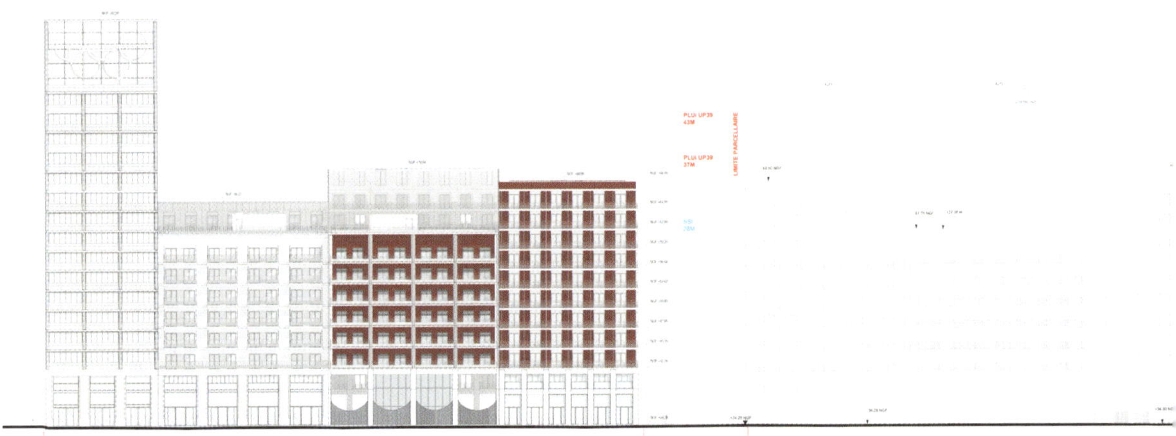
PLUI UP39
43M
PLUI UP39
37M
LIMITE PARCELLAIRE

#661# AMBITION 12

CHORAL ARCHITECTURE

Urban cohesion
Saint Denis. Allée Seine - Sector A.
Élévations - détails.

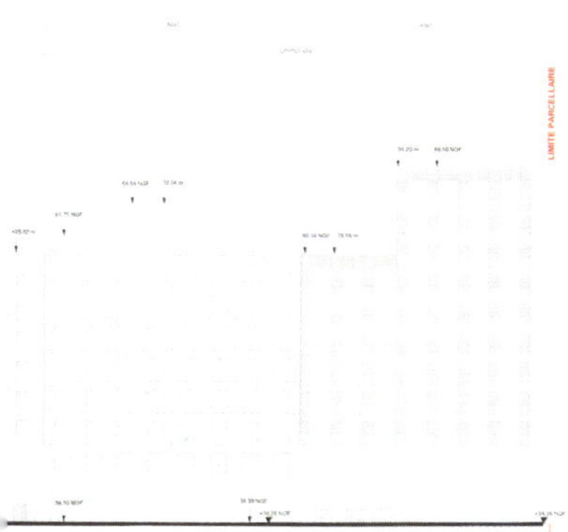

EXISTING BLOCK

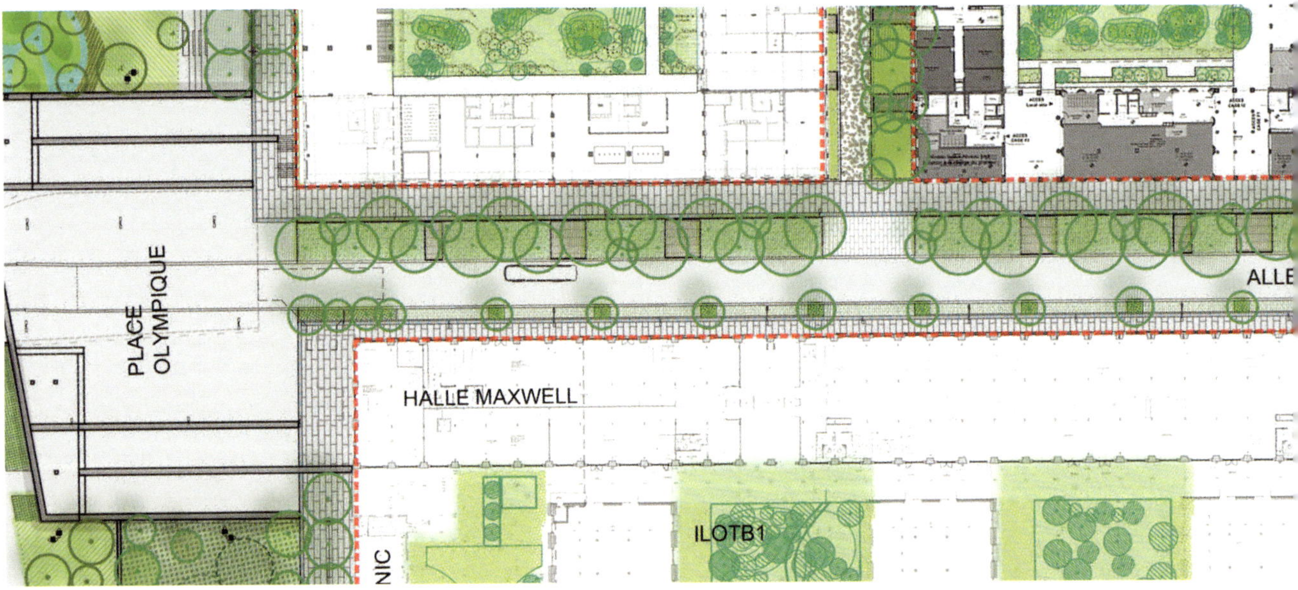
PLACE OLYMPIQUE
HALLE MAXWELL
ILOTB1
ALLE
NIC

#663# **AMBITION 12**

CHORAL ARCHITECTURE

Urban cohesion
Saint-Denis, Allée de Seine -
sectors A + B. Elevations - details.

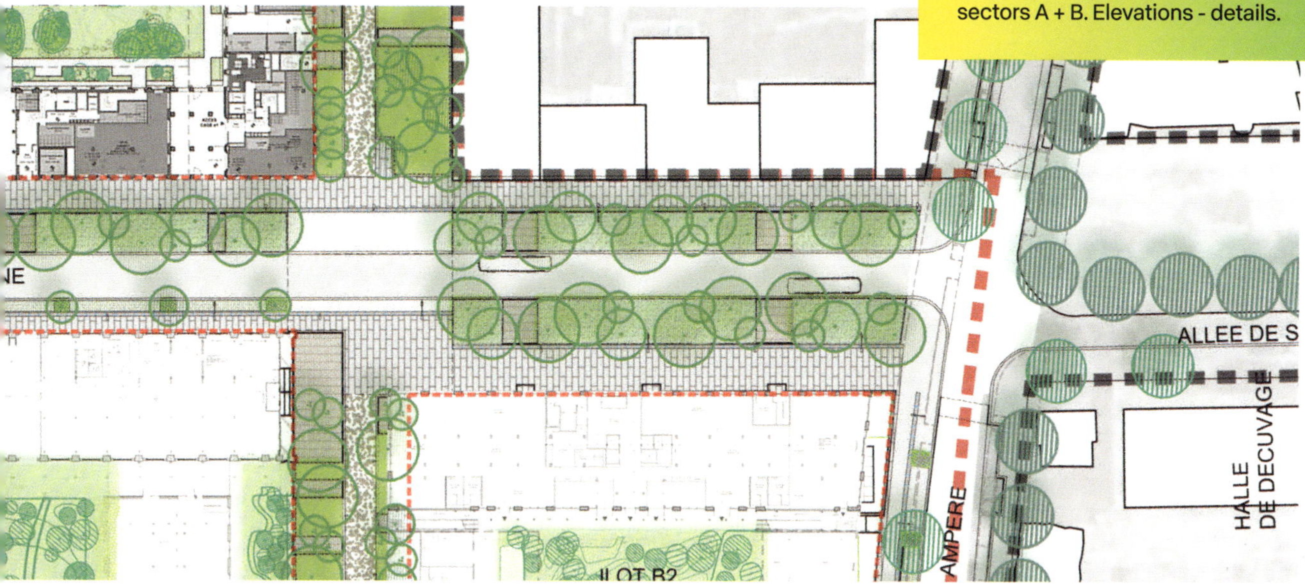

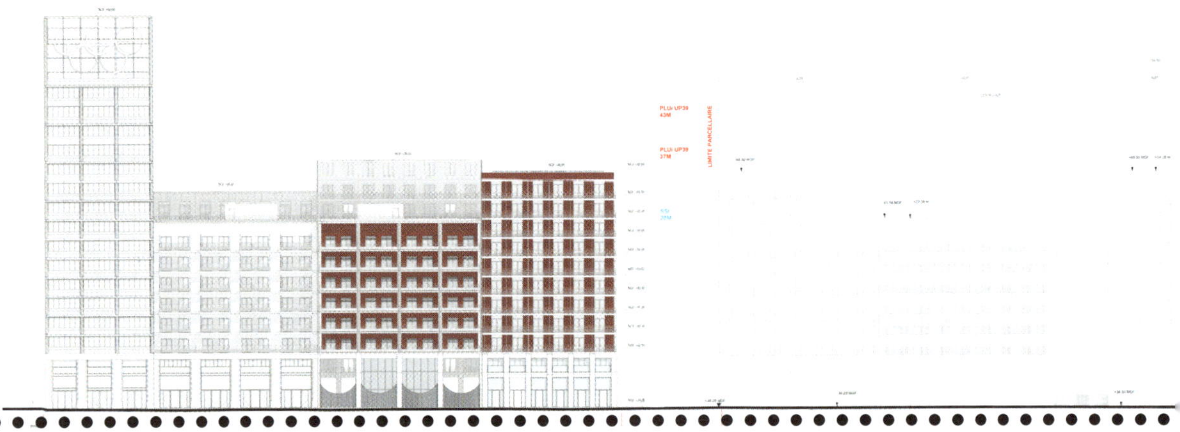

Sector B

#665# **AMBITION 12**

CHORAL ARCHITECTURE

Urban cohesion
Saint-Denis, Seine Riverside
Colorimetry.

Sector A

EXISTING BLOCK

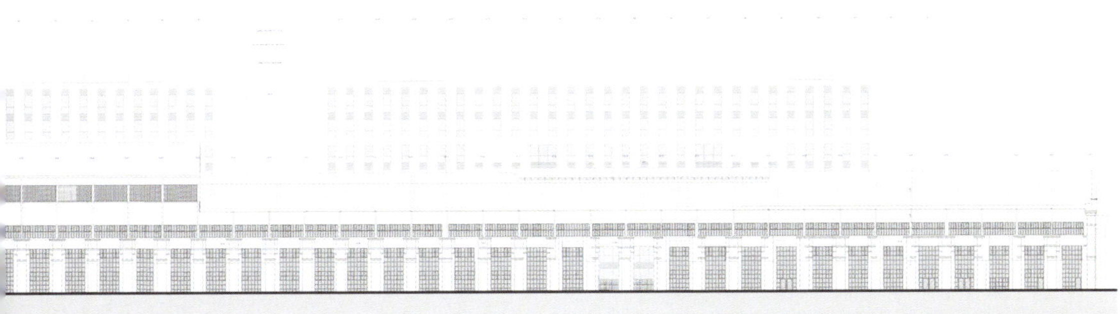

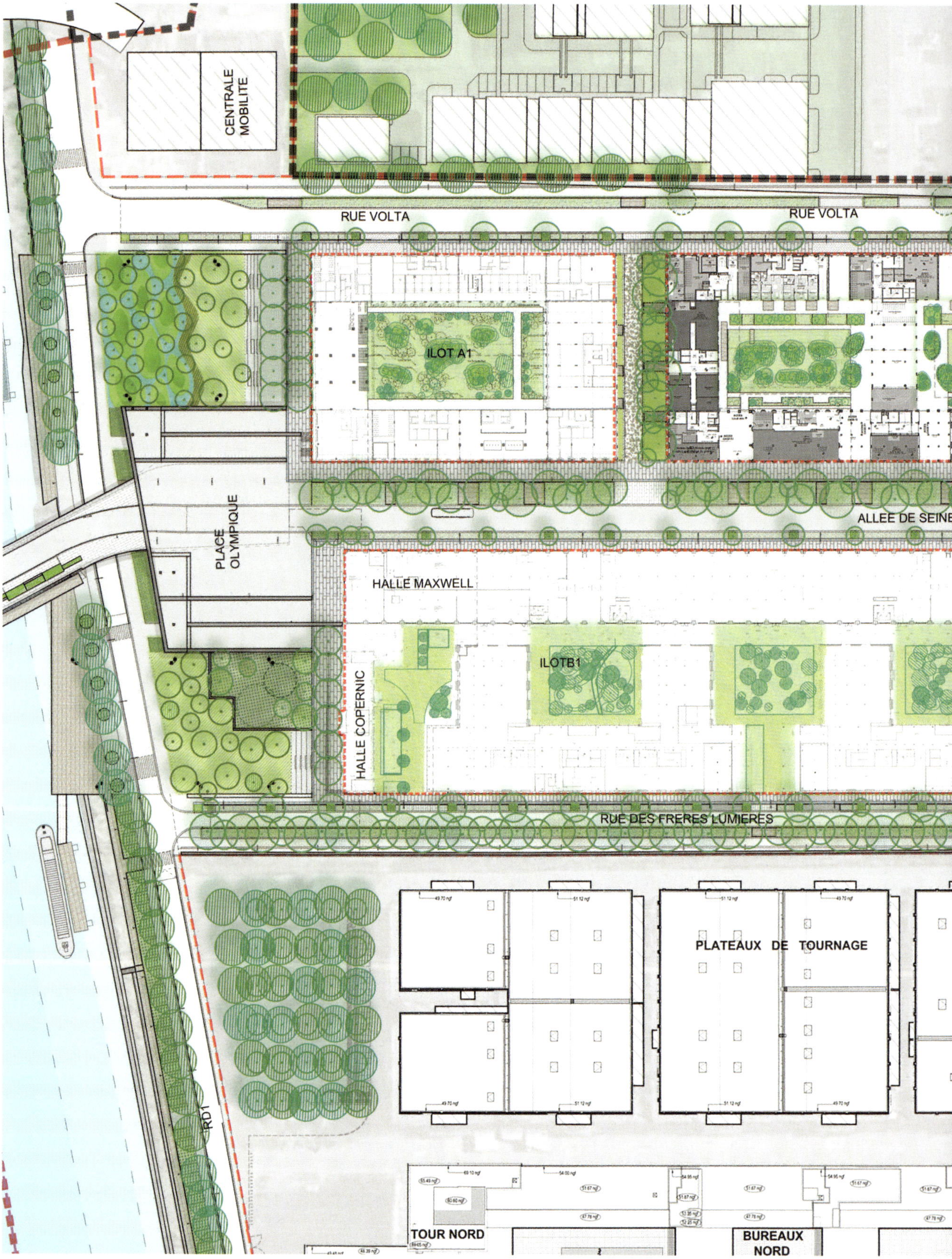
CENTRALE MOBILITE
RUE VOLTA
RUE VOLTA
ILOT A1
PLACE OLYMPIQUE
ALLEE DE SEINE
HALLE MAXWELL
ILOTB1
HALLE COPERNIC
RUE DES FRERES LUMIERES
PLATEAUX DE TOURNAGE
RD1
TOUR NORD
BUREAUX NORD

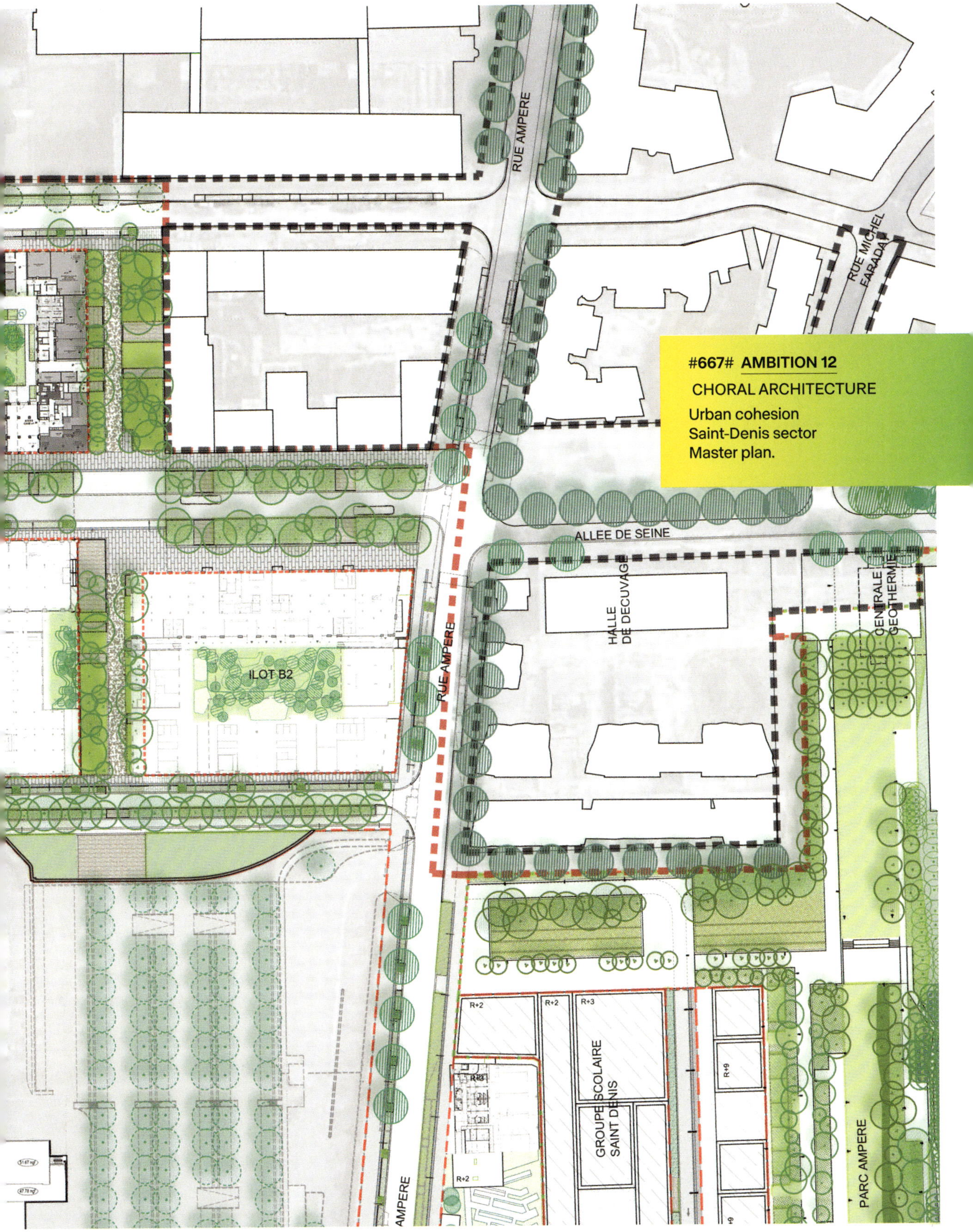

#667# AMBITION 12

CHORAL ARCHITECTURE

Urban cohesion
Saint-Denis sector
Master plan.

#669# AMBITION 12

CHORAL ARCHITECTURE

Urban cohesion
Saint-Denis, Allée de Seine
Sector B. Elevations and details.

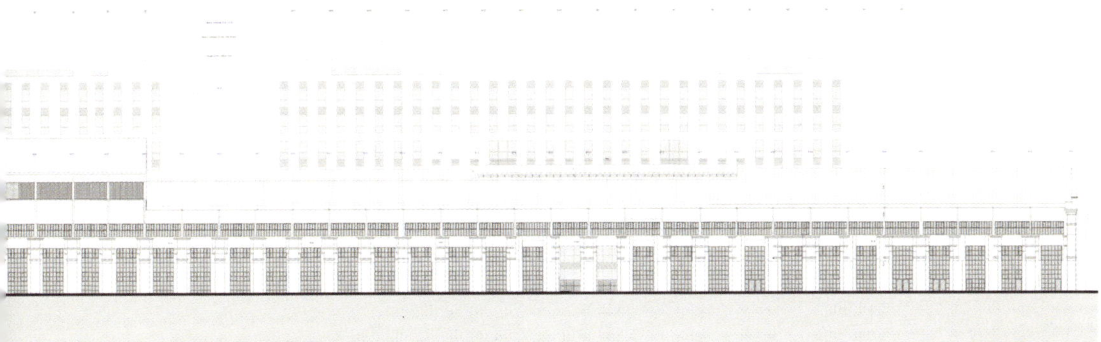

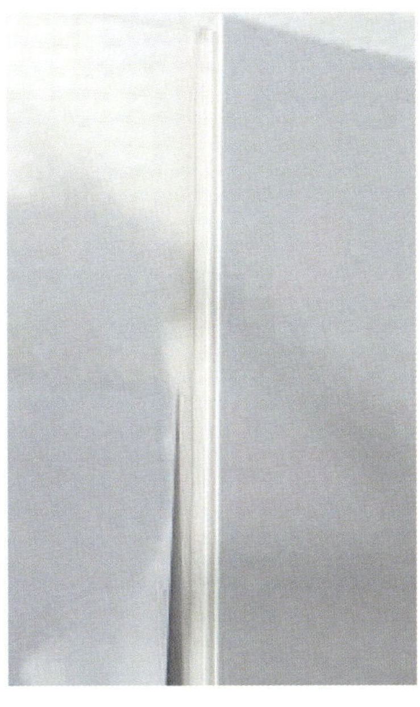

#671# AMBITION 12

CHORAL ARCHITECTURE

Urban cohesion
Saint Denis. Allée Seine - Sectors.
A + B Vis à vis. Élévations - détails.

MAXWELL
CAFÉ

#673# AMBITION 12

CHORAL ARCHITECTURE

Urban cohesion
Saint Denis-Allée Seine
Pedestals.

Block E
Cord: KOZ

Block E
Cord: CoBe

Block D
Cord: UAPS

#675# AMBITION 12

CHORAL ARCHITECTURE

Ateliers Workshop
Saint-Denis. Elevation, rue Ampère.

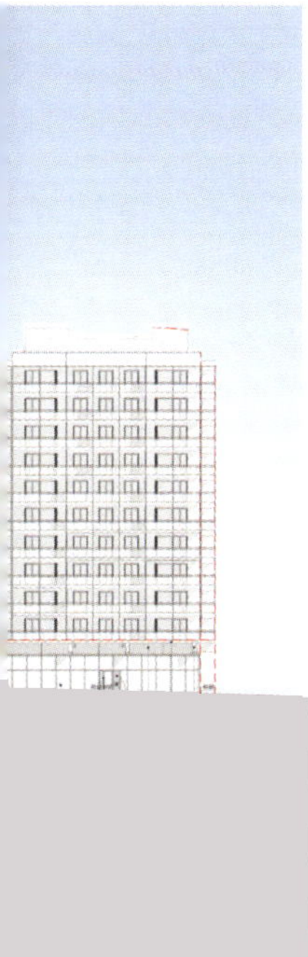

Block C
Cord: Cité du Cinéma

Block B
Cord: Chaix & Morel

E2
SAINT DENIS
PLACE
AMPÈRE
R+6
R+5
R+7
ÎLOT E3

#677# **AMBITION 12**

CHORAL ARCHITECTURE

Urban cohesion
Saint Denis - Place Ampère.
Master plan and public spaces.

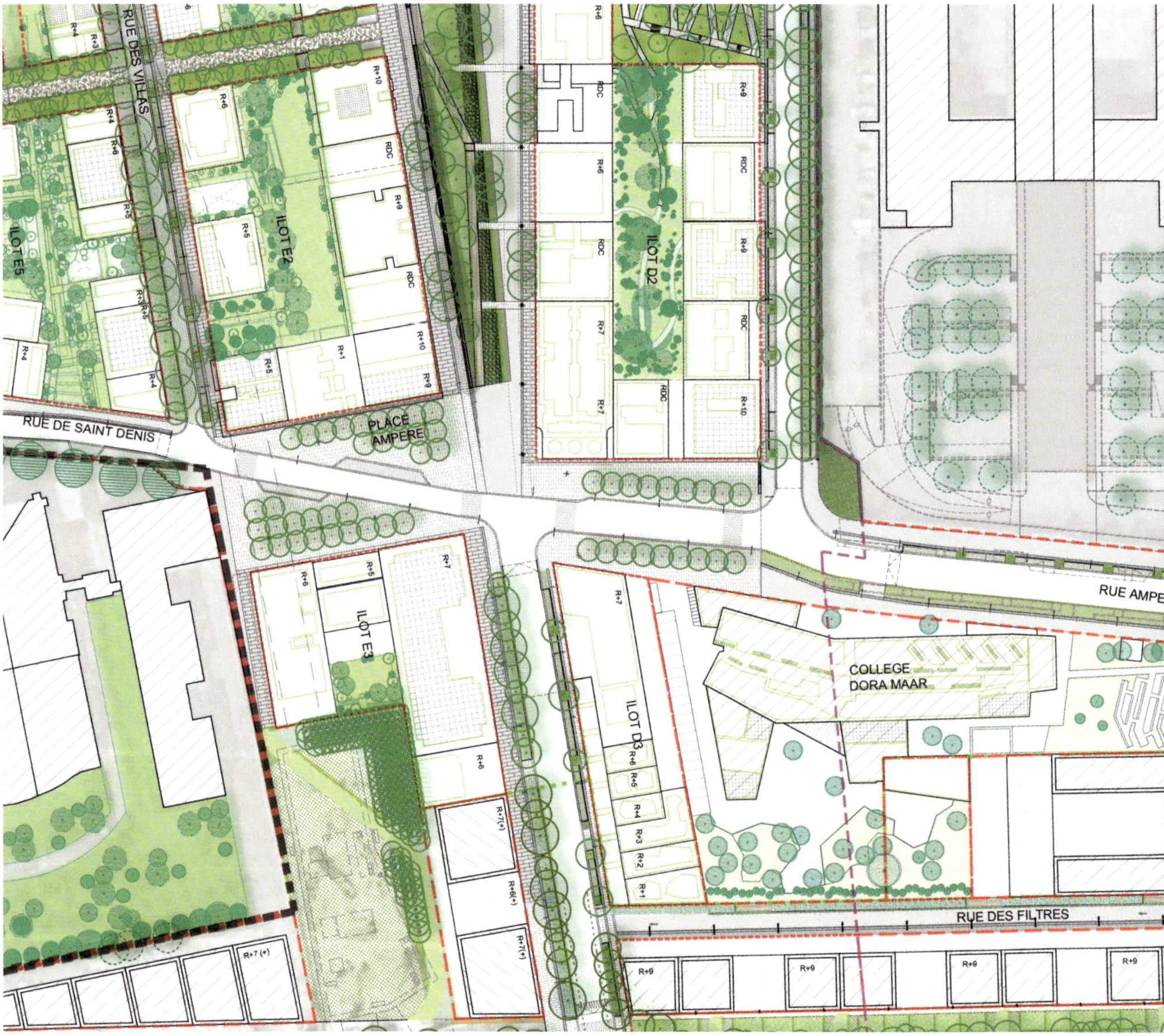

RUE DES VILLAS
ILOT E5
ILOT E2
ILOT D2
RUE DE SAINT DENIS
PLACE
AMPERE
ILOT E3
ILOT D3
COLLEGE
DORA MAAR
RUE AMPER
RUE DES FILTRES

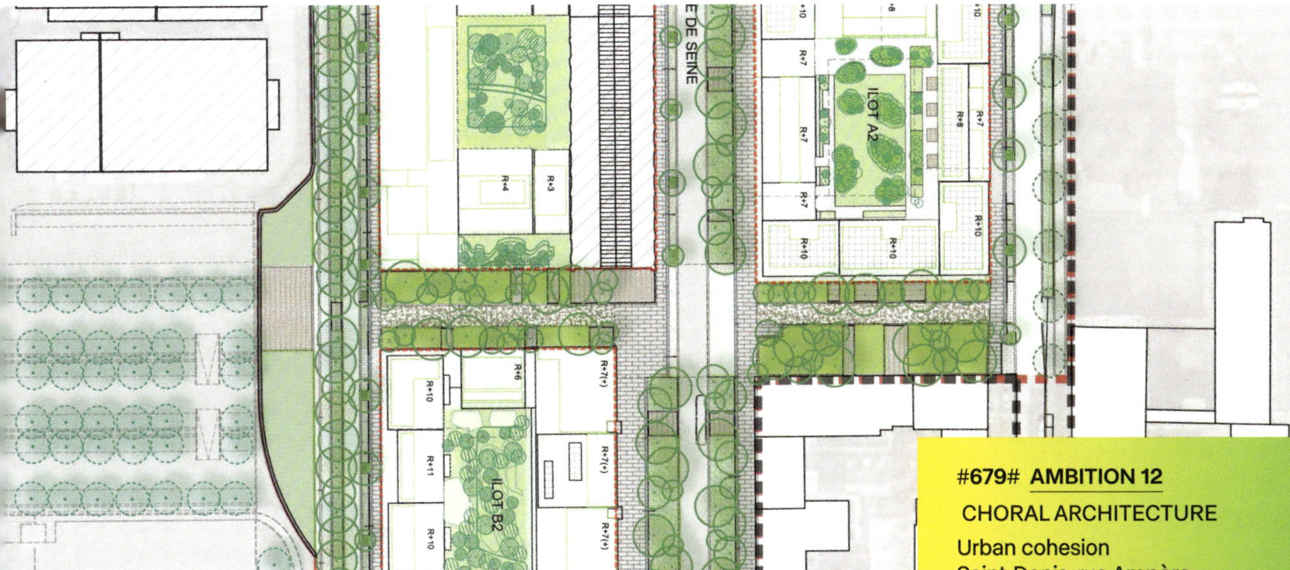

#679# **AMBITION 12**

CHORAL ARCHITECTURE

Urban cohesion
Saint-Denis, rue Ampère
Master plan.

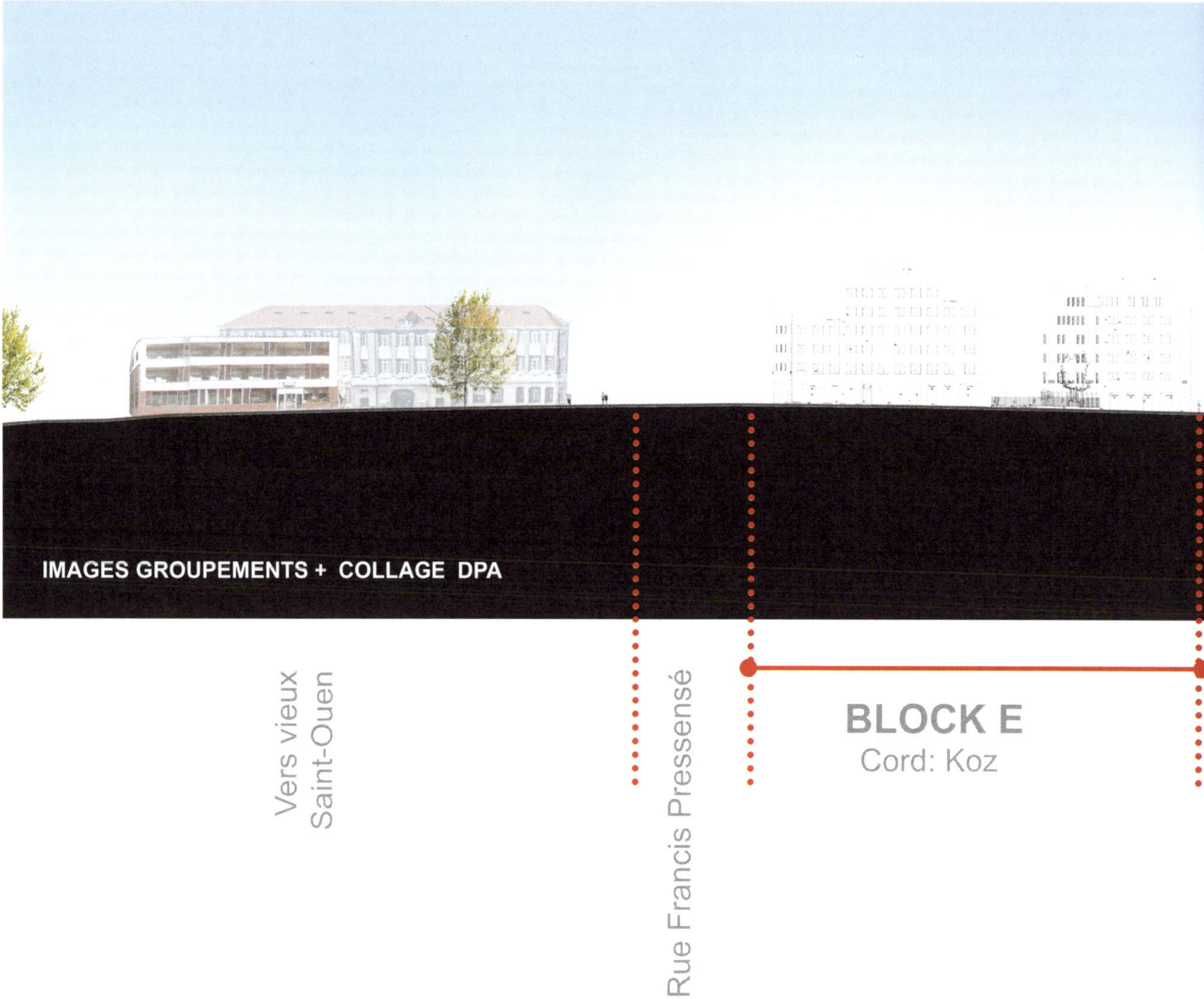
IMAGES GROUPEMENTS + COLLAGE DPA
Vers vieux
Saint-Ouen
Rue Francis Pressensé
BLOCK E
Cord: Koz

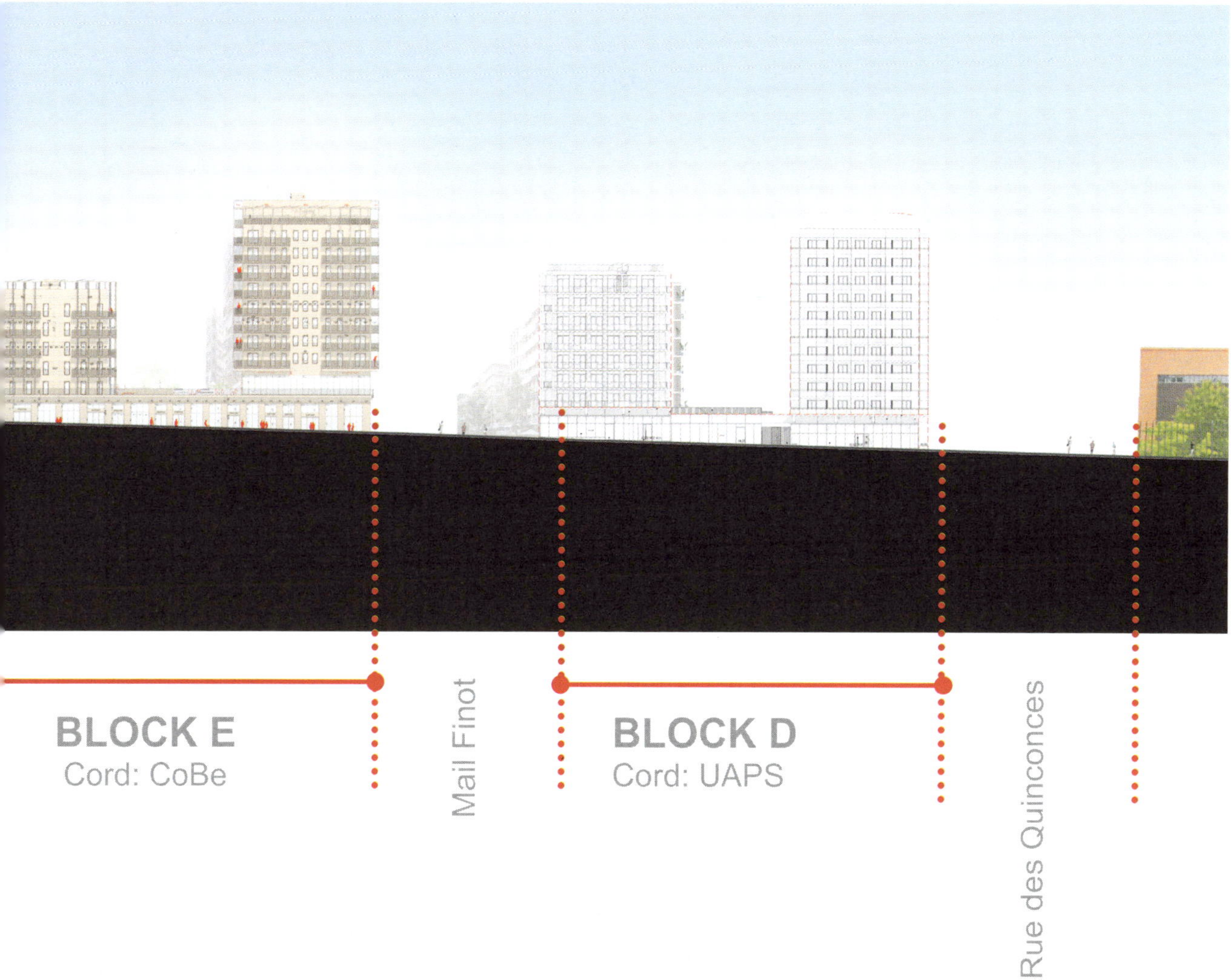

#681# AMBITION 12

CHORAL ARCHITECTURE

Ateliers Workshop
Saint Denis. Élévation Rue Ampère.
South detail.

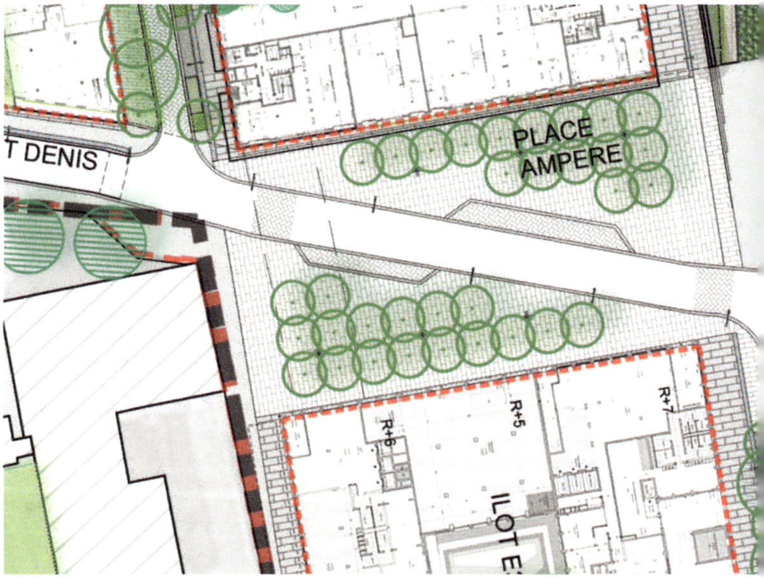

Sector E

#683# **AMBITION 12**

CHORAL ARCHITECTURE

Urban cohesion
Saint-Denis, Place Ampère.
Saint-Ouen Elevations.

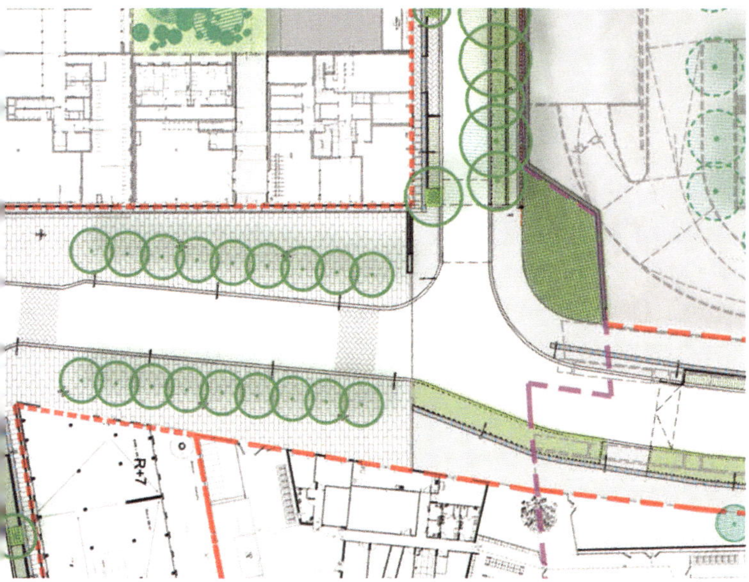

Sector D

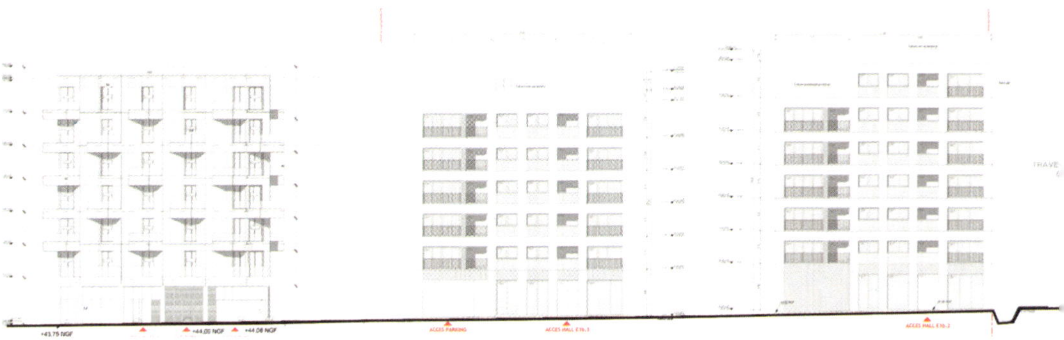

+43.75 NGF
+44.05 NGF
+44.08 NGF
ACCES PARKING

#685# AMBITION 12

CHORAL ARCHITECTURE

Saint-Ouen, Villas sector- details.

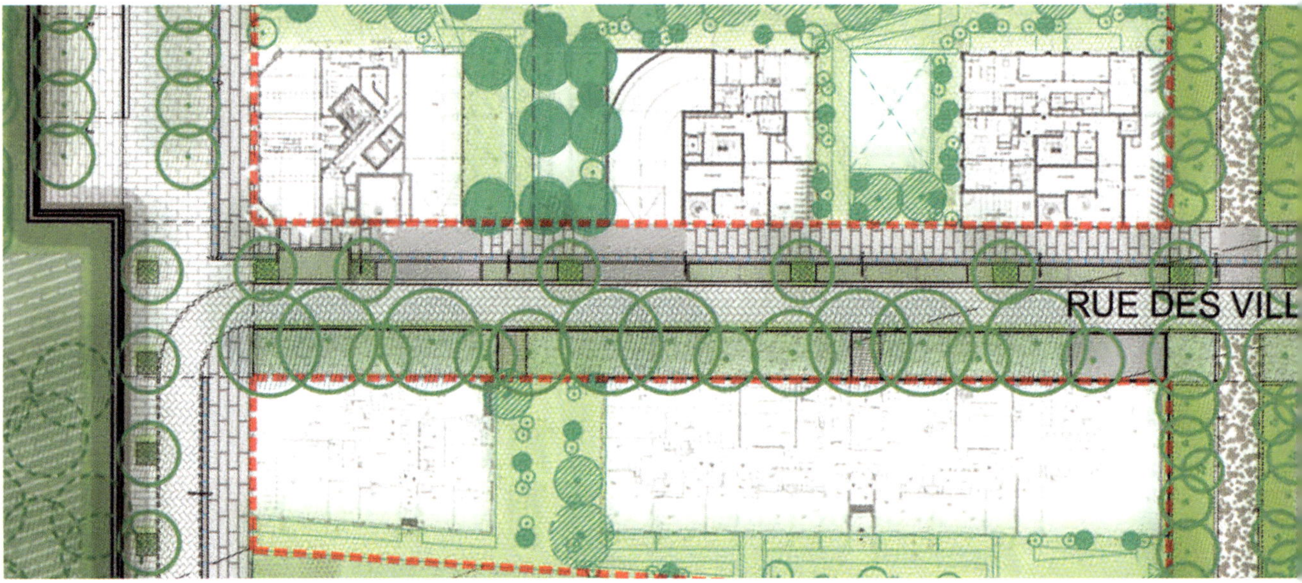
RUE DES VILL

#687# **AMBITION 12**

CHORAL ARCHITECTURE

Saint-Ouen, Villas sector - details.

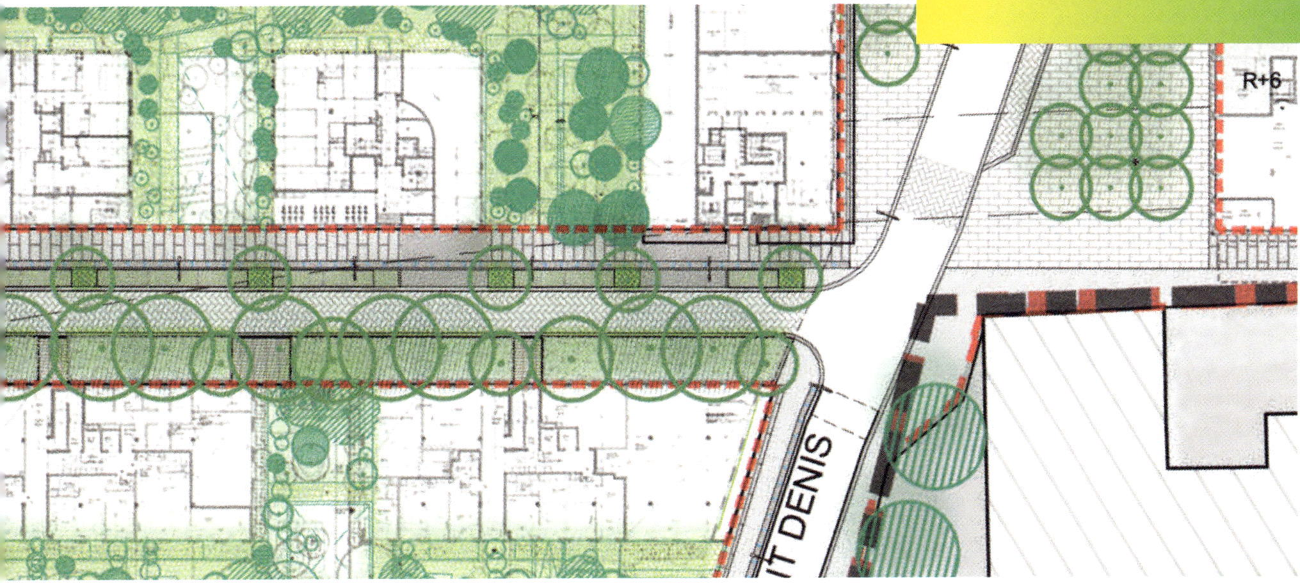

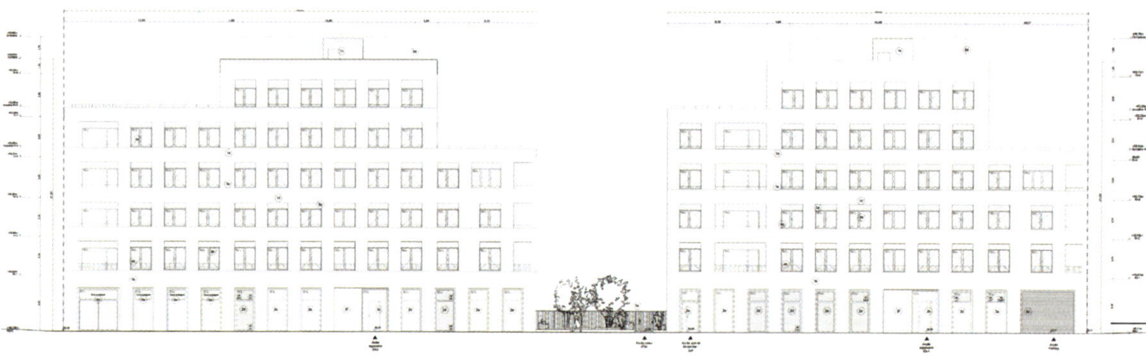

#689# AMBITION 12

CHORAL ARCHITECTURE

Saint-Ouen, Villas sector - details.

#691# AMBITION 12

CHORAL ARCHITECTURE

Saint-Ouen, Villas sector - details.

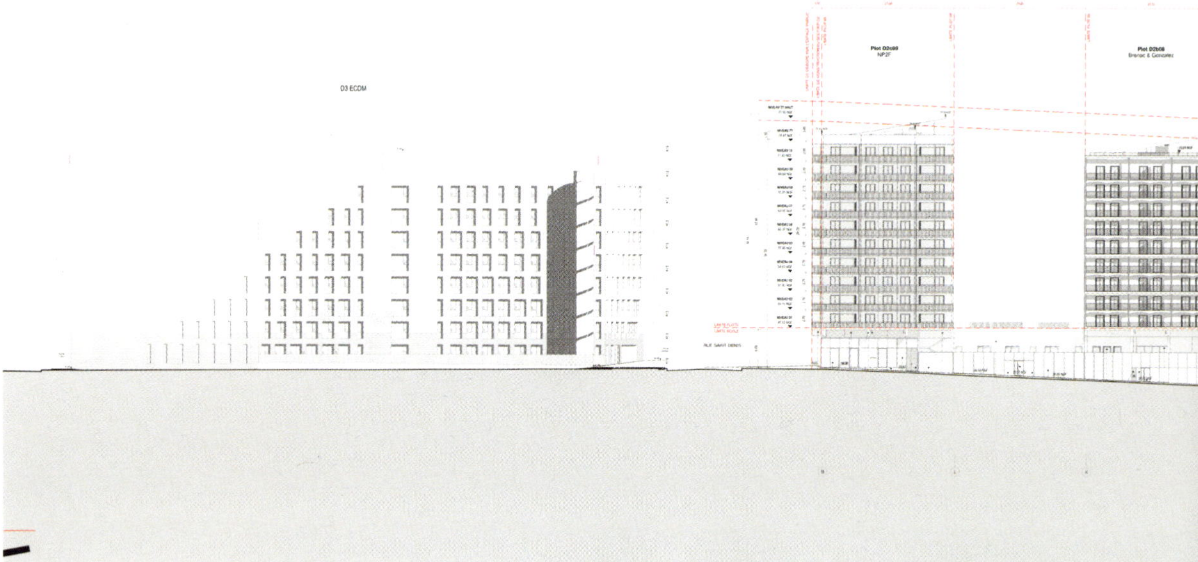
D3 ECDM
Plot D2c09
NP2F
Plot D2b08

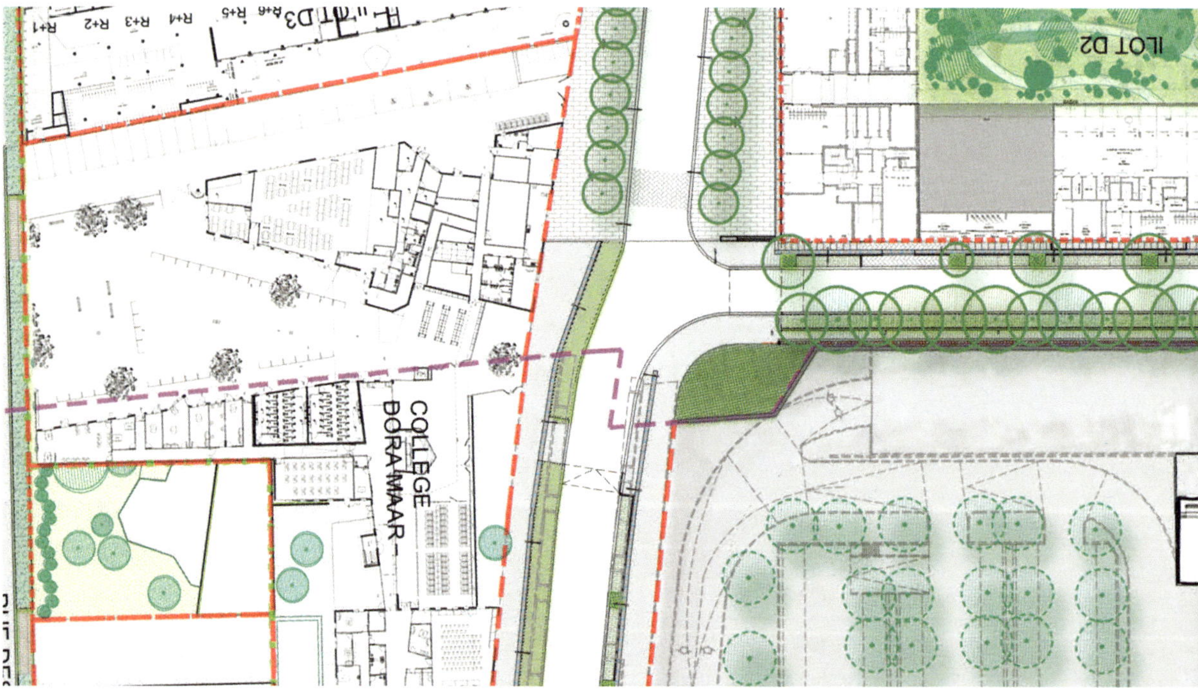
COLLEGE DORA MAAR
ILOT D2
R+1
R+2
R+3
R+4
R+5
R+6

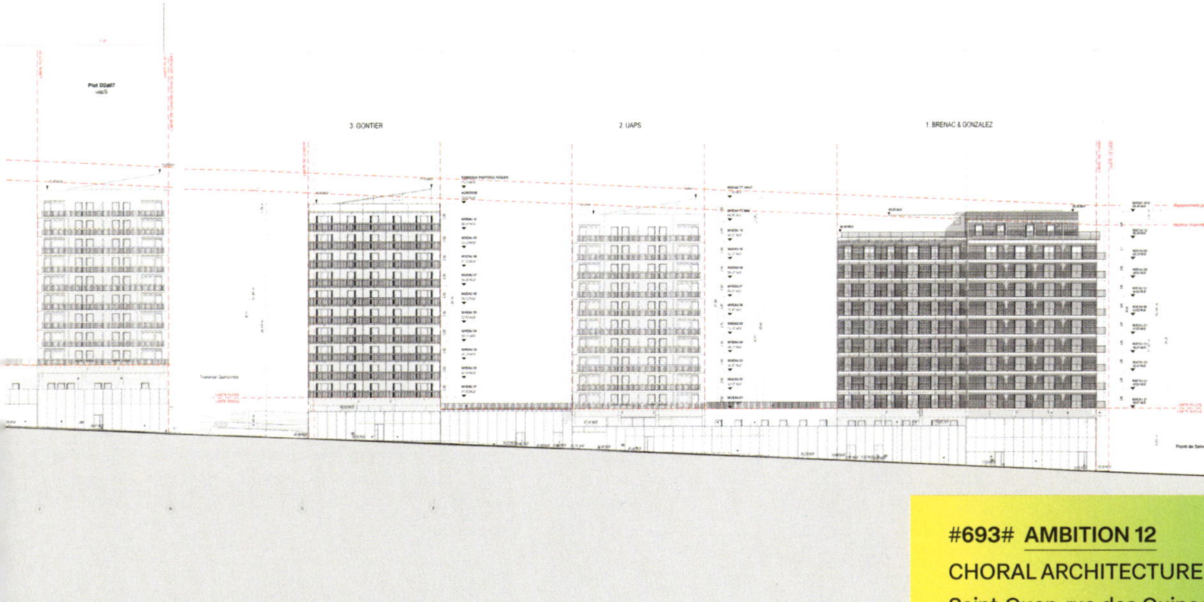

#693# **AMBITION 12**

CHORAL ARCHITECTURE

Saint-Ouen, rue des Quinconces - details.

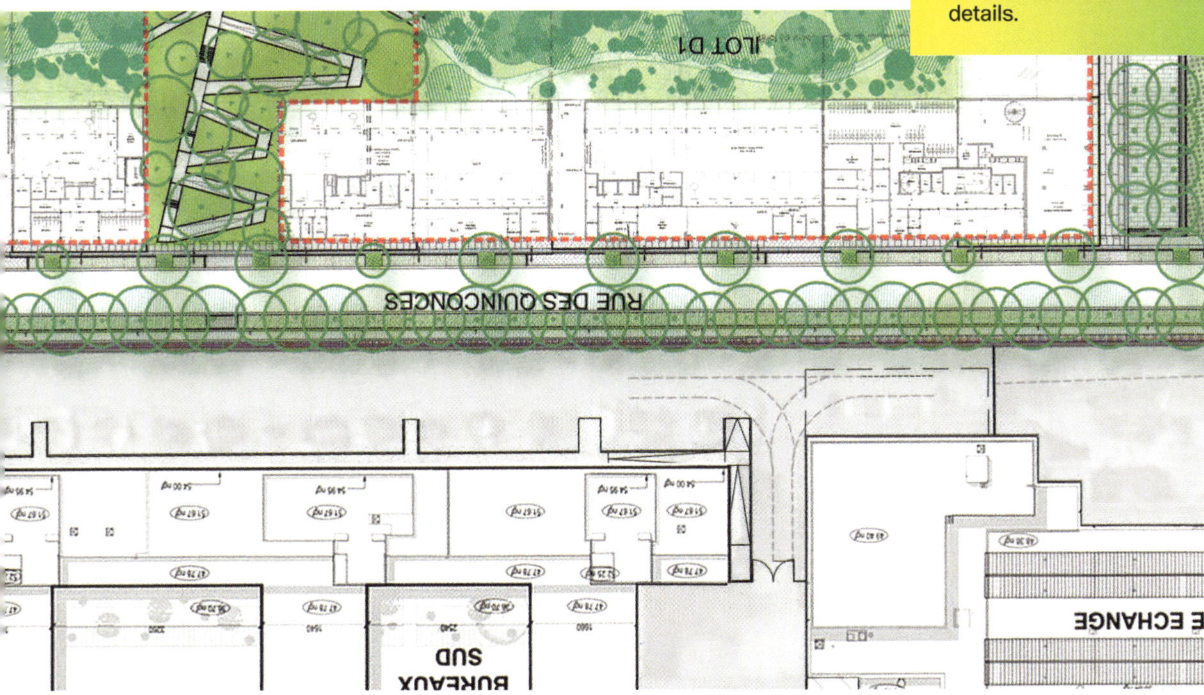

#695# AMBITION 12

CHORAL ARCHITECTURE

Saint-Ouen, rue des Quinconces - details.

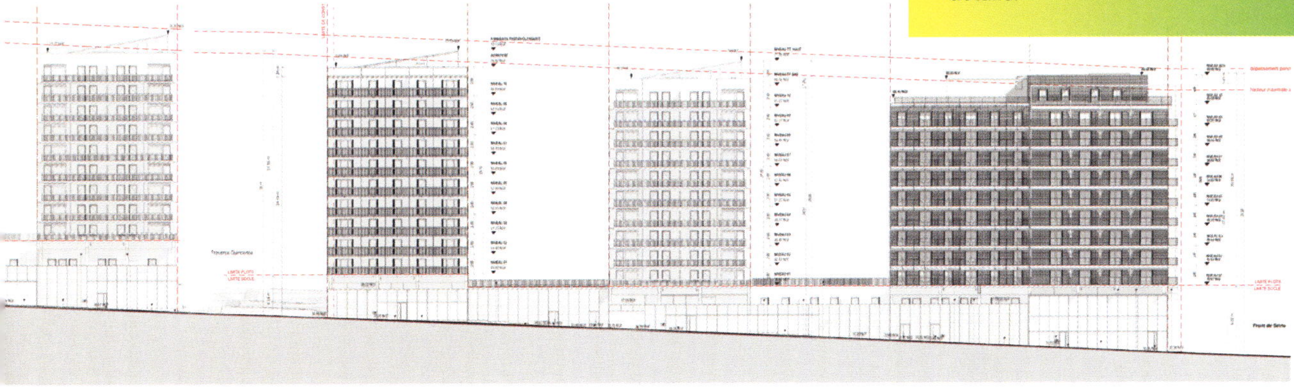

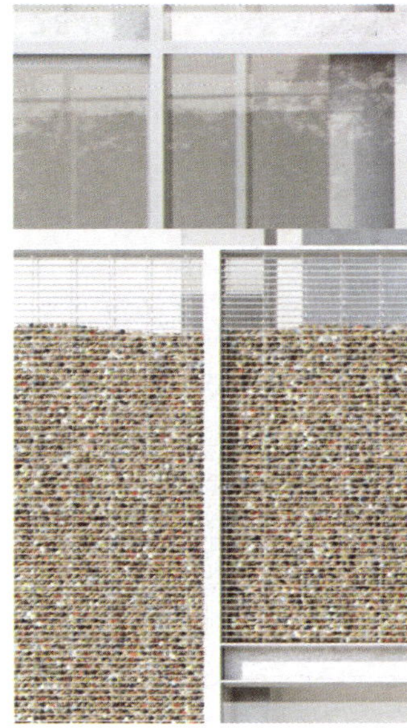

#697# AMBITION 12

CHORAL ARCHITECTURE

Saint-Ouen, rue des Quinconces - details.

#699# **AMBITION 12**

CHORAL ARCHITECTURE

Composition and materials.

Bright Grey
Gris perlé
Hellgrau

#701# **AMBITION 12**

CHORAL ARCHITECTURE

Composition and materials
Sector A.

#703# **AMBITION 12**

CHORAL ARCHITECTURE

Composition.
Colorimetry, Sector A.

#705# **AMBITION 12**

CHORAL ARCHITECTURE

Composition.
Colorimetry, Sector B.

06
07
10
09
08

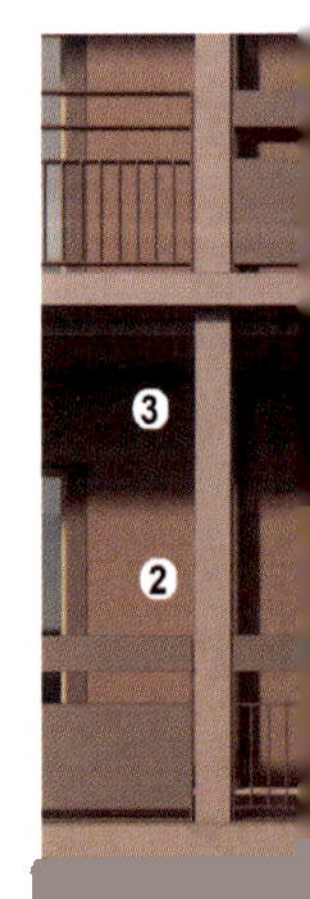
3
2

#707# AMBITION 12

CHORAL ARCHITECTURE

Composition.
Colorimetry, Sector D.

#709# AMBITION 12

CHORAL ARCHITECTURE

Composition.

Colorimetry, Sector E.

Typology_ Balconies Sector E

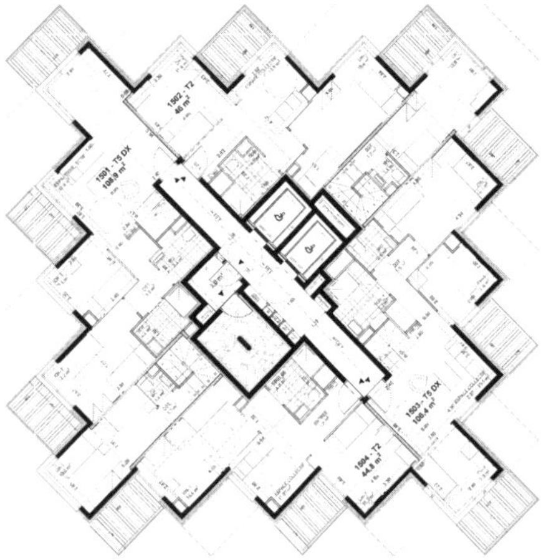

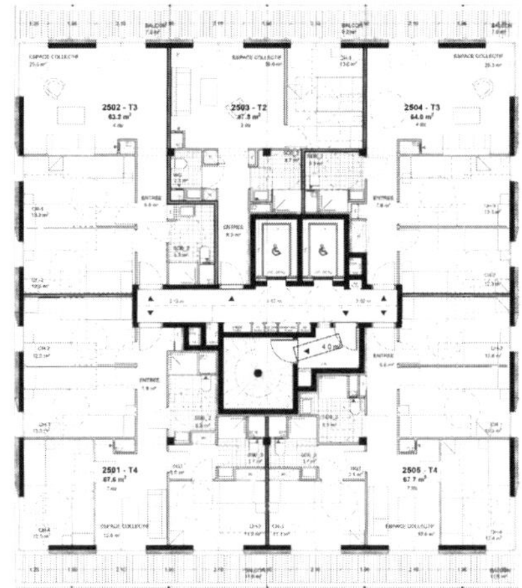

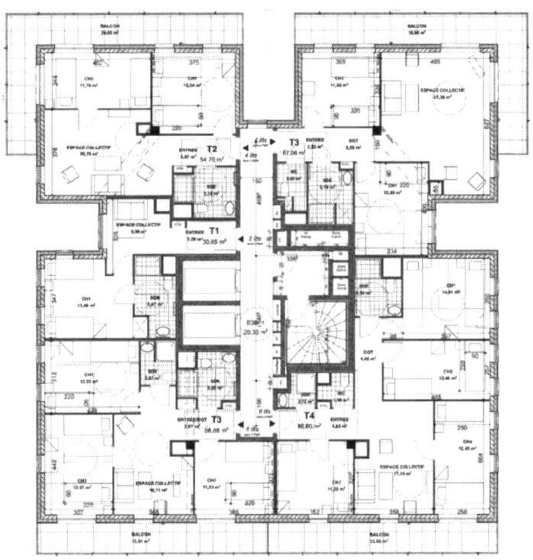

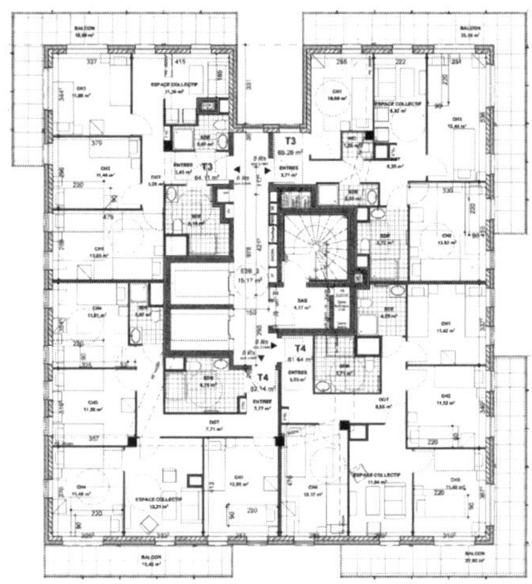

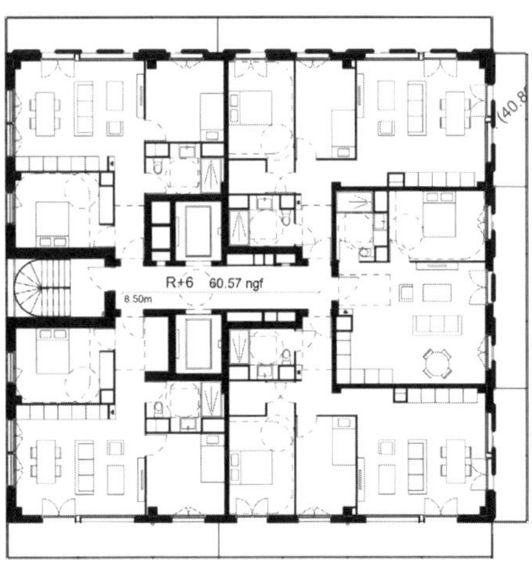

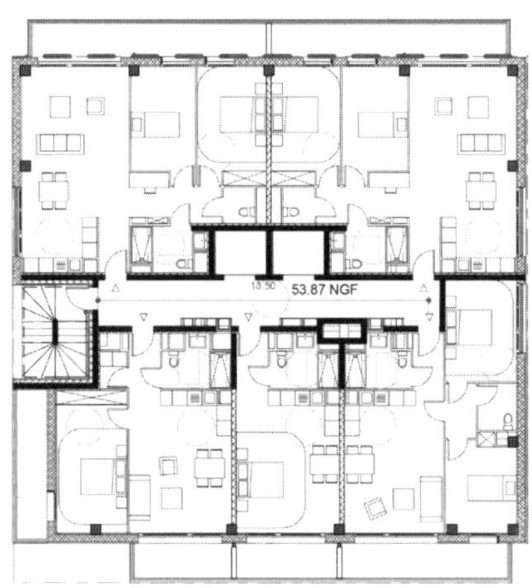

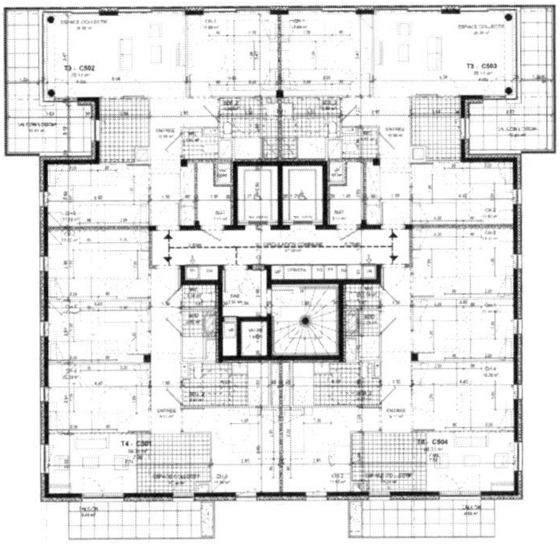

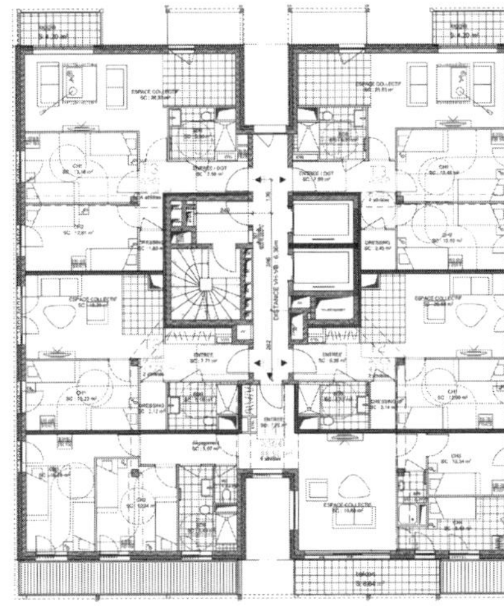

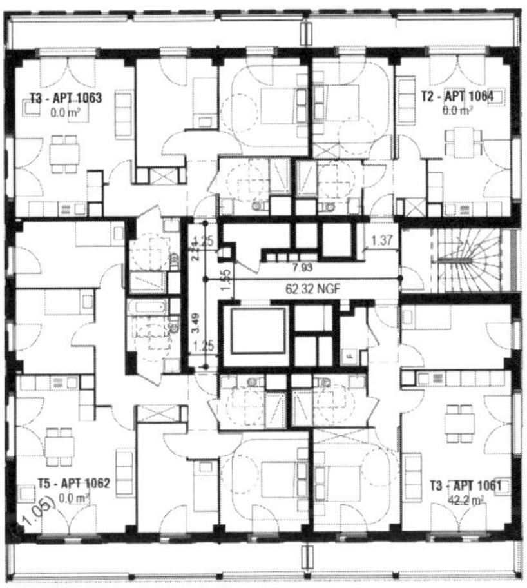
T3 - APT 1063
0.0 m²
T2 - APT 1064
0.0 m²
1.37
7.93
62.32 NGF
3.49
1.25
T5 - APT 1062
0.0 m²
T3 - APT 1061
42.2 m²

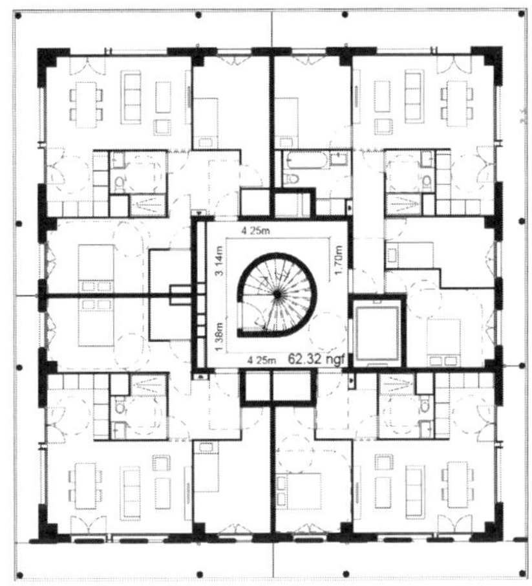
4.25m
3.14m
1.70m
1.38m
4.25m
62.32 ngf

2.29
5.67

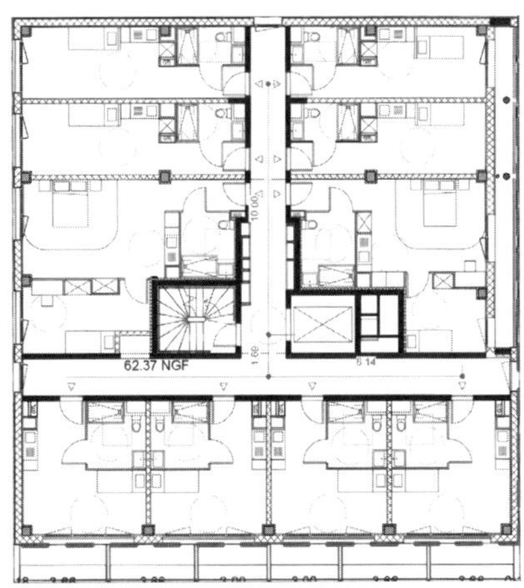
10.00
1.66
62.37 NGF
8.14

#713# AMBITION 12
CHORAL ARCHITECTURE
The Villas.

#715# **AMBITION 12**

CHORAL ARCHITECTURE

Belvederes.

#717# **AMBITION 12**

CHORAL ARCHITECTURE

Belvederes.

©GROUPEMENT ICADE

©GROUPEMENT ICADE

#719# AMBITION 12

CHORAL ARCHITECTURE

Les Quinconces.

#721# **AMBITION 12**
CHORAL ARCHITECTURE
Les Quinconces.

#723# AMBITION 12

CHORAL ARCHITECTURE

Verrières.

#725# **AMBITION 12**

CHORAL ARCHITECTURE

Universeine.

#727# AMBITION 12
CHORAL ARCHITECTURE
Universeine.

AMBITION 13

THE HEART OF THE HEART

Going "beyond the Athletes' Village" means going back in time to tell the story of the transformation of this piece of Seine-Saint-Denis with its rich industrial past, thanks to the Paris 2024 Olympic and Paralympic Games. This also means pushing back the geographical limits of this territory to observe its influence on the scale of a larger economic, social and cultural area. It's "going beyond the "moment" that the Athletes' Village constitutes in the life of this neighborhood.

Taking into consideration the ephemeral nature of the Olympic event in the design of the Village is the uniqueness of this project. Our approach also differed from previous Olympic experiences because it did not propose the construction of a Village ex nihilo but of a mixed neighborhood whose soul was already present.

This district, in fact, would have been similar to others if what was "already there" had not been exceptional: the river to which the old site turned its back while the roads of the future district will converge in its direction, the natural resources of the soil or even the Cité du Cinéma and Maxwell Hall. So many parameters which still require us to question the planning of the district as well as the "common" production of the city.

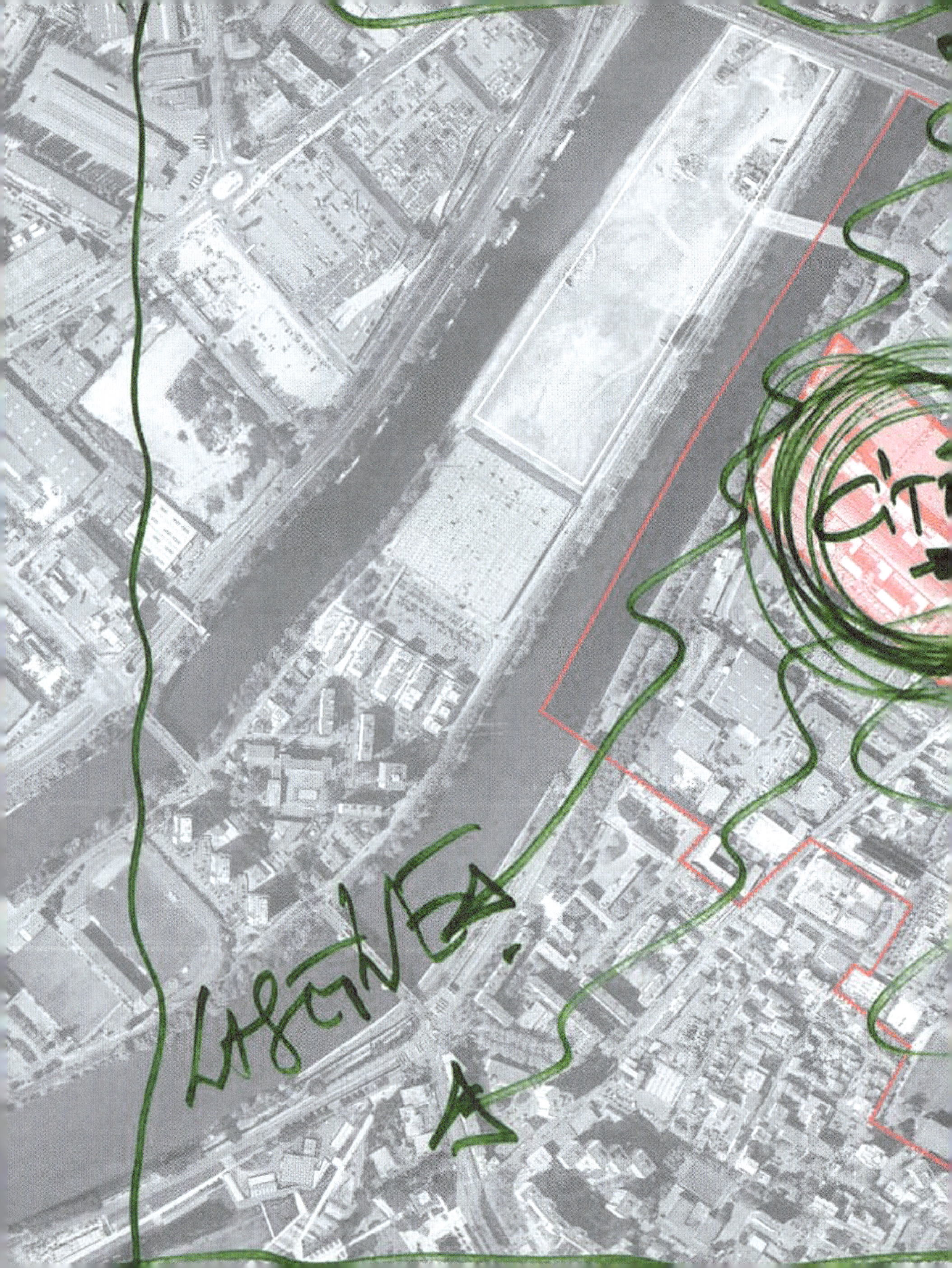

#731# AMBITION 13

THE HEART OF THE HEART

The Cité du Cinéma will make the neighborhood shine beyond itself.

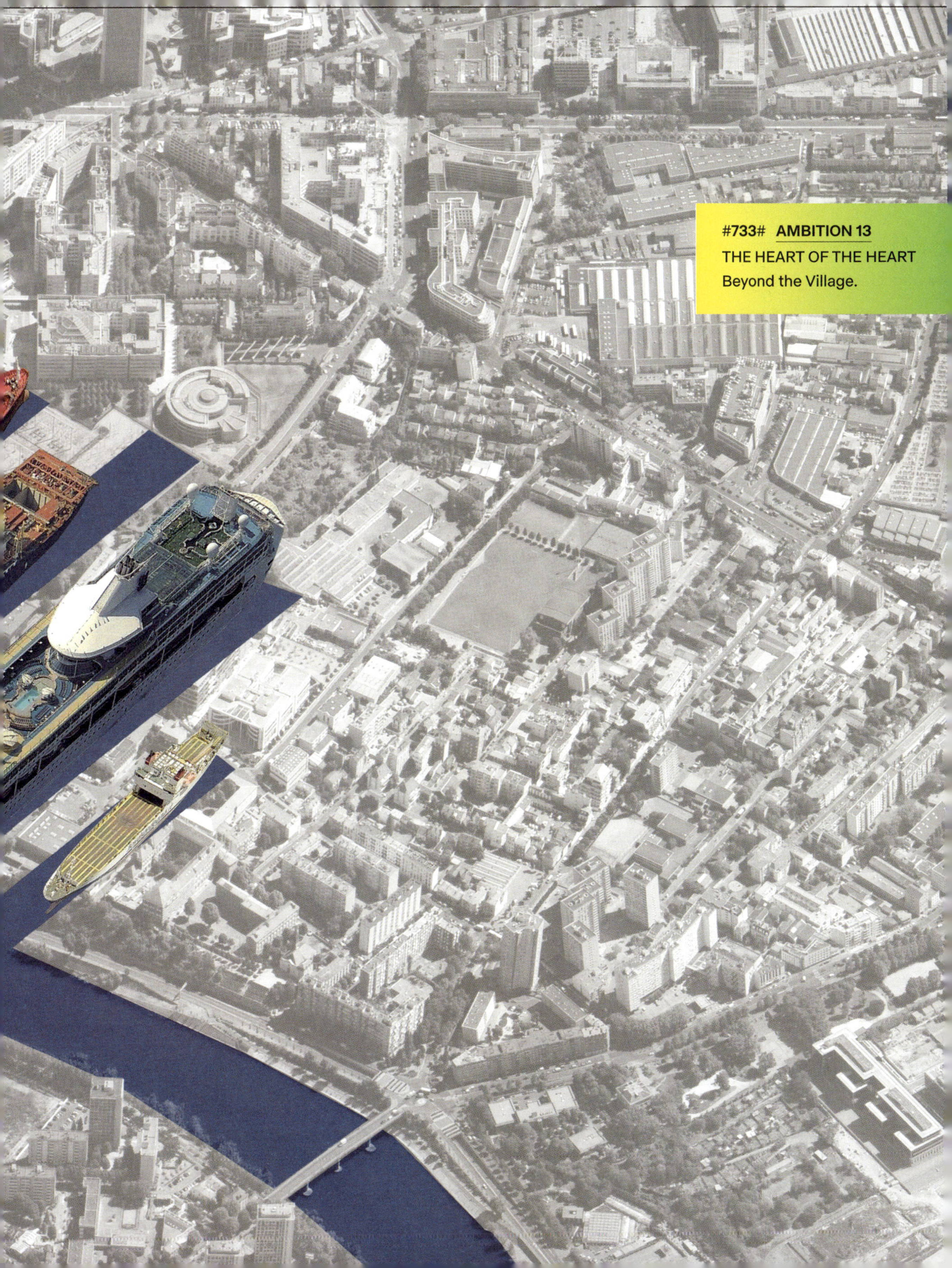

#733# **AMBITION 13**

THE HEART OF THE HEART

Beyond the Village.

#735# **AMBITION 13**

THE HEART OF THE HEART

At the heart of the district, the current Cité du Cinéma is intended to be an integral part of the legacy of the Paris Games.

It is located on the enclosed site of a former thermal power station built in 1930, which is inaccessible to the public. The fictions created by our agency transform this space into a new central facility that, in the future, will contribute to the metropolitan influence of the district, help to make Grand Paris a reality and anchor the “city-region” in the “world-city”.

#737# **AMBITION 13**

THE HEART OF THE HEART

Designing an urban square.

7 ha SEINE + 6.5 ha Ile-Saint-Denis +31 ha ZAC Outside Cité du Cinéma +6.5 ha Cité du Cinéma = 51 ha TOTAL

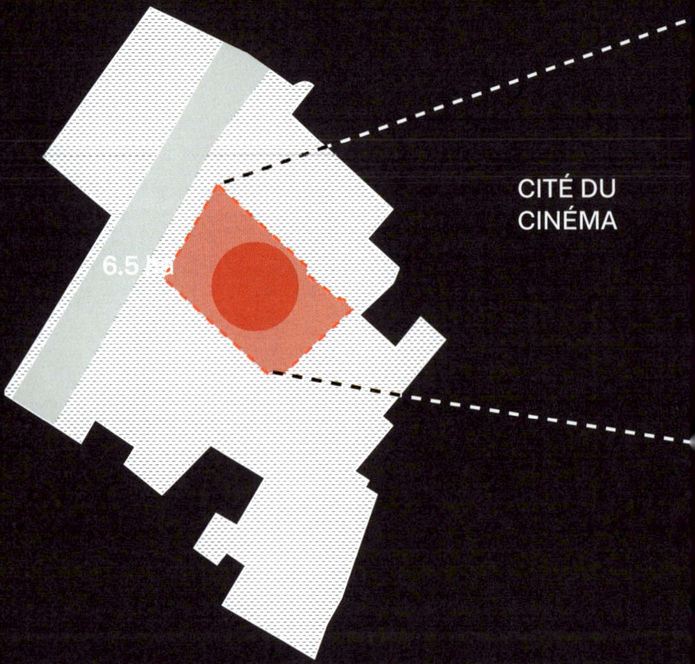

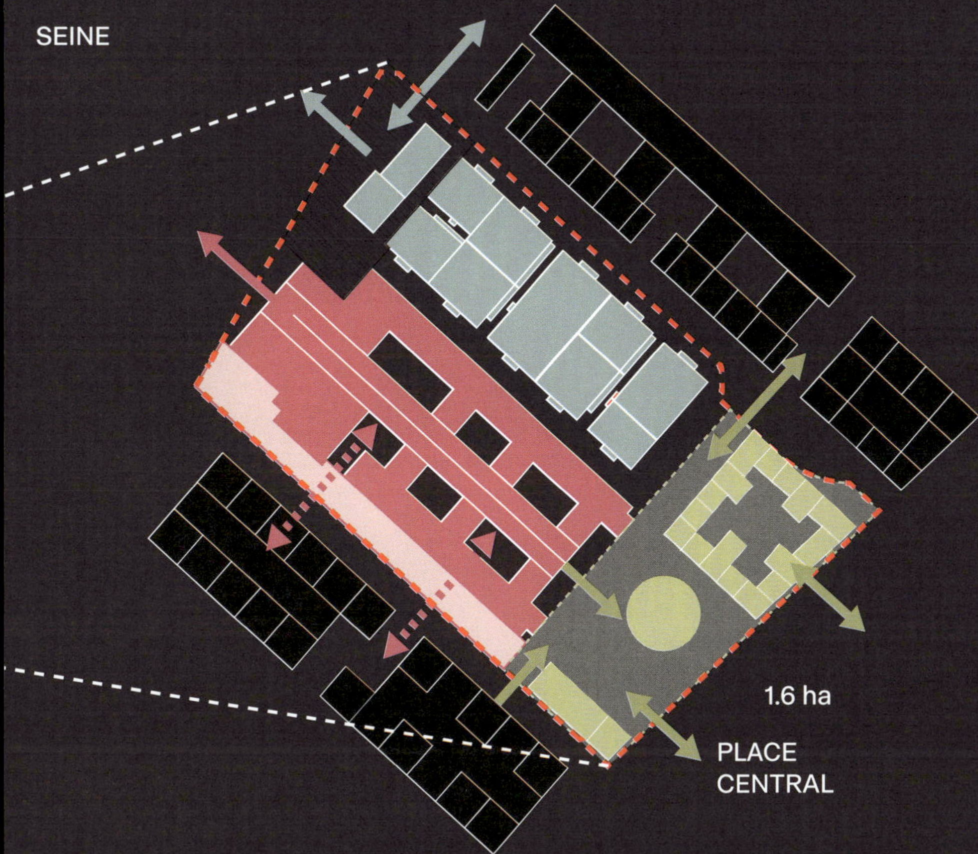

#739# **AMBITION 13**

THE HEART OF THE HEART
At the heart of the district: the Cité du Cinéma

Located on the banks of the Seine and covering almost seven hectares, the Cité du Cinéma complex needs to be re-imagined to give the district a real urban character and identity; in other words, a strong marker for the transformation of the site.

To date, it has been the "forgotten" part of the urban planning process.

How can this enclave be transformed into a major metropolitan facility, an exceptional object for the greater Seine-Saint-Denis area?

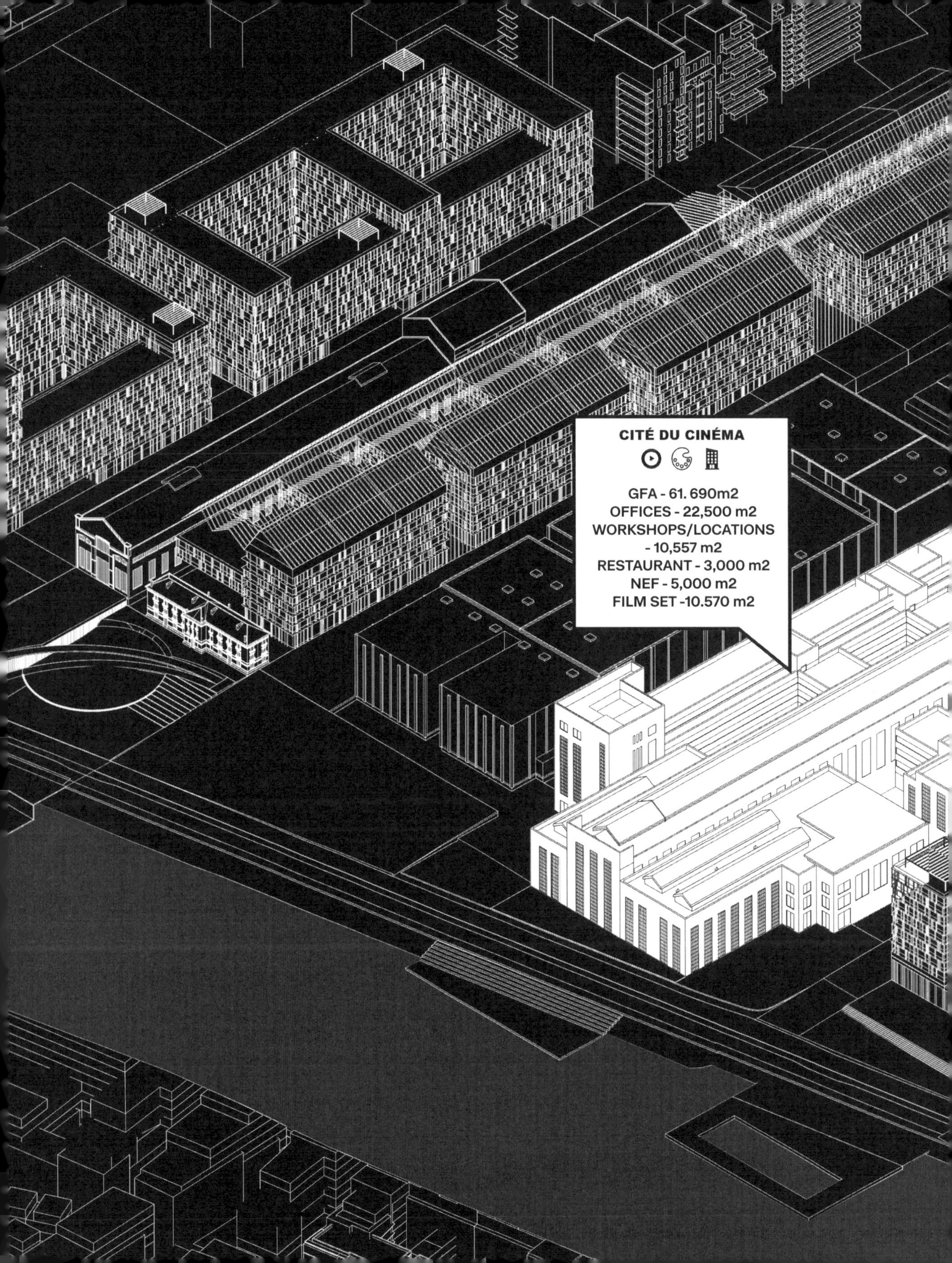
CITÉ DU CINÉMA
GFA - 61. 690m2
OFFICES - 22,500 m2
WORKSHOPS/LOCATIONS
- 10,557 m2
RESTAURANT - 3,000 m2
NEF - 5,000 m2
FILM SET -10.570 m2

#741# AMBITION 13
THE HEART OF THE HEART
Cité du Cinéma.

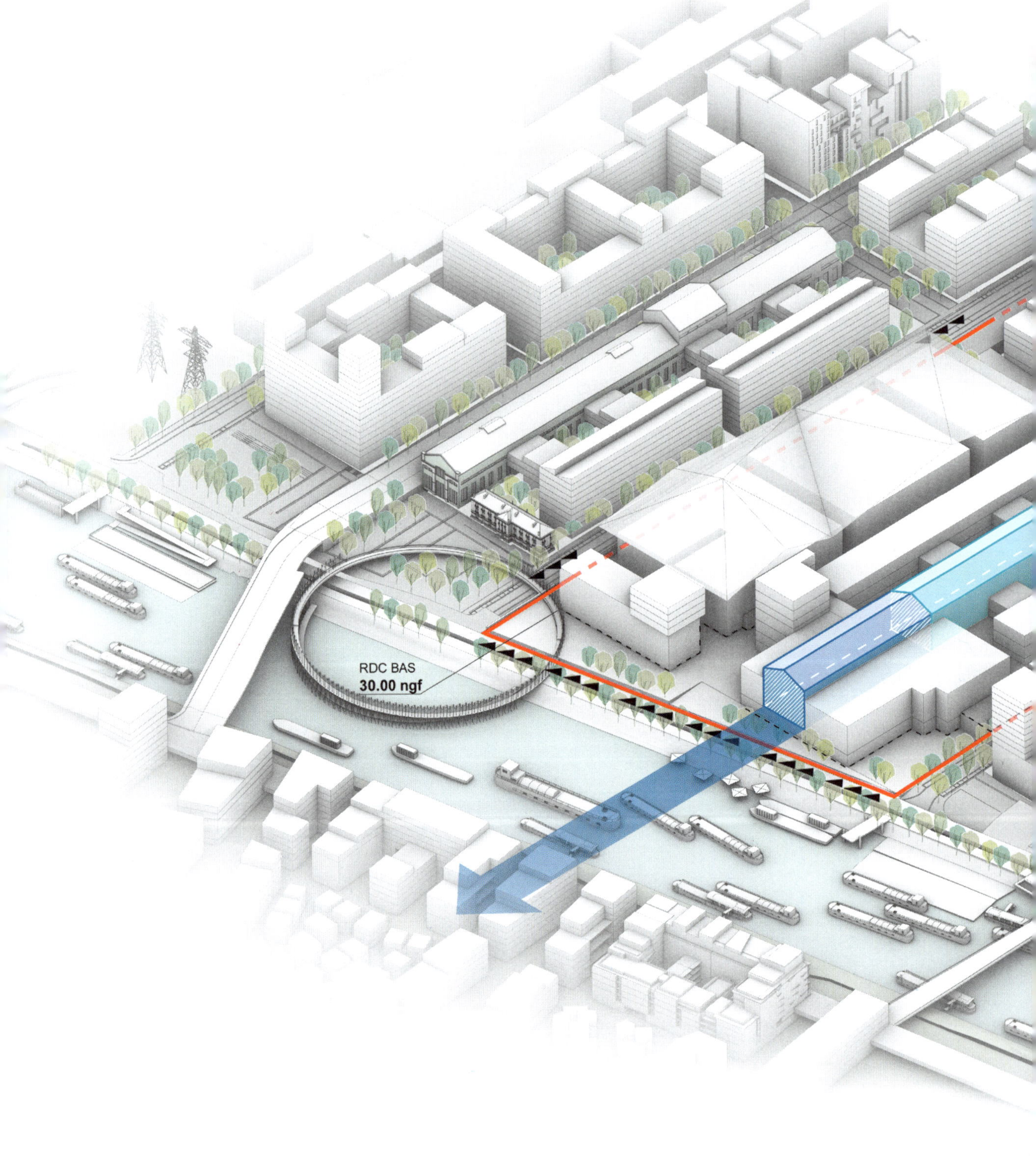
RDC BAS
30.00 ngf

#743# AMBITION 13

THE HEART OF THE HEART

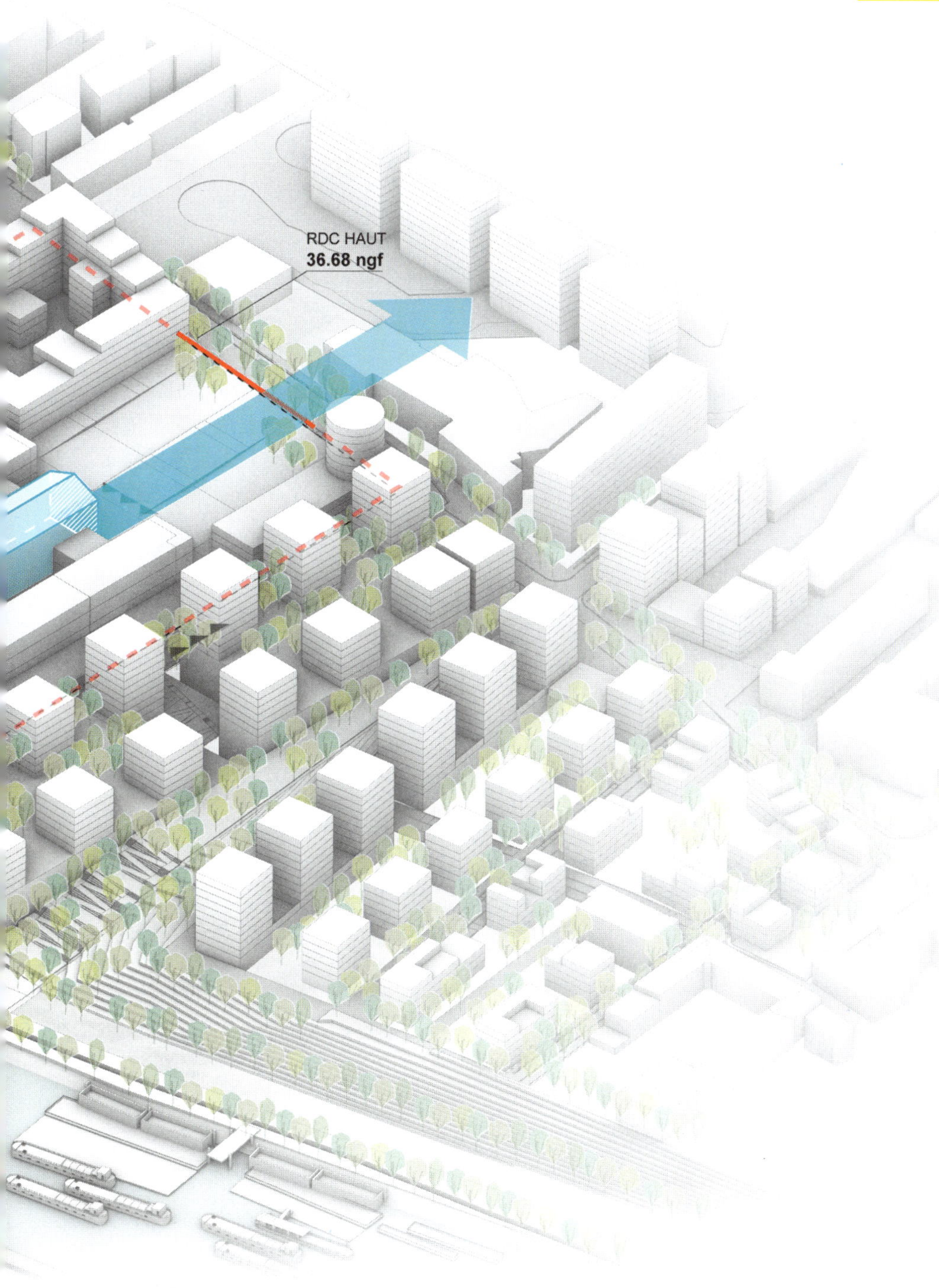

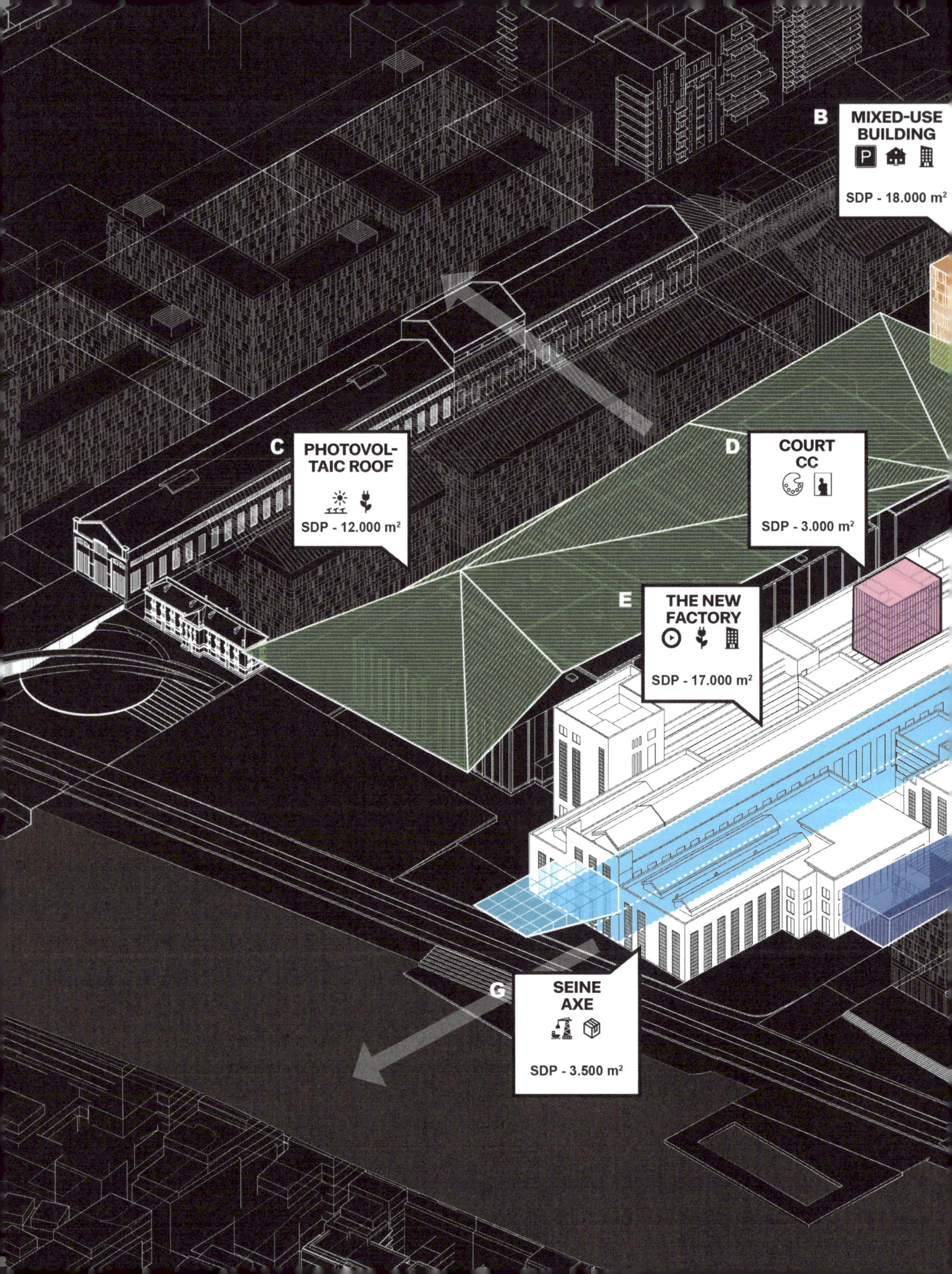

B
MIXED-USE BUILDING
SDP - 18.000 m²
C
PHOTOVOL-TAIC ROOF
SDP - 12.000 m²
D
COURT CC
SDP - 3.000 m²
E
THE NEW FACTORY
SDP - 17.000 m²
G
SEINE AXE
SDP - 3.500 m²

#745# AMBITION 13
THE HEART OF THE HEART
Cité du Cinéma.

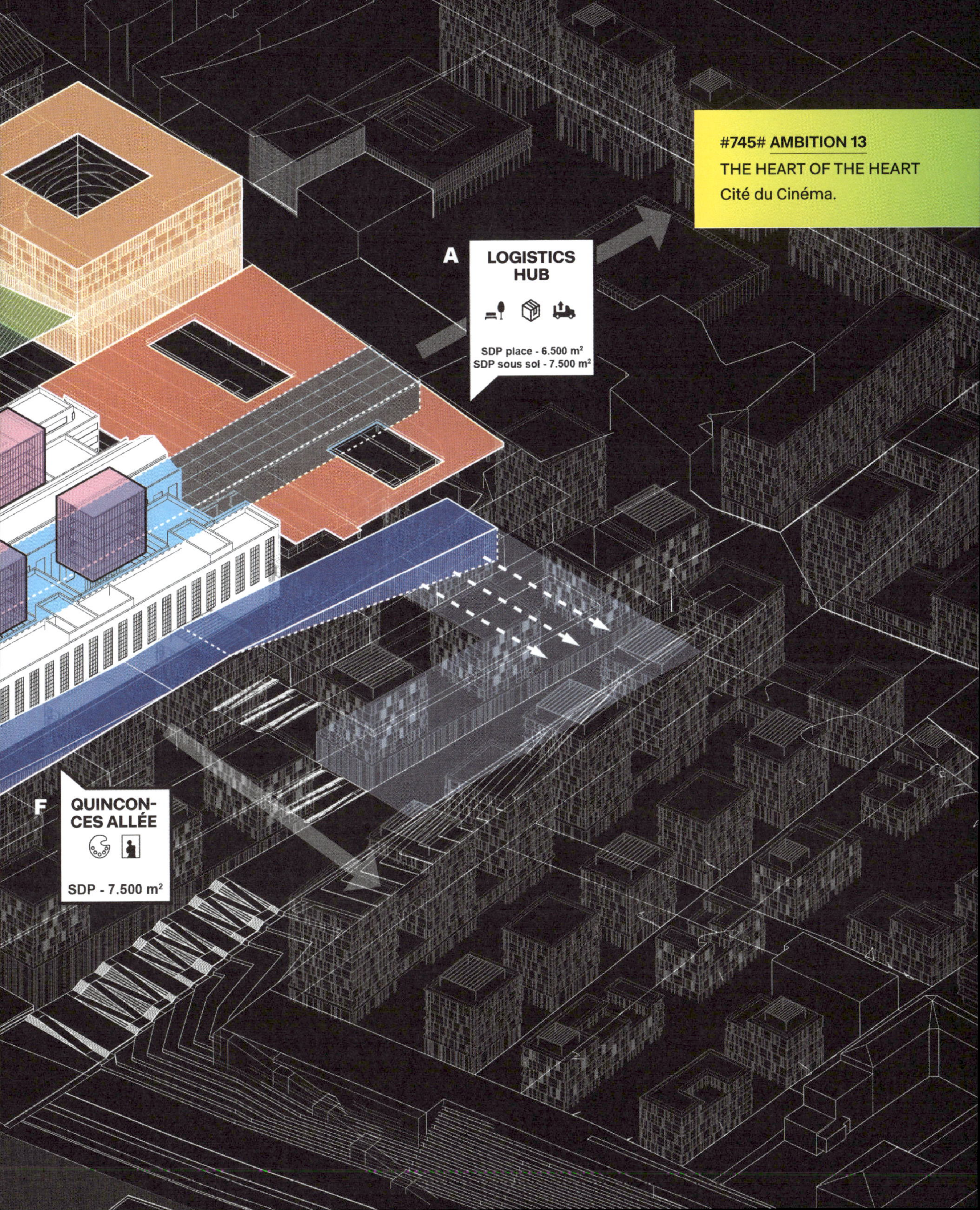

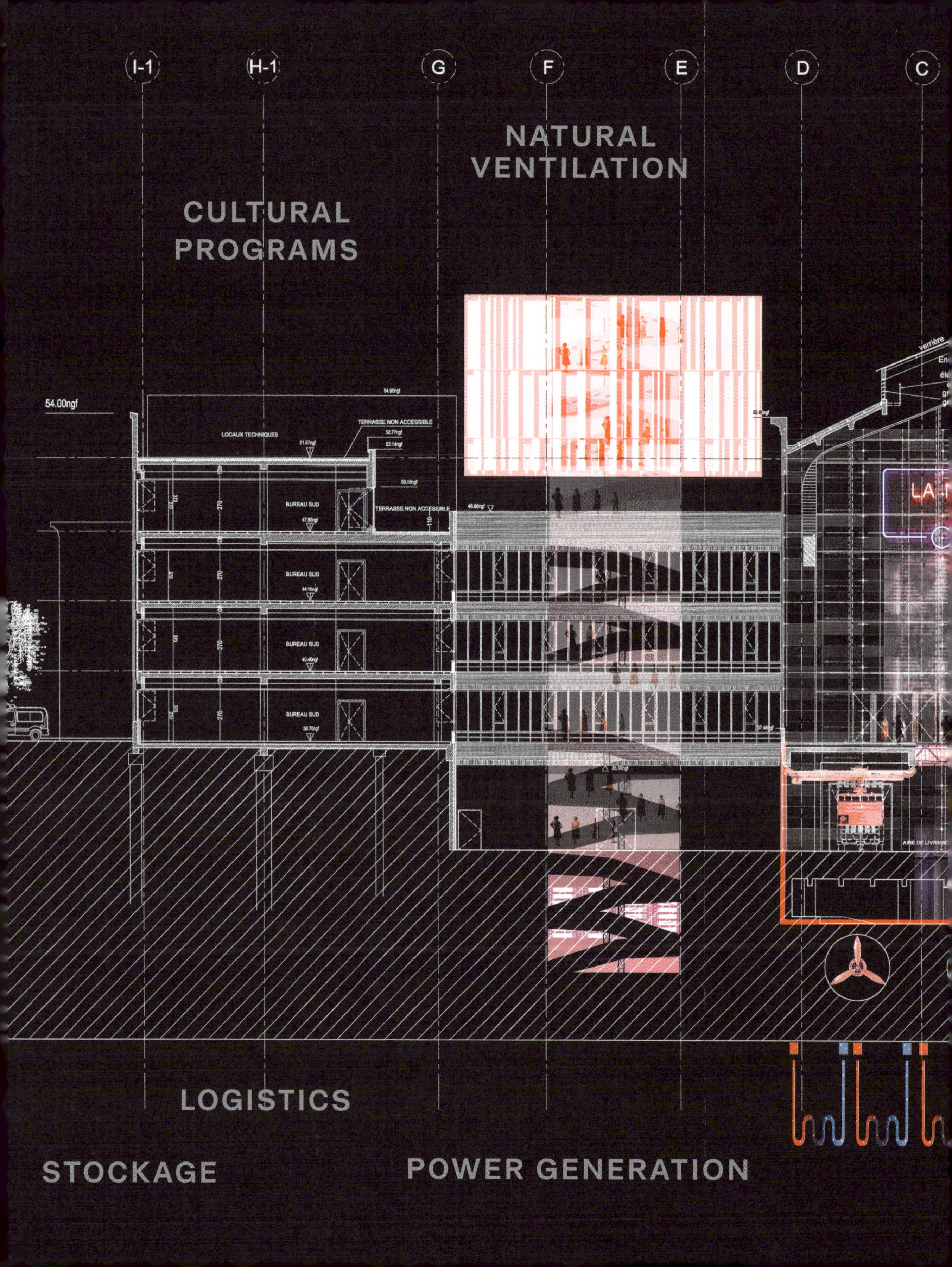

I-1
H-1
G
F
E
D
C
NATURAL VENTILATION
CULTURAL PROGRAMS
54.00ngf
LOCAUX TECHNIQUES
TERRASSE NON ACCESSIBLE
TERRASSE NON ACCESSIBLE
BUREAU SUD
BUREAU SUD
BUREAU SUD
BUREAU SUD
LOGISTICS
STOCKAGE
POWER GENERATION

#747# AMBITION 13
THE HEART OF THE HEART
Cité du Cinéma.

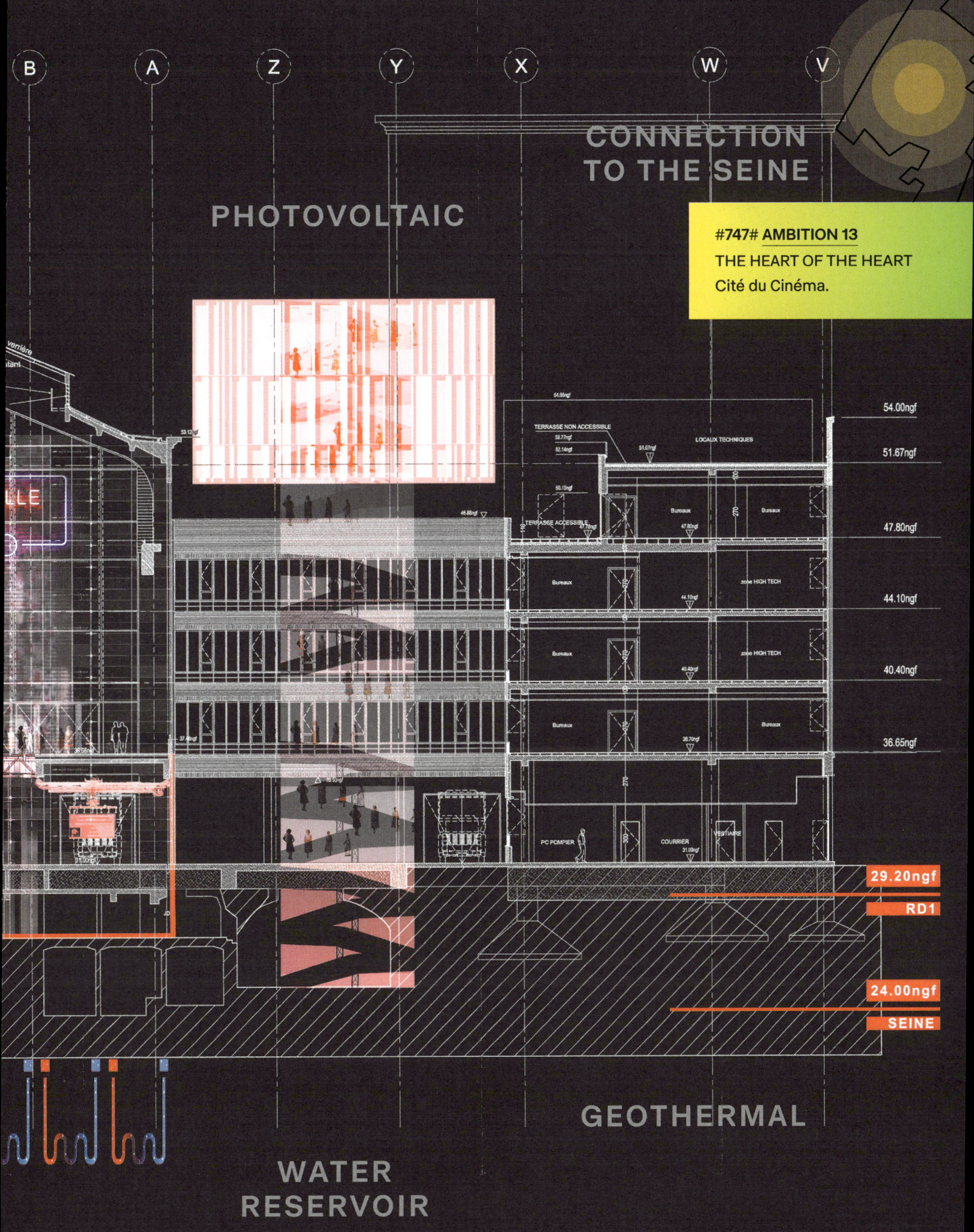

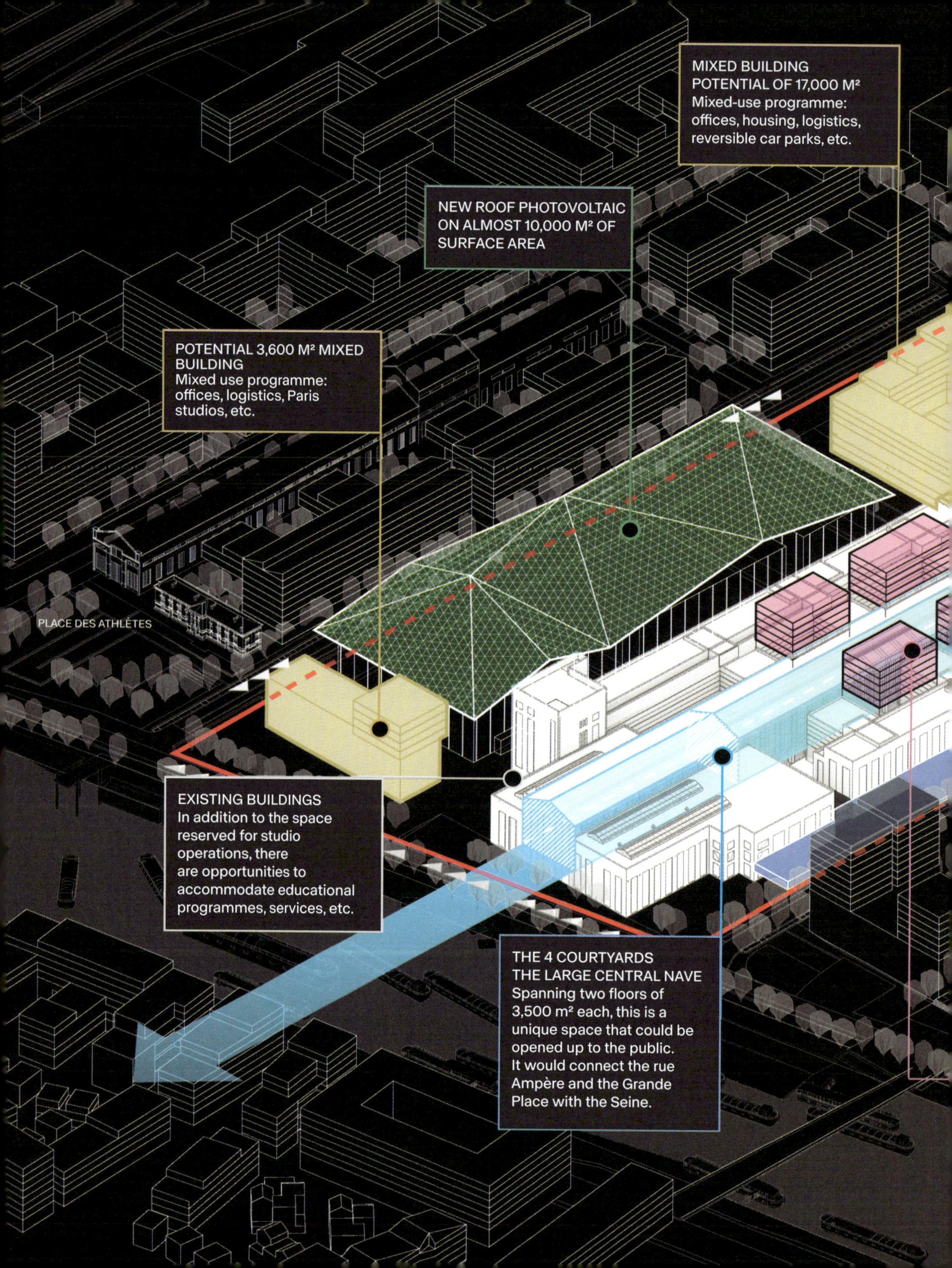
MIXED BUILDING POTENTIAL OF 17,000 M²
Mixed-use programme: offices, housing, logistics, reversible car parks, etc.
NEW ROOF PHOTOVOLTAIC ON ALMOST 10,000 M² OF SURFACE AREA
POTENTIAL 3,600 M² MIXED BUILDING
Mixed use programme: offices, logistics, Paris studios, etc.
PLACE DES ATHLÈTES
EXISTING BUILDINGS
In addition to the space reserved for studio operations, there are opportunities to accommodate educational programmes, services, etc.
THE 4 COURTYARDS
THE LARGE CENTRAL NAVE
Spanning two floors of 3,500 m² each, this is a unique space that could be opened up to the public. It would connect the rue Ampère and the Grande Place with the Seine.

#749# AMBITION 13

THE HEART OF THE HEART

From one city to another

The transformation of the Cité du Cinéma, which is the subject of fictions here, will be an opportunity for a large project open to the public. From reclaiming underground parking lots to reprogramming this former thermal power plant, to the construction of new mixed-use buildings or the installation of a logistics platform for the neighborhood, the possibilities are numerous.

In the large nave, for example, almost twice as long as that of the Tate Modern in London, various cultural, sports, and educational programs could be accommodated. Residents would also can reclaim a unique industrial heritage and cross the nave to reach the waterfront.

Like the esplanade of the Centre Pompidou, which it shares the shape and dimensions with, the square becomes a sloping forecourt that stages the Cité du Cinéma and creates a space open to the city, a large public square.

In addition to existing programs - the Louis Lumière film school, production studios, and offices - the site has a strong potential for developing new programs.

The first "gesture" of the project aims, while maintaining existing functions, to create a unique place in the metropolis combining arts and sports, private and public, those from here and those from elsewhere.

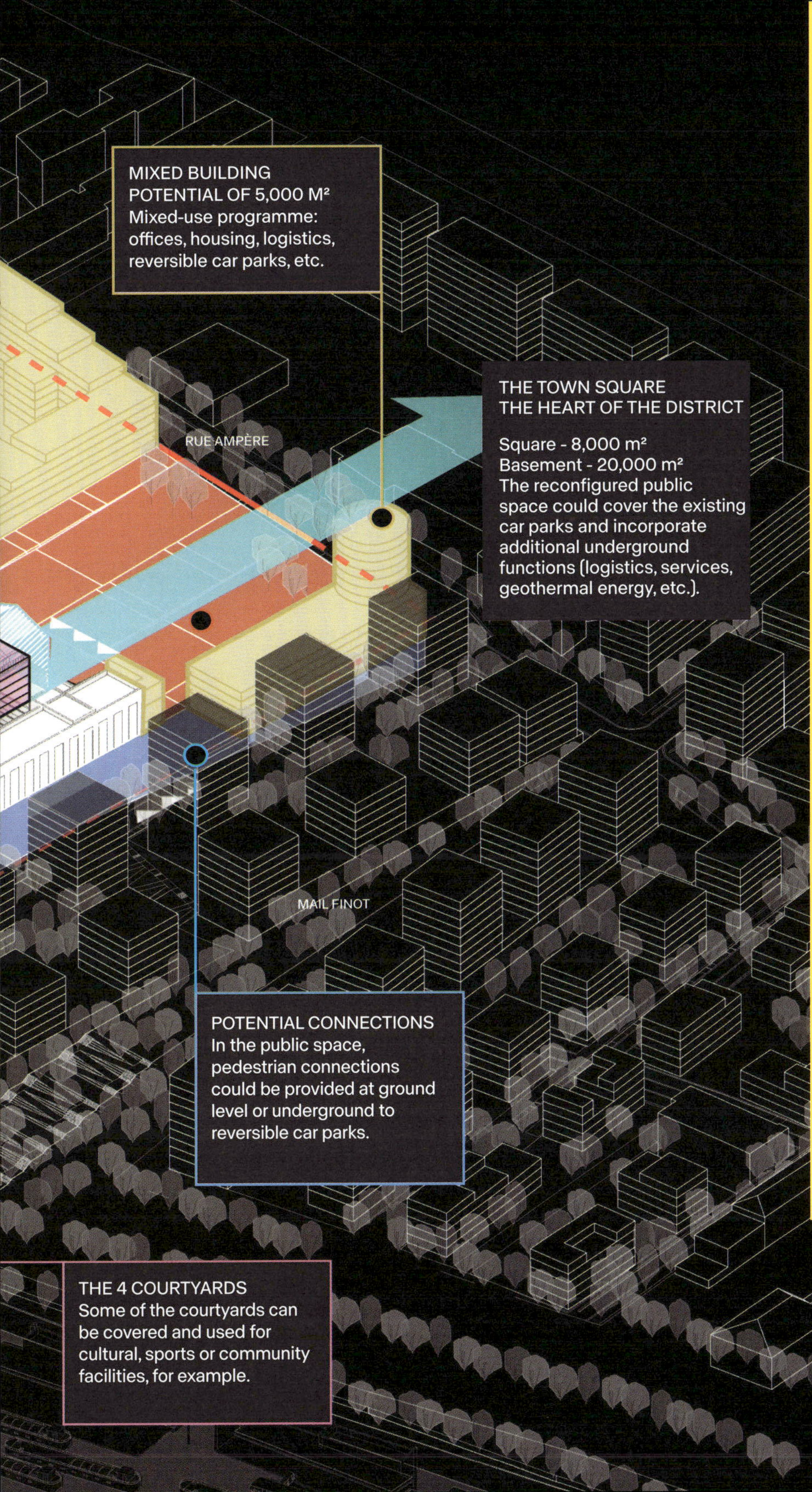

#751# AMBITION 13

THE HEART OF THE HEART

Cité du Cinéma.

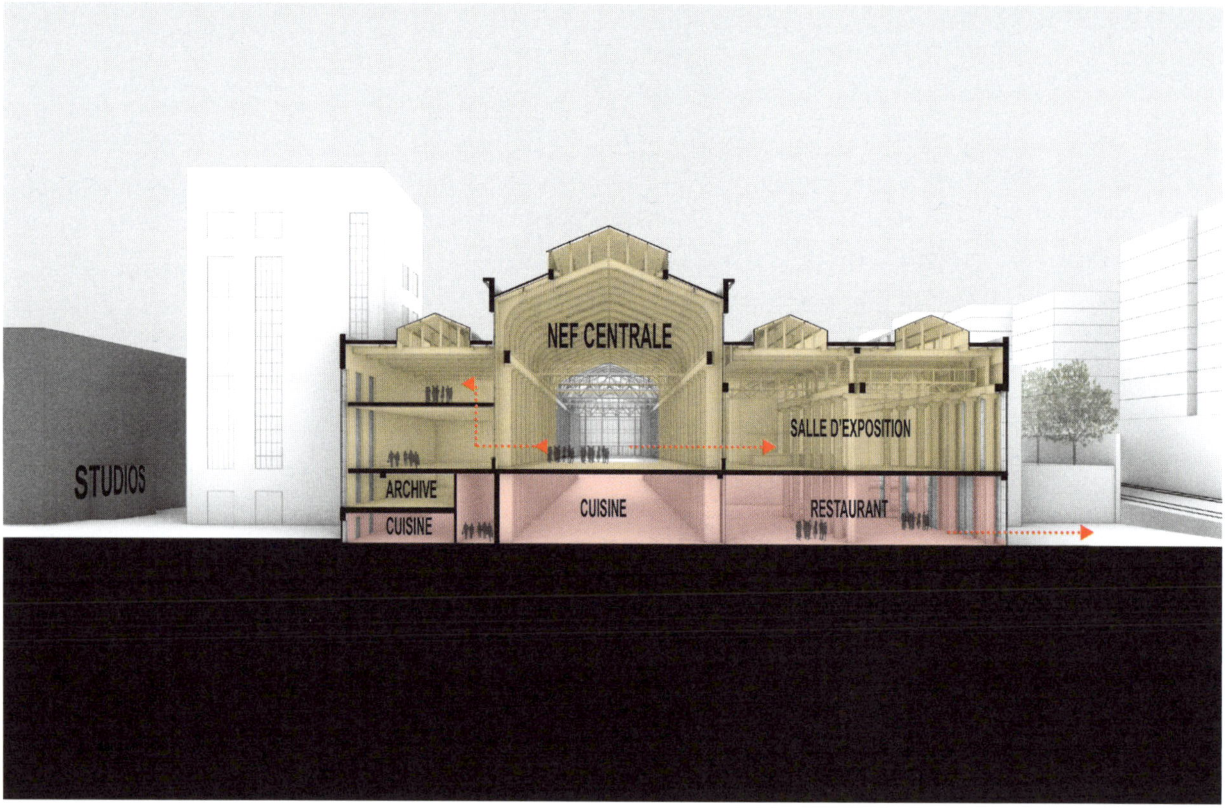
NEF CENTRALE
SALLE D'EXPOSITION
STUDIOS
ARCHIVE
CUISINE
CUISINE
RESTAURANT

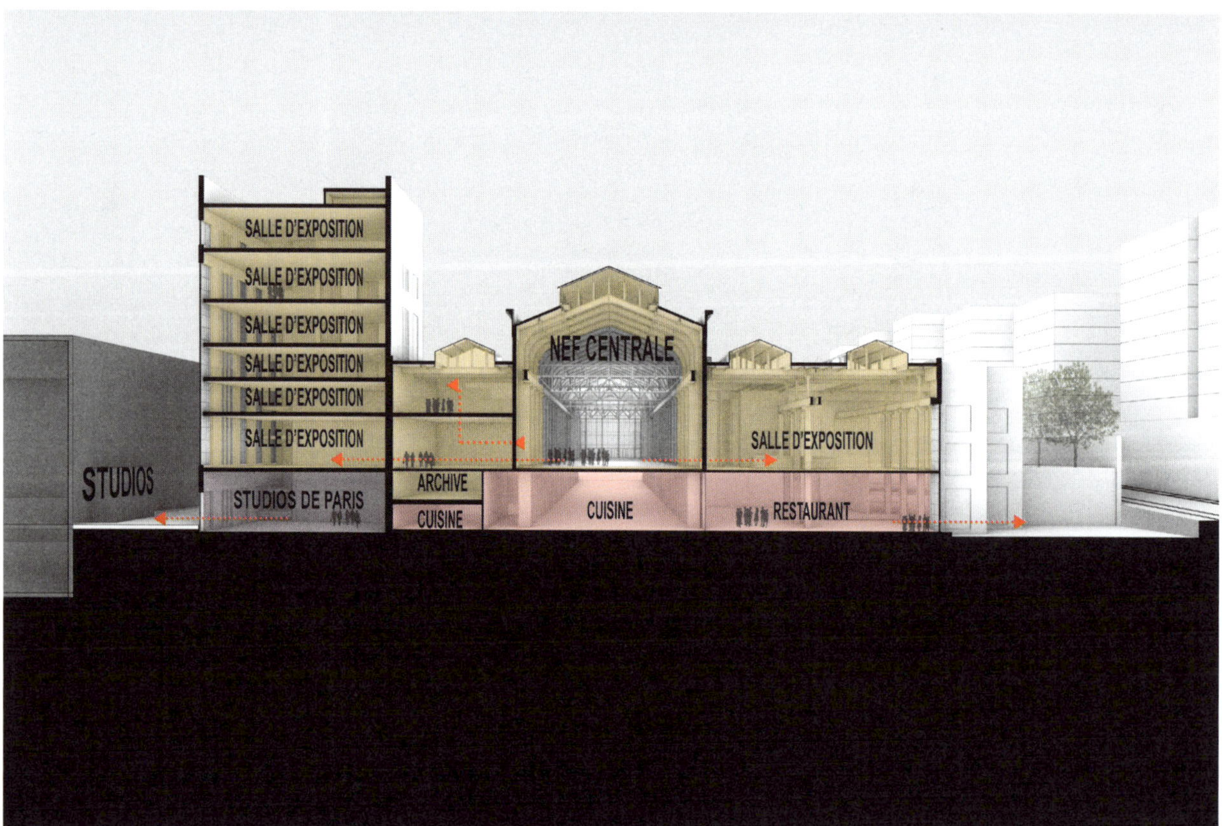
SALLE D'EXPOSITION
SALLE D'EXPOSITION
SALLE D'EXPOSITION
SALLE D'EXPOSITION
SALLE D'EXPOSITION
SALLE D'EXPOSITION
NEF CENTRALE
SALLE D'EXPOSITION
STUDIOS
STUDIOS DE PARIS
ARCHIVE
CUISINE
CUISINE
RESTAURANT

#753# AMBITION 13

THE HEART OF THE HEART

Cross-sections.

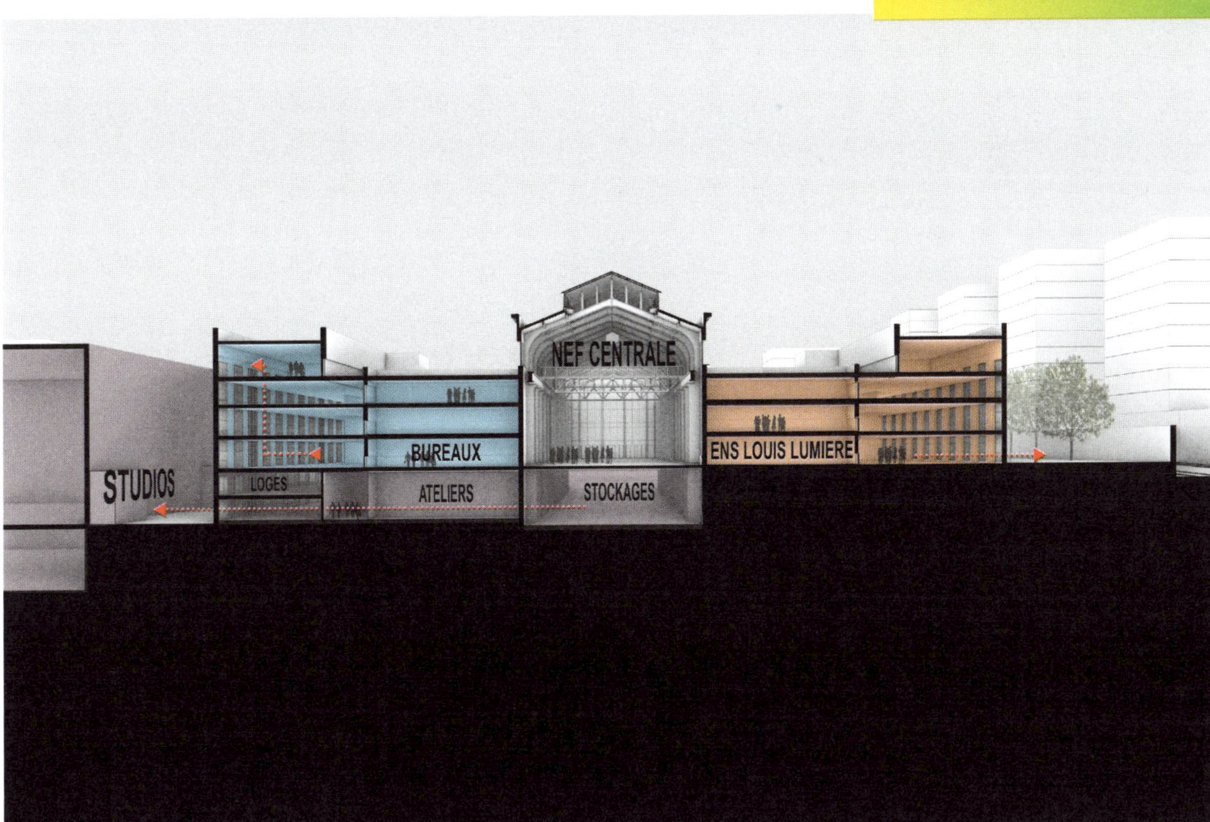

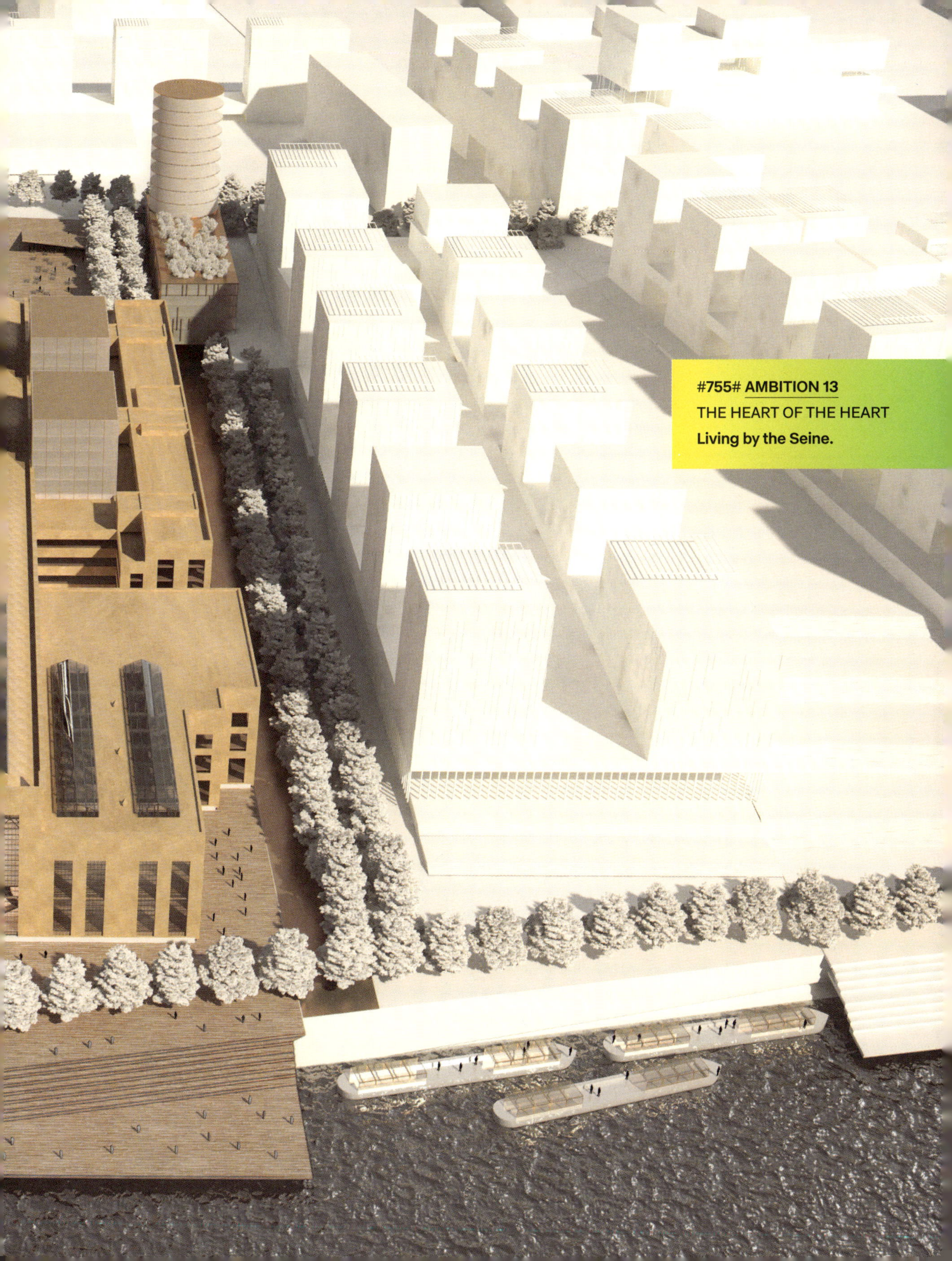

#755# AMBITION 13
THE HEART OF THE HEART
Living by the Seine.

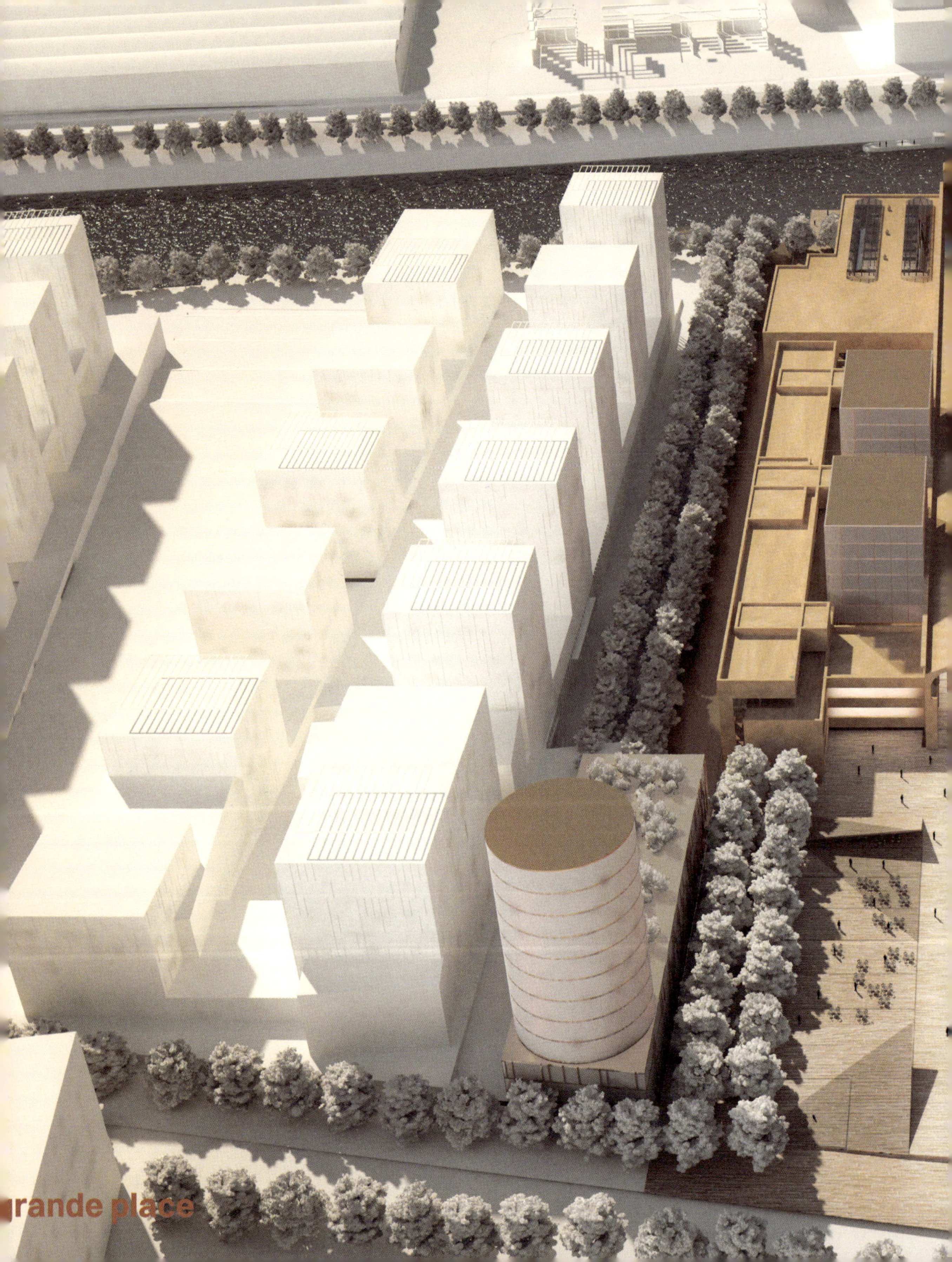

rande place

#757# **AMBITION 13**

THE HEART OF THE HEART

Living by the Seine.

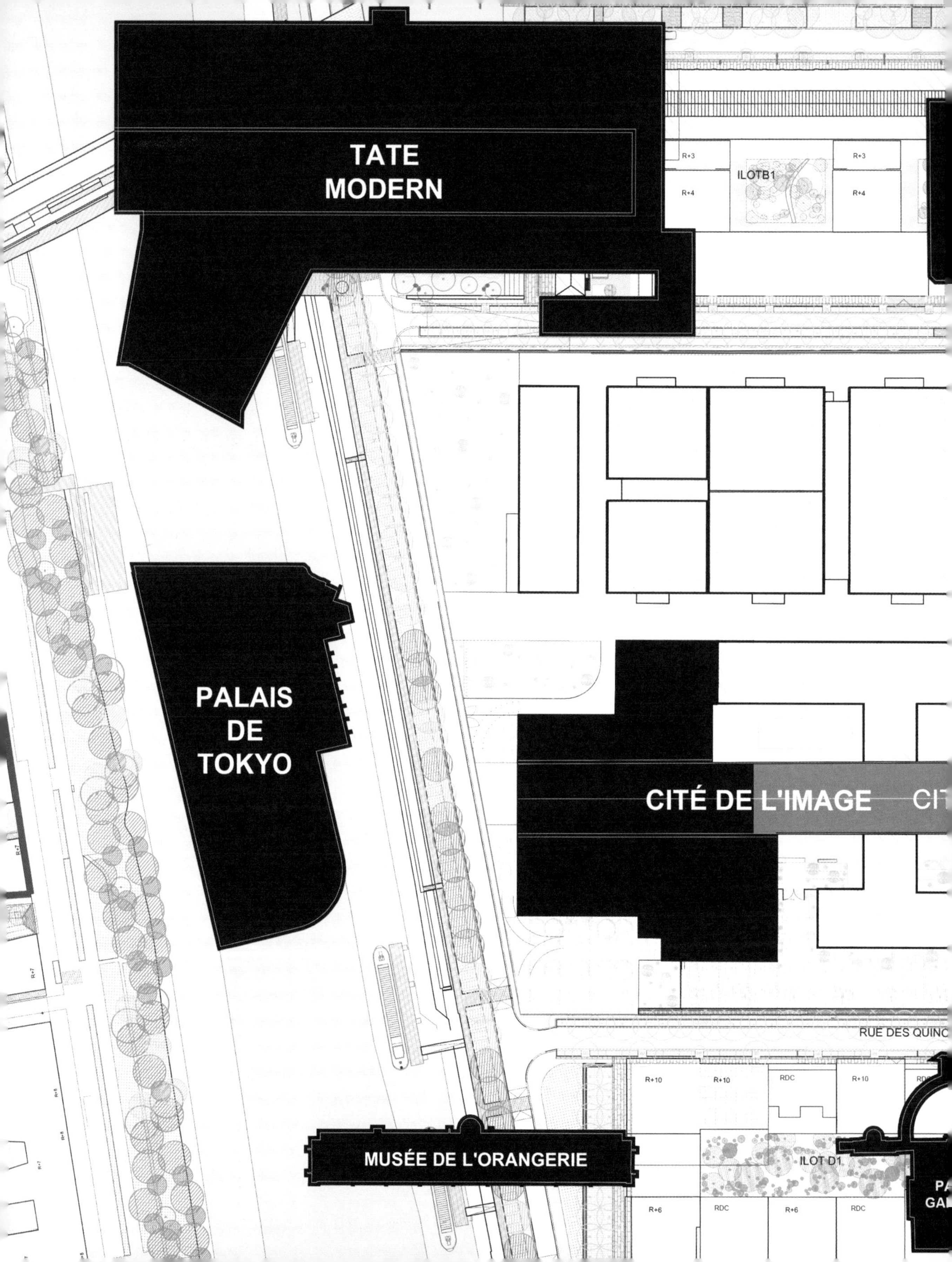
TATE
MODERN
R+3
ILOTB1
R+3
R+4
R+4
PALAIS
DE
TOKYO
CITÉ DE L'IMAGE
RUE DES QUINC
R+10
R+10
RDC
R+10
ILOT D1
MUSÉE DE L'ORANGERIE
R+6
RDC
R+6
RDC

#759# AMBITION 13
THE HEART OF THE HEART
Comparing exhibition spaces.

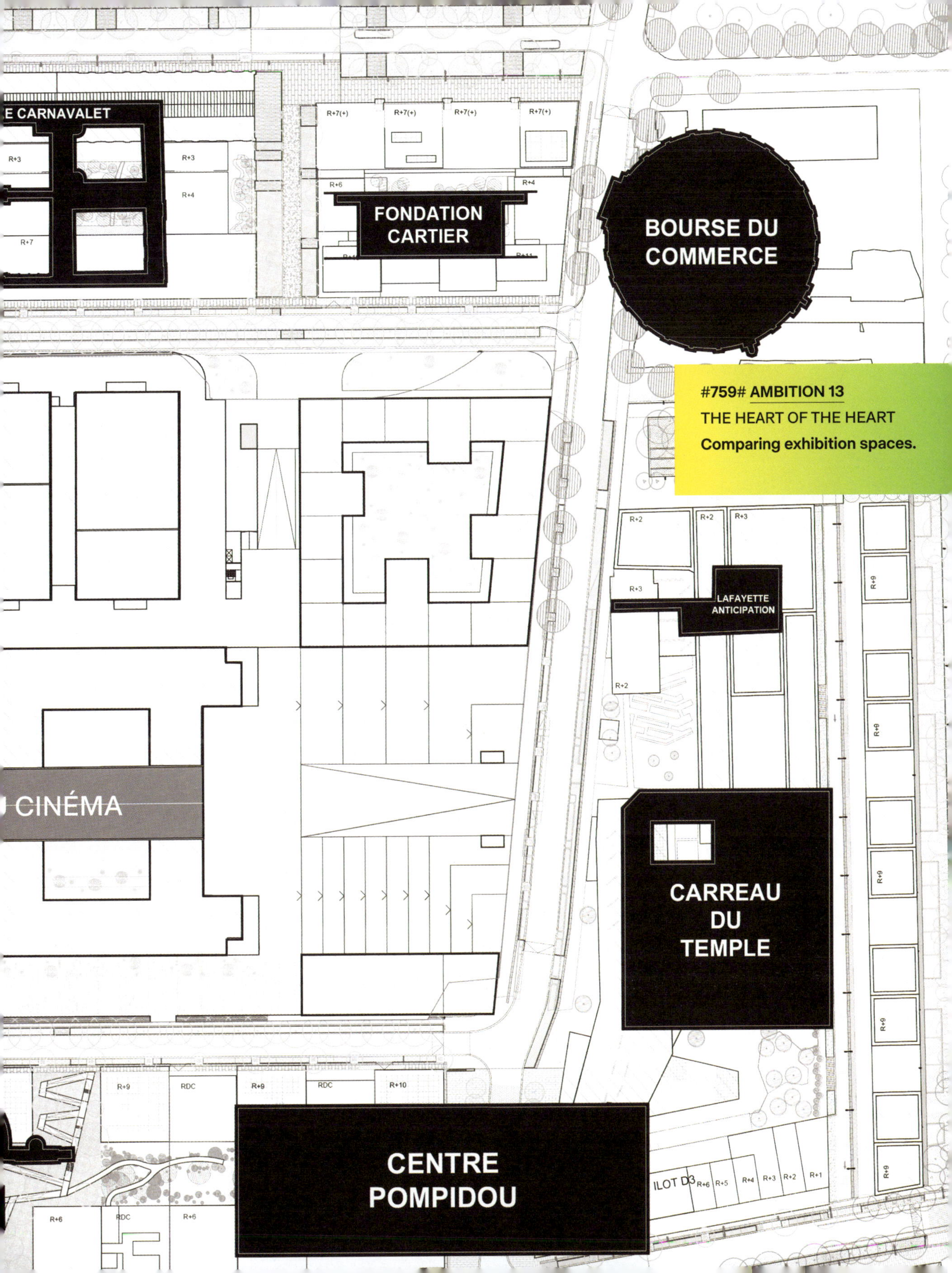

#761# AMBITION 13

THE HEART OF THE HEART

The great sports hall.

#763# **AMBITION 13**

THE HEART OF THE HEART

The great nave of culture.

#765# AMBITION 13

THE HEART OF THE HEART

The great nave of culture.

a village and its double

#767#

Postace

Dominique Perrault

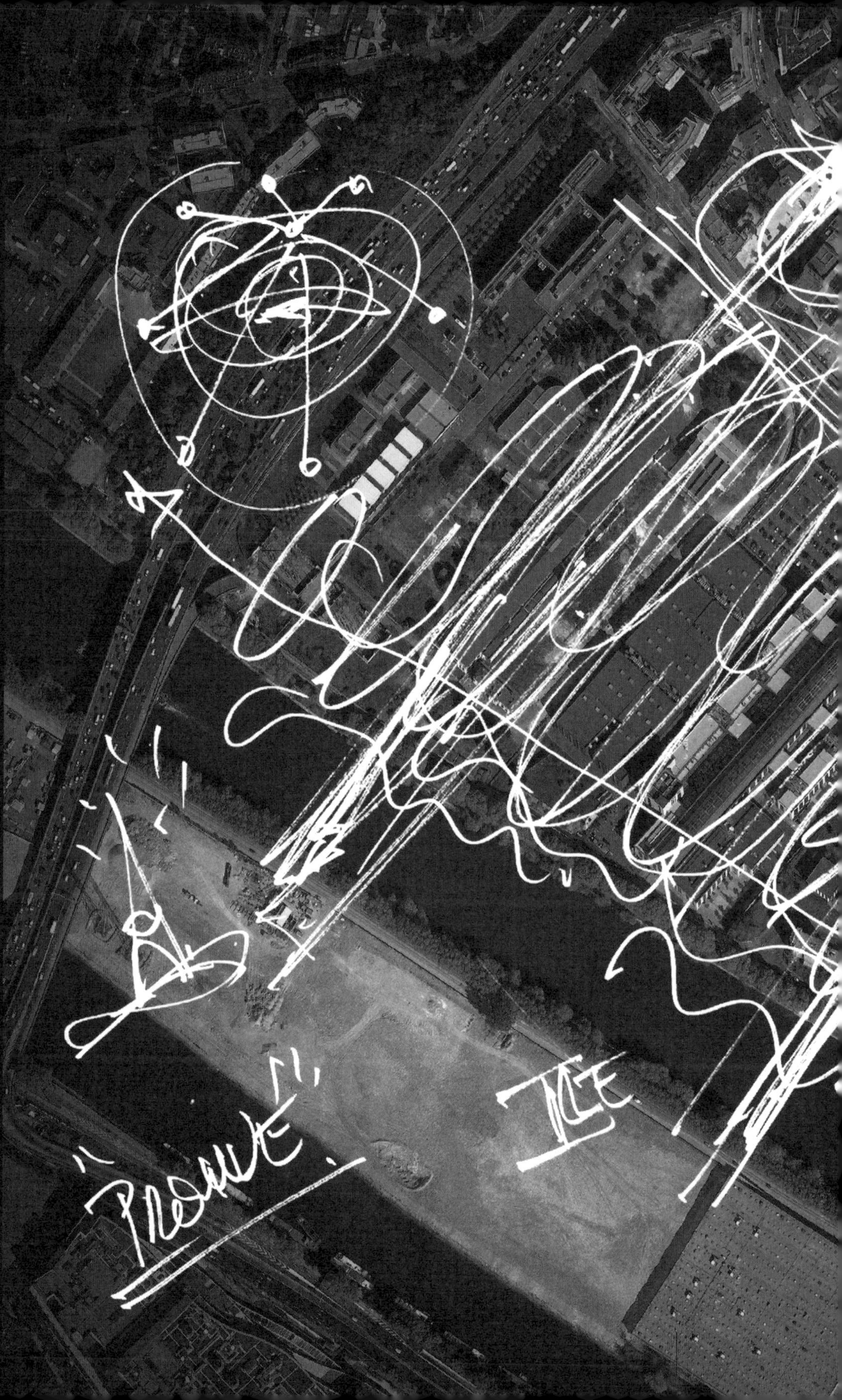

#769#

Athletes' Village, Paris 2024 Olympic and Paralympic Games
Sketch by Dominique Perrault

a village and its double

Dominique Perrault

The title "Urbanism, a manual" evokes a précis of biology.

The Village encodes two heredities: the site proper – its geography, history, what was already there – and my past research on the metropolis.

The manual augments the biological material of the Village with drawings, collages, maps, and models. Its genome and its intellectual matrix determine the first level of heredity. The second heredity is the one that this entirely new district is going to exert on the cellular tissue that receives it. I am speaking of its programming language.

The heredity of the Village plays its own partition in the construction of the metropolis. The ambivalence of the term seems to flow from a double bind contained in the very fact of inheriting, i.e., to conserver what one has received and at the same time to take ownership of it. One only really acquires something by taking hold of it. The influence of a heritage extends beyond itself. To confine the Village within the development of a few hectares would be to place blinders on its view of things, and to imagine the metropolis as merely a mosaic of hermetic projects. The Village is not a collector's piece.

Every heritage is situated at the interface of two heredities, the one of the transmitter and the one of the receiver. In the specific case of the Village, the synthesis of the two can only function if urbanism and the public authorities are integrated - the integration of vision and planning of the two cultures involved in the project. We observe a deficiency on the part of public authorities on the subject. The lack of planning in a country that in the past excelled in this domain is symptomatic. Thus, to avoid compromising the heritage of the Village, the state must rediscover its own heritage to avoid in turn compromising the heritage of the Village.

Urbanism and planning require wide-ranging consideration of the physiology of the territory of the city, in a rapport with its organicity and its growth. Time exerts its effects on every place where something lives. The city and the territory impose patience.

The Master plan and guide that we developed envisages a completely new district of the city for the region of Ile de France but this vision cannot be achieved without adequate public planning to meet the challenges involved.

Hence, arises the question of the very dimensions and meaning that we wish to give to the notion of heritage. Without a vision, neither the Village nor the possible synergies developed between it and its territory will be achieved. It seems to me that the Village even raises the question of the Greater Paris project itself: is the state counting on the development programs and infrastructure to spontaneously generate a coherent territory without further planning?

From the Village project's inception, we explained the necessity to place id within the extended system of relations, linked with all the other major projects under development in its area of influence. But we were not heard or understood. And yet this is precisely where heritage comes into play. A project of this breadth must participate in a broader territorial and national vision. Here we are talking about what in twenty years will be an El Dorado for the Ile-de-France.

We are in a shrunken geography- for now. From the Porte de la Chapelle to the Olympic and Paralympic site in Saint-Denis–Saint-Ouen, we identified dozens of projects. Each one is being developed with an inward focus, thereby forming an archipelago. The notion of shared city and metropolis planning is not achieving unity. The future metropolitan district of the Village was imagined as a piece of the city open to its environment and available for any mutation, as both an encoding and receptive urbanism. But this urban rootstock must be extracted from its pot and replanted in the ground.

Urbanism intervenes on the urban with its own material. The logic must be precise, structuring, and in a permanently unfinished state. If this process becomes frozen, something may decline or collapse. This constantly open and eternally unfinished work is a sign of robustness. In urbanism, like in architecture, nothing can be definitively designed or written. A district, like a building, must be able to function in the present and to be perceptively adapted to changing uses.

The program for the Village is neither linear nor unidirectional. Like an open book, it engenders an identity that is both perfectly defined and freely interpretable. The fictions and hypotheses developed in this manual of urbanism envisage the possibilities encoded in the genes of the future district.

The current state must never be separated from its potential. It is what we have call 'the Village and its doubles.' To reduce these projects to their perimeter without the ability to develop ties with their surroundings is to squander the organic material of the city and the territory. To cut the Village off from its zone of influence is tantamount to chopping its heritage down to the dimensions of a superblock. If we wish to experience our metropolis differently, planning must consider a much larger format. Apart from the major public works sector – with projects like the Grand Paris Express – there are no longer any large-scale developers capable of undertaking projects the size of a city district in relation with the city. When there is no vision, the capacity to enable the full range of populations, territories, and uses to live together declines.

The future district we are speaking about is intended to produce thriving urban life based on what is specifically metropolitan. It takes responsibility for its area by reconnecting it to itself and by making a great number of apartments available to its inhabitants. By 2025, some 2,500 new units will be completed as well as tens of thousands of square meters of offices and services. 6,000 inhabitants and as many professionals are expected, based on current projections. We have seen nothing like it since the 1970s period of new towns. That there is an acute shortage of housing in Ile-de-France is well-known. The notion of welcome is essential, and the most beautiful heritage. Urbanism is a political discipline oriented toward what is shared.

Nowadays, public commissions have declined significantly. In this regard, the program for a district like the Village is rather exceptional. However, the state ought to possess resources required to use this commission as a lever of prospection and experimentation for deploying a vision of what the future Grand Paris can be. A change of perspective is required to achieve this. In other words, an end to narrow parameters and ad hoc, opportunistic and self-regarding development policies.

The place in the Village joint-development zone dedicated to the Cité du cinéma is a revealing example of a deficient and piecemeal vision of the city. What future can this 7-hectare parcel have in the very heart of a 40-hectare site? This former "electric cathedral" is a powerful aspect of the site's physiognomy and its roots, conditioning its identity. And yet it has been excised from the urban plan, disappearing from the map. Indeed, the very heart of the Village is excluded from the project. Thus, the Village is deprived of what gives the site much of its substance and character. Heritage has been amputated. The future of the Village will depend on the necessary reappropriation of the Cité du cinéma. It must participate in the district's metropolitan influence. Here again, the notions of heredity and heritage intertwine.

Urbanists must come armed not only with patience but also cutting pliers. When necessary, they must cut things out in order act with precision at the right moment in the right place.

Other district goals figuring in the application file and in the Masterplan for development are currently held back owing to a lack of relays, willpower and quality of attention paid to the territory. The Seine is a good example – like everything around the spatial edges of the de project. Currently, this heritage is failing.

For the Village to advance toward the river via pedestrian and cyclable streets, the traffic on the departmental route requires revision. If the project were to succeed, the Village could provide the impulse, elsewhere on the territory, for other fruitful interfaces with the riverfront. The heritage of the Village is also in play regarding the ability to activate and stimulate other solutions that are just waiting to be expanded across all municipalities. One can clearly see that if the policy process offers no overall analysis, how can citizens fully play their role in discussions of planning issues? The construction of Grand Paris is first and foremost political.

Digital intelligence is the other stage of the rocket. The city of today is an immense generator of data, which form the basis of its program.

In the development masterplan that we designed for the Chinese city of Handan, we apply and even extend the concept of Hôtel Métropole presented at the Atelier International du Grand Paris. The concept is one of a temporary residence for populations of varying profiles: students, foreign researchers, newly formed households, business tourists, and mobile workers. It is imagined as an incubator of urbanity.

The study in question spoke about migrations versus movements in Ile-de-France and of setting up a network of points (Hôtels Métropoles) that could settle these migratory movements by establishing a new mapping of uses. This idea was premonitory of the coworking and co-living phenomena. The Olympic district possesses all the features to become a Hôtel Métropole. These programs evolve and today an unexpected supply of student housing is emerging in the zone of the future district. This approach allows us to test the potentials of the urban fabric by gently infiltrating the urbanity we seek to facilitate rather than to impose an a priori model of a city. At its scale, the Hôtel Métropole models the idea of the open data city. To ensure that the Hôtel Métropole can be achieved through the activity of its transitory residents, a computerized collection system and database are required.

The data serve collective intelligence. Artificial intelligence, at the service of the city and its uses must rely on citizen acceptance.

Its jurisdiction and its challenge are first and foremost human as regards the public space. Today, digital intelligence allows us to manage an ensemble like the Village in fruitful collaboration with the precise notion of the availability of places, of reversibility, and of receptivity.

Like development genes, the emerging metropolitan district ties its future to the organic quality of the life one can experience there and of its urban structures. Its code is agility-ready. The Village is designed to think with its times.

#779#
Construction work, November 2020.

#781#
Construction work, Mars 2021.

#783#
Work in progress,
March 2022.

#785#

The Athlete's Village completed, January 2024.

#787#

French President Emmanuel Macron inaugurated the Athletes' Village district on February 29, 2024.

#788# Acknowledgments

Dominique Perrault would like to express his gratitude to Anne Hidalgo, President of the Société de livraison des ouvrages Olympiques (Solidéo); Nicolas Ferrand, CEO of SOLIDEO; Tony Estanguet, President of Paris 2024; Jean Castex and Michel Cadot, successively Interministerial Delegate for the Olympic and Paralympic Games, for the trust they have placed in him.

These thanks also extend to Patrick Ollier, President of the Greater Paris Metropolitan Area, and Valérie Pécresse, President of the Ile-de-France Region. Stéphane Troussel, President of the Seine-Saint-Denis Departmental Council, Patrick Braouzec, and Mathieu Hanotin, successively President of Plaine Commune (with Mathieu Hanotin being Mayor of Saint-Denis), Karim Bouamrane, successively Mayor of Saint-Ouen-sur-Seine, and Mohamed Gnabaly, Mayor of Ile-Saint-Denis.

He would also like to extend his warmest thanks to all those involved in the unique adventure of designing a district of the Grand Paris that will be home to the Athletes' Village in the summer of 2024.

Contracting Authority

The organisation

Olympic Delivery Company (Solidéo)
Anne HIDALGO, Mayor of Paris, President
Nicolas FERRAND, Managing Director

Organising Committee for the Olympic and Paralympic Games Paris 2024
Tony ESTANGUET, President

Interministerial Delegation for the Olympic and Paralympic Games
Jean CASTEX (2017-2020)
Michel CADOT (since 2020)

Métropole du Grand Paris
Patrick OLLIER, President

Ile-de-France region
Valérie PECRESSE, President

Department of Seine-Saint-Denis
Stéphane TROUSSEL, President

Plaine Commune public territorial entity
Patrick BRAOUZEC, President (2005-2020)
Mathieu HANOTIN, President (since 2020)

SEM Plaine Commune Développement
Stéphane TROUSSEL, President

Town of Saint-Ouen-sur-Seine
Karim BOUAMRANE, Mayor

Town of Ile-Saint-Denis
Mathieu HANOTIN, Mayor

Town of Ile-Saint-Denis
Mohamed GNABALY, Mayor

Urban project management

Dominique Perrault Architecture DPA

Dominique PERRAULT, urban planner
David AGUDO, architect
Louis HENAUX, engineer
Marine OUDARD, urban planner

Une Fabrique de la Ville
Jean-Louis SUBILEAU, urban planner
Guillaume HEBERT, urban planner

Ingérop
Simon DUMOULIN, director of the urban planning and development division

CITEC
Franco TUFO, chief executive

TER
Henri BAVA, landscape designer

Urban Eco
Marine LINGLART, director

GLP Design
Gaëlle LAURIOT-PRÉVOST, architect and designer

AVELAC
Jean-Paul LAMOUREUX, acoustician

Experte accessibilité
Françoise FOLACCI, architect

Expert sécurité
Denis THÉLOT, architect

Les Belvédères / Les Villas
Lot E, Saint-Ouen

Nexity
Eiffage
CDC Habitat
Project owners

COBE
Coordinating architects
Alexis CHARLOT ETIENNE
Valérie DUMONT
Alexandre JONVEL
Laetitia PIERI

KOZ
Coordinating architects
Christophe OUHAYOUN
Julie STEINMYLLER

LAMBERT LENACK
Architects
Adrien LAMBERT
Etienne LENACK
Lorenzo SANTOSUOSSO

DREAM
Architects
Dimitri ROUSSEL
Julie SIOL

BARRAULT PRESSACCO
Architects
Darius CHAMBRIN
Cyril PRESSACCO

SOA
Architects
Vincent JAULNEAU LABARRE

ATELIER GEORGES
Architects – Landscape designers
Aurélien DELCHET
Mathieu DELORME
Chloé PICCARD
Raphaël ZEPHIR

Les Belvédères / Les Villas
Lot E, Saint-Ouen

Icade
CDC
CDC Habitat
Project owners

UAPS
Coordinating architects
Anne MIE DEPUYDT
Charlotte PINI

BRENAC & GONZALEZ
Architects
Emmanuel PERSON

ATELIER PASCAL GONTIER
Architects
Pascal GONTHIER
Frédéric MAIRE

FAGART & FONTANA
Architects
David FAGART
Line FONTANA
Quentin SIMONIN

ECDM
Architects
Emmanuel COMBAREL
Benjamin FERRER

NP2F
Architects
Théophile CHATELAIS
François CHAS

TN+
Landscape designers
Andras JAMBOR

Universeine A / Les Cours
Lot A, Saint-Denis

Vinci Immobilier
Project owner

CLEMENT VERGELY ARCHITECTES
Coordinating architects
Mary BRAVARD
Clément VERGELY

BEAL & BLANCKAERT ARCHITECTES
Architects
Antoine BEAL

ATELIER PASCAL GONTIER
Architects
Pascal GONTIER
Frédéric MAIRE

LINA GHOTMEH ARCHITECTURE
Architects
Lina GHOTMEH

GAËTAN LE PENHUEL ARCHITECTES
Architects
Gaëtan LE PEHNHUEL

WAGON LANDSCAPING
Landscape designers
Camille BOURGEOIS
François VADEPIED

Universeine B / Maxwell
Lot B, Saint-Denis

Vinci Immobilier
Project owner

CHAIX & MOREL
Coordinating architects
Jan HORST
Aurélia LECLERC

TRIPTYQUE ARCHITECTURE
Architects
Esther QUENEHEN
Charlotte MUGNIER
Guillaume SIBAUD

TAKTYK
Landscape designers
Sébastien PENFORNIS
Thania SAKELLARIOU

Group Scolaire
Saint- Ouen

SOLIDEO
Project owner

ARCHI 5
Architects

Shared database - Police headquarters, Saint-Denis

SOLIDEO
Project owner

NTSA
Architects
Nicolas TOURY

Dora Maar, College extension Saint-Denis Lot E4b

Conseil départemental
de la Seine-Saint-Denis
Project owner

PLATANE ET ILIC
Architects
Platane BERES
Milan ILICS

Student residence Lot E4b

CDC Habitat
Project owner

ATELIER MARTEL
Architects
Stéphane CACHAT

Le Village Insulaire
L'Ile Saint Denis
Lot PA

Pichet Immobilier
Légende Immobilier
Project owner

PHILIPPON-KALT
Urban planners

CHARTIER-DALIX
Coordinating architects

PETIDIDIER PRIOUX
Coordinating architects

EGA-ERIK GIUDICE
Coordinating architects

MG-AU MICHEL GUTHMAN
Architects

HARDEL LE BIHAN
Architects

NP2F
Architects

NEBBIA
Landscape designers

GAËTAN LE PENHUEL ARCHITECTES
Architects
Gaëtan LE PEHNHUEL

ATELIER FABRICE COMMERCON
Architects

N'DOYE ARCHITECTES
Architects

NZI ARCHITECTES
Architects

LAVIGNE & CHERON
Architects

FARID AZIB
Architects

AAVP
Architects

INUITS
Landscape designers

The Dream Team

Dominique Perrault pays tribute to all those who have contributed to the design of the Olympic district, Paris 2024.

Camille ABEILLE
Midia ADAB
Andreea ADAM
David AGUDO
Quitterie AMIEL
Stella ARMELLI
Henri BAVA
Herve BESSOU
Marcello BIFFI
Marie BODENES
Augustin BOURGEOIS
Carmelo CAGLIANO
Carl CANTIN
Tulio CATHALA
Ilaria CAZZATO
Sophie CHARLOTTE HOLMLUND
Ana COLMENERO
Joana COSTA
Berenice CURT
Fabienne DELANDEMARE
Anastasia DELINASIOU
Soetkin DEVOLDER
Divya DHANDAPANI
Sofia DISTEFANO
Vincent DULOUP
Simon DUMOULIN
Maia DURAND
Martina FABRIS
Anais FERNON
Francoise FOLACCI
Andrea FORTUNATO
Gabrielle FOURNIER
Julien FUENTES
Philippe GASSER
Pierre GIROD
Ramon GONZALEZ LOPEZ
Lea GORRA
Bernardo GRILLI
Chuan GUO
Guillaume HEBERT
Louis HENAUX
Amos HOUEWATONOU
Alexandra HUYNH-LENHARDT
Helena IRIART
Nanako ISHIZUKA
Myrlande JEAN PIERRE
Kariane JEAUROND
Paola JIMENO MARTINEZ
Sana KAMOUN
Jean-Paul LAMOUREUX
Gaëlle LAURIOT-PREVOST
Shawn LAW
Wafa LIMEM
Marine LINGLART
Jean Louis SUBILEAU
Frederik LYKKEBERG
Tiago MADEIRA
Baptiste MAGNIN
Stephania MARIANO
Bartetlomiej MARKOWSKI
Claire MARRACHE
Carlotta MAZZI
Remi MERCHAT
Alan MOQUET
Benedicte MOREL
Alexandre MORET
Patrice MORISSET
Louis MOUROT
Richard NGUYEN
Clement NICOLAS
Thierry NOBLESSE
Misaki NOZAWA
Marine OUDARD
Giulia PACE
Brigitte PAILLARD
Carlos PANTANELLA
Aurelie PAQUOT
Lea PELLETERET
Morgane PERNOT
Dominique PERRAULT
Camille PETIT
Sebastien PETITEMBERT
Emanuele PIENSANTI
Noel PINAUD
Julien PRINGUET
Celine RANDAZZO
Paolo RIGHI
Taehoon RO
Marina Alves ROSA
William ROTH
Sacha ROY LUMPP
Dolores RUIZ
Enrico SALVO
Matheus SARTORI
Loic SEITE
Polymnia SKORDA
Anne Sophie DELAVEAU
Denis THELOT
Simon THIROT
Ernesto URQUIZAR
Silvia VALENCIA
Nicolas VALLADON
Francesco VINCI
William YON

A Village and its Double
Urban Planning Manual for the Olympic and Paralympic Games Paris 2024

Credits

Every effort has been made to identify and credit the authors and copyright holders of the documents reproduced in this publication. However, we regret that some credits may have escaped our attention.
For the general views of the Athletes' Village, credit is given to the Société de livraison des ouvrages olympiques (Solidéo) and all the urban and architectural project management groups detailed above.

Opening

Photographs : DPA / Francesca Avanzinelli / Arthur Jan
Images: DPA / Francy

Ambitions 1, 2

Photographs : Archives départementales de la Seine-Saint-Denis
Images: DPA / Luxigon
Documents : Vinci Immo / Icade Group / Nexity Group /
Diagrams and maps : IGN / APUR / Zefco / Archives départementales de la Seine-Saint-Denis /
Drawing: Didier Ghislain
Drawing: Didier Ghislain
Layout: Patrice Debois

Ambitions 3, 4, 5

Photographs: 1924, IOC
Images: DPA / Plaine Commune / Paris 2024 / Luxigon
Diagram, maps : Plaine Commune / Zefco / Agence TER / Ingerop

Ambitions 6, 7, 8

Images: DPA / Icade / Nexity / Luxigon / Kreaction
Diagrams, maps : UFV / CITEC / Agence TER / Ingérop
Drawing: Didier Ghislain

Ambitions 9, 10, 11, 12, 13 and postface

Photographs: Tiago Madeira / Potion Médiatique / SOLIDEO
Images: Kreaction / Vinci Immo / Groupement Nexity / Icade / CDC Habitat
Diagram, maps : DPA / Agence TER / UFV

Archives and documentary sources

Plaine Commune
Saint-Denis municipal archives
Archives of the Seine-Saint-Denis Departmental Council
Paul Eluard Museum of Art and History, City of Saint-Denis
International Olympic Committee
and,
Martin Citarella, Comité Dép. Olympique et Sportif de Seine-Saint-Denis
Thomas Hervé Studio
Frederic Serrurier, Connexion Sport Urbain

A Village and its Double
Urban Planning Manual for the Olympic and Paralympic Games Paris 2024

Author
Dominique PERRAULT

Texts
Dominique PERRAULT
Frédéric PROT

Editorial coordination
Marga GIBERT
Ramon PRAT
David AGUDO
Marie BODENES
Tulio CATHALA
Kariane JEAUROND
Gaëlle LAURIOT-PREVOST

Edition
Actar Publishers

Graphic concept
Ramon PRAT
Marga GIBERT

Corrections and proofreading
Rina KENOVIC

Traduction
Gammon SHARPLEY

Printing and binding
Arlequin, Barcelona

Distribution
Actar D, Inc. New York, Barcelona

New York
440 Park Avenue Sud, 17e étage
New York, NY 10016, États-Unis
T+1 2129662207
salesnewyork@actar-d.com

Barcelone
Roca i Batlle 2-4
08023 Barcelone, Espagne
T +34 933 282 183
eurosales@actar-d.com

Index
ISBN English : 978-1-63840-130-8
PCN : Library of Congress : 2023952174

Publication date: April 2024